FRANCE DIVIDED
The French and the Civil War in Spain

The Cañada Blanch / Sussex Academic Studies on Contemporary Spain

General Editor: Professor Paul Preston, London School of Economics

Germà Bel, *Infrastructure and the Political Economy of Nation Building in Spain, 1720–2010.*

Gerald Blaney Jr., *"The Three-Cornered Hat and the Tri-Colored Flag": The Civil Guard and the Second Spanish Republic, 1931–1936.*

Michael Eaude, *Triumph at Midnight in the Century: A Critical Biography of Arturo Barea.*

Soledad Fox, *Constancia de la Mora in War and Exile: International Voice for the Spanish Republic.*

Helen Graham, *The War and Its Shadow: Spain's Civil War in Europe's Long Twentieth Century.*

Angela Jackson, *'For us it was Heaven': The Passion, Grief and Fortitude of Patience Darton – From the Spanish Civil War to Mao's China.*

Gabriel Jackson, *Juan Negrín: Physiologist, Socialist, and Spanish Republican War Leader.*

Sid Lowe, *Catholicism, War and the Foundation of Francoism: The Juventud de Acción Popular in Spain, 1931–1939.*

Olivia Muñoz-Rojas, *Ashes and Granite: Destruction and Reconstruction in the Spanish Civil War and Its Aftermath.*

Linda Palfreeman, *¡SALUD!: British Volunteers in the Republican Medical Service during the Spanish Civil War, 1936–1939.*

Cristina Palomares, *The Quest for Survival after Franco: Moderate Francoism and the Slow Journey to the Polls, 1964–1977.*

David Wingeate Pike, *France Divided: The French and the Civil War in Spain.*

Isabelle Rohr, *The Spanish Right and the Jews, 1898–1945: Antisemitism and Opportunism.*

Gareth Stockey, *Gibraltar: "A Dagger in the Spine of Spain?"*

Ramon Tremosa-i-Balcells, *Catalonia – An Emerging Economy: The Most Cost-Effective Ports in the Mediterranean Sea.*

Dacia Viejo-Rose, *Reconstructing Spain: Cultural Heritage and Memory after Civil War.*

Richard Wigg, *Churchill and Spain: The Survival of the Franco Regime, 1940–1945.*

Published by the Cañada Blanch Centre for Contemporary Spanish Studies in conjunction with Routledge / Taylor & Francis

1. Francisco J. Romero Salvadó, *Spain 1914–1918: Between War and Revolution.*
2. David Wingeate Pike, *Spaniards in the Holocaust: Mauthausen, the Horror on the Danube.*
3. Herbert Rutledge Southworth, *Conspiracy and the Spanish Civil War: The Brainwashing of Francisco Franco.*
4. Angel Smith (editor), *Red Barcelona: Social Protest and Labour Mobilization in the Twentieth Century.*
5. Angela Jackson, *British Women and the Spanish Civil War.*
6. Kathleen Richmond, *Women and Spanish Fascism: The Women's Section of the Falange, 1934–1959.*
7. Chris Ealham, *Class, Culture and Conflict in Barcelona, 1898–1937.*
8. Julián Casanova, *Anarchism, the Republic and Civil War in Spain 1931–1939.*
9. Montserrat Guibernau, *Catalan Nationalism: Francoism, Transition and Democracy.*
10. Richard Baxell, *British Volunteers in the Spanish Civil War: The British Battalion in the International Brigades, 1936–1939.*
11. Hilari Raguer, *The Catholic Church and the Spanish Civil War.*
12. Richard Wigg, *Churchill and Spain: The Survival of the Franco Regime, 1940–45.*
13. Nicholas Coni, *Medicine and the Spanish Civil War.*
14. Diego Muro, *Ethnicity and Violence: The Case of Radical Basque Nationalism.*
15. Francisco J. Romero Salvadó, *Spain's Revolutionary Crisis, 1917–1923.*
16. Peter Anderson, *The Francoist Military Trials. Terror and Complicity, 1939–1945.*

Also by David Wingeate Pike

Vae Victis! (Ruedo ibérico, Paris, 1968)
Les Français et la guerre d'Espagne (Presses Universitaires de France, Paris, 1975).
Latin America in Nixon's Second Term, ed. (Bennett & Starling, London, 1982).
Jours de gloire, jours de honte (Sedes, Paris, 1984).
The Opening of the Second World War, ed. (Peter Lang, New York, 1991).
In the Service of Stalin (Clarendon Press, Oxford, 1993).
Spaniards in the Holocaust (Routledge, London, 2000).
The Closing of the Second World War, ed. (Peter Lang, New York, 2001).
Españoles en el holocausto (Random House, Barcelona, 2003, 2004, 2006).
Mauthausen, L'enfer nazi en Autriche (Édouard Privat, Toulouse, 2004).
Betrifft: KZ Mauthausen: Was die Archive erzählen (BuchVerlag Franz Steinmassl, Linz, 2005).
Franco and the Axis Stigma (Macmillan, London & New York, 2008).
Franco y el Eje Roma–Berlín–Tokio: Una alianza no firmada (Alianza Editorial, Madrid, 2010).
Crimes against Women, ed. (Nova Science Publishing, New York, 2010)

FRANCE DIVIDED
The French and the Civil War in Spain

DAVID WINGEATE PIKE

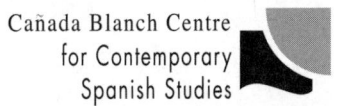

Copyright © David Wingeate Pike, 2011.

The right of David Wingeate Pike to be identified as Author of this work has been asserted in accordance with the Copyright, Designs and Patents Act 1988.

2 4 6 8 10 9 7 5 3 1

First published in 2011 in Great Britain by
SUSSEX ACADEMIC PRESS
PO Box 139
Eastbourne BN24 9BP

and in the United States of America by
SUSSEX ACADEMIC PRESS
920 NE 58th Ave   Suite 300
Portland, Oregon 97213-3786

and in Canada by
SUSSEX ACADEMIC PRESS (CANADA)
8000 Bathurst Street, Unit 1, PO Box 30010, Vaughan, Ontario L4J 0C6

Published in collaboration with the
Cañada Blanch Centre for Contemporary Spanish Studies.

All rights reserved. Except for the quotation of short passages for the purposes of criticism and review, no part of this publication may be reproduced, stored in a retrieval system, or transmitted, in any form or by any means, electronic, mechanical, photocopying, recording or otherwise, without the prior permission of the publisher.

British Library Cataloguing in Publication Data
A CIP catalogue record for this book is available from the British Library.

Library of Congress Cataloging-in-Publication Data
Pike, David Wingeate.
France divided : the French and the Civil War in Spain / David Wingeate Pike.
   p. cm. — (The Cañada Blanch/Sussex Academic studies on contemporary Spain)
Includes bibliographical references and index.
ISBN 978-1-84519-490-1 (h/b : alk. paper)
ISBN 978-1-84519-531-1 (pbk. : alk. paper)
 1. France—Politics and government—1914–1940. 2. Spain—History—Civil War, 1936–1939—Social aspects—France. 3. Spain—History—Civil War, 1936–1939—Press coverage—France. 4. Spain—History—Civil War, 1936–1939—Foreign public opinion, French. 5. France—Public opinion—History—20th century. I. Title.
DC389.P46 2012
946.081'10944—dc22   2011016461

Typeset & designed by Sussex Academic Press, Brighton & Eastbourne.
Printed by TJ International, Padstow, Cornwall.

Contents

The Cañada Blanch Centre for Contemporary Spanish Studies	xii
Preface	xv
Acknowledgements	xxi
List of Illustrations	xxiii
List of Acronyms: Groups, Organisations and Political Parties	xxiv
Author's Remarks	xxvi

Introduction   1
The Popular Fronts
The Second Spanish Republic between 1931 and 1936—Events in France between 1920 and 1936, and the confrontation between the extremes—The Soviet position—Spain's place in Europe—French foreign policy—Relations between Germany and Spain and between Italy and Spain—The triumph in France of the Front Populaire and its repercussions—The triumph in Spain of the Frente Popular and its aftermath—The Spanish military uprising and its semi-failure

PART ONE
The Limits of Intervention

1 The Call to Arms   9
The message from Giral to Blum—Blum's first reaction—The modification in Blum's position, following his visit to London and the reaction of the Senate—First dispatch on 2 August of French arms—The French proposal of non-intervention in Spain—The other Powers reply—Blum suspends French aid on 8 August—The fall of the Giral government

2 The Revolt of the Generals   13
The slogans of the adversaries: 'Order and patriotism' against 'Liberty and justice'—The first reactions of the French press on left and right—The question of legitimacy—The conflict expands

3 The Appeal of Giral — 18
Blum's initial promise of support—Opposition from the Right, the Radicals, and the British Government—The Cot formula suspended—Suspicions, accusations, denials—The legality polemic—The arguments of the Right: the Spanish Government of tomorrow, and a new defence line—Refutations from the Left—The fear of escalation—German–Italian preparations and financial aid

4 Italo-German Intervention and the Cot Formula — 29
Italian intervention: denial and proof—French interests in Morocco—The reply of the Right—The hesitations of the Radicals—The attitude of reserve of the Spanish Republicans—Pressure from the Left and French intervention

5 The Delbos–Daladier Formula — 37
British reaction as cause of the French volte-face—Support for the new policy—Opposition from the Left—Opposition from the Right—Frontier incidents

6 Mediation Appeals and Fascist Consolidation — 48
Appeals for international mediation: the South American initiative—Fascist aid to Franco: the German–Italian objectives—France in Europe: an analysis of its position

7 The London Committee — 55
Twenty-four nations participate—The Portuguese position—Accusations and counter-accusations—The Delbos Plan: new support and opposition—Contradictions between Soviet policy and the activities of the French Communists—The reply of *L'Humanité*—Division within the SFIO—The decision of the British Labour Party—Reaction of the Right and French aid to Franco

8 The Soviet Ultimatum and Intervention — 66
Soviet policy—The French 'Trotskyists'—The ultimatum of 7 October—The London Committee steps back—The effect on French policy

9 The Foreign Volunteers — 71
Blum agrees to the departure of the volunteers—The first arrivals—Franco's response—Travel restrictions—The International Brigades move into formation—Opposition to their formation and to their recruitment in France—Foreign volunteers for the insurgency

10 Axis Recognition of Franco 79
The 'preventive counter-revolution' against the mere idea of a Catalan republic—Franco's failure before Madrid: its repercussions on Axis policy—Relations between Hitler and Mussolini: the common front—Blockade and recognition: repercussions on the democracies—Reflections on the granting of belligerent status to Franco—The Pan-American Conference—A socialist delegation visits London

11 The Three Anglo-French Peace Initiatives 88
The 'Soviet' proposal for an international control (23 October)—The Committee approves it on 12 November— Further violations—The Delbos Plan for a 'Gentlemen's Agreement' (27 November)—Reaction from the Right and Left—Hostility to the Delbos Plan from both sides in Spain—The 'German' Plan (4 December)—The question of the volunteers—Accusations of bad faith—The attitudes of Hitler and Mussolini

12 The Democracies Outmanoeuvred 94
The initiatives of the Committee—The possibilities of general disengagement—The role of France—The antifascists dejected by fascist falsifications—Hitler's policy—Mussolini's policy—The democracies mark time

PART TWO
The Comedy of Non-Intervention

13 The Committee Implements Control 105
Malaga: its effect on morale—New calls for the granting of belligerent rights—The foreign volunteers—Frontier control and violations—Control of the coast

14 Guadalajara and Fascist Reaction 112
The Italian defeat and Italian morale—Mussolini sends reinforcements—The effect on German policy—Mediation plans proposed

15 Gernika'ko Arbola and the Catholic Agony 117
The destruction of Guernica—Outrage on the Left and in the Centre, indifference on the Right—Denials by Franco and the right-wing press—Irrefutable proof of German responsibility—The attitude of the Church—The Christian crusade: the Catholics divided—The Vatican grants recognition to Franco—Its influence on the religious dispute—The Vatican's apprehensions

16 The Pamphlet War and the Battle of the Minds — 130
Palmiro Togliatti—Jean-Richard Bloch—Daniel Guérin—Thomas Mann—Camillo Berneri—'Max Rieger'—Jacques Bardoux—Robert Brasillach—Georges Rotvand—Henri-Massis—André Malraux—Jean-Paul Sartre—Simone Téry—Drieu La Rochelle—Romain Rolland—André Gide—Literary congresses and art exhibitions

17 Incidents in France — 136
France and the Republicans violate non-intervention—The Nationalists violate French sovereignty—Right-wing activities—False information and conflict within the press

18 British Mediation and the *Deutschland* Incident — 146
The 'May Days' in Barcelona—Largo Caballero and Blum replaced by Negrín and Chautemps—The democracies respond to the blockade—Public opinion in Britain—The mediation proposal is submitted—Reaction in the French press—The attack on the *Deutschland* and the shelling of Almería—The fall of Bilbao—Its effect on British policy—The Committee at an impasse

19 The Nyon Arrangement — 158
First anniversary of the war: its goals newly assessed—Fascist aid to Franco—Comparing the foreign forces of intervention—Axis policy after Bilbao— The 'mysterious sinkings'—The Nyon Conference and the Nyon Arrangement—French and British policy after Nyon

20 The London–Burgos Exchange of Agents — 166
The Republic before and after Gijón—Analyses and prognoses of the war—Britain and France open representation—Differences between French and British policy

21 The Threat to French Security — 173
Teruel taken and retaken—New Year 1938 and new prognoses—The Anschluss and the second Blum Cabinet—French security in the Western Mediterranean and in North Africa—The danger from the Pyrenees—The Axis consolidates its position in Spain

22 The Daladier–Bonnet Formula — 182
Italian propaganda against France—Bombing of Spanish cities and Republican threats of reprisal—Air attacks on French territory—The Daladier–Bonnet formula: the closing of the frontier

23 The Republic in Isolation 192
The second anniversary—German policy *vis-à-vis* the Anglo-Italian Agreement—The Spanish gold—Seasonal exegeses

24 The Shadow of Munich 199
The Berchtesgaden talks and their effect on morale—Auriol visits Barcelona—The campaign to recognize Franco—The London Plan and belligerent rights—The International Brigades disbanded—The Nationalist offensive resumes—Perspectives for peace

25 The War at the Gates of France 208
Italian irredentism, Spanish Nationalist hostility toward France, and French reaction—Renewed talk of aid to the Republic—New attempts at mediation

26 Anglo-French Recognition of Franco 217
The Bérard mission—American isolationism—The Republican government arrives in France—Pétain and de Lequerica nominated as ambassadors

27 The End of Hostilities 225
Casado's coup d'état—Republican troops and matériel enter France—Marty explains to the Senate—Spain in Europe

Conclusion 232

Epilogue: The Fate of the Journals and the Journalists 241

Appendices
APPENDIX I	Principal Characters	264
APPENDIX II	The Five French Cabinets of 1936–1939	269
APPENDIX III	The Four Cabinets of the Frente Popular	272
APPENDIX IV	The French Consulates in Spain	274
APPENDIX V	Trans-Pyrenean Rail and Road Links between France and Spain	277
APPENDIX VI	Spain and the Pyrenean Border	279
APPENDIX VII	The French Press, 1936–1939	280

Notes 306
Bibliography 388
Index 407

The Cañada Blanch Centre for Contemporary Spanish Studies

In the 1960s, the most important initiative in the cultural and academic relations between Spain and the United Kingdom was launched by a Valencian fruit importer in London. The creation by Vicente Cañada Blanch of the Anglo-Spanish Cultural Foundation has subsequently benefited large numbers of Spanish and British scholars at various levels. Thanks to the generosity of Vicente Cañada Blanch, thousands of Spanish schoolchildren have been educated at the secondary school in West London that bears his name. At the same time, many British and Spanish university students have benefited from the exchange scholarships which fostered cultural and scientific exchanges between the two countries. Some of the most important historical, artistic and literary work on Spanish topics to be produced in Great Britain was initially made possible by Cañada Blanch scholarships.

Vicente Cañada Blanch was, by inclination, a conservative. When his Foundation was created, the Franco regime was still in the plenitude of its power. Nevertheless, the keynote of the Foundation's activities was always a complete open-mindedness on political issues. This was reflected in the diversity of research projects supported by the Foundation, many of which, in Francoist Spain, would have been regarded as subversive. When the Dictator died, Don Vicente was in his seventy-fifth year. In the two decades following the death of the Dictator, although apparently indestructible, Don Vicente was obliged to husband his energies. Increasingly, the work of the Foundation was carried forward by Miguel Dols whose tireless and imaginative work in London was matched in Spain by that of José María Coll Comín. They were united in the Foundation's spirit of open-minded commitment to fostering research of high quality in pursuit of better Anglo-Spanish cultural relations. Throughout the 1990s, thanks to them, the role of the Foundation grew considerably.

In 1994, in collaboration with the London School of Economics, the Foundation established the Príncipe de Asturias Chair of Contemporary Spanish History and the Cañada Blanch Centre for Contemporary Spanish Studies. It is the particular task of the Cañada Blanch Centre to promote the understanding of twentieth-century Spain through research and teaching of contemporary Spanish history, politics, economy, sociology and culture. The Centre possesses a valuable library and archival centre for specialists in contemporary Spain. This work is carried on through the publications of the doctoral and post-doctoral researchers at the Centre itself and through the many seminars and lectures held at the London School of Economics. While the seminars are the province of the researchers, the lecture cycles have been the forum in which Spanish politicians have been able to address audiences in the United Kingdom.

Since 1998, the Cañada Blanch Centre has published a substantial number of books in collaboration with several different publishers on the subject of contemporary Spanish history and politics. A fruitful partnership with Sussex Academic Press began in 2004 with the publication of Cristina Palomares's fascinating work on the origins of the Partido Popular in Spain, *The Quest for Survival after Franco: Moderate Francoism and the Slow Journey to the Polls, 1964–1977*. This was followed in 2007 by Soledad Fox's deeply moving biography of one of the most intriguing women of 1930s Spain, *Constancia de la Mora in War and Exile: International Voice for the Spanish Republic*, and Isabelle Rohr's path-breaking study of anti-Semitism in Spain, *The Spanish Right and the Jews, 1898–1945: Antisemitism and Opportunism*; 2008 saw the publication of a revised edition of Richard Wigg's penetrating study of Anglo-Spanish relations during the Second World War, *Churchill and Spain: The Survival of the Franco Regime, 1940–1945*, together with *Triumph at Midnight of the Century: A Critical Biography of Arturo Barea*, Michael Eaude's fascinating revaluation of the great Spanish author of *The Forging of a Rebel*.

Our collaboration in 2009 was inaugurated by Gareth Stockey's incisive account of another crucial element in Anglo-Spanish relations, *Gibraltar: A Dagger in the Spine of Spain*. We were especially proud that it was continued by the most distinguished American historian of the Spanish Civil War, Gabriel Jackson. His pioneering work *The Spanish Republic and the Civil War*, first published in 1965 and still in print, quickly became a classic. The Sussex Academic Press/Cañada Blanch series was greatly privileged to be associated with Professor Jackson's biography of the great Republican war leader, Juan Negrín.

Our publications in 2010 were inaugurated by the fascinating study by Ramón Tremosa i Balcells of the economic future of Catalonia and of the role being played in that future by the region's ports. They were continued with *Catholicism, War and the Foundation of Francoism: The Juventud de Acción Popular in Spain, 1931–1939* by Sid Lowe. This dealt with one of the least known elements on the road to civil war in Spain. The mass Catholic youth movement, the Juventud de Acción Popular, contributed to the polarization of politics within the Second Republic. After the right-wing defeat in the elections of February 1936, a large proportion of its militants went over to the overtly fascist Falange. They played a crucial role in the Falangist militias, both in frontline fighting and in rearguard repression.

This year, 2011, promises to take the series to new heights. Two remarkable and complementary works, Olivia Muñoz Rojas, *Ashes and Granite: Destruction and Reconstruction in the Spanish Civil War and its Aftermath*, and Dacia Viejo-Rose, *Reconstructing Spain: Cultural Heritage and Memory after Civil War*, have opened up an entirely new dimension of the study of the early Franco regime and its internal conflicts. They are followed by Richard Purkiss's analysis of the Valencian anarchist movement during the revolutionary period from 1918 to 1923, the military dictatorship of General Primo de Rivera and the Second Republic. It is a fascinating work which sheds entirely new light both on the breakdown of political coexistence during the Republic and on the origins of the violence that was to explode after the military coup of July 1936.

The publication of *France Divided: The French and the Civil War in Spain* by David Wingeate Pike is greatly to be welcomed. It makes available in a thoroughly updated edition, and in English for the first time, one of the classics of the historiography of the Spanish Civil War. It remains astonishing that the reaction of France to the conflict beyond its southern borders has not, until now, been the subject of a major study in English. That alone would make this an important work, but the meticulous nature of Professor Pike's research and the clarity of his prose will ensure it a place of honour in the overcrowded bibliography on the war.

PAUL PRESTON
Series Editor
London School of Economics

Preface

This work sets out to analyze the tragic schism in French public opinion during the Spanish Civil War that served as the catalyst in sundering France's national unity, exacerbating the deep division between Left and Right that was already wracking French society, especially after the riots of February 1934. That division was to prove fatal to France in the catastrophe of 1939–1940. The present work makes no claim to be a new history of the conflict, or even of the international events surrounding it. It touches only cursorily upon the events in Spain proper. It considers only tangentially French public opinion in regard to the two Spains. Even the pamphlet war of 1937 is disregarded except where it touches directly on the international question.

The international imbroglio surrounding the Civil War, and the position of France in the middle of the imbroglio, is therefore the focal point. In the foreground, the reaction of French opinion to the situation. In the background, in relating events at home or close to the frontier, the author has based his information on materials in the archives of the Midi-Pyrénées and the *départements* of Pyrénées-Atlantiques, Ariège, Aude and Pyrénées-Orientales, in particular the correspondence between the five frontier Prefects and Paris. Further information derives from the Berneri Collection, to call it so; these old suitcases, the property of the Italian anarchist philosopher Camillo Berneri, passed to his widow Giovanna after his murder in Barcelona in 1937. Giovanna died in 1964, and the suitcases passed into the hands of the Federazione Anarchica Italiana in Genoa. It was there, in 1965, that I was given not only access to the collection but also permission to keep parts that I selected.

The central interest, French public opinion on the international question, immediately raises a question which drew a remark from Charles Micaud: 'In spite of the importance of public opinion in contemporary history, most scholars have been hesitant in facing its study, fearing that it would be vague, elusive, and necessarily unscientific.'[1] The term 'public opinion' is itself worth examining. Indeed it defies any precise definition, even if it seems to refer to the manifold reactions of the general public. It seems reasonable to seek these reactions in what was then the only tangible evidence, the press. It should be remembered that there were no opinion polls or any other instrument of scientific precision in measuring public opinion, nor did radio commentary have any of the influence it gained later.[2*] It can be argued, certainly, that journalists are not the only guides to public opinion, that men and women of equal influence can be found in the business world, in the Church, in the universities, or in Parliament itself. It still remains true that in so far as each of these elements expressed opinions different from those of the rulers, those opinions were expressed primarily in the press: each had its newspapers. As for Parliament, no one questions its importance as a barometer of public opinion, but debates on foreign policy were not numerous in the Chamber, while in the Senate, composed of members elected indirectly, the impact on foreign policy was less. As a result, during the interval between debates, it was the press that was largely responsible for the diffusion of ideas. Despite the remark of Jacques Kayser that 'in the present state of information science, it is practically impossible to evaluate the influence of newspapers on public opinion,'[3] it is not unreasonable in our opinion to assimilate public opinion in the 1930s with the ideas expressed in the press.

It is true that the role of the press as a gauge of public opinion is subject to controversy on another basis, that of ethics.[4*] To believe Georges Boris in *La Lumière* and many others, the venality of the press was such that one could doubt its authenticity. 'The French press falls into two groups,' wrote Zola; 'the group that sells itself and the group that we call "incorruptible" because this group doesn't sell itself except in exceptional circumstances and at a very high price.' Thus, according to a widely held belief, most French journals were in the hands of corrupt owners who sold their columns to the highest bidders. But this is an absurd exaggeration. All things considered, newspapers are in business either to make money or to wage crusade; neither group can afford to ignore the reactions of its readers. Albert Thibaudet has claimed that the first group, comprising the news journals or the front-runners, followed public opinion more than it fashioned it. Alain, the philosopher of radical socialism, asked the question: 'And for whom exactly is this big journal intended? For the individual that expects it to say just what he thinks, but better than he can say it himself.'[5] Julien Benda wrote in similar vein that the public is becoming aware of its power: 'The newspapers will be their valets or they won't exist. Besides, valets can be quite arrogant on the palace steps of their masters and go at one another with a vengeance.'[6]

It seems reasonable therefore to say that the press truly serves as an exact reflection of the climate of political opinion in a given country and is an invaluable assessment of the thinking of an age. The documents contained in the archives of the Quai d'Orsay, Whitehall, the Wilhelmstrasse, the Palazzo Chigi and other places where foreign affairs were weightedly conducted can never explain a situation in its entirety. Such documents can never reconstitute the effect that the atrocities of Guernica or Barcelona, in photographic form, had upon the public. Such feelings, such impressions are so fugitive, so much a matter of time and place, that it is not easy to recapture them or to find any concrete traces, even a short time after the event. And yet these subtleties of thought and feeling take on special value when it comes to recreating the decor where the action took place.

In France, more than in any other country in the world, journalists counted among the elite. The most eminent writers collaborated with the press. Articles in the press were often quoted in Parliament. The influence of the Paris press, together with certain lions (and lionesses) among those commentators on foreign policy, was widely disseminated throughout the country. In the case of Spain, the press fulfilled a double function. Up to 1936, no press, in any country, had ever played so large a role in hostilities. Never before had so many celebrities, whether authors or journalists, become personally engaged, taking unequivocal part and providing moral—and sometimes material—support to one camp or the other. Hugh Thomas chose to remark upon this role of the press:

> The 1930s were the great age of the foreign correspondent. From the end of July [1936] onward, for two and a half years, the greatest names in world journalism were usually to be found south of the Pyrenees. Distinguished writers were hired by news agencies to represent them at the Spanish War. . . .[7]

This unprecedented public interest, and the profusion of the correspondents in Spain, led to a great number of interviews with the leaders on both sides. Their statements were often off-the-cuff, ill considered and hasty in judgment; they are none the less valuable—the more rash, perhaps the more valuable—in assessing the ulterior motives of these men, even when allowance is made for the misstatements, sometimes deliberate, of the correspondents.

It is a truism to say that truth is the first victim of war. All the news bulletins dispatched by French journalists in Spain had to surmount three obstacles: the journalists' own vulnerability to error, the Spanish censors, and the possible interference of their editors in France. The correspondents themselves were, of course, sometimes open to blame; they might see reality through distorting mirrors, or they might transform it knowingly. Beyond that, most newspapers were more or less ready to tinker with reports in furtherance of their own political ends.

The intermediate obstacle, censorship, had already been developed in the First World War to the highest level, making it virtually impossible to know anything about events on the other side of the front. The war in Spain, however, was the first in which radio played a role. Not that Spanish radio was widely disseminated,[8*] but its very existence made censorship less effective. This new method of communication was immediately adapted both to the dissemination of news and to the falsification of news; indeed, radio had made its entry less to serve as a means of information than to serve as a means of disinformation and misinformation.[9] Did this weapon serve to make demoralization and brain-conditioning harder or easier? It is an open question. If it made it easier, the responsibility fell the heavier on the journalist. Certainly the correspondents never stopped deploring the obstacles against them in their efforts to collect and transmit the news.[10*] Telephone and telegraph communications in Spain encountered enormous difficulties.[11*] The result was that many correspondents preferred to hold their dispatches until they had crossed the frontier and could telephone them to their base.

If news reports had been the subject of this study, some form of statistical analysis would have proved necessary. The analysis could have tried to evaluate what importance each journal gave to each news report. But the primary interest in this book lies in the editorials. All the news reports were long ago corroborated or rejected to the satisfaction of most historians. Editorials, on the other hand, lie on the other side of mathematical proof, because they belong in the domain of conjecture. Conjecture over what historians generally ignore: the motivations of the actors on the stage, the intimate thoughts that they never expressed or dared to express in written form, and the considerations which moved them to action or held them to inaction as they sprang from hope or fear.

Ideas thus taking centre stage, historical facts remain in the background, or reduced to the minimum necessary to an understanding of what here is the primary interest. Little is provided from secondary accounts, even those published at the time, unless they spurred a special interest in the press of that period. Those secondary works produced at that time that appear in the bibliography are included not for reasons of their value but for reasons of their impact on the press.

The work is divided into two parts, the chronological hiatus coming at the end of 1936. This is explained by the policy which the democracies then formulated and which did not deviate much thereafter; sufficiently strong, perhaps, to deter the Axis from all-out intervention in Spain, but weak enough to allow them to pursue with impunity a victory by attrition. Dante Puzzo has written:

'The weeks and months between January 1937 and April 1939 produced no fundamental changes in the respective policies adopted by the great powers toward the Spanish conflict during the summer and autumn of 1936.'[12]

This is to say that the periodic opening and closing of the French frontier played no decisive part in the outcome, since French aid to the Spanish Republic was insignificant compared with Axis aid to the Nationalists. Certainly nothing has been omitted from the catalogue of aid to the Republic by France or by Frenchmen or through France that was found officially recorded. Against this evidence, almost nothing has been said here of Axis aid to the Nationalists, since that is outside the purview of this work, and since the huge superiority of the one over the other is already well established.

It may be asked if this work is impartial, perhaps in the same figure of speech in which Berlin and Rome asked if Paris was neutral in Spain. In an attack upon K. W. Watkins—whose *Britain Divided* does for British opinion what the present work attempts *grosso modo* to do for French—Sir Arnold Lunn offered the sound advice that it is more honourable to admit to a bias than to dissemble one. The present author believes that the only bias his own work presents is aimed at misrepresentation. This would not have satisfied Sir Arnold, who opposed the equation of Republican and Nationalist atrocities in the war. 'There was a very real difference,' he wrote in the September 1963 edition of *The Month*, 'between Spanish Nationalists who sometimes killed without justification and the Republicans who frequently tortured.' He cites the admission by the Republic's Embassy in London of atrocities committed by Republicans. In point of fact, it was not hard to find Republicans in authority who confessed to Republican crimes. It was a far harder thing to find Nationalists who were prepared to do the same in regard to their own. The attempt to deny the evidence of German guilt in the Guernica crime lasted to the end of the century.[13]

As for nomenclature, no distinction is made among the terms 'rebel,' 'insurgent,' and 'Nationalist.' Such terms are used here interchangeably. Franco's forces objected more and more to the use by the press of the first two terms, and the last certainly became more common in the course of the war; but strictly speaking, under international law, a rebellion that is denied the status of belligerency—as this one was by France and Britain until almost the end—remains an insurrection. Again, while the moderate and the left-wing sections of the English-language press generally referred to the Azaña cause as 'Loyalist,' the same sections of the French press referred to it as 'government' or 'Republican,' and despite the right-wing's preference for 'Red,' it is 'Republican'—as the choice of the majority—that is the term used here.

With these reservations, the author has sought to give an airing to every single shade of political opinion. While he realizes the significance of extreme opinion, he has also weighed his selection on the scales of the thought's market, in terms of reader circulation. And since this selection cannot satisfy all, he takes comfort with Johnson, in the preface to his *Dictionary*, that when it shall be found that much has been omitted, let it not be forgotten that much likewise has been performed. If the selection, then, can be called impartial, the impartiality of the presentation is harder to defend. Here the author can only plead: *qui tacet consentire videtur*, for to reproduce an argument without comment is to imply that, in the recorder's opinion, that argument is well taken. It must be remembered also that editorials are often of an emotional character. In the French press of the time, they usually appeared in the first column of the front page and were in many cases the chief attraction. What those columns presented was a far cry from what K. W. Watkins presented in

Britain Divided. When Britain was divided over Spain, there were heated arguments whenever the sides met for tea and watercress sandwiches. France Divided was something else. This was a long-flowing, receding, resurging hatred between two women: Jeanne and Marianne, with half of France almost wishing the other half dead. Wherever the tone has been carried over into the present work, the author admits, not to prejudice, but only to sadness and some palpitations of the heart to think that the suffering here endured by Spain would very soon be visited on France.

D.W.P.
Paris, 30 October 2010

Acknowledgements

The author wishes to thank the following people for the kind help that he received over several decades:

Albertí i Gubern, Santiago: publisher and lexicographer, Barcelona.
Allain, Jean-Claude: Secrétaire-Général aux Publications de la Sorbonne, then Professeur á l'Universite de Paris.
Andrade, Juan: former leader of the POUM, Paris.
Arquer i Saltor, Jordi: writer and archivist, Perpignan.
Berch, Victor A.: director, Brandeis University Library.
Bertaux, Pierre: former Commissaire de la République ; former Director General, Sûreté Nationale, Sèvres.
Bertier de Sauvigny, Père Guillaume de: Professeur à l'Institut Catholique, Paris.
Bolloten, Burnett: historian, Stanford University.
Brademas, John: US Congressman (Dem. Indiana), later President, New York University.
Burdick, Charles: Professor at California State University at San José.
Carbonell, Olivier: Professeur à la Faculté des Lettres et Sciences Humaines, Université de Toulouse.
Cassou, Jean: author; director of National Museums, Paris.
Chessa, Aurelio: editor of *Volonta* (Genoa) and custodian of the Federazione Anarchica Italiana (Genoa).
Defourneaux, René: Professeur à la Faculté des Lettres et Sciences Humaines, Université de Toulouse.
Duroselle. Jean-Baptiste: Membre de l'Institut de France, Paris.
García Durán, Juan: Fondren Library, Rice University.
Godechot, Jacques: Doyen de la Faculté des Lettres et Sciences Humaines, Université de Toulouse.
Guérin, Daniel: anarchist author, Paris.
Guy, Alain: Professeur à la Faculté des Lettres et Sciences Humaines, Université de Toulouse.
Hilton, Ronald: Professor Emeritus, Stanford University, and President, World Association of International Studies..
Irujo, Manuel de: former Spanish Republican Minister of Justice, Paris.

Jong, Rudolf de: Internationaal Instituut voor Sociale Geschiedenis, Amsterdam.
Latapie, Daniel: archivist, Toulouse.
Leval, Gaston: anarchist author, Paris.
London, Arthur (with Lise): former Czech Deputy Foreign Minister ; author, Paris.
Michel, Henri: Directeur, *Revue d'histoire de la Deuxième Guerre mondiale,* Paris.
Mikhaïlov, Marie-Christine: Centre International de Recherches sur l'Anarchisme, Lausanne.
Miller, Persis: Unitarian Universalist Service Committee, Toulouse.
Moch, Jules: French former Minister of the Interior, Paris.
Montseny, Federica: anarchist author and activist, Toulouse.
Nicoletis, Colonel John: archivist, Bourg-la-Reine.
Planes, Jordi: director, CEHI/FIEHS, University of Barcelona.
Puig, Juan: archivist, Toulouse.
Renouvin, Pierre: Membre de l'Institut de France, Paris.
Riquelme, Doña Manuela Ruiz de: widow of General José Riquelme, Paris.
Rubio, Javier: historian, Paris ; Spanish Ambassador to Budapest.
Semprún, Jorge: author, Paris; Spanish Minister of Culture.
Sermet, Jean: author, Professor of Geography, Université de Toulouse.
Southworth, Herbert Rutledge: historian, Paris.
Steiner, Prof. Dr. H.: Dokumentationsarchiv des österreichischen Widerstandes, Vienna.
Tillon, Charles: former PCF député; author, Paris.
Valera, Fernando: Prime Minister, Spanish Republican Government in exile, Paris.
Wiesenthal, Simon: Director of the Dokumentationszentrum, Vienna.

Finally, my thanks go to the secretarial staff who assisted me in the production of the present work: Adriana Barillas-Batarse, Maria Mancuso, Irina Massovets, Dawn Osakue, and Paula Prince.

List of Illustrations

Plate section is after page 100.

A demonstration at the Mur des Fédérés (commemorating the 1871 Commune) in the Père Lachaise cemetery. Paris, 24 May 1936. *Roger Viollet.* Ref: 3352-16.
The leaders of the Front Populaire. Paris: Place de la Bastille, 14 July 1936. *LAPI/Roger Viollet.* Ref: 2377-3/ LAPI-12039.
Warning poster (to report any sighting of three Nationalist warships). Barcelona, 1937. *DWP Collection, courtesy of Giovanna Berneri, Genoa.*
'Le fascisme rouge.' Anarchist reaction to the May Days, Barcelona, 1937. *DWP Collection, courtesy of Giovanna Berneri, Genoa.*
Cardinal Pacelli, the Vatican Secretary of State and future Pius XII, signs the Livre d'Or. Paris: Arc de Triomphe, 14 July 1937. *Bibliothèque Nationale*
André Marty visits the International Brigades. Albacete, 1937. *Keystone.* Ref: 7241/33.
The Blum Cabinet. Paris, March 1938. *Keystone.* Ref: K3003644.
Reopening of the Chambre des Députés, 3 October 1938. *Bibliothèque Nationale.*
The British leaders visit Paris, 24 November 1938. *Bibliothèque Nationale.*
Spanish Republican refugees mass at the French frontier, January 1939. *Associated Press.*
Spanish Republicans cross the frontier, reopened on the night of 27-28 January 1939. *Associated Press.*
Franco's troops in triumph at the French frontier. February 1939. *DWP Collection, courtesy of Juan Puig, Toulouse.*
A scene at the frontier: wounded Republicans and a Senegalese guard. Le Perthus, February 1939. *DWP Collection, courtesy of Juan Puig, Toulouse.*
Crippled Republican children approach the French frontier. February 1939. *DWP Collection, courtesy of Juan Puig, Toulouse.*
A Spanish refugee family in distress, February 1939. *Roger Viollet.* Ref: RV 66.366.

List of Acronyms: Groups, Organisations, and Political Parties

AIT	Association Internationale des Travailleurs: Bakunist, adhering to the First International.
CASPE	Comité d'Action Socialiste pour l'Espagne.
CEDA	Confederación Española de Derechas Autónomas: conservative bloc grouped around Gil Robles.
CGT	Confédération Générale du Travail: Socialist labour union congress, incorporating the CGTU after the fusion of 1936.
CGTU	Confédération Générale du Travail Unitaire: Communist labour union.
CNT	Confederación Nacional del Trabajo: Anarchist labour union, adhering to the First International.
CSAR	Comité Secret d'Action Révolutionnaire: Cagoule (right-wing terrorist organisation).
FAI	Federación Anarquista Ibérica: Anarchist ideological society, adhering to the First International.
HISMA	Compañía Hispano-Marroquí de Transportes: Spanish trading company in association with the German Government.
IOS	Internationale Ouvrière Socialiste: adhering to the Second International.
JARE	Junta de Auxilio a los Republicanos Españoles.
LAPE	Líneas Aéreas Postales Españoles.
OJT	Office de Justification des Tirages.
OVRA	Organizzazione per la Vigilanza e la Repressione dell'Antifascismo.
POUM	Partido Obrero de Unificación Marxista: anti-Stalinist Marxist party, adhering to the Fourth International.
PPF	Parti Populaire Français: the party of Jacques Doriot.
PSF	Parti Social Français: the party of Colonel François de La Rocque.
PSOE	Partido Socialista Obrero Español: adhering to the Second International.
PSUC	Partido Socialista Unificado de Cataluña: the united Socialist-Communist party of Catalonia.
SDN	Société des Nations.
SERE	Servicio de de Evacuación de Refugiados Españoles.

List of Acronyms

SFIO   Section Française de l'Internationale Ouvrière: the French Socialist Party.
SIFNE   Servicio de Información de Fronteras del Norte de España: Franco organization.
SIM   Servicio de Investigación Militar: the Soviet secret police.
SIM   Servizio di Intelligenza Militare: Italian fascist organization.
UGT   Unión General de Trabajadores: Socialist labour union.
USR   Union Socialiste Républicaine.

Author's Remarks

1 Certain superscripts in the text are followed by an asterisk. This indicates that the corresponding endnote contains supplementary information and not merely the source references or cross references.
2 With reference to the value of the French franc in this period, its purchasing power in 1936 was roughly equal to 0.68 Euros in 2010, while a franc in 1939 was roughly equal to 0.44 in 2010.[1] As for the exchange rate, in July 1936 one pound sterling was worth 76 FF, and one US dollar was worth 15 FF. Following the devaluation of the franc in October 1936, the franc fell to 176 to the pound and 38 to the dollar.
3 Place names: The following place names only have been anglicized:
Andalucía—Andalusia
Cataluña/Catalunya—Catalonia
La Coruña—Corunna
Lyon—Lyons
Mallorca—Majorca
Marseille—Marseilles
Menorca—Minorca
München—Munich
Navarra—Navarre
Reims—Rheims
Sevilla—Seville
Zaragoza—Saragossa
Geographical locations of minor importance, including small towns, are identified in the Index by their *département* or province.
4 Journals: The term 'epigraph' is used in reference to the permanent motto appearing in each issue below the title of the journal. The term 'slogan' is used when referring to the message in the top right-hand corner of the front page for certain journals, which changes from issue to issue.

1. National Institute of Statistics and Economic Studies, 'Purchasing power of the euro and the French franc'. www.insee.fr

To
Jeanne Margrethe du Luart
and Carol Lynn Tjernell

Others helped. But none gave help like theirs.

Introduction

The Popular Fronts

The Second Spanish Republic between 1931 and 1936—Events in France between 1920 and 1936, and the confrontation between the extremes—The Soviet position—Spain's place in Europe—French foreign policy—Relations between Germany and Spain and between Italy and Spain—The triumph in France of the Front Populaire and its repercussions—The triumph in Spain of the Frente Popular and its aftermath—The Spanish military uprising and its semi-failure

The Second Spanish Republic was proclaimed on 12 April 1931, after impressive Republican victories in the municipal elections had induced King Alfonso XIII to "suspend deliberately the use of [his] Royal Prerogatives, until the nation speaks."[1*] During the next four and a half years the Republic passed through two Biennia, the first progressive, the second reactionary. Under the presidency of Alcalá Zamora, the liberal Republican-Socialist coalition of Azaña and Largo Caballero was replaced in 1933 by the Radical-right wing coalition of Lerroux; the four major measures introduced by Azaña to correct abuse (military reform, agrarian reform, separation of Church and State, and the statute of Catalan autonomy) were soon rescinded. On the last day of 1935 Cortes was again dissolved. In the ensuing elections of 16 February 1936, the Frente Popular won a resounding triumph.

The French experience during this time was comparable. In France there were constant changes of government between 1929 and 1936. At the Congress of Tours in 1920, the majority of the Socialist SFIO had voted to adhere to the Third International founded by Lenin in Moscow the previous year. This decision, reached largely though the efforts of Frossard who had led the SFIO's pacifist minority in World War I and became its secretary general in 1918, reflected the frustration felt by so many French Socialists at their own repeated failure and the triumph of Socialism in the Soviet Union. The result was the creation of the French Communist Party, under the leadership of Cachin and, from 1930, of Thorez, who kept it in total isolation from corrupting bourgeois influences until 1932. Meanwhile, the other Socialists elements grouped around Blum, Bracke, Longuet and Faure emerged from the schism of Tours in considerable dejection, until the elections of 1932 offered the forces of the Left the opportunity to coalesce in the Cartel des Gauches.

The result was the return to power of the Left. Financial crises (the delayed effect of the Depression) and the Stavisky scandal (in its importance akin to the *straperlo* scandal in Spain in 1935) touched off the riots in Paris of 6 February, which aimed at the very life of the Third Republic. These riots were promoted by such surgent Fascist groups as Maurras' Camelots du Roi, Taittinger's Jeunesses Patriotes, Bucard's brown-shirted Francistes, La Rocque's Croix de Feu, and Renaud's Solidarité Française, the last two financed by François Coty. This reactionary movement was defeated only by a 24-hour strike on 12 February, organized by the Socialist CGT and the Communist CGTU in unison. The subsequent pact on 27 July 1934, between the Communists and the Socialists, and their coalition with the Radicals at the Salle Bullier meeting in Paris on 18 January 1935, laid the foundation of the Front Populaire. A demonstration in Paris was called by the Comité Amsterdam-Pleyel for 14 July of that year, and the Radicals, heeding Daladier rather than Herriot, decided to participate. The meeting resulted in the formation of a Comité d'Organisation du Rassemblement Populaire, comprising SFIO Socialists, independent Socialists, Radicals and Communists, as well as the CGT, the CGTU, and four militant groups: the Comité Amsterdam-Pleyel, the Ligue des Droits de l'Homme, the Mouvement d'Action Combattante, and the Comité de Vigilance des Intellectuels Antifascistes. This last had been formed in Paris in March 1934 by the philosopher Alain and Professors Paul Rivet and Paul Langevin, with the purpose of unifying the forces of the Left. Control of the new Comité was entrusted to Victor Basch, president of the Ligue des Droits de l'Homme. The CGT and the CGTU now issued their first joint declaration on 24 July 1935, and the reunification of these two labour unions into the CGT was adopted by the Congress of Toulouse on 2–5 March 1936.

In the meantime, the Soviet Union was gaining a certain respectability. In 1933, the same year that the Soviet Union was finally recognized by the United States, the Soviet Union and the Spanish Republic exchanged de jure recognition[2*] and appointed ambassadors.[3*] In September 1934 the Soviet Union entered the League of Nations. On 2 May 1935, France and the Soviet Union signed a mutual assistance pact,[4*] and in August of the same year the Seventh World Congress of the Third International formally endorsed the Popular Front movements.[5*]

Much has been said of Spain's isolation from the mainstream of European affairs, of her historic immunity to change, from the Reformation to the Industrial Revolution. History has shown, however, the strategic importance of Spain to Europe, a fact not lost on Rome when Punic forces first crossed the Ebro. It has shown too that every major conflict in Spain has involved the European powers. At no time were foreign powers more involved in Spain economically than they were in 1936. Great Britain, France, Belgium, Canada, the United States and several others had substantial interests in the Peninsula. Though Germany's holdings were less important, she had a sizeable colony in Spain of some 16,000, of whom 6,000 were living in Barcelona. France, for her part, controlled the silver mines at Peñarroya (Córdoba)[6*] and the copper mines of San Plato (Huelva).[7*]

Overall French policy was to maintain her military hegemony in Europe by containing Germany within a ring of countries in alliance with France. French opposition to this policy expressed its disgust that France could be drawn into conflict in the event that Hitler's *Drang nach Osten* were released. Meanwhile, the two totalitarian powers which, in the first three months of the Spanish conflict, were to adopt the term Axis, had steadily been cultivating their relations with the right-wing elements in Spain. Alfonso XIII visited Vittorio Emmanuele III in Rome in 1923, allegedly introducing his attendant dictator, Primo de Rivera, as 'my Mussolini.' In March 1934 Mussolini pledged his support to the Spanish Monarchist leader Goicoechea in a conspiracy to restore the Spanish Monarchy by force. Again, the Duce's appetite for a new adventure was no doubt whetted, on the eve of the Civil War in Spain, by the League of Nations' decision of 15 July 1936 to rescind the sanctions imposed on Italy during the Abyssinian campaign.[8*] Relations with Germany had also prospered, if not officially. In defiance of the Treaty of Versailles, Admiral Canaris, chief of the Abwehr, arranged with the Echevarrieta shipyards in Cádiz for the construction of submarines to be delivered to Germany.[9] Canaris also organized the arms sales to the Carlist leaders, the regent Francisco Javier de Borbón-Parma and the lawyer Manuel Fal Conde.[10*] Sanjurjo and José Antonio Primo de Rivera visited Germany in February 1936 and reportedly received a promise of support for a military insurrection against the Spanish Republic, including air transports if needed for ferrying troops across the Straits of Gibraltar.[11*] A month later, on 7 March 1936, Germany threw down her first unequivocal challenge to the peace treaty and the democracies in her remilitarization of the Rhineland.

The victory of the Frente Popular in February 1936 was the prelude to the triumph of the Front Populaire in the general elections of 26 April–5 May 1936. The strikes and the seizure of the factories by the workers on and after 26 May was followed by Blum's formation of his first Cabinet on 4 June. This Cabinet was composed of Socialists and Radicals—who in 1936 re-elected Édouard Daladier as their leader—and was supported, on the outside, by the Communists. Subsequently, management and labour delegates met at the Hôtel Matignon, residence of the Premier, where their differences were settled in the Accords de Matignon.

Big business was never to forgive Léon Blum for his electoral victory and the demands (backed by strikes) that followed for collective bargaining, a 40-hour week, and paid vacations, all of which were adopted by the new

Parliament in its first month. Violence sponsored by reactionary elements increased. Blum himself had been the victim of an assault on 14 February. The result was the dissolution of the Ligue d'Action Française, the Fédération Nationale des Camelots du Roi, and the Fédération Nationale des Étudiants d'Action Française. Charles Maurras was charged on 16 February with inciting to murder. His *Action Française* and other journals of the Right attempted to laugh off the affair, publishing photographs of a bandaged Blum with captions that mocked the gravity of the assault. He was nevertheless sentenced on 22 March to a term of imprisonment,[12*] and in further measures taken on 18 April and 19 June all the Fascist leagues in France were declared dissolved.

Meanwhile, the Frente Popular was experiencing the same difficulties from widespread disorder. Two major differences obtained between the two Popular Fronts on their arrival in power. Azaña, unlike Blum, was given no time to prepare his government but had to form it almost immediately, on 20 February. Second, while the government of the Front Populaire included Socialists and had the outside backing of the formidable Parti Communiste, the government of the Frente Popular was composed entirely of Liberal Republicans, with no Socialist and with even less deference shown to the negligible Partido Comunista.[13] On 7 April, the same say that the Socialist UGT[14*] and the Anarcho-Syndicalist CNT formed a coalition, Alcalá Zamora was removed by the Socialist Prieto from the presidency of the Republic, a move that allowed Azaña to take his place on 10 May. The failure of both Prieto and the moderate Republican Martínez Barrio to form a Cabinet resulted in the formation on 13 May of a Cabinet under the moderate Republication Casares Quiroga. Casares proved powerless to end the wave of strikes that engulfed the cities of Spain from May onwards. The entire country was now a tinder-box. The spark it awaited came on 12 July, when Lieutenant José Castillo of the Republican Guardia de Asalto was murdered by right-wing elements. In reprisal the following day, a left-wing group assassinated the Alfonsist leader Calvo Sotelo. Four days later, on 17 July, General Franco raised the standard of revolt in Spanish Morocco. Garrisons rose against the government throughout Spain, but the insurrection failed in Madrid, Barcelona, Valencia, Bilbao and Málaga, which is to say in all the major cities except Seville, while some two-thirds of rural Spain also remained in Republican hands. So too did the Spanish Navy and Air Force. When Martínez Barrio failed to stave off war by forming a government of conciliation on 18 July, President Azaña the following day entrusted the survival of the Republic to the left-wing Republican José Giral. The failure of the rebellion in Madrid and Barcelona brought the masses into the street demanding arms, and after delaying as long as he dared Giral yielded to the pressure. Thus the military rebellion spawned the revolution, but against the one-third of Spain held by the Nationalists the Republicans lacked the organization and arms to drive home their huge superiority in numbers.

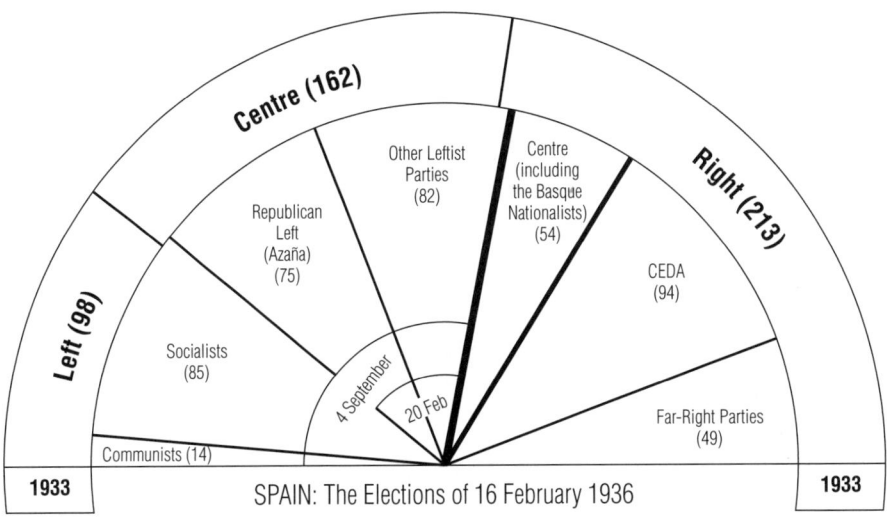

SPAIN: The Elections of 16 February 1936

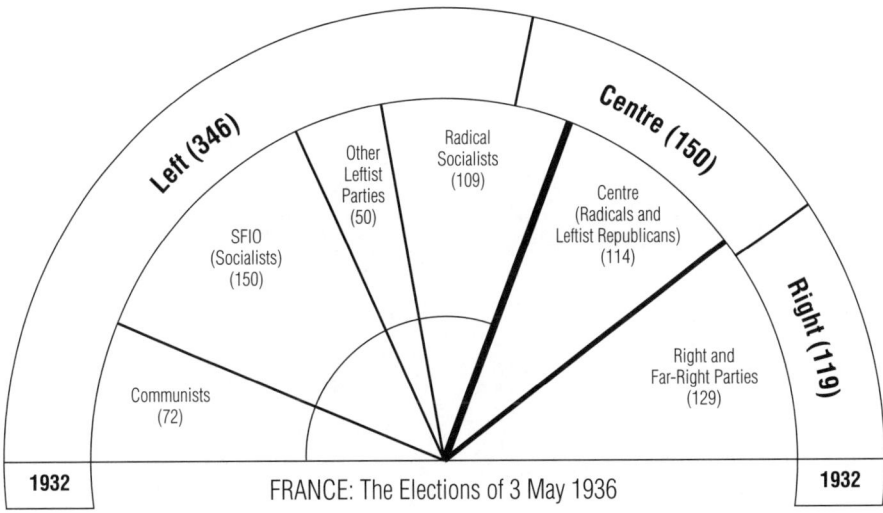

FRANCE: The Elections of 3 May 1936

The fluctuating alliances, both in Cortes and in the Chambre des Députés, gave rise to a vast number of combinations in the formation of blocs in the two Assemblies. The differences stem mainly from the alignments adopted by the centrist and independent Députés and Diputados.

In the case of Cortes, there were always a certain number of vacant seats, for various reasons, which explains why the total number of members (473) is not complete. Cortes, following the 1936 elections, was composed as follows: Frente Popular, 266; Centre, 54; Frente Nacional, 153. According to Jackson (**Spanish Republic**, 193), the Left had won 4,700,000 votes, the Right 3,997,000, the Centre 449,000, and the Basque Nationalists 130,000.

PART ONE

The Limits of Intervention

1
The Call to Arms

The message from Giral to Blum—Blum's first reaction—The modification in Blum's position, following his visit to London and the reaction of the Senate—First dispatch on 2 August of French arms—The French proposal of non-intervention in Spain—The other Powers reply—Blum suspends French aid on 8 August—The fall of the Giral government

On the evening of 19 July 1936, the French Socialist Premier, Léon Blum, leader of the Front Populaire, received a telegram from the Spanish left-wing Republican Premier, José Giral, leader of the Frente Popular. The message, transmitted *en clair*, read: 'Are surprised by dangerous military coup stop beg you to help us immediately with arms and planes stop fraternally yours Giral.' Blum called a meeting the following day with Édouard Daladier, Vice-Premier and Minister of National Defense, Yvon Delbos, Foreign Minister, and Pierre Cot, Air Minister. Blum at once showed himself to be fully in favour of complying with Giral's request and instructed Cot to proceed with the dispatch, in the shortest possible time, of a certain number of planes and artillery units.[1*] This decision, reached on 21 July, was not publicly announced. Two events arose to force Blum by 25 July to modify his attitude: his visit to London, and the reactions of the Senate and the right-wing press.

The visit to London, which took place on 23–24 July, had been planned long beforehand. It was not motivated by the crisis in Spain, but obviously this was a principal subject of discussion. Stanley Baldwin, the Conservative Prime Minister, and Anthony Eden, the Foreign Secretary, did not conceal their fears of the Frente Popular nor their strong disapproval of any French military aid to Madrid. Delbos, who already shared their feelings, was particularly impressed. Even Blum, whose foreign policy was pivoted upon a reconciliation with Britain after the estrangement of preceding years—without which reconciliation no *rapprochement* with the Soviet Union would be possible for him—was sensitive to, and affected by, the pressure exerted by the British leaders.

The French Senate, under the constitution of the Third Republic, held the right to overthrow the government, but it had nevertheless voted all the social legislation of the Front Populaire. It had done this quite against its wishes and its judgment, but its hand was forced by the gravity of the strike movements.

Its ill-temper would now be expressed in regard to the aid to Spain. It was not alone the general fear in the Senate of the Anarchist, Communist and Socialist masses now triumphant in Barcelona and Madrid that determined its attitude; it was also the new position taken by the strong moderate wing of the Radical Party. These moderates were influenced by their own former Minister, Louis Malvy. Malvy had lived in Madrid and frequented Masonic circles, and there he had formed a close friendship with Francisco Franco. 'I can assure you,' he would tell his fellow Radicals, 'that Franco is neither a Fascist nor a cleric but a republican general who simply wishes to put a stop to disorder and anarchy.'

Blum, an expert jurist, had scrutinized the Franco-Spanish treaty of 1935 and found a clause providing for the sale of war matériel to Spain, if indeed any special authorization were required for a sovereign state to export arms to the legitimate government of another state. By the end of the month too, the fact of Italian intervention had been established.[2*] The French Government's dossier was, in any event, in order, and Blum's first action deferred to Cot's desire for immediate intervention—if the sending of aid under such circumstances can be so termed—, and not to Delbos' counsel for a more cautious policy. The first shipment of aid to the Republic left on 2 August,[3*] without prejudice to two measures of double indemnity taken by Blum on the preceding and the following days: on 1 August the French Government first proposed that the principal Mediterranean powers (Great Britain, France and Italy) formally agree not to intervene in Spain;[4] and on 3 August, the French Ambassadors to Rome, Berlin, London and Moscow began to present the French plan for non-intervention.

In the week that followed, on 4 August the British Government agreed in principle to the French proposal, which was, after all, British in origin. On the same day, Germany's Foreign Minister von Neurath scoffed at the suggestion that Germany would intervene in the affairs of another state, but indicated that Germany would cooperate in a non-intervention agreement if all the interested powers, especially the Soviet Union, were to participate.[5*] The Soviet Union announced on 5 August her agreement on three conditions,[6] but even if her agreement had been unconditional it would still not have satisfied Neurath, who objected that the Comintern would not be bound by the official attitude of the Soviet Government.[7] On 6 August the Italian Government also agreed, but also on certain conditions.[8]

The French shipments of aid to the Republic from 2 August could not possibly have eluded the observations of the French right-wing press. It was at once a secret to no one. The British Conservative Government made its intentions plain, threatening on 4 August to free itself of its obligations toward France under the Treaty of Locarno unless France desisted from her current attitude. The threat brought an abrupt change to Blum's policy. From 8 August Blum officially suspended all export of war matériel to Spain, while attempting to persuade the other powers to do likewise or, in the more confident parlance of the day, 'while expecting the compliance of others.'

In an interview by *Le Nouvel Observateur* thirty years later, Cot expressed the view that the fear of war with Germany played little part in Blum's decision. German rearmament was still at an early stage, and Spain simply supplied the terrain for the new Wehrmacht's grand manoeuvres. While the situation for the French Army was far from easy, continued Cot, there were many officers, such as Lattre de Tassigny on Weygand's staff, who thought that Germany should not be allowed to install herself in Spain; and even Admiral Darlan had acted with loyalty when entrusted with an assignment to the British Admiralty.[9]* The dual opposition of the British Government and of the French Senate and right wing, concluded Cot, could not have been overcome by playing once again on popular pressure.

> But there was obviously a great risk to be taken. Léon Blum preferred to sail between the rocks. In retrospect, I think that his policy of non-intervention on condition of reciprocity was perfectly defensible. But it would have been necessary then to see what exactly the reciprocity was. It was not in August 1936 that the game was really lost. It was some months later, when Franco, having failed before Madrid, received massive supplies of aid from Italy and Germany which these powers would certainly have hesitated to provide if they had believed France capable of reacting with more vigour.[10]

In the fluctuations in Blum's policy during the first two weeks of the crisis, three separate phases can therefore be distinguished: the agreement on the part of Blum–Cot to supply Giral with war matériel, without the decision being implemented; the discovery of Italian aid and the actual dispatch of the French matériel; and the reversal of the Blum–Cot formula in favour of the Blum–Delbos–Daladier formula. It must be remembered, however, that neither the French public nor the press was fully informed of all these events and that the press consequently adhered to its respective preconceived opinions. The Cabinet and the pro-Blum press, therefore, chose to present the government's policy as constant and faithful to the principle of non-intervention.

The failure of Giral to secure aid from France, though he had little enough to say in the decision, was to cost him the presidency on 4 September. It was also to cost the Republic the war, unless the democracies could show in the ensuing months, by refusing to allow the violation of the non-intervention agreement on the part of the Fascist states, that what they sought in Spain was peace and not appeasement. Meanwhile, Giral's remark, on hearing of the French decision to ban shipments of arms to Spain, had the gift of prophecy: 'By forcing the hand of Paris, [London has] committed more than a crime, they have committed an enormous ineptitude for which sooner or later they will have to pay.'[11]

2
The Revolt of the Generals

The slogans of the adversaries: 'Order and patriotism' against 'Liberty and justice'—The first reactions of the French press on left and right—The question of legitimacy—The conflict expands

When news of the military insurrection first reached France on 18 July 1936,[1]* the two wings of the French press seized at once upon the events as a vehicle of doctrine. Their cries were the cries of the belligerents: 'democracy and the people against tyranny'; 'order and fatherland against anarchy.' Setbacks and defeats were ignored by both, when they were not presented as victories. Restraint held no appeal: the Right instantly claimed a successful *pronunciamiento*, the Left its speedy suppression; they were, in fact, merely repeating the claims of Nationalist and Republican headquarters.

Within a few days, however, it was obvious to both that the affair was no longer a coup d'état but a full-scale civil war. The leftist press bitterly regretted the laxity through which the Spanish Government had allowed the generals to manoeuvre. In *La Dépêche*, J. Félicien Court recalled that the leaders of the revolt had sworn on the colours of Spain an oath of loyalty to the Republic.[2] The Socialist press wrote in its legend: 'Once again the people have shown themselves to be too indulgent, this time the Spanish people that won the elections. Ah! if only they had tightened the screws on some generals and advanced thinkers.'[3] Similarly, *L'Humanité* deplored the failure of Azaña to 'cauterize the disease of Fascism.'[4] In *Le Peuple*, the Italian Socialist Pietro Nenni declared: 'It was the *liberal* revolution which caused the treason of the army.'[5] But in *Le Midi Socialiste*, André Leroux drew a parallel with the French Revolution and the threat to the young Republic from the treachery of the officer corps, and looked for the same result, no compromise being possible.[6]

To the right-wing press, the uprising never was a mere *pronunciamiento* but a national movement of revolt against a régime controlled by Moscow. It was a revolt of 'aversion,' wrote *La Journée Industrielle*, rather than a revolt of 'cause,' by a composite group knowing better what it was fighting against than what it was fighting for.[7] In *La Victoire*, Gustave Hervé described the rising in cavalier terms: 'Confronted with this rabble, this base anarchy, and in accordance with the Spanish tradition, the army rose to try to save the dying country; and for some days now we have witnessed one of the most beautiful wars that Spain ever had.'[8] For French Ambassador Count Saint-Aulaire, the victories of Franco represented the triumph of 'mind' over 'matter,' of 'idealism' over 'the basest instincts,' of 'intellect, heart, intelligence, faith and creative love' over 'destructive hate.'[9] By saving Spain from Bolshevik anarchy, wrote Guèze in *L'Express du Midi*, the generals were serving not only Spain but her neighbours too.[10] In *La Revue Hebdomadaire*, Le Grix explained to his readers that a Soviet victory in Spain would result in communism in Paris, while the triumph of Franco could bring 'the hour of French regeneration.'[11] Such was the burden of Franco's statement in Tetuán, made on the eve of receiving German and Italian aid, to the correspondents of the London *News Chronicle* and widely reproduced in the French press:

> The Spanish Civil War is becoming one of the forms of the great world struggle between the forces of disintegration and anarchist tyranny on the one hand, and those of order, freedom and discipline on the other.[12]

> Europe must see that Spain cannot become a second Communist state in Europe, making use of her strategic position to spread Red propaganda in Morocco, Algeria, Tunisia, and even in America. The major powers must understand that, France must understand it.[13]

Two days later Franco declared to the Reuter Agency: 'We would have taken Madrid already if it had not been for the lack of patriotism of the Marxist government in fomenting anarchy in every province where its influence was strongest, in arming the unruly masses and in spurring them on to unbridled revolution.'[14] The *pronunciamiento* was thus presented as a contest with certain ground-rules: the struggle was strictly between the government and the army; the army could accept volunteers, but the government was required to fight with only those forces it had immediately available. Another officer at Nationalist headquarters was interviewed by Rieu-Vernet of *La Dépêche*:

> Lenin declared that Spain would be the second country to install a Soviet. Our preventive revolution has no other purpose than to prevent the execution of the prophecy. In so doing, we believe that we are performing an invaluable service to all the democracies.[15]

The moderate press proceeded to refute the propaganda of both extremes. *Le Petit Journal* replied to the 'revolt of aversion' theory of *La Journée Industrielle* by terming it 'not even a revolt of opinion but a mere pretorian revolt' and finding a parallel in the events in Danzig on the same day:

> The two events are without direct relation, but both reflect the *mal d'époque*.

The young Spanish democracy had found its Vendée in Andalusia. It remains to be seen if it can produce both an Hoche to bear a trusty lance and a centralized authority to ensure the public safety.[16]

The Catholic *L'Aube*, too, expressed its preference for the system of universal suffrage, 'a system so derided in these times,' over the so-called modern methods to 'reawaken' the nations.[17]

The question of legitimacy was central to the argument. Months later, when Franco had expanded his conquest, writers such as Henri Rochefer in *L'Express du Midi* referred to the Caudillo's 'visionary powers' which had won him election by his peers. This, explained Rochefer, and not the suffrage of the ignorant, was truly the test of legitimate election.[18]

There were other points of view. Fernando de los Ríos, acting Ambassador to Paris, based his appeal to France on the score that 'there is only one legitimate government of Spain, and that government is backed by the nation's will, expressed in the ballot boxes.'[19] Yvon Delbos also referred to the 'legitimate government of Madrid.'[20] The occupation of a given territory was irrelevant to the question of legitimacy, as *Le Petit Journal* pointed out.[21] The more plausible argument was that of the right to revolt, invoking the doctrines of apologists from Plato to Lincoln.[22] A theory submitted to the League of Nations by Armindo Monteiro, the Portuguese Foreign Minister, suggested that 'if the tradition, the culture, the strength, the desire for order and justice, the aspirations to unity and grandeur, in a word *the wealth* of a given country, rise up against a government, that government is no longer legitimate.'[23]*

The Spanish delegation to the League included Eduardo Ortega y Gasset (the brother of José) and Angel Ossorio y Gallardo. The latter, a Catholic and an eminent jurist, proceeded to pulverize Monteiro's theory. In order to establish, declared Ossorio, that the forces representing tradition and the rest have the right to revolt against a government which claims to represent the will of the people, it is necessary first to define those forces, to specify where they lie and how they can be identified, for quite obviously each individual can define them as he sees fit:

> We arrived by elimination at the only conclusion acceptable in law and in conscience. Legitimate power lies in him who is elected in accordance with the laws of the people . . . For us, Spanish Republicans, a government is legitimate if it has fulfilled its duty under the constitution of presenting itself before Cortes and obtaining its confidence . . .
>
> Here is a simpler definition: the Spanish Government and the Cortes supporting it have emerged from elections which they contested with the parties holding the majority in the last Cortes . . . The elections were held in

conditions of sufficient liberty to allow the majority the right to affirm that it represents the will of the people . . .

Once a people accepts as a principle of legitimacy the sovereignty of the people, once it acknowledges that the only legitimate source of authority is invested in the representatives of the people, then it can no longer escape the consequences; legitimate government is that which obtains the support of the majority of the people in elections that are sufficiently free and fair.

All the inevitable objections, concluded Ferrero in his résumé of Ossorio's address to the League, would be fewer than the objections to the illegitimate government or the usurper. A legitimate government can rectify its faults and improve itself to a certain degree, but an illegitimate government, unable to maintain itself except by terror, graft, and an appeal to the mystical, is doomed to grow ever worse.[24]

When, then, is a rebellion legitimate? Thomas Aquinas listed four justifying circumstances,[25] worthy of study by Christian Crusaders. Georges Scelle in *La Dépêche* condensed them into one, calling the act of rebellion legitimate only in the case of an oppressed people who, having no other constitutional means of making its voice heard, finds itself compelled to resort to force.[26] It remained for such overnight experts in constitutional law as old General Cabanellas to show that the oppressed nation that was Spain had no recourse except to force.[27]

It was becoming more evident each day that for lack of mobility neither side could force the issue. All the while, inside the two zones the deepening hatreds and the will to win were expressed in the 'mopping-up' of the respective opposition. The Nationalists were far more successful in concealing their operations. Much was made in the right-wing press of the enthusiasm shown for the Army by the people in the Nationalist zone. *L'Intransigeant* published Franco's claim to the sympathies of the Moroccans,[28] a claim strongly denied by the Socialist press, which insisted that the colonial troops were incited only by terror and the promise of rapine in 'White' Spain.[29] The use of Moorish levies against the national government reminded Socialists of 'the ancestors of the French Fascists invading their country with the help of the Prussian and Austrian armies.'[30] Senator and former Minister Aimé Berthod expressed a similar disgust in *La Dépêche*: 'I can find nothing to attenuate the hideous crime committed by the rebels in arming foreign mercenaries against their compatriots.'[31]

Again in *La Dépêche*, Rieu-Vernet observed that the struggle would be the more desperate since one half of Spain was pitted against the other in equal force,[32]* resulting in a 'long, atrocious and inhuman war.'[33] Four days, later, *La Dépêche* was writing of the war almost in retrospect, predicting the imminent victory of the Republicans 'at the end of one of the bloodiest civil wars in modern times.'[34] Such optimism was shared by the Socialist press, which was confident that the critical period had now passed.[35] 'A rebellion still unsuccessful at the end of ten days,' it wrote, 'has lost the game.'[36] The same press, however, reported a disquieting remark by Indalecio Prieto:

> If the struggle continues another month, the consequences will be grave indeed. If all is not over in two months, we have at present no yardstick to measure what the political and economic life of Spain will then be.[37]

The Catholic *L'Aube* also feared the effect of the conflict not only on Spain's material wealth and economic progress but also on her artistic heritage and even more so on her moral unity.[38] In the Radical press, both *L'Ordre* and *Le Quotidien* pointed to the dangers immanent in the victory of either extreme: if the rebellion succeeded, the repression would be beyond description, faced as it would be by the entire working class and a general strike; if, on the other hand, the rebellion failed, all counterweight to the extreme Left would be eliminated and the result would be a dictatorship of the proletariat, in liaison with Moscow or not.[39]

It can therefore be said that the conflict in Spain went through three essential phases: a coup d'état, thwarted in 48 hours; a purely civil war, ground into stalemate in ten days; and finally, with both sides forced by their immobility to seek supplies from abroad, a war of international ideology, aided and abetted by outside nations. Without foreign aid, the probability is that the rebel movement would have remained at the point it was, neither able to advance nor needing to retreat.[40*] Spain would thus have been partitioned, until eventually the mobilization of Republican industry, the introduction of an entire new officer corps and the Republic's huge superiority in numbers would have turned the scales in favour of the government.

It can safely be assumed that the leaders of the revolt envisaged no more than a coup d'état. The second step, that of civil war, would be taken reluctantly, but it would be taken. So too, when this failed, would the third step. The offer of German and Italian aid had been received. Now, since there was no alternative, it would be accepted.[41*] The Socialist press attached the greatest seriousness to Franco's remark, during his interview by the *News Chronicle*, that to achieve his goal he was prepared to sacrifice half the people of Spain, and that if he failed in his enterprise he would be 'tempted to provoke an international incident of the utmost gravity.'[42*]

3
The Appeal of Giral

Blum's initial promise of support—Opposition from the Right, the Radicals, and the British Government—The Cot formula suspended—Suspicions, accusations, denials—The legality polemic—The arguments of the Right: the Spanish Government of tomorrow, and a new defence line—Refutations from the Left—The fear of escalation—German–Italian preparations and financial aid

The possibility that the conflict could develop into a general war had been appreciated from the outset, and the danger was growing from day to day. Those foreign powers with investments in Spain[1] already viewed the possible consequences with grave concern. A Nationalist communiqué on July 20 announced that 'the interests of Spain are not alone at stake as our trumpet call sounds across the Straits of Gibraltar.' It was apparent, at least to *Les Echos*, that the situation was already more than a domestic conflict.[2] In *Candide*, Jean Vertex stated the opinion that, while Germany was thinking about the Canaries, Britain was thinking about Ceuta, and Portugal, Britain's oldest ally, might be nursing the thought of taking over the administration of Spanish Morocco, by arrangement with Britain.[3] Within a week warships had been dispatched to Spanish waters by France, Italy, Britain and the United States. 'Capital investments are at stake,' explained *Les Echos*, 'and neither London nor New York is prepared to watch them go down the drain.'[4]

Although Blum decided, on 21 July, to heed Pierre Cot and respond to Giral's appeal for aid, he allegedly stated in London, even at the time of his *arrival* on July 23, that he did not dare supply this aid openly. Whether the aid was supplied overtly or covertly, however, was not the issue in Paris, but whether it was supplied at all. During the Premier's absence from the capital, the Spanish Military Attaché, Antonio Barroso, had leaked the story to Henri de Kérillis of *L'Écho de Paris* that Blum had decided to aid the Republic, and Kérillis splashed the news across his edition of 24 July. The report caused widespread consternation. Raymond Cartier in the same newspaper, and Maurice Pujo in *L'Action Française*, added their denunciations. Blum's Radical Ministers announced immediately that they would not endorse any such undertaking without the assurance that France was supported by Britain, at the same time that Blum, in London, was receiving the very opposite assurance. On his return to Paris, Blum was forced to make certain modifications[5] to his plan, but on 25 July all was ready for the immediate shipment of aircraft and other matériel. In the meantime, however, difficulties arose at the Spanish Embassy.

After he had delivered the order of aid on behalf of the Giral government,[6] the Spanish Ambassador to Paris, Juan Cárdenas, submitted his resignation in accordance with his Nationalist sympathies. On the following day, Fernando de los Ríos, the former Minister and representative at the League of Nations, arrived in Paris in the capacity of acting ambassador. De los Ríos held no official position, however, until he could submit his credentials to the French President. For this reason he had to ask the Chargé d'Affaires in Paris, Cristóbal del Castillo, to sign the necessary papers and the check covering payment to the French Government for the first four planes due to leave Madrid that same day. Del Castillo refused and resigned from his position. So too did Barroso. Both ex-officials now recounted everything to the press. The result, in the Paris evening press of 25 July, was pandemonium.

The outcry was sustained in the press the following morning. The Spanish request, it was reported, was not merely for planes, weapons and ammunition; Giral was also asking France to supply the Republic's fleet and to grant Madrid the use of French air bases in Morocco.[7] *L'Echo de Paris* in particular published sensational articles on the 'arms traffic,' while *L'Express du Midi* printed a statement by Del Castillo: 'If I leave my post, it is because my conscience forbids me to collaborate in the dispatch of arms intended to kill my unfortunate compatriots.' According to *L'Express*, de los Ríos, in order to get the check signed, had next called on Cruz Marín, whom Madrid had just appointed as its diplomatic agent in Paris, his signature was worthless and the check remained unsigned.[8*]

Into this raging polemic now stepped the influential figure of François Mauriac, whose Catholicism was not untainted by anti-Semitism. His first pronouncement on the war was hastily dictated by telephone from Vichy to a correspondent of *Le Figaro*. The article, entitled 'The International of Hatred,' referred to 'a France governed not by statesmen but by gangsters' and to the 'secular rancour gnawing at the entrails of partisan Blum, . . . burning with the desire to intervene.' Mauriac concluded with a threat to the Premier: 'Take care. We shall never forgive you for this crime.'[9] If Mauriac soon had second thoughts, *Le Figaro* did not. Editor Wladimir d'Ormesson stressed that the Republic had imbrued its hands in blood, inciting the mobs to violence and then finding itself powerless to control them. 'But that,' added d'Ormesson, 'is the internal drama of Spain. It affects us. It grieves us. We can all draw whatever conclusions we believe true. But it does not concern us.'[10] Later he added: 'We want neither a crusade nor a stratagem. We demand caution and reason,'[11] by which he meant absolute neutrality.[12]

Meanwhile in the Palais-Bourbon, the presidents of the two Chambers, both of them Radicals, had confirmed the attitude of their party in consultations with Blum. 'Above all, dear boy,' Herriot told him, 'Just don't go poking your nose into this.' Without the support of the Radicals, the Front Populaire was doomed.

So it was that after the Cabinet meeting of July 25 a communiqué was issued to the effect that France would not execute any delivery of war matériel to Spain, either directly or indirectly. Under the latter clause, the government '[would] not authorize' the supply of arms by French private industry, 'as it [was] entitled to do.' The ban applied to reconnaissance planes as well as combat aircraft but excluded commercial aircraft designed for passenger or freight transport. *La Dépêche* quoted *députés* 'usually well informed on government opinion' who gave their assurances that the French government was unanimous in its intention to adhere to its traditional policy of non-intervention in the internal affairs of foreign nations. But another statement made by a government spokesman after the Cabinet meeting reflected the apparent intention of the government to leave itself a loophole: 'It is false that the French Government is resolved to practise a policy of intervention.'[13] Under this open-door policy, the government, once 'resolved,' could reverse its policy without contradicting itself.

Certainly the communiqué gave cause for argument. The government had reserved the right to authorize the dispatch of non-military aircraft by the private sector. Since the French arms industries had been nationalized, the approval of the Cabinet was therefore required not only for the export of this matériel but also for its purchase. The 'strict export regulations' consisted of the requirement of two export licenses, one from the Air Ministry and the other from the Foreign Ministry. Since Cot's Ministry would presumably find no objection to an application, great importance attached to whether or not Delbos was prepared to allow the private sector to do what he discouraged the government from doing. In any event, the Foreign Ministry was authorized to act at its discretion, on the recommendation of the technical departments concerned. The distinction between government and the private sector was thus being preserved on a purely academic plane. Such ambiguities, and such clauses as 'without prior consultation,' led even *La Dépêche* to remark that the communiqué was far from a categorical denial of all possible arms for trafficking.[14] In *L'Express du Midi*, Guèze saw in the statement the ulterior purpose of the government to make use of every camouflage.[15] In *Le Journal de Toulouse*, Arnaud-Bernard affirmed that private industries had already dispatched artillery and bombs to Spain by roundabout routes.[16] Another report referred to a munitions train en route for Spain. Although the communiqué made no mention of this, *La Dépêche* published a categorical denial of this report by government officials.[17] In point of fact, Blum could justly deny the dispatch of arms until 2 August.

The communiqué of 25 July asserted the government's right to permit the arms traffic.[18]* The Spanish Government was a regular legal government. If it wished to buy arms from France, and if the French Government and French industrialists wished to sell them to it, the entire matter was above reproach. *La Dépêche* quoted the opinion of the jurist Gaston Jèze:

> From the point of view of international law, no objection can be made to the supply by France of arms to the Spanish Government. Has the government been regularly constituted? Yes. Have we recognized it? Yes. Does any other European state have any rights to impose on Spain? No. In that case, it is a simple matter between two neighbour governments, a matter which is nobody's business but theirs. Only if France were to provide arms to the rebels would she be acting in violation of international law. This much is clear and simple logic.[19]

The liberal *Manchester Guardian*, in an article widely reproduced, agreed that the supply of arms to a legally constituted government could not be termed interference in the internal affairs of another state. It nevertheless discouraged such action on another count:

> The situation in Spain at this time constitutes a special problem. In principle, it is a civil war waged between the legal government and a rebel army. However, there exists on both sides of the barricade considerable forces which submit to no control. We are therefore free to wonder whether arms dispatched to the Spanish Government would fall into the hands of extremists who, through fighting the insurgents, show no obedience to the central authority . . . In conclusion, it would be preferable to see the minimum amount possible of arms in Spain, and it would be equally desirable to avoid all international complications.[20]

At the end of July, Yvon Delbos, the reluctant Radical in this matter of arms, expressed the same opinion:

> The government might have [provided arms to the Spanish Government] since it constituted a regular government. It has not done so for reasons of doctrine and humanity, and also in order not to provide a pretext for those eager to send aid to the rebels.[21]

At the moment that the Foreign Minister expressed this sentiment, Italian warplanes were on their way to Morocco.

Whatever may have been the modification of Blum's policy on 25 July, the revision won no acclaim in the right-wing press, whose pressure campaign against any form of French involvement[22]* showed no sign of abating. This campaign was led, in the influence they commanded or in the intensity with which they fought, by *L'Action Française, L'Echo de Paris, L'Ere Nouvelle, Le Figaro, Le Jour, Le Journal, La Journée Industrielle, Le Matin, L'Ordre, La République, Le Temps* and *La Victoire*. It was in vain that Blum appealed to this press in the name of national interests. It was in vain that he exhorted France to sustain a government in Spain which would facilitate, in the event of war, communications by sea with French North Africa. His true motive, suggested *Le Figaro*, was to supply the Frente Popular with arms.[23] *La République* expressed the fears of the Radicals in its belief that Blum would sustain the Frente Popular even if it were the insurgent.[24] Its editor Dominique saw in the very equilibrium of the two Spains a danger of accelerating the collision between France, the Soviet Union, and the Spanish Republic, on the one hand, and Germany, Italy, and the Spanish rebels on the other.[25] In mid-August, Dominique still opposed all export of arms to either Spain;[26] in October, it was the same cry: 'Not a man, not a machine, not a centime.'[27] Nor was any distinction made between aid provided by the government and aid supplied by the private sector. In fact, it was suggested that the government had forfeited its freedom of action. In *Le Journal*, Anatole de Monzie insisted that the government could not do what it instructed private citizens to do on their own behalf. 'We are going to think of the Rhine rather than the Ebro,' he added, 'of Vienna rather than Madrid.'[28] In *La Tribune des Nations*, Monzie denounced the attitude of those who hitherto had preferred civil war to foreign war and were now quite ready to unleash international war in the interests of a civil war.[29]

One of the favourite arguments of this press campaign was that artfully expressed by *L'Action Française*:

> The French people forbid the Blum government to supply [this aid to Madrid]. Not because the Spanish insurgents are 'Fascists,' but because the Spanish insurgents, if they are victorious, will be the Spanish Government of tomorrow.
>
> Through the fault of the Front Populaire, we have lost the friendship of Italy. That is enough. Let us not make an enemy of Spain.[30]

L'Express du Midi followed suit. Gaston Guèze conceded, disingenuously, that a government owes its neighbour loyalty and may extend it its sympathy; nevertheless, insisted Guèze, it must reserve the same loyalty, if not the same sympathy, for the régime which circumstances may put in its stead.[31]* In *Le Petit Bleu*, G. de Marcilly took a wide route to the same conclusion. Earlier he had suggested that the events in Spain presented an opportunity of special appeal to the French people, the opportunity for moral commitment. Since there were only two countries in the world governed by Popular Front, it was natural for a sister republic to observe these events 'with real, if sober, interest.'[32] Within days Marcilly was writing of 'this despicable affair for supplying arms to a party in a foreign land which is in danger of being swept out of power by a friendly party which would then take power itself.'[33] In *L'Oeuvre*, Léon Archimbaud maintained that third-party States had to honour their commitments to the regular government, without waiting for the end of hostilities. The attempt of *L'Oeuvre* to present French aid to Madrid as legitimate was assailed by *L'Express*, which termed it an 'inadmissible transaction, creating a dangerous precedent and showing the hand of the Freemasonary which binds the two governments of Popular Front'[34*] In the same paper, Roger Parant added in mid-August that it was impossible to predict the final result of the conflict and that, if France were to support either one of the belligerents, she would take on the appearance of an enemy in the eyes of the other which might then take power in Madrid.[35] Radical journals (other than *L'Oeuvre*) and even one Socialist shared this sentiment. *L'Ere Nouvelle* reflected the concern of the Radicals appealing for caution and circumspection: 'Let us take care not to embark on any adventure which could turn out badly.'[36] Even in *Marianne*, Emmanuel Berl considered the 'only certainty' to be the ultimate reconciliation of all Spaniards, who would then feel the more xenophobic the more foreigners had contributed to their war of fratricide.[37] D'Ormesson in *Le Figaro*, and Dominique, in *La République*, put forward the same argument.[38*] The former remarked that on the day of their recovery, all Spaniards, whichever side they had taken, would ask themselves why the *Deutschland* showed so much zeal that day at Ceuta;[39] and he reminded his readers that between Spaniards and Italians there had always been a relentless rivalry in the Mediterranean.[40] Dominique, for his part, reminded his readers, and Germany, that the rebel generals were attempting a revolution which they themselves called 'national' and that these insurgents would agree with Giral himself in their desire that the Spain of the future remain the Spain of today, entire and intact, with the Balearics and Morocco, and ceding not one village or islet; and the rebels 'would resent, as a national insult, one round of gunfire aimed by foreigners at a Spanish town.'[41] Finally, *Le Matin* argued for neutrality for the opposite reason to Berle. For the conservative daily, it was very probable that if the rebels won, it would not be long before they fell to fighting among themselves, while if the Loyalists won, such a sequel would be even more likely.[42*] 'That is why,' concluded *Le Matin*, 'France must on no account interfere in a civil war which is none of our business.'[43*]

Another argument centered upon the possibility of a new line of defence for France. In *L'Action Française*, Léon Daudet expressed his concern that in the event of hostilities France would have to defend the Pyrenees frontier, to the prejudice of the defence of her frontier to the east.[44] This consideration troubled also Pierre Bernus of *Le Journal des Débats*. If the government were so foolish as to carry out its project of supplying arms, wrote Bernus, Spain could one day show her resentment at such unwarranted interference in her affairs by confronting France along a frontier long undefended.[45] In *L'Express du Midi*, Guèze was equally concerned lest 'a Fascist Spain, aligned against France through the fault of Blum, should force France to keep watch on a new frontier.'[46] In *L'Indépendant de Paris*, Henry Lémery observed that Germany had always exerted considerable influence in Spain and the insurgents looked to her. If they won, they would establish a régime to the southwest of France in close liaison with the régime to the northeast. If they lost, they would still retain power over the whole of Spanish Morocco; they would proclaim its autonomy and place it under the protection of Germany.[47] *Le Petit Journal* also warned against the establishment in the southwestern frontier of a Italo-German dominion, where the two Fascist states would begin by exerting their influence until they had set up their headquarters and their military bases.[48] These fears were to be confirmed in November, when Jaume Miravitlles, a councillor in the Catalan Generalitat, was interviewed by Armand Salvan of *La Dépêche*. According to Miravitlles, a document in German which had just come to light described a future system of fortifications along the Pyrenees.[49]

The anxiety of the Left was not the less profound for being more subdued. Against the surging chorus of hostility to the attitude of Blum, the press of the Left presented a feckless and divided front. In regard to the possibility of a new frontier to defend, Péri in *L'Humanité* expressed the same reservations as the Right: 'It is not a matter of unconcern to us that France may have a frontier to defend tomorrow on the Southwest.'[50] The Socialist press published old pacifist dicta of Léon Blum: '*Esprit de guerre* is not to be overcome by developing *esprit de guerre*';[51] 'everything that contributes to intensifying and impassioning national feeling, to investing it with suspicion and animosity contributes thereby to creating the environment in which Fascism can thrive.'[52] Setting its course by such doctrine, the press of the SFIO shunned the slippery slope: 'We refuse to be contaminated by the virus of the Tricolore or slumber in the hope of national reconciliation when the guns of Spain show it as nothing but a dream.'[53]

Thus the reaction of the press of the Left during these days of waiting was cautious and defensive. It spoke most clearly when it rebuked the Right for its hypocrisy. Paul Faure, Minister of State and secretary general of the SFIO, protested in *Le Populaire* against the servile flattery shown by the French Fascists toward the Spanish rebels:

> You would imagine, perhaps, that our defenders in France of law and order would shudder and protest. Not a bit . . . The felon officers and the generals in revolt take on the appearance in their eyes of servants of order.[54]

To the cry of 'An end to the spirit of Coblenz,' Faure warned that if the rebels won the day, an anti-French government would rule Spain.[55] On behalf of the CGT, Jouhaux berated as anti-French any demand for a neutrality which aimed at rewarding Spanish Fascism. 'The idea of the national interest,' he wrote in *Le Peuple*, 'is completely lost on those engaged in this campaign.'[56] The Radical Socialist and Radical press shared these sentiments. *La Dépêche* asked if the events in Spain did not serve as a pretext or an opportunity for political campaigns inside France, more precisely for campaigns of political revenge.[57] *L'Oeuvre*, after incurring the wrath of the Socialist press by reporting that the French leaders were resigned to the victory in Spain of a 'military dictatorship, more or less Republican,'[58] now regained favour with the Front Populaire. *L'Oeuvre* pointed out the irony of seeing the French right wing grandly proclaim the principle of absolute neutrality and of non-intervention in the internal affairs of another country, when their own organs were the least qualified to speak on such an issue.[59] For *L'Oeuvre* also, the defeat of Madrid would be a defeat not only for French Republicans but for the entire French people.[60]

The fear of possibly having one more frontier to defend was not, however, the main cause for reservation for the majority of the French press. The main cause was quite simply the fear of escalation. Before the second week of the war was out, nobody was any longer in doubt that the events for which Spain provided the theatre were part of a larger conflict waged by the 'dissatisfied' powers, Germany and Italy. 'Beware the fearful conflict which would result,' wrote *L'Aube*, 'the day when a Fascist holy alliance and an anti-Fascist holy alliance confront each other, over a single country or over the entire continent. Beware, for the two sides are near to being formed.'[61]

The right-wing press continued to do its best to discourage all intervention. For *L'Echo de Paris*, French intervention would have the effect of provoking the intervention of other countries, transforming Spain into a tiltyard where the two Internationals seeking to divide up Europe would be locked in mortal combat.[62] This would be the beginning of the European conflagration so desired by Moscow, wrote Pierre Gaxotte in *Candide*: 'The Soviets are doomed to perish, hanged in the Nippo-German noose, unless they can provoke, and very quickly, a war in the West that would free their frontiers and submerge Europe into bloody chaos.'[63] If the French Government, argued Guèze in *L'Express du Midi*, aided the Azaña régime, there was no reason why Hitler and Mussolini should not supply arms to the rebels: 'If the conflict is to be internationalized and turned into a struggle between the democracies and Fascism, that is the logical result.'[64] In *L'Action Française*, Léon Daudet also pointed out that Blum, by 'violating neutrality,' was giving Germany and Italy the pretext to do the same in favour of the Spanish Nationalists, 'regarded today as rebels, but who could well be the government of tomorrow.'[65]

The danger of counter-intervention was of equal concern to the moderate and centrist press. In the opinion of *La Dépêche*, Germany and Italy were eager to find the smallest pretext to supply the rebels with arms, 'contrary as that is to *jus gentium*'.[66] The *Manchester Guardian* made the similar observation that if the democracies sold arms to one party, other nations, namely Germany and Italy, could send arms to the other.[67]

While the entire press was discussing the morality of supplying the Spanish Government with French arms, the Fascist régimes were hastily preparing to arm the rebels, at the same time that they were issuing categorical denials. The French press for one began to express its suspicions from 21 July. Even the conservative *Le Journal* announced that plans had been drawn up 'several weeks' earlier. On 21 July the decision was allegedly taken to run the risk of action at once. 'Non-Spanish' pilots took off for Madrid with a staggering consignment of 500 million francs, presumably intended to reward a successful insurrection in the capital. Despite the failure of the uprising in Madrid, the pilots, according to *Le Journal*, accomplished their mission.[68] In *L'Humanité*, Marcel Cachin predictably demanded to know the identity of this 'non-Spanish' agency which had allowed so large a loan to the insurgents.[69]

The possible suppliers were certainly not very numerous, and among them there were some who reacted with an uneasy conscience. The reports that Italy had sent aircraft to Franco via Hamburg were indignantly denied by the Duce's puppet press. 'The reports,' wrote *Il Giornale d'Italia*, 'are false and stupid; they seek to compromise both Italy and Germany, Fascism and National-Socialism together.'[70] The French Socialist press remained suspicious. A dispatch written on 24 July by the special correspondent of *Le Populaire* in Antwerp confirmed that a financial transaction had just been closed in Hamburg. According to his 'highly reliable source,' it consisted of a payment in gold, on behalf of Franco, to cover the purchase from Italy of 24 planes.[71] *L'Express du Midi* labeled the report 'a king-size *canard*, . . . given out in the hope of justifying Blum's unwarrantable plan to supply the Communist forces in Spain.' Denying categorically that Italy had supplied arms to Franco, *L'Express* continued: 'It does not require genius to see in this report the very essence of news stories fabricated anywhere, by anyone, on anything.' Noting the alacrity with which the Italian press had denied this 'ingenious invention,' *L'Express* hoped that the denials of Delbos' Ministry would carry as categorical a tone.[72]

The Socialist press was unimpressed, and it proceeded at once to spell out its accusation:

> We have never asserted that the delivery by Italy of 24 planes to General Franco would be made from Hamburg. Our correspondent in Antwerp was careful to inform us that it is the financial transaction—the payment—which will be settled in Hamburg.[73]

Thereafter, the reply of the right-wing press began to assume the tone of 'why not?' In *Le Jour*, Léon Bailby urged Blum to start by setting an example of neutrality and abstinence if he found foreign intervention 'intolerable.' That, wrote Bailby, was the opinion of the Palais-Bourbon and of the French people, 'irrespective of party.'[74] In *L'Action Française*, Charles Maurras finally replied to the prevailing 'rumours':

> Well, then. If it is true, the more such recklessness is shown abroad, the more restraint should be shown by an experienced government here. It should refrain above all from political measures which can be interpreted in a bad light. Such is the price of peace. The preservation of peace requires, not the strict, inflexible exercise of legal formulae, but on the contrary their careful, cautious and exact application ... We are for peace. Any government worthy of the name is for peace. Its purpose is to forbid, others of course, but itself first, everything that can drag it from off the path of peace.[75]

The article suggests that Maurras sincerely considered the policy of Hitler and Mussolini to be 'reckless,' and that their action in supplying arms could suffice to provoke a general war. The fact remains that the peace invoked by Maurras was no different from the peace of the cemetery.

The Italian denial was no more successful in convincing *Le Quotidien*. This Radical paper harboured no doubt that a military government in Madrid would be favourable to Italian interests in the Western Mediterranean. In respect to German 'neutrality,' *Le Quotidien* quoted from the *Völkischer Beobachter* to the effect that the conflict was henceforth between Communism and 'national forces' and that the outcome could have international repercussions if the Civil War should give birth to a Soviet. *Le Quotidien* referred also to reports published in Britain that the rebels were importing arms across the Portuguese border and from Moroccan ports,[76] but nevertheless counselled strict neutrality for France.[77] The Socialist press also borrowed from the British press, notably the *Manchester Guardian*, which had discovered that Nazi emissaries had arrived in Spain several weeks earlier from the Balearic Islands; their object was to reach agreement with Spanish Fascists on the aid to be given in exchange for a naval base which would be guaranteed to Germany once a Fascist government was installed in Madrid.[78]

In Barcelona Nazi activities attracted the attention of Jean Vidal, the special correspondent of *La Dépêche*. According to Vidal, documents collected in the course of recent searches of the homes of notorious Fascists in that city revealed that the German Consulate had encouraged the uprising of 19 July by the direct action of its associations, namely the Germania Club and the Frente del Trabajo, which comprised a thousand card-carrying members.[79]

In *L'Écho de Paris*, Henri de Kérillis was proud at this time to champion the cause of Germany, whose desire to swallow up the world, he wrote, was gradually giving way to the desire to save the great principles which had given Germany her grandeur. Countries with no liking for Fascism, he added, were turning toward Germany in their horror of Bolshevism, while Britain and all the Anglo-Saxon peoples of the world were turning away from France, who would then find herself in isolation.[80]

La Dépêche now had the feeling that 'certain countries' were simply looking for a pretext and awaiting an opportunity to turn Spain into a battlefield.[81] Against this impatience to intervene, the attitude of the French Government, in the view of *La Dépêche*, was 'of a propriety open to no misunderstanding: in its respect for absolute neutrality it [had] abstained and [would] continue to abstain from any donation, sale or delivery of arms, munitions and war matériel.'[82]

It was at this moment that Franco himself hinted at the imminent widening of the conflict, both in his interview by the *News Chronicle*[83] and in another by the Reuter Agency's correspondent in Tangier. In the latter he said:

> The question is not simply national, it is international. Great Britain, Germany and Italy must certainly look upon our purposes with sympathy. For myself individually, I am utterly disinterested. If the insurrection is of benefit to Spain because it drives Communism out, I would be satisfied, but I have no desire whatever to inflict upon her unnecessary severity. After all, they are not all Communists.[84]

The threat expressed to the *News Chronicle* of provoking an international incident was testimony to the fact that the movement was at a standstill without foreign aid. But foreign aid was already on the way, and when the time came the rebel leaders made no excuse for it. 'The aircraft we receive,' they said, 'are in compensation for those which France has supplied to the Frente Popular.'[85] The policy of Blum had failed utterly; it was a far cry from the 'propriety open to no misunderstanding.' On the one hand, by hesitating to supply arms to the Republic he had prevented it from suppressing the revolt; on the other hand, his indecision and vacillation had provided the Fascist regimes with the pretext to intervene which *La Dépêche* had feared, a pretext slim but sufficient. 'It matters little,' commented *L'Ordre* bitterly, 'whether the story of the French supplies is fact or fiction.'[86] The rumour alone had sufficed.

4
Italo-German Intervention and the Cot Formula

Italian intervention: denial and proof—French interests in Morocco—The reply of the Right—The hesitations of the Radicals—The attitude of reserve of the Spanish Republicans—Pressure from the Left and French intervention

Reports of German military aid to Franco were basically accurate from 29 July. On that day, Operation *Feuerzauber* went into operation: twenty Junkers transport planes, with an escort of six fighters, carrying in all 86 men, arrived at Franco's headquarters. On the same day, the visible proof of Italian intervention was available in the French Sahara. In the first delivery of Savoia bombers from Sardinia, two had to make a forced landing at Berkane in French Morocco, and one crashed at Saïda in Algeria.[1] The official investigation conducted by General Denain of the French Air Force showed that the planes were military, armed, flown by Italian airmen, and on their way to Spanish Morocco. Moreover, these planes were prepared for departure on 17 July, the day of the uprising. According to Peyrouton, in *L'Écho de Paris* of 1 August, the Italian airmen had received their flight orders as early as 15 July.

The Italian Government denied collusion right up to the last minute. The rumours concerning the imminent departure of Italian planes, which even as cautious a journal as *La Dépêche* took seriously, were haughtily dismissed in Rome. On 30 July, even in the teeth of a report that Italian aircraft had landed in Morocco, Italian spokesmen issued fresh declarations of strict neutrality and non-intervention.[2]

On that same day, while Spanish Nationalist officers were making no attempt to dispute the evidence,[3] the Italian Government published the following communiqué:

> The Italian Government remains loyal to the principle of absolute neutrality in regard to these events. It is, however, a safe presumption that Rome expects this same principle to be followed by all the interested powers, for if the Italian Government should feel itself offended in any way, there would be reason to fear the possibility of international complications.[4]

The arrival of the Italian planes in Morocco spotlighted a situation which concerned France directly. On 27 November 1912, France had signed a treaty with the Sultan establishing a French protectorate over all Morocco. At the same time, France had signed a 'sub-lease' treaty with Spain, under which she surrendered a part of this protectorate to the latter. Under the terms of the treaty, Spain could not permit the installation of any foreign powers in this part of Morocco nor could she arm the population. When reports were received that Franco had decided to conscript Moroccans, France was thus already entitled to protest.[5]* If at the end of July it was units of the German and Italian Air Forces that Spain had invited to the north coast of Morocco, the matter was no longer an internal affair of Spain: it was now an international question. The French left-wing press at once cried out that French territorial integrity had been violated beyond a doubt. Many right-wing papers, for their part, affected a total indifference: *L'Écho de Paris*, *Le Matin* and *Le Petit Parisien* did not print a single word of the protest.

The right wing had paused only to catch its breath. When it resumed, Blum was still responsible for everything. He had shattered the solidarity achieved at Stresa, wrote *L'Express du Midi*, and allowed the Triple Alliance to re-form after twenty-five years; 'and now what extravagances and complications is France going to let herself be dragged into?'[6] In *L'Action Française*, Maurice Pujo went so far as to accuse Blum and Cot of treason,[7] although the 17 Potez-25 aircraft earmarked for Spain and readied for take-off still stood on the airfield at Étampes-Mondésir (Seine-et-Oise). In the same paper, Charles Maurras declared himself for neutrality whatever the circumstances. The affair of the Italian planes was for Maurras a case of 'violating municipal, or if you wish, international air traffic ordinances,' and should be settled as such.

> If Italy wished to intervene, that is Italy's affair. Germany? Germany's affair. There is not one iota of our interests at stake in all this, that is the sole comment that makes any sense to Frenchmen. As for the cause of justice, even that can be served in this marvellous debate: did not the first aid to the Spanish belligerents come from Russia? We have said it, we have written it, we have repeated it, we would have even sung it ten days ago! And we were not looking for any quarrel with Russia on this subject. In the same way, let France be the first to let other nations alone![8]

In *L'Indépendant de Paris*, Henry Lémery was as little concerned as Maurras by the Italian intervention but repeated his fears of Germany.[9] In *L'Ami du Peuple*, Pierre Taittinger continued to treat as romantics those who wished to sustain the Republic, an attitude that had already received a stinging rebuke from *L'Oeuvre*.[10] Taittinger now asked how many days it would take before human lives became a factor along with open credit and weapons of war. His counsel was still to maintain an 'absolute and total' neutrality as the only way to avoid general mobilization.[11] He gave a warning to both sides, however, that though everyone spoke of neutrality, no one observed it. 'What then is this comedy that can end in drama?'[12]

In *L'Echo de Paris* too, Pertinax now admitted that Italy was participating openly in the Civil War.[13] His first reaction was indignation. Pertinax demanded of Franco absolute respect for the Franco-Spanish Treaty of 1912 and for the Agreements of 1923 and 1928 in respect to Tangier; he even called for the use of force if necessary to back such a demand and to show that no change in the balance of power in the Mediterranean would be tolerated.[14] This was perhaps the last anti-Franco sentiment expressed in *L'Echo*. Pertinax followed it immediately with a warning that France had everything to lose and nothing to gain by intervention.[15] Henri de Kérillis considered it an error or a lie to present civilized Europe in two blocs, one (including the Soviet Union) democratic and the other Fascist, for Britain 'certainly prefer[red] the Hitler régime to the Stalin régime.' Thus, according to Kérillis, in a war in which Spain were the point of departure, conservative, imperial Britain would be more or less opposed to France.[16] In the same daily, Raymond Cartier took it upon himself to expose the violations of neutrality committed by the French Government. When the French diplomatic and consular representatives in Spain asked the French Government to place three transport planes at their disposal for the repatriation of French nationals, the government first obtained an assurance from the Spanish Government that these aircraft would not be requisitioned.[17] According to Cartier, however, the planes were seized, requisitioned and put into service by the Republicans. Moreover, wrote Cartier, volunteers for Spain were being recruited at the offices of the Secours Rouge International in Paris, and especially at the head office of the French Communist Party at 8 Rue Mathurin-Moreau.[18]* Pointing out that this attitude profited France nothing in compensation for the fury it aroused among the Nationalists, Cartier called for a 'total, absolute and scrupulous neutrality.'[19]

A conservative journal such as *Le Figaro* expressed a more volatile reaction to the event of 30 July. Wladimir d'Ormesson acknowledged at first that the French Government found itself in a most difficult situation. The SFIO was, after all, a pacifist party. If it acted, it would be said that it was motivated by panic; if it failed to act, it ran the risk of being the victim of its inaction.[20] He then regretted that the Premier had not made, on the first day, an unreserved and unequivocal declaration that France would observe strict neutrality, so that 'all this unpleasant—and dangerous—international intrigue might have been nipped in the bud.'[21] France, continued the editor of *Le Figaro*, must observe hermetic neutrality in respect to all Spaniards regardless of this affiliation; her only means of maintaining her position in the Mediterranean and elsewhere was by keeping her self-control, by pursuing only her higher interests and by 'avoiding like the plague any confusion between French policy and revolutionary propaganda.'[22] At the end of the year, d'Ormesson analyzed in his fashion the Italo-German intervention. If the Fascist states had intervened, he now argued in a harder tone, it was because, on the one hand, the Frente Popular had allowed an 'abominable mess' to develop in Spain which could only have provoked a violent reaction, and because, on the other hand, the Frente Popular had long indulged in insulting Fascism and Nazism. D'Ormesson concluded that 'the worst enemies of France in Spain were those who, incapable of governing, incapable of resisting the oncoming revolution [*sic*], have clung to our apron-strings when their errors, or perhaps their crimes, have forced them to defend themselves.'[23] The Socialist press remarked that d'Ormesson had assumed hitherto a certain Briandism; 'but Briandism is no longer in fashion, and now his cry is: "What we want is Hitler".'[24] Julien Benda commented in *La Dépêche* that the position taken by this self-styled 'right-thinking press' (*presse bien pensante*) was exactly the position it had taken a year earlier in regard to the war in Abyssinia. 'A section of French opinion,' he concluded, 'is not content simply to practice *primum vivere*, it makes a virtue of it.'[25]

Among the moderates, though they advocated caution, *L'Aube* showed how much a rebel victory would be contrary to French interests.[26] *Le Petit Journal* expressed the opinion that if the Nationalists were victorious the worst enemies of France would be in control of Spain: 'The Francos and the Molas are prisoners of the Germanophile lobby which presided joyfully over the destruction of our submarines during the Great War.'[27]*

It was in the vacillation of the Radical and Radical-Socialist press at this point that the vacillation of Blum himself during these first three weeks of the war was so clearly reflected. While *Le Quotidien* counselled strict neutrality[28] and *La République* congratulated Blum on his 'cautiousness,'[29] *La Dépêche* expressed all sorts of inner convulsions.

The first reaction of *La Dépêche* to the event of 30 July revealed almost a split personality. How should the French Government act, it asked:

> Certainly, if we follow only the impulses of the heart, if we allow ourselves to be guided only by our reactions of sympathy, we would say: 'Well, since General Franco is the representative and the agent of the Fascist forces, our duty is to fly to the aid of the Spanish Republicans with all the resources we can muster.'

But then, in the same curious hesitation, the same obstinate questioning of Hamlet's whispered 'he goes to Heaven,' *La Dépêche* propounded the advantages of doing nothing:

But wait. Is it not to fall into the trap prepared for us? Is it not to join in the game of the Fascists themselves? Is it not utterly to disserve, as a result, the interests of our friends, the Republicans of Spain?

We strongly approve the attitude of caution adopted by the French Government, an attitude which perhaps offended, at first, our deepest feelings and natural generosity, but which appears, on careful consideration, to be the only policy capable of counteracting the drive of the reactionary and Fascist forces and of thwarting their provocations. Politics are not played with sentiment but with reason.[30]

France, therefore, had only one desire, one aim, according to *La Dépêche*: not to intervene in a fratricidal struggle, to assist in bringing it to a quick end, and above all not to draw advantage from it.[31] But a day later, the mood had changed: the French could have their preferences for one party or the other, it wrote, but they had to realize that it was in the interests of France that the rebel generals be defeated.[32] To top the confusion, no less a writer than Julien Benda expressed a judgment he was long to regret, calling naïf those who imagined that the Fascist powers would come to the aid of a party 'that [had] already proved itself once and for all to be the weakest in substance; as if it were not the exact opposite of their doctrine.'[33]

Writing in retrospect of this period, Emile Buré, in *L'Ordre*, felt in 1937 that London and Paris should have informed Rome and Berlin, on the very first day, that they would not tolerate intervention. Buré did not accept the view that such an action would have made war inevitable. 'Obviously,' he wrote, 'a nation determined to defend its interests always runs the risk of angering those who seek to destroy it. The real question is whether it gains by pretending not to see their designs and by allowing them to manoeuvre to bring about its defeat.'[34] In 1938, Théodore Balk described the Italo-German invasion as the opening of the Second World War. At that time, wrote Balk in *La Dépêche*, many people thought that it was nothing more than a *pronunciamiento*, but within a few months the real nature of the conflict had become evident to the whole world except for a few French and British diplomats.[35]

Within 72 hours of the arrival of the Italian aircraft in Morocco, the French Government began to implement the Cot formula. Curiously, it was from this moment that the Spanish Republican leaders began to express a more reserved, independent and self-sufficient attitude. Perhaps it reflected a deliberate policy of camouflage, for the French Government certainly did not announce the measures it was taking. Martínez Barrio declared: 'We ask all nations to observe absolute neutrality.'[36] Fernando de los Ríos expressed the same sentiment: 'We do not seek the intervention of France. I ask France to provide moral support.'[37] When French policy had officially changed on 8 August, in favour of the Delbos–Daladier formula, this mood was still maintained. Azaña himself expressed it in an interview by Andrieu: 'We ask for nothing but your sympathy, but this sympathy we deserve.'[38] Even to the fire-eating *Solidaridad Obrera*, organ of the CNT and after the outbreak of war the largest-selling daily in Barcelona,[39*] the French policy of non-intervention was considered natural: 'The sequel to Sarajevo cannot be forgotten so easily.'[40] According to *Le Quotidien*, even Giral, on behalf of the Spanish Government, was seeking in September nothing more than a strict neutrality observed by all.[41]

General Walter Krivitsky, chief of Soviet military intelligence in Western Europe, writes that 'the Comintern, of course, made a great deal of noise [in response to Italo-German intervention], but none of us practical men took that seriously.'[42] Demonstrations in Moscow and Paris increased in size and frequency, to the cry: 'Planes for Spain!'[43*] The planes demanded by the crowds in Moscow, however, were French, and if the French crowds continued their outcry after 2 August it attests to the covert method as well as the inadequacy of the delivery of matériel by the French Government. The method employed was understandably the use of the private sector, and it served to satisfy the volatile Radical press. In reply to the indignation of the right wing, Cléon appealed in *La Dépêche* for 'a little more good faith, a little more national feeling.' These actions, Cléon argued, were not the actions of the government, and they were certainly less serious than the dispatch of military planes to the rebels.[44]

Meanwhile, and throughout the week following Blum's decision of 2 August, the French Government did everything in its power to conceal its operations.[45*] The Spanish Government's order was presented by a Spanish subject, Andrés García de la Barga, residing at 1 Rue Mérimée in Paris. The order, to be debited to another Spanish subject, Andrés Ramírez, residing at Calle Formentor 21 in Madrid, consisted of the purchase of 20 aircraft to be delivered in small quantities to Francazal Airport in Toulouse, beginning on 4 August.[46]

L'Express du Midi, already suspicious, revealed on 6 August that 13 Dewoitine-D.372 fighters and 6 Potez-54 bombers, all without registration numbers, had reached Francazal from Villacoublay during the previous 48 hours. Predictably, *L'Action Française* published the following day an exposé of its own, in the form of a document intended to prove the destination of 8 Dewoitine-D.372 and 6 Potez-570 at Francazal; their armament and ammunition were stored inside the aircraft, and Spanish pilots were en route to Toulouse to take delivery.[47] It would appear that the document was accurate in every detail, even the last. As a result of the opposition of Delbos, alone among Blum's Ministers to hesitate in sending aid to Giral, French pilots were to fly the planes only as far as Perpignan, where Spanish pilots would take delivery. Nevertheless, the left-wing press chose to contest the whole affair, and the account published by *L'Action Française* gave rise to a protracted battle in the Toulouse press between Hudelle of *Le Midi Socialiste* and Lalande of *L'Express*.[48*]

On the same day that *L'Express* published its exposé, application was made for a license to export 14 Dewoitine-D.372 (valued at 8,540,000 francs) and 6 Potez-54 (valued at 9,810,000 francs), together with 400,000 francs' worth of accessories and spare parts. Authorization was immediately granted by the Ministries involved, under license number 436 dated 6 August. The license served to legalize (if so secret an operation would need to be legalized) a series of deliveries which had already begun. Pierre Cot insisted, before the Senate's Air Commission, that the 14 Dewoitine fighters delivered on 4–6 August corresponded to orders received prior to the neutrality agreement. Within one week of Blum's implementation of the Cot formula, no fewer than 38 French planes left Francazal for Barcelona.[49*]

It is indicative of the secrecy surrounding the Cot formula that while the highest echelons of the French Government were thus authorizing the supply of French aircraft to Madrid, the five border Prefects remained under those instructions which the public understood to be the government's actual policy. The Prefect with the heaviest responsibilities, Frédéric Atger of Haute-Garonne, was nevertheless aware, through rumour and not through any official communication, that the aircraft standing at Francazal were being readied for transit across the frontier. At 11.10 p.m. on 6 August, Atger received a telephone call from the Sûreté Nationale, instructing him to keep close watch on the Toulouse airport. Naturally assuming, from the communiqué issued by the government, that the watch demanded by the Sûreté meant the prevention of all unauthorized flights bound for Spain, without any need for confirmation, Atger at once posted policemen at the airport with instructions to prevent such flights and at the same time possible sabotage to the aircraft. The police inspection on duty at Francazal had received identical orders. The following day, 7 August, Atger received a circular from the Sûreté, dated 5 August, giving similar instructions, and warning the Prefect of reported attempts to enlist French civilian pilots both as ferry pilots and as belligerents, especially at private airfields in the Southwest.[50*]

Some hours before Atger received this circular, however, a telephone call reached him at 1 a.m. from Verlomme, *chef de cabinet* at the Ministry of the Interior, authorizing the departure of the planes in deference to the demonstrations in Paris protesting against the embargo. The reply of the inspector at Francazal was that no embargo existed, since none of the pilots had sought authorization to leave, apparently because the 20 planes had not yet arrived in Toulouse. Atger at once informed Verlomme that the instructions of the Cabinet were totally at variance with those he had received from the Sûreté. Verlomme replied that Charles Magny, Director General of the Sûreté, would himself confirm the instructions. Accordingly, Magny telephoned at 2.30

a.m., explaining that this was a special case and that any licenses received by the pilots could be processed. Atger was then informed by the inspector at Francazal that he had received the licence to cross French air space, issued by the Aeronautical Office, together with the export licence pursuant to Law 35. Atger next consulted the Chief Customs Officer in Toulouse, who informed him that export of the planes was forbidden by law and that exception could be made only at the request of the Superintendent of Customs of the Ministry of Finance, and with the agreement of the Ministries involved, chiefly Air and Foreign Affairs; a provisional license had been received and had been issued to García de la Barga. Atger then received a further call, at 3.30 a.m., from Jean Moulin, *chef de cabinet* at the Air Ministry and destined later to become the embodiment of the Resistance. Moulin confirmed that the consignment of planes was in order and ruled that the police were wrong in preventing their departure. At 4 a.m. Atger again telephoned Magny to apprise him of the papers now held by the pilots; Magny replied that in the circumstances there was no objection to their departure. The Chief Customs Officer phoned Atger at 4.20 a.m. to inform him that a representative of the purchaser had arrived at Francazal, bearing the necessary documents to take delivery of the planes. Atger had no choice but to confirm the authorization to the Customs Officer and the police inspector. In summarizing these events in a report sent to Verlomme, Magny and Moulin, Atger ended tersely:

> It appears from all these incidents that the Prefect of Haute-Garonne has been excluded from all consultations concerning these planes; it would be desirable if, in future, the Ministries involved kept the Prefect informed as to his exact duties in his *département*.[51*]

5
The Delbos–Daladier Formula

British reaction as cause of the French volte-face—Support for the new policy—Opposition from the Left—Opposition from the Right—Frontier incidents

We have seen that the principal factor in the sudden change of policy of the Blum Cabinet on 8 August was the disapproval of the Baldwin government, based upon the unanimous desire of the British people for non-intervention. No important group in British political circles stood in opposition to that desire, despite the claims of the French left-wing press: among such claimants, Jean Longuet insisted in the Socialist press that England hoped for a Republican victory,[1] while Cachin, in *L'Humanité*, contended that the British Socialists had undertaken to send all possible aid to the Spanish workers[2]—at the very moment that the Labourites were voting unmistakably for non-intervention. Arnaud-Bernard of *Le Journal de Toulouse* was closer to the truth in his belief that if British opinion at this time found Fascism repugnant, it found Communism even more so.[3] Nevertheless, the existence of a Fascist Triple Alliance would represent a greater and more immediate danger to British hegemony in the Western Mediterranean than all the naval power of the Soviet Union, which would be inadequate to the extension of its communications. As *L'Oeuvre* pointed out, an England which in 1926 had thwarted the application of the treaty between Mussolini and Primo de Rivera to promote their friendship and collaboration in the Mediterranean would certainly assure France that she would not permit, in 1936 any more than in 1926, the slightest Italian intrusion in the Balearics, and that she would make such a forbearance on the part of Italy a *sine qua non* condition of the expected 'Gentleman's Agreement.'[4] Such would explain the comment made in October by Gaston Guèze, that the situation in Spain was not the concern of the British Parliament.[5]

In point of fact, the British Government announced, through Lord Cranborne, Eden's deputy, that it would act 'in strict accordance with the laws in force.' The laws in force, as we have seen, allowed at least the private sector to engage in commerce within the terms of contracts previously signed and of international agreements. According to the Chief Inspector of Special Police in Toulouse, the British Government agreed to the sale of French aircraft to the Republic and awaited the dispatch of the planes before agreeing to collective neutrality;[6] this must be considered, however, high-echelon rumour rather than fact, to which the Chief Inspector could hardly have had access. Nevertheless this policy, rumour or fact, and the alacrity of the free press, whose right to comment at will was too much for Queipo de Llano's understanding, infuriated the 'Radio General' who replied threateningly: 'Nations which treat the Spanish military movement in this fashion[7] can expect similar treatment from us in the near future.'[8]

The failure of the Blum–Cot movement to commit French and British aid to the Republican cause was concealed by the government and subsequently by the press, both of which attributed the government's change of policy to the government's confidence that the doctrine of non-intervention would be accepted by all the Powers. Thus, whether or not he knew the truth, Wladimir d'Ormesson professed his satisfaction in *Le Figaro* at Britain's favourable reply to the French proposal.[9] *L'Oeuvre* congratulated the Quai d'Orsay on its success in aligning Britain with France.[10] *L'Ere Nouvelle* expressed its pleasure that the British Government should stress its close accord with France;[11] for 'only through their cooperation would peace be assured.'[12] It was left to *L'Ordre* finally to perceive the truth. It was enough to read the last article by Sir Austen Chamberlain, it observed, at the beginning of November, to be absolutely sure that England had refused to make common cause with France.[13]

Meanwhile, the first patrol of the Garde Républicaine Mobile arrived in Toulouse on 8 August and took up its position at Francazal. No watch, however, was yet kept on the neighbouring airfield of Montaudran, which was in the private ownership of Air-France. Later reports of the Chief Inspector of Special Police show that a maximum of 56 planes left Toulouse for Spain between 9 August and 14 October. All 56 planes were seen to land at Montaudran.[14*] The collusion of Air-France, or at least that of its personnel, would in itself have reduced the effectiveness of the Government's control.[15*] But doubts remain as to the intentions of the government during these weeks. A handwritten memorandum, emanating from the War Ministry on 4 September, addressed to General Ménard, commanding the 17th Region (Haute-Garonne), but signed illegibly, was presumably intended to limit the efficacy of the Garde Républicaine Mobile. On 9 November the GRM patrol was withdrawn from Francazal to Paris by the War Ministry, with the approval of the Ministry of the Interior, a move which, as Prefect Atger complained, made further control of Francazal impossible.[16]

The Delbos–Daladier formula: no ideological crusades, was welcomed by the majority of Parliament, from conservatives to Socialists; two among them publicly expressed their support of the Ministers, despite their sympathies with the Madrid government. The Moderate conservative Paul Reynaud declared at the end of July: 'Embroilment in a fight to the death with one or other of the two halves of the Spanish people would be a grievous error for the security of France.'[17] Socialist Senator Aimé Berthod (Jura) pointed out that there was some objection to allowing too close an assimilation, in world opinion, between the Front Populaire and the Frente Popular, since the internal situation in France was totally different from that in Spain; this difference could be seen in the position of the French Communist Party which, unlike its Spanish counterpart, explained Berthod, had no choice but to assert its respect for the republican system and its concern for the nation's defence.[18]

The majority of the press gave the Delbos formula similar support. *Le Quotidien* stressed the duty of supporting the government in its efforts toward moderation[19] and congratulated it later for having kept its promises.[20] In *L'Intransigeant*, Gallus paid tribute to the French initiative,[21] noting at the same time that it was precisely the most ardent supporters of the government who were urging it to abandon the position it had adopted.[22] To *L'Oeuvre*,[23] *Le Temps*,[24] and *La Concorde*,[25] the Blum government had worked diligently to preserve international peace; in *L'Oeuvre*, Victor Basch, president of the Comité International d'Aide au Peuple Espagnol (formed in Paris on 31 July at a meeting of the Secours Rouge International), explained that their hearts went out to the Spanish Republicans 'but the interests of peace preclude all interventionist policies,' while at the same time he called pessimistically for measures which would allow the forces of peace to postpone the cataclysm.[26] J.B. Sévérac, Assistant Secretary-General of the SFIO, acknowledged the difficulties of the task that the government had assumed to disperse the thunderclouds of war: 'We put our trust in the government.'[27] 'What we can do for them [the Republicans],' he added, 'is indeed very little.'[28] Again in *Le Midi*, Emile Farinet thought that the best solution lay in whatever action carried the least risk to the French working class.[29] In *La Dépêche*, Georges Scelle considered neutrality as a 'practical necessity': otherwise the conflict could unleash not only international war but also civil war in every country involved.[30] Aware of this danger, André Mureine in *Le Midi* warned the militant Socialists that the position taken by their delegates in power forbade their raising any polemic which might jeopardize internal or international peace. Mureine insisted, without any basis in fact, that 'total agreement' had been reached between the Communist leaders and the Socialist representatives in the government.[31] G.-J. Gignoux was closer to the truth in stressing, in *La Journée Industrielle*, the contradiction between the official government position and that held by the 'constitutive forces' of the Front Populaire.[32] The Internationale Ouvrière Socialiste published a manifesto denouncing the lack of unity and the inaction of the forces of the Left.[33]

Conscious of this new danger, Roger Deleplanque posed in *Le Petit Bleu* this 'frightening question': did the government understand neutrality in the same way as the representatives of the extreme Left? If it did, it was, in the opinion of Deleplanque, extremely serious:

If the witness to a dispute who encourages one of the antagonists by word and gesture can be called neutral, is he not more neutral still if he places a dagger or a revolver in the hand of the combatant of his choice? Is not our government 'ultra neutral' toward the Frente Popular? Let us be cautious. Let us on no account use neutrality as it is understood by the Left. Let not Europe sink into general neutrality.[34]

Deleplanque's sardonic comment seemed to be a warning to the all-important Radical press, in which Buré insisted that neutrality did not mean indifference.[35] But the Radical press fluctuated widely in its criticism. Buré also counselled the government to 'rush into nothing and so forfeit nothing,'[36] for 'to bet is to risk.'[37] For the Radical-Socialist *L'Ere Nouvelle*, intervention would be 'an act of weakness,'[38] which could expose France to a new Agadir Incident.[39] When, after a month of hostilities, the Republic had proven itself capable of resisting 'unaided' the rebel movement despite its foreign aid, *L'Ere* called this all the more reason why France should insist upon the neutrality agreement which would deny the rebels this aid: 'Such is the best reply to the senseless reproof of our interventionalists.'[40]

This admonition by the Radical-Socialist organ was obviously addressed to *L'Humanité* and *Le Peuple*, which were pursuing their campaign in favor of intervention and the end of sanctions against the Madrid government. *L'Humanité* published the appeal of González Peña, a Socialist *député* and UGT leader, to Jacques Duclos, secretary of the French Communist Party, and to Jean Zyromski, a member of the executive committee of the SFIO: 'What we want are weapons, more weapons. The miners defending Oviedo have one rifle for every five men.'[41] In *Le Peuple*, Léon Jouhaux announced in the name of the CGT that neither the French people nor the French working class could be neutral in the present drama.[42] Sévérac's praise of the Blum government was intolerable to Harmel, who declared in the same daily: 'He who is not with us is against us.'[43] Denouncing the 'crocodile tears' of those like Sévérac 'given up to flight and shameless treason,' Harmel turned to Bracke, who had replaced Blum in the political leadership of *Le Populaire*: 'Bracke, are you going to let your readers think that Sévérac represents the opinion of French Socialists?'[44] *Le Peuple* then published the appeal of Pietro Nenni: 'The Spanish working class demands of the international proletariat . . . above all things else . . . an international action capable of preventing Germany and Italy from sending aid to Spanish Fascism . . .[45] In response to Nenni, Jouhaux wanted to go even further, like *L'Humanité*: he advocated not only the prohibition by the democracies of all shipments of arms and munitions to the rebels but also the delivery of necessary supplies of war matériel and foodstuffs to the Madrid government.[46]

Certain voices in the Blum press supported this viewpoint: 'The French

Government had decided to show an example of neutrality. We do not approve.'[47] Rosenfeld found it 'tragic' that the search for peace should be tied to the supply of planes, 'but whose fault,' he asked, '[was] that?'[48] While predicting the final victory for the Loyalists, *Le Midi Socialiste* asked what would be the response of those champions of non-intervention, such as Joesph Caillaux in *L'Ere Nouvelle*, if the outcome were otherwise.[49] Bracke himself found neutrality 'immoral'[50]* in the face of a triple Fascist threat. In the same press Louis de Brouckère, president of the Internationale Ouvrière Socialiste, urged France and Britain to intervene 'to safeguard peace.'[51]

The danger to the peace of Europe was underscored meanwhile in *Claridad*, the Madrid organ of Largo Caballero, leader of the left-wing Socialists. In the event that the rebels were successful in Spain, he wrote, France would find herself surrounded by Fascist states: 'War, which international Fascism has been long preparing against the great democratic republic, would break out the moment it could count upon the support of a Fascist Spain.'[52] It was in the national interest, repeated *L'Oeuvre*, to prevent agents of Italian and German Fascism from installing themselves on the southwest frontier.[53] To *Le Midi Socialiste*, the Spanish Republicans were the only friends France had or had ever had on the other side of the Pyrenees.[54]

Confronted with this certain danger, the 'interventionists' staked out the limits of the action they advocated. Longuet, who was also a member of the executive committee of the Internationale Ouvrière Socialiste, did not go so far as to demand that the Front Populaire come to the aid of the Frente Popular. The 40,000 citizens chanting 'Planes for Spain!' at the Vélodrome d'Hiver, he explained, were simply demanding that the legal government of Spain, in accordance with international law, be given on cash payment the planes it had ordered.[55] *La'Dépêche*, too, remarked that if Madrid asked Paris, on a strictly commercial level, to allow the execution of transactions provided for by treaty, Paris would be hard put to deny Madrid the exercise of its right.[56] It was a matter not of intervention, explained Vaillant-Couturier, but of normal commerce with a legitimate government:

> The prevention . . . of a regular and friendly government from trading as it wishes constitutes . . . an impingement upon the sovereignty of that state, in short, intervention. Because it is a Popular Front government, the Spanish Government is made to suffer sanctions . . . which none dares apply to Italy . . .
>
> The French masses . . . do not accept this humiliation. They do not demand any 'intervention' by the French Government. But they refuse to allow the friends of France in Spain to be strangled.[57]

Non-intervention, added Jacques Duclos in the Communist organ, was becoming synonymous with blockade.[58] In *Le Peuple*, Harmel declared that absolute neutrality could only be a fraud since it would be unilateral.[59] Neutrality was no longer sufficient either for Gabriel Cudenet of *Le Petit Journal*: placing the constitutional government and the insurrection on the same footing was tantamount to imposing unilateral neutrality.[60] And in this event, thought Cudenet, when the dictators' claws had hooked upon the Balearics, the Canaries, Tangier and Gibraltar, practically nothing would remain of Spain.[61]

The Socialist press, for its part, now began to demand immediate control, 'unless they want us to do the very same thing, in favour of the other side.'[62] Though Bracke admitted that non-intervention was possible if it were authenticated by control—which would ensure, he thought, a Republican victory—he echoed the point made by Vaillant-Couturier: 'Would it not constitute "intervention" to deprive the legal authority of the means of survival and of the resources to sustain its people to which it is at all times entitled?'[63] Indeed, none ventured to refute this argument. On the contrary, Léon Archimbaud agreed in *L'Oeuvre* that international law permitted France to supply arms to the Loyalists. The international ruling in question, adopted in 1900 by the leading jurists of Europe, expressly forbade any power at peace with a given independent state from hindering the measures taken by that state to restore internal tranquillity. No point of law, concluded Archimbaud, allowed the French Government to deny the right of the legal government of Spain to place its orders for war matériel with French firms.[64] When it was apparent that France, in her declaration of neutrality, had renounced her own rights, *Le Peuple* invoked the only freedom of action which was not compromised by this neutrality: that of French citizens to sell—or give—the Spanish Government anything it needed.[65] André Malraux, for one, had already in August opened a subscription fund to buy planes and other matériel[66] and, with other other pilots, delivered the first twenty French planes to Madrid on 13 August.

Writing of this period from the coign of vantage of the spring of 1937, the Radical Pierre Dominique argued that if France had intervened in Spain in August 1936 it would have meant immediate war.[67] At least two prominent Leftists, Jean-Richard Bloch and the Belgian Socialist Émile Vandervelde, wrote in a different retrospect, the former in *Espagne! Espagne!* and the latter in *La Dépêche*. 'I am quite satisfied in my own mind," wrote Vandervelde, 'that the danger of war would have been virtually null if the French Government had waited for the other nations involved to do likewise, and for control to be made effective, before proceeding to ban the export of arms and munitions.'[68]

The opposition of the Right to the Delbos formula was based upon its 'hypocritical' or 'equivocal' character. In response to the position adopted at the Cabinet meeting of 8 August, predicating the neutrality of France upon the neutrality of others, *L'Action Française* affected a grave concern over 'this game of morality, of *pundonor*, of points of law':

> It runs against all political wisdom.
> Political wisdom insists: do not intervene. And if others intervene, then intervene even less. And the more others intervene, the more France must take care not to intervene, for the very simple reason that others may fight to some purpose and even to their advantage, whether among themselves or with Spain, but our France can only find that she is fighting against all. She cannot take sides without setting everybody on her back![69]

In *Candide,* Pierre Gaxotte echoed this sentiment: in 1914 France had been attacked and she had allies; but this time, the French would be alone and Europe would hold them responsible in advance. 'The inanities committed by the Front Populaire,' wrote Gaxotte, 'place France in a difficult position.'[70]

In *L'Echo de Paris,* Jean Hutin also considered that the form of the French communiqué of 8 August was not free from ambiguity. The view that French neutrality was not absolute but conditional was being expressed openly in government circles, and if Germany or Italy continued to supply arms to Franco the French Government would resume its freedom of action; this, insisted Hutin, was precisely what the communiqué did not state.[71] In an interview granted in late August to the special correspondent of the paper, Queipo de Llano levelled another charge at France: 15 planes bearing French markings had flown over the Irún battle area on 21 August. The charge related probably to the incident at Tolosa (Guipúzcoa), a town which had been bombed on 22 August by French-built aircraft, some of which, according to General Kindelán, still bore French markings. For *L'Echo*, this incident revealed the 'insane conduct of the French Government in attempting to conceal its moral and material support behind a veil of neutrality.' And *L'Echo* concluded that the French position vis-à-vis the Burgos junta ran the risk of irremediable compromise, and it called on the government to recognize the junta.[72]

For the extremist Bailby in *Le Jour,* the Blum Cabinet had blundered once again. As Bailby saw it, the government, 'incapable of making a sincere and valid commitment to non-intervention,' was cancelling its earlier appeal to the great Powers and disclosing its willingness to abide by a simple undertaking on the part of each state not to arm officially one or other of the belligerents.[73] In point of fact, Blum was at this very moment on the point of submitting his resignation, but he continued to prepare the groundwork for what was to become the London Conference. The right wing continued to hand the Premier gratuitous advice, such as the remark of Guèze that none of the powers was reluctant to participate in a neutrality convention, but in order for France to expect compliance she must first be beyond reproach herself.[74]

It was the opinion of certain neutral observers, such as the U.S. Consul in Bordeaux, who had inspected the whole length of the frontier, that by the end of August France was indeed beyond reproach. First of all, it was the Spanish Republicans who had taken the initiative, closing the frontier on 13 August to all the French. Irún was out of bounds to all visitors. A week later, orders were issued at the French frontier to prevent anyone from crossing in, orders that the Republican authorities called unjustifiable. Relations on the frontier were falling away. On 18 August a photo was published of the frontier post at the international bridge in Béhobie, where Gardes Mobiles, Carabineros and militiamen were seen to be on neighbourly terms. By the end of the month, under the stress of the situation, the Spanish Basques were visibly angry with the French. The attitude of the summer tourists on the French side, who viewed the agony of the Basques as some kind of entertainment, added to the rancour. *La Dépêche* described it as '"a tawdry-looking fair,"[75*] reminiscent of those gawking crowds lining the streets around La Santé on the mornings of executions.'[76] In Béhobie and Hendaye, as Mola tightened the noose around Irún, numerous incidents took place on the frontier bridges. The gravest concerned the French ambassador, Jean Herbette. Since Herbette was a supporter of the Republican Government, he did his best to downplay the affair, and even to deny it, but the incident quickly became known.

The ambassadors to Madrid of Great Britain, the United States, Germany and Italy—all of them except for the American Claude Bowers supportive of the rebel cause—had set themselves up in Hendaye at the beginning of August.[77*] From there they moved to Saint-Jean-de-Luz, while Madrid did all it could to lure them back to the capital.[78] Ambassador Herbette, for his part, had moved to San Sebastian and did not reach the frontier until early September. Accompanied by his wife, he had offered a place in his car to a certain Caballero, of Spanish origin but of French nationality and holder of a French passport. At the international bridge, a Spanish frontier guard, having stopped the diplomat's car, considered the passenger 'suspicious' and ordered him to dismount. Naturally, the ambassador intervened, whereupon the guards at the bridge became abusive. Herbette reminded them of his position, which then led to an exchange.

—Now suppose we just give you a short burst? said one of the guards.

—Do so, Señor. Shoot if you dare at an Ambassador of France!

The French squad, on the other side of the bridge, seeing the ambassador in a delicate situation, then advanced across the bridge, thus allowing Herbette's car to cross into France with all its occupants.[79*] As a result of this and similar incidents, the Prefect of Basses-Pyrénées gave orders that all combattants crossing into France were to be held and prevented from returning to Spain.[80*]

The border on the French side was now sealed at every point, with the possible exception of Hendaye, while the traffic in arms by sea had been nearly eliminated by the presence of Italian aircraft and submarines.[81] Even at Hendaye, the outcome of the battle for Irún on 3 September attested to the sincere efforts of the French Government to prevent aid from reaching the defenders. Although André Marty[82*] and a number of French and Belgian Communist technicians, together with some Catalan Anarchists, succeeded in crossing the border, the French authorities refused to permit six freight cars loaded with war matériel from Catalonia to continue to Irún,[83*] where the defenders' desperate shortage of ammunition facilitated Mola's capture of the town on 5 September.[84*]

Following the fall of Irún, the frontier remained closed until 19 September, at which time refugees began to return to Guipúzcoa. The bridge at Hendaye, reported *Le Midi Socialiste*, was guarded by Moroccans,[85] and from 23 September by five Falangists permanently assigned to the post.[86] According to Gaston Dumestre, the Franco authorities were taking care to look extremely well behaved, with the aim of showing that life had returned to normal; the capture of Irún was now to be celebrated monthly.[87] On the bridge at Béhobie, on the other hand, it was the Requetés who were in command, and *La Dépêche* reported that courtesy was nowhere to be seen.[88] Incidents took place that resulted in the closing of the road to Biriatou from 9 p.m. to 7 a.m.[89] The cause, insisted *L'Express du Midi*, was the way that Spanish refugees lined up on the banks of the Bidassoa were taunting the Nationalist sentries 'to the breaking point,' shouting and singing the *Internationale*, with gunfire breaking out on each side.[90] The eye-witness André Miramas added a new note: French citizens on the left bank of the Bidassoa were hailing the victors with the fascist raised-arm salute and the cry: '*Arriba España!*'[91]

Incidents multiplied everywhere. At Canfranc, when those working at the international station felt that they could no longer cooperate with the Nationalists who had taken control of the region, they asked the French Government to close the frontier,[92] and this was done. At Hendaye, the son of the Republican mayor of San Sebastian was lured to the bridge, where he was beaten up by fascists who tried to kidnap him; he was saved only by the forceful intervention of the French gendarme.[93] Provocative acts were daily life. *Le Midi Socialiste* wrote of parades, of cries of 'Long live Hitler!' in the face of French officials, and when a French gendarme was assaulted by Spanish Carlists, *Le Midi* called for the immediate closing of the frontier.[94] Even *L'Express* admitted to the 'lamentable' incident in which three Spanish Falangists brutalized a French customs officer after three others who had 'strayed across into France' had been arrested and disarmed.[95] In Hendaye, officials and rail workers held a meeting to protest the lack of security; it was attended, wrote *La Dépêche*, by a 'large part' of the population. A vote was taken 'condemning the actions of the Spanish fascists and calling on the French Government to close the frontier.'[96] Such an action was superfluous when the Franco authorities themselves closed the frontier.[97] At the end of November, Burgos insisted that this was to be only a 'limited action.'[98]

On the higher level—the interdiction of arms to Spain—control was patently effective, but reports or rumours continued to circulate that here and there the French authorities were considerably lax in their duties. With or without the machinations of the extreme Right, the Delbos formula acquired an aura of duplicity. Symptomatic of this was an incident in Comminges, where a group of inhabitants posted a notice at Saint-Martory (Haute-Garonne) and in all communes of the district. The notice, reproduced in *La Petite Gironde*, was a complaint that 'dozens' of Spanish planes had refueled in Toulouse and that 'numerous' French planes had been sold to Madrid and Barcelona. The notice also complained about the situation at the frontier, which was allegedly closed only at Canfranc (against the Navarrese), while the Toulouse-Bayonne railroad line was reportedly at the disposal of the Republicans, who continued to transfer militiamen and munitions between the Basque front and Catalonia.[99]* A further complaint was directed at the government's policy toward refugees: it was stated that the 'Whites' were being evicted from Pyrénées-Orientales while the 'Reds' were permitted to remain in Hautes-Pyrénées and Basses-Pyrénées.[100]

Given the fact that communications within Spain between Catalonia and the Basque Country had been rendered impossible from the first day of the war, and that the terrain along the Pyrenees was barely accessible, Toulouse had been converted into the main communications centre between the two zones at war. The Ville Rose had been famous from the time of Jean Jaurès for its left-wing tendencies, and for *L'Express du Midi* it was 'long known as the reddest city in France.'[101] For the Republican Government, wrote *Il Giornale d'Italia*, it was 'a veritable centre for recruitment and arms supplies.'[102] Indeed, barely two weeks after the uprising, an announcement in Spanish was placed in *La Dépêche* calling for moral and material help to the Republic.[103]* As for the Spanish consul in that city, Ángel de Tuesta was of Basque origin, and having been appointed to that post by Madrid, he refused to yield his *exequatur* to Lluhí i Vallescà, the delegate nominated to the post by the FAI and by the Generalitat of Catalonia. The Prefect of Haute-Garonne, following instructions from the French Government, yielded to Catalonia, threatening Tuesta with expulsión *manu militari* if he did not vacate the consulate. Under such a threat, he had no choice but to give up his post.[104]

The first Catalan militiamen sent by the FAI passed through Toulouse on

15 August, bound for Irún to fight with the Republican troops. To back their statements, they showed passports that were perfectly in order. But for *L'Express du Midi*, it was already intervention. 'What would Monsieur Blum say,' it asked, 'if the Carlists did the same? Is it not in violation of neutrality to allow such troops to pass through French territory?'[105] *L'Echo de Paris* agreed that in authorizing the transit of these militiamen across France from one front to the other, the French Government was betraying its commitments to neutrality.[106] What is more, trucks belonging to the FAI were carrying munitions from Madrid to Hendaye, crossing the international bridge at Latour-de-Carol (Pyrénées-Orientales) by making a detour across French territory.[107] A dispatch from Agence Havas exposed the transfer to San Sebastian of several munitions trains coming from Barcelona.[108] Basque militiamen, mobilized in Catalonia, were returning to France in December through Cerbère. Interrogated on their arrival in Bayonne, several of them stated that they had received orders to make for Bilbao to serve on the Basque front. 'The one concession, and a hypocritical concession it is,' —protested *L'Express*— 'that the French authorities are making to neutrality is to ask the Marxist combatants transiting our country to remove their insignia from their uniforms.'[109] *La Dépêche* agreed that militiamen were heading across France to the front in Navarre.[110] A migration in the opposite direction was also noticed. Orders from Madrid specified that all Spaniards who had taken refuge in France after the fall of Irún were to move at once either to Barcelona or Bilbao.[111] The first refugees from Irún, of whom a thousand were militiamen,[112]* passed through Toulouse, bound for Barcelona, on 4 September.[113]

The accusations spelt out in the poster put up in Saint-Martory were not therefore without foundation. When the local Prefect solicited legal advice on the subject, he received a letter in reply which illustrates the degree to which the French Government had compromised its image:

> In order to establish that a crime has been committed, it would be required to show the falsity of the facts reported, the bad faith of the accused, etc.
>
> It would appear that at least some of these elements are lacking in this case. Rumours circulating prior to the appearance of this poster attest to some measure of truth in the charges; these charges are further vindicated by the action of the government in tolerating recent demonstrations in Paris in support of the Frente Popular.
>
> The Assizes would probably reach a verdict of acquittal, which in turn would offer the opposition useful and gratuitous publicity.
>
> My counsel would be to refrain from investigation.[114]

6
Mediation Appeals and Fascist Consolidation

Appeals for international mediation: the South American initiative—Fascist aid to Franco: the German–Italian objectives—France in Europe: an analysis of its position

Among the numerous appeals for international mediation which were issued from August onward, none was more interesting, or less likely to succeed, than that by José Castillo, Professor of Roman Law at the University of Madrid and Director of the Spanish National Foundation for Experimental Reform, who propounded in London the following suggestions:

> When one of the two camps has more or less destroyed the other, a dictatorship will be established. Whatever the political persuasion of this dictator, it will in no way satisfy the whole of Spain and revolts will resume.
>
> Catalonia already constitutes an independent unit. The Basques have voted for similar autonomy. The northwest provinces will opt for the same.
>
> I should like France, Britain and the other powers to propose through diplomatic channels the application of autonomy on a general basis.
>
> One region may be Fascist, another Communist, another Socialist, another Republican, and all may live in peace.
>
> The people should be permitted to travel freely from one territory to another. In this way, they will settle in the province under the régime of their choice.
>
> In a few short years, Spain will have understood which system is the best and the others will be abandoned.[1]

The press, too, was pregnant with suggestions, the majority emanating from the centre forces. In *La Dépêche*, Georges Scelle remarked: 'We are all tenants of the same mansion . . . We have the *right* and the *duty* . . . to try to extinguish the fire. To do nothing is to be an accomplice of the incendiaries.'[2] Romier urged that something be done for the hostages.[3] He and Mauriac, in *Le Figaro*,[4] and Milhaud, in *L'Ere Nouvelle*,[5] sought a softening of the passions and an emphasis on whatever the combatants held in common which could lead to a reconciliation. To Mauriac, who reminded his readers that he was born between the Pyrenees and the Garonne, the problem of intervention was now wrongly posited. What was needed, he explained, was a plan of action in which all parties in all countries would agree to intervene. Non-intervention, he now maintained, resembled complicity, given the new intensity of the conflict. 'Help the hostages, protect the prisoners on both sides,' was now his nonpartisan conclusion; 'on that issue all Frenchmen would become interventionists, at least all those with sufficient imagination to picture the meaning of that simple headline in an evening paper: Badajoz taken.'[6*] Similarly, Victor Basch called in *L'Oeuvre* for action by the League of Nations, under Article 11 of the Covenant,[7*] and by the World Court in The Hague.[8] Cooperating for once, Léon Daudet of *L'Action Française* went further: the League was duty-bound to intervene.[9*] *L'Express du Midi*, in supporting Daudet, rebuked the League for its inability to end the atrocities.[10] But in the same daily, at the end of the year, Guèze was to describe the conflict as an internal dispute outside its jurisdiction.[11]

This appeal for a solution even in the form of dictation by outside powers was elaborated notably by Scelle, who pointed out the difference between neutrality and non-intervention. It was possible to intervene, wrote Scelle, while remaining neutral, if the object of the intervention was not to favour one of the parties but to restore public order, the breakdown of which was a threat to the general peace.[12] Over and above the dangers of such a theory, which could be applied to justify any foreign intervention in the name of peace—such as that of Louis XVIII in Spain in 1823—the difficulty lay in finding a mediator who did not arouse the distrust of the other governments. The United States would probably have provided the most effective intervention, but there was little hope that the U.S. Senate would accept the risks, however slight, of such an undertaking. Indeed, so splendid was the isolationism of the United States that her neutrality precluded her participation even in a committee of non-intervention.

It was therefore on the initiative of the Ambassadors of Argentina and Uruguay that a series of conferences was held from the end of August at Saint-Jean-de-Luz, their object being to draft a mediation plan. In spite of the participation of international figures such as the Spanish historian Américo Castro,[13*] the conference failed, less as a result of the absence of precedent or the lack of prestige of the South American republics than because of the indifference displayed by the United States toward their proposals and because of the intransigence shown by the combatants themselves. Alcalá Zamora, at the time of his arrival in Paris from Berlin on 11 August, had announced, with a supercilious air which irritated the Socialist press: 'I do not think that the two sides would accept my mediation.'[14] Again, while the conferences were in session, the former President of the Republic added debonairly: 'Neither mediation from the outside nor settlement from the inside has much chance of success. One side or other will win the field.'[15] What is more, at this same moment the Spanish Ambassador to Paris requested *La Dépêche* to deny, once again and categorically, the report that the Madrid government had invited the great Powers to mediate.[16]

With the failure of the conference at Saint-Jean-de-Luz, attention turned toward 'humanizing' the conflict; if the war could not be stopped, perhaps it could be made less barbarous. Reference was made to the Hague Convention of 1907, signed by 44 nations, and to its Articles 23 (relative to the treatment of prisoners-of-war) and 50 (prescribing reprisals on vanquished peoples). Even the right-wing journal *Journal de Toulouse* suggested the immediate opening of a public subscription fund, the proceeds of which would be donated in exactly equal amounts to the Red Cross in Madrid and the Red Cross in Burgos.[17] Even that did not please Jean Longuet, who in the Socialist press inexplicably denounced the 'hypocrites' of the Red Cross for favouring intervention 'on behalf of the hostages.'[18] In the next breath, the Socialist press was deploring the 'great blight in these events in Spain: the unconcern of the international organisms responsible for implementing, and impeding, international decisions.'[19]

Meanwhile the supply of aid to the rebels by the Fascist states slackened not a whit. For once, all factions of the French press merged in their reaction to German aspirations. Wladimir d'Ormesson traced these aspirations back to the time of Alfonso XIII, whose sympathies toward France owed less to his Bourbon lineage than to the annoyance he felt over German intrigue in the Spanish Rif, especially in relation to the mines.[20] According to Henri de Kérillis, Germany was preparing an offensive against Czechoslovakia even at the beginning of July 1936,[21] but when the curtain rose on the Spanish drama she realized the advantage she could draw from a war in which territorial conquest would be concealed behind a crusade against Bolshevism in the West.[22] Geneviève Tabouis reported that among the papers found on the body of General Sanjurjo[23*] was a plan endorsed by Germany, under which Germany would share with Italy the Mahón base in Minorca, thus threatening the direct line of communications between Marseilles and Algiers.[24] André Marty denounced German intrigue vehemently, on the basis of British[25*] and German reports,[26*] and of a manifesto published by a group of the Commission Européenne d'Aide à l'Espagne (comprising Jean Zyromski, Eugène Henaff and Senator Branting[27*]), which declared: 'The Spanish people would have already suppressed the Fascist rebellion if the rebel leaders had not been able to obtain, and did not still obtain, war matériel from international Fascist organizations.'[28] The organ of the CGT expressed a special indignation: 'The facts are staring us in the face. It is said that non-intervention has now been achieved. It is false! The provision of the rebels continues via Morocco, despite the denials of Queipo de Llano to the *News Chronicle*.'[29] *Le Peuple* had been one of the very few French journals to reserve judgment on the sincerity of Italy's declaration of neutrality, and now it called upon the uncommitted press to open its eyes.[30] The Socialist press provided the evidence: according to the British consul at Vigo, a seaman from a British vessel anchored in this port had witnessed an Italian ship unloading 24 aircraft bound for the rebels.[31] According to *Le Petit Journal*, the Fascist states were not waiting for the rebels to become the uncontested masters of Spain but only for them to disturb the Republic sufficiently to create a chaotic situation which would justify their intervention.[32] In this new War of the Spanish Succession, ran its argument, Spain would loan its soil and its ports to the powers aspiring to replace France both in the control of the Mediterranean and in the responsibility for the future of North Africa, and one day would play the role, on behalf of these powers, of 'an ally in reverse.'[33] Only the fear of a long war, asserted Lucien Romier, with remarkable optimism, could repel the Fascist states, which would collapse in such a war.[34] And on behalf of the Radicals, Pierre Dominique, after upholding the contrary argument,[35] published certain disclosures made to him by the Spanish delegation headed by Marcelino Domingo, the Minister of Education: the rebel leaders had undertaken, in the event of victory and in return for the financial aid received, to cede Spanish Morocco to Germany and the Balearics to Italy.[36] According to Leroux in *Le Midi Socialiste*, a Fascist Spain would allow Italy the use of both, resulting in an eclipse of the military importance of Gibraltar.[37]

The manoeuvres now preoccupied all the right-wing press. In *L'Echo de Paris*, Pertinax warned against another target of German aspirations and intrigue: the Canaries.[38*] According to Jean Vertex in *Candide*, Germany was eying not only the Canaries but the sphere of influence in Spanish Morocco, while Italy would take control of the naval base and the first-class airfield in the Balearics.[39] In *L'Action Française* too, Léon Daudet acknowledged that the cession by Franco to Hitler of a fragment, however small, of Spanish Morocco in return for German collaboration in whatever form would resuscitate to Berlin's benefit the question of Germany in Africa, left in abeyance in 1905.[40] Even Pierre Taittinger, in his *L'Ami du Peuple,* now conceded that the events in Spain were serious because they had provided Germany with the opportunity to recover a place in the Mediterranean.[41] And the affairs of southwest Europe and North Africa, remarked *L'Ordre*, were no longer the concern of Germany; thus her participation, at the request of Italy, in the initial international talks, was seen as a serious embarrassment for France.[42]

It appeared, from the German press, that Germany was on the watch for any pretext to justify the dispatch of military forces. *La Dépêche* believed that Berlin was quite ready to intervene at the end of July.[43] Hitler's policy, however, remained undecided. Confronted with the laissez-faire attitude of Britain and France, the Nationalist-Socialist Party was eager to take advantage of the opportunity, while the Wilhelmstrasse was reluctant. Geneviève Tabouis considered that Hitler would strike only if he felt that the Frente Popular would win.[44] Meanwhile, the celebrations for the *Deutschland* at Ceuta, where on 3 August Franco fêted the officers and crew, presaged nothing but ill for France.

Following a vague announcement by the Madrid government on 16 August concerning a type of blockade, a Republican vessel boarded the German steamship *Kamerun*. The German press immediately magnified the incident into a sensational event. While *Paris-Midi* considered that the Madrid government had committed an incredible blunder by not informing the powers of the precise objectives of its intended blockade,[45] *Le Petit Journal* attributed the German reaction to sheer spite.[46] The Socialist presse carried the slogan: 'AT A PINCH, A NEW EMS TELEGRAM WILL BE DRAFTED, UNLESS HITLER REDUCES THE INCIDENT TO ITS PROPER PROPORTIONS.'[47] Though acknowledging that Hitler was adopting an ever more arrogant attitude, Rosenfeld thought that this attitude was beginning to alarm Italy; Mussolini's acceptance on 21 August of the French non-intervention proposal 'without conditions or reservations'[48*] misled Rosenfeld into thinking that the Duce no longer believed in a Nationalist victory.[49] However, in an identical naval incident which took place on the following day, the Republicans boarded the British steamship *Gibel Zerjon*. The composure with which the British Government reacted to the incident led Rosenfeld to present it to Germany as a fine example to follow.[50]

In the absence of a solution through international mediation, the press concentrated on an examination of French policy in the light of the balance of power.[51*] In *La Journée Industrielle*, Jean Pupier called upon Europe's moderate and liberal states to fulfill their historic destiny by forming a union against extremism in whatever form.[52] Louis de Brouckère, president of the IOS, used this argument to justify intervention: 'Once the Republican troops are beaten, the Western democracies will be beaten with them.'[53] In *Le Petit Journal*, Gabriel Cudenet asserted that Hitler saw nothing in the French neutrality proposal but a confession of weakness and resignation. It was more than ever indispensable, insisted Cudenet, for Paris, London, Moscow, Prague and Brussels to form a 'human front.' The successes of Fascist policy, he thought, were due to the fact that it had a backbone; the policy of the free peoples had not.[54] In the face of an Anglo-Franco-Belgo-Soviet alliance, repeated *L'Ere Nouvelle*, Germany and Italy would be quickly brought to their senses; but to achieve that alliance, added the Radical-Socialist organ, France must first be without sin.[55]

In *La Dépêche*, Senator Aimé Berthod thought that, if the worst came to the worst, France could defend herself at less cost against a Bolshevik domination of Spain than against a Nazi victory.[56] Jaume Miravitlles weighed in with what was obviously the propaganda line of Largo Caballero, who had by now replaced Giral as Prime Minister.[57] German documents found on rebel prisoners, wrote the Catalan councilor, revealed that Franco's plan aimed far beyond Spain; it aimed at the Fascist encirclement of France by lining a third frontier; it aimed at Britain, for the cession of bases to Germany and Italy left disgruntled the chauvinism to which the Nationalist movement appealed, and this discontent could be dispelled only by fabricating an irredentist cause, directed at Gibraltar[58] or Tangier.[59] Augusto Barcia, the former Foreign Minister under both Casares Quiroga and Giral,[60] and Guglielmo Ferrero[61] wrote similar warnings. The alliance of Spain, thought Ferrero, could be of decisive importance if a war should break out on the morrow for the control of the Mediterranean, the future of which was thus being determined at the gates of Madrid.

On the left, Stolz considered in the CGT daily that the war was also a competition for control of the new market which Spain would offer Europe in the future. The SFIO press pointed to the announcement by Queipo de Llano at the end of 1936: 'We offer Germany appreciable trade preferences and advantages of another kind.'[62] Georges Duhamel contributed an article to the leftist weekly *Marianne* entitled 'France in Mortal Danger,' whose argument impressed such unimpressionable figures as the Marquis de Palaminy and Gaston Guèze of *L'Express du Midi*.

These two writers, like most of their colleagues on the right, had upheld a very different argument in this regard. Even in the latter half of November, *L'Express* declared: 'As for the Fascist peril, Monsieur Bracke will simply have to get used to it. In a few months he will have Messrs. Hitler, Mussolini and Franco for his neighbours. No doubt the propinquity will cause some discomfort to the revolutionaries of *L'Humanité* and *Le Populaire*, but we personally find the prospect as pleasing as the comrades find it depressing.'[63] Nevertheless, by mid-December, the tone of *L'Express* had softened for the nonce. Guèze now considered it 'fully justified' that Blum should view Axis infiltration in Spain as a threat to Anglo-French sea routes in the Mediterranean.[64] The editor-in-chief, for his part, now feared that many a Frenchman would fall for the ploy of a crusade against Communism, which was simply 'a Germanic feint to divert the attention of France from the frontier of the Rhine.'[65]*

Perhaps the most clear-sighted exposé of the situation in Europe in the autumn of 1936 was that presented by Azaña himself. Having stated his views to François Andrieu of *La Dépêche* at the beginning of August, the President of the Republic elaborated them in a statement to Andrée Viollis of *Le Petit Parisien* in October:

> Over and above the liberty and independence of the Spanish people, the stakes contested in the apparent 'Civil War' are the balance of power in the Mediterranean, the control of the Straits of Gibraltar, the use of Spanish naval bases in the Atlantic and of the raw materials in which the Spanish subsoil is so rich: copper, mercury, lead and potassium. Such is the prize presently in dispute in this opening scene of a new World War, which is not officially declared, but which stamps so cruel an imprint in Spain.[66]

7
The London Committee

Twenty-four nations participate—The Portuguese position—Accusations and counter-accusations—The Delbos Plan: new support and opposition—Contradictions between Soviet policy and the activities of the French Communists—The reply of *L'Humanité*—Division within the SFIO—The decision of the British Labour Party—Reaction of the Right and French aid to Franco

The Non-intervention Committee had to wait for the agreement of all the participants to the prohibition of all exports of war matériel to Spain and Spanish possessions. We have seen that, in their reply to the French proposal, the Soviet Union, on 5 August, and Italy, on 6 August, imposed conditions.[1] The three Soviet conditions were that Moscow not be held responsible for the activities of the Comintern[2] and other such international organizations, that aid to the Spanish rebels cease forthwith, and that Portugal adhere to the non-intervention plan.[3] Italy's objection to 'ideological and spiritual' intervention, meaning support of the Republic by private organizations and individuals, was apparently satisfied by Blum's adoption of the Delbos–Daladier formula on 8 August and by Chambrun's assurance to Ciano on 14 August that the subscription of funds and the recruitment of volunteers in France would be prohibited. The German objection to the freedom of action for the Comintern[4] and the Soviet claim against Germany's intervention served for the present to cancel each other out. On 23 August, the Soviet Union adopted the official notification of agreement signed by France and Great Britain on 15 August, and on 24 August Germany and Italy followed suit.[5]* In all, 27 nations formally put their signaure to the Non-Intervention agreement. Of these, only 24 attended the inaugural meeting held at the Foreign Office in London on 9 September, under the chairmanship of W.S. Morrison, soon to be replaced by Lord Plymouth. The most important absentee had been the subject of one of the Soviet conditions, namely Portugal, who had been duly invited by Britain and France on 7 August and had given her agreement on 13 August.

Portugal at this time offered the rebels their only permanent and semi-official contact with the diplomatic corps. The Portuguese attitude underlined, in the eyes of the SFIO, the need to organize international control seriously, without which the execution of the Non-intervention Agreement would be impossible. This control, the Socialist press contended, was the more urgent in the light of rumours in early September concerning the delivery of fresh German aircraft, transported to the rebels by ship, mainly through Portuguese ports.[6] In *L'Intransigeant*, Jean Antoine reported that the matériel unloaded in Lisbon on 21 and 22 August from the German freighters *Kamerun* and *Wigbert*, and thence routed northeastward, was intercepted despite such precautions at the railroad station of Setil (Cartaxo), thirty miles northeast of Lisbon, as a result of British intervention. Greater care, added Antoine, was taken thereafter to conceal such operations.[7]* *Le Peuple* also remarked on the apprehensions felt in London over this Luso-German cooperation, and expressed the indignation of the CGT over the 'collusion of the Jesuit Salazar' with the dictator who warred on the Church in his own country.[8] *L'Oeuvre* similarly deplored the fact that Lisbon seemed to be heeding Berlin more than London.[9] *L'Humanité* accused Portugal of being, more than ever, the headquarters, the arsenal and the marshalling yards of the insurgents.[10] On the other hand, the conservative *Le Journal* disclosed, in spite of itself, certain problems facing the Salazar regime, highlighted by a mutiny of the crews of two Portuguese vessels who were eager to lend assistance to the Spanish Republicans. This mutiny, *Le Journal* contended, proved that Soviet agents had been highly active in the country and it explained why the Portuguese Government had recently launched a campaign against Communism.[11] The Socialist press was more blunt. Leroux, in *Le Midi Socialiste*, considered Salazar 'a sort of Portuguese Schuschnigg whom the Vatican uses to prolong the war.'[12]

Portugal finally joined the London Committee on 24 September. Thus all the powers supplying or attempting to supply one or other of the two camps in Spain were assembled to proclaim their allegiances to the neutrality pact. Léon Jouhaux of the CGT expressed the thought of everyone in his remark: 'Neutrality remains a fraud; the Committee, a smoke-screen.'[13]

Each side, however, was eager to surpass the other, through its press organs, in the contest of integrity. 'Portugal,' *L'Express du Midi* contended, 'scrupulously respects the agreement, while it is uncertain that the Soviet Union observes it as strictly.'[14] In Lisbon, confidence in Franco's imminent victory[15] was now such that on 23 October the Portuguese Government broke relations with Madrid. In the Committee itself, the participants were treated to a lively confrontation between the Italian and Soviet delegates. According to Grandi, the charges and evidence submitted by Kagan were 'unfounded' and 'inadequate,' a method of defense which at least one French right-wing paper considered 'brilliant, masterfully putting the Soviet delegate in his place.'[16] In *Le Jour*, Bailby presented Italy as the defender of friendly powers unjustly accused of intervention by Russia. The pro-Fascist editor then described how Grandi, 'dismissing the more or less controlled press reports,' had proven with facts that it was Russia herself who had supplied Madrid with gasoline, 'and that freely.'[17] This no doubt sounded strange to Kagan, who knew well enough that the Soviet Union never gave anything for nothing and would demand payment in the gold of the Bank of Spain for all aid provided. But Grandi played on, describing (accurately) the dispatch of forty Soviet specialists, among the 150 who in fact arrived in Alicante on 13 October, the day after he spoke, and (less certainly), among the catalogue of arms he listed, the shipment of thirty dismantled Soviet aircraft via Warsaw and Toulouse. Grandi did not fail to cast suspicion on Kagan's desire for haste in the Committee and to accuse the Soviet delegate of wanting to break its rules of procedure. In point of fact, Italy was temporizing, confident in the fall of Madrid, as was the French right-wing press. Guèze wrote of the 'slightly Byzantine aura of the discussions in the Committee, on the eve of Franco's entry into the capital.'[18] In his reply, Kagan could still say with truth: 'Not a single Soviet cannon or plane or pilot is to be found in Spain.[19*] If the Committee is incapable of strictly enforcing the agreement, let it say so.'

Kagan had already handed Plymouth, on 7 October, a note resembling an ultimatum.[20] Consequently, a coordinating committee was set up to examine the charges submitted by both sides. Meanwhile, the first Soviet arms arrived in Spain on 15 October, the first Italian troops on 23 October. From this the Committee found the Soviet Union guilty of violation on three counts and Italy guilty on one. The Committee also examined the explanation presented by Germany and found them satisfactory, except for two or three points requiring further details. Obviously, such disregard for the facts could have only one result: the Soviet Union resumed her freedom of action. Then, at the very time that Russia withdrew from the Committee, Lord Plymouth, faithful to the formula 'too little, too late,' proposed the stationing of observers in Spanish ports as a means of international control.

Despite the farce of the Non-intervention Committee, which in Ribbentrop's phrase should have been called the Intervention Committee,[21*] Blum strove to maintain his course, regain the support of the majority and hold his Front Populaire intact. On 6 September, at a Socialist mass gathering in Luna-Park outside Paris, the Premier responded to his critics with a declaration of pacifism:

> I do not believe, I shall never admit that war is destined and inevitable . . .
> The cause, then, is understood. Far be it from a government of the Left, whose whole object is the maintenance of peace, to throw France into a preventive war. The policy of non-intervention represents for the government the unalterable course toward peace.

Thus the centre elements in France continued their support of the Blum–Delbos–Daladier formula into September and beyond. Henry Austruy in *La Nouvelle Revue*,[22] and C.-J. Gignoux, in *La Journée Industrielle*,[23] applauded the 'good sense' of the French Government in seeking to contain the conflict. When in the same week Blum received Dr. Schacht, the German Finance Minister, in Paris, the Socialist press lauded this return to the spirit of Locarno.[24] *La Dépêche* congratulated the government on avoiding the trap set by Berlin[25] and on forcing Fascist aid underground.[26] Both *La Dépêche*[27] and *Le Petit Parisien*[28] wrote of the wisdom of never interfering in a Spanish quarrel. In *Vendémiaire*, Emile Buré considered non-intervention a national duty.[29]

The Spanish Embassy in Paris continued to present the war as a bitter struggle between two ideologies, contending that the war was the symbol of future wars and that to intervene on behalf of the Republic would be no more than to hasten the day of reckoning. To this appeal, *L'Ere Nouvelle* replied bluntly that those who preached intervention and clamored for 'planes for Spain' were 'the spit and image of the heroes of the Crusades, the Inquisition, and the *jihad*.[30]* We ourselves have evolved a little.'[31] The Radical-Socialist organ congratulated Blum on adopting the argument of the Radicals, an argument which, it added, had not wavered.[32] Blum's policy, conclude *L'Ere,* would have no chance now to revert to the Cot formula.[33]

In adopting the cause of the Radicals, however, Blum also compromised the Radicals in the eyes of the Right. Gustave Hervé, in the National Socialist *La Victoire*, washed his hands of the Radical Party. It was the Radicals, contended Hervé, who had abandoned their country, in France as in Spain, 'to the two Marxist revolutionary parties to try to save their Masonic concept of a republic, rather than revise their doctrine.'[34]

Blum's further turn toward the policy of the Radicals came at the time of the inaugural meeting of the London Committee, on 9 September. Only days before, Bracke had been writing in the Socialist press of the 'immorality of neutrality.' Now even Sévérac was saying that to continue to authorize supplies to Madrid was at the same time to give a semblance of right to the Fascist governments to extend de facto recognition to Burgos and then supply the rebels openly, and decisively. Rather than that, Sévérac upheld, strictly limiting both camps to their own resources in Spain would give Madrid the clear advantage.[35] A similar view was taken by *député* François Camel (Ariège), who argued that even if France had aided the Republic, she certainly could not, in her isolation, have assured its victory and she would have surely jeopardized world peace.[36] Even the Internationale Ouvrière Socialiste considered in mid-October that the maximum that could be done for Spain was to persevere in the government's policy since its transition to the Delbos formula.[37] And although *Le Peuple* called periodically for French reconsideration of its non-intervention policy, in the light of Fascist violations,[38] the CGT in December pronounced in turn against any crusade in Spain, whereupon the press, almost in its entirety, applauded the new attitude of Jouhaux.

The attitude of these Radicals and Socialists could not have been farther removed from that of the French Communist Party, which continued to wage an active campaign, distributing pamphlets, posting bills and arranging meetings to the tune of 'Planes for Spain!' The posters, sometimes in five colours, were printed in quantity and quality. In *L'Humanité*, Vaillant-Couturier[39] and Cachin[40] stated emphatically that they did not accept the choice posited by Sévérac: either neutrality or war. None was more opposed to intervention than the Communist Party, insisted Vaillant-Couturier: 'but to blockade, in point of fact, the sole regular government of Spain, when the whole world knows and sees the Fascist powers supplying the rebellion, is, properly speaking, to intervene against our friends the Republic.'[41] The French Communist Party, he explained in November, demanded neither crusades nor interventions. It demanded simply free trade with democratic Spain, and it demanded above all that France 'stop playing a ridiculous and odious role which, far from guaranteeing peace, [brought] the danger of holocaust closer daily, by the incentive it gave to Fascist insolence, in France as well as abroad.'[42] To Léon Blum the Communist organ gave this warning: 'Those who commend you are precisely those who yesterday commended Laval; and they support you because the policy of blockading Spain is akin to the policy of torpedoing the sanctions against Italy.'[43]

The Radical *Le Quotidien* was quick to note this contradiction between the activities of the French Communists and the policy of the Front Populaire government, at the very time that the powers had agreed to the latter's proposed measures of neutrality. 'The prestige of France,' wrote *Le Quotidien*, 'which the French initiative had enhanced, is thus diminished by the duality of action of the parties forming the Front Populaire.'[44]

Apart from this contradiction between the activities of the French Communists and the declared policy of the Front Populaire government, there was another contradiction, even more curious, to be seen between the former and the attitude of the Soviet Government. It was again *Le Quotidien* that asked if the French Communist Party, in its campaign against neutrality, was obeying the directives of the Third International. If it were, the Radical journal observed, it would be necessary to explain why the Soviet Union had imposed an embargo on arms to Spain.[45] In the same way, *Le Matin* wondered why it was that Muscovites no longer gathered in Red Square to chant as they did in Paris: 'Planes for Spain!' 'What are they waiting for? What are they afraid of?' it taunted.[46] In *L'Echo de Paris*, Kérillis found it very strange that the French Communists should have to do more than the Russians.[47] *Le Populaire* had asked the French Communists the same question, before the SFIO modified its policy: 'We demand planes for Spain, but we should like to hear the same demanded in Moscow.' In point of fact, the publication of resolutions and subscription lists had been banned in the entire Russian press from 7 August.[48]

Moscow, *La Dépêche* contended, was fully aware that any ambiguous move could only serve the rebel cause.[49] Moscow, noted *Le Populaire*, had therefore yielded to Hitler's condition which it had previously termed 'unacceptable.' In so doing, the Soviet Union had become the only non-Fascist country to interdict all demonstration of sympathy with the Spanish Republic. 'May we ask why it is,' wrote Bracke, 'that the French Communist Party, being so incensed at its own government, does not direct its demands for a "lifting of the blockade"—albeit in a gentler tone—to a government with which it is in close relations, both ideologically and organically.'[50]

The question could hardly have been more embarrassing to the French Communists;[51*] and hard pressed for an answer, *L'Humanité* strove to divert attention to a different topic: Jacques Duclos would support the Union Nationale proposed by Paul Reynaud.[52] Four days later, the Communist organ believed it had found an escape, in denying any parallel, in the circumstances, between the Soviet Union and France. 'It is the French Government,' it explained, 'which took the initiative of proposing the embargo. The confidence which it thus showed in the Fascist powers has been betrayed by their actions. Experience is the best teacher. The hoped-for neutrality ended in the blockade of the sister republic, in the massacre of our Spanish brothers. Patience has limits.'[53] None of such palliatives had any validity in the view of the Socialist press; even in December *Le Midi* carried this legend: 'WHEN THE SOVIETS HAVE OFFICIALLY ADOPTED THE ATTITUDE WHICH OUR COMMUNISTS DEMAND OF OUR GOVERNMENT, AND WHEN WE HAVE SEEN THE RESULTS, THEN OUR ALLIES [the Communists] CAN TALK TO US AGAIN ABOUT AFFAIRS IN SPAIN.'[54] It was in the hope of finding a solution to this predicament that Thorez made his celebrated visit to Moscow on 21 September.[55]

The cause of *L'Humanité* did hold the support of certain Socialist elements and even a few Radicals such as Pierre Mendès-France, who called for an end to the blockade.[56] A Franco-Spanish committee was formed in Paris on 1 September, under the patronage of Professor Paul Langevin, Jean-Richard Bloch and André Chamson.[57*] The committee requested the Socialist press to insert its two articles of faith: 'Frenchmen unite to end the blockade of Republican Spain! Frenchmen unite lest peace be lost again!'[58*] Zyromski upheld that the lifting of the embargo could not be termed intervention but simply the application of international law.[59] Zyromski, who represented the 'untouchable' faction in this federation, inveighed against the Quai d'Orsay for 'stubbornly clinging to its attitude in defiance of the Soviet initiative.'[60] He submitted a resolution calling for 'the re-establishment of free trade for the Spanish Republic' and advocating 'action by the working class to check the arming of the rebels'[61] and he drew attention to the appeal of the Spanish Socialist Party to the French Socialist Party to denounce the Non-intervention

Agreement.[62]* To insist on conclusive proof of Fascist violations was pure sarcasm, said the party of Largo Caballero, when every government was kept fully informed of these by its consular representatives. It called on France to correct the 'ghastly error' committed in proposing the pact by taking advantage of the Soviet charges to resume her own freedom of action.[63]

Indeed, those Socialists who thought otherwise were now branded by the Communist Party as cowards. The Socialist press reacted to this insult by taking, paradoxically, the argument of the right-wing elements:[64]* 'Among these signatories, are there any Frenchmen?'[65] In reply to Duclos, Deputy F. Roucayrol (Hérault) declared himself an opponent of the Front Français advocated by the Communists as an answer to Hitler, with the words: 'We refuse point-blank to accompany our Communist comrades on this path.'[66] The role of France, continued Sévérac in *Le Populaire*, was to alleviate the suffering of the Spanish Republicans and to offer the refugees both asylum and the maximum of material and moral comfort and assistance. 'But more than that is not neutrality.'[67]

Another claim by the French Communist Party provided their opponents with another chance for riposte. On 27 August, the same day that the French veterans' association announced its unconditional approval of the policy of neutrality, the British Labour Party reached an identical decision.[68] *L'Humanité* did not fail to point out in early September that two of the most important leaders of the Labour Party and the British trades unions had categorically denounced 'the farce of one-way neutrality.'[69] The report of the Communist daily was not false, and indeed, on 9 October, the Labour Party was to support the Soviet ultimatum. But for the moment, the sympathies of the British working class were moving in the opposite direction. As *Le Matin* pointed out, the vote at the Trades Union Congress held on 10 September ran 2,978,000 to 51,000 against intervention in the affairs of Spain.[70]*

The great public debate now raging on this point served to clarify the general issues. *La Dépêche* considered that Blum's attitude spoke for the great majority of French republicans and that *L'Humanité* was merely exploiting 'the unthinking generosity of popular feeling.'[71] *L'Aube* pointed out, however, that if the French Communists were intransigent in their demand for intervention, they were nonetheless careful not to compromise either the fate of the government or the basis of the Front Populaire.[72] But to Bracke in the Socialist press, that was precisely what Thorez was doing by urging the government to intervene and thus pushing France into isolation.[73] Bracke in fact had made a volte-face; he now wrote: 'There is no blockade except in respect of the arming and supplying of the Spanish rebels.' In the view of *Les Echos* too, the Communist Party had shown no desire since September, or even earlier, to ease the task of the government. It incessantly found fresh pretexts to oppose it. It appeared to *Les Echos* that even if the Communist Party repressed its desire to see the government fall, it was nonetheless harassing it in such a way as to weaken it.[74] The prospect of a split in the Front Populaire was not displeasing even to the moderate conservative press, which thus incurred the scorn of *La Dépêche* for 'nearly wanting to congratulate the Communists.'[75]

At the beginning of November, Kérillis remarked in *L'Echo de Paris* that the conflict between Blum and the Communists must be viewed as a struggle transcending the purely parliament sphere. Very probably Blum would resign, wrote the conservative, since he had always said that he would not wish to govern without the support of the Communists. Added Kérillis: 'We shall not mourn his departure.'[76]

Quite clearly, the parties of the Right made capital out of the disarray in the Front Populaire. The French Communist Party compromised everything, wrote their journals, at the same time that they enjoyed the deleterious effect this had on the government and while they attacked the Delbos formula themselves. In *Le Journal*, Clément Vautel tried to show that the declarations of neutrality of the French Government could evoke such reactions as: 'Yes, but are they really neutral in Paris? What about those subscription funds, those meetings, that reception given to the Spanish agitator [La Pasionaria], that impassioned speech of M. Perrin. There's nothing very neutralist about all that. So what double-cross are you playing?'[77] *L'Echo de Paris* and *L'Express du Midi* continued to deplore the 'cynicism'[78] and the 'two-faced behaviour'[79] which they attributed to Roger Salengro, the Minister of the Interior. The former accused the French Government of violating neutrality by authorizing and facilitating the transit across southwestern France of Spanish militiamen moving from one front to the other;[80] the latter charged Salengro with opening the airfields while Delbos talked non-intervention.[81] In *Le Journal de Toulouse*, Victor Lespine, while confessing total ignorance of Franco's means of supply, denounced the French authorities for allegedly allowing trains loaded with war matériel to pass daily through Toulouse and cross the border at Cerbère.[82] In *Le Jour*, Bailby charged that French suppliers, provided with special immunity, had been noticeably constrained and slowed as a result of the 'neat trick played by Italy on Blum and his *mouscoutaires*.'[83] In *L'Action Française*, Maurice Pujo accused the government, even in October, of sending planes to Spain.[84] As a result, he was taken to court.[85]* The same daily created a sensation in December with the publication of de los Ríos' letter of 25 July to José Giral, which referred to Blum's promise to effect delivery of the aircraft through private channels.[86] In *Le Figaro*, Philippe Rolland listed the results of the 'detailed inquiry' he had carried out in Toulouse and Perpignan. Since Rolland's figures for the first eight days in August were actually lower than those shown in official records,[87] and since he provided the points and times of take-off, his information on the aid to the Republic, 'approved by Blum' even after the transition to the Delbos formula, can be considered probably correct:

26 August 1936	1 Bloch-210
27 August 1936	1 Potez-54
3–7 September 1936	5 Loire-46 C.1
18–20 October 1936	7 Potez-54
21 October 1936	1 Dewoitine-371[88*]

L'Express, for its part, followed its policy of using anything to embarrass the Blum government. To this end it reproduced an article from *El Sembrador*, an Anarcho-Syndicalist journal in Puigcerdá, which attacked France vehemently for following a policy of 'belligerent neutrality.'[89] Obviously, the 'belligerent neutrality' about which *El Sembrador* complained concerned not the violations authorized by Cot and Salengro[90*] but others, better concealed, committed by rightist elements themselves.

French aid to the rebel cause took both a material[90*] and a moral[91] form. Spanish right-wing leaders had been setting themselves up since February in French frontier towns. Reporters from *La Dépêche* had been following their activities in Hendaye, Biarritz and Bayonne, and at the frontier observing the precautions taken to prevent capital flight.[91] *L'Humanité* protested against the presence in Biarritz—'the headquarters of the insurrection'—of the 'seditious leaders' Gil Robles, head of the CEDA, and the financer Juan March. A printer in Biarritz had produced a long manifesto, signed by the 'Junta Militar Suprema,' calling on Spain to rebel; copies were being dropped by plane on the other side of the Pyrenees.[92] Following the discovery of these tracts, the French authorities asked Gil Robles and March to leave the city.[93] Two other conspirators, Gabriel Ártica and Francisco Rodríguez, implicated in the affair, were also ordered out.[94] Further Franco agents in Biarritz, who remained there during the month of August to act as recruiters, included the Duke of Los Andes, the Duke of Saint-Cyr, and Matilde Jiménez, the mistress of Juan March. The two dukes were expelled in late August. In *Le Midi Socialiste*, Paul Lenglois reported that monarchists, mounted on mules, were crossing the Basque forests to bring arms to their Carlist friends, while Nazi officials in uniform, accompanied by Philippe Henriot, a journalist and president of the Jeunesses de la Fédération Républicaine, were in the area of Bayonne, where they had gone aboard German merchantships and torpedo-boats. The same journalist reported that señorita María del Pilar Castillo, daughter of the former Spanish ambassador to Peru, was performing her own little work of recruitment among Carlists in the frontier region of Soule.[95] In Saint-Jean-de-Luz, a monarchist agency was uncovered in October; it was engaged particularly in the manufacture and delivery of false passports.[96] Lucien Sampaix, in *L'Humanité,* reported three trucks crossing the Irún frontier on 15 October, loaded with explosives for the insurgents. Gauthier Charentier, of the Union Commerciale Bordelaise in Bassens, shipped 200 tons of rice to

Béhobie, similarly addressed. Colonel de La Rocque himself arrived in Mauléon in late October to facilitate the traffic.[97]

There was constant talk of imminent revolution in France.[98*] Even Charles Magny reported in October that certain bishops, including those of Versailles and Montpellier, fearing a revolutionary movement, had instructed members of the clergy to get hold of passports and civilian clothes in order to be ready if necessary to move instantly abroad.[99] Also in October, a certain Lieutenant-Colonel Gabet made the remark: 'Similar events could very well happen here in France. On that day, I don't know which side I shall be on.' He was awarded 30 days at hard labour and reassigned.[92] In the same month, in the Salle Pleyel in Paris, a meeting was held of the leaders and staffs of the dissolved seditious leagues, under the presidency of Pierre Taittinger; after preaching a sort of international of the parties he called 'national,' Taittinger announced that he was sending, in the name of all French Nationalists, a telegram of solidarity to Franco and Mola.[93] Acting on the inspiration of Henri de Kérillis, *L'Echo de Paris* opened a subscription fund to offer a sword of honour to one of the rebel generals.[94] Two months later, Franco having been selected as the recipient, Taittinger was photographed in Paris holding the sword while a Spanish bishop, Monsignor Palmer, gave it his blessing.[95] Senator Pierre Laval (Puy-de-Dôme) wrote to Franco assuring him that not all France stood with the Front Populaire and that good Frenchmen, such as he, backed the Spanish rebels.[96] In reply, Franco sent Laval a brief which the latter expounded before the Senate Commission; Laval added that he personally favoured the creation of a Holy Alliance of dictators and a definitive break with Britain.[97] There were reports that even official French circles were lending assistance to individual Nationalists. Lieutenant-Colonel Augusto Muñoz Grandes, the former chief of the Guardia de Asalto which had largely remained loyal to the Republic, had been arrested in the first week of the war.[98*] He escaped, took refuge in the French Embassy in Madrid and was given shelter in the French Lycée. In July 1937, again with the assistance of the French Embassy, and accompanied by his adjutant, Major Batalla, he boarded the *Hyméréthée* anchored in Alicante by using a false name, and so escaped to France. The French Embassy in Madrid, again using the French Lycée, also gave shelter in October 1936 to General Espinosa de los Monteros until he too could be evacuated in July 1937.

There was further aid to the Nationalists from the French private sector. In the offices of *L'Echo d'Indre et Loire* in Tours, a four-page pamphlet went on sale which recounted, from the reports of special correspondents in Spain of several French and foreign journals, the atrocities committed by the Republicans.[100] *L'Express* invited its readers to address their donations to Roussillon, 9 Rue Foy, Perpignan.[101] A committee formed in Toulouse and elsewhere of gifts of money or in kind, to be donated to the 'saviours of the country'; donations were to be addressed to *L'Express*.[102] In December, Kérillis and six other Deputies, all National Republicans, who had just returned from a fact-finding visit to Nationalist Spain, published the following manifesto: 'The abstention of France from supplying war matériel to the Nationalists . . . allows the situation to develop in a way harmful to the long-range interests of France.'[103]* Thus, concluded *La Dépêche*, the French Right had supported non-intervention only as long as it believed that to do so was in the interests of the insurrection.[104] It was a fitting testimony to the failure of the rebel cause at the end of 1936.

8

The Soviet Ultimatum and Intervention

Soviet policy—The French 'Trotskyists'—The ultimatum of 7 October—The London Committee steps back—The effect on French policy

Stalin's foreign policy in the nineteen-thirties had all the intricate and interwoven patterns of a Persian rug. In regard to Spain, it supported the Republic from 1931 insofar as it applauded the end of the Monarchy. It supported the July Revolution insofar as the Revolution increased the power of the Spanish proletariat. It supported the transition from Giral to Largo Caballero insofar as the transition was a move toward the left and represented a stiffening of the Republic's will to resist—only to find that Largo Caballero was of minimal use to the Kremlin's purposes. In domestic affairs, the revolution he preached had an odious ring of independence to it. And in foreign affairs, his revolutionary image threatened to lose him the sympathies of the middle-classes in France and Britain, without whose support the Soviet Union could not achieve her ultimate goal: a confrontation between the Western democracies and the Fascist states, sufficiently internecine to allow Russia finally to enter and pick up the pieces.[1]*

The French transition to the Delbos formula was therefore a blow to Soviet policy. But in order not to endanger her pact with France by alienating the French bourgeoisie, Russia reluctantly accepted the fact that she would have to take the lead herself in supplying the Republic. As Puzzo and others show,[2] her main objective was not to defend the Republic as such, but to prolong the war so as to widen the gulf between the democracies and the Fascist states and so preclude any return to the spirit of Locarno which would restore Russia to isolation. On the other hand, while the Soviet Union desperately strove to delay a Fascist victory in Spain, her assistance to the Republic was necessarily limited, partly because she could not afford to antagonize the democracies, and partly because she could not hope to match the aid supplied by the closer Fascist states or afford to denude her own defences in the face of a dual threat from Germany and Japan. To this end, the Soviet Union sought in France as in Spain two objectives which sometimes seemed to conflict. In Spain, Stalin was providing the Republic with sufficient aid to survive, but not sufficient to win. In France, the USSR was discouraging the spirit of appeasement while holding together the Front Populaire. In pursuing these objectives, Stalin's policy was in fact in tandem with Hitler's: both were strangely self-contradictory. Both sides wanted to keep their Spanish pawn on the chess board and prevent their opponent from winning; at the same time, both sides hesitated to provide their champion with the power necessary to score checkmate, because too large an engagement in Spain was contrary to both their interests.[3*]

The tendency in the French press was to oversimplify this Soviet policy. In *L'Action Française*, Charles Maurras contended that the Kremlin aimed at grouping the nations of Europe not on the basis of national interests—which, thought Maurras, would align France with Britain, Belgium, Italy, Poland and the Petite-Entente[4*]—but on the basis of ideology: the friends of 'democracy' against the friends of Fascism, 'in the dream of attracting into the revolutionary camp conservative, aristocratic, monarchic Britain!'[5]

The curious 'contradiction' between the Soviet Union's declared policy and the activities of the French Communist Party[6] led Bracke to repeat a generally accepted tenet that the French Communist is a Frenchman first and a Communist second. The reply of the Right, however, that 'Russian Communists and French Communists are of the selfsame mind,'[7] had much to commend it. It is quite certain that the French Communist Party was still taking its orders from the Kremlin, for the Party represented the last chance of committing the Front Populaire to an interventionist policy. And in the event of failure or embarrassment, the Kremlin could still call the French Communists Trotskyists.

Trotskyists, in fact, was the term used by *L'Ere Nouvelle* to describe them. If they condemned direct intervention, contended the Radical-Socalist daily, these French Trotskyists continued to support Madrid in every possible form. *L'Ere Nouvelle* added, with a straight face: 'The Soviet Government, which has wisely and admirably understood that Trotskyist methods lead to foreign war and which proclaims its resolute attachment to the cause of peace, has condemned these methods, with what energy we know!'[8] The real Trotskyists, however, were known very well to *L'Humanité*; they were those Communists who wished to see the Soviet Union adhere to the bequest of Lenin: 'Revolution everywhere!' Whether or not Lenin would have held in 1936 to a view expressed in 1917 is open to question, but *L'Humanité* was satisfied he would not. Vaillant-Couturier thus excused the Soviet Union for her neutrality: 'Otherwise it means the isolation of the Soviet Union . . . It would require the soul of a Trotskyist *provocateur* not to see that or to wish a catastrophe [such as the intervention of the Soviet Union] on the proletariat.'[9]

As we have seen, the Soviet Union, instead of intervening, directly or indirectly, opted for the neutrality agreement, announcing its acceptance on 23

August and interdicting the export of all matériel to Spain on 28 August. Nevertheless, motivated either by fear of the Fascist states or by duplicity, or by a combination of the two, within three days it set up an organization for the supply of Communist, but not Soviet, arms. On 21 September, Stalin took the decision to send aid to the Republic; on that same day, Krivitsky arrived in Paris to begin the organization of international aid.[10]* Meanwhile, the Soviet delegation in the London Committee could complain with justification that no change was to be seen in the policies of Italy and Germany. *Le Peuple* as well as *L'Humanité* adopted the Soviet point of view: neutrality continued to be expressed by the incessant reinforcement of the rebels while the Spanish Government was subjected to a blockade. 'What was at first a fraud,' wrote the CGT organ, 'is now simply a lie.'[11] Indeed, *Le Petit Journal* asked the same question, and in a headline: 'WAS IT NOT CLEARLY UNDERSTOOD THAT NEUTRALITY WAS NOT TO BE A ONE-WAY STREET?'[12] The Communist organ, for its part, presented the Soviet point of view in these terms:

> France spoke as follows [on 8 August]: 'My purpose is to prevent the provision of the rebellion. To obtain my end, I am undoubtedly placing the Republic and the rebels on the same standing, but in return I am impeding the latter from obtaining aid from international Fascism. The quicker the peace-loving nations friendly to the Republic adhere to my initiative, the more certainly I shall obtain this result. It is the more necessary that no peaceful power provide by its abstention a pretext for Germany and Italy to withdraw.'
>
> It can easily be imagined to what degree the Soviet Union would be reproached if after that she refused her adherence. The Soviet Union has therefore subscribed to the initiative taken by a friendly nation, without concealing the fact that this initiative seemed to her unjust and constituted a dangerous precedent in her eyes. On this understanding, the Soviet commitment, like the French proposal itself, was of a conditional nature. It was valid only insofar as non-intervention would be effective.[13]

The trajectory of Soviet policy through the month of October monopolized the attention of the press. Having failed in her plan to involve France, the Soviet Union could no longer defer her decision. Never perhaps since the march on Warsaw, wrote Raymond Cartier in *L'Echo de Paris*, had Soviet Russia experienced so decisive a moment.[14] The quasi-ultimatum submitted by Kagan on 7 October, threatening Russia's withdrawal from the Committee unless violations of the Agreement ceased immediately, evoked an editorial reaction which, in the main, considered that a satisfactory solution was still possible. *L'Ordre*, in particular, expressed relative optimism, pointing out that the Soviet Union had committed nothing yet irreparable and that she would give her full support to the formation of a commission of inquiry.[15] *La Dépêche* wondered if this move would succeed at least in slowing the intensive provision of the Nationalist armies by Portugal and in galvanizing the spirit of resistance of the Loyalist forces.[16] Neither the one nor the other, replied *Le Matin*: 'Russia has already lost her campaign in Spain.'[17] What the Soviet Union demanded in her last try was not, however, any different in principle from the proposal submitted to the Committee by Lord Plymoth two weeks later:[18] 'We require the Committee to establish a control of the Portuguese ports, through the agency of the British or French fleet, or of both fleets together.'[19] These 'odious demands of the Kremlin,' as *L'Express du Midi* described them,[20] were reportedly not even taken into consideration in political circles.[21]*

On 28 October, the Soviet Union, refusing to be bound 'in any greater measure than any of the other participants in the Agreement,' withdrew from the London Committee. Her action evoked no surprise in the press. Although the move was justifiable insofar as the Agreement lacked the force of a treaty, was loosely binding, and depended upon the goodwill of each signatory state, it was generally considered a desperate action that was bound to evoke angry criticism. *La Dépêche* remarked that Moscow could not have failed to understand that its decision could consummate the collapse of the Spanish Republic, unless, by its decision, the Soviet Government still hoped to force the hand of the French Government, whereby the latter would render the help that Russia's own remoteness prevented her from giving effectively. The fact remained, added *La Dépêche,* that the Franco-Soviet pact, concluded within the framework of the League of Nations, was not intended to revive the age of the Crusades but to maintain peace.[22] Thus the question resolved itself into this: did the Soviet move affect France under the Franco-Soviet pact? The reply of the Right was predictable, but the Radicals and moderates were divided. No, answered Roche and Dominique.[23] Yes, replied *L'Oeuvre*, and her support of the Soviet Government would thus ensure the European balance.[24] No, retorted Frossard in *Marianne*: France was certainly not failing in her obligations under the pact by adhering to the Non-intervention Agreement in Spain, bearing in mind that the contrary attitude would not only fail to provide decisive aid to the Republicans but would also risk escalating the war. 'Unless we fall into thinking,' added Frossard, 'that we shall have to fight sooner or later and therefore the sooner the better. Unless we fall into believing in the inevitability of war and unless we want a "preventive war"!'[25]

The reaction of the press of the Centre and Right to the Soviet move was varied. For *L'Ere Nouvelle*, none of the European governments had the right to renounce the principle of non-intervention. The organ of Herriot argued naïvely that any violation of the Agreement would provoke such a storm of public protest that it was hard to believe that the denounced infringements could possibly have taken place. *L'Ere* thus considered the Agreement, in the current circumstances, as 'the guarantee of European order.'[26] The Russian move was similarly described by *Le Figaro* as 'a diplomatic offensive to undo the concord of the powers.' The Soviet decision, *Le Figaro* contended, necessitated a fresh examination of the question of non-intervention, to which the Socialist press replied that the examination might well commence with an investigation of the charges presented at Geneva by Álvarez del Vayo.[27] *Le Figaro* further asserted that the Soviet decision, coinciding 'as if by chance' with a new approach to the British Government by British Labour Party members, could have disastrous effects on the maintenance of peace in Europe,[28] an argument which the Socialist press described as 'the whole gamut of Nazi blackmail.'[29]

Other right-wing journals scoffed at the motivation and implications of the Soviet withdrawal from the Committee. Guèze reacted predictably in *L'Express du Midi*: 'The attempt of the Soviets to torpedo the Conference was a piece of theatre, as untimely as it was uncalled for . . .[30] It was sufficient for the Soviet Union to claim, without any basis in fact, that Germany and Italy had dispatched three muskets to the Nationalists.'[31] In *La Victoire*, Gustave Hervé called it bluff: 'And so what? Moscow arrives on the scene like a petty customs officer . . . The Frente Popular is in full retreat. The fall of Madrid is now a mere matter of days. The most that Moscow can do is to send some ships to Valencia to pick up the fugitives.'[32] Pertinax, in *L'Echo de Paris*, also disbelieved that the break-up in the London Committee could change the course of events: 'It comes too late. No Socialist country or Popular Front can any longer prevent the collapse of the Madrid government.'[33] The French military attaché in Madrid, Lieutenant-Colonel Morel, also thought that the fall of the capital was imminent.[34]* Indeed, even Largo Caballero gave Madrid up for lost: on 6 November, the Republic transferred its capital to Valencia.

9
The Foreign Volunteers

Blum agrees to the departure of the volunteers—The first arrivals—Franco's response—Travel restrictions—The International Brigades move into formation—Opposition to their formation and to their recruitment in France—Foreign volunteers for the insurgency

For the political forces surrounding Cot, still searching for a formula for aid acceptable to the majority of the French people, another possibility presented itself. If the government were constrained by the need for caution, Jouhaux pointed out in the CGT journal, the peoples and organized labour remained free to 'show their active sympathy' with those fighting on their behalf. *L'Oeuvre* described the issue as an appeal to idealism. For the Radical daily, France was a country whose people would never be stopped from rallying to a noble cause, and rallying to it so much the more if the cause seemed for a moment compromised:

> If there are Frenchmen who join the Spanish Republicans to help in the defence of their freedom, and if there are others who provide them with the means to defend that freedom, they are simply repeating a gesture which has left its mark in history and which we have never had a cause to regret: the gesture of Beaumarchais and La Fayette.[1]

On the other hand, *Le Temps* reproached the Republican Government for accepting such aid, and the French Government for permitting it.[2] Another French journal carried the headline: 'LET US BE NEUTRAL! IT IS NOT GRANDIOSE, BUT IT IS SAFER.' Vandervelde replied in *La Dépêche*: 'To avoid greater evils, it is necessary to resign oneself to many things. Non-intervention can concern only governments. Individual or collective action, in the nature of things, remains free.' In free countries, added the Belgian Socialist, the working masses would never be stopped from 'giving evidence of their active sympathies' with those defending democracy against those intent on destroying it.[3] The words were written in the same month that the British Labour Party replied with a declaration of non-intervention.

It must be remembered that France had not extended Franco the rights of a belligerent. But even if she had, Article 6 of the Hague Convention (V) of

1907, respecting the rights and duties of neutral powers and persons in case of war on land, stipulates that 'the responsibility of a neutral power is not engaged by the fact of persons crossing the frontier separately to offer their services to one of the belligerents.' Thus, Blum was entirely within his rights in authorizing, at the beginning of August, French and foreign volunteers to leave France, on condition that they held a regular passport and travelled unarmed.[4] A group of some fifty Spaniards living in Toulouse had already formed in the Place du Capitole at 6 a.m. on 29 July; they were driven off by coach.[5*] Within ten days, Georges Naychent, of *La Dépêche,* had observed in Barcelona that the workers' militia were assuming more and more the appearance of a foreign legion; Italians, Portuguese and Brazilians were already in evidence.[6] The first French volunteers reported for duty on 15 August having entered via Irún.[7] On the following day, *La Dépêche* reported that a former Italian senior officer, who had taken asylum in France, would take command of a foreign contingent, composed mainly of French and anti-Fascist Italian and German volunteers.[8] At the same time, the first medical assistance teams reached Barcelona and Madrid; the first of these was provided by the Comité de Vigilance des Intellectuels Antifascistes, under the direction of Georges Rul,[9*] followed by the first British mission, which passed through Toulouse at the end of August.[10]

The reaction of the rebels was instant and emphatic. *Le Matin* published this message from Franco:

> It is with surprise and sorrow that we learn that France is permitting the enrollment of combatants whose intention is to join the troops of Madrid.
>
> If France, the gentle France whom we love, should so forget her duties and persist in her error, she will have dug a deep trench between two nations who were sisters and whose destinies in history were often bound together.
>
> France, there is still time to avoid the catastrophe! Frenchmen, think of your future![11]

Once the rebels had installed themselves along the Basque frontier, the only means for Republican Spain to communicate with France by land were the rail routes Narbonne-Cerbère-Portbou and Toulouse-Latour de Carol-Puigcerdá; the latter was in bad condition, which made it useless for heavy traffic. Traffic by road, for its part, could not in any way replace rail traffic, given the scarcity of vehicles in Spain. The Port-Bou station thus took on such importance for the Republican cause that, in the words of *La Dépêche,* once that station was destroyed it would mean famine for the Republic.[12] The Port-Bou tunnel thus became a major target for Franco's saboteurs. Immediately after the closing of the Irún frontier, two Nationalist volunteers were assigned to dynamiting both the tunnel and the Colera bridge. Their poor knowledge of the Catalan language proved fatal to them; they were quickly arrested. Two further attempts were made. The first to try was a German who was arrested carrying explosives into the tunnel. The second was a Catalan Requeté who was completely out of luck. In reporting on this in *La Dépêche*, Rieu-Vernet stressed that it was the imminent arrival of the foreign volunteers that worried Franco most.[13] Even if the Nationalists were to succeed in destroying this rail line, they could hardly expect to block the Perthus road. In any case, in order to put an end to further attacks on these routes, the tunnel pass and the Cerbère-Port-Bou road were closed in mid-September by the French authorities.[14*]

In the subsequent vicissitudes of Blum's policy, the French authorities imposed certain restrictions in respect of the passage through France of foreign volunteers. Most of these volunteers arrived from Brussels, conducted to the Franco-Belgian border by what *La Dépêche* termed an international Anarcho-Communist organization in the Belgian capital. At the border, those whose documents were not in order were sent back by the French authorities.[15*] However, the closing of the Basque frontier resulted in an increase in the ranks of the volunteers entering Catalonia. Two hundred passed through Perpignan in a single day in October.[16*] A complete train transporting four hundred volunteers was reported passing through the town on 10 November; four hundred others, the majority of them Polish, allegedly reached Perpignan in taxis.[17] Another eight hundred volunteers were reported passing through Perpignan on 25 November.[18*] Meanwhile, some two hundred and sixty volunteers left Marseilles for Valencia.[19] According to Dominique, from 12 December a party of one hundred and thirty French volunteers left the Paris-Austerlitz station for Barcelona at 10.17 p.m. daily. 'It is impossible to obtain any further information,' added Dominique; 'the station employees are under orders not to reply to any question on this subject, and yet a regular departure of this kind cannot be carried out without the consent of the railroad administration.'[20] *Le Matin* joined the voices on the far right demanding that the government stop all volunteers from passing through France.[21] The volunteers, however, seemed to experience greater difficulty in entering Republican territory where the FAI (Federación Anarquista Ibérica) was in control. Passage across the Catalan border had passed into the authority of the FAI from the outbreak of war. No one passed into France without its authorization. Nor into Spain either. To do so required a safe-conduct pass issued by the antifascist committees in Perpignan, Cerbère or Bourg-Madame, depending on whether one approached the frontier at La Junquera, Port Bou or Puigcerdá.[22] Clara Candiani even reported that the FAI authorities in August 1936 demanded from her a pass issued by the FAI in France; she explained to them that the FAI did not exist in France.[23*] It was the fear of losing its hard-won influence that led the FAI not only to oppose general mobilization in Catalonia but to try to restrict the number of foreign volunteers, on the pretext that they might spread defeatism. Thus, of 600 volunteers who reached the border in mid-November, the FAI sent 150 back to Perpignan.[24]

There was at the same time a certain traffic in the opposite direction. Many young Catalans were crossing the frontier daily, for one of three main reasons: first, the mobilization order announced in October by the Generalitat; second, a fascist propaganda unit, set up in Ripoll (Gerona), that was fairly successful in offering bribes to those who deserted;[25] and third, the terrorism of the FAI, that had a serious effect on morale. *L'Express du Midi* made much of the reign of terror in the Val d'Arán (Lérida) and in Andorra, whose only access that was constantly open was on the Catalan side. Faced with the threats of the anarchists and the provocations of the fascists, the muncipalities in Le Perthus and Andorra asked the Prefect to close the frontier across the entire line.[26*] Andorra, under the joint sovereignty of the President of the French Republic and the Bishop of Seo de Urgel, finally asked[27*] for the protection of France, which at once sent a detachment of Gardes Mobiles.[28] Entry into France was also denied, in early December, to the President of the Generalitat, Lluís Companys. When Companys reached Cerbère, the Prefect of Pyrénées-Orientales, Raoul Didkowski, who was formerly head of the Sûreté Nationale, welcomed him on to French soil, but he also informed him that the French Government was averse to his taking part in the demonstration in Paris on 5 December. He was asked not to attend and to postpone his journey, whereupon Companys returned to Barcelona.[29]

His saboteurs having failed, Franco now entrusted the destruction of the Port Bou station to his air force. On 16 December four Junker bombers encroached on French airspace in order to bomb the station. The population of the town entered the tunnel to take refuge in Cerbère. Many of the inhabitants of Port Bou and Colera then stayed in villages on the Roussillon coast. For *La Dépêche*, this air attack followed 'a premeditated plan of provocation' whose aim was to close down all rail communications between France and Spain.[30] The Socialist mayor of Cerbère, Julien Cruzel, asked for air protection against the rebel planes and boats. Blum replied by sending a torpedo-ship.[31] The station's main building was now draped in two huge tricolore flags, 'so that the Junkers and Caproni make no more mistakes.'[32] But in effect the 'premeditated plan' had some success, because as a result of this bombing attack French trains no longer entered Spain but stopped at Cerbère.[33]

Apart from the volunteers, what Franco feared seeing, entering Spain through the only frontier gap that remained open, was of course the supplies. If, in the winter of 1936, there were grave violations of neutrality on the part of France, it is certain that the right-wing press did not find them. In *L'Express du Midi,* Guèze fulminated in December about suspicious convoys encumbering the roads in Aude and Pyrénées-Orientales,[34] but gave no evidence. The accusations against the Blum government were baseless.

Meanwhile, the International Brigades, first described in the press as the 'foreign corps'[35] or even the 'international legion,'[36*] went into the line on the Madrid front on 11 November, four days after the opening of Franco's first assault on the capital. The strength of these Brigades was deliberately exaggerated by the right-wing press as by Nationalist propaganda, 'to give an impression that the whole Republican Army had been taken over by the Brigades.'[37] *L'Express du Midi* even claimed that there was not a *madrileño* or a Catalan left in the whole Loyalist Army.[38] *Le Figaro* estimated that the number of Russians and the 'mercenaries from all countries' who had entered the fray by February 1937 amounted to 70–75,000, of which 20–25,000 were French.[39] Even Ambassador Herbette reported in November that the combatants included 21,000 Russians.[40] Even Rieu-Vernet twice calculated the number of Loyalist volunteers at fifty battalions,[41] when the total never exceeded more than five brigades or 18,000 men, of which 60 percent was required to consist of Spaniards (though this percentage was later reduced to 12 or 15). In early 1938, Émile Vandervelde visited the XIV Brigade. He found that its components were 70 percent Spanish, most of the remainder being French or Belgian, while Russian representation was minimal.[42*] Nonetheless, in April of that year the very partisan General Toussan contended that the Republican Army, 'equal in strength to the Nationalists in July 1936,'[43] had since received as many troops again from abroad.[44*] Meanwhile, according to *Le Matin*, the Soviet Ambassador to Madrid, Marcel Rosenberg, had made it clear that Soviet aid was predicated upon the condition that command of this force be given to Soviet officers.[45] In point of fact, though almost all the International Battalions were placed under Communist commanders, none of these was Russian. Political discipline was entrusted largely to three French commissars: Marty and Vidal-Gayman,[46*] from Paris, and Billoux, from Marseilles.[47]

In the transit and departure of volunteers, two other legal aspects must be considered: their formation and their recruitment. The free assembly of volunteers is as unassailable as their crossing the border singly. Nevertheless, the authorization given by the Blum government to the formation of groups, which naturally won the warm approval of *L'Humanité*,[48] served to galvanize the opposition of the right-wing press. Pertinax, in *L'Echo de Paris*,[49] and Bailby, in *Le Jour*,[50] protested vehemently. *Le Matin* termed it a provocation,[51] while *Le Journal* asked if it was compatible with neutrality.[52] Anatole de Monzie deplored in *La Tribune des Nations* the readiness of some to volunteer for service in the Civil War when they would refuse to take part in a regular war, who were willing enough to die fighting, but for the party, not the country.[53] In *L'Action Française*, Georges Gaudy expressed his grief to see so many French lives sacrificed to a cause which was 'not their concern at all.' These men, he added, 'willingly or reluctantly enrolled,' might have been at his side, dressed in sky-blue.[54*] In affecting compassion for the Republican volunteers, in depicting them as lambs led willy-nilly to the slaughter, Gaudy presumably hoped to imbue them with terror.[55*] However, as a good Nationalist, he took pains to exalt the prowess in arms of the French combatants at the expense of their Spanish comrades. Thus, while the Frenchmen brought to the battle 'their hereditary virtues,' their Spanish companions, 'seized with fright at the sight of the tanks or planes, often abandon[ed], on the approach of these machines, the positions where the French [hung] on and [were] thus overrun, a serious matter in a conflict in which none show[ed] quarter.'[56] The Marquis de Palaminy was also 'deeply grieved' to see Frenchmen dying in Spain in the belief that they were saving humanity from the Fascist yoke. As Palaminy and his *L'Express du Midi* neared the end of life, his ideas were more confused, his ideals less relevant:

> Where, then are the Fascists, if not in the ranks of those who wage revolution to insure the worst of dictatorships?
> Those young Frenchmen . . . would do better to work on the repopulation of France.
> These are the wages . . . of the search for emancipation, . . . of the efforts to snuff out the stars of Heaven.

'Frenchmen have lost their taste for service,' concluded the Marquis on a feudal note.[57] *L'Express* continued to deplore the 'unspeakable traffic in French cannon-fodder' passing through Toulouse.[58] The same journal reported that, in the Barcelona suburb of Vallvidrera, volunteers who had refused to leave for the northwestern front had been executed.[59] By mid-December, without stopping to consider the charges and demands made by Álvarez del Vayo at Geneva,[60] Guèze was calling for an end to 'this odious crimpage'[61] and even for the dissolution of the Brigades,[62] a testimony to their worth.[63*] *Député* and former Minister Louis Rollin (Paris) demanded that all Frenchmen who served as volunteers in Spain forfeit their French citizenship. 'It is important to protect young Frenchmen,' he explained, 'against the sway of passions all too generous.'[64] A French veterans' association also allegedly protested against Frenchmen enrolling in the Spanish forces.[65] Even among the Radical Socialists, *L'Ere Nouvelle* objected to the transit of volunteers as well as their recruitment.[66]

Article 4 of the aforesaid Hague Convention of 1907 stipulates that 'corps of combatants cannot be formed nor recruiting agencies opened on the territory of a neutral Power to assist the belligerents.' The mere formulation of volunteers in small groups could be construed as individual action. Their recruitment and organization on French soil was quite a different matter, and some journals who had failed to make much impression in their opposition on the first now concentrated on the second. According to *L'Echo de Paris*, arrangements to recruit French volunteers for the Republic were made in Paris as early as 24 July, nearly two months before the arrival of Krivitsky.[67] Two Spanish Communist leaders, Juan Robertico and Fernández Peña, allegedly visited French Communist leaders to request them to recruit a battalion of volunteers as a token of Communist solidarity. The Politbureau was reported to have given its consent.[68] In *Le Jour*, Bailby accused Spanish Ambassador Araquistain of being a 'recruiting sergeant.'[69] The Ambassador replied that, on the contrary, he was making every effort to prevent or discourage applicants from 'spontaneously leaving for Spain to fight an enemy . . . whom they consider a potential enemy of France.'[70] In December, André Marty and Pietro Nenni published an appeal to help the Brigades.[71] The existence of recruitment centres in Paris and Marseilles was now common knowledge.[72*] The British Conservative Member of Parliament Alfred Denville announced that he had personally witnessed, in southeastern France, the recruitment of Frenchmen to be sent to Barcelona, an operation which the right wing press instantly branded a violation of neutrality.[73] Even more serious for the Blum government was the charge that minors had been enrolled as combatants. Even before the departure for Barcelona of the sons of Alcalá Zamora,[74] the Minister of the Interior was apprised of a number of complaints of such enrolments. The Minister consequently instructed Prefects to prevent this practice and to insure that the departure of volunteers did not assume an organized or collective character.[75]

There was also the question of foreign volunteers for the rebel cause. Apart from the obviously 'organized and collective' character of Italian and German combatants, there were others, admittedly insignificant, who genuinely volunteered in the democracies.[76*] At the beginning of September, Mola grandly announced that he would proceed to the enrolment of foreigners wishing to find service in his cause.[77] Two months later, however, he stressed in an interview with Nicolas of *L'Express du Midi* that there were necessarily few Frenchmen in the Nationalist ranks, 'since we have never sought to attract foreign volunteers, on account of the national character of the movement;'[78] all this in the very same month that Cerruti confided to Ambassador Bullitt in Paris that Franco's effectives were 'insufficient to enable him to conquer the whole of Spain,'[79] and in the same month too that Ramón Franco was negotiating with Mussolini for a massive intervention of Italian 'volunteers'.[80] In any event, French volunteers had enrolled in the 'White' forces, according to *Le Figaro*, in time to take part in the triumphant entry into San Sebastián.[81] In fact, the French contingent was a major disappointment. There had been talk of a French 'Tercio'. Instead, the 'Jeanne d'Arc' was little more than the size of a company. Their number did not exceed 300, even when some Belgians and some Swiss are included.[82] Other Frenchmen had allegedly volunteered to serve in the Republican ranks in order to commit acts of sabotage.[83] In December, *L'Action Française* explained the reason for the 'insignificant number' of foreign volunteers in the Nationalist ranks. According to Georges Gaudy, the ratio was in keeping with Franco's 'orders.' 'Why would he want to recruit combatants among the French?' asked Gaudy. 'His reserves are enormous . . . There would be no purpose in the French offering him their services. Trust Spain to work out her salvation with her own.'[84*] Apart from service freely and individually offered, the matter of recruiting volunteers was in turn raised by the Left with reference to the activities of pro-Nationalist agents in France, including a White Russian general.[85] In any event, certain Frenchmen fighting on the Nationalist side confessed to a private resentment: a pro-Fascist Paris journal deplored Germany's distraint of Spain, asserting the 'these brave volunteers fighting like good sportsmen' could not abide the contact with the Germans into which circumstances forced them.[86]

10
Axis Recognition of Franco

The 'preventive counter-revolution' against the mere idea of a Catalan republic—Franco's failure before Madrid: its repercussions on Axis policy—Relations between Hitler and Mussolini: the common front—Blockade and recognition: repercussions on the democracies—Reflections on the granting of belligerent status to Franco—The Pan-American Conference—A socialist delegation visits London

Meanwhile, the governments of Hitler and Mussolini were pursuing what their apologists called their 'preventive counter-revolution,' providing Franco with 'the means of defence.'[1*] According to Leroux, Hitler and Mussolini were encouraging Franco to persist *at any price*. The more Spain was ruined, thought the Socialist editor, the greater the chance for Berlin and Rome to derive advantage, for Franco would have to turn to them for the reconstruction of the country.[2] Some voices on the Right disclosed the same fears, notably the ever less germanophile Henri de Kérillis. The Paris *député* no longer looked on the Führer as the disinterested crusader and defender of civilization, nor as the little St. Joan dreaming of saving from the slaughter all the frightened bourgeois of the world. Instead, Kérillis had reached two conclusions. The first was that Germany was preparing to colonize Spain, even though Italy was as much opposed to the prospect as were Britain and France. France, in her turn, would be caught in the pincer movement, 'the historic collusion between the Germanic and the Iberian worlds.' His second conclusion was that Hitler was treating Spain as he would treat France if another revolution should break out there.[3] *L'Express du Midi* also felt a growing anxiety over the international repercussions[4*] and the possibility of escalation, in the event that the Nationalist cause failed and Rome and Berlin decided to continue their aid.[5*] *La Dépêche* offered some reassurance at the beginning of December with the reminder that neither Italy nor Germany was sufficiently affluent to underwrite the whole of Franco's cause, the expenses of which amounted to six million pesetas a day.[6]

The failure of the Madrid offensive, even the failure of the first assault, resulted in the visit of Ramón Franco to Rome. This visit reminded Leroux[7] of Franco's earlier threat to arrange an international incident in the event of failure.[8*] Even the right-wing press failed to obtain any information on this visit. When the correspondent of *L'Express* asked Ramón Franco a question in Naples, the Caudillo's brother termed it 'very indiscreet. We are at war and we cannot disclose details of either our directives or our objectives.'[9] There was no mystery about Italian objectives, however; the goal was supremacy in the Western Mediterranean and the fragmentation of French military forces. After a visit to Italy, Jacques Maxence reported in *La Griffe* the hint by Rome that Spain under Franco would provide an outlet for Italy's redundant manpower as well as several naval and air bases, though these would remain under Spanish sovereignty.[10] In response to the reaction of the British Government, which showed its complaisance in everything save the prospect of the Italian bases, Grandi reassured Eden of Italy's disinterestedness in regard to the Balearics. According to Geneviève Tabouis, Grandi was dangling the offer to Britain of sharing the Balearics as a sphere of influence, provided that the Republic did not overcome Franco, in which case Italy 'would have her word to say in the struggle.'[11] Meanwhile, Mussolini's attitude hid behind the proclamation that Italy was 'unwilling to permit the establishment of a Soviet republic, either in Spain or in Catalonia alone.'[12] This presumption of a power of veto, which both Mussolini and Hitler arrogated to themselves in the event that a Catalan republic were constituted,[13] offended Cudenet of *Le Petit Journal*. By what right, he demanded to know, did two countries without any common frontier with Spain forbid Spaniards to settle their own affairs. It was proof positive for Cudenet that Franco's insurrection had been, and continued to be, the work of Berlin and Rome.[14]*

The talks at Berchtesgaden in late November seemed to *La Dépêche* to show that Franco was unable to overcome the Republic on his own.[15] According to the *News Chronicle*, a German diplomatic mission sent to Spain at the beginning of December had informed Berlin that Franco's unpopularity was such that victory was impossible without fresh reinforcements of troops and arms.[16] Hitler, according to Leroux, had been contemplating a more direct intervention since a secret meeting held in Berlin in mid-November.[17] A month later, Hitler had decided to send five divisions.[18] The objectives of the Führer were now more clearly delineated. His interest, as Heinrich Mann pointed out in *La Dépêche*, lay in acquiring not military bases, the cession of which might demoralize the insurgents, but the subsoil wealth: copper, mercury, and above all, iron-ore.[19] It was believed, even in mid-October, thanks to a radio message intercepted in Madrid,[20] that a decree of the Franco government gave Germany monopoly rights to the utilization of the minerals of Spanish Morocco, a monopoly hitherto reserved for Britain, France and the Netherlands. Only copper, however, was mentioned for utilization. According to *L'Oeuvre* also, it was the use of the copper mines of Ríotinto, now to be ceded to the Reich, and the impotence of Franco to refuse, which London found particularly galling: Minas de Ríotinto had supply contracts with important British firms, and considerable British capital had been invested in this enterprise.[21] However, according to *Juventud* of Madrid, it was *iron-ore* which interested Germany most. Thus, four German vessels which had arrived in Cádiz in October with war matériel departed for Bremen with 12,000 tons of iron-ore. Several German ships would reportedly call in January 1937 to load a further 600,000 tons; it was estimated that the Rif mines alone would supply Germany with 800,000 tons of ore in the space of eight months.[22] As for the utilization of the Moroccan mines, this was not merely a source of irritation and humiliation for the democracies but, once again, a violation of the resolutions of the Algeciras Conference of 1906.[23*]

Relations between Hitler and Mussolini were still on an experimental level. Hitler wanted, above all, Mussolini to be involved in Spain to the maximum, in order to drive deeper the wedge between Italy and the Entente Cordiale. The French press, in turn, generally sought to find conflicts of interest between the two totalitarian states, the right wing usually sympathizing with Italy. *L'Excelsior* contended that Rome had no interest in seeing the Mediterranean swarm with aircraft and submarines of the Third Reich.[24] The Italian Government might therefore better resist the temptation of the Balearics in the knowledge that Germany was equally tempted by the Canaries.[25] According to *Les Echos*, Berlin had grown impatient by Christmas over what it considered Rome's breach of promise and almost threatened to 'go it alone from now on.'[25] Meanwhile, the Italian Ambassador in Madrid, Orazio Pedrazzi, pointed out 'very delicately' to his French counterpart that if Italy was backing German policy in Spain, it was precisely to provide a balance to German expansion in that country.[26] Few then were the hopes expressed in the press of a possible split between the Fascist powers in regard to Spain. Indeed, it was precisely the Civil War that made them allies and it was in that very autumn that Mussolini first launched the term 'Axis.'[27*] *La Dépêche* noted that if either of the Fascist nations were to embark on a large-scale colonial war, the other would necessarily follow; neither could allow itself to be overtaken by the other. There was every reason to suppose, thought *La Dépêche*, that Germany considered Spain as her own Abyssinia: 'She intends to use Franco as Italy used that ras Gouxa, the son-in-law of the Negus and a traitor to his country.'[28] In the Socialist press, the hope of disintegration in the Axis front had been abandoned by the end of 1936. Leroux acknowledged, on New Year's Eve, that Mussolini had decided to maintain his 'single front' with Hitler, above all in matters concerning Spain.[29]

This single front was revealed on 18 November in the first combined action of the Axis: the simultaneous de jure recognition[30*] of Franco by the two governments.[31*] The date has a certain importance. Leroux had written in October that there was little likelihood that German and Italy would recognize Franco until he had taken Madrid, unless the Soviet Union withdrew from the London Committee.[32] The Soviet move of 28 October admittedly served as a useful pretext. The most probable motivation of the Axis decision, however, was the expected outcome of the battle of Madrid, and not the hope that the capital would soon be invested but the fear that it would not be. Recognition was extended not in the first flush of Franco's advance on 7 November but eleven days later, when Madrid had withstood the full brunt of repeated and relentless attacks;[33]* indeed, four days later Franco definitively abandoned the hope of taking the city by assault. It is equally plausible that the announcement by Franco the day before, to the effect that Nationalist forces would in future attack even foreign vessels in Republican ports, forced the Axis leaders' hand. It is at once evident that Franco's naval forces were inadequate to a blockade of the Catalan coast, still less the entire Republican coastline. Only the massive cooperation of the Italian and German fleets could achieve his purpose. The Axis' grand plan, remarked Leroux, was therefore to attack the Catalan and Levantine coast.[34] Italy at once took charge of preparing the blockade, clearly violating Article 10 of the Covenant of the League of Nations to which Italy was still officially bound: 'The Members of the League undertake to respect and preserve as against external aggression the territorial integrity and existing political independence of all Members of the League.'

The nexus, at least, between the announcement of 17 November and that of 18 November was soon obvious. As Léon Archimbaud noted in *L'Oeuvre*, the attempt was being made to present the blockade as the legitimate act of regular government, and to pretend that Franco was committing no infraction of international law by opening fire on Soviet vessels.[35] Moreover, the whole question of non-intervention would now be turned inside out. According to the new Fascist argument, France of the Front Populaire had become the sustainer of the rebels, while Germany and Italy could invoke the principles of international law to supply Franco with arms and interdict the Soviet Union from rendering the same service to the Republic. In *La Dépêche*, Maurice Ajam foresaw clearly the approaching danger. In the event that a Soviet vessel attempted to run the blockade, the Italian and German Governments, upholding the absolute validity of the blockade, could claim that the vessel was legally at fault; and if the Soviet Government should then take reprisal action, the casus belli would be established.

The democracies were thus confronted with a travesty, even a parody, of international law. Whether the reasons they invoked to explain their inaction, wrote Archimbaud, were fear of war or respect for law, the fact remained that France was being encircled.[36] For the Socialist press, the combined action of 17–18 November signalled the point of departure. Almost its next headline ran: 'THE WAR HAS BEGUN.'[37]

For the right-wing press, the Axis move was both predictable and desirable. According to *L'Echo de Paris*, Whitehall was aware, even at the beginning of November, that Germany, Italy and Portugal, and even Brazil and Uruguay,[38*] were preparing to recognize the Burgos government,[39] but even *Le Matin* did not expect it to be more than a simple de facto recognition.[40] The applause given to this news by the French pro-Fascist press scandalized not only the Socialist organs but even the moderate journals such as *La Dépêche*, which denounced *Le Jour* in particular. In this Bailby wrote: 'The joy and pride which the people of France will feel at the news of Italian and German recognition is easy to imagine. The friends of the Spanish Nationalists in France congratulate them!'[41] In *Le Petit Parisien*, Lucien Bourguès contended that Rome and Berlin, by their action, had rendered a service to world peace. The Germans and Italians, explained Bourguès, could now 'assist [Franco] in a more active manner and with less risk of complications,' for their aid would now be addressed to 'a regular government and no longer to rebels.'[42] Other journals sought to minimize the importance of this action. Guèze tried to show that the recognition of Franco by Hitler and Mussolini did not signify their support; rather, the position of Germany and Italy in relation to Franco would be identical to that of France and Britain in respect to the Republic. 'The policy of non-intervention,' wrote Guèze, apparently quite satisfied with the new perspective, 'can therefore continue.'[43]

Le Petit Parisien to the contrary, there can be no doubt that the danger of war in late November 1936 was greater than ever. Ambassador Bullitt reported on 25 November that the French Government was extremely concerned over the possibility of general war.[44] Perhaps it was the fear that Soviet policy aimed at bringing about war between the Western democracies and the Axis[45] that induced the French Government to pursue a policy more conciliatory than ever. As for the British Government, the Axis gamble left it apparently unperturbed.[46]

It seemed to the public at the time that the two democracies, Britain especially, preferred to temporize. But more than that, the French press did not know what to think. Several journals believed that neither London nor Paris would recognize Franco even after the capture of Madrid. *L'Ordre* thought that the Nationalist Government would remain in their eyes a rebel government so long as its authority fell short of the entirety of Spain and so long as the government currently recognized as regular continued to exist.[47] Even *Le Petit Parisien* pointed out that France was not bound to recognize the government so long as another recognized government existed in Spain.[48] Other journals believed that the Axis move would weigh heavily upon the policies of the democracies. *L'Echo de Paris'* London correspondent thought, even prior to the action of 18 November, that the British Government was leaning toward a recognition of Franco, the more so since it knew[49] that the Fascist states were preparing to do the same.[50] In *Le Journal des Débats*, Pierre Bernus considered it an 'extraordinary motive' to refuse to recognize Burgos for the sole reason that the latter had not achieved a victory in free elections. 'Spain' wrote Bernus, reviving an old argument of the Right, 'considers France as a country hostile to its reconstruction.'[51] Henri de Kérillis responded to the Axis move by regretting that France had not done the same on the very first day. 'If she had [flown to the aid of Franco],' he wrote, 'she would have gathered all the advantages of the situation and at the same time brought to an immediate end the martyrdom of a great people . . . In short, she would have pulled of a great moral victory and rescued her essential interest.'[52] If only France had had a 'National' government, he added in December, these complications would have been avoided. 'The Nationalists,' Kérillis explained again, 'are in no way "rebels," for the good reason that in unhappy Spain, shaken for several years by revolutionary convulsions, there was no longer any legal authority, or at least any authority capable of quelling anarchy and murder.'[53]

The Axis declaration recognizing the Franco regime had followed so closely Franco's announcement of the blockade that any French or British reaction represented a reaction to both. British policy was motivated above all by the desire to remain outside the conflict.[54*] To this end, the British Government would have liked to extend Franco belligerent rights, were it not for two considerations: the opposition of the French Government, and the effect of such a decision on the blockade.

On 13 April 1937, Anthony Eden presented in Commons the dilemma facing the British government. Its position was again enunciated by Lord Plymouth before the London Committee, namely, that in normal circumstances a conflict of the nature and scope of that present in Spain would justify the recognition of both sides as belligerent; 'the circumstances, however, have not been normal.'[55] Indeed, up to now, in a conflict of this size and danger to world peace, no refusal to grant belligerent status had ever been so long withheld. No State would in fact grant belligerent rights to either side in the first two years of the conflict. Germany and Italy, in their communiqués of 18 November 1936 granting Burgos de juré recognition, mentioned nothing about granting belligerent rights. All the powers refused to do so, for two reasons. They all sought to deny the two Spanish camps the exercise of rights on the high seas that could be prejudicial to their interests; and they all wished to protect the delicate balance of their policy of non-intervention. To disturb this balance could only help the rebels, whose naval forces were now superior; it was a perspective that found no support in any of the powers, for reasons that were peculiar to each. Besides this, the public statements of the highest government officials referred to all operations in Spain and in Spanish waters as acts of 'civil war.'

According to generally accepted practice in diplomacy, an outside State confronting a civil war passes through various stages: recognizing the state of insurrection, granting belligerent rights, establishing official de facto relations, and granting de jure recognition. The granting of belligerent rights and the de facto recognition of a new regime as a regular government have always been considered as separate actions. Thus the Axis decision to refuse the second while granting the third and the fourth was not in violation of established practice.

The non-intervention system already represented, by itself, the recognition of an insurrection.[56*] It is often in this form that a foreign State gives its first official indication that in its eyes the insurgents hold some probability of success, and it generally does so for humanitarian reasons. In reality, one is recognizing a fact: the country that is granting recognition considers the insurgents as legal opponents and not simply as outlaws, but it concedes to them no rights on the high seas nor over commerce nor over the rights of outside States; not even in their own territorial waters, and although the insurgents have the right to interdict supplies from reaching the opposite camp, they cannot treat as an enemy a foreign merchantman navigating in these waters. In the same way, the foreign State is not assuming any of the rights or obligations of a neutral power: it retains all its freedom of action, including the freedom to supply arms to the regular government, but under no circumstances to the insurgents, because to do so would amount to an intervention. The recognition of belligerency, on the other hand, places the rebel camp, vis à vis the foreign State, on the same footing as the regular government in its intercourse with other countries and its handling of the war.

To sum up, so long as a state limits the recognition it confers on another to that of insurgency, it recognizes only that revolt exists and does not accord belligerent standing to the insurgents. If, however, a state recognizes the belligerency of parties to a civil war, it binds itself to assume a position of neutrality toward those parties and accords to each the rights and duties of a power engaged in regular or foreign war. Thus it confers a status whereby the grantee is guaranteed the protection of international laws and usages of war, as those laid down by the Hague Convention of 1899. Among these usages of war is the right, automatically conferred on the belligerent—and withheld from the insurgent—to visit and search neutral vessels both on the high seas and in the territorial waters of the enemy. So long as France and Britain withheld from Franco the title of belligerent, their merchantmen could carry arms to Spain from foreign ports and could demand naval assistance if interfered with, provided that the interference occurred on the high seas and not in Spanish territorial waters, where foreign warships were of course forbidden to enter. Since such interference would be made legal with the granting of belligerent rights, the insistence of French right-wing partisans that to recognize Franco as a belligerent was in no way to recognize him as head of the legal government was quite beside the point. On the other hand, some journals had become lost in the confusion.[57*] When Clement Attlee called upon the British

Government to respond to Franco by treating attacks on British vessels as acts of piracy, *L'Ere Nouvelle* reported a reply (which is attributed to Eden) that Britain preferred to refrain from any move or attitude which could involve his country in the internal affairs of Spain.[58] But it was precisely by treating the attacks as acts of piracy that Eden was able to avoid any international incident.[59*] This was apparent at least to *L'Humanité*'s Gabriel Péri, who considered it 'indispensable that the French Government dissociate itself publicly from the indecent statement of Mr. Eden.'[60*] The 'indecency' in Eden's policy, adopted by Blum, rested then in its refusal to confer the title of belligerent on either of the two camps, thus allowing Britain and France to label their acts of war as acts of piracy and to take appropriate—and limited—action. So it was that, in the view of the extreme Left, Fascist warships could commit acts which constituted, strictly speaking, casus belli, without evoking from the British and French Governments any more serious protest than what was proper to an act of piracy. One other aspect of the situation was noted by *L'Oeuvre*. According to the latter, Franco had informed Berlin and Rome that if Britain and France were indeed to maintain the international blockade impartially, the Nationalist cause would inevitably be lost.[61]

Notwithstanding the insistence by Buenos Aires that no South American state intended to recognize Burgos,[62] certain Central American dictatorships now proceeded to do so: Guatemala and El Salvador on 8 November, and Nicaragua on 4 December. On the occasion of the opening of the Special Inter-American Conference for the Maintenance of Peace held in Buenos Aires at the beginning of December, Álvarez del Vayo reminded Roosevelt, in *La Dépêche*, of four reasons why such a recognition was out of order. In the first place, under the Washington Treaty of 7 February 1923, Costa Rica, El Salvador, Guatemala, Honduras and Nicaragua undertook not to recognize any government conceived of a coup d'état so long as the legal government continued to exist. In the second place, the declaration of the nineteen American states in 1932 decreed the non-recognition of territories acquired by force of arms. In the third place, under the Saavedra Lamas Treaty of 10 October 1933, the signatories renounced military intervention in other countries. And in the fourth place, Article 8 of the resolution passed by the Pan-American Conference held in Montevideo in December 1933 (the Montevideo Convention) stipulated that no state held the right to intervene in the internal (or external) affairs of another state.[63]

The recognition of Franco by the Fascist states did not cease to disturb the French Left. A French anti-Fascist delegation left for London, including Victor Basch, president of the Ligue des Droits de l'Homme,[64*] Professor Paul Langevin of the Collège de France, *député* Longuet and Senator Morizet. *L'Express du Midi* was quick to sneer that the German and Hungarian origins of Longuet and Basch hardly qualified them to speak in the name of France.[65]

Indeed, the latest turn of events had scattered the optimism of the French Left that had just been compacted by the successful defence of Madrid. The blockade of the Catalan ports led, in mid-December, to the first provocative bombing-raid on the frontier village of Port-Bou. The French Socialists still sought a middle road. Hudelle wrote in *Le Midi Socialiste:* 'Between an excessive sensitivity, which betrays nervous tension, and an overlong indulgence, which smacks of cowardice, surely there is a place for firmness.'[66]

11
The Three Anglo-French Peace Initiatives

The 'Soviet' proposal for an international control (23 October)—The Committee approves it on 12 November—Further violations—the Delbos Plan for a 'Gentlemen's Agreement' (27 November)—Reaction from the Right and Left—Hostility to the Delbos Plan from both sides in Spain—The 'German' Plan (4 December)—The question of the volunteers—Accusations of bad faith—The attitudes of Hitler and Mussolini

The Soviet Union herself was therefore the first to suggest international control to the London Committee, although the Russian plan advocated—significantly—a control which would be limited to the Luso-Spanish frontier. At the same time, the Republican Government would be invited to substantiate its charges that Germany and Italy had violated their neutrality. The two nations, predicted Hudelle in the Socialist press, would cry insult; they would threaten to break the agreement if the Committee as much as hinted that the charges were true.[1] Indeed, ten days later Germany dismissed the charges as totally false and unacceptable.[2] Socialists now expressed a reaction bordering on despair at the democracies' inertia. Hudelle considered that the Soviet motion should have been submitted by the democracies in unison two months earlier; it was now so late it was sterile.[3] Sévérac wrote provocatively that if it were found that Germany and Italy had not violated the agreement, it would be the Republican Government that would lose face in the affair, having proffered false or unfounded charges:

> But this over-simple and all too human fashion of settling such differences is quite unworthy of the better part of the diplomats and heads of state. Rather than fall to that expedient, they will prefer to strike an attitude and speak loftily of national honour wounded and loss of face. Though how that honour and prestige could suffer from the confirmation that they had kept their promises passes our understanding.[4]

The grounds for Sévérac's bitterness were promptly substantiated by the black humour of the German press and the vituperation of Dino Grandi before the London Committee.

The plan, suggested by the Soviet Union and formally submitted by Lord Plymouth, was approved by the Committee on 12 November. It was handed to the Spanish Governments on 2 December. The Valencia Government accepted it in principle on 16 December; the Burgos authorities replied on 19 December with questions. The system of international control, as drawn up at the end of 1936, provided for no less than 75 or 80 control commissions (whose staffs would be selected from among the neutral states) of 17 persons each, stationed at every possible entry-point into Spain, on land, at sea, and in the air. The cost of this operation, estimated at 500 million francs per year to be shared pro rata among the Committee members, was considered slight by such as Rieu-Vernet, who reminded readers that peace was worth infinitely more, and that the costs of the world war it might avoid would be upwards from 500 billion.[5]* Nevertheless, the *Dépêche* columnist conceded that the Axis, caught off balance, was seeking to gain time to recover its position.[6]

While the Soviet-Plymouth proposal was still on the table, Delbos submitted his plan for a 'Gentlemen's Agreement.' It called for a cessation of the arms traffic and then for mediation. The French plan, at once supported by Britain, subsequently received the approval of Germany, Italy, Portugal and the Soviet Union. The press began once again to express some hope. It was observed that as the war dragged on, there were signs of lassitude; the forces were evenly balanced; the assurance now that they would receive no further aid could exert a decisive influence on the leaders. It could entice them, thought *Le Journal*, to accept a free national constitution if it were possible to organize the preparations.[7] In *L'Aube*, Georges Bidault entertained the hope that the spiritual power of mediation would prevail even upon the Fascists, if Spanish and non-Spanish democrats alike harassed them in the name of peace until they yielded.[8] *La Dépêche* considered that neither Franco nor Largo Caballero nor the Barcelona authorities—an involuntary concession to the right-wing argument concerning Republican political disintegration—could refuse to call off the slaughter if Europe in general had the will to demand it; the continuation of the conflict could not be justified by reason.[9] Apart from mediation by the European powers, Albert Milhaud of *L'Ere Nouvelle* revived interest in the possible role that Latin America could play in exerting irresistible moral pressure on her blood-brothers. The United States, wrote Milhaud, was clearly in favour of mediation.[10]* With Christmas approaching, the Vatican was reported to be also in favour, and its intercession would be a decisive influence on Spanish Catholics.[11]

The hopes of a solution by mediation, however, were not seriously entertained by the Left. Hudelle contended that mediation would be rejected by whichever Spanish camp considered itself the strongest. Even if it were not, added the Socialist editor, Hitler would refuse to allow a referendum in Spain if it were to be conducted honestly; if it were not to be conducted honestly, then the proven methods of the Spanish Right would insure it a sweeping victory.[12] In *L'Ouevre*, Geneviève Tabouis also thought that there was little chance for mediation, since Franco was confident of victory and feared elections more than he feared anything, knowing that popular sentiment in Spain was opposed to an authoritarian regime. The best proof of this, added Mme Tabouis, was the fact that, despite all the efforts deployed in the 'reconquered' provinces, Franco had never been able to mobilize any forces on the spot.[13]

While the moderate elements fluctuated between hope and despair, the prospect of an armistice followed by a plebiscite inspired the extreme Right with horror and the extreme Left with contempt. The former was galvanized in December by the publication of Giral's telegram to Blum of 19 July. This was the signal for the *Berliner Börsen-Zeitung* to announce: 'There is no longer any Red Spain; there is only a Red Army fighting on Spanish soil.'[14] The Spanish Nationalists offered their own curious advice to the democracies: 'If you supply Madrid . . . , we Nationalists will have to seek help from other countries.'[15] As for the plebiscite, it was a dangerous expedient which, in the phrase of *L'Express du Midi*, 'would serve only to inflame the passions.'[16]

In the initial view of *L'Humanité,* the plebiscite would serve no purpose whatever, since the Spanish people had expressed their will not one year earlier in free and proper elections, conducted by a Conservative Cabinet.[17] By Christmas Cachin had changed his mind and now welcomed the suggestion for another election, defying the opposition to follow suit and obviously confident of the result.[18]

Meanwhile, the two Spanish camps considered the proposition. Suspicion was uppermost in their minds. In the Republican camp, a Madrid journal attributed the Delbos plan to the rebel camp, of which France and Britain, it maintained, were the agents.[19] In the Nationalist camp, Merry del Val, Franco's representative in London, labelled the initiative 'an invitation from Moscow which reaches the London Committee via Paris.'[20] In point of fact, it was *against* the advice of Paris that Largo Caballero resorted to the League in early December, even if the Spanish Premier explained, with ill-fitting *machismo*: 'The government will go to Geneva without asking anything from anyone.'[21]* In mid-December, however, according to Dominique, Valencia was leaning toward peace, while Burgos and Barcelona defended war:

> The chances of the spirit of Valencia reclaiming Spain are slim indeed today.
> Yet it is possible to imagine a Spain in which various parties live together without exterminating one another, in which free men seek power without forgetting that lawful opposition is necessary.
> But let once Burgos win the field and an entire ideology—and the men upholding it—are condemned to die. Thus the voice of freedom—or what

remains of it—murmurs: 'Let us make peace!' But Lenin said: 'Let us make war!' And Torquemada commends it highly.

Dominique's conclusion to that was that Spain had not completed her suffering, and that the liberal nations held the destiny of Europe in their hands. 'If they stand fast,' wrote Dominique, 'against the dual religious spirit of Moscow and Berlin, peace can be saved. If they abandon one another, if they capitulate, Europe sinks into the morass.'[22]

In *La Dépêche*, Rieu-Vernet agreed with Dominique that the Delbos plan was shown the cold shoulder, especially in Catalonia. The Anarchists and the POUM[23*] wanted none of it.[24] *L'Excelsior* reported that it was no more popular in Valencia.[25] This negative attitude on the part of both the governments in Spain was due to their concern not to appear diffident of victory: the mere consideration of the plan exposed them to the danger of demoralizing their troops and of comforting the enemy. Whether or not the leaders on both sides, in their heart of hearts, favoured the plan to put an end to the war, it was nevertheless probable, as *L'Excelsior* pointed out, that the stubborn fury of the forces engaged in combat was not shared by the civilian populations far from the battle. *L'Excelsior* was therefore astonished that this very human consideration had influenced so little the response of Italy and Germany. For, according to *L'Excelsior*, Berlin and Rome were already set on repudiating their acceptance of the 'Gentlemen's Agreement,' justifying their withdrawal on the grounds that the Republicans and the Nationalists in Spain had equally rejected the idea of foreign mediation.[26] Portugal, for her part, according to the lusophile *L'Express du Midi*, would refuse her agreement both to mediation and a plebiscite, since she considered them bound to fail.[27*] The only success to celebrate was on a local level: *L'Express* reported a truce between the Basque and Navarrese camps, though even this was limited to Christmas, reflecting therein the religious and traditionalist character shared by the two peoples in their battle of the North.[28]

If the Soviet Union could claim the credit for being the prime mover of the first proposal (the control of supply), it was Germany who was responsible for introducing a third proposal.[29*] Indeed, Germany had raised the disturbing question of volunteers on 24 August, on the day that she decided—officially—to cease all exports of war matériel to Spain.[30*] On 4 December then, Lord Plymouth submitted to the Committee his plan to banish foreign volunteers. Once again the proposal was championed by France and Britain. There were now three proposals on the Committee's table, and all of them were the subject of heated discussion.

The possibility of the mass enrolment of authentic volunteers in the democracies had for long disquieted Mussolini as well as Hitler. In reply to Italy's call for total neutrality, which would extend to private commerce and even public demonstrations, even Guèze had acknowledged that there would still be the matter of 'individual' intervention, whether or not it served as camouflage for government action, for no government could be held responsible for the actions, gestures and speeches of its nationals.[31] *Le Petit Parisien* was similarly sympathetic to Blum in this respect, when Paris reminded Rome that under French law the government had no power to prevent the dispatch of private subscriptions or the departure of single volunteers, while at the same time it would not tolerate organized recruiting on French soil.[32]

The proposal to ban foreign volunteers was favourably received by the French press in general, while Grandi's refusal to consider the matter of volunteers separately from the other problems of non-intervention was carefully vindicated by his champions in France.[33] In *La Dépêche*, Rieu-Vernet advocated 'bolting all the gates of Spain.'[34] In *La République*, Dominique expressed deep concern over the possibility of direct conflict between French and Italian combatants, for according to information received by *La République* and *L'Ouevre*, French troops were to be positioned by the Largo Caballero government exactly at the point where an Italian offensive was expected.[35] At the same time, false reports were circulating: Britain and Belgium were said to have prohibited the departure of all volunteers for either camp.[36] Such reports were based on a reference in the House of Commons, reproduced in the British press, to the Act of Parliament of 1870 forbidding all British subjects to participate in the Franco-Prussian War. A similar bill of the U.S. Congress, ratified in 1811 and prohibiting all U.S. citizens from enlisting in foreign armies, was also reported under scrutiny, but with no noticeable effect on reinforcements for the Lincoln Brigade.

No sooner had the press welcomed the new proposal than its anxieties were expressed in charges of bad faith. According to *Le Matin*, at the very moment that the Soviet delegate in London was calling for a halt, Moscow was ordering haste in the dispatch of the volunteers.[37] According to *L'Humanité*, it was violating the letter and the spirit of the proposal by preparing the dispatch of sixty thousand men.[38] Even the right-wing *L'Ami du Peuple* agreed with *L'Humanité* that the Fascist states were striving to gain time. General Faupel was reported to have informed Hitler, on the ambassador's return to Berlin, that the German expeditionary corps required a minimum contingent of sixty thousand men to insure a Nationalist victory.[39] The *Times'* Berlin correspondent reported that Hitler's only alternative was to recall all German forces from Spain.[40] With greater accuracy, Hudelle of *Le Midi Socialiste* pointed out that Germany was not yet ready for general war,[41] and *Le Petit Parisien* surmised that after her initial hesitations Germany had now decided against open intervention.[42] *La Dépêche* replied that Hitler was merely waiting for Franco to produce some decisive victories in order to minimize his risk.[43] The opposite view was propounded by the *Daily Telegraph* and *L'Express du Midi*. According to the Conservative London daily, Hitler did not want to send Franco sufficient troops to enable him to take Madrid. The Machiavellian plan of the Führer, ran its argument, consisted of dragging out the war by all possible means, to give Germany sufficient pretext to maintain her troops along the Pyrenees frontier.[44] It was this last consideration which alarmed the French Right. 'Certainly,' wrote *L'Express*, 'it would be very difficult for Germany to invade France from this side, but the threat of German invasion from the Basque ports would be sufficient to immobilize 300,000 French troops on the southwest frontier.' The concomitant prospect of German air bases in Spain was equally perturbing: even *L'Express* now published maps to show how the entire industrial areas of the French Midi would then be within the target range of Hitler's bombers.[45] *L'Echo de Paris'* Kérillis was equally disturbed by the prospect that any colonization camps that Hitler should establish in Spain would only be the camouflage for something much more serious: the maintenance of an entire army ready in case of need to invade France through the Pyrenees.[46]

The revival of interest in the question of volunteers renewed the conflict within the Front Populaire. With the Nationalist offensive against the capital essentially in abeyance from 22 November, *L'Humanité* ran the headline a month later: 'MADRID ATTACKED BY THE REICHSWEHR.' The French Government's new regulation governing the departure of volunteers[47] was construed by the Communist organ as evidence that French policy was dictated by Franco through the agency of Kérillis and Tixier-Vignancour.[48] The reply of the Socialist press was prompt and predictable. Reminding his readers that the Communist Party had promised its loyal support to the Front Populaire, Rosenfeld described the remarks of *L'Humanité* as 'an almost outrageous form of argument.'[49]

The Socialist editor Hudelle had qualified his optimism by a single condition, that Rome had not secretly promised Franco further support at the conclusion of Ramón Franco's visit.[50] The news from Italy was for the moment encouraging. Propaganda for the recruitment of volunteers had quietened almost to silence. *L'Oeuvre* reported that the decision not to pursue intervention was more evident every day.[51] Paradoxically, it was *L'Express du Midi* which detracted from the Christmas optimism, warning that any demand by Italy that the banning of volunteers be made retroactive—which was to say that all foreign combatants already in Spain be recalled—would jeopardize whatever chance the initiative still had.[52] *L'Express* had only to quote from an article in Italy's controlled press. The Anglo-French initiative, wrote Signoretti in *La Stampa*, 'seems principally intended to rescue the Republicans. The reply of the Italian Government is expected to represent *grosso modo* ... its acceptance of the form and its rejection of the substance.'[53]

12
The Democracies Outmanoeuvred

The initiatives of the Committee—The possibilities of general disengagement—The role of France—The antifascists dejected by fascist falsifications—Hitler's policy—Mussolini's policy—The democracies mark time

In spite of the three initiatives submitted to the London Committee by France and Great Britain, the Committee, as Gabriel Péri showed in *L'Humanité*, had proved itself incapable of enforcing a single effective measure of control.[1] The chances of all three seemed 'weak' to *Le Journal des Débats*,[2] 'slender' to *L'Information*.[3] As for applying the sanctions, Georges Scelle of *La Dépêche* considered that it was not desired, because this time it would certainly mean war.[4] The initiatives earned at least the approval of *Le Temps*.[5] *L'Aube* remarked that nobody dared to voice open opposition to the peace proposals. Instead, everybody was obviously trying to deceive, to gain time, to take shelter against the probability of failure. Care was taken not to say no, it pointed out: 'Small consolation, you will no doubt say, but it may well depend upon their perseverance if the peace-loving powers are to drive home their advantage over whichever nations feel pangs of conscience about prolonging the war.'[6] Rieu-Vernet of *La Dépêche* thought that if the Committee's actions satisfied neither of the camps in Spain it could well prove that it was on the right track. While acknowledging that each was trying to deceive the other, Rieu-Vernet insisted that world peace depended upon the success of the Committee.[7] Meanwhile Franco, according to *La Dépêche*, was striving to find a solution before the proposals of Paris and London were successful.[8] Any solution, perhaps, was being considered, which reminded everyone once again of the promise Franco had made in July, to the effect that he might provoke an international incident in the event that the rebellion failed.[9] Kérillis wished however to show that the leaders in Burgos and Salamanca were perfectly aware of the 'fearful, phenomenal' character which the war had assumed in their unhappy land.[10]

Optimists on both sides thought that the time had come for a general withdrawal. *L'Ordre* suggested, now that the fortunes of the war had for some weeks inclined less favourably to Franco, that Rome and Berlin might find some way of extricating themselves without dishonour from the extreme position they had taken.[11] *La Dépêche* thought that it might be the perfect opportunity for both the Soviet Union and Germany to cut their losses with the least damage to their prestige.[12] Gaston Riou, however, though his Radical outlook was never in question, did not share this opinion in *La République*. To Riou, Russia was the only nation which could want a future war to be waged in the West and not in the East, where she had good cause to fear it.[13] *L'Express du Midi*, for its part, sang its old refrain: how could the Fascist governments be asked not to intervene in the Peninsula when the Soviets were sending massive daily supplies to the Republic?[14*]

Certain journals considered that France was contributing nothing to a détente. *L'Ami du Peuple* remarked that the French Government lacked the moral authority to invite other nations to desist from supplying aid to their champions in Spain.[15] To *L'Express* too, France fortified such authority by the 'reprehensible and scandalous partiality' she had continually shown toward the Republicans.[16] As for *La Victoire*, it had the impression that the Blum government submitted its non-intervention and mediation proposals only to save its brother, the Frente Popular.[17] It was at this moment that the seven French right-wing *députés*, headed by Kérillis, paid their visit to Franco.[18] The argument of Kérillis ran as follows: France should help Franco achieve a speedy victory because that was the only way of freeing him from Hitler. The refusal of France to supply matériel to the Nationalists simply allowed other nations to acquire considerable strategic and commercial advantages for themselves. If, on the other hand, France were to contribute to a Nationalist victory in a direct and vigorous manner, she would have a claim to their gratitude, which would spare France the worry of having an additional frontier to defend.[19] The frivolity of such a suggestion caused *L'Aube* to shudder, mindful of Kérillis' huge public. 'A political leader,' wrote the Catholic daily, 'should, it seems, have judgment, wisdom, and a memory.'[20]

While this moderate journal thus criticized the Right, the Radical-Socialist *L'Ere Nouvelle* still aligned itself against the Left, denouncing again[21] the belligerent attitude of Zyromski in *Le Populaire*[22] and, with *Les Echos*,[23] calling for total non-intervention: the banning of all exportation of arms, the freezing of Spanish gold held in France,[24*] and the prohibition of recruitment and transit of volunteers.[25]

The French right-wing press maintained a steady barrage of criticism of the activities of Republican sympathizers in France. In *L'Action Française*, Maurice Pujo described the part played by a British pharmacist named Dutt. According to Pujo, Dutt had received a visit in London on 29 December 1936 by the Spanish Naval Attaché Navarro, who suggested that he contact Major Bolaños, a member of Cortes serving as the new Military Attaché in Paris. On New Year's Eve, Dutt, Bolaños and an engineer named Salsas met at the Embassy's Chamber of Commerce at 27 Avenue George V. Dutt was then invited to serve the Republic. At a further meeting at 3.30 p.m. on 5 January, held in the Collège de France, continued Pujo, Dutt was instructed in his mission: he was to organize the dispatch to Valencia of poison gas and explosives. Production of poison gas would also begin at the three factories in Republican territory equipped for such work: in Barcelona, at the Flix electrical and chemical plant owned by the Sociedad Anónima Cros on the Barcelona-Saragossa highway, and at Cartagena.[26] Pujo's exposé evoked the scorn of *Le Populaire*, which supplied the names of some of the 'anonymous technicians' present at the meeting in the Collège de France: Professors Joliot-Curie and Langevin.[27]

The response of *Le Populaire* was indeed clumsy, for Edward Eric Dutt[28] was a master of imposture. A friend of Salsas, the renowned engineer Colonel John Nicoletis,[29] attended a meeting with Bolaños and Salsas at the same Chamber of Commerce on 3 January. The meeting was hurriedly called, and Nicoletis had travelled overnight from Bardonnechia to attend it. The purpose of the meeting was to question Dutt, who was offering his services to the Republic. Dutt claimed to have a laboratory in Switzerland and expertise in the field of chemical warfare, notably explosives and radio-activity. He further claimed that he was in close contact with the British Intelligence Service. Dutt proposed not only to manufacture cyanamid (an explosive well known but little used) but also to introduce artificial radio activity as a war weapon. In return for his collaboration, he requested enormous sums. A further meeting was held on 4 January at Nicoletis' office at 14 rue Jean-Goujon. At the end of it, Nicoletis advised Bolaños that the Republican Government should make no change in the programme he had recommended to it and which was already about to start: the large-scale production of explosives from nitrate of ammonia. At the same time, although Dutt's ideas on radio activity seemed to others to be somewhat fanciful, Nicoletis wanted, out of scientific curiosity, to have them examined by a specialist on the question. He therefore suggested the matter to his friend Marcel Courtines, head of the experimental physics laboratory at the Collège de France. A meeting was then held at the Collège on 5 January, when Courtines and Nicoletis introduced Dutt to Professor Joliot-Curie. The latter, who had been warned by Nicoletis that Dutt was most probably an impostor, pointed out to Dutt that only heavy gases could be used in warfare, and that artificial radio activity had never so far produced anything more than light elements. Joliot-Curie pointed out to Dutt, with all due politeness, that his experiments were false, based as they were on calculations that were out of order by the positioning of a comma fourteen places out of line, and he summoned him to repeat his experiments in the laboratory. Faced with this rebuke, Dutt remained impassive. It seems, however, that after this meeting Dutt went directly to the offices of Action Française, near the Place de l'Alma. He also went to see Count Quiñones de León, the former ambassador of Alfonso XIII, who had taken residence in the Hotel Meurice. The count recommended that he offer his services to a nationalist leader in Spain. Subsequently, without informing Dutt, *L'Action Française* published, in its issues of 10 and 15 January, the phantasmagorical findings of Dutt, embellished even further by the imagination of editor Pujo. Rebutted by the Franco camp, which no less considered him an impostor, Dutt made his way to Tangier to offer his services once again to the Republic. Republican authorities invited him to Valencia, where he was arrested and imprisoned.[30*]

Meanwhile, posters throughout Paris in February proclaimed a meeting entitled 'Writers for Peace,' held at the Palais de la Mutualité under the patronage of Professor Langevin and Léo Lagrange, Assistant Secretary of State at large. The guest speaker was André Malraux, billed as 'squadron leader in Spain.' In *Le Figaro*, Wladimir d'Ormesson conceded the right of Malraux and Langevin to express their views but considered 'scandalous' the participation of the Cabinet member.[31]

At the same time that it called upon France to adhere more closely to her announced policy, *L'Ere Nouvelle* and other journals added that their patience was at an end with regard to the policy of Germany. It was a question of knowing whether or not any action was intended, wrote *L'Ere*,[32] repeating the expression of the *Sunday Times* of London. For Leroux, in *Le Midi Socialiste*, Germany, and possibly Italy, now knew that neither Paris nor London could allow this comedy to be performed again.[33] Buré, of *L'Ordre*, while urging caution, nevertheless feared that the German Government would prolong the negotiations until the right moment arrived to provoke the casus belli it was waiting for.[34] To Buré, Germany would let go her Spanish prey only if she were forced to do so; Hitler considered it the best of bases for the revanchist war he was planning.[35] The speech made at this moment by Schacht, the German Minister of Finance, who was generally considered the most cautious of the Nazi Ministers,[36*] showed in fact that Germany would release her grip only in exchange for real colonial indemnities.[37] Meanwhile, whoever emerged the victor, France would have cause to fear the actions of Germany in the Peninsula. If Largo Caballero were to win, Hitler would say, as Mussolini was saying: 'I shall not tolerate a Bolshevik Spain.' If, on the other hand, the winner were Franco, Hitler would demand concrete proof of his allegiance, to the detriment of France. Obviously, Buré concluded, Franco could welch; but as his power, attained through foreign aid, would probably be precarious, could his revolt succeed?[38]

In point of fact, Hitler's policy at this moment was vacillating between three possible solutions: continuing his aid at the present level; withdrawing his aid, in preference to being drawn in further, and thus cutting his losses; or increasing his aid. The problem was aggravated by a polarization of political thinking in Germany. *L'Oeuvre*, as early as October 1936, had observed an ever-widening split between the National-Socialist Party, whose sentence was for open war in Spain, and the rest of Germany: the Reichswehr, the economists, and the fraction of public opinion, if such a thing still existed. These last considered that the Führer now had sufficient securities in Spain—in the form of rights to the subsoil, to bases in the Canaries, and to disembarkation in Spanish Morocco—to allow him, albeit with the help of economic and financial aid from London and Paris, to close his account in the Peninsula.[39] Pierre Dominique also alluded, in *La République*, to this great quarrel waged between the Nazis and the Reichswehr, with the latter supported by Schacht and the industrialists, who preferred to wait.[40] Together with the Wilhelmstrasse, as Lucien Bourguès pointed out in *Le Petit Parisien*, these circles saw a very grave danger of isolation in pursuing the Spanish adventure further.[41] *L'Oeuvre* quoted from an article by General Ludendorff condemning Hitler's policy. Germany should not have intervened or even taken sides, wrote Ludendorff, because Franco would not defeat the Republicans. Ludendorff, who was the sworn enemy of the Pope and Catholicism, considered moreover that Franco's ties with the Vatican presented a danger almost as great as that of Communism, while he deeply distrusted the ambitions of Mussolini.[42] The Nazi Party remained, however, in favour of a headstrong policy of erecting an outpost of Hitlerism on the ruins of Spain. It was the Nazis, wrote Dominique, who were trying impatiently to force the Führer's hand.[43] And as *L'Oeuvre* pointed out, the decisions he took were always aimed at satisfying the party which had set him in power.[44]

It was prestige, thought *L'Excelsior*, even more than self-interest, which would determine the attitude of the Reich. The German leaders were only too aware of the technical difficulties involved in a massive intervention in Spain. France and Britain would retain mastery of the seas, and Germany could not count even on Italy to favour a German occupation of the Peninsula.[45] It was not, added *L'Excelsior*, in the considered interests of Hitler to repeat the error of Napoleon; but for reasons of prestige the German Chancellor would undoubtedly insist that France and Britain, and especially the Soviet Union, be the first to submit to control.[46] The question of course was wrongly posited: Germany knew well enough that the two democracies—and even the USSR—were quite ready to comply. The Soviet Union, Leroux pointed out in *Le Midi Socialiste*, would certainly consent to non-intervention being made general and effective by precise agreements and by a genuine control. She would ask only that the comedy of August, when the Fascist governments signed the Agreement only after shipping massive supplies of arms, should not be re-enacted.[47]

The essence of the problem was to know at what point Hitler would unleash general war in order to extricate Franco. The arrival of three hundred Germans in Spanish Morocco on 7 January elicited an immediate protest by Blum, who invoked the Treaty of 1912. Even the Marquis de Palaminy was now gravely concerned by Hitler's policy, though it had no noticeable effect upon the scope of his vision. Germany, he wrote in his valedictory to 1936, would not abandon the bases she had acquired, while the French Government, 'bound by its pro-Jewish, one-world sentiments,' had backed the wrong horse.[48] For Albert Bayet of *L'Oeuvre*, war would be inevitable if Germany were to install herself in Spain and Spanish Morocco, or if France were to be surrounded.[49] Georges Scelle of *La Dépêche* did not share this opinion. It seemed to him that it would be difficult to mobilize France on the grounds of defending the legal government of Spain, that Germany knew this well, and that the situation would change only if France were directly attacked.[50] In any event, thought Bayet, if France and Britain agreed to state flatly that they would not permit the Reich to lay its hand on Spain, Hitler's manoeuvre would be defeated and peace would be saved.[51]

The statements of the German leaders and those of the controlled German press continued to provide endless speculation on the intentions of the Führer. His favour seemed to vacillate between the party and the military. The execution of a German citizen, Lothar Guedde, in Bilbao in early December provided the war party with a suitable casus belli. But the reaction was four weeks in coming. The *Völkischer Beobachter*, Hitler's mouthpiece, hardened its tone, telling the Basques that they would soon know they had challenged the entire German people.[52] Again, *Le Journal's* Berlin correspondent, Georges Blun, reported the sudden disgrace and dismissal of Admiral Forster, German Chief of Naval Staff, who had favoured a refusal to Franco's request for further aid. Only a clear warning from the British Admiralty, added *Le Journal*, could now deter Germany.[53] In a subsequent report, Blun believed that the Reich would go to the water's edge. The German leaders were confident, he wrote, that the British would not condemn them and that Britain was turning against Valencia.[54] In another move to isolate France, the German press congratulated the British Government on its recently concluded Mediterranean agreement with Italy, while at the same time the German press intensified its attacks on the Front Populaire.[55] Strategically, Germany was now engaged, according to *L'Humanité*, in fortifying Ceuta with 155-mm and 240-mm cannon.[56] Hitler's objective, explained *Le Petit Journal*, was empire, and no colonies were more appetizing than the French. Once he had installed himself in Spanish Morocco, the Führer could offer to vacate in exchange for a colony elsewhere. The future of France, concluded *Le Petit Journal*, was thus being fought in the Spanish sierras.[57]*

On the other hand, the German General Staff expressed its concern to Hitler at the meeting at Berchtesgaden on 9 January 1937, urging him to caution in his Spanish adventure. Certain French editorialists considered that he heeded their advice. Pertinax thought in *L'Echo de Paris* that he could detect a reduction during the month that followed in both the German and the Italian involvements in the Peninsula. His reasons were several: the alleged desertion of many German soldiers, the inadequacy of certain German war matériel,[58] and the unsatisfactory results of the last Mussolini-Göring meeting in Naples. Pertinax held to the belief that Spain was never anything more than a diversion in the Führer's grand scheme.[59]

As for Italy, Buré thought that Mussolini had nothing to gain in Spain and that he was hesitating at that moment to follow Hitler.[60] Such was also the opinion of Geneviève Tabouis, who explained in *L'Oeuvre* the reason why the Italians wanted to extricate themselves from the Spanish trap, namely that Italy was more and more the prisoner of her conquest of Abyssinia.[61*] According to *La Dépêche*, Franco was moving with the greater haste the more it seemed that the Italians had decided to withdraw from the Balearics and to remain genuinely neutral.[62] However, the press which had best access to official Italian sources gave quite a different account. To *Le Matin*, Italy seemed less than ever prepared to detach herself from Germany; she would not accept, any more than the Reich, the installation of a Soviet government in the Mediterranean, 'whether or not it were camouflaged.'[63*] She would comply, thought *Le Matin*, with all the measures taken by the Non-intervention Committee to limit the risks of war, but never at the cost of giving Russia a kind of option on Spain.[64] This position was now clearly delineated, in view of the fact that Soviet policy now aimed at replacing the intransigent Largo Caballero by someone more in sympathy with Russian aspirations.[65] *L'Express du Midi* also found, in Italian political circles, confirmation of its earlier statement that acceptance of the Anglo-French request would, in the Italian view, be playing the Communists' game.[66] When at the end of 1936 Great Britain joined France in presenting a reminder to Italy, their action was interpreted, according to *L'Express*, as an attempt to alter the status quo in Spain to the advantage of the Reds, a policy which *L'Express* could promise did not curry universal favour.[67]

In *Le Midi Socialiste*, Leroux aligned himself with those who did not subscribe to the theory of Buré and Mme Tabouis. Mussolini, thought Leroux, sought in Spain a government which would pursue his policies and which would participate in the Axis offensive against the League of Nations and against the Mediterranean pact. He sought to nullify the military value of Gibraltar by erecting a Fascist hinterland behind the rock.[68] For this, it seemed to Leroux, there was no need at all for the Balearics to be annexed to Italy; it would suffice if Franco merely allowed Mussolini the use of the Balearics as a base for his submarines. Thus, by announcing that they had no territorial ambitions, Hitler and Mussolini were renouncing what in fact they had never wanted; 'so great a sacrifice will be so gratefully acknowledged that they will be invited to take everything they really want.'[69] Just like Hitler, added the Socialist writer, Mussolini would stop only before the assurance that France

A demonstration at the Mur des Fédérés (commemorating the 1871 Commune) in the Père Lachaise cemetery. Paris, 24 May 1936.
In the middle row, from left to right: Jean Zyromski, André Morizet, Maurice Thorez, Léon Blum, Marcel Cachin, Thérèse Blum, Marcel Gitton, Jacques Duclos. Behind Morizet, in profile: Jules Moch. On the extreme right: Marceau Pivert.

Roger Viollet. Ref: 3352-16.

The leaders of the Front Populaire. Paris: Place de la Bastille, 14 July 1936.
From left to right: Thérèse Blum, Léon Blum, Édouard Daladier, Maurice Thorez, Albert Paulin, Roger Salengro, Maurice Violette, Pierre Cot, unidentified.

LAPI/Roger Viollet. Ref: 2377-3/ LAPI-12039.

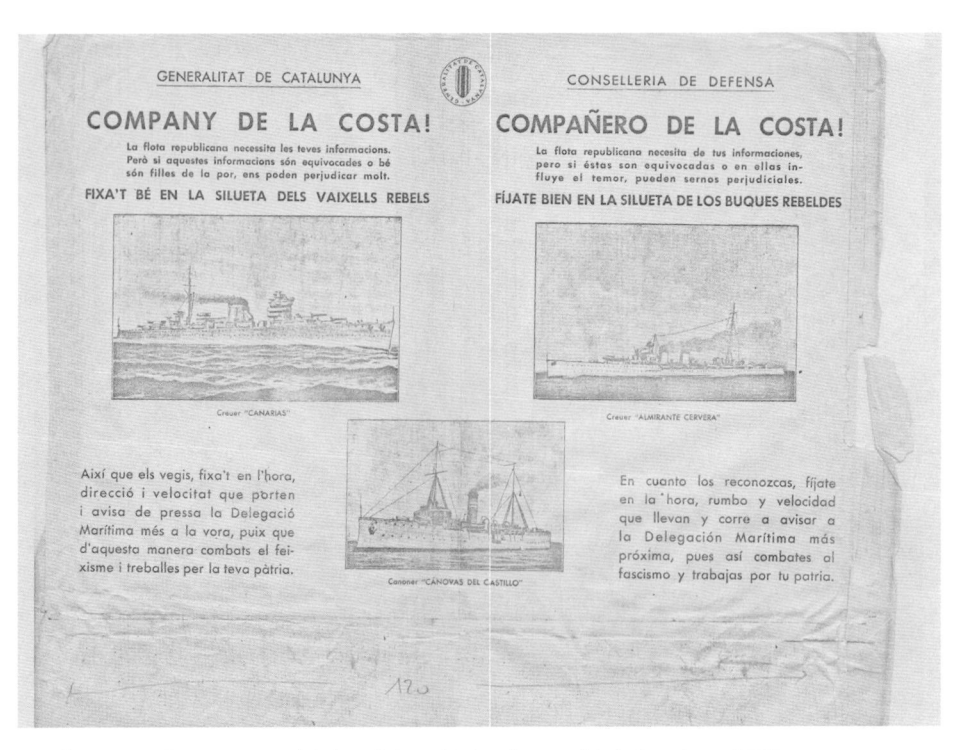

Warning poster (to report any sighting of three Nationalist warships). Barcelona, 1937.

DWP Collection, courtesy of Giovanna Berneri, Genoa.

'Le fascisme rouge.' Anarchist reaction to the May Days, Barcelona, 1937.

DWP Collection, courtesy of Giovanna Berneri, Genoa.

Cardinal Pacelli, the Vatican Secretary of State and future Pius XII, signs the Livre d'Or. Paris: Arc de Triomphe, 14 July 1937.

Bibliothèque Nationale.

André Marty visits the International Brigades. Albacete, 1937.
On Marty's left, Luigi Longo.

Keystone. Ref: 7241/33.

The Blum Cabinet. Paris, March 1938. Directly behind Blum (left to right): Dormoy, Lebas, Auriol, Mendès-France, Lagrange, Moch; On Blum's right: Albert Sarraut. On Blum's left: Viollette, Paul-Boncour.

Keystone. Ref: K3003644.

Reopening of the Chambre des Députés, 3 October 1938. Daladier at the rostrum.

Bibliothèque Nationale.

The British leaders visit Paris, 24 November 1938.
From left to right: Bonnet, Halifax, Daladier, Chamberlain.

Bibliothèque Nationale.

Spanish Republican refugees mass at the French frontier, January 1939.

Associated Press.

Spanish Republicans cross the frontier, reopened on the night of 27–28 January 1939.
Associated Press.

Franco's troops in triumph at the French frontier. February 1939.
DWP Collection, courtesy of Juan Puig, Toulouse.

A scene at the frontier: wounded Republicans and a Senegalese guard. Le Perthus, February 1939.
DWP Collection, courtesy of Juan Puig, Toulouse.

Crippled Republican children approach the French frontier. February 1939.
DWP Collection, courtesy of Juan Puig, Toulouse.

A Spanish refugee family in distress, February 1939.
Roger Viollet. Ref: RV 66.366.

and Britain were opposed to any Italian or German mortgage on Spain.[70] According to Marcel Pays, in *L'Excelsior*, Italy had no more desire that France or Britain to see Germany installed in the Mediterranean.[71] Together with the Soviet Union and the Balkan Entente, which had everything to fear from German hegemony, with Poland and the Petite-Entente, and with Switzerland, Belgium and the Netherlands, who had bitter memories of Austrian and Spanish occupation, they would form an all-powerful bloc.[72] The imperative, in the words of Leroux, was once again to speak firmly and unequivocally, 'and thus disperse the fog of Fascism.'[73]

The adoption of a firm attitude on the part of France and Britain, added Augusto Barcia, writing in *L'Oeuvre*, was in their own direct self-interest. The progress in air communications between Europe and America would give Spain a considerable strategic importance which neither democracy could overlook in planning its colonial development. Indeed, Barcia continued, a strong and independent Spain was essential to Western Europe.[74] Nor was the prospect for the democracies very difficult, implied Romier in *Le Figaro*, arguing persuasively that Germany would be as hopelessly out-classed as Russia if she attempted to maintain sea-routes to the Peninsula, and that therefore strategic speculations about Spain in Europe led to nothing.[75] Georges Boris in *La Lumière* considered the danger now greater and more clearly defined than in August, with the Fascist powers intent on the annexation of Spain and the Spanish rebels reduced purely and simply to tools in their hands. Like Leroux, Boris called upon France and Britain to show firmness, while the dictators themselves would be forced to heed the voices of dissent in their own official circles.[76]

That no such firm attitude was adopted by the democracies was the triumph of the Rome–Berlin Axis, which continued to thwart a full rapprochement between London and Paris by playing upon the distaste of the British people for any risk of war. According to *L'Oeuvre*, the opinion was now being expressed in British parliamentary circles, and even by certain Cabinet Ministers, that the only way to prevent in Spain a Franco-Hitler victory over Britain was for Britain herself to join forces with Franco.[77] Ambassador Corbin in London reported a growing sympathy on Fleet Street with the Nationalist cause: 'Whether it be Garvin [editor in chief of *The Observer*], or the *Evening Standard*, or the *Morning Post*, or the *Daily Mail*, or the *Evening News*, what is noticed in all of them is the same readiness to blame the Soviet Union as primarily responsible for the war in Spain, and on the other hand to treat Germany and Italy with indulgence. The same journals frequently show hostility toward us, even though they were entirely on our side on the Abyssinian question.'[78] *Le Figaro* saw the same trend in Westminster, but attributed it to the repulsion felt in Britain toward anarchy and toward the propaganda campaign recently launched by the Republican Government; London considered Franco more and more kindly in proportion as the status quo in the Mediterranean was respected and as the Nationalists gave Spain 'a liberal government acceptable to the masses.'[79] *L'Aube* expressed a Christian disgust with the diplomatic hypocrisy on both sides.[80]

The speech of President Azaña in Valencia on 22 January 1937 echoed the old sentiments[81] that the Spanish conflict were best left to the Spaniards to decide, and that the Republicans would have found the issues clearer and their morale higher if they had drawn their ideals and based their cause in the Spanish soul alone. In praising this contention, Count Sforza added in *La Dépêche* that the support given by Hitler and Mussolini would ultimately harm the Nationalist cause just as much as Marxist formulae were already harming the Republican.[82] Among the controlling elements in the democracies which felt that there was much to be said for and against, such arguments were a comfort and encouraged them further in the policy of doing nothing.[83*]

PART TWO

The Comedy of Non-Intervention

13
The Committee Implements Control

Malaga: its effect on morale—New calls for the granting of belligerent rights—The foreign volunteers—Frontier control and violations—Control of the coast

Badajoz, Irún, San Sebastián, Málaga. Four straight victories without reply gave a growing confidence to the Nationalist cause and to the press supporting it. *Le Journal* could not hide its glee to see Madrid cut off from Valencia; the old capital, it crowed, which was so easy to defend in the streets and which it was so foolhardy to attack frontally, would soon be surrounded and would then fall like an overripe plum. *Le Journal* then examined the internal situation in Nationalist Spain, in an ironic echo of the recent words of Unamuno[1]: victory lies not in conquering but in convincing, in reconciling the people. This, wrote *Le Journal*, was what the Franco régime was achieving by providing order. Such order, it continued, could not be based upon terror for it would require one soldier behind each citizen. *Le Journal* denied point-blank that any government, however powerful, could dispense with the general consent and argued that, in the case of Nationalist Spain, one simple sit-down strike would paralyze transport and supplies and endanger the entire campaign.[2]

The fall of Málaga revived *L'Humanité*'s indignation at the growing presence of the Fascist powers in Spain, which nullified the resolutions formulated by the Front Populaire at Lyon and Châteauroux. Germany and Italy, it repeated, were resolved to forestall any type of control until they had won a decisive military advantage, and the inaction shown by the Quai d'Orsay and the Foreign Office constituted, no longer laissez-faire, but actual intervention against the Republic.[3] It was a far cry from Blum's former dictum: 'It is necessary to accept the possibility of war in order to save peace.' Another who thought so was Marceau Pivert, whom Blum had appointed special information officer for cinema and radio and who now in February 1937 resigned his post in protest.

The left-wing press now saw, in the defeat of its cause in Spain, an omen of further mischief elsewhere. *L'Oeuvre* joined *L'Echo de Paris*[4] in its conviction that Hitler, satisfied that France would not move to aid Czechoslovakia, despite a mutual assistance treaty between these nations, was already preparing another *coup de force*. *L'Humanité* observed a mounting political and diplomatic offensive against Prague from January, and warned that only by stopping Hitler in Spain could Czechoslovakia be saved.[5]*

There was a growing demand, led by Wladimir d'Ormesson in *Le Figaro*, that France grant belligerent rights to both sides.[6] Even in the neutralist *Le Journal des Débats,* Pierre Bernus thought that such recognition would reduce the risks of war.[7] The right-wing *Le Journal* trusted that the imminent capture of Madrid would leave Spain with only one régime for France to recognize in any form.[8] *L'Echo de Paris,* which in the opinion of Buré had become Franco's mouthpiece,[9] also urged recognition of Burgos. *Le Jour* published an interview with Robert Valéry-Radot, a government spokesman, who implied that Burgos had approached Paris with just such a request.[10] In *L'Ordre*, Buré denounced the right-wing press for its demands, which were the more improper in international law since Franco had informed Pironneau of *L'Echo* that he was still undecided between a monarchy and a republic.[11] In reply to Jacques Bardoux,[12] Buré remarked that the recent alliance in Bucharest between Fascists and Spanish Nationalist leaders showed that it was Berlin, not Moscow, that was waging an ideological crusade.[13] Or, as *L'Oeuvre* put it, the real issue was not Bolshevism but the Mediterranean.[14]

As a result of Málaga, however, the London Committee finally reached a decision to implement border control. And the question of foreign volunteers was one that had long cried out for a solution.

The Soviet solution was that a line had to be drawn between volunteers acting upon personal motivations and volunteers who were drafted, willingly, as in the case of most of Hitler's men, or reluctantly, as in the case of most of Mussolini's men.[15] *Le Peuple* supported the Soviet attitude.[16] So too did *Le Figaro*, while at the same time it blamed the USSR as well as Germany for sending volunteers of the latter group.[17] With the question of the recruitment and transit of volunteers now before the Chamber of Deputies, *L'Humanité* countered that the volunteers for the Republic represented only a minute fraction of the army's strength, which now rested upon a military discipline and training sufficient to wrest victory from the best German or Moroccan troops.[18]

There were several reports of dissatisfaction in the International Brigades. Even *La République*, and as early as December 1936, Eugène Frot underscored the disillusionment felt by the volunteers face to face with reality. 'I know some who left,' he wrote, 'with the sublime enthusiasm of their burning faith. Alas! the rare and discreet news that they can still get through to those they have left behind reflect a grievous disenchantment.'[19]* In early January 1937, Jean-Baptiste Barbier, counsellor at the French Embassy now removed to Valencia, reported that certain French volunteers wanted to return to France.[20] The majority of them had not signed any document of enlistment, but a good many of them had been robbed of their identity cards. *Le Figaro* reported that, by mid-February 1937, 279 French volunteers had returned home through the assistance of the French consul in Valencia; they complained that chiefs like André Marty preferred cruising around Albacete (headquarters of the International Brigades) in big cars rather than appear at the front.[21] In March, Ambassador Herbette wrote that French and Belgian volunteers had been sentenced to death for wanting to leave, and their lives were saved only through the intervention of the consul Marcassin.[22*] *Le Jour* asserted that three hundred French and a hundred Belgian volunteers were imprisoned in the Alliance Française in Valencia. *Le Jour* also reported that two Belgian officers who had served in the Brigades returned complaining that they had not been paid.[23*] However, an international incident which occurred in late January 1937 suggested that certain defections among the Loyalist volunteers were the result of outside interference. The Baron de Borchgrave, the Belgian Chargé d'Affaires in Madrid, was believed to have persuaded several of his compatriots in the Brigades to desert. He was found murdered in the outskirts of Madrid.[24*] The incident left Émile Vandervelde, leader of the Belgian Socialist Government, with the choice of taking a position against Largo Caballero's Socialist government by issuing a formal rebuke, thereby risking a turmoil in Belgium which could enable the Monarchists to take power, or resign. Under an agreement between the Belgian Government and Álvarez del Vayo, Vandervelde resigned. In the French Socialist press, Rosenfeld expressed his satisfaction with the agreement and stressed that the Spanish Socialists, far from being disappointed with Vandervelde, admired his courage, while del Vayo, by yielding to the demands of the Belgian Government—left undefined by Rosenfeld—had given proof of Socialist solidarity.[25]

As for the Italian anti-Fascists, they received heavy censure for the poor account they had given of themselves. Following a philippic they received from Major Jover at Huesca, and the engagement at Carrascal on 7–12 April, the Italians deserted. In Barcelona they received the same from Major Ceva, whereupon they refused to fight; they were promptly disarmed. What the haughty Spanish Anarchists failed to understand about their Italian comrades, complained the Italian Anarchist leaders later, was the enormous differences in traditions, culture and even temperament between Spanish and Italian Anarchism.[26]

On 23 December 1936, the French and British Government had joined in an appeal to all states[27*] to prohibit the departure of further foreign volunteers. The British Government announced on 10 January 1937 that the Foreign Enlistment Act remained in vigour and that it applied specifically to enlistment in the Republican or Nationalist forces. On 19 January, a French decree prohibited the passage of volunteers into Spain. *L'Humanité* now called louder than ever for full international border control. The recent statement by

Hitler's General Ludendorff that victory for the rebels was impossible[28] was reproduced with alacrity. Delay in applying control, added *L'Humanité,* would not prevent the rebels' defeat but it would serve to prolong the war.[29] Four days later, with the fall of Málaga, *L'Humanité* changed its tune: delay now favoured Franco.[30] As for Portugal, it had rejected on many occasions the idea of an international control on her Spanish frontier. Consequently, the simultaneous arrival in Lisbon in mid-February of the British battleship *Resolution* and three French motor torpedo boats was viewed by the Portuguese government as an attempt at moral pressure. On 16 February, the Non-intervention Committee, under the pressure of the French initiative, agreed to ban recruitment of volunteers as from 21 February and to institute border control as from 7 March, though it was not until 20 April that such control actually went into effect.[31*] *Le Figaro* affected the greatest pleasure at the news, deploring only that seven months had elapsed before the agreement had been reached.[32]

The London Commission, as agency of the London Committee, was placed under the direction of the Dutch Admiral De Graaf, while his second in command, his compatriot Vice Admiral Van Dulm, was given overall control. Van Dulm was assisted by two chief administrators (*Agents-chefs*): Rear Admiral Van der Schatte Olivier, also Dutch, responsible for maritime control (with a hundred and eleven observers), and the Danish Colonel Christian Lunn, responsible for territorial control in France, hence the entire Franco-Spanish frontier. Lunn, resident in Paris, was assisted in the surveillance of the frontier by his compatriot Colonel Oels, who set up his headquarters in Tarbes. The frontier was divided into three zones. Zone I consisted of the *département* of Basses-Pyrénées; Zone II Hautes-Pyrénées, Haute-Garonne, and Ariège; and Zone III Pyrénées-Orientales and Andorra. Each Zone was placed under the control of an Agent, the duty falling to the respective Prefect of the *département*; in the case of Zone II it fell to the Prefect of Haute-Garonne. Each of the five frontier Prefects was assisted by an outside administrator: for Basses-Pyrénées, the Swedish Captain Gyllenran; for Hautes-Pyrénées, the Norwegian Colonel Wettre; for Haute-Garonne, the Finnish Lieutenant-Colonel Wallden; for Ariège, the Latvian Captain Reinhards; for Pyrénées-Orientales, the Dutch Colonel Palm.

The two wings of the French press were quite equal to the task of accusing Frenchmen of bad faith, without any help from abroad. According to *Le Matin*, Miguel Valdez, the former secretary general of the Catalan Communist Party and now a member of the central committee of the Communist-controlled PSUC,[33*] had arrived in Paris to discuss measures to increase recruitment.[34] Doubts were expressed as to the effectiveness of the border surveillance. *Le Petit Parisien* published an article by a reporter who, while admitting that he had had to limit his investigations to a small area in order not to arouse suspicion, remarked that six sentries on foot could not police the air.[35] The article drew an angry retort from the Chief Inspector of Special Police, who termed it 'fanciful, false and deceitful. No aircraft has left or can leave the Montaudran airfield in Toulouse without my being informed.'[36] Under a decree of 18 February, Air-France was instructed not to issue any more tickets for Spain or for points beyond until the passenger's passport had been checked and found in order. Tickets could only be issued in Toulouse, and only planes belonging to a regular airline, and recognized as such, could in future take off for Spain.[37*] Two French pilots, Louis Raymond Delarbre and Georges Cornez, were therefore prosecuted for flying Dutch Koolhoven aircraft from Toulouse on 9 March and landing, not at Perpignan as scheduled, but at Prat and Barcelona respectively; they were returned to Toulouse the following day by Air-France. The prosecution of the pilots, however, was conducted apparently for propaganda purposes alone. In a handwritten postscript to his report to the Minister of the Interior, the Prefect of Haute-Garonne added: 'I have just heard that M. Eldin, Inspector of Special Police at Francazal Airport, has been instructed by an anonymous official of the Sûreté Nationale "not to cause the pilots any anxiety".'[38]

The law of 21 January and the decree of 18 February prohibited all persons French or foreign, with the single exception of Spanish citizens, from entering Spain through French territory. Nevertheless, the French consul general in Barcelona reported in mid-March that several thousand Spanish passports had been sent by the Catalan authorities to the Comité Antifasciste in Perpignan, in order to camouflage the identity of the volunteers crossing the frontier.[39]

L'Action Française now posted a correspondent to Perpignan, from where he reported, *inter alia*, a convoy of taxis transporting sixty volunteers across the border in early April. The correspondent also described the standard itinerary. The party would leave Perpignan at 9 p.m. by way of Pollestres, Ponteilla, Fourques, Llauro, Oms and Taillet, where they would get out and cross the Tech River by a railroad bridge between Céret and Amélie-les-Bains. Passing through the forest of Céret, they would then cross the frontier and, after a journey of 15 miles on foot, finally reach Massanet de Cabrenys, where buses would be waiting.[40]

In the same paper, Pierre Héricourt exposed another route: from Cerbère to Requeséns, Massanet and Molló. The column would then re-form at Camprodón and Figueras and proceed, via Ripoll or Gerona, to Barcelona. It was important to avoid the international patrols. It was an easier affair with the Socialist Mayor of Cerbère, Julien Cruzel, who turned a blind eye on the traffic. According to Héricourt, the organization of the supply line was in the hands of Soviet agent Roger Tolera, whose headquarters was the Bar Continental in Perpignan. Among his agents was Gaston Silla, Commissar of the Libertad Column in Barcelona.[41*] Between early February and April 1937, Silla allegedly took across some 2,800 volunteers.[42] These accusations were corroborated by a retired Lieutenant-Colonel of the Gendarmerie, Prosper Claire. A former leader of the Croix-de-Feu in Ariège, Claire was now the top militant of the PSF in that *département*, and in Foix he declared in public that the French authorities in that region had allowed volunteers to cross into Spain. A certain Pédoussaut, a Belgian who had been assigned to the frontier at Aulus as an observer, had allegedly protested with such vehemence that he had come to blows with Colonel Claire.[43]

As for those bearing US passports, visas granted for Spain by the US authorities were no longer taken into consideration since the United States was not party to the Non-intervention Agreement. In May, 29 Americans who attempted to cross the border to participate in the war were sentenced in Muret (Haute-Garonne) to 40 days' imprisonment. *Le Petit Parisien* remarked that the sentence was not merciless but neither was it lenient. It was sad to think, it though, that courage and the spirit of self-sacrifice should be made a misdemeanour punishable by imprisonment. *Dura lex sed lex*, it concluded, and non-intervention demanded the strictest observance.[44]

Certain incidents were now causing embarrassment to the French Right. *Le Petit Journal* reported a centre of espionage based in the Bar Basque at Saint-Jean-de-Luz. The group, headed by a certain Jean Guimera, was believed responsible for the Nationalist naval action in March against the Republican vessel *Galerna*. The ship was intercepted and boarded, the crew and all but two of the passengers were shot. Converted into a Nationalist armed trawler, the *Galerna* was immediately involved in an attack on the Republican coaler *Mar Caspio* in Bayonne, an inland port.[45] Even *Le Journal* conceded that the Republican vessel was protected by the international law of the three-mile limit, and it reminded Burgos that an unrecognized belligerent could claim no rights of war.[46] Another furore involved Lufthansa, which was currently operating a mail service between Marseilles and Burgos every two days, and between Marseilles and Lisbon once a week. The mail planes flew at low altitude, serving to guide German warplanes following at 16,000–18,000 ft. The warplanes, taking off from Milan with two reserve fuel tanks and meeting the Lufthansa mail en route, thus avoided the need to fly over French territory, the direct route to Burgos passing over Turin and Toulouse. This diversion lengthened the flight to 850 miles, which would just be within the capacity of three-engined Junkers.[47]

In *L'Ordre*, Buré continued his campaign against the policy of the right wing which was contrary, he insisted, to the present interests of France.[48]* At the same time, Buré attacked those anti-Fascists in France who regretted finding themselves in alliance with the Soviet Union. The editor of *L'Ordre* declared that, in his private opinion, the only friends of France were those who had a personal interest in being so, and that among these at the present time was Joseph Stalin.[49]

The Committee Implements Control

Despite opposition from the Axis powers, the London Committee invited the Soviet Union to participate in the surveillance of the Spanish coastline. Russia nevertheless declined. Ambassador Maisky explained to the Committee that his government was temporarily waiving its rights, since it had no political or other reason to dispatch its naval forces to the Mediterranean or the Atlantic. The Soviet concern, as *Le Populaire* accurately pointed out, lay in the danger incurred to Russia's own naval defense.[50] It was therefore disingenuous of *L'Humanité* to present Russia's reluctance in the headline: 'THE SOVIET UNION WILL NOT PARTICIPATE IN THE FAKE BLOCKADE,'[51] and it drew angry comment from Blum's press.[52]

The coastal control measures went into operation on 6 March 1937. By this time the left-wing press had taken a pessimistic view of the struggle for hegemony in the Western Mediterranean. If the war in Spain were such a struggle, remarked *L'Oeuvre*, France at least did not claim the area for herself; she was, however, committed, and so was Britain, to resisting any power which so tried.[53] In *L'Humanité*'s view, neither had resisted at all, and the entire Mediterranean was already an Axis lake.[54] The Communist organ intensified its protest when, on 4 March, Radio Salamanca[55*] announced the text of a note sent by Burgos to the governments subscribing to the Treaty of Algeciras, to the effect that France had violated the treaty by fomenting disorder in Spanish Morocco in order to find a pretext to invade the Spanish zone.[56] It would appear that the Nationalist note was intended to maintain the utmost pressure on the democracies in the light of the Republican note they had received in February. This note, the inspiration of Comintern agents, offered to transfer Spanish Morocco to Britain and France—ignoring the fact that the zone was already in the hands of Franco—in exchange for their guarantee to prevent further Italo-German intervention. As Bolloten suggests, the agreement of Britain and France to this plan would have risked precipitating an international conflict,[57] but a conflict confined to Western Europe and with the Soviet Union, according to her grand design, uninvolved.

14
Guadalajara and Fascist Reaction

The Italian defeat and Italian morale—Mussolini sends reinforcements—The effect on German policy—Mediation plans proposed

Guadalajara provided the Republic with its first major victory of the war. The rout of the Italians on 12 March 1937 took placed in the same week that Franco categorically denied the presence of foreign units in his army.[1*] Following the rout, *L'Oeuvre* reported that 950 officers and men had defected with their equipment. It added that they were soon singing 'Bandiera Rossa' and were most happy to be prisoners,[2] though joy is not the expression on their faces in a photograph published by *La Dépêche*.[3] They had possibly been informed of the Duce's immediate outburst that no Italian would return home until the war had been won. Again in *L'Oeuvre*, Geneviève Tabouis reported that letters found on dead Italians outside Madrid showed how deep ran antifascist sentiment in Mussolini's forces. According to information given by prisoners of war, Italian officers had attempted to check the obvious decline in morale by promising them the same solution as had been adopted in Abyssinia: the use of African troops to provide a frontal shield.[4] Other leftist journals openly gloated over the Duce's defeat. So too, in the opinion of *Le Figaro,* did the British press, whose 'rather unnecessary exaggerations,' it felt, served only to further exacerbate Italian pride.[5] *L'Aube* shared the desire of *L'Oeuvre* not to offend this pride. The essential thing, explained *L'Aube*, was to prevent all *further* intervention; if that could be obtained, the Fascist powers would soon want to recall all of their volunteers[6]—a remarkably optimistic view. *Le Petit Journal's* remarks were more direct. Mussolini's only solution—in Spain as in Abyssinia—would be mustard-gas.[7]

Mussolini's actual solution, if we may believe Geneviève Tabouis, was almost as draconian. His reply was an order to the Italian General Staff in Spain to proceed with the execution of the officers responsible for the débâcle. Only the intervention of the Spanish General Staff prevented the order from being carried out.[8] Madame Tabouis' accounts, however, were not always reliable. She reported that General Bergonzoli, the Italian commander, had anticipated Rome's order by dying the Roman fool. In point of fact, he lived to repeat his defeat in Cyrenaica.

The restraint advocated by *L'Oeuvre* and *L'Aube* was obviously less evident in the Spanish Republican press. *El Diluvio* of 21 March wrote of 'open season for Italian rabbits' and of 'Mussolinian eunuchs.' When Ezechiel Enderiz wrote of Italian cowardice in *Solidaridad Obrera* of 20 April, Camillo Berneri in *Guerra di Classe* was moved to reply, quoting letters found on Italian prisoners.[9]* One such, written by a soldier to his fiancée, read:

> You were right when you told me not to leave home. I thought we were going to work in Africa, as the draft card said. And so I joined up as a volunteer, not to fight but to work and earn 40 lire a day, as everybody in Italy said. Instead of that, it's all been a lot of hogwash . . .

The Italian Fascist defeat at Guadalajara, continued Berneri, was a victory of Italian antifascism. He referred to reports in *La Vanguardia*, the organ of the Esquerra and the largest selling daily in Barcelona,[10]* which ascribed the Fascists' defeat to the Italians' lack of enthusiasm and conviction,[11] and in *Le Petit Journal*, which recorded an interview with Ambassador to Paris Luis Araquistain, who remarked:

> The conduct of the Italian army in Spain, far from bringing discredit upon it, does it honour . . . Mussolini's troops are men first, and soldiers second . . . Why should they fight? Fighting would be the real crime.
> Italy can feel proud and not humiliated by such an army . . . The Latin race cannot produce robot-soldiers, and that is its virtue.[12]

L'Oeuvre, too, quoted a certain Major Silva who, upon capture, remarked: 'If the soldiers of the Italian Army call it quits and the militiamen of the Garibaldi Battalion have stood their ground for four months in Madrid, it is because the Italians understand what side peace and freedom are on.'[13]*

The optimism of *L'Aube* was disappointed. According to *Le Populaire*, Grandi remarked that Italy could not withdraw her troops 'after what [had] just happened,' because the honour of her flag was at stake, an attitude which the Socialist mouthpiece called 'undeniably grave.'[14] *Le Petit Journal* noted that, while the Führer had heeded the advice of his generals, concerned over the inferior quality of German war matériel,[15] and had decided not to send in troops, the Duce had committed his prestige, and Italian volunteers were drawn by lots by the village podestas.[16] Even *Le Petit Parisien*, which had moved progressively to the right, conceded that the arrival of further Italian units would constitute a breach of the London Agreement.[17]

Further units were now reported arriving. *L'Humanité* observed that nothing had changed in the Duce's policy, as 10,000 fresh Italian troops disembarked in Cádiz between 22 and 24 March.[18] The chief of militia Pollastrini was now recruiting two new army corps for Spain; they would be sent whatever happened and probably in broad daylight, once Italy had denounced the Non-intervention Agreement. Meanwhile, a Black Shirt division had been created to serve partly in the militia and partly in the regular army.[19] In Majorca, an air base was under construction to accommodate 100 fighters and heavy bombers, and a General Staff with 3,000 troops had been situated there, 'like a spider on the French communications web with North Africa.' Nor was Italy acting alone, according to *L'Humanité*. Two German battleships had just discharged troops and matériel in Seville and Málaga[20]* in preface to an imminent advance on Almería.[21] *L'Humanité* was opposed to the very form of the control system which was victimizing the Republic and allowed the presence of German and Italian naval units off the Republican coasts. Documents found on captured Italian officers allegedly showed that German and Italian vessels, camouflaged as Nationalist ships, had already carried out bombardments prior to a massive naval attack on the Republican shoreline.[22]

Whatever the fluctuations of January 1937 in the Führer's policy,[23] journals of various political persuasions began to believe that Moloch was now losing to Mammon in the formulation of that policy. Corroborating the opinion of *Le Petit Journal*,[24] both *L'Echo de Paris* and *L'Oeuvre* ascribed Hitler's hesitations over any deeper involvement, or 'open war,' even after Málaga, to the discovery that German matériel was indeed deficient. In *L'Echo de Paris*, Pertinax reported that though the artillery was excellent, tanks were too light, armor having been sacrificed to speed.[25] *L'Oeuvre* added that the tanks were found to be badly constructed and had earned the name of 'self-propelled coffins' and 'Black Marias.' All of them allegedly failed at a ditch three feet in depth. The heavy tanks were the most dangerous, but only for the crew. They were virtually unprotected and could easily be scaled or put out of action by throwing tar at the sight-vane, which consisted of small perforations.[26] Pertinax had earlier pointed out deficiencies in certain aircraft.[27] *L'Oeuvre* added that new models were now under construction at Warnemünde and Marienden, where work continued around the clock. Morale in the German units was therefore reported very low, especially in the tank corps, and there were allegedly cases of troops refusing to advance.[28] The last is highly unlikely, since no German infantry units were involved in Spain, but the report was corroborated by no less a figure than Heinrich Mann. Mutiny in German units was not infrequent, he wrote in *La Dépêche*. Even in the spring of 1937 the German people were still being kept in ignorance of the destination of the departing volunteers. Officially, Germany was still not engaged in any war, not even an expedition. Every month the Minister of War issued reassurances to every family concerned, to the effect that their son was safe and well; these assurances would continue even after next of kin had been advised of a soldier's death. The only real news Germans heard, Mann assured his readers, reached them by clandestine radios.[29]

L'Echo de Paris also quoted an article from the *Berliner Tageblatt* which implied that Málaga was the exception in the catalogue of incompetence committed by the Nationalist General Staff. The fact that such an article was not censored by the Nazi authorities, thought *L'Echo de Paris*, was proof positive that Hitler was now heeding the Wehrmacht rather than the Nazi Party.[30] In *L'Oeuvre*, Geneviève Tabouis thought that Hitler was now getting the same advice wherever he turned; from information they had received from observers, the Ministries of Foreign Affairs and of War considered that Franco had lost. Faced with the prospect of losing his entire investment, Hitler was prepared to cut his losses, and no further German aid would be dispatched, concluded Madame Tabouis, after the consignments currently on order.[31]

L'Ere Nouvelle remarked upon a curious coincidence. As soon as peace proposals were discussed or put into effect, there was a sudden increase in inflammatory reports. Was it mere chance, asked the Radical-Socialist paper, or was it design? In any event, it concluded, it was well to distrust news reports more than ever.[32] In *La Dépêche*, Georges Scelle was also less than sanguine about the possibility of mediation.[33] So was *La Journée Industrielle*, which saw no desire for mediation in either camp nor any preparation for eventual reconciliation. Both camps were acting as though resigned to the indefinite presence of their foreign champions. The stirring, patriotic slogans of the rebel generals in July had given way to urgings to greater savagery, regardless of military advantage, which could result only in the death or exile of Spain's best-tempered spirits. Such a prospect, concluded *La Journée Industrielle*, would hardly deter those for whom Spain was merely a field for political combat, but it asked whether true Spanish patriots could remain indifferent.[34]

The two camps, Scelle observed, had equal confidence in ultimate victory.[35] At the end of April 1937, General Miaja granted a special interview to Rieu-Vernet, also of *La Dépêche*. The war, he said, could end only through the attrition of the enemy and the demoralization of his rear; if the rebels had succeeded, he added confidently, France would have suffered the tragic consequences.[36] And thus the two camps, remarked Scelle, felt the same necessity to annihilate the other and the same aversion to reconciliation. Besides, he added, even after a compromise peace guerrilla war would still last for eternity.[37] Not so, replied *L'Aube* and *L'Oeuvre*. To the former it was becoming more and more clear that, without massive intervention, Spain could not be conquered either by Fascism or by Communism or by Anarchism. Only the mediation of Europe in general could bring a solution, by restoring power to the true moderates, the men of liberty and reconciliation who had been dispossessed of all influence.[38] Even in *L'Oeuvre*, however, Albert Bayet admitted that the Republic would indeed have been conquered by Fascism by the spring of 1937 had it not been for Soviet aid.[39] Former Premier Martínez Barrio expressed the same view in *La Dépêche*.[40]

In London, a mediation plan was proposed in April by Winston Churchill. It called for collective intervention and the establishment of a centrist government. Moderate journals such as *La République* praised the initiative,[41] but *Le Populaire* had already repudiated it[42*] and it met, at home, with limited approval, in Berlin, with skepticism and sarcasm, and in Rome, with reserve. While Rome, according to *La République*, now favored a plebiscite, both Nationalists and Republicans remained totally opposed to any transaction.[43]

There was certainly little encouragement to be drawn from Largo Caballero. 'All entente is impossible,' he told *Le Temps*. 'We shall fight to the end. We shall import all the arms we can, whatever happens.'[44] Even out of office, the Socialist leader continued to do his best to involve the democracies. In September 1937 he visited Paris. Interviewed by *Le Matin*, he admitted openly that his purpose was to request 'more active' support by the democracies, urging the French Government to reach an agreement on the recall of foreign volunteers and then to allow the Republic a free hand in the purchase of war matériel.[45] 'If the League of Nations refuses to act,' he declared, 'we will call a new meeting of the Second and Third Internationals and force the democracies to act.'[46] 'Nothing will force us to act,' replied Stéphane Lauzanne blandly in *Le Matin*.[47] Martin-Mamy, in *L'Echo de Paris*, was more direct: 'What Largo Caballero needs is not so much a commentary as a doctor's prescription.'[48]

Meanwhile, talks were being held in Rome between Mussolini and Göring. *L'Oeuvre*, with its customary private access, real or imagined, to the Palazzo Venezia itself, reported that Göring had made it plain that Germany wished to engage no further reinforcements in Spain, where it considered the game was lost except in the realm of diplomatic manoeuvres. The Reichsmarschall added, however, that Germany was prepared to continue the supply of war matériel, since the present control system would make the operation perhaps even easier than before. The Duce reportedly concurred, as agreement was reached to pursue Axis activity more energetically on another level, not only by seeking mediation as early as possible, but also by magnifying to the fullest any reported violation of the Non-intervention Agreement by France and Britain, and by continuing the hate campaign in the press.[49]

15
Gernika'ko Arbola and the Catholic Agony

The destruction of Guernica—Outrage on the Left and in the Centre, indifference on the Right—Denials by Franco and the right-wing press—Irrefutable proof of German responsibility—The attitude of the Church—The Christian crusade: the Catholics divided—The Vatican grants recognition to Franco—Its influence on the religious dispute—The Vatican's apprehensions

The destruction of Guernica was a watershed in the story of the French press and the war in Spain. Things were never quite the same again afterwards. Fascism, as *L'Humanité* said, had beaten all its records. On the other hand, the Guernica incident was doubtless a propaganda blessing to the same political group that felt not a shred of compassion over the fate of Marshal Tukhachevsky, Chief of Staff of the Red Army, who that very month found himself and his staff the victims of another Stalinist purge.

The dive-bombing of Guernica by the German Condor Legion[1*] took place on 26 April 1937. The little Basque town was invested by the Nationalists two days later.

No foreign correspondent was in Guernica at the actual moment of the air attack, on the afternoon of the 26th, but that evening and night four foreign correspondents reached the town: George L. Steer, of *The Times*; Noel Monks of the *Daily Express*; Christopher Holme of Reuter's Agency, and Mathieu Corman, the Belgian correspondent of *Ce Soir*.[2*] *Ce Soir* was thus the only francophone journal to offer a report on 27 April.[3*] Havas, which was the only French press agency, had a correspondent in Bilbao, but the Havas version of events did not appear in the French press until 28 April, and was manifestly lacking in detail. Some other foreign correspondents based in Nationalist territory, including another correspondent of *The Times* who made his way from Vitoria, left at once for Guernica, but in all cases they arrived there at least five days after Guernica was captured. From the Republican lines, Georges Berniard, of *La Petite Gironde*, arrived on the day after the attack. Shortly afterwards he was arrested by the Nationalists, who treated him roughly. While acquitted of charges of spying, he was accused of something equally serious:

the Nationalists had decreed the death penalty for any journalist who had filed reports from Nationalist Spain and was later captured in the Republican ranks. The Nationalist authorities transferred him to Vitoria, where they forced him to sign a curious statement corroborating their own version of events concerning Guernica, as if they could trust him not to write the truth once he was freed. Whatever their reasoning, the two pro-Franco communiqués that made use of this testimony left nothing in doubt to their own listeners and readers.[4*]

The attack stirred a wave of indignation in the European press, indeed throughout the world. The outrage expressed in the left-wing press was fully to be expected.[5*] It is more significant that its indignation was shared by the moderate press. The Catholic *L'Aube* spoke for those whom partisan passions had not blinded, remembering Guernica, and Durango,[6*] not as victory or defeat but as crimes against humanity.[7] It reproduced the formal statements, first published in *La Dépêche*, of a Basque Catholic priest who had been an eye-witness of the bombing.[8] *L'Ordre* recalled that Guernica was the little town where Ferdinand and Isabel had sworn to respect Basque liberties.[9*] It called its destruction 'a butchery coldly prepared and coldly executed,' which could not but reduce the chances of mediation; 'so abominable and gratuitous a slaughter will engender hatreds precluding forever the possibility of Spaniards freely submitting to a Mola or a Franco or a Queipo de Llano, for the time has passed when a dictatorship could be erected upon the corpses of thousands of innocents.'[10]

If there was general agreement in the moderate press that the town had been destroyed by bombs and not by Anarchists' mines, there was doubt as to the identity of the attackers. *La Dépêche,* first attributed the crime to Italian and Nationalist planes.[11] A week later it published a special interview with Manuel de Irujo, the Basque Minister of Justice, in which he said that the German action was an act of vengeance for the assistance given by the Basques to the Royal Navy during the 1914–1918 War.[12] *L'Oeuvre* saw the action as a rehearsal of a new form of 'total war,' in which the spreading of terror among the civilian population would be the means to a rapid solution.[13]

The first reaction of the French right-wing press was less indifference than total silence. The raid's initial effect upon *L'Express du Midi*, for example, was to wipe the war right off the front page and off its page 2 to boot. Even then it contained no reference to Guernica. It described the road to Bilbao jammed with refugees, which might have given its readers cause to wonder why this should be so, with their redemption so close at hand. Eibar, meanwhile, had been relieved; 'unfortunately, the arson committed by the Anarchists tempered the joyful pride of the Nationalist troops.'[14]

L'Echo de Paris put on a braver face. 'Numerous military objectives,' it reported, 'have been bombed by Nationalist pilots, notably the village of

Guernica.'[15] This report was no doubt based upon a communiqué issued by the Agencia España to the entire press on the evening following the raid. This communiqué recorded the last public address by General Mola before his death on 3 June 1937, in which he declared: 'We shall raze Vizcaya, and its bleak and desolate site will rob Britain of all desire to sustain the Bolshevik Basques in arms against us. We must destroy the capital of a perverted people who dare to defy the irresistible cause of nation.'[16]

At the very same moment, Franco's headquarters in Salamanca, more mindful of the backlash which could result from such bombast, were denying any complicity and were issuing frantic communiqués of reassurance.[17*] Indeed, when looked at from a military point of view, Guernica was no more than a modest communications centre with a factory close by that produced light arms and which, according to Steer, was left untouched by the bombing.

Accordingly, *L'Echo de Paris* reversed its story, proclaiming that the destruction of Guernica was 'not the work of the Nationalists.'[18] Harold Cardozo of the *Daily Mail*, who was 'indignant at the success [the report] was having in England [and who] was in Guernica immediately *after* [italics added] its occupation by the Nationalists,'[19] ascribed the destruction of Guernica and Eibar to the same Republicans who had previously set fire to Irún. Vilmorin of *Le Jour* similarly blamed the action on Asturian Anarchists, allegedly engaged with the Communists in a battle against the Basques; the Anarchists placed sticks of dynamite in every building.[20] Meanwhile, more than Cardozo were indignant over the reports in the British press. Berlin, wrote *L'Ordre*, evinced anger over the publication of what it termed 'Bolshevik lies intended to distract attention.'[21] It was less necessary for Berlin to attack the same reports in the French press, since there was no lack of French right-wing journals ready to do so. 'The press of the Front Populaire,' wrote *L'Express du Midi*, 'persists in its lies concerning the destruction of Basque villages, despite all proof to the contrary. It is beyond all shadow of doubt that the burning of Guernica was the work of the defenders of the town. Most of the buildings to which the Loyalists set fire were blown up as well by volunteers of the Asturian Battalion, which formed part of the garrison.'[22]

Fresh attempts were made to discredit the ubiquitous accounts of Nationalist responsibility for the destruction of Guernica. The right-wing press readily accepted the communiqué from Salamanca denying that any Nationalist planes took off 'on the day the bombing was reported to have taken place.' It denounced too the 'hypocritical indignation of the pro-Republican French and British presses regarding German planes over Guernica.' To counter such calumnies, it was reported, Franco had adopted the most correct procedure: he had invited the entire foreign press, regardless of political ideology, to visit Guernica. The journalists that accepted the invitation, continued the same press, went everywhere and questioned everyone. At the end of a meticulous search, they all agreed that not one bomb crater was to be seen nor any other trace of bombs.

The campaign of the Right to refute everything, whatever the evidence, was nowhere better served than in *Le Journal de Toulouse*. Under the headline: 'IT WAS THE REDS WHO BURNED GUERNICA JUST AS THEY BURNED IRÚN,' it continued:

> When will the press of the Front Populaire stop trying to brainwash us?
>
> Echoing the lies of the Anarchists of the Frente Crapular, they claimed that Guernica had been horribly bombed by the foreign air force in the service of the Nationalists. They showed us German planes machine-gunning, at point-blank range, women, children and old folk fleeing from their stricken town. In this manner they inscribed in the minds of civilized men an indelible image of cruelty on the part of Franco and Mola. Mola has indeed reacted rigorously. Foreign journalists have been invited by him to visit the smoking ruins of Guernica. They have acknowledged that the fire, far, far from having fallen from the sky, arose from the earth, that the smoke-blackened walls had been drenched in gasoline, while not a trace was found of bomb-craters or other evidence characteristic of air bombardment.
>
> The Quai d'Orsay at once opened an on-the-spot inquiry, and our colleague Cyrano informs us that the French Consul in Bilbao has sent the Ministry of Foreign Affairs a detailed report on the annihilation of the little Basque town. We may assume that the Quai d'Orsay is fully informed. In any case, representation was made this week to M. Yvon Delbos by some *députés* of the Extreme Left. When the *députés* asked the Minister to protest in the name of France against the destruction of Guernica, the Minister allegedly replied: 'Gentlemen, if I have any good advice to give you, it is not to speak any more about this miserable affair. For it may have some unpleasant surprises in store for you.'
>
> *L'Humanité* passed over this incident in a few discreet and non-committal lines. But what really proves the point is this.
>
> *The Times*, the great British daily, whose sympathies for the governments in Valencia and Barcelona are well known and which was the first to impute the destruction of Guernica to the Nationalists, has the courage and honesty to acknowledge its error[23*] and to make amends for it by a new report, better documented, which it received from its special correspondent in Vitoria. 'It is the Basques,' it states, 'who are responsible for the burning of Durango and Eibar. In these towns which suffered heavy shelling during their resistance, it is indeed to be noted that fire broke out only at the moment of the evacuation, that is to say when the Red fugitives sought a dual objective, to leave nothing behind them but ashes and to charge their pursuers with an imaginary crime.'

This correction has been reproduced by the Agence Havas, but of course the press of the Front Populaire has taken care to ignore it.[24]

In *L'Express du Midi*, the 'pitiless cruelty' of whose lines had already been denounced by its Toulouse confrère *La Dépêche*,[25] Gaston Guèze waited two weeks after Guernica before writing his first editorial. Following a preamble to the effect that 'the hardest hearts are those who appear ready to shed the most tears,' Guèze declared that no one any longer dared to lay Guernica 'unqualifiedly' to the charge of Franco, though he omitted to specify where better the blame should lie.[26] In *L'Action Française*, Pierre Héricourt had a similar impression, scouring Guernica, Eibar and Durango for several days without detecting a scrap of undesirable evidence:

> Guernica is in ruins, but as a result of arson.
> The myth of the German planes . . . is revealed even to the least observant.
> The paved outskirts of Verdun, even after three weeks of heavy bombardment, did not present the mournful look of this town where destruction was systematically organized and where gasoline was poured along pipelines in order to ensure that the fire would reach whole blocks of buildings.
> On the roads that still exist, we looked in vain for traces of shell bursts. But on 1 May, at the time of my first visit, we could still smell the gasoline and material was still burning in some places under the stones and tiles.
> In the whole of Guernica, to which I returned several times, I was not able to discover more than five large craters, which anyway could have been caused by mines just as easily as by heavy bombs. The reason why I consider they were caused by mines is that the surrounding trees and walls are not pockmarked by shrapnel.
> However, a simple observation will suffice to reveal the criminal responsibility of the Reds: in order to reduce such a town to ashes in a matter of hours, it would have required a powerful squadron and thousands of bombs. How can anyone explain why not a single bomb fell on any of the roads which converge on the town from all directions? How can anyone explain the miracle of Franco's pilots scoring a bull's-eye on all the houses on each side of a street without damaging the pavement?
> This single observation, which can be applied to every street, and which is open to everyone to make, is sufficient to reveal the premeditated crime of the Anarchists and the Communists, who nevertheless, in deference to their Catholic allies, decided to spare the famous Biscay archives and the symbolic tree[27*] above the sacred town, as well as Santa María Church which they had converted into a barracks.[28*]

It was Noel Marks of the *Daily Express*, reproduced in *Le Petit Journal*, who tossed the charge straight back again. On his return to London after a lengthy stay in Bilbao and Guernica, Monks replied:

> I swear that it was the German pilots under Franco who bombed Guernica and killed a thousand peaceful inhabitants. And for saying so, the Reuter correspondent, another London newspaperman and I, who were there on the spot, were branded liars by Franco, who would have us believe that we never saw thirty Junkers heading toward Guernica at 4 p.m. on 26 April. Franco has declared before the world that on that day[29*] none of his planes took off on account of bad weather. And I declare before the world that his planes did take off. I saw them. My colleagues saw them. Six thousand inhabitants of Guernica saw them. Moreover, Monday 26 April was the sunniest day I ever spent on the Basque front. I do not say that Franco is a liar. Perhaps he did not know that the Germans had taken off that day.[30]

The Christian agony was never more acute than in this raging conflict between the Christian Basques and the Christian Carlists. From the moment that the Basque people, whom even its enemies called 'the most Christian people in Spain,'[31*] aligned itself with the Republic, to the cry of 'God and our ancient laws,' Catholic opinion was no longer ecumenical. In a letter written to the Bishop of Pamplona on 7 June 1937, Cardinal Gomá y Tomás, Archbishop of Toledo and Primate of Spain, acknowledged the fact that a mood of hostility toward the Nationalist movement undoubtedly existed among foreign Catholics, especially in England,[32] France and Belgium. Even in those circles which were the more favourable to Franco, added the Primate gloomily, opinion was strongly in favor of a settlement of the war by agreement between the opposing camps.[33] Indeed, the majority of the French Catholic press remained either skeptical of the concept of the Holy Crusade or downright critical. This majority included the semi-official organ of French Catholicism, *La Croix*, the Dominicans' *Sept* and *La Vie Intellectuelle*, Gay's *La Vie Catholique*, and Mounier's *Esprit*.

Within a month of the insurrection, *Sept* had published an article entitled 'The Right to Rebellion.' Calling the Republic a tyranny for the sake of argument, the article quoted from *De Regimine Principium*'s ruling, itself based upon the teachings of St. Thomas Aquinas,[34] that if such tyranny were not 'excessive,' it were better to endure it temporarily than to risk graver dangers than tyranny itself. Before resorting to armed resistance ('the solution of despair'), continued *Sept*, all means of conciliation, of protest and of non-violent resistance must have been exhausted. Rebellion would naturally be more difficult to justify in a state upholding freedom of speech, of the press and of propaganda. Moreover, the revolt must be the action not of leaders, whatever their office, but of the common people ranged against tyranny. Again, the rebels must hold such guarantee of success as may afford a moral certainty. It must be remembered also that the man for whose sake the people have driven out the tyrant may well assume tyranny along with power, and for fear of sharing the fate of his victims he may impose an even heavier burden of slavery. *Sept* observed that in the nineteenth and twentieth centuries the Church had never given its blessing publicly to those who took up arms in its cause, whether it were the Polish insurgents, the Irish Sinn Feiners, or the Mexican Cristeros.[35*] *Sept* concluded as follows 'If in theory rebellion may be legitimate against a government whose tyranny is such that every citizen can consider himself in grave danger, it must be stated that in practice and in general all sedition is illegitimate, because the anarchy and disorder which it habitually engenders are usually worse than the wrongs which it seeks to remedy.'[36]

In *La Vie Catholique*, Jeanne Ancelet-Hustache echoed this sentiment, that it was a rare war indeed that put an end to as many ills as it brought forth. In reply to the concept of the holy cause, she observed that the early Christians martyrs were indeed resigned to the spilling of blood, but the blood was only their own. Against the opposing cries for Order and Country and for Justice and Liberty, concluded Madame Ancelet-Hustache, the compelling need was to remember the meaning of the word Charity.[37]

Esprit denounced the execution of Basque priests.[38] In *La Vie Intellectuelle*, Père Duployé described an earlier message from Gomá y Tomás, published in Paris in pamphlet form,[39] as merely a letter and in no way a pastoral letter.[40] Victor Montserrat, in *La Croix*,[41] and Georges Hoog, in *La Jeune République*,[42] denounced the myth of the disinterested, anti-Bolshevik crusade as long as it employed disciples of the Crescent. To Montserrat, the war had a single objective: extermination. *La République* suggested that the Vatican should take the initiative in proposing an armistice, to take effect first in the Basque country.[43] In general, however, appeals addressed to the Holy Father sought a blessing on the cause or a curse on the enemy's.[44] In *Le Journal*, Bernoville invoked the Pope to give open support to Franco. The congregations of bishops of Vizcaya and Guipúzcoa, he complained, had disobeyed their respective bishops of Vitoria and Pamplona who had allegedly condemned Basque resistance.[45] The denunciations of Gomá y Tomás,[46*] who was not only Primate of Spain but the Vatican's official Chargé d'Affaires in Burgos, would hasten the day, thought Bernoville, when the Basque Nationalists whose lives had been centered for centuries around their parish church would be faced with a terrifying choice: orthodoxy, and with it repudiation of the alliance with the Communists, or heresy.[47]

Bernoville's arguments were directly challenged by Jean Caret in *La Croix*, who insisted that the Church had no business taking sides or any role other than that of peacemaker and bearer of the divine injunction: 'Love one another.'[48*] A similar response came from a group of leading Catholic intellectuals, some of whom proceeded to form the Ligue Internationale des Amis des Basques, with its centre in Paris. The league's honorary committee consisted of Jean Cardinal Verdier, Archbishop of Paris, Édouard Herriot, president of the Chamber of Deputies, Mgr. Maurice Feltin, Archbishop of Bordeaux, and Louis Gillet of the Académie Française. Mgr. Clément Mathieu, Bishop of Dax, was elected president, and Mgr. Fontanelle and Jacques Maritain vice-presidents; among the league's members were François Mauriac and Georges Hoog.[49*] In February 1937, a group of French Catholic intellectuals—with Maritain at their head but Mauriac not taking part—had issued a manifesto in favour of putting an end to the conflict while placing the responsibility for opening it squarely on the Spanish military.[50] In the early spring, Maritain and Mauriac together issued a pro-Basque manifesto, which was also signed by Georges Bidault, Claude Bourdet and Maurice Merleau Ponty. Shortly after Guernica, these 'Chrétiens Rouges,' as the Right now dubbed them, published a further manifesto:

> Whatever opinion one may have on the quality of the parties face to face in Spain, it is incontrovertible that the Basque people are Catholic people and that public worship has never been interrupted in the Basque country.
>
> In these circumstances, it behooves Catholics, irrespective of party, to be the first to raise their voices to spare the world the pitiless massacre of a Christian people. Nothing justifies, nothing excuses the bombing of open towns like that of Guernica.
>
> We address an anguished cry to all men of goodwill in every land to bring an immediate end to the massacre of non-combatants.
>
> Postscript: this appeal is published after some of the above signatories presently in Paris, namely Fumet, Isvolsky, Lacombe, Madaule, Marcel, Maritain, and Meer de Volkeren, were able to hear the evidence on Guernica given by Chaplain Onaindía y Zuluaga, who was on the spot at the moment of the bombing.[51*]

Subject only to the findings of an international body of inquiry as to the complicity of any other elements in the aforesaid destruction, this evidence concludes that Guernica, a town without defence, was indeed bombed for three hours without respite and that the aircraft pursued the fugitives with machine-gun fire.[52*] The statement of 3 June by General Mola, which showed that he at least suffered from no such qualms after Guernica, had been by now widely reproduced in the press. In the Catholic *L'Aube*, Don Luigi Sturzo described Mola's threats as an offensive to civilization. 'It is the Germans,' wrote Don Luigi, 'who in a European war tomorrow will apply their methods of destruction to open cities like Brighton, Grenoble, Basle, Cardiff, Antwerp, Lyons, or Ostend, creating a hecatomb of women, children, helpless old folk and unarmed men.'[53] Don Luigi next confronted all those who believed that to speak of peace 'on the eve of Franco's victory' was to betray the cause not only of order and national unity in Spain but of Catholicism too. Don Luigi noted that such reasoning had been propounded in November 1936 (prior to the first offensive against Madrid), in March 1937 (prior to the drive on Guadalajara), in June 1937 (prior to the capture of Bilbao), and now in August 1937. In three short months, Don Luigi reminded Franco's partisans, the icy winds would howl across the plateau of Madrid in a winter even worse than the last.[54]

A veritable battle of the pens now raged in France. Francisque Gay published *Dans les flammes et dans le sang*, in which he rejected the notion that the conflict could be presented as a Holy War. Paul Claudel, the only major French poet to side with Franco, published his famous ode 'Aux martyrs espagnols,' originally as a verse preface to a pro-Nationalist tract by a Nationalist agent in Paris.[55*] Both Mauraic and Maritain replied, the former in a preface, published in *Le Figaro*, to a book by Victor Montserrat,[56*] the latter in a preface, published in *La Nouvelle Revue Française*, to a book by Alfredo Mendizábal, a former professor of the University of Oviedo. Mauriac, himself a Bordelais, reminded Catholics that the Church teaches above all else obedience to the established temporal power, 'however feeble and bad it may be':

> One does not exterminate an old Christian people such as the Basques simply because they believed they were not duty-bound to revolt.
>
> If they have committed an unpardonable fault by refusing to deliver up to Germany the minerals of Bilbao, may the French, at least, show them forgiveness. One day perhaps we shall understand that this poor people suffered and died for us. God grant then that we do not find their dead on the very spot where we shall have to bury our own.

Mauriac invited Claudel to add a verse, in the next edition of his 'unfinished poem,' in honour of 'the thousands and thousands of Christian souls whom the chiefs of the 'Holy Army' . . . [had] dispatched to eternity.'[57] This consciousness that the Nationalist movement had compromised Christ led Mauriac to despair. In a later article he added:

> We no longer have the right to be happy.
> Between the victims torn to pieces by the mobs or executed by the leaders of the Frente Popular, and the victims of premeditated bombing, carried out by foreign mercenaries in cold blood, with neither hatred nor delight, which would you say stirs most pity in the heart of God?
> Who knows? Perhaps the saints know . . .

Ah! If only a voice were to be raised at this moment, a single voice! But the saints no longer speak.[58]

Maritain, one of the first in the 20th century to urge a Christian compromise in temporal matters, was already the symbol of a new Christian humanism, saying that the Church, without sacrificing its theological principles, should give active support to democracy and to social reforms. Now president of the Comité pour the Paix Civile et Religieuse en Espagne, Maritain struck at the very basis of the Nationalists' pretensions, with a direct reference to the Collective Letter of the Spanish Bishops, an edition of which had also been published in Paris. Christianity, declared Maritain, would be remade by Christian means or it would be utterly undone; its cause could never be advanced by the sword. Maritain mocked the claim that God had no other means to save mankind than through the intercession of the Nationalists and their allies, and poured scorn upon the award of Sacred Heart medallions to the Moorish levies. He pointed out that if there were any difference between atheists who murdered priests and Christians who murdered the poor, it lay in the sacrilege inherent in the latter crime. Although Maritain took care to dissociate himself from the Republican cause, saying that his repudiation of the one did not imply his endorsement of the other, his article[59] was in turn attacked by Vice-Admiral H. Joubert, who published a pamphlet in which he expressed his anxieties over the replacement of 'historical Christianity' by such novel exegeses of the Gospel as Maritain's. It was in vain, wrote Joubert, that 'this ardent convert,' as he cruelly referred to Maritain, should deny the findings of the international inquest into the events at Guernica. Dismissing his opponent as an 'ill informed malefactor,'[60]* Joubert continued his campaign along these lines, giving three lectures in early 1938 and publishing their synthesis.[61]

On 28 August 1937, the Vatican accorded de facto recognition to Franco, altering this to de jure recognition on 3 May 1938. Catholics of similar political persuasion did not hesitate to remind neutral or pro-Republican Catholics that they were now technically in rebellion against the Pope. Thus the dogma of 1870 gave an entirely new dimension to the argument. The stigma of heresy, no more noxious by definition than 'to make one's choice,' was once again applied, in Bossuet's phrase, to anyone with an opinion.

Such support of the Nationalist cause may not have been quite the intention of the Vatican. The Pope's personal anguish was revealed on 30 November 1937, the Feast of St. Andrew. Since St. Andrew was the patron saint of the Solidarité des Ouvriers Basques, the Archbishop of Bordeaux, Mgr. Feltin, observed the occasion by celebrating the Mass with the Basque refugees at Cadaujac. In his address, Mgr. Feltin announced that he had received an audience with the Holy Father only a few weeks earlier; the Pope, he said, had inquired about the Basques with great interest and, in listening to the Archbishop's report, showed by his expression his compassion for their suffering.[62*]

The religious conflict which ensued took the argument out of the realm of politics,[63] but politics kept creeping back. While Maurras in *L'Action Française* presented the Church as the only real International, Mauriac continued his articles in sympathy with the Republic, and especially with the Basque Nationalists, notably two articles in *Le Temps Présent*[64] and *Le Figaro*.[65] On 21 March 1938, Mauriac and Maritain met in Paris with Gabriel Marcel and Père Bernardot. According to Hélène de La Souchère's report on the meeting, Père Bernadot denounced Franco's invocation of Christ in the bombing of Barcelona.[66] Marcel declared that in all temporal matters a Catholic still retained his freedom of conscience and could not be forced as a Catholic to side with any clan in conflict with another. Maritain inveighed against the pseudo-realism which would fight evil with evil. Mauriac stressed that Christ was at the service of no party or leader.[67] Mauriac's subsequent article in *Le Figaro*, which opened with a defence of Maritain against Serrano Suñer,[68*] amounted to a palinode of Mauriac's position in the first week of the war. Mauriac explained that when the news reached him in Vichy on 19 July 1936, he reacted as a political Rightist and dictated his article[69] in haste; 'but then came the presence of the Moors, the massive Italo-German intervention; total war was waged by the generals against a poor people, their own people; and then the sufferings of the Basques, guilty of the crime of non-rebellion.' What determined his group's subsequent attitude, continued Mauriac, was the pretension of the Spanish generals that they were waging a Holy War. The disastrous result was the confusion of Christianity with Fascism, and for millions of Spaniards it was no longer possible to hate the one without hating the other. It appeared to Mauriac that this compromise of Christianity was perhaps more alarming to French Catholics than to any others, for France had experienced since 1918 a unique revivalist movement which might not have been observed abroad: a Catholic renaissance among the working classes, with the creation of Catholic trades unions and Catholic workers' youth organizations. With the victory of the Nationalists, concluded Mauriac, the rule of force would begin. 'And the force which makes use of the Church is the greatest evil which can befall a Christian people. It is also the greatest betrayal of the doctrine that God is love.'[70]

Meanwhile in *L'Aube*, Georges Bidault and Luigi Sturzo continued to deny the war the character of a crusade. Sturzo wrote: 'The Church does not curse its persecutors, it prays for them. It does not kill them, it binds up their wounds. It does not take up arms or give arms to others, it urges peace for all. This, and only this, is the Church.'[71] In *La Croix*, a daily of vast influence, François Veuillot cried out: 'No! No! Believe me, dear Spanish Catholics, it is not in this way that religion will triumph!' The same journal responded with indignation when, in March 1938, General Martínez Anido prohibited the use of Basque in the Mass.[72] And when Maurras, himself under excommunication, visited Spain as the guest of Franco,[73] *La Croix* took occasion to express its grave concern over the deepening relations between the Nationalists and the pagan racists of Nazi Germany.[74] At the same time, Georges Bernanos published *Les Grands cimetières sous la lune*. This vivid indictment of Nationalist repression in Majorca was the more effective in that the author was both a Catholic and a Monarchist and that his book was based upon his experiences while living on the island in July 1936.[75*] In reviewing the book, *L'Aube* remarked that this 'Christian Crusade' revealed the same hypocrisy and dearth of compassion as were evident to Cardinal Mercier, Archbishop of Malines and Primate of Belgium, who on being asked after a visit how he found Christian Spain replied, after a long silence: '*Chrétienne, l'Éspagne? Vous trouvez?*'[76] It was far beyond the feckless powers of François Maret to attempt a rebuttal.[77*]

In December 1938, Mendizábal gave two addresses in Lille and Roubaix. After the meetings, the following motion was adopted:

> In respect of the Spanish tragedy, Catholics as such remain free to express their preference and extend their sympathy to either camp. At the same time, they may express their disagreement with either cause, especially in the matter of the methods of warfare employed.

L'Osservatore Romano replied:

> That does not, however, mean denying the difference between good and evil. It is idle to ask Catholics to deny reality and to disobey their bishops in order to follow the stupefying proposition of Professor Mendizábal.
>
> The methods of the two belligerents are so dissimilar from the Christian point of view that it is pointless to compare them.[78]

Thus the spirit of Christian humility shown by Lincoln, who did not claim that God was on his side but prayed to be on His, was nowhere even in the very organ of the Church. Despite such editorials in the Vatican's semi-official daily, there was a growing awareness by the Holy See that its unqualified support of a cause in Spain that owed so much to Nazi Germany compromised its own struggle against the State in Germany. On 18 March 1938, when Theodor Cardinal Innitzer, Archbishop of Vienna and Primate of Austria, together with the bishops of Austria proclaimed their adhesion to the Anschluss, both *L'Osservatore Romano* and Radio Vatican responded on 1 April by denouncing 'political Catholicism' and in particular the attitude of the Austrian hierarchy. These remarks were reproduced in *La Croix* on 2 April but not in any organ of Nationalist Spain. As the Civil War progressed, Pius XI seemed to be less attentive to the conservative counsel of his Secretary of State Eugenio Pacelli. In January 1939, on his return from Rome, the Cardinal-Archbishop of Lisbon denounced the 'myth of the Spanish Crusade to annihilate the infidels.' According to the Brussels *Soir*'s Vatican correspondent, F. Cochin, this statement accurately reflected the opinion of the Pope.[79*] On 16 February 1939, the same day that Georges Bidault cried out in *L'Aube* against Franco's treatment of Basque and Catalan Christians,[80*] the Vatican protested to the Franco government that a recently proposed cultural agreement between Spain and Germany violated the Spanish-Papal Concordat of 1851, and the protest, backed by the Spanish clergy, succeeded in limiting subsequent Nazi cultural influence in Spain. The death of Pius XI, however, and the election of his Secretary of State Eugenio Cardinal Pacelli, turned the balance in favour of the Nationalists. At the time of the final victory of Franco, and on the morrow of the German–Spanish treaty of friendship signed in Burgos, the new Pope Pius XII was to send the Caudillo the following telegram: 'Raising our souls toward God, we join Your Excellency in giving Him deepest thanks for the victory of Catholic Spain.'[81*]

16

The Pamphlet War and the Battle of the Minds

Palmiro Togliatti—Jean-Richard Bloch—Daniel Guérin—Thomas Mann—Camillo Berneri—'Max Rieger'—Jacques Bardoux—Robert Brasillach—Georges Rotvand—Henri-Massis—André Malraux—Jean-Paul Sartre—Simone Téry—Drieu La Rochelle—Romain Rolland—André Gide—Literary congresses and art exhibitions

Apart from the question of Christianity applied or misapplied, intellectuals in France had long since joined the struggle in other fields of discord. Their activities consisted of giving frequent lectures, writing articles, compiling pamphlets, and often producing their arguments later in book form.

As far as the international aspects of the war were concerned, one of the first pamphlets to appear in France was that by the Italian Communist leader Palmiro Togliatti, who used his nom de guerre, Ercole Ercoli, as his nom de plume. His *Particularités de la révolution espagnole*, which appeared shortly after the outbreak of hostilities, stressed the solidarity of the antifascist forces in Spain. Jean-Richard Bloch was another eye-witness to the events in Spain during the early days, when in Barcelona and Valencia, and later in Madrid, he obtained interviews with Companys, Prieto, Largo Caballero, Álvarez del Vayo, and Azaña, the President urging him to remind the French leaders of the trade agreement between France and Spain covering the supply of war matériel. These personal experiences were the subject of innumerable lectures and articles, which appeared in condensed form in October 1936 under the title *Espagne, Espagne!* In the name of the Anarchists, Daniel Guérin warned from 1936, in his *Fascisme et grand capital,* against underestimating the chances of fascist victory.

Among other such writers in 1937, Thomas Mann published in French the first edition of his work based upon his articles in *La Dépêche,* under the title *Avertissement à l'Europe,*[1] to which André Gide contributed the preface. *Paris-Soir*'s Louis Delaprée was no sooner killed in an air-crash than his memoirs appeared under the titles *Le martyre de Madrid* and *Mort en Espagne.* Another victim of the war, the Italian Anarchist philosopher Camillo Berneri, received the same homage as Delaprée, his articles in *Terre Libre* up to the month of his murder in May 1937 being reproduced in pamphlet form under the title *Guerre de classes en Espagne*.

Berneri, who considered himself a 'moderate' Anarchist, felt even in November 1936 that the war had taken a dangerous turn both for the Republic and for Spanish Anarchism. He was opposed to the two extreme positions currently held by the majority of Anarchists, the one in favour of 'ministerialism' and militarization, the other hostile even to a unified command. In direct opposition to the Marxists, he felt that a compromise solution to this problem, which would still save the Revolution from being subordinated to the struggle against Fascism, would alone ensure the military victory of the Republic. For the dilemma facing the Republic was no longer that of war or revolution but that of victory through revolution or defeat. Turning to the democracies and Russia and their obsession with non-intervention, Berneri imputed a heavy share of the blame to Gabriel Péri, who despite his previous posturing in favour of French aid to the Republic had since led the French Communists in their submission to Blum, and so effaced 'one of the few bright pages in the story of the French Communist Party.'[2] Meanwhile, none could put his trust in 'the paralytic on Lake Leman's shore.'[3] And if the battle today were in the skies above Madrid, tomorrow it would be above Barcelona, and the day after above Paris,[4] for the triumph of Fascism would make war inevitable in the very near future.[5] If, on the other hand, Britain, France and Russia were moved to intervene, as well they might be, at the moment that the Republic was in the throes of death, their intervention might save Spain from the Axis grasp but it would take care too to snuff out the fires of the July Revolution.[6]

Max Rieger was the nom de plume of the Comintern Propaganda Department. In 1938 a tract appeared under the name entitled *Espionnage en Espagne*, in the preface to which the Communist and pseudo-Catholic poet José Bergamín[7*] cleverly described the author as a Socialist and an International Brigader, 'not a writer.' The entire tract was an attack upon the POUM and justification of Stalin's persecution of this slightly Trotskyist party. Bergamín described the POUM as 'a highly effective instrument of Fascism'[8] and 'a spy network in the hands of Franco.'[9] 'Max Rieger' described it as the party selected by Fascism for the task of disorganizing the Frente Popular,[10*] and provided the names and addresses of Nin's 'agents' in Perpignan. Significantly, the tract refrained from any direct attack upon the Anarchist rank and file. In fact, it did not dare even to mention them by name, referring to them instead as 'uncontrollable elements' disowned by the CNT-FAI. In sum, the Comintern's tract lacked the exciting duplicity of Fascist propaganda; instead, it droned on through all its 230 pages of the inadequacy of language wherewith to paint the ignominy of the POUM.

Among the right-wing writers engaged in propaganda, the most influential, apart from Charles Maurras and Paul Claudel, were Jacques Bardoux, Robert Brasillach, and to a lesser extent Maurice Bardèche, Georges Rotvand, and Henri Massis. Bardoux concentrated on exposing, in periodical and pamphlet, an alleged Russian plot to subvert France and Spain in May and June 1936. The plot, disclosed to *Gringoire* on 9 October 1936, was first discovered through the alleged seizure by the Nationalists of a document in Majorca. Another document in French, published by *L'Echo de Paris*, was purportedly the battle order for the uprising in France, first scheduled for 1 May 1936, but postponed at the request of the Communists, who were not yet prepared. The date was then set for 10 June, and was again postponed until 29 June. Again the signal was withheld, until the events following the assassinations of July provided their own opportunity.[11] Writing in the *Revue des Deux Mondes*, Bardoux contended that a meeting had also been planned for 10 June, or thereabouts, in Madrid, to be attended by such ill-assorted persons as Auriol, Cachin, Díaz, Dimitrov, García Oliver, Largo Caballero, Pestaña and Thorez.[12] This unprecedented assembly of Socialists, Communists and Anarchists would be followed, according to Bardoux's exposé, by the creation of a Spanish soviet under the presidency of Largo Caballero. Bardoux attempted to substantiate his charges in a pamphlet entitled *Le chaos espagnol: éviterons-nous la contagion?*, which drew from articles already published in the right-wing press. The author, however, did not fail to berate the negligence of the League of Nations in failing to guarantee states against foreign intervention and in permitting the revival of jungle law in Europe, to the detriment of every treaty and undertaking. Bardoux held that the failure of the West to impose an effective blockade had now made it impossible to end the war by means of a ban on further foreign volunteers, and that Western diplomats were deluding themselves in thinking that a war could be extinguished by stages, like a fire. The only solution open to France and Britain, concluded Bardoux, lay in arranging an immediate armistice and total withdrawal, both to be imposed and controlled. Russia, whom Bardoux considered to be the power, and the only power, opposed to this solution, would be forced to concur through her fear of total isolation if she refused.[13*]

Brasillach, a conservative Catholic like Bardèche (his brother in law) and Claudel, revealed his fascination with Hitlerism in an article he wrote for *Revue Universelle* in October 1937, following a four-day visit to the Führer.[14] In July 1938 he visited Franco, describing his impressions in the same journal.[15*] *Revue Universelle* also began publishing extracts of his *Histoire de la guerre d'Espagne*, in which Bardèche only lightly collaborated.[16*] Brasillach had not forgotten his own Catalan origins, but he chose not to take part in the conflict. It is reasonable to ask why. According to Bardèche, taking part would be meaningless: all Franco needed were technicians to repair the German planes.[17*] The new Spain was the subject of a tract produced in that year by

Georges Rotvand who also visited Franco. Rotvand considered that the 'July Movement' would restore to Spain her rightful place in the world, a place which she had forfeited only through the hesitant policies of the last few years.[18] Spain, Franco told Rotvand, welcomed this movement; the generals had simply obeyed the national will.[19]

Several other right-wing figures, from Maurras and Massis to Doriot and Gaxotte, paid their respects in Burgos and Salamanca at this time, in celebration of the second anniversary of the insurrection. Maurras, immediately following his controversial election in June 1938 to the Académie Française, visited Salamanca where he received the courtesies usually reserved for a Head of State. In the same month of July, Massis was received in Burgos. A Monarchist with a poetic approach to history, Massis presented in his subsequent *Chefs* a treatise which contained hardly a line of factual observation or even an opinion supported by an example. The burden of *Chefs* was to show the difference between Hitler, a dictator only of things (*custos rerum*), and the Latin dictators, who were defenders of the human person. He insisted for this reason that order reigned in Nationalist Spain without the police making their presence felt.[20] In his interview with the Caudillo, he was told that in Spain a man was Catholic or he was nothing.[21] As for intellectual free trade, Franco told him that Spain had no need to import anything,[22] and that the Nationalist cause was sworn 'to hurl back into darkness, whence it should never have emerged, all the foreign mischief which has so grievously misled certain of our intellectuals.'[23] Franco further expressed to Massis his indignation at the 'propaganda of the lie,' in pursuit of which, he said, Republican sympathizers imputed to the Nationalists crimes they did not commit. His own best arms, he maintained, were 'victory and truth.'[24]

In the realm of *belles lettres*, whether or not propaganda was the author's intent, the propaganda value was considerable. The most important novel to emerge from the war was André Malraux's *L'Espoir*, selected extracts of which appeared in 1937–1938 in *La Nouvelle Revue Française*.[25] Drawing from his own experiences both as an air-gunner and as a squadron-leader of the Republican Air Force, Malraux presented the conflict from a point of view which, though fiercely Republican and not unfriendly to Communism, declined too close a collaboration with Marxist dialectics, to the point that Trotsky wrote of him—albeit in regard to *Les Conquérants*—that 'a good dose of Marxism' would have solved the author's problems.[26] The Marxist belief in historical necessity, however, held little attraction for Malraux, and there were other prophets besides Marx who denounced the hedonism and easy optimism of the bourgeoisie, among them not only Nietzsche but Bakunin. If he shows the Anarchists as half-Christians sharing the thanatolia of the early martyrs, Malraux does not condemn the libertarians' sublime if futile gesture, and the Communists emerge rather worse as some new class of priests. Nonetheless, it is because the latter are intent on *doing* something, and not merely *being* something, like the former, that the author's hero is the Communist Manuel. The propaganda thesis of the novel thus holds to the Communist doctrine that comradeship and self-sacrifice alone do not win wars, but in a larger sense the the book contrasts the values shared by the Republican forces with those that they opposed: on the one hand, the human element, the horror of humiliation, and the desire to give to all men a sense of their own dignity; on the other, the taste for humiliation, the denial to the enemy of the quality of man, and the cynical outlook which, when coupled with a zest for action, bespeaks the full-grown Fascist.[27*]

Jean-Paul Sartre's short story *Le Mur*, also published in *La Nouvelle Revue Française*,[28] analyzes the behaviour of a trio of International Brigaders who have been captured and sentenced to death by the Nationalists. *La Porte du soleil*, by Simone Téry, is a love story based upon the author's experiences in Spain as a war correspondent for *L'Humanité*.[29*] On the other side of the barricade, Drieu La Rochelle marched as to war in the person of his eponymous hero Gilles, a French Nationalist volunteer in Franco's army, fighting for a cause which he and his author fondly believed to be that of France. But Drieu was markedly unstable. Despite his aristocratic name he came from the lower bourgeoisie. In the First World War he had been wounded three times. His nostalgia for the heroism and fraternity of the trenches drew him to seek these virtues in fascism and to become in 1936 the theoretician of Doriot's PPF, but his first response to the outbreak of the Civil War was to call Blum weak for not intervening. In August of that year, Doriot's weekly *L'Emancipation Nationale* sent him on mission to Spanish Morocco, then to Cadiz and Seville, where he interviewed Queipo de Llano, then back to Morocco. His tour of Spain was all over in weeks. Then, in total self-contradiction, Drieu appeared on 13 January 1937 at the Théâtre Municipal in the Paris suburb of Saint-Denis and called for the repatriation of the French pro-Franco volunteers.[30] In 1938, just after Munich, Drieu broke with Doriot on an ideological dispute, only to return to him in 1940.[31]

The case of Drieu La Rochelle reflected the new polarization of political thought, with the choice reduced to the simple alternative of Fascism or Communism. Characteristic of this trend was the predicament of Romain Rolland, who had turned from Communism in his aversion to the excessive practices of Stalin, only to return to it again out of his horror and fear of Nazism. The disenchantment with Communism of André Gide, however, was more enduring. Gide had earlier supported the Communists, and in 1935 he had presided at the Congrès des Écrivains Révolutionnaires in Paris. He was invited by the Soviet Union to visit Russia, and in his *Retour de l'URSS*,[32*] on page 67, he summed up his impressions: 'I doubt that in any other country today, not even in Hitler's Germany, is the spirit more strangled, the mind less free, more crushed, more petrified, more vassalized.'[32] It was partly to denounce Gide that the Communists organized a writers' congress in Madrid in the summer of 1937.[33] The congress attracted not only the major Spanish poets of the war—Rafael Alberti, José Bergamín, Miguel Hernández and Antonio Machado—but many prominent foreign writers, including Ernest Hemingway, André Malraux, W. H. Auden and Stephen Spender, and a speech by Bertolt Brecht was read to the delegates.[34*] In Paris, the great names of the Spanish art world took part in the International Exposition to show their solidarity with the Republic. Picasso presented *Guernica*, y Miró, *El segador*, a scathing satire on war; the fresco has since been lost. Another international writers' congress, organized by the Comité de Vigilance des Intellectuels Antifascistes, was held that year in Valencia, where the principal speakers included Julien Benda, André Chamson and Ilya Ehrenburg. The choice of Spain as venue for the committee's 1937 congress reflected the fact that Spain was the focal-point of its interest.[35*]

17
Incidents in France

France and the Republicans violate non-intervention—The Nationalists violate French sovereignty—Right-wing activities—False information and conflict within the press

It was not difficult for the Axis or the French right-wing press, in pursuit of a set policy,[1] to fasten on to smaller or larger violations of the Non-intervention Agreement by France or the Spanish Republic. On 8 May 1937, 15 warplanes bearing the red, yellow and violet colours of the Republic landed on the Air-France airfield at Montaudran outside Toulouse.[2] The aircraft consisted of nine French Brack fighters, powered by Wright or Katiuska engines, and six Russian MM3 bombers. Air-France personnel, led by a certain Jean-Marcel Blanc, a member of the SFIO, were apparently expecting the planes for refuelling, for tanks were in place several hours before the aircraft arrived.[3] Captain Valle, commanding the Spanish Republicans, explained to Colonel Lunn, Chief Administrator of the International Board of Control, that the aircraft were en route from Valencia to Bilbao via Pau, but without written orders. The orders he now received, from Minister of the Interior Marx Dormoy, were to leave French territory forthwith and at the point the aircraft entered it. To this the Spaniards now replied that they entered France from Bilbao! At 7a.m. the following morning, the planes left Montaudran escorted by a French squadron, which led them in the truer direction of south-southeast.[4*] A place was reserved in the French squadron for the Finnish Lieutenant-Colonel Wallden, attached to the International Board and responsible for Haute-Garrone.[5] This and other incidents did not fail to attract a lively curiosity. *Le Jour* sent its special correspondent Gaston Gélis to investigate the landing at Pau of 17 Spanish Republican planes, en route from Catalonia to Bilbao.[6] Henri de Kérillis was flying his private aircraft over Toussus airfield near Versailles when he noticed several large U.S.-built transport planes being serviced by Gardes Mobiles. There was no doubt, wrote Kérillis in *L'Echo de Paris*, that these aircraft were earmarked for Spain.[7] On the frontier, the Italian Fascist agent Filiberto Smorti was assigned to observe the activities of the International Board.[8*]

On May 27 the International Board informed the French Foreign Military that clandestine shipments of arms were passing through the private airfield of the Latécoère aviation plant in Toulouse, at the rate of two a week. The arms were reportedly brought to the airfield in ambulances, thence transported by plane to Bilbao. In a letter from the Ministry of the Interior to the Prefect of Haute-Garonne, the signature to which appears to be that of Charles Magny, the Ministry instructed the Prefect to take all necessary measures '*pour en éviter le retour*,' an ambiguity which the Prefect decorated with some handwritten question marks.[9]

According to Pierre Héricourt in *L'Action Française*, supplies passing through Cerbère in the first four days of June amounted to 174 trucks, 25 automobiles, 35 tons of spare parts, 22 tons of steel, 26 tons of nickel, 13 tons of heavy oil, 11 tons of chemical products, and 56 tons of footwear.[10] A high-ranking Nationalist officer informed Héricourt in July that Franco's chief enemy was foreign aid, not only French and Soviet but U.S., Mexican, Czech and British. It should be pointed out, however, in vindication of Eden's flat denial that any British arms had been exported in any form whatever, that the British cannon listed by Héricourt were 1914-model 4.5-inch howitzers, better suited to the Imperial War Museum than to an up-to-date army. Héricourt continued to supply elaborate statistics: at Le Perthus he counted 233 trucks and 63,360 gallons of gasoline passing into Spain between 17 July and 19 July. He was rather less observant in Nationalist Spain: a tour of the entire territory failed to bring to light the presence of a single German or Italian weapon.[11]

As for the transit of foreign volunteers during this period of mid-1937, it would appear that the Non-intervention Agreement was honoured by France more in the observance than in the breach. The only communication in this matter from the Ministry of the Interior to the border Prefects concerned a strong protest from the Netherlands Legation in Paris over the transit of some sixty Dutch volunteers during the first half of June. The route followed by the volunteers ran from Antwerp via Roubaix, Paris and Alès to Sète, where they embarked on a Greek vessel bound for Catalonia.[12] The vessel in question was probably the small Greek ship *Varko*, the subject of complaint in *El Heraldo de Aragón* on 5 December. On this subject—the violation of the Non-intervention Agreement by clandestine shipments by sea, from ports north of Pyrénées Orientales—other evidence attests to it. The Prefect of Aude reported that 'large numbers' of volunteers were being transported from Narbonne to Port-La-Nouvelle by car and then loaded at night on to motor launches. The launches left immediately for Port-Bou, Llansa, Palamos or other ports in Republican Spain. The man entrusted with this traffic was a certain Hernáez, a well-known anarchist whose brother had been sentenced to three months' imprisonment for trafficking in arms. He also had at his disposal five boats each with two high-powered engines and a special appliance for firing torpedoes.[13] This report of the Prefect, however, was not entirely borne out by an official investigation. The special investigator in Carcassonne confirmed that five boats had recently arrived at the port; they were certainly equipped with two 150 horsepower engines, but not with an appliance enabling them to fire torpedoes; that assertion, he said, was far fetched. The boats, he concluded, had nothing to do with the departure of volunteers for Spain, nor with arms traffic, but it was quite likely that the traffic involved smuggling.[14]

Articles had appeared in *Le Jour* and *L'Émancipation Nationale* in January and February 1937 concerning pro-Republican activities in Toulouse. Colonel Lunn subsequently reported that the Bar Opéra and the Bar Gambetta in that city were being used as arms depots; packages, believed to contain arms, were being conveyed to and from the bars in municipal ambulances, escorted by municipal police. The Prefect of Haute-Garrone strongly denied the charge.[15] Nevertheless, at the end of July the Chief of Police in Toulouse informed the Prefect that the Bar Gambetta was indeed a headquarters for gun-running and a focal point for Soviet agents. The bar was owned by the mistress of Jean-Marcel Blanc, now a representative for two airlines: the newly created Compagnie Air-Pyrénées and the Líneas Aéreas Postales Españoles. Blanc was in close relations with officials at the Air Ministry, whom he called frequently from the bar's telephone booth; several of these calls were partly overheard. This indiscretion, and the manner in which he flaunted his sudden wealth, had led to an investigation.[16] No subsequent action, however, was reported.

The suppression of the anarchist revolt in Barcelona in May 1937[17] was to have repercussions beyond the frontiers of Spain. The French intelligence services intercepted several letters to French anarchists from an anarchist centre in Zurich. These letters, if authentic, disclose the new policy of anarchist organizations worldwide: 'to profit from this mournful experience and do everything possible so that the communist reactionary movement in Barcelona serves as a wake-up call proclaiming a world anarchist revolution.' Comrades must therefore get to work to provide money and arms for the CNT-FAI in Spain.[18*] A centralized information service was entrusted to the delegate in Barcelona, Antonio José Irigoyen. Chief Inspector Porterie, at the Francazal airport, picked up certain information concerning the assembly points and itineraries for the passage of arms and volunteers. In Haute-Garonne, at Saint-Béat, a certain Boulineau had taken charge of passage through the Val d'Aran, crossing the frontier to the east of Pont-du-Roi. At Burgalays, a certain Maudinat was in charge of the convoys to Bausén; depots had been set up at Cierp and Marignac; the route passed the Pic de Burat, crossing the frontier at the Pic de la Hage. At Mayrègne, a certain Paco also guided convoys to Bausén, passing through Cier-de-Luchon and the mountain roads toward La Cabaña on the Bosost plain. At Bagnères-de-Luchon the same function was performed by a certain Moulin, routing his convoys to Bosost through the Portillon de Burbe.

In Ariège, an assembly point had been set up in Castillon-en-Couserans, to make for Montgarri through the Pic de Girette. In Pyrénées-Orientales, at Prats-de-Mollo, the guide was a certain Pruja who was directing the arms traffic to Molló through the Collade de Prats. The centre at Arles-sur-Tech was headed by a certain Sala; his route passed through Saint-Laurent-de-Cerdans and the Bouja pass to Albañá. In Montalba, a certain Martimat led the convoys to Tapis through the Périllou pass.[19]

It was at this time, in mid-1937, that several more border incidents took place which could be construed as a violation of French sovereignty. On 26 May, after the machine-gun strafing of Cerbère and the shooting in Hendaye, a plane belonging to Air-Pyrénées and operating between Bayonne and Bilbao was shot down over the Basque country by six Heinkels. *L'Humanité* at once ruled out the possibility of accident or error, declaring that Franco had already announced that he would destroy the plane and that Major Troncoso, the Nationalist Military Governor of Irún and Commandant of the Requetés in Guipúzcoa, had stated before witnesses in Hendaye on 17 May that action was imminent. Moreover, added the Communist organ, the plane had at no time entered Nationalist air space. But while *L'Humanité* described the aircraft as a mail-plane,[20] Héricourt in *L'Action Francaise* claimed that the sole function of the new airline was to supply the Basque Nationalists and enable Vaillant-Couturier to commute between Biarritz and Bilbao.[21]

The left-wing press was no less diligent than the right in unearthing plots and exposing spy networks. In June 1937, *L'Humanité* denounced the activities of Count Quiñones de León, a former Ambassador of Alfonso XIII, who, it alleged, was publicly issuing passports to Nationalist Spain in the Hôtel Meurice in Paris. The Count was also described as head of a spy network in direct liaison with Franco; each evening two couriers, working in rotation, left the Gare d'Orsay in Paris in the sleeping-car to Hendaye, their reservations being held in the name of Quiñones de León; from Hendaye they continued to Burgos and Salamanca. *L'Humanité* invited the police to confirm its findings.[22]

Indeed, the French authorities were making their own discoveries. After a long surveillance in the port of Sète, the special inspector unmasked the activities of José Antonio Batlle, Agent 45 in the service of the Spanish Nationalists. Batlle was arrested at the moment he was boarding a train for Marseilles. He was carrying with him certain papers addressed to his superior José Camps, residing in Marseilles at the Hotel Colonna and in Sète in the Villa Aimée. Camps was responsible for all intelligence collected whether in Republican Spain or in the French frontier *départements*.[23] The documents found on Batlle included an identity card issued by José Bertrán y Musitú, head of the SIFNE organization in Salamanca,[24] and a letter from Camps reporting on the secret information that Prieto had recently divulged to his cabinet ministers on the subject of the possible manufacture and use of poison gas.[25]

Official investigations were also conducted into the sailings of the yacht *Carmen*. The yacht had remained anchored at Port-Vendres for six months before sailing for Port-La-Nouvelle. According to the frontiers inspector in Nice, the owner of the *Carmen* belonged to Franco's intelligence services and was specifically assigned to the watch on all vessels sailing from French ports to Spanish Republican ports.[26] It is a measure of the confusion in the French intelligence services that Special Inspector Imbert, assigned to Narbonne, reported that not one of the charges against the owner of the yacht was based on fact.[27*]

Equally barren of fact, according to Ambassador Herbette, were the suspicions surrounding the Marquis de los Andes, head of the House of Alfonso XIII and resident in France. Even if it were shown, wrote Herbette to the Quai d'Orsay, that the activities of the marquis in Biarritz went a little beyond his diplomatic function (consisting of analyzing French and foreign newspapers, checking on the motives of persons wishing to enter Spain, and of classifying information on the activities of Franco's adversaries in France), that did not justify forcing all Spanish nationals in Biarritz to migrate to other regions of France, and even worse to north of the Loire. Such a measure was to no purpose, insisted Herbette, and neither was the policy of preventing Spaniards from returning to Spain via Hendaye or Béhobie. He had been assured, he added, by the French Consul General in San Sebastian, that the Spanish authorities were determined, if need be, to force French citizens resident in cities such as San Sebastian and Bilbao to move their homes to other regions, such as south of the Guadiana. Indeed, on 29 August the president of the French Chamber of Commerce in San Sebastian and two other French nationals were asked to leave the city. Herbette warned that the Spanish authorities could go as far as expelling from Nationalist Spain the majority of the French consuls.[28*]

The circumstances surrounding the entry of Spanish submarines in French territorial waters was a matter of general embarrassment. Back on 2 August 1936, the French Navy had issued the following secret instructions to all authorities concerned:

> In the event that a Spanish warship shows up in a French port without your having received prior clearance from this office, you are to take the following action. Prohibit all communication between the vessel and the shore, except with the Spanish consul. Prohibit any delivery of arms; order the ship to stand ready to set sail within six hours or face arrest and internment. The Spanish consul is held responsible for reporting the situation of the vessel in relation to the regular government of Spain. Action taken is to be reported by tele-

graph to the Minister of the Navy, and the above instructions are to be followed until new instructions are issued.[29]

Such instructions were not followed with much precision. A Republican submarine, damaged by a Nationalist fighter-plane, managed to reach the roadstead at Blaye and was authorized to undergo repairs in the naval shipyards in Bordeaux. Another case caused acute embarrassment to the press on Franco's side. In September the Spanish Republican submarine C-2 entered the commercial port of Brest. Investigations into this by the Sûreté Nationale, now under the direction of Moitessier, showed the existence in France of terrorist organizations in the pay of Franco that were linked to the Doriotistes and the Cagoulards.[30] Major Troncoso, Franco's governor of Irún, was arrested in Bayonne after a man who confessed to being Troncoso's agent stated that he had been instructed to bomb either the Paris Exposition or the Marseilles labour exchange, which was known as a recruitment centre for foreign volunteers for the Republic. The action was then to be blamed upon the FAI, which was widely reputed to be capable of any action, however irrational. Troncoso in turn confessed to the French police that he was the leader of a team that included his personal servants, a French officer belonging to the PSF, and the commanders of the C-2 and its sister ship, the C-4; the two Spanish naval officers, Ferrando and Las Haras, were arrested in Bordeaux. It was discovered that Troncoso's 'chauffeur,' who went by the name of Parella, was none other than the Marquis de Maravellés. Another grandee of Spain, the Marquis of Linares, who used the pseudonym Antonio Martín Montis, was arrested in Brest. The target of the team was to hijack the C-2 in Brest and the C-4 in Bordeaux.[31]*

The report created a sensation in the press. *L'Express du Midi* called it 'dumbfounding'.[32] *L'Echo de Paris* denounced Dormoy for 'recklessly arresting one of the most important intimates of Franco' and for 'compromising relations with the Spain of tomorrow.' Such action, it asserted, with curious foreknowledge, could provoke reprisals against the French consuls in Salamanca and San Sebastián.[33] *La Dépêche* linked the affair to sixteen attempted assassinations in the Midi.[34] According to *L'Humanité*, Troncoso received his orders from two Gestapo agents, Major von Orsten and Captain Karl Brandt.[35]* At the same time, *L'Humanité* saw a possible connection between the Troncoso case and the recent disappearance of the White Russian General Evgeny Miller, who in actual fact had been kidnapped by NKVD agents in broad daylight on the Champs-Élysées. Since it was common knowledge, argued *L'Humanité*, that Miller had been active in recruiting volunteers for Franco, his kidnapping may well have been staged to avoid his being implicated in the Troncoso affair. Reminding its readers that White Russian groups in France had already raised a Gorgulov to carry out the assassination of President Paul Doumer, it charged that these groups were providing Franco with terrorists and provocateurs and that, by now accusing the Communists of kidnapping Miller, they were 'pulling off a double.'[36]

Le Populaire, which had already reported the presence in southwestern France of an entire network of spies at the service of Franco,[37] identified its mastermind as Troncoso, who indeed now warned the French authorities that the French consul in San Sebastián would be held as hostage against his release.[38] The very next day, Franco responded by imposing house arrest on the French consul in Málaga, Desmartis, and on 4 January 1938, by arresting and imprisoning the French consular agent in Irún, Ducourau. A further immediate reaction against France was staged by Italian naval personnel in Tunis, who were reported organizing a 'punitive expedition.'[39]

The report was taken seriously by *Le Populaire*, which proceeded to expose the Mancini plan, named after the Italian general responsible. The plan allegedly aimed at the invasion of the French Basque *départements*. On the night of 8 October 1937, armed French Fascists, aided by Spaniards resident in the Basque country, would disembark along the coast at high tide, occupy strategic points, and close National Highway 10 linking Béhobie with Paris. At the same time, motorized columns would cross the frontier at Béhobie and Hendaye. Armed groups would move in from La Rhune to aid in the task of inciting the people to insurrection. Barges and lighters concentrated at Fuenterrabía would disembark troops at Saint-Jean-de-Luz and various points unknown. These armed units would attack the defenders of Hendaye and Béhobie from the rear if they should offer strong resistance. This plan, added *Le Populaire*, had been carefully prepared in Fort Guadalupe at Fuenterrabía in the presence of Spanish and German officers, and would have been executed resolutely had it not been exposed.[40]

Noting that Franco's spy ring had been only partially dismantled by the arrest of Troncoso, *L'Humanité* gave warning, in February 1938, that Franco had entrusted the task of rebuilding it to the Marquis de Montago.[41] The Sûreté, for its part, was focusing its attention on the activities in the Midi of Romero de Luque, son of the Marquis José de Luque. Resident in Perpignan, he called himself a journalist, but in reality he spied for Burgos.[42] Marx Dormoy followed up by distributing a list giving the names of 89 persons hired by the CNE 'Pro Movimiento Nacional' to collect money in France for the Franco cause.[43] Another Nationalist agent, Carlos de Arellano, was engaged in recruiting volunteers, especially technicians, for the rebel army.[44] Dormoy had already written an article on the possible collusion of these agents with the Italian and German secret services. *L'Humanité* then accused a French citizen by the name of Lambressat of being the agent in Irún of the German and Italian spy rings attached to Franco's headquarters,[45] and at the end of 1938, the French police reported the arrival in France of two leading members of OVRA, Mussolini's secret police. They had entered France through Irún, accompanied by a Franco agent, the Duke de Gamero Cívico, whose purpose was to introduce them to Franco agents who were already operating in the Côte d'Azur region.[46]

Meanwhile, a notice, issued by the Comité national d'Entente contre la Guerre with the simple aim of discouraging French peasants from supporting the Communist Party in the next elections, was now displayed on the walls of every canton in France.

FRENCH COUNTRYMEN:
Those who want to send you away (for the Red Czar Stalin) are the 300,000 Communists who will cry "Go to it!" and who will stay in the shelter of the factories and earn a hundred francs a day. As for you, you will earn ten rounds a day in the trenches, and if by any chance you bring your hide back from this red crusade:
As a conqueror, you will be bolshevized, and you will find your home, your land and your wife at the feet of the Reds.
Conquered, you will be *bochisé* and you will find your home, your land and your wife at the feet of the Boches.
Peace before anything! *Vive la France*!
DOWN WITH WAR![47]

Perhaps the most serious attempt by the Right to seize power in France took place in November 1937. After the leagues had been dissolved in 1936,[48] Eugène Deloncle, a member of Action Française, at once formed a secret Fascist organization called the Comité secret d'Action révolutionnaire, popularly known as the Cagoule, whose avowed objective was to prepare a conspiracy to overthrow the Third Republic. With the aim of setting a military figure in power, the leaders of the Cagoule approached Marshal Pétain, but since he declined the invitation it was passed to Marshal Franchet d'Esperey. The plot was to be concealed under the pretext of preventing a coup d'état by the extreme Left. In November 1937 the plot was discovered. Dormoy took immediate counter-measures, Deloncle was arrested, and the conspiracy was nipped in the bud.

Meanwhile, in the hate campaign in the press encouraged by the Axis,[49] among the dailies only *L'Action Francaise, L'Écho de Paris, Le Jour,* and to a certain degree *Le Journal* were taking a sympathetic part. *L'Écho de Paris* now took pleasure in publishing a letter from Queipo de Llano to Miaja, the commander of the Republican forces in Madrid, which was presumably motivated my Miaja's interview with *La Dépêche*.[50] The letter enclosed a wooden sabre and ran as follows:

Dear old pig,
I know that you are distressed to learn that the French have sent Moscardó a fine sabre of honour. To console you, I send you this one as a perfect symbol of the valour of your army.

It has another merit: its hilt is in the form of a cross. We can therefore place it on your coffin when we have had you shot. Thanks to this cross, which will ennoble your filthy carcass only slightly, you may even enter Paradise, if God decides to forget your crimes.

Quiepo de Llano[51]

La Dépêche reproduced the letter as the expression of a quite extraordinary mentality.[52] *L'Écho* next crossed swords with *L'Humanité,* which published an allegedly official Nationalist document showing that Kérillis had relations with the Falange.[53] Kérillis labeled it an odious lie and engaged Albert Naud to take proceedings against the Communist organ.[54] In reply, *L'Humanité* described Kérillis as "thrashing about like the devil in a stoup,"[55] and cried out grandiloquently: "They shall not pass, ever, here any more than in Spain."[56]

It was at this time that the right-wing forces in France found themselves deeply divided. In November 1936, the congress of the Parti Démocrate Populaire (liberal Catholic) had admitted that the Right was evolving toward an anti-republican and authoritarian position. That was a trend that the PSF of La Rocque[57*] had no intention of following. The next month, during its first national congress on 18–20 December, the PSF published a pamphlet entitled *Une mystique, un programme.* It declared itself 'firmly attached to those Republican principles of freedom that are the crowning glory of France; principles that rule out fascist dictatorship, Hitlerian absolutism, or the inhuman slavery of Soviet Marxism.' La Rocque thus refused to join the Front de la Liberté created by the fascist PPF of Doriot with the aim of unifying the Right in an anti-Marxist crusade. This refusal reflected the new strategy of the PSF: win over the moderate elements on the Right, at the expense of the extremists tied to the party of Doriot.[58*] These extremists, under the direction of André Tardieu, who had become the grand critic of the French parliamentary system, responded with a campaign of calumny against La Rocque that was intended to ruin him politically, to the advantage of Doriot. At the moment that La Rocque was purchasing *Le Petit Journal*, Doriot was buying up the floundering *La Liberté* in the hope of gaining an advance on his rival. His campaign against La Rocque was fully supported by *L'Action Française*, *Gringoire* and *Le Jour*.

For *L'Ami du Peuple,* too, the difficulties were financial, but more dramatic on the Right was the resignation of Henry Simond from the administration of *L'Écho de Paris.* Although *L'Écho* published a front-page statement by Francois-

Edmond Blanc to the effect that Simond had resigned for purely administrative reasons,[59] his resignation was immediately followed by that of Kérillis and the majority of the senior staff members.[60] In the first issue of *L'Époque*, their new National Republican journal, Kérillis explained the reason for the mass withdrawal: 'A journalist cannot be put up for sale in the public square, nor in the Stock Exchange along with his journal's shares, like sacks of lentils sold in the market.'[61]

In *L'Ordre*, Buré spoke for all the centre forces in denouncing the lies published by both extremes in their coverage of the war in Spain. He called the attention of some leading journals of the Right to the fact that the armies of Franco were not unfamiliar with defeat in battle, while he reminded some prominent organs of the Left that the same armies had been known to win the field.[62] The vehemence of the two extremes of thought resulted in further litigation. An article by Georges Suarez in *Gringoire* entitled 'Les Russes à Paris: Pertinax,'[63] in which the author accused Pertinax of having fabricated a story about Germans landing in Spanish Morocco in order to bring about a general war, led Pertinax to sue Horace de Carbuccia for libel. Yvon Delbos testified by letter that Pertinax had written nothing that did not conform to the truth in the government's archives. The judges awarded Pertinax an uncommon ruling: 30,000 francs in costs and damages, with a fine on top of it. The defendants did not dare to appeal.[64]* Action for libel was also taken by Léon Daudet of *L'Action Francaise* against Louis-Martin Chauffier and the managing-editor of *Vendredi*,[65]* in respect to articles published on events in Spain. Another such action was taken by Daudet, Maurras, and Pujo against Georges Valois and *Nouvel Age*.[66]* In this case the plaintiffs failed to win their case, but the left-wing press was suffering financially: *Sept* went into liquidation on 27 August 1937, and *Vendredi* followed suit on 10 November 1938.

No improvement was noticeable in the subsequent quality of the reportage. The left-wing press continued to downplay or even ignore Republican setbacks. Conversely, when at the end of 1937 the tide of battle turned temporarily against the Nationalist cause,[67] *La Dépêche* took to task not only the French pro-Fascist press but even the majority of the general information dailies, for either ignoring a news item or presenting it in a questioning or dubitative manner,[68] in sharp contrast to the massive structure of their headlines proclaiming the precedent victories of Franco,[69] and in contravention of the Caudillo's own injunction.[70]

18

British Mediation and the *Deutschland* Incident

The 'May Days' in Barcelona—Largo Caballero and Blum replaced by Negrín and Chautemps—The democracies respond to the blockade—Public opinion in Britain—The mediation proposal is submitted—Reaction in the French press—The attack on the *Deutschland* and the shelling of Almería—The fall of Bilbao—Its effect on British policy—The Committee at an impasse

In the Republican camp, as Rieu-Vernet observed in *La Dépêche*, two forces were headed in opposite directions.[1] What the loss of Málaga had served to fuse, the victory of Guadalajara served to sever. Communists and Anarchists alike could now see the war only through the prism, or indeed the prison, of their respective ideologies.

In France, the right-wing press had contended from the outset that power in Republican Spain was in the hands of the Communists.[2*] Few writers on the right understood the irreconcilable differences between the two ideologies. Few even pointed out, as d'Ormesson pointed out in *Le Figaro*,[3] that Spanish Anarchism was independent of Soviet influence. Ironically, by suggesting that the two groups shared a common purpose, they were serving the turn of the Communists, for by March 1937, the Third International had set out to divide the Anarchist movement, presenting the moderate Anarchists, who were prepared to collaborate, as the true voice of the movement and the remainder as traitors. This lent a curious ambivalence to editorials in the Communist press. Thus, while Cachin wrote in *L'Humanité* that Anarchists in authority were increasing their efforts to achieving unity and that their appeals were receiving more and more attention from the Anarchist rank and file,[4] *Pravda* and *Izvestia* were intensifying their attacks upon the Anarchists in general, portraying them as the saboteurs of anti-Fascist unity.[5*] In this work of deception, the Stalinists were assisted by the ingenuous and over-generous character of so many Anarchist intellectuals like Kaminski.[6] If a left-wing Socialist like Zyromski could see that the Spanish Revolution was in grave danger, it was only a few like the Anarchist philosopher Berneri who perceived that what threatened the Revolution was not simply foreign efforts to mediate in the war but the Anarchists' recent entry into the Republican Government. The hour had come, he wrote in *Guerre des Classes*, to ascertain whether the Anarchists had joined the government to be the guardians of a flickering flame or whether their sole purpose henceforth was to serve as a Phrygian cap for politicians flirting with the Fascist enemy or with the forces bent on restoring 'the Republic of all classes.'[7]

Meanwhile, the moderate press was flirting with the thought that real Communist participation in the government,[8*] if it were only given the chance, might be of benefit to the Republican cause. *La Dépêche* reported in January, with obvious sympathy, that the major concern of the Ministry of the Interior was to restore the authority of the State over that of groups and uncontrollable elements, whatever their origin.[9] On May Day itself, Georges Scelle, who still felt that time was on the Republican side, berated those who 'in their blindness' feared the advent of Communism in Spain. Peace could not be won except through order, wrote Scelle, and order could not be restored in Catalonia or anywhere else except by a strong government. He added clairvoyantly: 'It could be said that the hour has come.'[10]

The civil war within the Civil War erupted on 3 May 1937. Although it did not appear in the French press until 6 May, it came as a welcome relief to the cause of Nationalist propaganda which was now reeling from the worldwide effects of Guernica. In fact, the French Right could not hide the pleasure if felt. Guèze referred to it as the fundamental issue of the war: 'In Nationalist Spain order reigns,[11*] while in the Red zone anarchy reigns . . . Is that not sufficient to determine on which side the criminals are?'[12]

The curious aspect of French reaction was that all the major journals ascribed the collision to what *Le Journal* called 'the fury of the Anarchists burning with revenge.'[13] The national papers of the Centre and Left, without exception, took the Republican—and thus the Communist—side, against the Anarchists. The Communist invasion of the CNT-held Telefónica building in Barcelona was described in *La Dépêche* as 'another Anarchist uprising.'[14] The moderate *L'Aube* felt that if the FAI won the struggle, or if it were even allowed to continue in operation, the collapse of the Republic was certain.[15] *L'Ordre* called eponymously for order and for a strong hand in Catalonia.[16] *Le Peuple* accepted Valencia's version of events in good faith, attributing the disorder to the work of 'irregular elements, Fascist auxiliaries perhaps.'[17]

In point of fact, the Communist provocation reflected Stalin's conviction that Russia and the Communists must support the republican and bourgeois revolution, and not the revolution of the proletariat, because feudal roots were still too strong in Spain. Now, having imputed the fault for the disorders to the Anarchists, and having suppressed the uprising in the name of the Republic, the Communists set about consolidating their new position. 'This victory,' said one to Rieu-Vernet, in terms curiously reminiscent of those that Millán Astray had addressed to Unamuno,[18] 'will allow us to cauterize the cancer that gnaws at our entrails. It will be painful, but it will restore the rear to health and ensure victory over Fascism.'[19]

The cancer gnawing at Stalin's entrails was thus all parties in Spain to the left of his. The subsequent suppression of the POUM was in fact no more 'painful' to the Communists than their earlier persecutions of the Anarchists in Kronstadt and Petrograd.[20*] As for Largo Caballero, all hope of working with him had long been abandoned, and the aftermath of recrimination that followed the 'May Days' provided the occasion for his removal, an action which had been planned, according to Scelle of *La Dépêche*, as long ago as January.[21] The same plan called for his replacement by one of Prieto's moderate Socialists, who controlled the executive committee of the Frente Popular. In announcing the formation of the new government of Juan Negrín, *La Dépêche* carried the headline: 'LARGO CABALLERO COLLIDES WITH COMMUNIST INTRANSIGENCE.'[22] The Toulouse daily now saw, in the words of Rieu-Vernet, that the Communists had chosen 'democracy without adjective' as the means of achieving their Soviet aims.[23] The official Stalinist line still carried the old duplicity: 'It is by no means necessary that all members of the new government share the same doctrines. The common will to triumph over Fascism is all that is necessary.'[24] But at a press conference given in June, the Spanish Communist leader Jesús Hernández was still blaming Largo Caballero for everything except the recent spring floods. Rieu-Vernet who attended commented wryly that with the old Socialist out of the way, the Communists could assume the heavy responsibility of winning the war quickly.[25*] Colonel Morel, however, saw it differently. As French military attaché in Valencia, and the only French military officer in Spain, he wrote to Daladier: 'The die is cast. If the Republican Government were to lose this war, it would not be for tactical or technical errors. It would be for having squandered the only strength it had, the revolutionary élan of the army.'[26]

If the Republic intended to win the war, the help of France seemed more necessary than ever. In June, Negrín and his foreign minister, José Giral, left for Paris to confer with Camille Chautemps,[27*] who had just been called upon to form a new Cabinet, Blum having resigned as prime minister. The Spanish leaders wanted to put an end as soon as possible to non-intervention, or at least to frontier control. The dangers of putting an end to the non-intervention agreement were of course obvious: if there was no longer an agreement, then Germany and Italy could give their aid officially to the Franco government that they had recognized, while France and the Soviet Union could do the same, officially, to the government that they recognized. The two groups of Powers could claim the same, that they were helping the legal government of Spain to suppress a rebellion. The risk of seeing the conflict extend to the rival powers supporting one or other of the camps would be therefore much increased.

While there was no change in the attitudes of the French Right and Left, the all-important Centre followed an uneven approach. In *La République*, Pierre Dominique argued that French intervention in August 1936 would have meant immediate war. If now, in the early summer of 1937, France signed any agreements to *refrain* from supplying a belligerent, it would serve to postpone the war a little, but it would be war none the less. If the French Communists failed to involve France in war, explained Dominique, Stalin would have only one recourse: to abandon the French Communists to their fate as he had already abandoned the Spanish Communists, and then, with or without the services of Marshal Tukhachevsky, throw himself into the arms of the German General Staff. Stalin was thus choosing between 'world revolution [and] a knouto-Germanic empire.'[28] Apart from Dominique's confusion between the Stalinist and Trotskyist attitudes toward revolution, no clearer prophecy was written on the imminent fate of Poland. On the other hand, in another Radical-Socialist daily, *La Lumière*, Georges Boris revived the demand for honest dealing. Either non-intervention was to be observed equally by all, wrote Boris, and with that its indispensable corollary, the prompt withdrawal of volunteers, or the agreement was a dead letter and all states had an equal right to send supplies to Spain.[29]

Much hinged upon the credibility of each contestant's victory propaganda. Among the journals that were less committed to either side, *L'Oeuvre* had confidence in the Republic. The situation at the League of Nations, wrote the Radical daily, was now reversed. The mention of Franco's name allegedly evoked derisive smiles: he was considered the loser.[30]

L'Oeuvre devoted considerable time to such assessment of public opinion, particularly British opinion. Albert Bayet described British opinion at the outbreak of hostilities as cool to the Republic, with Conservative circles showing an unmistakable reserve toward 'the Reds.' However, added Bayet, the massacre in Badajoz, the bombing of Madrid and Guernica, and the executions in Salamanca had produced a change of heart, and all England cheered the crew of the *Seven Seas Spray* who braved the Nationalists' would-be blockade and delivered supplies to the people of Bilbao.[31]

This matter of the blockade was a direct result of the nature of the non-intervention agreement. As already stated, each signatory State was committed to prohibiting all dispatch from its territory of arms, munitions and any other war matériel to one of other of the camps in Spain. This agreement amounted, without a doubt, to a recognition of the insurrection. The signatory State did not deny to one camp or the other the right to regulate navigation within its own waters or the right to prevent, again within its own waters, help from reaching the enemy. But what the signatory State certainly did deny to the camps was the same right on the high seas wherever belligerent rights obtained. Both Spanish camps acted, however, as if they had secured belligerent rights, the better to win the recognition of such rights by the foreign Powers.

It was the Madrid government that had been the first to provoke, when it attempted, with its two proclamations of 9 and 11 August 1936, to mount a blockade. The British Government had promptly declared that the action was illegal, since it came from a party that did not hold belligerent rights.[32*] As a result, the British Government would not permit any interference with its merchantmen outside territorial waters, and it ordered its warships to 'train their guns' on any Spanish warship that attempted to put such a blockade into practice. Germany, for its part, had dismissed the Madrid proclamations as 'Red piracy,' and when in December 1936 the *Palos* was arrested on the high seas, Germany retaliated by arresting and holding two Republican merchantmen.

Meanwhile, the Burgos authorities had similarly announced, on 17 November 1936, their intention of interdicting the traffic of war matériel to Barcelona 'by all military means.' On 9 April 1937, Franco warned the British Government that his forces were organizing a total blockade of the Basque ports, and that he would use force against any attempt to break through the blockade, whatever the consequences that might ensue. On 28 November 1937, Burgos issued a new proclamation, this time without mincing matters: 'Any ship that attempts to enter government ports will be attacked.'

To all these communiqués, the responses of the British, French and US Governments were identical. To Franco's proclamation of November, the State Department in Washington declared that the United States had not recognized and had no intention of recognizing the belligerency of either camp. In the House of Commons, Anthony Eden declared the same: 'As a result, His Majesty's fleet will, if necessary, protect British merchantmen on the high seas against any interference by the Spanish navy, whether the government's or Franco's.' In almost identical terms, it was announced in Paris that 'French merchant ships would submit to the control of local authorities within territorial waters, in accordance with international law. But outside this zone, the French Government would not tolerate any of its ships being arrested, boarded or captured by either one of the Spanish fleets.'[33*] At the moment of the siege of Bilbao, in April 1937, Prime Minister Baldwin repeated the warning: an absolute protection would be given to every British vessel up to the three-mile limit, and the responsibility for any damage incurred would redound on General Franco. That statement was put into practice in the weeks that followed.

The exploit of the *Seven Seas Spray* thus came as a direct challenge to Nationalist claims of a right to blockade. The case was not unique. On 22 April, under the protection of the battle-cruiser HMS *Hood,* three other British cargo ships—*MacGregor, Hamsterley* and *Stanbrook*—entered Bilbao, despite the efforts to intercept them by the Nationalist cruiser *Almirante Cervera* and the armed trawler *Galerna*. The 5,000 tons of provisions carried by these vessels gave an enormous boost to the morale of the populace which was thus supplied with foodstuffs for more than a month. Nevertheless, on 30 April, in response to a communiqué from the Basque Government, the British Government decided to cooperate in the evacuation of Bilbao's civilian population, while Franco, angered by the unfavourable publicity spawned by the Guernica incident, strove to prevent the Basques from leaving their capital en masse. Describing this exodus as 'a ruse of the Russians in command of Bilbao,' he offered to create, as an alternative, a 'security zone' between Bilbao and Santander; he would organize the evacuation of Basque women and children to Salamanca, 'except for those guilty of crimes.'[34] 'Only thieves and murderers will be prosecuted,' he added, 'but quite without hatred.'[35] Dark allusions followed, however, as to what Bilbao could expect if it did not abandon in time its 'separatist folly.'[36]

None of Franco's offers was accepted. France was now aligned with the British position, albeit apprehensive over the vulnerability of the French naval forces currently engaged. They consisted of a single warship, the destroyer *Terrible*, which, according to Ambassador Herbette, was not in a condition sufficient to measure itself against the *Almirante Cervera*.[37]* Herbette urged the French Government to move at once on a separate matter, that of 'repatriating the involuntary volunteers,' by persuading Valencia to allow France to withdraw those Frenchmen in the International Brigades who wanted to leave Spain but who were prevented from doing so.[38]

As for British public reaction to the current situation, Geneviève Tabouis was pleased to inform her readers in mid-May 1937 that both political parties in Britain now strongly supported Valencia, while the partisans of Franco had melted like the snows of yesteryear.[39] In *La Dépêche*, former British Home Secretary Sir Herbert Samuel endorsed some of Madame Tabouis' impressions. British public opinion, wrote Sir Herbert, was not formulated in the long run according to government decisions: on the contrary, government decisions had to conform to public opinion. Sir Herbert agreed that the consensus of British opinion hitherto uncommitted had turned against Franco as a result of the bombing of Madrid and Guernica, while his recent declaration proclaiming military rule as the future regime in 'reconquered' Spain was repugnant to the British people. Nevertheless, he maintained, the British people clearly understood that the conflict was for the Spanish people to decide. At the same time, Sir Herbert commended Winston Churchill's recent mediation plan,[40] while pointing out that its success would depend essentially upon the readiness of all Spaniards to accept a compromise in preference to a continuation of the conflict.[41] Churchill was out of office, but it was at this time that the British Government submitted a plan for mediation. And Britain, *Le Figaro* remarked, was the only major power not to have dirtied its hands in intervention.[42]

On 15 May 1937, Eden informed the German Ambassador in London, Joachim von Ribbentrop, that the British Government intended to work, through normal diplomatic channels, for a cessation of hostilities in Spain. The British plan, presented two days later by the British Ambassador in Berlin, Sir Neville Henderson, in a note to the German Foreign Minister, Constantin von Neurath, envisaged an attempt by all the interested powers to arrange a truce in Spain which would permit foreign volunteers on both sides to be withdrawn from the Peninsula. A similar proposal was submitted to the Italian Government.[43]

Almost before the Fascist powers had time to squash the proposal, many a voice in the French press had repudiated it. *Le Petit Journal* expressed its opposition to mediation if it meant rewarding the aggressor.[44] Recalling the words of Lamartine expressed almost exactly a century earlier, *Le Petit Journal* considered the question of such intervention untimely, whether too early or too late. At the same time, poet and paper warned that it was in the interests of France to prevent a civil war in Spain from dragging on, dishonouring Europe and weakening France, for French security required a Spain free from foreign domination.[45] *L'Humanité* objected that the question of mediation arose every time the tide turned against the Nationalists or there was the possibility of action by the League of Nations.[46] Insisting that the more organized and cohesive Republicans were gaining ground each day on the economic as well as the military level, *L'Humanité* claimed that Salamanca was secretly in favour of mediation, since a ceasefire proposal implied the recognition of the equality in law of the two parties and the conferral of belligerent rights on Franco. The Communist organ denounced handing Franco such an advantage or entrusting the matter to the London Committee, where Spain was not represented; the Committee, it said, had already proven its inability to check Fascist aggression and it was the responsibility of the League, where Spain *was* represented, and which was not apprised of the Committee's inefficacity, to put an end to the war.[47] *Le Matin* replied that all that had been or would be achieved in the cause of mediation in Spain had been performed through the energy of the London Committee and not through the 'effete Byzantinism' of the League of Nations.[48] *Le Journal* felt that there was no hope of mediation while the fate of Bilbao hung in the balance, or until one side or the other was exhausted.[49] In *La Dépêche*, though Georges Scelle also considered that the time was not psychologically ripe for mediation,[50] Manuel Chaves Nogales maintained that the war was now approaching the end. The reason for his optimism was 'the defeat, already visible, of both armies in combat.' Both, he felt, were now convinced of the impossibility of crushing the other. Both sides had thus proceeded to eliminate the extremist factions which in combination had provoked the war in the first place; the arrest by Franco in April of the Falange chief Hedilla had been matched by the suppression of the FAI and the POUM, while the new government of Negrín spelt the end, thought Chaves, of Communist aspirations in Spain.[51] In the same issue, the editors of *La Dépêche* dissociated themselves from their contributor's viewpoint.

The fate of Bilbao was central to the problem. According to Álvarez del Vayo, Germany, concerned with the needs of her own rearmament program, insisted that the Nationalists give priority to the conquest of the iron-rich Basque country.[52] Whether or not the British initiative was prompted, as Franco implied,[53] by concern for the fate of Britain's own interests in that area, the British were soon disabused of their hope. As *L'Oeuvre* put it, Italy was 'not yet resigned' to the defeat of Franco, and neither Italy nor Germany would come to the bargaining table until they had either achieved a definite victory or abandoned all hope in the Nationalist cause.[54] In *L'Ordre*, Buré suggested that Hitler and Mussolini were indeed losing hope, and if they had only known what troubles Franco would see they would never have recognized him. The two Axis leaders were now committed, but they were looking everywhere for an avenue of escape that would not entail a loss of face.[55] According to *Le Journal*'s Berlin correspondent, the advice of Neurath had sufficed to persuade Hitler at the end of May not to send several additional brigades to Spain.[56] On the other hand, *L'Oeuvre*'s Rome correspondent reported in early June that Mussolini was now ready to resume sending reinforcements, but with this difference: in future, divisions would be fully trained and fitted out in Italy, not in Spain.[57]

It was this moment that an international incident arose which again evoked the spectre of global war. On the morning of 29 May 1937, the German battleship *Deutschland* was deliberately attacked off the Nationalist-held island of Ibiza by Republican aircraft. Two days later, on 31 May, the *Deutschland* bombarded the south-coast town of Almería in reprisal.

Just sufficient time elapsed between the two incidents to allow distinctions to be drawn in editorial reaction. Before the news of Almería had been received and analyzed, *Le Journal* even spoke of the legitimacy of Berlin's anger.[58] In *L'Écho de Paris,* Pertinax denounced Valencia but in a blind and mechanical fashion, attributing the incident to three causes for which the Republican Government could hardly be blamed: firstly, the failure to complement international control with the withdrawal of foreign volunteers; secondly, the indignation expressed in London and Paris by the Republican authorities at the inequity in the maritime control, claiming—quite justly, in point of fact—that the German and Italian navies were applying the sanctions on the Republican coastline with maximum severity, while the British and French fleets cruising debonairly off the Nationalist coasts were often turning a blind eye on the blockade-runners; and thirdly, the formal charge by Valencia that

Italian warships were transporting war matériel to Palma.[59] *L'Humanité* replied by showing the *Deutschland* wrong on two counts: firstly, the German battleship was in the French zone of control and not where it should have been, patrolling Spain's southeast seaboard; and secondly, it was inside Spanish territorial waters, thus forfeiting its freedom of the high seas.[60]

In the moderate press, *La République*'s Dominique considered that such an incident was bound to happen, given the confused situation in the Western Mediterranean, with Majorca and Ibiza in Nationalist hands and Minorca in the control of the Republic.[61*] *L'Oeuvre* feared the danger of escalation, as a result of unconsidered reflexes: the inexorable drift from reconnaissance to attack, from attack to reprisal, from reprisal to ultimatum—the whole sickening incline.[62] *L'Ere Nouvelle*, however, denounced Valencia for what it termed another deliberate attempt to extricate itself from its predicament by unleashing general war, and warned that such action, far from assuring its safety, compromised its cause.[63*]

As for the shelling of Almería, the right-wing press at first barely knew to which saint to pray. *La Victoire* was the exception: Gustave Hervé wrote on 1 June: 'Well done the Germans!' *L'Humanité* seized the initiative by demanding that the Franco-Soviet mutual assistance pact be invoked in favour of Valencia.[64] Predictably, the demand served to ignite the right wing, notably Léon Daudet in *L'Action Française*, Paul Marion in *La Liberté*, Wladimir d'Ormesson in *Le Figaro*, and even Pierre Bernus in *Le Journal des Débats*. *La Journée Industrielle* considered that Valencia could have precluded the bombardment of Almería by taking disciplinary action against the bomber crews responsible for the attack on the *Deutschland*.[65] A new twist was added in October by Jacques Bardoux, who contended in *Revue des Deux Mondes* that the planes over the *Deutschland*, though painted in republican colours, were not only of Russian manufacture but manned by Russian officers. Bardoux even reported their names. The raid, he concluded from this premise, was a snare laid by Stalin to trap Hitler, and Hitler fell headlong into it, bombarding Almería while the world observed.[66*]

Few incidents showed more clearly the effeteness of the League of Nations and the democracies' failure of nerve. *Le Petit Journal*, in its closing months under a liberal administration, understood this. The coup which succeeded at Almería, it wrote, would succeed tomorrow in Prague; 'nothing brings war on faster than the passive reaction of the great democracies to a gesture of defiance of a Fascist state.'[67] Georges Boris observed in *La Lumière* that the successful evacuation of refugees from Bilbao proved that the Fascist bluff would collapse before energetic and united action by Britain and France.[68] In *Le Journal*, however, Saint-Brice expressed his faction's anxiety over the proposal to submit the Almeria incident to the League of Nations for collective action. 'Setting the League's wheels turning in an emergency action,' wrote

Saint-Brice, paying the League an unmerited compliment, 'could have been extremely dangerous, since it might have led the League to draw hard and fast conclusions from a situation which in reality is nothing but a chain of inconsistencies.'[69] A week after Almería, Gabriel Péri declared bitterly in *L'Humanité:* 'We were told after Almería, "Now for a *détente.*" Well, there's no *détente.* Instead, there's the capitulation of the democracies.'[70] The Communist organ proceeded to attack Blum and Delbos, while an identified Communist *déeputé* and member of the Foreign Affairs Committee accused the Quai d'Orsay of being a branch of the Wilhelmstrasse.[71]

A paper with a better claim to speak for the democracies, *Le Petit Journal*, appealed for an understanding of the basic issues. What was at stake, wrote the organ of Patenôtre, was no longer ideological affinities or demonstrations of friendship toward a sister republic, but the life or death of France. Echoing again the sentiment of Lamartine, *Le Petit Journal* reminded Frenchmen that whatever regime had ruled France, whether kingdom, empire, or republic, the independence of Spain was a necessary condition of the national security of France.[72]

Bilbao fell to the Nationalists on 19 June 1937. Hitler openly exulted at its capture. His reference to the Basque subsoil as if it were already German property exasperated *Le Petit Journal. Le Peuple* wrote bluntly of the Führer's reaction: 'The truth is that the war waged in Spain by the two Fascisms is the preparation for another world war.'[73] In *La Dépêche*, Georges Scelle observed after the fall of Bilbao that no diversionary action had been attempted on the part of Barcelona to relieve the northern front, or even the southern.[74] Barcelona apparently had other commitments or had not learnt its lesson, for two weeks later Santander fell. With the capture of Santander, the French right-wing press luxuriated in the 'wild, unforgettable joy' of the inhabitants as the Nationalists entered. In reply, *Le Peuple* made an apt allusion to the 30,000 additional Basque refugees who were at that time disembarking in the French ports between Bayonne and La Rochelle.[75]

Reports differed as to the current state of Republican morale. If Prieto, convinced of the Republic's incapacity to continue the struggle after the May Days in Barcelona, had asked Blum in Paris to arrange an immediate armistice,[76] it is uncertain what backing he had among Republicans in general. For now, even with the defeat in the North, Valencia was reported by *Le Petit Parisien,* which described its source as 'totally reliable,' to be no more interested than Salamanca[77]* in a mediation plan aiming at reconciliation.[78] The effect of the fall of Bilbao, according to Rieu-Vernet of *La Dépêche*, who sounded the opinion of ambassadors, was to strengthen world opinion in favour of the Republic,[79] although Georgi Dimitrov's subsequent appeal in *L'Humanité* to the French and British masses to rise against their governments[80] hardly encouraged such a trend. Sir Herbert Samuel, for one, disagreed with his colleague on *La Dépêche*. After Bilbao, the victory of Fascism in Spain seemed to Sir Herbert and, he professed, to British opinion, the most probable result, but he still maintained that neither extreme ideology could be imposed on Spain undiluted; if either side were to apply dictatorial methods in restoring peace, it would soon find, the ex-Home Secretary believed, that Spain was ungovernable.[81]

By August 1937, in the similar view of *La République*'s Dominique, the British Government had switched its bet to Franco and was acting accordingly.[82] The Radical-Socialist journal repeated this sentiment in a November headline: 'BRITAIN BETS ON FRANCO.'[83] By that time even *L'Oeuvre* had formed the same impression. For Geneviève Tabouis, British policy had indeed swung in favour of the Caudillo and aimed at separating Franco from Mussolini.[84] In another exclusive article for *La Dépêche*, Sir Herbert Samuel declared that the consensus of British opinion still favoured 'a friendly intervention by the Mediterranean powers in order to establish a centrist regime of pacification and reconstruction, with no reprisals.'[85] Guglielmo Ferrero replied to Sir Herbert's thesis in the same column: if Britain thought that there were still any centrist, moderate or liberal reserves in Spain from which to establish such a regime, wrote Ferrero, then Britain was living in a world of dreams.[86] More realistically, David Lloyd-George, Britain's Liberal Prime Minister from 1916 to 1922, wrote in *L'Oeuvre* that Chamberlain seemed so eager to win the Duce's favour that he seemed ready to pay any price. He added what was to prove a sad irony: 'I have, however, the greatest esteem for Daladier and his attachment to democratic principles.'[87] The time was now eleven months to Munich.

Amid the cross fire of recriminations, the interested powers and the press sometimes lost sight of the basic recommendations of the British proposal: the repatriation of foreign volunteers. This was the one point, observed *Le Petit Parisien*, on which the two Spains would agree whenever they were ready to make peace.[88] Even *L'Echo de Paris* was now calling for the withdrawal of all foreign volunteers.[89] The character of the war in the Basque country was no doubt responsible for the mellowing of Kérillis, who in his last month with *L'Echo de Paris* wrote of 'the heroic struggle on both sides' and added his support to the appeals of the moderate elements for mediation, peace and an end to foreign intervention. In so doing, he denounced the opposition of Vaillant-Couturier[90*] to mediation, warned against a peace that would 'strangle the Spanish people in order to stanch the hemorrhage,' and applauded the prospect of ending all Soviet, German and Italian intervention in Spain, which Kerillis now found equally distressing.[91] In his new paper *L'Époque*,[92] Kérillis freely expressed his growing fears: 'We only want to live in peace with Germany. But our pride cannot accept that *Mein Kampf* be taken as the Bible of the Reich.[93*] German activity in Spain and Morocco is taking more and more the form of a threat to France.'[94] In the same journal, however, General Édouard de Castelnau argued that the Western democracies would carry a heavy responsibility if they failed to ensure the victory of Franco. After describing the Republicans as dominated by the Anarchist factions—this after the POUM had been liquidated and the FAI repressed by the Communists—Castelnau summed up his opinion: 'Democracy in Spain is good. The peace of the world is better!'[95]

Le Figaro now made the suggestion that Nationalist Spain should replace Italy in the London Committee and offer its agreement to the repatriation of all foreign volunteers in exchange for belligerent rights. 'The hour has come,' wrote d'Ormesson, 'for Franco to show that he is neither a puppet nor a prisoner.'[96] To *Le Figaro*, the London Committee was the Wimbledon Centre Court, with the ball bouncing back and forth as the totalitarian rivals shuttled the blame.[97] The Soviet Union was now saying, in effect, that she would agree to the granting of belligerent rights to Franco on condition that volunteers were first recalled. Germany, on the other hand, was demanding that belligerent right be granted as prior condition of recalling volunteers. Both projects, as *Le Populaire* pointed out, were contrary in letter and spirit to the British proposal.[98] The whole question of volunteers, observed the Socialist organ, cynically but at least half-accurately, would be debated by the Committee so fully that the volunteers would surely remain in Spain to the very end.

19
The Nyon Arrangement

First anniversary of the war: its goals newly assessed—Fascist aid to Franco—Comparing the foreign forces of intervention—Axis policy after Bilbao—The 'mysterious sinkings'—The Nyon Conference and the Nyon Arrangement—French and British policy after Nyon

In July 1937, for the first time since the outbreak of war, and presumably to celebrate the first anniversary of the insurrection, Franco received members of the foreign press. *L'Express du Midi* made the refutable remark that the Caudillo had first given these representatives full liberty to scour Nationalist Spain and to visit the various fronts.[1] The burden of his address was the matter of truth:

> I ask you to report the truth. The truth is our only ally in this struggle that is for us the fulfilment of an international mission, that of fighting Communism, and of a national mission, that of saving Spain from chaos.
>
> We seek a Western civilization. We seek to establish order and justice everywhere, that and nothing else.[2]

Just three days earlier, on 12 July, Franco had signed a secret commercial protocol with Nazi Germany.

The first anniversary and the search for 'truth' inspired the entire press to redefine the issues. Pierre Dominique of *La République* saw the conflict as more and more a battle of ideas. 'The real loser,' he wrote, will be either Germany-Italy or the Soviet Union. That is why the conflict drags on.'[3] In *L'Ordre*, Buré agreed that Europe was in full ideological crusade but warned that it was not the crusaders of democracy who were gaining ground. The Fascist powers, he said, were growing the more dynamic the more they felt that the democracies were, by their very principles, remaining static, and the hope that the position would improve once Britain had rearmed ignored the fact that by then the position could be beyond remedy.[4] This static attitude on the part of the democracies evoked the scorn of Augusto Barcia. In an exclusive article for *La Dépêche*, Spain's former Foreign Minister expressed his amazement that the leaders of the great European democracies could make the 'unpardonable' mistake of thinking that the Spanish conflict concerned none but Spain. 'After Agadir,' he wrote, 'it was the Great War. After the

London Committee, . . . some years may elapse perhaps, but the conflict will be only the more terrible.'[5]

The French right-wing press continued to feel no such involvement. So devoted was it to Fascist causes, Buré pointed out, that in the summer of 1937 it at once began to applaud Japanese victories in China.[6] As for its support of Mussolini's plan to re-establish the empire of Augustus in Africa, and at the expense of France, the editor of *L'Ordre* considered its behaviour not only mistaken but criminal.[7] Buré made a special exception for *Le Figaro's* d'Ormesson, whom he complimented on the fact that, though he cordially detested both Popular Fronts, he was not one of those who would appeal to foreign intervention in order to crush them.[8] Indeed, *Le Figaro* now reacted strongly to the Axis suggestion, prompted no doubt by Hitler's 'triumph' at Almería, that naval control be abolished while territorial control be maintained. The suggestion, replied *Le Figaro*, was 'a joke, but a joke in the worst taste.' Control, to be effective, had to be absolute; it was all or nothing.[9]

The first anniversary also brought a major appeal for reconciliation from Salvador de Madariaga, the Republic's former representative in the League of Nations, in a letter to *Le Temps* dated 15 July 1937. Madariaga introduced himself as a Spanish citizen who had remained equally removed from both sides and who had the bitter advantage of exile and distance, an advantage he recommended to the leaders of both sides. All these leaders, wrote Madariaga, were men of vision. If they looked beneath the surface of popular enthusiasm, however sincere it might be, they would reach the same conclusion as he: the need for peace through reconciliation:

> Both sides must understand that moral victory is inaccessible to both, because the victory of either will be no more than a military victory achieved with foreign arms, a victory without intrinsic meaning to the history of Spain. The real Spain will reap nothing from a victory which, whoever may be the victor, will remain a foreign victory. Whoever wins, Spain will lose . . .
>
> Both sides are fighting for an ideal, that of saving Spain from tyranny or of saving her from anarchy, as they call them. But what tyranny and what anarchy are worse than those brought by civil war? . . .
>
> Both sides must see that their actions are not only dangerous but sterile. Spain will never be either Communist or Fascist. Her foreign policy is governed by geo-political and economic realities. It will remain essentially the same, whichever side wins.

Thus Madariaga reminded the ultimate victor that the goodwill of the people was essential to his rule and could not be imposed by force. At the same time, Spain's cultural contribution to the world lay above all political ideologies, which were nothing but 'ephemeral and uncertain forms of our vacillating human thought.' Meanwhile, Spain continued to suffer as the sacrificial victim of the European civil war hitherto avoided.[10]

Reports appeared sporadically concerning the origin of foreign aid to Franco. In May 1937, *L'Humanité* announced the dispatch from Germany of 400 Benz artillery-transport trucks.[11] The Sûreté Nationale took the report seriously and instructed the Prefect of Haute-Garonne to investigate.[12] Official French sources reported two loans negotiated by Franco in the early summer. The first was for 2 billion francs, the source of which was unknown. The second was in the amount of 5 billion francs from three sources, which French Intelligence identified as the British group Mintz & Fletcher, the Banque Lazard, and La Séquannaise. Franco allegedly offered 125 percent in pledged guarantees both in customs and in certain other commercial concessions.[13] Furthermore, the leading purveyors in France to the Nationalist forces were identified as the South American Dibos brothers, the Austrian Egler, and the German Dr. Scholl, all resident in Paris.[14] As an example of this provender, *L'Ordre* reported that in the single month of May 1938, and by the Hendaye rail route alone, some 400 tons of various material entered Nationalist Spain. This material, dispatched mainly from Germany, Switzerland and the Netherlands, included automobiles, trucks and spare parts.[15*]

General Armengaud, Inspector General of Defence in the French Air Force, wrote a series of articles for *La Dépêche* in 1937 on the military lessons to be learnt from the Spanish conflict.[16*] He quoted a secret report of a German officer to the effect that anti-tank weapons had shown themselves to be better developed than the tanks themselves.[17] In subsequent articles, General Armengaud stated that the side would win that succeeded in obtaining the greatest amount of foreign aid, especially aircraft, delivery of which the international patrols would remain powerless to prevent.[18] The general later made a study of all aircraft engaged in Spain, which included the following main types:[19*]

	BOMBERS	FIGHTERS
Italian	Caproni Savoia 79/81	Fiat
German	Dornier 17 Junker 52	Heinkel 51 Arado 68 Messerschmitt 109
French	Potez 54 Bloch 200/210	Dewoitine

Soviet	Katiuska	I-15
		I-16
British		Fairey

Armengaud attested to the superiority of the Heinkel and Fiat at high altitudes, while the Soviet fighters were the fastest and their pilots the best trained. Among the bombers, the German, Italian, and especially the French were of poor quality: they were slow and heavy, and easy targets for the best anti-aircraft weapons, the German 88 mm and the Swiss pom-poms. The best bombers were the Katiuska and the Dornier. The Katiuska, though designed as an interceptor, with a speed well in excess of 250 mph, was being used for certain bombing missions, while the newly arrived Dornier rivaled the fighters in speed and thus needed no escort. General Armengaud attached the greatest importance to air power and attributed the Republican debacle in Majorca to the Nationalists' control of the skies. The general added that the Soviet Union could claim general superiority in quality in mid-1937, but that any such lead was likely to be ephemeral.[20] In *Vu-Lu*, Maurice Fontenay estimated that the Soviet aircraft were more than one year ahead of the rest of the field, the German models coming last. In an analysis compiled on the basis of actual combat experience, Fontenay considered the best current fighter to be the Russian I-16, which he praised for its combat manoeuvrability and accredited with a speed of 300–320 mph.[21]* *La Liberté* reported that both the Katiuska and the I-16 were equipped with special rapid-climb devices, retractable undercarriage, and supercharged engines which put them on a par with the latest French prototypes. The fact that the Soviet Union had already delivered some 140 of these aircraft to the Republicans meant that the Russians were already mass-producing a model which in France was still on the drawing board.[22] In any event, the arrival of the Messerschmitt in late 1937 altered the balance of quality. With a speed of 250 mph, wrote Armengaud, it was a match for any.[23] By November, government sources in Valencia were admitting that the newest German and Italian aircraft had regained supremacy over the Russian.

On 12 July 1937, the French Government put an end to the international control along the Pyrenees frontier. The next day the frontier was tacitly reopened to contraband traffic in arms and men. The question throughout July 1937 was whether or not France and Great Britain had conserved sufficient credibility in their will to resist to deter further Axis aggrandizement, or to what extent was the French Right aware of the danger of the Axis. In *L'Echo de Paris*, Pertinax was satisfied that the Axis powers fully understood that there were ineluctable limits to Anglo-French compliance; he added that they were probably in no position to risk a warlike venture, and yet the game they were playing was fraught with danger.[24] Pertinax subsequently expressed grave concern over recent reports of German consolidation in the Western Mediterranean and even the Atlantic. German air and naval bases had been established at Melilla, Alhucemas, Ceuta, and Larache, as well as in Ifni, the Canary Islands and Río de Oro. Each base contained a submarine shelter, an airfield, a fuel depot, a radio station and a power station, and the Ceuta base also included gun batteries that complemented those at Algeciras to cover the Straits of Gibraltar. France, concluded Pertinax, a little belatedly, must not be duped.[25] In a subsequent appeal for national unity, he explained that it was not in the interests of France to side with Valencia against Salamanca, but it *was* in her interests to look to her communications in the Mediterranean and to see that international treaties were respected. These treaties, added Pertinax, even more belatedly, were violated in Spanish Morocco the moment that foreign troops were called to the rescue. In a quite disingenuous conclusion, Pertinax claimed that such had been the policy of *L'Echo de Paris* ever since the end of July 1936.[26]

In that same month of July 1937, debates were held among the French leaders on the subject of the readiness of the French economy in the event of war. The distinguished engineer John Nicoletis, who was now consulted, showed his relief that those in authority were taking the matter seriously. At that time one of the elements for the manufacture of all gunpowder and of almost all explosives was sulphuric acid. France, however, could not produce more than small quantities of sulphur, notably in areas outside Narbonne; French sulphuric acid was consequently based almost entirely on pyrites. Certainly, as a result of the development of concentrated synthetic nitric acid, the dependence on pyrites could be reduced for an equal production of arms, but even so, the need would still require 100,000 tons per month, and indeed, during the war of 1914–18, France had needed double that quantity. The fact remained that France could not hope to draw from its pyrites mines, even at their fullest production, more than 50,000 tons per month. It was thus necessary to import the rest. The pyrites producers to which France could apply in time of war were few and far between. They were primarily Spain, Portugal, Norway and Greece. The pyrites produced in Norway and Greece, however, was of inferior quality, being too hard to crush. From Portugal French imports of pyrites almost tripled in 1936, reaching not less than 326,000 tons for the year, at the same time that France imported vast quantities of sulphur. That still left Spain as the indispensable provider. Some of the more clairvoyant French leaders understood, from the moment that the Civil War opened in July 1936, that this source could come to an end. During the last six months of that year, the import of Spanish pyrites was accelerated even while France searched the earth for other sources. With the help of the huge British enterprise Imperial Chemical Industries (ICI), recourse was now made to gypsum as a source of material. France could thus take it better in stride when, in

February 1937, Franco issued a proclamation forbidding the export of pyrites to France or to any country that would re-export the material to France, but the problem was still unsolved. Most of the detonators manufactured in France were produced with mercury fulminate. Obviously, if war were to break out, France could not count on Italian mercury, or on importing mercury from Central Africa or Mexico or Australia. In this state of affairs, even if lead nitrate could, at a pinch, partially replace mercury fulminate, France was nonetheless once again thrown back on a single source: Spain.[26*]

The ominous significance of August became of special concern to *Le Figaro*'s Romier, who observed that for the last three years August had produced an international crisis: first Abyssinia, then Spain, and now Shanghai, while the League of Nations had ingeniously arranged not to open its annual sessions until September.[27] In the second half of August, reports began to appear in the world press concerning 'mysterious sinkings' not only of Republican ships in Spanish waters but also of other vessels far from the Spanish coasts. The judgment of *L'Aube*, immediately following the sinking of the British merchantman *Woodford* near Valencia, best represented the free inquiry of the unbiased press. The Catholic daily proceeded by elimination. It first exonerated Salamanca which had only two submarines, both reportedly in the Bay of Biscay; moreover, these two vessels alone could not have accounted for so great a number of losses inflicted in so wide an area. *L'Aube* next eliminated Valencia, whose eight submarines had remained out of commission for lack of skilled crew able to replace the officers massacred in July 1936; even if the deficiency had now been made good by the use of qualified volunteers, the fact remained that the Republic would have no good reason to torpedo its own ships. As for the Soviet Union, *L'Aube* dismissed as too Machiavellian the theory that Russia would destroy her own ships at a distance of up to 1,200 miles from the Spanish coast. This left Italy, and public opinion in Britain was almost unanimous in laying it to her charge; in France and elsewhere, majority opinion was of the same conclusion, if slightly more restrained. The Palazzo Chigi responded with an emphatic denial, which the Wilhelmstrasse corroborated.[28*] *L'Aube* defied both to address their denials to the British Admiralty. Such denegations, added *L'Aube* scathingly, would once have been accepted without question, but the Italian treachery at Santander[29] had eroded the credibility of declarations from Rome.[30]

At the suggestion of the British and French Governments, a conference was opened at Nyon on 10 September 1937, its purpose being to put an end to piracy in the Mediterranean. All states except Spain bordering on the Mediterranean, together with Germany and the Soviet Union, were invited to attend. Italy and Germany refused to do so. Italy had apparently been trapped by Litvinov into making another angry denial of a Soviet charge which could not have been substantiated at Nyon,[31] thus hoisting her bad conscience with the petard of her indignation. Germany declined on the grounds that the matter could be dealt with—by which she meant ignored—in the London Committee. The other three European powers, together with Bulgaria, Egypt, Greece, Romania, Turkey and Yugoslavia, attended the conference, under the presidency of Yvon Delbos. Within four days, on 14 September, an agreement was reached which became known officially as the Nyon Arrangement. The action which Britain and France now reserved the right to take, with the backing of the other signatory nations that could not or dared not do likewise, was open to no misunderstanding: their fleets were under orders to 'counter-attack and, if possible, destroy' any submarine that attacked a non-Spanish merchant-ship or whose presence in the vicinity of such an attack merely aroused their suspicion. Three days later, on 17 September, these orders were extended to cover piratical attacks by any surface vessel or aircraft. The two fleets were instructed not to allow those engaged in piracy even the protection of Spanish territorial waters.

Even before the Nyon Arrangement had been communicated to the League of Nations, the moderate *L'Ere Nouvelle* was already calling for an international police force to protect the free movement of maritime trade in the Mediterranean, noting that Anglo-French offers to provide such a force were evoking every 'if' and 'but' on the part of the absent Axis.[32] *Le Populaire* cheered the Arrangement as a practical application of the principles of collective security, even if it was limited to states bordering on the Mediterranean and the Black Sea. The Socialist organ also noted with satisfaction a change of attitude in the British Admiralty. When the French Government shortly before proposed a mixed Anglo-French squadron to counteract Axis efforts to terminate international naval control of the Spanish coast, the Admiralty had declined; now, for the first time, the two fleets were operating together.[33]

As Puzzo lucidly shows, the disarray in the Fascist camp immediately following the Nyon Conference proved that if Great Britain and France had continued thereafter to act with such unity of purpose and resolution, 'Nyon could have marked the beginning of the end of appeasement.'[34]* The reasons given for the democracies' subsequent failure were that Nyon had a deleterious effect upon the recent Anglo-Italian 'Gentleman's Agreement' and that it encouraged the Left to demand the reopening of the frontier. In this the latter were successful, the frontier being reopened at the beginning of November for the passage of arms by night, with the French Cabinet itself involved in the contraband.

It was in the nature of things that the French Left would pursue in a moment of triumph a campaign it had waged in defeat and rejection. In *L'Humanité*, Péri cautioned the democracies that Mussolini, checked at sea, would be more eager to resume his intervention on land. France and Britain, he wrote, now had enough trumps in their hand to insure that their success at

Nyon spelt an end to policies of violence and adventure.[35] In *Le Peuple*, Harmel warned that the battle was lost unless the two democracies pressed home their advantage and understood, from the telegram of the Duce and the speeches of the Führer at Nuremberg, that the war in Spain was directed against *them* and that the Fascist states had used the Non-intervention Agreement as long as it served their turn.[36*]

20
The London–Burgos Exchange of Agents

The Republic before and after Gijón—Analyses and prognoses of the war—Britain and France open representation—Differences between French and British policy

On 25 September 1937, former Premier Portela Valladares returned from asylum in France[1] via Port-Bou to Republican Spain. According to elements of the right-wing press, his purpose was to arrange a settlement,[2] by which they presumably meant their readers to think of mediation. But in *La Dépêche*, Rieu-Vernet quoted the former Premier as saying: 'I believe we shall prevail,'[3] and the hoped-for settlement was explained as a rapprochement between the Valencia Government and Portela's Centre Party.[4] In the same paper, Díaz Alejo recounted verbatim an interview he had with the former Premier:

> From the moment I left Spain until now, I have abstained from making any political statement. Those which have been attributed to me are completely false, invented in accordance with partisan or professional necessity. If today I consent to breaking silence, it is because two new facts have arisen to completely alter the physiognomy of Spain.
>
> The first of these is that the government of the Spanish Republic is acting as a government of order, authority and respect for law, and conducts itself in accordance with the Constitution. The rights of citizens are guaranteed. The more or less arbitrary control committees have disappeared. The sole authority is the authority of law, before which all citizens are equal. The second fact is that past events have been investigated, and crimes committed in a period of lawlessness have been brought to judgment.
>
> I was, and I am still, a believer and a practicing Catholic, and the whole of my public and private life has always been guided by a respect for the freedom of all within the law. I consider that the civil authority must have supremacy over all parties, organizations, and military, clerical, or any other groups.
>
> So it is that we look back to that period prior to 19 July 1936 as the most flourishing, the richest and the happiest in Spanish history. Reason one day will resume its onward march, and when it does, severely will it judge those

men who preferred solutions of violence to the peaceful solutions of democracy.[5]

Portela Valladares was accompanied by former Minister of the Interior Miguel Maura, who made his own news. *La République*'s Dominique remembered moderate conservative Maura as the false prophet of August 1931, when he told the Radical editor: 'Nothing serious will happen. Communists? No, sir. The Spanish people are not Communist . . . A riot, perhaps; a revolution, never.'[6] After narrowly escaping execution in Madrid in the first weeks of war, Maura was thereafter reported in and out of exile.[7*] According to Buré, Maura corroborated Portela's claim that there was now more order in the Republican camp than in the Nationalist.[8] *La Tribune des Nations*, however, did attribute Maura's return to a peace design. Maura reportedly considered that the two belligerents were in a military deadlock, for neither side could annihilate the other; it was an auspicious moment for the two sides to make peace by adopting in Spain a 'liberal dictatorship.'[9]

On 28 September, Álvarez del Vayo requested the League of Nations to declare once and for all its recognition that Spain was the victim of aggression. Either the Charter was applied or it was violated, he said; if applied, the rights which had been denied the Spanish Republic must be restored; otherwise, it must be understood that the League was abetting the aggressor. The mere reproduction of this address in the left-wing press was labeled by the Right 'an aggravation of the tension.'[10] The same misrepresentation was shown to Kérillis of *L'Epoque*, of whom it said that he 'spurned taking the tragic view,'[11] when in fact he was urging vigilance and a special distrust of subsequent Italian activities.[12]

As the ring closed around the Basque Nationalists still resisting in the North, great importance attached to the port of Gijón, firstly as the last bastion of defense, and secondly as a point of evacuation. The French pro-Republicans demanded that a French squadron sweep Franco's ships from the area and enable the Asturians to make for the open sea. *L'Homme Libre* objected that if the Nationalist ships fired on the French ships, France would find herself virtually in a state of war and in circumstances which would exempt Britain from involvement, as she had already advised the French Government. In regard to the anticipated massacre of the Asturian miners by the Nationalists, *L'Homme Libre* felt that the only means of preventing it was to have Britain, and if possible, Italy, persuade Franco that such unnecessary cruelties could only harm his cause, discourage those in favor of granting him belligerent rights, and deepen the gulf dividing Spain and the rest of Europe. It was certainly not by insults, concluded *L'Homme Libre*, not too coherently, that a victorious army could be persuaded to exercise a modicum of humanity.[13]

On 20 October 1937, Gijón was invested by the Nationalists and resistance in the North was at an end.[14*] In *La Dépêche*, General Armengaud alluded to the decisive role played by Germans in Franco's Air Force: of the thirty or forty Nationalist planes shot down in the North, all the crews were found to be German.[15] In *L'Humanité*, Gabriel Péri remarked bitterly that Mussolini had kept open the London Committee session long enough to take the last Basque town.[16] In *Le Jour*, Jean Rey gloated over the victory which marked, he said, 'this time definitively,' the collapse of the Republican Government. With Catalan industry deprived of its Basque raw materials, Rey reasoned, and with non-intervention now becoming stricter, the Loyalists would have no means of obtaining arms.[17] *L'Oeuvre* put forward a dilemma for the Right. Marshal Badoglio, wrote the Radical daily, had arrived in Spain incognito to assess the military situation for the Duce; he allegedly informed the Caudillo that the capture of Madrid before the winter would involve another 150,000 casualties, an estimate which was said to leave the Generalissimo understandably disconsolate.[18]

The loss of Gijón, the suppression of the last resistance in the North, was a severe blow to Republican morale. The Basque *gudaris* (militiamen) were scions of a stock which—at least according to Basque legend—had defeated the Romans, stopped the Moors at Tolosa, turned back Charlemagne, and repulsed Napoleon at Vitoria. The history they were now repeating was that of the Abrazo de Vergara.[19*] For the moment, defeatist attitudes would still be muted. Fernando de los Ríos, now Spain's Ambassador to Washington, would cry grandiloquently that the future of twenty American peoples was a stake,[20] and Zyromski would continue through 1937 to express in the Socialist press his confidence in a Republican victory.[21] The pro-Republican press would still call for resolution in the face of disaster. But there were some jarring notes now to be heard. In *La Dépêche*, although its administration was careful to dissociate itself from such pessimism, its guest editorialist Chaves Nogales could recognize the current trend of the war as fatal for the Republic. 'Henceforth,' he wrote, 'it can be said that the sacrifices of the Spanish people are utterly sterile . . . The war is now quite without meaning.' Chaves Nogales' point was that both Spanish camps had lost sight of their cause; all that kept the forces of Franco fighting was the fear and hatred of a supposed Soviet domination, while the Republican forces continued to resist what they believed to be the Italo-German occupation of their homeland.[22] Even a Liberal Republican like Gregorio Marañon, a historical biographer and a giant in the field of medicine, wrote an article entitled 'Liberalism and Communism' for *La Revue de Paris* which set out to vindicate the use of Moorish troops[23] in the defense of Western values. 'On the Red side today,' wrote Don Gregorio, 'there is not a man who does not feel closer to the Moors fighting against him than to the semi-Asiatic Russians piling up behind him.'[24] And in the new Toulouse daily *La Garonne*, the Count of Saint-Aulaire also stressed the tendency of the Republic to downplay respect for civic rights. The former ambassador explained that Liston Oak, head of the American section in the propaganda department of the Republican government, had just left Spain with a parting statement: 'I'm leaving because none of this has anything to with a democracy.'[25]

Again in *La Dépêche*, two other important European figures were attacking the question on the most basic level. The Italian historian Guglielmo Ferrero considered it the greatest scandal in European history. The Hague Convention of 1907, Ferrero pointed out, had been signed by 44 states, including both Germany and Italy. The very first article of Convention III relative to the opening of hostilities stipulates that no state may engage in hostile acts against another state unless it issues 'previous and explicit warning, in the form either of a reasoned declaration of war or of an ultimatum with conditional declaration of war.'[26] The Belgian Socialist Émile Vandervelde quoted from André Chamson's recent *Retour d'Espagne*,[27*] criticizing those in power who had drawn up a complicated system of so-called control, full of falsehood and guile, and whose purpose was to insulate the evidence and shelter every State from the suffering of reality. 'But who,' asked Vandervelde, 'even from the point of view of dirty self-interest, still believes in the value of such a system?' He concluded in these terms:

> Face to face with the Meistersinger of brute force, the nations desiring peace form a potential strength enabling them to be steadfast in the cause of right, without incurring the risk of hostile reactions and without needing to meet force with force. Such firmness in the right cannot be disclaimed. And even now it is not too late.[28]

Rather more prosaically, Émile Buré maintained that it was Maisky who was talking sense at the meeting of the London Committee on 25 October, when he called for the immediate and unconditional withdrawal of all foreign combatants.[29]

The editor of *L'Ordre* was assailing not the faint hearts among the pro-Republicans, for he was no staunch defender of the Frente Popular, but rather the defeatist outlook of the 'Coblenzard'[30*] Right. Among more moderate elements of the pro-Franco press, doubts were now expressed as to the purpose of the war. In *Le Figaro*, Lucien Romier saw the Spain of the future, irrespective of the outcome of the war, as doomed to a totalitarian austerity and submission to the foreign powers that had financed the war and that would afterwards be needed to finance reconstruction. The point had been forgotten, added the editor of *Le Figaro*, that civil war brings neither freedom at home nor independence abroad.[31] In a subsequent editorial, Romier referred to a double error being committed simultaneously by both the Fascists and the

Communists. In their vain hope of ever being adopted by Spain, wrote Romier, both ideologies were oblivious to two other conflicts that would ensue: that between centralism and regional autonomism, and that between authoritarian corporative bureaucracy and Spanish individualism.[32]

In much the same vein, *L'Homme Libre* reminded Franco that his régime would face a 'silent confederacy of all hatreds and all sorrows' and that the vanquished would seek to avenge themselves at the first opportunity. Even among the victors, added *L'Homme Libre*, the only factor uniting Alphonsists, Carlists, Army and Falangists was opposition to the Republicans; if and when the Republic succumbed, such unity would dissolve and Spain would revert to her traditional solution, the *pronunciamiento*.[33] That the present solution to civil disorder was brutal suppression was now tacitly admitted even by *L'Express du Midi*, whose advice seemed to be addressed to the Caudillo. Justice in Nationalist Spain, it wrote, must be in no way an instrument of repression or politicking, but rather an instrument of 'spiritual impartial purification.'[34]

British consuls, unlike their French counterparts,[35] had stayed in Nationalist Spain, while a British diplomatic agent plied between Salamanca or Burgos and the British Ambassador in Hendaye. Early in October 1937, *L'Oeuvre* explained that Sangróniz, Franco's shadow Foreign Minister, had travelled to Hendaye for talks with Chilton and French Ambassador Herbette. It was reported that he was asking Chilton for a loan of 10 million pounds, under an exchange guarantee that 9.5 million of this amount would be spent in purchases of heavy British industry[36] Early in November 1937, the British and Franco Governments exchanged representatives, Sir Robert Hodgson going to Burgos and the Duke of Alba (who was also Duke of Berwick) moving to London. This diplomatic action was not emulated by either Paris or Washington. Although France did not have the vast commercial interests that Britain had in what was already Nationalist territory, the French Government was nonetheless under mounting pressure from French business circles to establish at least commercial relations with Burgos. Instead of that, when the Republican Government evacuated its seat from Valencia to Barcelona on 31 October 1937, the French representative followed—'willy-nilly,' as Dominique described it[37]—and the Chautemps government even seemed to celebrate the occasion by sending Eirick Labonne as its new ambassador, an action which in its turn drew no parallel from the British Government. In *La République*, Dominique berated the government for such conduct at a time when France had withdrawn her ambassador from Rome.[38]

In the same Radical daily, Emmanuel Berl defined the current difference between French and British policies. France, wrote Berl, claimed to be with Britain. But for Britain, non-intervention meant impartiality; for France, it had to work in favour of the Spanish Republic. The Front Populaire claimed that Negrín represented Spain's only regular government. Unfortunately for

Blum, reported Berl, Negrín would become the less 'regular' the more he lost, and Franco the more legitimate the more he won. The French Government liked to speak of Franco's 'failure.' They were wrong, replied Berl. If Franco was to lose, it would have been at the start. Britain, thought the Radical editor, did not wish him to fail, and Germany, Italy and Portugal would not allow him to fail.[39*] The question of the Mediterranean, concluded Berl, certainly worried the British, but it was separate from the Spanish question.[40]

In *Le Figaro*, d'Ormesson shared Berl's view and praised Eden for his realism. Britain remained neutral in word and deed, but she could see which way the wind was blowing and had taken action accordingly. The same absolute neutrality, added d'Ormesson, could not be accredited to the Front Populaire, since it continued to give vocal support to the Republic even if it could be said to have suspended overt aid.[41] That Delbos should take a page out of Eden's book was the advice also of *L'Ere Nouvelle*, which stressed the latter's proposal 'to live on friendly terms with Spain, whatever the result of the conflict may be.' This, added the Radial daily, meant refraining from supplying the other side.[42] It meant even more than that, thought another Radical daily, *L'Oeuvre*. The desire for peace meant refusing all involvement, including the granting of belligerent rights to Franco, on the grounds that his foreign support disqualified him from such recognition.[43] Thus parted from the rest of the Radical press, *L'Oeuvre* moved closer to *Le Populaire*, which viewed the British action as one of 'astonishing optimism which historians of the future may well call blindness.'[44]

A new dimension to British policy was added in December 1937, with the visit to Republican Spain of Clement Attlee, leader of the Labour Party opposition, accompanied by Dr. Ellen Wilkinson and Phillip Noel-Baker. While Major Attlee was careful not to make any official statement on behalf of the Labour Party, it was left to Noel-Baker to make a sensational disclosure, whether or not he was leaking his party's policy. According to Rieu-Vernet, Noel-Baker condemned the conciliatory spirit of Prieto[45*] and urged Republicans not to lose heart and to hold on until the next British general elections, which the Socialists, he said, would win. The new government would then reverse British policy and provide the Republic with the help it deserved. Would this aid be sufficient to decide the issue in the Republic's favour, he was asked. 'I won't go quite so far as to say that,' replied Noel-Baker. 'Decisive aid would require the dispatch of British military and naval forces, and I can't answer either for the possibility of collective action. But personally, I am inclined to think that it would be decisive.'[46]

Victory, however, fell not to the Labour Party but to the incumbent Conservatives, now under Neville Chamberlain. The state of British politics which ensued was described by Vandervelde as a split between Chamberlain and the rest, encompassing not only Attlee's Labour Party and Lloyd George's

Liberals but also the many Tory supporters of Winston Churchill.[47] It would seem, however, that the differences within the government party were less pronounced on the subject of the Spanish Republic. In an exclusive article for *La Dépêche*, Nobel Peace Prize winner Sir Norman Angell[48*] conceded the importance of Spain to British imperial security, a fact which was borne out by Britain's participation in two Peninsular wars, in the cause of maintaining Spanish independence.[49] Sir Norman's analysis of the current trend of British opinion pointed, however, to the fact that in probably every Commons debate on Spain, the Conservative Party had expressed its antipathy toward the Republic.

21

The Threat to French Security

Teruel taken and retaken—The New Year 1938 and new prognoses—The Anschluss and the second Blum Cabinet—French security in the Western Mediterranean and in North Africa—The danger from the Pyrenees—The Axis consolidates its position in Spain

The fall of Gijón and the collapse of Republican resistance in the North was followed, not by an intensification of the war on the eastern and southeastern fronts, but by a lull. Among the reasons suggested to account for the delay in the expected Nationalist offensive, *L'Oeuvre* submitted a boner: Mussolini had ordered the evacuation of 40,000 troops to Libya until the Commission of Inquiry currently in Spain had completed its investigation and had left the Peninsula.[1]

In *La Dépêche*, Pierre Mille considered that the war dragged on because the defence had shown itself stronger than the attack.[2] The truer reason for the lull was given by the pro-Franco, anti-Axis *L'Époque*, which surmised correctly that Germany and Italy were in no hurry to end the war in Spain. They suspected that war in Europe would break out in the course of 1938. In that event, it was paramount that they still held their strategic positions in the Balearics, the Canaries, Morocco, and south of the Pyrenees. If Franco sought to hasten the end, the Axis did not, and since it paid the pipe-lines it would call the tune.[3]

In the absence of a Nationalist offensive, the Republicans launched one of their own, and on 21 December 1937, they captured the town of Teruel. For days afterwards, the French right-wing press refused point-blank to surrender it. 'TERUEL STILL HOLDING OUT,' ran the headline in *L'Express du Midi* on 25 December and even 29 December. Readers would piece together the truth only in January 1938 by reading about the Nationalist drive to 'recapture' the town and by noting, as did *L'Humanité*,[4] the importance the pro-Franco press attached to the counter-offensive.[5]* On the other hand, the gravity of its subsequent loss to Franco on 22 February is best understood by the applause in the pro-Republican press at the time of the Republic's December victory, which was only its second (after Guadalajara) of the war. At that time *Le Peuple* described Teruel as a 'key position of the highest importance, one of Spain's few great natural communications junctions, and a bridgehead which had caused the gravest anxiety to the Republic.'[6]

At the beginning of 1938, General Armengaud estimated the relative strength of the forces in conflict, from information he had gained on the spot. The total number of men under arms, he wrote, amounted to some 1.5 million. Franco's forces totaled some 500,000 Spaniards and Moors, including 10–12,000 officers, plus 50–60,000 foreign troops. Republican strength, as a result of mobilizing all men between the ages of 20 and 28, amounted to some 50 divisions of 600–700,000 men, plus 10–20,000 foreign volunteers. Only three regular generals were at the service of the Republic. Armengaud found, however, that the new officer corps was, in the main, very Republican and distinctly anti-Communist.[7] The general later reported on relative naval strength. The two fleets, he found, were now roughly equal in power.[8*] Each had three cruisers: Franco, the *Baleares,* the *Canarias* (both launched since the outbreak of war) and the *Almirante Cervera*; the Republic, the *Libertad*, the *Cervantes* (both of the *Almirante Cervera* class[9*]) and the *Méndez-Núñez,* of an earlier class. While the Republican cruisers were of shorter range, they were faster and better armed. Thus, in an engagement between the *Baleares* and the *Libertad*, the former sustained seventeen hits before it could close with the enemy. (In point of fact, the speed of the *Libertad* was no higher than the 34 knots that the *Baleares* could attain, in spite of the difference in their respective displacements (7,475 tons against 10,000 tons), while the Nationalist cruiser boasted eight pieces of 203 mm and eight of 129 mm against the eight pieces of 152 mm and four of 102 mm of the *Libertad*.) As far as destroyers were concerned, General Armengaud saw a clear advantage lying with the Republic: of fifteen in its service ten were operational, against only three or four in the service of Franco. The use that the Republic made of its destroyers was of the greatest importance, for while the Loyalists had only one submarine still in service, Franco had several, including at least six Italian and an unspecified number of German midgets.[10*]

Another and equally important comparison was made in the financial field, and here the Republic appeared in a far less favourable light. Despite the absence of gold in July 1936 to back the Nationalist peseta, by the end of that year it was quoted internationally at twice the value of the Republican. By 1 February 1938, reported Ernest Vincent in *Le Journal des Finances*, the Burgos peseta was worth 1.62 French francs on the European markets, while the Valencia peseta, in spite of the guarantee of 15 billion francs in gold in the Bank of Spain, had fallen to 0.35 French francs.[11] In April 1938, the Nationalist peseta was quoted at 0.15–0.20 Swiss francs, while the Republican peseta had fallen from 0.31 Swiss francs in 1936 to 0.05 Swiss francs.[12*]

The New Year opened, however, with both camps in Spain expressing a certain optimism, while in France Chautemps was forced to form a second Cabinet without the participation of any Socialist Minister.[13*] In his New Year address, Franco referred to 'these historic days in which we are forging our

Imperial Spain.' He described the Nationalist economy as 'already flourishing, with bread for all.' The New Year, added the Caudillo, would restore to Spain 'the glory, the power and the rank that she deserves.'[14] The New Year, replied Buré with a greater gift of prophecy, would be the democracies' very last chance and would decide the fate of Europe. For years, he wrote, the democracies had taken the ostrich's relief from reality.[15] France and Britain had sacrificed their principles and their prestige, and they could not even be sure that their sacrifice would be rewarded.[16] Buré continued to point out the misjudgements that were leading to a holocaust. Hitler's genius lay in his ability to camouflage pan-Germanic revanchism as a crusade against Communism, and to present himself as the champion of every little frightened bourgeois. In the very countries marked by the Führer for destruction, national spirit was subordinated to class spirit, and Franco's victories were applauded by a large section of France's 'stupidly conservative bourgeoisie and by a mendacious press passionately employed in the service of Berlin and Rome.'[17] Buré was now convinced that it was in Spain that the future of Europe and the world was being decided. Peace or war would come of it, according as France and Britain carried out their role as peacemakers. Buré also corrected the fallacy held by Franco sympathizers in France that the Spanish Nationalists were kindly disposed toward their northern neighbours, simply by quoting from the Spanish Nationalist press. The Bilbao Falangist daily *Hierro* of 6 April 1938, wrote:

> The real France is dead. Only this can explain the villainy of forcing Spanish refugees to return to the Red zone. Poor France, how dearly will she pay for what she has done!

Hierro of 8 April 1938, added:

> Ethnic and geographic groups mean nothing in themselves, and among the sad examples of peoples who have ceased to be there is the case of France, who was our neighbour in times gone by, and today is nothing more than contiguous to us, like some foul and stinking hovel [*casucha infecta y mal oliente*] at the end of our fair patio.[18]

If further evidence were needed, Buré quoted from an interview of a Spanish Nationalist general by the *Berliner Börsen-Zeitung*:

> Our sympathies with Germany are particularly strong. Each time the two nations have marched together, the world has seen great actions. From the economic point of view, the natural resources and the products of the two countries complement each other and allow for still more active exchanges. From the political point of view, above all, in the light of the struggle against

Communism, the similarity of the two régimes is another sign of our rapprochement and our collaboration.[19]

Curiously, the same stratagem was employed by the Right in France: that of showing that the Spanish Left was Germanophile and not Francophile. Spain's former Minister of Labour, Eduardo Aunós, wrote in *La Garonne* that Spain's leftist intellectuals were saturated with the worst Germanic philosophy—by which he meant Kant, Hegel and Krause—whereby they had proceeded to infect the country. Aunos recalled that Sanz del Río, the precursor of 'that nursery of the Left' the Institución Libre de Enseñanza,[20]* received his intellectual formation in Germany before introducing Spain to the idealistic pantheism of Krause. Among other intellectual leaders of the Left who had foresworn *Esprit* in favor of *Geist* were Alcalá Zamora, Azcárate, Besteiro, Marañon, and Ortega y Gasset. These Republicans, wrote Aunós, were ostensibly Francophile, but the Republic they had introduced in 1931 had copied every imperfection of the Weimar Constitution.[21]

Le Populaire, for its part, quoted from *Raum und Volk im Weltkrieg*, a work published in 1931 by Professor Ewald Banse, the leading Nazi theoretician on military affairs.[22]* In this book, Banse recalls that Spain is the natural ally of Germany against France and insists that it is in Germany's interest to restore Spain to a position of power,

> For the importance to Germany of Spain, Italy, the Netherlands and Switzerland is this: the frontier which France would be called on to defend, which at present stretches only from Luxemburg to a point facing Karlsruhe, would thus be considerably extended.[23]

The enthusiasm on the Republican side, which had been revived by the initial victory at Teruel, was not entirely dampened by the subsequent reversal. In *La Dépêche*, Vandervelde expressed his conviction, less than a month before Vinaroz,[24] that Franco could not reach the Mediterranean, any more than Hindenburg and Ludendorff could reach the English Channel in 1918.[25] Republican confidence had been boosted, ironically, by Hitler's annexation of Austria.

At the same time, the Anschluss of 11 March 1938 gave momentary pause to the French Right. The latter's cause, however, was reactivated by a French Cabinet crisis two days later. Chautemps, who had shown no real initiative in the face of mounting foreign and domestic problems, had forfeited his remaining Socialist support by reclosing the southern frontier in January. On 13 March the government fell. Blum resumed the premiership, appointing Joseph Paul-Boncour as his Foreign Minister and entrusting a newly created Ministry of Propaganda to Ludovic-Oscar Frossard. In the light of another visit to Paris by Negrín,[26*] it now appeared that France might discontinue her subordinance to Britain in her policy in Spain. Exasperated at the Axis' failure to comply with the Non-intervention Agreement, Paul-Boncour was 'prepared to permit' a steady flow of war matériel to cross the Pyrenees.[27*] On 17 March Blum signed a confidential order in council—not for publication in *Le Journal Officiel*—authorizing the transit of French arms to the Republic.

In *Le Journal des Débats*, Jacques Bardoux claimed that on 16 March the Spanish Embassy in Paris informed the Quai d'Orsay that thirty or forty thousand German troops had disembarked at Cádiz and Pasajes. The news was certainly false, but without awaiting confirmation several French Ministers allegedly approved a suggestion to send three divisions to Catalonia, despite technical objections from General Gamelin and Marshal Pétain. Some *députés*, led by Augustin Michel (Haute-Loire), who had been informed of this, protested to Herriot, president of the Chambre des Députés, whom they found 'prostrate.' The British Ambassador had called twice at the Quai d'Orsay with an official warning that such a decision, contrary to the Non-intervention Agreement undertaken by the French Government, would result in the dissolution of the Entente, the isolation of France, and war between France and the Axis. Bardoux reminded France that she had 36 divisions with which to resist 100 Axis divisions, and 1,050 obsolete aircraft to pit against Germany's up-to-date 3,000 and Italy's 2,000. The French aircraft were 50–60 mph slower than the Axis, and French aircraft production was at best 40 per month, against 300 in Germany and 200 in Italy.[28*] A similarly incendiary exposure was made over radio in June by Pierre-Étienne Flandin, former Prime Minister and former Foreign Minister, who now revealed that on 17 March Blum had reopened the frontier.[29*]

French security in the Western Mediterranean and North Africa had become a question of deepening anxiety and was now the principal subject of editorials in the press. The journals, however, still made careful distinctions in regard to the precautions necessary. These ranged from direct military intervention in Spain to the fortification of the frontier.

It was now understood, even by *L'Humanité*, that the most that could be expected of the new Blum government was permission to supply arms to the Republic. Accordingly, it again demanded 'only that France respect international law, no more, no less,'[30] meaning that international law provided for the supply of Spain's freely elected, established and recognized government. It is evident that Blum's action of 17 March was either so moderate as to escape the attention of the press or else so secret that even the SFIO organ was unaware of it or cleverly concealed it. For the best that *L'Action Française* could produce was a report that twenty Bloch aircraft had taken off from Toulouse's Francazal Airport on 5 April, bearing—of all things—Soviet markings.[31] And in April *Le Populaire*, which had been split in 1936 on the subject of aid,[32] finally joined the chorus of those demanding, with greater vehemence than ever, the reopening of the frontier.[33] There was, however, at least one important Socialist dissentient: on 18 March Postmaster-General Lebas spoke at Roubaix to the effect that non-intervention was essential to peace.[34]

Inevitably, such a cause was still opposed tooth and nail by the entire press to the right of *Le Populaire*. In *L'Action Française*, Delebecque wrote that it was intervention, and not the triumph of Franco, that endangered French communications with North Africa. As a sop to current indignation over the recent bombing of Barcelona, Delebecque described it as 'a terrible thing,' but asked if anyone in France wanted it to be the preface and foretaste of the bombing of Paris.[35] Kérillis also hoped for an end to the bombing of civilian populations but decried intervention as less than ever the answer.[36] In *Le Jour*, Bailby was pleased to inform his readers that the victory of Franco was now only a matter of weeks and that French aid to the Republic could delay it for a few days at the most.[37] *L'Ère Nouvelle* also suggested abandoning the Republic to its fate in order to hasten the end,[38] an attitude denounced by another Radical-Socialist paper, *La Dépêche*, as contrary both to justice and to French interests.[39] Contrary or not, by the end of May a new committee had been formed under the name of Solidarité d'Occident, the purpose of which was to support the cause of Franco in France.[40]

The question of the Pyrenees was viewed more carefully. In *L'Époque*, Kérillis deplored the fact that France, by not aligning herself with Franco, was faced with the formation of a 'major military state,' irrespective of the outcome of the war, behind a frontier which had caused France no concern for more than a century.[41] Kérillis conceded that a risk of encirclement existed but held that it was a hypothesis and not a certainty; in any event, he added, the only way to reduce the risk was to negotiate with the 'conqueror.'[42] *Le Figaro* was equally concerned about the threat of attack from over the Pyrenees, but not from an exhausted Spain which would hardly be inclined to embark on foreign adventures. The only real danger, wrote *Le Figaro*, lay in the concealed air and naval bases that France had 'stupidly permitted' the Axis powers to construct and which, in the event of war, would present the gravest difficulties.[43] The seriousness of these problems was underscored in *La Dépêche*, which reported the anxiety felt in French West Africa regarding Axis installations in Río de Oro and the Canaries.[44] Kérillis subsequently expressed his approval of fortifying the frontier.[45] So too did *L'Écho de Paris*, which quoted Marshal Lyautey: 'Strength should be shown, so that force need not be used.'[46] So did not *Le Jour*, where Bailby disagreed that France need ever defend her southern frontier, provided that she did not 'commit the folly of supporting the Reds.'[47]

No sooner had *Le Figaro* raised the subject of Axis bases south of the Pyrenees than its editor Lucien Romier all but dismissed the danger. The structure of the Pyrenees, wrote Romier, protects France from invasion from Spain.

Romier conceded that in 1813–1814 Wellington crossed the Bidasoa, gained the highway to Bordeaux, repulsed the French forces moving up from Orthez and Tarbes, and defeated Marshal Soult at Toulouse. Romier attributed the success of this invasion, however, to a series of defeats already suffered by the French on the other side of Pyrenees and to the support given the Iron Duke by the British fleet cruising unchallenged off shore. Even assuming that the French armies were held to the defensive, concluded Romier, it was only along this coastline that an enemy could conduct a quick and decisive operation, *a fortiori* if the enemy were not Spanish and had to transport its troops to the Peninsula along vulnerable sea routes.[48]

In *La Dépêche*, General Armengaud considered the question from a point of view that Romier had ignored: the use of air power. The problem, wrote the Air Force general, was serious. Fascist air bases south of the Pyrenees opened up a radius of attack which encompassed Bordeaux and Marseilles. Of even greater importance was the construction of air and submarine bases in the Balearics and, in the foreseeable future, along Spain's eastern coast. In the event of war, wrote Armengaud, France would need to transport some 1.5 million troops and workers in both directions between southern France and North Africa. Already Italian air and naval power would require that such convoys sail under cover of darkness and even then ply to the west of the Balearics. In the event that Spain became hostile to France, even these measures would prove useless: the Western Mediterranean would be virtually closed to France. Convoys to and from North African ports would have to use Bordeaux, a route which would take up to three or four times as long. Such a restriction on French sea routes revived the need to construct the long delayed Canal des Deux Mers.[49]

In *L'Oeuvre*, Senator André Morizet (Seine) shared Armengaud's concern over France's new vulnerability to air attack. Already in 1937, Colonel John Nicoletis had expressed his concern, in the course of his meeting with President Lebrun, over the vulnerability of French war factories to air attack. Certainly, defensive measures were being undertaken by evacuating arms factories, but the measures were being taken as if there was no risk of attack from the air. Certain factories of vital strategic value had been found impossible to evacuate and remained in very exposed positions. Others which had indeed been evacuated were not necessarily in a safer place. It was now necessary—and this was a new element entirely—to think of the poorly defended frontier in the south-west, where privately owned industries evacuated from the Paris region, the north and the east had been set up. Beyond that, a good number of large French war factories, such as those in Toulouse, Bergerac, Angoulême and Saint-Médard were also situated in this region. In the event of war across the Pyrenees, one of these factories was in an exceptionally precarious situation: that in Toulouse, not only because of its manufacture of powder, but also because it was the site of one half—the other was in the North—of France's production of ammonia-based nitric acid, of such vital importance, as we have seen, to national defence.[50] To this argument Senator Morizet added that the distance between the general axis of Franco's airfields, lying along the Ebro between Logroño and Saragossa, and the summit of the Pyrenees was between 60 and 100 miles. This meant that a bomber taking off from the Ebro had not exceeded one fifth of its range at the time it crossed into French air space. It was significant, added Morizet, that although these airfields were of no further value in the war against the Republicans, being located in areas where further hostilities were unlikely, work was still being carried out to improve them. Moreover, if these airfields were intended for use in Franco's operations against the remaining Republican territory, why would bases be constructed between Saragossa and San Sebastián unless it was intended to take advantage of the circumstances and prepare an offensive front against France?[51]

The question of Axis entrenchment in Spain was now receiving growing attention, especially in the light of the expected finalization of the Anglo-Italian Mediterranean Agreement. This agreement, reached on 2 January 1937, but since then held in abeyance pending detailed negotiations, affirmed the independence of Spain and freedom of passage through the Mediterranean. Kérillis urged that France do nothing to jeopardize this agreement since it was in the interest of France. Chamberlain, added the editor of *L'Époque*, had shown that he did not wish to get his fingers burnt in the Spanish conflict, while Italy and Germany had denied they would send further reinforcements and Franco had given France guarantees for the future.[52*] *Paris-Midi*'s Jean Devau reported from Rome that Italy would withdraw her volunteers if France and the Soviet Union would do likewise,[53] a cynical ploy that could deceive hardly anyone. In *L'Action Française*, Maurras urged the withdrawal of all non-Spaniards from Spain before an incident sparked world war and France found herself attacked in the rear through the Pyrenees. Abetting the resistance of the Reds, added Maurras, served to prolong the war, and prolonging the war served to prolong the Axis' time to manoeuvre in their operations between Burgos and Toulouse.[54] It represented no small concession on the part of Maurras to admit that such a danger existed.

Not long afterwards, Buré insisted in *L'Ordre* that the Germans and Italians were militarizing the Pyrenees border.[55] Héricourt countered in *L'Action Française* by making a tour of inspection; he found no such evidence and offered one million pesetas to anyone who did.[56] There was no reply from Buré until July,[57*] when he simply quoted a statement by General Kindelán, the Chief of Staff of the Nationalist Air Force:

> In the first week of a war with France, we could pulverize Bordeaux, Toulouse, Marseilles, Biarritz, and Bayonne and disrupt the French railway system. A

war with France would develop our fighting spirit, and would assure us the support of the ancient enemies of that country, who remember the hatred of times past. We can view a war against France with optimism, for the Spanish Army, made up of several hundred thousand veterans, could be massed on a single front, and our adversaries would be hard put to resist it. A world war would have the certain result of reducing France to the level of a third- or forth-rate power.[58]

It was almost too much for *La Garonne*, whose answer was presumably addressed to Burgos: 'It would help if such statements were denied. The Marxist press can turn such imprudent talk to its advantage, whether it finds it, or invents it.'[59]

In fact, the report by Buré was corroborated at that moment by the plan handed over to Senator Morizet on 25 May 1938 by the Republican air force authorities in Barcelona, at a time when Morizet was heading a French parliamentary inquiry into German air force activities in the Nationalist zone. In a report to Guy La Chambre, the minister of aviation, Lieutenant Colonel Quir-Montfollet, air attaché at the French Embassy in Barcelona, underscored certain military measures, 'not justified by the present conflict', that were underway in Nationalist territory. He mentioned several projects under construction, among them the intensive work on airfields situated to the east of Vitoria (on the road to San Sebastian) and at Recajo (Logroño), amounting to an entire system of airfields intended for use by heavy bombers, on a line closely following the Ebro. Conspicuous in this system of air bases were those between Saragossa and Tudela. The Germans were thought to have a plan of penetrating the Cerdagne valley along the line of Lérida—Seo de Urgel. From January 1938, an air base had been set up in San Sebastian, and no unauthorized person could visit the nearby airfield at Lasarte which contained, according to the same report, huge underground hangers. The unloading point for most of the German matériel was Pasajes, which had been 'perfectly set up as a military port', and all this within 10 kilometres of the French frontier.[60]

22
The Daladier–Bonnet Formula

> Italian propaganda against France—Bombing of Spanish cities and Republican threats of reprisal—Air attacks on French territory—The Daladier–Bonnet formula: the closing of the frontier

On 10 April 1938, two days after Indalecio Prieto resigned from the Republican Government in disgrace over his efforts to win a compromise peace, the leader of the French Radical-Socialists, Édouard Daladier, was appointed Premier. Five days later, on 15 April, Nationalist forces reached the Mediterranean at Vinaroz, cutting the Republican forces in two. On the following day, 16 April, the Anglo-Italian Mediterranean Agreement was finally concluded. Under this agreement, Mussolini undertook not to make any territorial claims or seek to obtain political or economic privileges in Spain or in any of her possessions. In return, Chamberlain acknowledged the Duce's right to retain his Legionnaires in Spain until the Republic was defeated.

For the moment, Mussolini was satisfied to attack on the propaganda level, accusing France of desiring a Red victory. *L'Époque* promptly replied that the Roman realist knew well enough that what mattered in politics was not desires but facts.[1] *L'Oeuvre* pointed out that if France and her governments had really desired a Republican victory, it would probably have been achieved long ago. France, added *L'Oeuvre*, despite the opposition of a considerable segment of the nation, had maintained the non-intervention which she had been the first to propose. If Mussolini had taken his place on one side of the barricade, the most that he could say of France was that she was on the other side of the Pyrenees.[2] As if in reply, *Il Corriere della Sera* became more specific:

> Certain ambiguities are not to our liking. Supplying the Reds with arms and combatants with which to massacre our Legionnaires is hardly the best preamble to diplomatic talks between Italy and her neighbour republic.[3]

L'Humanité at once fastened on to this blatant confession, calling on the French Government to take action against these insults of describing the Italian presence in Spain as regular and normal and of crying scandal whenever efforts were made to free Spain from foreign intruders.[4]

The question of atrocities was resumed with the bombing of Barcelona and other towns in Catalonia, especially Granollers. Between 7 and 18 March 1938, Barcelona was subjected to no fewer than ten attacks that altogether lasted 32 hours. The result, announced in a very detailed report by the mayor of Barcelona that was published in the Catalan press of 27 March, amounted to 875 dead (512 men, 245 women, 118 children) and some 1,500 hospitalized.[5*] This high level of dead and wounded was due in part to the lack of air raid warnings, which was due in turn by a device much used by bombers approaching Barcelona of cutting their motors at the point at high altitude that they calculated they had entered the listening radius, and from this planning their approach to the target; they thus gained time on any intercepting aircraft, and twice achieved their goal of reaching their target totally unmarked. The Catholic *L'Aube*, which had previously denounced Republican atrocities, felt justified in decrying the bombing of Barcelona.[6*] On 25 May, Nationalist planes bombed Alicante, inflicting another 300 dead and a thousand wounded. The air attack of 2 June on Granollers, a small town of no military importance, caused several hundred more deaths, and came at a time when the British Government was again trying to find some formula for compromise. This did not surprise *L'Oeuvre*, which noted that the attack followed the pattern of 'pirate blackmail,' creating a climate of international anxiety whenever the London Committee was about to reconvene.[7] When Nationalist headquarters denied responsibility for the raid, even *Le Jour* was moved to suggest that it should declare what its military targets were to avoid charges of intentionally bombing defenceless towns.[8]

The fact is that in June 1938 a change was manifest in the attitude of the right-wing press. It now withheld its approval of Nationalist air raids and presented them as the sole responsibility of Franco's allies and as acts carried out against the Caudillo's wishes. In a raid on Alicante on 27 June in which the British steamer *Farnham* was sunk, the five attacking aircraft were identified by Reuter's as Junkers. At first, Kérillis held to the argument that the Republicans had used five captured Junkers in a Machiavellian attack upon their own city, as a last desperate attempt to provoke the world war which alone could save them.[9] Even *L'Oeuvre* believed that the British and French Governments responded with a warning to Barcelona that any attempt it made to 'internationalize' the conflict would not be binding on Britain and France.[10] *La République*, however, considered that the provocation was the work of Berlin;[11] and two weeks later, Kérillis himself had changed his mind. The intensification, he wrote, in the bombing of open cities both in Spain and in China seemed to presage even more hideous massacres.[12] *La République* shared the belief that Franco was no longer commander but commanded; if he refused this air raid or that massacre, he would find himself bereft of supplies, 'and so the wretch obeys!'[13] But another Radical-Socialist daily, *La Dépêche*, reminded such sophists that the whole thesis of Nationalist Spain would collapse if it were shown that Franco was at the mercy of foreign invaders, invited or not.[14] The tendency of the right-wing press thereafter was to urge Franco not to alienate the sympathies of the civilized world.[15*]

According to *Le Journal*, the Spanish Ambassador to London, Pablo de Azcárate, at once informed Lord Halifax, who on 20 February had replaced Eden as Foreign Secretary,[16*] that if such raids continued the Republican Government might decide on reprisals.[17] A subsequent note from Barcelona included the more specific threat of a reprisal on an Italian target each time that an open town was bombed by the Nationalists, a threat which justified on its own, wrote *Le Matin*, the total closing of the frontier.[18] To Georges Scelle of *La Dépêche*, however, the Republican Government would be well within its rights to carry out reprisals, even against Italian air bases. If it refrained from doing so, it was in deference to world peace.[19]

It is incontrovertible that the Republic was now staking heavily, if not everything, on a general European war which would involve the democracies in their defence. Prieto's *El Socialista* of Madrid wrote in August 1938 that a general war could not but help the cause of the Republic.[20] But it is equally certain that the French right-wing press was fabricating all sorts of plots. In November 1937 Le Roussillon had written in *Le Journal de Toulouse*: 'Incredible as it sounds, we can affirm that the Generalitat and Valencia are preparing, in the greatest secrecy, the bombing of our coastline from Cerbère to Port-Vendres, as well as attacks on the Port-Vendres-Algiers-Oran air service.' The operation would be performed by downed Fascist planes, which had been repaired and repainted. In what Le Roussillon claimed was evidence, the paper published a photo of Marxists in leather flying-suits grouped around Italian planes.[21]

In the spring of 1938, several raids were carried out on French border towns and villages. The first, on Cerbère, involved no casualties, and the only damage incurred was the rupture of the local power cable. The raid on Orgeix on 5 May was more serious: apart from the destruction of the château, two persons were injured.

Curiously, neither *Paris-Soir*, nor *Le Temps*, nor *La Liberté* carried news of the Orgeix incident in their issue of the evening of 5 May. Indeed, throughout May not only the right-wing press but even the 'information' press downplayed, or even attempted to suppress, news of any violation of French sovereignty. *La Liberté* finally responded, with Paul Marion scoffing at the indignation of the Left, calling for further measures of military protection along the Pyrenees, but attributing the blame for the attacks to the traffic in arms with the Loyalists and demanding an immediate cessation.[22] Predictably, *Le Journal* dignified a communiqué from Burgos charging the Barcelona authorities with having staged an act of provocation.[23] *La Garonne* followed suit,[24] but most of the press preferred to await the findings of an inquest ordered by the military and civil authorities.

On 5 June, three flights of unidentified foreign aircraft, totaling nine planes, again violated French territorial sovereignty, flying at a height of 3,000 ft. over Ariège and Cerdagne and dropping bombs on hamlets between Ax-les-Thermes and Orgeix. *L'Humanité*,[25] *Le Populaire*,[26] and *Le Peuple*[27] at once identified the planes as Axis or Nationalist. *La Dépêche* referred to it as 'criminal aggression, the gravity of which could not be exaggerated.'[28] *L'Ordre* called it an 'intolerable provocation on the part of Franco' and ruled out the chance of error; it demanded the immediate installation of anti-aircraft batteries on the Pyrenees frontier and the dispatch of fighter squadrons, with orders to shoot down without hesitation the next foreign military planes crossing into French air space. This, concluded *L'Ordre*, would automatically preclude further 'navigational errors' by Nationalist pilots.[29]

The reaction of the right-wing press was initially an embarrassed near-silence. *Le Journal* limited its report to a single column of eight lines.[30] *L'Époque* clung to the consolation that the aircraft were of 'unknown origin.'[31] *L'Action Française*, currently organizing a pro-Franco meeting in Paris, did not hesitate to identify them as Red.[32] Both *Le Jour* and *Le Figaro* strove to divert responsibility from Franco by asking what possible interest he could have in alienating France and Britain, 'in the moment of his approaching victory,' as Bailby put it.[33] While admitting that Franco's Air Forces included foreign volunteers who would not be averse to creating an international incident, *Le Figaro* asked what real objection was there to identifying the aircraft as Republican, sent out with the simple mission of 'whipping up excitement.'[34]

On the following day, 6 June, the action was repeated: nine aircraft again violated French sovereignty by flying over Cerdagne. A considerable section of the French right-wing press now accepted the version from Berlin that the planes were Red. *Le Journal* insisted that this time ground witnesses recognized the colours and registration letters of the Republic,[35] but otherwise *Le Journal*, together with *Le Jour* and *Le Matin*, minimized the incident, displaying what *La Garonne* called an 'inexplicable discretion.'[36] *Le Jour*, after all, had been announcing for the last three weeks that the Reds were planning to bomb a French town in order to provoke an incident, and that this plan was known to the Minister of the Interior. *Le Matin* only vaguely accused the Republicans; it ventured no more than to rule out the possibility of error, noting that the combat formation was the same in both cases.[37] The reaction of *Le Figaro* was similarly evasive: after first accusing the Reds,[38] Wladimir d'Ormesson flatly ignored the question of responsibility, turning instead to France's 'disrespect' for her own frontier.[39]

L'Époque, in harmony with its pro-Franco, anti-Axis policy, tried deftly to shift the blame to the Italians. Admitting that the raids over French territory may have been perpetrated by the same agency that had bombed open towns and torpedoed British ships, *L'Époque* nonetheless suggested that the actions were ordered by Italian officers against the wishes of the Nationalist authorities. Franco, it explained, was no murderer and he certainly did not seek diplomatic embroilments, but he was at present unable to detach himself from the influence of his allies who, *L'Époque* now freely admitted, were extending him considerable aid.[40] None of this seemed to displease Berlin. The *Berliner Börsen-Zeitung* congratulated the Right in France on its perspicacity in identifying the authors of this 'act of piracy arranged with the usual malignity and refinement.'[41]

The thanks of the Nazi press were especially due to *L'Action Française* and *La Liberté*. In the former, Théo Ripoull blamed the action on the Reds and accused them of having selected religious holidays: Ascension Thursday for the bombing of Cerbère, and the Feast of Pentecost to strafe aircraft at Ax-les-Thermes. While even *Le Matin* had attested to clear visibility in the area on 6 June,[42] Ripoull alleged that the Reds had 'conducted their nefarious trade under cover of mist, just as the first time they had operated under cover of dark.'[43] In *La Liberté*, Jacques Doriot even identified the planes as three-engined Blochs delivered to the Republic by Pierre Cot. Franco, explained Doriot, far from wishing to provoke France, sought instead the closing of the frontier in order to cut off the Republicans' supply; any act of provocation would have the opposite effect of tempting France to increase her aid.[44]

La Liberté's concern over the Republic's supply routes lent credence to the argument of *La Dépêche*: the fact that the planes had reconnoitered for two hours over the Ax-les-Thermes-Toulouse railroad, which the Italo-German press had itself marked as one of the Republic's supply routes, was prima facie evidence that Franco's forces were responsible.[45*] *Le Petit Parisien* also ruled out the possibility of error, observing that this time the planes had not stopped over the plateau of Chioula but had continued as far as Tarascon-sur-Ariège, an incursion of some forty miles into French territory; moreover, the points at which the bombs fell suggested that the raid had been carefully planned and that the targets were the viaduct at the entrance to the Orgeix tunnel and the hydro-electric plant at Orlu near Foix, for which the pilots had mistaken the Château d'Orgeix.[46]

Since Daladier hesitated to accuse any state, the Radical press showed caution, with *La République* and *L'Ère Nouvelle* writing only of 'unidentified aircraft.' The only exception, apart from *La Dépêche*, was *L'Ordre*, which ridiculed the rightist claim that the planes were Republican disguised as Nationalist and that such camouflage had deceived all but the sharp eyes of Franco and *L'Action Française*.[47] So too did *Le Populaire* on behalf of the Socialists, asking to know why the Republicans would want to destroy the railways still linking Catalonia with France.[48] To this *La Garonne* retorted that the aircraft in question had not attempted to destroy anything; they had not taken aim at the railway tracks nor tried to cause casualties or damage, but instead had deliberately dropped all their bombs on the mountainside, the purpose being 'not to cause harm but to stir things up.'[49]

If *Le Journal de Toulouse*, *Le Jour* and *La Garonne* attributed the raids to a Republican plan, *L'Humanité* traced them instead to a Nationalist plot—not only premeditated but announced for weeks beforehand in the Burgos and Salamanca press—to 'plug the Perpignan gap.'[50] *Le Populaire* felt that the subsequent embarrassment in the Italian press was proof enough of where the responsibility really lay.[51] The Socialist organ analyzed the increasing incidence of torpedo attacks on shipping and of raids over French territory as evidence that the Fascist states hoped to intimidate France and force a new international control of the Pyrenees border at the earliest possibility. The voice of the SFIO strongly urged Daladier not to yield to such blackmail.[52] Even *La Garonne*, in publishing an account of an interview granted by Franco to Senator Henry Lémery,[53] had pondered in print whether Franco's purpose in bombing Cerbère and Orgeix could be any other than the intimidation of France.[54] In response, Brigadier General Gambier was appointed on 24 July air defence commander for the Pyrenees and set up his headquarters in Perpignan.

In all the logomachy of diplomatic warfare, some editorialists were able to draw some general conclusions. In *Le Petit Bleu*, Georges de Marcilly traced some characteristics of national methods of diplomacy. Germany acted, then talked; Italy talked, then acted; Britain talked little and acted hardly at all; and France acted never and talked endlessly.[55]

Another distinction was now evident, especially to Lucien Romier in *Le Figaro*, between those nations with interests in ending the war and those nations which considered it in their interests to prolong the conflict to the maximum.[56] It was generally understood that Mussolini desired such a prolongation no more than Franco.[57]* In the opinion of *Le Populaire*, the Duce was increasingly disillusioned over his Spanish adventure. Germany continued to enjoy a prestige among the old Spanish aristocracy which Italy, despite all her aid, could not hope to match. According to René Bonjean, the French chargé d'affaires in Madrid, the comportment of the Germans was winning them ever greater admiration with the public. On the other hand, the loss of prestige suffered by the Italians following the rout at Guadalajara had only increased: 'Their affectation, their pose as conquerors, their haughty airs in their treatment of their comrades in the National army or the civilian authorities or the public have cost them whatever goodwill they enjoyed at the beginning of the war. They had come to be known in fun as the troops of non-intervention, because they intervened as little as possible; or by the name of *cien pies* (centipedes), by analogy to their speed of movement, or *reculantes* (advancing backwards).[58] Chaves Nogales believed that if Mussolini were to dispatch another massive and decisive contingent to Spain, it would run the risk of igniting the hostility of the Nationalist Army, 'secretly proud of the courage and heroism of the Republicans and more disposed, if the choice were necessary, to a victory of the Reds than to an Italian victory.'[59] Even Kérillis wrote of the resentment widespread in Nationalist Spain at the arrogance and pretentiousness displayed by the Italians,[60] and even the italophile *La Garonne* reported it.[61*] Mussolini was said to feel that he had served merely to pick Hitler's chestnuts out of the fire.[62] Franco's recent losses, however, reported as very heavy by the *News Chronicle*,[63] called for further reinforcements; as the only member of the Axis that sought a quick end to the campaign, Italy had either to send more troops or persuade the French Government to reclose the Pyrenees frontier.

At the same time, the importance of the German presence in Spain was made clear in April 1938 by von Stohrer, the German Ambassador to Salamanca. Count Jordana, the Spanish Foreign Minister, had assured him, said Stohrer, that Franco counted on holding on to the German volunteers right up to the moment of victory.[64] In May Stohrer added: 'Franco is asking to keep the German volunteers for some time more. He thinks he still has to face up to a dogged resistance by the Reds. . . . Only when it comes to the "small war" (at which point only can we start to talk about police action) will the moment have arrived for Franco to safely dispense with his German volunteers.'[65*]

In the formation of Daladier's Radical Cabinet in April 1938, Paul-Boncourt was replaced by Bonnet as Foreign Minister. Pierre Cot refused to participate, and in fact no member of the SFIO was included. An immediate cooling of the French Government's attitude toward the Republic might therefore have been expected. A detailed report by French customs purported to show that material imported into Catalonia by the three routes open during the month of April represented a reduction of more than 60 percent below the figures for March. Nevertheless, Daladier informed Bullitt at the beginning of May that he had opened the French frontier as wide as possible, and Flandin, a junior member of the new Cabinet, later revealed that 25,000 tons of war matériel crossed the border in April and May. These shipments consisted mainly of 300 Soviet aircraft which Stalin, in the interests of anonymity, and anxious no doubt not to add to his losses incurred from Italian submarines in the Mediterranean, dispatched via the North Sea to Bordeaux on condition that the French Government undertake their transit across the Midi. This Daladier did, and he also opened the Canal du Midi to allow the Republic's smaller vessels to pass from sea to sea.[66*] Accordingly, the Axis press, assisted by some organs of the French extreme Right, raised a chorus of complaints that contraband traffic through the Pyrenees had been intensified under the Daladier government. In *La Garonne*, Pierre Taittinger charged the government in June with having supplied the 'last gangs of Spanish Anarchists' in every conceivable way since April, thereby enabling them to 'bomb, strafe and dynamite Spanish homes offering shelter to women, children and old folk after two years of terror.'[67] Such articles aroused even *Le Matin*, which felt no love for the Republic, to decry the campaign to deceive the public. The publication of such lies, it wrote, could only jeopardize the cause of peace.[68] *La République* added a point of its own: Franco was also free to obtain his supplies in France and did not deprive himself of the opportunity.[69*] Nevertheless, it seemed that Hitler still hoped to turn the question of the Pyrenees frontier to further advantage. The Berlin correspondent of *The Times* wrote that the Führer hoped to see the Spanish question divide Britain and France; if, on the other hand, Paris were to yield to London to the extent of closing the Pyrenees frontier, its action would seriously weaken the Franco-Soviet pact.[70]

The frontier was reclosed on 13 June, Daladier issuing his order in council just after the Assembly recessed.[71*] The Premier's action raised considerable criticism in the press; even the right-wing papers considered that it was unnecessarily surreptitious, akin, they thought, to Blum's method of opening it. But as Republican resistance stiffened behind the Ebro, the Right directed its ire at Blum as the man who had rescued the Republic from defeat in the Teruel counter-offensive. Laval and Flandin charged Blum, before the Senate Committee and the Lower House Committee respectively, with having willfully prolonged the Civil War by several months and with having added tens of thousands to the death toll. In *La Garonne*, Pierre Taittinger displayed the kind of ready submissiveness which was to make him Hitler's choice as puppet mayor of Paris. 'Wherefore resist?' cried Taittinger. 'To what end? To save what, to defend what? The revolution was over in Spain the moment that Britain shifted her weight to Franco's side. Just how, since then, could the worst ideologues of the Front Populaire imagine for one second that their point of view could prevail.'[72] In the same paper, Maurice Legendre accused the Republicans of having 'criminally prolonged the war through their stubbornness.' Besides, snarled the voice of reaction, the Frente Popular was a cause unworthy of any sacrifice at all.[73*]

Nevertheless, Blum contended, with his usual dignity, that France had met her obligations throughout 'with the most scrupulous precision,' supporting this with the official report of Colonel Lunn, Chief Administrator of the International Board of Control.[74] At the same time, the Socialist leader conceded that the new control measures would suffice to end Republican resistance.[75] In a subsequent series of articles in *Le Populaire*, Blum believed that public opinion in France and Britain was evolving in opposite directions, the French swinging toward Franco—from a 'negligible' segment in 1936 to a 'considerable' segment in 1938—and the British swinging away from Franco.[76] In resuming his appeal for collective action, Blum proposed first an armistice to allow for the withdrawal of foreign combatants, then intervention or mediation to prevent a resumption of hostilities. There could be no prospect of peace in Spain without mediation, warned Blum, nor any mediation without withdrawal, nor withdrawal without armistice, nor armistice without the sincere collaboration of the Nationalists.[77] Since the collaboration which Blum advocated involved the lifting of the blockade, it was obvious, even in Franco's days of travail in early August, that the proposal had no chance of success. The only card that the democracies had left to play was the same that Blum himself had withheld in the summer and autumn of 1936: the only hope of enforcing the Non-intervention Agreement, wrote Blum, was for France to suspend her part of the agreement until the Fascist powers were compelled to cooperate.[78]

The cause of Anglo-French solidarity was therefore saved, but the price paid was temporarily obscured. Writing in *La Dépêche*, Yvon Delbos expressed the belief that this solidarity could be 'more effectively applied, in Spain and elsewhere, when maintained and strengthened in a common attitude,' and that therein lay the last, best hope of Spain.[79] This was Delbos' convoluted way of saying that France and Britain could be relied upon to do more or less nothing. In the same paper, Scelle far more accurately assessed the price as the deliberate sacrifice of the Spanish Republic.[80] The evidence was to be seen in Chamberlain's avoidance throughout 1938 of any unequivocal confirmation that the maintenance of the Mediterranean status quo, his object in the Mediterranean Agreement, was to be applied also in regard to Spain. Even though the Chamberlain policy would play for time to allow Britain and France to mobilize against the day when British and French interests would be directly threatened, Scelle disabused the Prime Minister of any hope of peace for their time. Three months before Munich, Georges Scelle posed the question to be forever tied to the city's name: 'Who really believes that peace can ever be won in such a way?'[81]

The Anglo-Italian Mediterranean Agreement, therefore, was now seen by the clear-sighted as a British show of weakness where the Nyon Arrangement had been an Anglo-French show of strength. The firmness shown in September 1937 had put an end to submarine piracy. The hesitancy displayed in April 1938 would fail to put an end to air attacks on defenceless cities and on a population in flight. Moreover, Chamberlain had guaranteed Franco's victory in the belief that Republican resistance would cease within a few weeks. The British Prime Minister, suggested Scelle, would find that his only advantage was narrowly national and temporary: Mussolini would ask Franco to refrain from further attacks on British shipping; the fact that the Caudillo's aircraft were Italian would make the request that much easier, and at least that much détente would be achieved.[82] But from that point on, Mussolini's actions in Spain would be ambivalent. The continuation of the Italian presence in the Peninsula would be contingent upon the continuation of some organized

Republican resistance. In a subtle analysis published in *Le Populaire*, Blum predicted that the Duce would seal his part of the bargain with Chamberlain by isolating the Republicans, but he would not yet administer the *coup de grâce* because a quick solution was no longer in his interest.[83]

23

The Republic in Isolation

The second anniversary—German policy vis-à-vis the Anglo-Italian Agreement—The Spanish gold—Seasonal exegeses

As the second anniversary of the insurrection approached, the Spanish question remained in the forefront of the world news, constituting still, in the opinion of *The Times* of London, the greatest obstacle to a general settlement in Europe.[1] The United Press produced some inflated casualty figures for the first 22 months of hostilities: 'perhaps' one million dead, one million in exile, and 'perhaps' one million prisoners, with material damage estimated at 100 billion pesetas in gold.[2] In reproducing these figures in *L'Aube*, Don Luigi Sturzo asked of what possible advantage could the war be to Spain.[3]

The Republic, in the eyes of *La République,* was still beset by disorder.[4*] The plight of the Republicans, wrote Dominique, was not due to any lack of men, not to want of courage, nor simply to lack of arms, for if the Republic lacked arms now, they did not (he claimed) lack them in July 1936. The failure lay in the deficiency in the officer corps. The best example of this, added Dominique, was in the balance of naval power: the Republicans' material superiority had given way to an inferiority marked by their inability to put to sea and manoeuvre their largest vessels, notably the battleship *Jaime Primero*.[5] The sinking—in March 1938—of the Nationalist cruiser *Baleares*, concluded Dominique, did not alter the situation.[6] *L'Oeuvre* was of a different opinion. The Axis powers, it wrote, were now anxious to strengthen Franco's naval power, but supplying naval units was a far more difficult matter than sending land-based reinforcements; for if his Navy were to expand suddenly, Franco would be hard put to deny Axis complicity. Meanwhile, the Nationalists' naval defeat off Cartagena militated against their hopes of obtaining belligerent rights.[7]

The Nationalist thrust to the sea at Vinaroz did not win much acknowledgment in the Socialist press, although Vandervelde's previous prediction that such a thrust would never succeed[8] may have made the Socialist gloom ineffable. Bracke bravely suggested that French military experts considered the thrust 'unwise.' In any event, the editor of *Le Populaire* stressed that Republican resistance was very far from exhaustion and that their courage was based upon the will never to resume the yoke they had shaken off. Negrín's latest appeal for aid, added Bracke, was not the cry of the desperate but a call for solidarity to all who valued their freedom.⁹ To this Dominique replied that Negrín, once he saw Republican Spain cut in two, should have installed his government in Valencia or Madrid; if it stayed in Barcelona, it was only out of fear that otherwise the Catalans would negotiate a separate peace.¹⁰

Shortly after Vinaroz, Franco granted the interview to Senator Lémery. Lémery published an account of his meeting in the pro-Franco *La Garonne*:

> General Franco spoke to me at length on the origins of this war. 'It is regrettable,' he said, 'that we talk of a Spanish Civil War. It is in fact a war between National Spain, or Spain *tout court*, and foreign intervention. This foreign intervention by the Soviets has unfortunately found traitors in Spain to abet it.
>
> National Spain made no appeal to any power. Only when Russian tanks appeared in Madrid, only when the illustrated journals of Barcelona showed the 'People's Army' parading under the leadership of Soviet officers, did the Generalissimo of the National forces decide to allow foreign volunteers to enlist.
>
> The first of these volunteers were the Irish, then the Italians, who formed side by side with the Spanish troops a legion comparable with the 'Garibaldini' who once fought in France.
>
> Later, faced with the fact that the Reds had at their disposal the bulk of the matériel, especially in aviation, and that they were receiving liberal supplies of bomber and fighter aircraft from the Soviets, the Nationals found themselves constrained to purchase aircraft abroad. They applied to Britain and to Germany—they could hardly have applied to the France of the Front Populaire. It was Germany who responded. And that is why in National Spain today there are German technicians and pilots. But the proportion of foreign troops fighting side by side with Franco's soldiers is negligible in comparison. Spain is working her own resurrection.
>
> General Franco confirmed what I had already heard from General Jordana during a previous visit I made to National Spain: the Franco-Spanish frontier is in no way fortified on the Spanish side, and there is no political, military or economic agreement tying National Spain to any state whatever . . . .
>
> General Franco gave a smile, and thanking the French for their understanding he added: 'I firmly believe that on my side I am going to help you.'¹¹*

It was at this time that Charles Maurras and Henri Massis also visited Franco.¹² Maurras paid tribute in *L'Action Française* to 'this admirable man of war and peace':

> All the superficial appearances of legality, which are false anyway, were against

Franco. What operated for him was the real legitimacy, deep-lying and unquestioned, and it is precisely that that the so-called rebel will establish in fact.[13]*

To Massis, according to the visitor's own evidence, Franco clearly contradicted himself on the subject of German aid. Having expressed his appreciation for this,[14] the Caudillo added a note of defiance which apparently escaped the Führer's attention until their meeting in Hendaye after the collapse of France: 'We owe nobody anything.'[15]

In May 1938 the right-wing press proclaimed that Franco's supreme offensive was imminent. Accordingly, *L'Époque* considered it unsportsmanlike that the Soviet Union should wish to galvanize Catalan resistance by responding with a parallel military effort, reinforcing the Republican Air Force with several hundred aircraft, of which a hundred had already arrived.[16] With the Republican counter-offensive due to begin within weeks, Stalin sent a telegram to the Spanish Communist leader José Díaz: 'The freedom of Spain . . . is not a private affair of the Spanish people but the common cause of all advanced and progressive mankind.' In *L'Humanité*, Dimitrov repeated that everything must be done to ensure victory for the Spanish people, though when he suggested that Spain, Czechoslovakia and China were three manifestations of the same aggression,[17] he drew the scorn of Dominique, who presumed that the Soviet Union would assign herself to the China question while assigning France to handle the problem in Spain and Czechoslovakia.[18] Meanwhile, the Nationalist press spelled out the price of peace: unconditional surrender, insisted *Unidad* of San Sebastián, and nothing less.[19]

Special consideration was again given to the dark intentions of the Führer. Dominique described Germany as the only true enemy of Spain, whatever her régime, because ever since the beginning of the twentieth century German ambitions had been directed toward Spain and Morocco, as the two territories controlling not only the Straits of Gibraltar but the British and French empire routes, Europe's air and sea routes to South America, and even Europe's winter routes—via the Azores—to North America.[20] Germany's policy, wrote Dominique, was aimed not only at Spain but at Portugal; Germany had eyed Portugal's African colonies before the 1914–1918 War, and the presence of a strong German colony in Brazil was especially important.[21] Even Kérillis acknowledged that Hitler and Mussolini, in their bitterness over their exclusion from the larger spoils of empire, viewed the Portuguese and Dutch possessions as particular anachronisms, and that their new diplomatic and military position in Spain would enable them to exert real pressure on Portugal.[22] Portugal, in turn, was described as 'violently hostile' to Hitler and Mussolini, though 'friendly' to Franco.[23] Dominique, however, referred to Portugal's natural sympathy with the cause of regional autonomy and her aversion to any Unitarian movement which would place all Iberia under a totalitarian centralism.[24]*

The Anglo-Italian agreement, with its restraining effect on Mussolini, was a setback to German policy. If the Duce's policy thereafter was to ensure victory but protract the war,[25] the Führer aimed one better: to thwart the Anglo-Italian agreement by reducing German assistance to Franco to the lowest possible level consonant with preserving final victory. Such a policy would shift back to Mussolini the onus of meeting Franco's further appeals for aid, which according to *L'Oeuvre* were now emanating daily.[26] In May, Field Marshal Mackensen visited Ciano in Rome, reportedly to propose Hitler's all-out support in Spain in exchange for Mussolini's unqualified backing in the impending adventure in Czechoslovakia. According to *L'Oeuvre*, it was decided differently: as soon as France had been persuaded to close the frontier—a necessary first step—the smothering of the Republic would proceed in a leisurely fashion, with neither Axis state contributing much help.[27]

Far from increasing his commitment, therefore, Mussolini was reportedly in favour of reducing it. The prospect of Italy withdrawing her combatants and leaving the field to the German technicians now struck terror in the heart of Charles Maurras. Once the Italians had left, wrote Maurras, there would be no effective counterweight to German influence in Spain, least of all in the technological fields where the Germans had made themselves both invisible and indispensable.[28]* Also, in *L'Action Française*, Delebecque quoted the London *Observer* to the effect that Germany, while continuing to castigate the Reds, would not contribute underhandedly to prolonging their agony:

> At the same time that German specialists are entrenching themselves in the Franco régime, Germany is bolstering the resistance to the Republicans, because she needs the struggle to last longer. Germany is even allowing the Communists subsidies.[29]

Léon Bailby presented the same thesis in *Le Jour*, giving a new slant to the case of the five Junkers which raided Alicante on 27 June. Where Kérillis had claimed that the aircraft had been captured by the Republicans prior to the raid, Bailby suggested that the planes had been supplied by Germany to Barcelona via Marseilles.[30]* While such a policy was not too Machiavellian for the capacity of Hitler, it was hardly an attractive proposition for Germany's wire-tight economy. But *L'Action Française* occasionally indulged such fears. Charles Maurras, whose ambivalent attitude toward Germany would one day win him a traitor's end, wrote at this time: 'Look beyond appearances for the hand that holds the strings of the Revolution and you will find Germany.'[31] Other voices of the Right were of the same persuasion. *Le Journal* sent a correspondent to an exhibition of captured Republican war matériel, held in

January 1939 in the Kursaal in San Sebastián. Although the Nationalists showed 'a necessary discretion,' they did not conceal in private their resentment that this matériel included late-model weapons of German manufacture, supplied to the Republicans through the agency of obscure Paraguayan and Guatemalan intermediaries.[32*] Tixier-Vignancour was equally convinced that German arms would be found among those brought into France by Republican troops fleeing from Catalonia.[33*] Chaves Nogales supported their argument in *La Dépêche*. If Hitler, he wrote, were to see in the Spanish Communists a useful tool in his drive against Britain and France in North Africa, he would not hesitate to support them any more than the Kaiser hesitated to support the Russian Communists in 1917. In the same way, if Mussolini had any hope of finding support for his expansionist claims among the Spanish Republicans, he would not hesitate to abandon Franco and his entourage of Catholic bishops and Jewish bankers.[34]

Geneviève Tabouis now presented another sensational exposé, with rather more credibility than usual. It purported to be a résumé of an address given by General Walter von Reichenau to a select committee in Germany. Reichenau reported that the German anti-aircraft and anti-tank guns had proven themselves first-rate. The role of infantry and the machine gun, trump cards in the German war machine, had been shown to be decisive. For the German High Command, the Spanish conflict had taught that in modern war petroleum and spare parts play as vital a role as ammunition. The general added that German pilots in the Condor Legion were being continually rotated in order to increase steadily the number of pilots with combat experience.[35*]

In July 1938 the question was raised concerning the 1.5 billion francs in Spanish gold deposited with the Banque de France.[36*] In *La Dépêche*, Georges Scelle discerned the fear of the French Government that if it were to deliver the gold to the Republic on demand, it could be called upon at a later date to make a second payment to the Nationalist Government.[37] Of course France should not hand it to the Republic, wrote Bailby predictably in *Le Jour*; France would indeed be obliged to pay the sum again, sooner or later.[38] *Le Matin* suggested that the gold be released only after all outstanding accounts had been liquidated. Of three mentioned by *Le Matin*, the first, a loan of 1,115 million francs contracted in 1931, should be repaid at the rate of exchange in gold of the franc at that time; the second corresponded to the expenditure by the French Government on the needs of Spanish refugees in France; the third covered indemnification of financial losses suffered as a result of the Civil War by French citizens resident in Spain. It would be not merely folly but treason, added *Le Matin*, for the government to ignore its opportunity.[39] In *Le Populaire*, Léon Blum, himself a jurist, pointed out that the judgment of the courts not only refrained from challenging the rights of the Bank of Spain but also expressed no prejudice. The gold would therefore be retained in France, not until the victory of Franco but until the courts announced a ruling.[40]

Even before the Republicans launched their counter-offensive across the Ebro on 25 July 1938, Franco was showing signs of impatience at the slowness of the Nationalist advance. 'The reason we have not yet won,' he announced on radio on the occasion of the second anniversary of the insurrection, 'is the presence in Spain of the International Brigades.' But how 'the scum of the earth,' as he described their members, could have offered such resistance went unexplained. Turning to the matter of atrocities, Franco was no more generous, or logical. 'I deny,' he said, 'that the crimes committed by the Republicans are the work of Spaniards. They are the work of the hunchback Rosenberg, of Marty, of Negrín and Álvarez del Vayo.'[41]

The effect of the counter-offensive on the Right was predictable. *Le Figaro's* d'Ormesson thought back nostalgically to the previous March when Prieto had applied his considerable influence to the cause of mediation. Those who rejected his efforts, d'Ormesson now wrote, would have a heavy reckoning to make.[42]

There was a seasonal increase in the number of exegeses of the issues and analyses of the situation. Buré agreed with Franco that this was no civil war, but from quite a different point of view, the Radical editor viewing it as a stage in a world war meditated by Führer, Duce and Mikado.[43] Buré referred to documents recently published, notably by O.K. Simon in his work *Hitler en Espagne*, proving to the author's satisfaction that Hitler and Mussolini had long planned the Spanish adventure, which would gain them Spain and, in the event of general war, impede French mobilization and cut British maritime communications.[44]* Buré referred also to a significant editorial in the *Frankfurter Zeitung* which recalled that 'Scipio too, after the war in Spain, transferred the theatre of war to Tunisia.' In a subsequent editorial, Buré repeated that these 'Reds,' so much maligned in France and Britain, were in fact the vanguard of the democracies in their struggle against the totalitarian states which had sworn to destroy them, referring the doubters to the Italian Fascist review *Gerarchia* and the latest speech by the Duce.[45]

Other editorialists, from Radical-Socialist to Conservative, shared Buré's sentiments. In *La Dépêche*, Chaves Nogales redefined the war as the work of a handful of dissatisfied militants who frivolously declared a *pronunciamiento*. 'This' he explained, 'is authentically Spain. All the rest is foreign, artificial, and arbitrary.' Spain now realized, he concluded, that anything was possible except Fascism and Communism. It might be that for many years Spain would not be able to afford the luxury of a democratic way of life; but this way of life would nevertheless become the strongest aspiration of the Spanish people.[46] *L'Europe Nouvelle* took note of the recent flight of Gil Robles from Nationalist Spain[47] and scoffed at the presentation of the Nationalist movement as national, counter-revolutionary and Catholic. The spurious threat of Bolshevism, wrote *L'Europe Nouvelle*, had been fabricated to enable the Spanish Army to defeat its own people; Spanish nationalism and the conservative classes had been used as pawns in a foreign manoeuvre which would ultimately replace Spain's subservience to Italy by a belligerent alliance with Germany.[48] Romier in *Le Figaro* agreed with Chaves Nogales that Spain could be neither Communist on the Russian pattern nor totalitarian on the lines first drawn up by Franco, and that if at the commencement the foreign powers had been better informed of the Spanish character and temperament, it would have spared them some cruel and costly mistakes. The difficulty, added Romier, would now lie in preserving a peace which would not give way, through financial instability and unconsidered opposition, to a resumption of hostilities in a matter of weeks or months.[49] *La République*, on the other hand, observed the operation of a classic phenomenon of conquest: the more the Nationalists advanced and incorporated Republicans, the more they assimilated Republicanism and Socialism themselves, willingly or not. Thus the Falange was growing increasingly anticapitalist as the beaten Republicans joined it in droves. Since the Nationalists' only alternative was the impossible one of liquidating all the Republicans, they were finding themselves the victims of their victory; a limited victory which shed less blood would be to their advantage.[50]

Again in *La Dépêche*, Vandervelde examined the international situation in the light of Bernanos' recently published work, *Les grands cimetières sous la lune*.[51] Bernanos, the Belgian Socialist admitted, had a weakness for Maurras.[52]* He even saw Léon Daudet as a man of destiny. He even fondly hoped that France would be saved from Hitler by the Duke of Guise. Despite all this, wrote Vandervelde, Bernanos held Marc Sangnier, the leader of the 'Jeune République' movement, to be the most despicable type of bourgeois; for Bernanos had a horror of the middle course, of the policy of choosing the lesser evil. If the democracies, concluded Vandervelde, were to allow international Fascism to pursue with impunity its work of destruction and death, they were merely postponing the universal cataclysm outlined in the Spanish tragedy, and made more horrible with each remission.[53]

The same warning and the same suggestion were expressed by Lucien Lehmann in *La Marseillaise*, the weekly organ of the Rassemblement Populaire:

> Would it not be better, when all is said and done, to face the risk of an immediate conflict—a small risk if the peace-loving nations agree to unite and speak up—rather than continue to live in the certainty of a general war sooner or later.[54]

Le Journal de Toulouse spoke for more than the far Right in replying: 'No! No! Peace! Peace!'[55]

24
The Shadow of Munich

The Berchtesgaden talks and their effect on morale—Auriol visits Barcelona—The campaign to recognize Franco—The London Plan and belligerent rights—The International Brigades disbanded—The Nationalist offensive resumes—Perspectives for peace

'Who really believes that peace can ever be won in such a way?' The question raised by Georges Scelle[1] was asked also by his colleague Émile Vandervelde. After his visit to Republican Spain in early 1938, Vandervelde wrote that they who persisted in a policy of concessions and capitulations, far from saving peace, were following a path leading straight to war.[2] Again, in March he warned against an imminent situation in which the only choice for the democracies would be between general war and surrender to Fascism without a shot being fired.[3] The danger was less evident to others. *Le Matin* described Chamberlain at this time as the best of the workers for peace and deserving of the whole-hearted support of all Frenchmen.[4]

If it is true that France was under no treaty obligation to come to the aid of the Spanish Republic in 1936, it was a very different matter in 1938 in the case of Czechoslovakia, whose integrity she had pledged to defend.[5] Face to face with its responsibilities, the French Government was deeply divided. Daladier's initial opening to the left, with the inclusion in his Cabinet of two independent right-wing Socialists, was reversed on 21 August. The two Socialists resigned, one of them, Frossard, being replaced by the more conservative Anatole de Monzie. As the Munich crisis approached, Daladier was sensitive to the counsel of centrists like Paul Reynaud and Georges Mandel, who urged him to show firmness. So propitiating, however, was the mood of the majority of the Radicals that Daladier appeared even hawk-like in comparison. Chautemps, Bonnet and Monzie advocated extreme caution, and it was the Foreign Minister's warning that the state of French preparedness did not allow France to follow a policy independent of that of Britain that persuaded Daladier to adopt their counsel. At the same time, the SFIO had purged itself of its left-wing element demanding a 'Front Populaire de combat.' At the Congress of Royan on 3–8 June, Marceau Pivert and other militants of the revolutionary Left were ousted from the Socialist party.[6*] This left the party in the undisputed control of its secretary-general Paul Faure, whose pacifist convictions were so strong that he had even opposed the war in 1914–1918, when the majority of the Socialist Party, and the country as a whole, supported it. The result was a widening split between Faure and Blum.

Chamberlain's decision to visit Hitler in Bavaria on 15 September 1938 was a break in British tradition. The Spanish Republican press considered the gesture sensational. *El Heraldo de Madrid* wrote: 'Traditions, principles, everything has been sacrificed in the cause of peace. If the offer meets with success, the name of Chamberlain will be listed among the great benefactors of humanity.'[7] Although some Republican journals doubted the chances of success of the talks at Berchtesgaden, the Socialist *Informaciones* reflected the consensus in calling the visit deserving of respect, whether fruitful or not.[8] The occasion was seized by the Euzkadi Government to declare its solidarity with France, who at that time still recognized the Basque Government. Five hundred Basque seamen had given their lives in the 1914–1918 War while shipping food supplies to France, and now the Basque refugees offered the French Government their services without reservation. Their chief offer was to place their trawler fleet, adapted to and trained in mine-sweeping, at the disposal of France for the protection of the Gulf of Gascony.[9*]

As the clouds of Munich gathered, Edouard Helsey in *Le Journal* had a premonition of disaster. 'All of us are responsible,' he found; 'but let us all put aside all personal partisanships, let us sacrifice everything to union.'[10] The phrase looked slightly bizarre in the columns of *Le Journal*, which had cared little enough hitherto about allaying the class passions which were tearing France apart. But in *Le Petit Bleu*, Marcilly felt no need of such restraint. 'The Front Populaire is to blame,' he wrote flatly, 'in aligning us against New Spain.'[11] The villains were MacDonald, Briand, Herriot, Blum and Sarraut, explained the guiltless *La Garonne*.[12] 'Put 'em on trial,' roared Henri Béraud in *Gringoire*, indicting not only Blum and Sarraut but Cot, Paul-Boncour, Auriol, Péri and Reynaud.[13] The sickness of the age was such that newspapers of the two extremes wrote only to themselves. The important thing was to accuse and ignore the answer.

The immediate effect of Munich was to seal the fate of Czechoslovakia, but it raised its ripples too in the Mediterranean. The French General Staff made it clear that, unless Franco declared his neutrality, there would be, in the event of war, an immediate attack on Spanish Morocco and across the Pyrenees. Franco's quick response, through his representative in London, was to reiterate the pledge of Alfonso XIII that in the event of war Spain would observe the strictest neutrality.[14] Meanwhile, Larralde reported in *La Dépêche* Germany's intensified military and economic consolidation in Spain.[15] There was no mistaking the new threat from Italy either, expressed in the jingoism of the crowds in Rome and Genoa.[16*] The consequent effect on the Right in France was to divide it down the middle.

Pierre Taittinger was quite satisfied that Munich was neither a humiliation for the democracies nor a Sadowa. The agreement, he thought, offered Hitler no encouragement:

> Hitler has no intention of attacking France, for he knows that French resistance will be united and total and that any attempted invasion will cost millions of German lives.
>
> Every remission of war, even if only temporary, means a definite saving of human life.
>
> In my opinion, a few square miles of territory or a few hundred thousand individuals scattered here and there count for far less than the chance to live, work, produce, and trade.[17]

The view so vividly expressed by Taittinger was shared by Bailby in *Le Journal* and *L'Echo de Paris,* by Saint-Brice in *Le Journal,* by Marcel Déat in *L'Oeuvre,* and *grosso modo* by Romier in *Le Figaro*. Bailby believed that the solution lay in 'resignation and reason.'[18] François Mauriac wrote: 'They were simply acting as human beings.'[19] As for the Ligue des Droits de l'Homme, on 1 November it had a poster displayed on public walls showing a telegramme that *député* Flandin, still a member of the Foreign Affairs Commission of the Assemblée, had addressed to Hitler on 30 September: 'Chancellor Hitler. Berlin. Please accept my warm congratulations for the maintenance of peace, with the hope that out of this historic act a collaboration of trust and cordiality will emerge among the four great European powers that met at Munich. Pierre-Étienne Flandin.'

The two principal opponents of these 'Munichois' in the press of the Right and Centre were Henri de Kérillis and Emile Buré. The burden of their answer was as follows:

> The problem is wrongly posed. It is not a question of the Sudetenlanders, nor of the Czechs, nor of Danzig, nor of the Poles. It is a question of the domination of Europe, that and nothing else. If we start by abandoning our allies to their fate, tomorrow it will be our turn and we shall find ourselves alone in defeat and dishonour.

'I should be very surprised,' wrote Kérillis in *L'Epoque*, 'if France and Britain have come away from Munich without having lost a great deal.' Kérillis reminded Taittinger and his colleagues of a testament called *Mein Kampf*, where on page 755 of the expurgated French edition its author set out an important first step: 'the isolation of Germany's mortal enemy France.'[20] 'It is not at this point,' wrote Kerillis, mindful no doubt of the leading part he himself had once played,[21] 'by bringing the guilty to trial and by investigating the mistakes, the faults and the crimes that we shall rise from the abyss, but in giving one another a hand to try to repair the terrible evil that has been done.'[22] 'We must rise above our ancient disputes,' he explained; 'France and Britain need Russia today more than ever.'[23] Kérillis found the support of Frossard in *L'Homme Libre*, André Tardieu in *Gringoire*, his former colleague Pertinax now in *L'Ordre*, and belatedly—and with certain reservations—Charles Maurras in *L'Action Française*. And within two weeks, even Taittinger had come to see that Munich was in the nature of a defeat.[24]

Franco's immediate response to Munich was, like Flandin's, the dispatch to Hitler of a telegram of congratulations.[25] The Republicans were now as dejected by the surrender of the democracies as the Nationalists were relieved. In *L'Humanité* Cachin expressed deep pessimism.[26] Blum referred to it as cowardly relief (*'lâche soulagement'*).[27*] *Regards* wrote: 'Let no one come to us saying that our policy was leading to war. The policy that is leading to war consists of continually giving in to blackmail and to strengthening those who dream of isolating France the better to beat it down.'[28] Munich had in fact completed what Spain began. The Front Populaire was all but dead with the fall of Chautemps' second Cabinet, but nobody could decide to give it the coup de grâce. At Munich, when it gave in to Fascism beyond the power of platitude to deny, it was quite, quite dead. It died because it had not lived up to its basic tenet: resistance to Fascism. It remained for the Radical Party, stung by the recriminations of the embittered Left, to announce its demise. The Radical Party Congress, which opened in Marseilles on 28 October, drew up the death certificate, imputing the blame—unfairly—to the Communists, while striving to maintain the Cartel des Gauches with the Socialists. On 10 November, the secretary-general of the Radical Party formally announced the withdrawal of his party from the Comité National du Rassemblement Populaire.

In the month that followed Munich, *La Garonne* published an account of a visit to Barcelona of the former SFIO Minister, Vincent Auriol. His purpose, stated *La Garonne*, was to submit to Negrín, on behalf of the French Government, a mediation plan which would entail the resignation of Negrín and the formation of a moderate government. When his intentions were understood, added the Toulouse daily, Auriol 'just had time to reach the door.'[29*] In the first of a series of letters addressed to *La Garonne*, Auriol described its account as 'faithful to its tradition of falsehood and false from beginning to end: an intervention out of comic opera.' The purpose of his visit, he explained, was not to discharge any missions for anyone but to see old friends and to acquaint himself with the current situation. This he described as excellent: a free government and a free people were united in the struggle against those who would 'extend the Rome–Berlin axis to Madrid and then encircle France according to the plan of *Mein Kampf*, closing her on the south and using the

Balearics to cut her off from her empire in Africa.' As for a mission of mediation, Auriol informed *La Garonne* that the Spaniards desired nothing else than to see the Italians and Germans follow the International Brigaders from their shores[30] and to be left alone to settle their destiny among themselves. This, concluded Auriol, would be Europe's best road to peace. Informing *La Garonne* that he was taking legal action against it, Auriol demanded that the paper publish his rebuttal.[31] When *La Garonne* delayed ten days before doing so,[32] Auriol wrote again in stronger vein, reminding *La Garonne* of the amicable relations which he had enjoyed with its predecessor, *L'Express du Midi*, and with such men of honour as its editors Victor Lespine and Gaston Guèze. That paper, wrote Auriol, knew what self-respect was, and it could therefore respect an opponent; the polemics between the paper and him were conducted with courtesy, exempt from civil hatred, and animated solely by concern for the public interest. Auriol accused *La Garonne* of forcing him to take legal action, not only for the delay but for an arbitrary division of the letter into two parts, published separately 'in order to drown the argument in a flood of immoderate comments and to shuffle dates, facts and figures in a manner not only perfidious but hypocritical.'[33] Auriol's action against *La Garonne* was a libel suit for damages of 100,000 francs. The case was heard on 23 December, the paper's counsel being Tixier-Vignancour. In their verdict, announced on 30 December, the judges imposed a fine of 100 francs on Lagarde, publisher of the daily, and awarding damages of 20 centimes in Auriol's favor.[34] *La Garonne* responded to the verdict with predictable sarcasm and intransigence.

Daladier's opening to the Right had revived the campaign to extend recognition to Franco. *Le Petit Bleu*, which in the week that Daladier assumed power had announced that the war was now all over, since within a few hours Franco would have cut off Barcelona's source of electricity, welcomed the chance of opening negotiations. *Le Petit Bleu* informed its readers that Franco strongly wished France to hold the Spanish refugees at his expense until further notice, meaning until the defeat of the Republican Army, when a 'humane solution' would be found for their repatriation.[35] Several other reasons were given to justify recognition. *L'Epoque* drew its conclusion from the raids on Ariège and Cerdagne,[36] evoking the scorn of Bayet in *L'Oeuvre* that so-called 'realistic' Frenchmen should side with Franco because he was thought the stronger.[37] Maurras invoked the fact that twelve States, including Great Britain, now had representation in Burgos; the resumption of diplomatic contact with 'Spain,' wrote Maurras, would preclude general war and spare France the need to fight on three fronts.[38] In *L'Eclaireur de Nice*, Léon Garibaldi also felt that the appointment of ambassadors to Burgos and Rome (the latter vacant since January 1938) would serve to prevent war.[39]

The Anglo-French agreement known as the London Pact and sometimes as the London Plan stipulated that Britain and France would grant Franco belligerent rights once all foreign combatants had been withdrawn from Spain: 10,000 from the Republican side, and 50,000–60,000 from the Nationalist. A total withdrawal of this kind was not included in the proposals of the Duce or the Caudillo, who suggested de-escalation on a one-for-one basis. The difference between the two proposals would have meant the difference between Republican victory in the space of a few months, as Geneviève Tabouis pointed out,[40] and a gratuitous Nationalist victory, as Chaves Nogales observed.[41] But the difference appeared to *Le Figaro* as pure sophistry. The fact that the Burgos government had refused to accept the terms of the London Plan, ran its argument, was no reason to suspend the plan or withhold the granting of belligerent rights. Facts, explained *Le Figaro*, count for more than form, and reality for more than points of procedure; and what France and Britain were doing here was to make use of procedure on their way to another stupid hypocrisy, that of denying the patent reality of Franco.[42]

The major advantage that would accrue to Franco by gaining belligerent rights was the right to blockade the Republic, and thus achieve by starvation what he had failed to achieve by force of arms. When spokesmen in London reported that the British Government was considering modifying the terms of the London Pact, it drew some angry comments in France. Blum reminded the British Government that, while it was free to draw up any pact it wished, it had no unilateral authority over the London Pact in whose application all the signatory powers had an equal voice. In this respect, wrote Blum, no concession or transaction was admissible which would expose the Republic both to foreign intervention and to blockade. Referring to the recent Radical Party Congress in Marseilles, Blum affirmed that the categorical resolutions adopted by that congress were fully endorsed by the SFIO.[43] In *La Dépêche*, Cléon dismissed the possibility of persuading French opinion to facilitate Franco's task in any way.[44] *L'Ordre* reported Negrín's own strong opposition to any attempt to modify the terms of the London Pact and to any proposal which, under the guise of mediation, sought the partition of Spain. The one point that all these proposals omitted, wrote *L'Ordre*, was the one condition of Negrín that was not negotiable: the liberation of Spain from all foreign intervention, thus allowing the Spanish people the chance to decide their destiny themselves.[45] 'Spain for the Spaniards!' repeated Buré in December. Recalling Negrín's assurance that there would be no Runciman[46*] between Franco and him, Buré was convinced that the Spanish people, enlightened by the experience of history's most hideous civil war, would soon come to terms among themselves.[47] Even greater confidence was expressed by *Le Petit Parisien*. The attempts at mediation, it wrote, which had hitherto met with rebuff, would now probably be welcomed by a people bone-weary of an inconclusive war; they would demand an armistice, and Franco no less than Negrín would find himself obliged to grant it.[48*]

Rather a different impression was given in an article by the Republic's Minister of Education, Marcelino Domingo, published in *L'Oeuvre*. While he shared Buré's sentiment in favour of a 'Spain for the Spaniards,' Domingo suggested the Spaniards would find no refuge from the force of their uncompromising pride.

> Accustomed like the French to depreciating themselves, Spaniards have discovered through this trial their higher qualities of heroism, self-sacrifice, and the capacity for self-discipline. This means that if there exists anywhere in Europe today a man who refuses to bow down to anyone, that man is a Spaniard. Despite all his sorrows, the Spaniard is proud of this: that he is Spanish.
>
> Between 1936 and 1938, Spain has discovered españolismo. In Burgos as in Barcelona, one idea holds sway: the independence of Spain. The Spain of the future will be of the Left or of the Right. But it will be one, single and sovereign.[49]

One of the effects of Munich was to persuade Stalin to withdraw his trusted agents from Spain while there was still time.[50*] This decision was translated into an announcement by the Republican Government that in order to set an example to the Axis powers it would disband its foreign volunteers unilaterally. Accordingly, the ten thousand International Brigaders currently in combat were withdrawn from the line in October 1938 and left the country.[51*] At the same time, Pierre Taittinger was spending a week in Nationalist Spain as the guest of Franco. Reporting on his interview with the Caudillo, Taittinger quoted his host as follows:

> Fifty thousand men[52*] of the International Brigades lie dead on our soil, having come here to fight in the cause of the bloodiest of revolutions. Ah! I beg you to go and repeat this to all Frenchmen, to those who know little about us, to those who disparage us, that if these fifty thousand had not fallen here, if their victory had been won without a shot being fired, it is among you in France that they would be at work today, with the same violence, the same methods of murder and terrorism. It would have been France, at this very moment, that knew in her turn the meaning of civil war, the destruction of her freedoms, and the devastation of her homes.[53]

Franco now responded to the Republic's act of good faith by announcing his opposition to any attempt at mediation.[54*] It was therefore the worst time, as Blum pointed out, to hear that the French Ambassador to Barcelona,[55*] Labonne, was under consideration to succeed Coulondre, the French Ambassador to Moscow,[56*] while no new ambassador to Barcelona would be appointed. It was inconceivable and intolerable, wrote Blum, that France should place her relations with the Spanish Republic on a level of 'negative equality' with her relations with Burgos, at the same time that France was reappointing an ambassador to Rome.[57] In December, Pierre Laval set out to alter the balance even more by again demanding French representation in Burgos before the Senate Foreign Affairs Committee. He received some useful support in *Le Petit Parisien* from Lucien Bourguès, who argued that the need to know what was happening in Nationalist Spain justified *ipso facto* the sending of a representative. Not to do so, he contended, was to invite Germany and Italy to pre-empt the field, and to leave France as the only country in Europe, apart from the Soviet Union and perhaps Finland, still to withhold such recognition.[58*]

The Nationalist offensive was renewed on 15 November 1938, and quickly threw the Republican forces into retreat. The high degree of mobility of the Italian forces was a decisive factor in the ensuing débâcle in Catalonia. Nevertheless, the old contradictions persisted concerning the attitude of Mussolini, whose withdrawal was central to the problem. D'Ormesson affirmed that the Duce was anxious to withdraw, since the campaign was both costly and unpopular in Italy. But precisely because the expedition was unpopular, added the editor of *Le Figaro*, in terms echoing the Italian press, Italy would not reduce her commitment to the minimum until she had gained a 'moral satisfaction,' by which she meant an international agreement granting Franco belligerent rights.[59] *Le Journal*'s special correspondent in Rome reported that Mussolini was trying for the fastest possible solution in Franco's favour.[60] The impending visit of Chamberlain to Italy in January 1939 gave Mussolini every conceivable reason to force the issue now and confront his guest with an impressive victory. Chaves Nogales therefore predicted in *La Dépêche* an intensification of the struggle in the coming weeks.[61] And *La République's* Dominique added pointedly that if the Duce should fail in Spain now it could be the end of him as well as the end of Franco.[62]

With the Republican forces already reeling from the Nationalist onslaught in Catalonia, it was curious to read in *L'Ordre* that a Nationalist offensive planned for 15 December and designed to occupy Barcelona before the end of 1938 had been abandoned when a Burgos staff colonel defected with the secret plans for this offensive.[63] The rest of the right-wing press followed with unconcealed satisfaction the course of the offensive, the speed of which was barely slowed by the intemperate weather. Kérillis nonetheless expressed his concern that, despite Franco's claims that his foreign aid had never been so slight, the Italian press should proudly trumpet the part played by the Italian corps in this operation.[64] The statement by General Miaja—oddly similar to that just made by Franco to Taittinger—that he was fighting for France, was given a special credence by Buré, who now faced up to the prospect of the Republic's final defeat. Such a result, wrote Buré, would be a great incentive to Mussolini's diplomatic offensive against France; when the time came for the Duce to lodge his claims, he would then have some aces to play which would give pause to his would-be partners in France.[65]

There was still one good reason left why Republican resistance should continue to the very end. Already in March 1937 the Caudillo had announced to his enemies, in *La Revue Universelle*, that the Nationalist movement would 'cleanse the country of all the putrefaction that had poisoned it.'[66] In the interview he gave on 7 November 1938 to the American journalist James Miller of United Press, Franco added: 'We already have two million names in our archives, together with the proof of their crimes and the names of witnesses.'[67] This kind of promised bounty, against the Caudillo's joyous day of victory, served to galvanize some resistance even now. *L'Ordre* retched at the prospect of seeing two million opponents of the Nationalist régime sent into concentration camps.[68] Meanwhile, there was less suggestion than ever of a compromise. Shortly before Christmas the *Berliner Börsen-Zeitung* announced the seasonal tidings that compromise was *ausgeschlossen*. There was no conceivable point of contact between the parties in dispute, it explained; and if an 'artificial' compromise were to be adopted, it would carry in the germ the basis of a new civil war that would be even more terrible.[69] The hope expressed earlier by Romier, that opponents of the next régime might refrain from impulsive action,[70] was dismissed by Pierre Mille in *La Dépêche*, who considered that the vanquished might obey the victor for a time, but they would not stop hating him, and sooner or later it would start all over again. And so a military solution would solve nothing.[71]*

There was a general suspicion, as the Old Year went out, that it was even more the Axis' round. Chaves Nogales called European war 'imminent' and believed that Franco, 'after myopically destroying his country for two years, now [understood] the harsh reality of the wider situation and now [hurried], cap in hand, to offer pledges of friendship to the same democracies that he [had] so mindlessly arraigned.'[72] The wry comment made three years earlier by *La Dépêche*, that 'things [would] go better in the coming year, better that is to say, than in the year after,'[73] seemed even truer now. In its slogan welcoming the New Year, *Le Midi Socialiste* could only wish 'more luck to Socialism, less to the dictators than in 1938.'[74]

25
The War at the Gates of France

Italian irredentism, Spanish Nationalist hostility toward France, and French reaction—Renewed talk of aid to the Republic—New attempts at mediation

According to Senator Aimé Berthod, French sympathies at the beginning of 1939 were regrouping around the Republic. Four reasons were given: Stalin's recall of André Marty in 1937 on suspicion of embezzlement had delighted many Frenchmen who detested him;[1*] the departure of the International Brigades, which seemed to spotlight the Republican forces as the last volunteers in the defence of democracy; the recent declaration of religious toleration in Catalonia;[2*] and the recent demonstrations of Italian irredentism directed at Nice, Savoy and Corsica, together with some provocative bombast published in the Italian press to the effect that the Italian forces might not stop at the Pyrenees.[3] This braggadocio found its expression too in the Spanish Nationalist press. 'Bearing in mind the imperial positions of fascist Italy,' wrote *El Diario de Burgos* on 18 December 1938, 'we need to find a definitive answer to the question of Tunis.' 'France oppresses Corsica, which is Italian and must be returned to Mussolini,' added *El Domingo* (San Sebastian) on 1 January 1939.

The Nationalist victory in Catalonia in January 1939—the result of the greatest concentration of war matériel since 1918—was essentially an Italian victory; and Mussolini missed no opportunity to say so. For two and a half years the Franquista cause had downplayed the role of the Duce's contribution. The smell of victory after frustration and defeat was now too sweet and strong for his vanity to resist. The *New York Times* was now permitted—we may assume Franco reluctantly concurred—to take photographs, which were reproduced in the French press, showing advancing Bersaglieri waving the Tricolore.[4] The significance of the fall of Barcelona, observed *L'Ordre*, could be seen in the demonstrations that followed in the streets of Rome, where the placards read: '*A Parigi! A Parigi!*'[5*] It could be seen too in a statement which appeared in the first subsequent issue of *Il Tevere* of Rome: 'Now, thanks to the Italian fleet, not a single French ship or soldier can cross the Mediterranean.'[6] Mussolini increased his bluster, now calling for the 'liquidation of all Republican forces, not only in the Peninsula but in contiguous territories,'[7] meaning Morocco and southwest France. Even as the war ended, and on the very day that France agreed to turn over to Franco the Republic's warships, Mussolini publicly declared: 'Let us hear no more about Latin sisters or about any other bastard relationship.'[8]

This new irredentism at the expense of France could not but influence the attitude of all sections of the French press in reviewing French policy after the Republican retreat from the Ebro. Yvon Delbos, out of office since the fall of Chautemps and back with his old paper *La Dépêche*, attributed the Duce's anti-French outbursts to his long-awaited rapprochement with Chamberlain, in which Mussolini undertook to withdraw his forces from the Peninsula after the victory of Franco in return for the continuation of British inaction.[9] In facilitating this victory, wrote Blum, Britain and France were only hastening the day when they would be face to face with Mussolini's imperial program, backed by Hitler's colonial program.[10] *L'Oeuvre* analyzed the opinion of the Italian in the street following Chamberlain's visit to Rome. According to *L'Oeuvre*, the average Italian considered that, since France and Britain had given way at Munich and were resigned to the fate of Czechoslovakia rather than risk war, the same policy and the same pressure as those applied by Germany would achieve the same results for Italy, provided only that Germany continued to give Italy her full support.[11] Thus the French Government, as *L'Ordre* pointed out, was relying upon the German Government, incredible as it seemed, to moderate the Italian Government.[12] But such a situation was quite temporary. Italy, added *L'Oeuvre*, had shown her hand too soon for the liking of Germany, who needed a few more months to prepare; Italy would therefore temporize until Germany was ready.[13] Both Fascist states, however, understood the strategic importance of Spain. In *L'Époque*, Jean Perrigault reported that the Canaries were now fully equipped to service Germany's Atlantic fleet.[14] The German High Command, wrote *L'Oeuvre*, was of the opinion that if war should 'suddenly and unfortunately' break out in Europe, it would be well to use the Pyrenees as a point of departure for a powerful air offensive against France.[15] By February even Maurras of *L'Action Francaise* had become concerned over the presence of German and Italian planes and Italian regiments on the other side of the Pyrenees.[16] The decision reached between Mussolini and Franco not to station Italian troops along the Pyrenees did nothing to reassure Senator Jean Odin (Gironde), who remarked:

> A fine assurance of security it is, to know that, in the event of another international crisis tomorrow, the Italian Army, instead of lining the frontier, is a whole hour's march away! And will the security of Corsica and the freedom of our maritime communications be guaranteed by the mere fact that the Italians will limit their annexation to Majorca, while Minorca will be manned only by authentic Spanish Fascists?[17]

One right-wing writer needed no such reassurance. Georges Segone pointed out in *Le Journal* that the Pyrenees decline rapidly on the French side, while on the Spanish side the mountain zone is extended far into the interior by numerous foothills. As a result of this, France is provided with a network of roads in proximity to the frontier, which, added to motorization, facilitates the movement of troops. In Spain, on the other hand, the logistics problem is acute: only six routes, linked by a single lateral, provide access to France along the entire length of the Pyrenees.[18]

Just as the Radical-Socialist *L'Ère Nouvelle* had moved to the right, the Conservative *L'Époque* had moved to the left. It was unthinkable, wrote the latter, that Italy would sacrifice billions of francs and tens of thousands of lives if she did not hope to derive some profit.[19] 'I consider,' now wrote the editor who had once presented a sword of honour to Franco,[20] 'that the victory of Franco in Spain, under the present circumstances, would be a real catastrophe for France.'[21] Kérillis asked whether, in the event that France were attacked in 1939, not only on her north-eastern frontier but also across the Alps and perhaps the Pyrenees,[22*] General Gamelin and Admiral Darlan, the Chiefs of Staff, could possibly prevail under the adverse conditions now facing France: the dissolution of her alliance with Poland and with the countries of the Petite-Entente, and the threat from Axis submarines and planes to her lines of communication, not only in the Western Mediterranean but on every sea.[23]

These gloomy forebodings were made more gloomy by certain articles and remarks published in the press of Nationalist Spain, which showed more and more hostility toward France as Franco's hopes of victory increased. Even François Maret admitted that Maurras' visit to Nationalist Spain in 1938[24] had met with a certain indifference.[25] Ernesto Giménez Caballero, one of the founders of the Falange, wrote in the weekly *Domingo* (San Sebastian) that he never read Maurras' articles, that Spain did not need the friendship of France, of the Right any more than of the Left, and that in the past, ever since François I and his alliance with the Turk, France had done grievous harm to Spain.[26*] 'In token of our gratitude,' Giménez added vindictively, 'we yearn for the chance of paying off this debt with interest and, once the war is over, of sending our friends in France, not a mere Hundred Thousand Sons, but two hundred thousand soldiers of Franco to spread the faith in the lovely, gentle countryside of France.'[27*] *La Voz de España* (San Sebastián) wrote bluntly: 'The victim of the next Munich will be France.'[28] In *Arriba España* (Pamplona) of 11 January 1939, Mariano Prado described France as 'the public enemy of peace in the Mediterranean,' and *El Correo Español* (Bilbao) expressed the same sentiments.[29]

This attitude inevitably served to stiffen Anglo-French pride. Daladier, more and more conscious that in regard to Munich he had listened to the wrong advice,[30*] contended that a nation as strong as France could respond to insults with calm and equanimity, while the French General Staff was believed ready, in alliance with Britain, to seize control of Republican-held Minorca, and even to march on Spanish Morocco, in the event that the Italians failed to withdraw from Spain after victory. On 7 February 1939, the British Government took action, sending the destroyer *Devonshire* to Minorca to make sure that the Italians did not take possession of the island.[31*] The attitude of the Italians and the Spanish Nationalists also had a visible effect upon the French right-wing press. Although *Le Journal* and *Le Matin* did their best to ignore the remarks, *Le Petit Parisien* and *L'Excelsior* were much more reserved in their treatment of Franco's final victories. Even Bailby in *Le Jour* was moved to appeal for national solidarity, though one may well wonder what contribution Bailby had made over the years in his reaction to progress and reform.

The argument of the extreme Right was that France had certain vested interests in Spain, the maintenance of which was vital to French security. In March 1938, Count Emmanuel de Peretti de la Rocca, who had served as French ambassador to Madrid from 1924 to 1929, travelled to Nationalist Spain. As the representative of a large number of French industrial companies, Peretti was there to seek ways to resume commercial ties with Nationalist Spain. He had known all the Spanish ministers for some time, and especially Jordana, with whom he had a 'long and cordial' conversation. In order not to give his visit too much of an acquisitive look, Peretti avoided talking about pyrites, but Jordana himself brought the matter up. 'When trade relations are resumed,' he said, 'you will find 100,000 tons of pyrites waiting for you at the frontier.'.[32] It was difficult, however, in 1939 to ignore the sentiment expressed in *El Diario Vasco* (San Sebastián) on 12 February, to the effect that if the New Spain needed any financial aid she would seek it from among her friends. It was those who had shared the cost and burden of war, added the expropriated Basque daily, who would be invited to 'reap from peace whatever benefits the Spanish people themselves cannot derive.'[33] It was over the supply of pyrites that Franco now exercised the heaviest pressure on the French Government, imposing conditions for future delivery which the latter found unacceptable. Léon Blum wrote that he was disclosing no secrets of national defence by saying that the government had found a substitute for pyrites without much difficulty. Franco, added Blum, had perhaps done France a favour, quite unknowingly, by ending her dependence upon Spanish pyrites, for it had now been discovered that sulphuric acid could be produced from other substances; stocks had been assembled and manufacturing processes readapted.[34] The relative unimportance of Franco *qua* Franco to the security of France was reflected in many of the cartoons of the period, in which the Caudillo was invariably drawn as a small boy holding the hand of the Duce, who in turn was half the size of the Führer.

Against this background of animosity toward France, the French press considered the question of whether France should allow aid to the Republic while there was still time. With the opening of the Italian offensive on 23 December 1938, and the breakthrough against General Líster on 3 January 1939, Ciano had understood the possibility of French intervention. But opinion in France was almost evenly divided between the desire to rescue the Republic and the fear of provoking war, while the speed of the Italian offensive allowed the National Assembly little time for debate. With the fall of Tarragona and Manresa on 14 and 24 January, the Assembly argued the question for a further week. Bonnet, whose growing fondness for appeasement now earned him a rebuke from Daladier, sat unmoved[35*] while Blum, on behalf of the entire Left, insisted that there was still time to save the Republic. But Daladier no less than Bonnet held that it was too late. One of the key factors in the debate was the credibility of the Republic's will to continue the struggle.

With the Ebro line cracked, Philippe Lamour had sounded the note of resistance and desperation in the Catalan journal *Messidor*: 'The armies hold on, but the stomachs cry out.'[36] The tribulations now facing the Republic were known to all. *L'Oeuvre* reported that Republicans were eating grass and that children everywhere were dying for lack of nutrition; mothers no longer had the strength to nurse their infants, and there was no condensed milk.[37] French milk happened to be the only product that still crossed the frontier, and even that was a subject of ridicule in the right-wing press.[38*] Radicals such as Roche and Dominique, of *La République*, and Buré, of *L'Ordre*, joined *L'Oeuvre* in invoking aid to the beleaguered Republic. *L'Oeuvre* and *La République* belonged to Daladier's own party, and all three were read by the Cabinet. With the whole Catalan front crumbling, Ángel Galarza, ex-Minister of the Interior under Largo Caballero, made a last desperate appeal to France for the right to buy arms.[39] Jaume Miravitlles made a similar speech in Toulouse on 23 January 1939. Three days later Barcelona fell.[40*] Although the collapse of the Catalan front had dumbfounded public opinion abroad,[41*] the fall of the city itself caused so little surprise that only *Le Jour* commented on it, with predictable relish.[42*] In an interview given in Figueres to Herrmann of the *Midi Socialiste*, Álvarez del Vayo gave his word for it that five thousand opponents of Franco had been executed in Barcelona in the first two days of the city's capture. 'I shall see you again in six months,' he added. 'I predict terrifying results for the destiny of Europe.'[43]

Meanwhile, the debate in the French National Assembly reflected the fatal division between the forces of peace at any price and those of intervention at any price. With Daladier's Radical-Socialists joining the peace group, despite the personal reservations of their leader, the vote against intervention now carried by 374 votes to 228. Whatever aid the French Government now decided to allow the Republic during the last days of the Catalan campaign, the French right-wing press curiously refrained from the indignant outbursts which had been so common in July 1936 and since. The growing chaos at the border might have allowed supplies to pass through unobserved, but such a theory is unlikely. The fact that *La Dépêche*, which had transferred its support from Blum to Daladier, omitted all mention of French supplies, suggests two possibilities: the operation was conducted in the greatest secrecy, and for the first time in the war the secrecy was preserved; or, which is more likely, the 'war materiel' to which Thomas refers,[44] never included more than medicines and foodstuffs, which was conceded even by the right-wing *Le Journal*, in an article by former Minister Louis Rollin.[45] Certainly the report by Herbert Matthews in the *New York Times* that the border had been 'opened just a little' puzzled other unbiased observers, and official circles in Paris did not deign to comment.[46*]

L'Humanité's headlines, it need hardly be said, still screamed for intervention. To help the cause, the facts were doctored not a little. 'SPAIN HOLDS ON, SPAIN RESISTS AND WILL OVERCOME,' ran one such headline, after the surrender of Barcelona. *Ce Soir* spoke of the 'splendid recovery of the Army of Catalonia.'[47] Prominence was given to sanguine statements by Republican leaders, several of whom still spoke of victory, whatever they may have felt. One such was Aguirre.[48] General Miaja also repeated his confidence in final victory to the correspondent of the London *Evening Standard*.[49] He followed this up with an announcement that the Republicans would fight to the last man.[50] Such was still the policy of Prime Minister Negrín, who called for a war to the death[51*] and whose differences with President Azaña on this matter were now public knowledge. It may not have been the counsel of Largo Caballero, who had refrained, however, from making any public announcement since his arrival in France. He broke this studied silence only to write a letter to *La Dépêche*, in which he refuted various statements published in his name.[52] Meanwhile, the French Socialist Party still called for further resistance and demanded that the government reopen the frontier[53]—further testimony that the frontier had remained closed. In Figueras, for eleven days the fourth capital of the Republic, Álvarez del Vayo informed *Le Midi Socialiste*'s correspondent Herrmann that the Republicans had no arms.[54*] One week later *Le Midi* was congratulating the Republican forces on saving the bulk of their matériel: 500–600 machine guns, more than 200 pieces of artillery, and their fighter-planes.[55*] The thought did not strike *Le Midi* that Franco would not only demand their immediate surrender but would be justified in so doing by international law.

Perhaps *Le Midi Socialiste* was still hoping, like many Republican leaders, for a miracle that would rob Franco of his victory. According to Pierre Taittinger, writing in *La Garonne*, Negrín had declared to French Minister

Jules Henry, at the time Negrín crossed the border on 9 February en route to Toulouse,[56] that the Republic's only hope now lay in the outbreak of a general war.[57] If this was the millennium awaited by these leaders, wrote *L'Oeuvre*, the visitation would be a catastrophe, not a miracle.[58] But by mid-February, the Republicans' hope was ebbing. Salvador de Madariaga joined Azaña in his desire for negotiations, in a letter to *The Times* which was widely reproduced in the French press.[59] *La Dépêche* now agreed that the struggle was useless, that further resistance was impossible, and that peace was necessary.[60] Blum, too, knew that the game was lost; he now discouraged French Socialists from inciting the Republicans to further resistance.[61] Not so the left-wing Socialist Zyromski, who still pleaded, even when all Catalonia had succumbed, that the Republic was not beaten. His demands in fact increased. He now called for French military assistance in regrouping the Army of Catalonia and for French naval assistance in transporting it to Valencia. What is more, he demanded what even *L'Humanité* had balked at: French occupation of certain positions in Spanish Morocco and even of enclaves on the Spanish coast opposite North Africa.[62]

Other journals called for a mobilization of French resources rather than for a specific involvement. *Le Peuple* asked the government whether, by continuing its present policy, it intended to make a wider conflict inevitable and to lose such a conflict—in which it would be the first victim—by simple default.[63] For Kérillis also, the choice was between mobilization now or capitulation later. France, he said, should not count upon a miracle: Mussolini's apoplexy and the dissolution of the Axis coalition were equally improbable.[64] *Les Echos* believed that a heavy responsibility rested with the United States, since the European democracies could not call the hand of the Axis states without American support. *Les Echos* referred to a letter written by former U.S. Secretary of State Henry Stimson addressed to his successor Cordell Hull, which the latter had until now declined to answer and which now appeared in the *New York Times*.[65] In it Stimson denounced the Neutrality Act of 1935, while at the same time he conceded that non-intervention had been—and still was—an ineluctable necessity for France.[66*]

Opposing the motion for involvement, even *L'Oeuvre* now expressed the opinion that the reasons valid in 1936 for doing nothing detrimental to the Anglo-French alliance were even more relevant in 1939.[67] *La République* reached the same conclusion by a different route: if only the two camps in Spain had never hearkened to the foreign tempter, they would already have found, on their own, the way to make peace, 'if only in their hearts.'[68] The Right liked *L'Oeuvre*'s argument best, what with the Catalan front crumbling. In the opinion of *Le Matin,* Mussolini had prepared the same trap that Hitler had laid in Czechoslovakia.[69] The trap, as described by d'Ormesson in *Le Figaro*, consisted of fostering an anti-French psychosis in order to provoke France into committing an indiscretion.[70] No right-wing paper dared any longer to defend Mussolini, and even *Le Journal*, in an article by Louis Rollin, denounced the Italians for openly flouting their pledge to the London Committee after the Republicans had disbanded their foreign troops and while the French frontier remained closed.[71] Nevertheless, *La Garonne* could still insist that it was not in Spain that the account with the Duce should be settled.[72] Its argument for a good-neighbour policy was answered by Stivio in *L'Ordre*, for whom the only good neighbour was one who remained his own master. 'My friends' friends are my friends,' added Stivio; 'but my friends' enemies?'[73]

An alternative argument was developed by Compère Morel in *L'Homme Libre*. Any military aid to the Republicans, he wrote in early January, would only prolong the war, since it would give rise to further foreign intervention. Besides this, it would be incongruous for the Front Populaire leaders who introduced the non-intervention policy in 1936, at a time when aid to the Republic might well have proved decisive, now to ask Daladier and Bonnet to reverse their policy in favour of a belated and perhaps ineffectual line of action.[74] Blum, however, now asked nothing so incongruous. The sending of war matériel, said Blum, could no longer stop the Nationalist avalanche. In the light of this, it was hard to suggest any longer that France should open the frontier simply to share in the Republic's defeat. Political passion, wrote *L'Homme Libre*, had fortunately not blinded Frenchmen to the point of losing sight of the national interests of France.[75]

The argument of *La République*, that left alone the Spaniards would soon make peace, helped to revive the interest in a possible compromise under a system of liberal monarchy. Significantly, *La Garonne*, the champion of far-from-free monarchy, had nothing to say. Chaves Nogales in *La Dépêche* considered that restoration would be less welcome in Nationalist Spain than in Republican Spain, where it would now offer an attractive solution in the eyes of the old moderates who now thought only of peace.[76]

An attempt was now made to further the cause of peace in the form of identical letters sent to Franco and Negrín by a certain Marquis de Cañada-Hermosa, allegedly representing the Asociación Monárquica Española. The letters, which were published in *Le Populaire*, called for peace and unity, for a Spain free from foreign extremist ideology, for Spanish neutrality in the event of world war, and for an amnesty and guarantee of no reprisals.[77] The Socialist press gave the letter the fullest coverage, as if restoration would indeed have been welcome to Spanish Republicans at this time. However, Count de los Andes, Master of the Household of Alfonso XIII, at once announced that no such association and no such marquis were known to the nobility of Spain.[78]* 'We might have known it,' ruefully remarked *La Garonne*, which had an unfortunate habit of following false leads, 'considering the source.'[79] But the Socialist press did not yield. *Le Midi* replied to the

Count's disclaimer with the report that the Marquis indeed existed but had been arrested by Franco in San Sebastián on 15 February, the day before the letter was written.[80] And there the matter rested, ending one more futile attempt to bring the war in Spain to a halt by compromise or mediation.

26

Anglo-French Recognition of Franco

The Bérard mission—American isolationism—The Republican government arrives in France—Pétain and de Lequerica nominated as ambassadors

Up until the fall of Barcelona, the press had been fairly equally divided on the subject of extending recognition to Franco. Now came a change, *Le Petit Parisien*, which was regarded at this time as the closest expression of the Daladier government, showed in its editorials how much the government had come to realize the need to recognize the Burgos authorities. Lucien Bourguès, who was one of the few to presage the imminent flood of refugees, wrote that to settle such a problem the only practical solution was to enter into direct contact with Franco, who would certainly wish to prevent a great number of Spaniards from leaving Spain, perhaps for ever.[1] Recognition of Franco, pointed out *Le Petit Parisien* later, implied neither approval nor disapproval of his regime, citing the example of French recognition of Lenin in 1924 which, if it came after long deliberation, still did not constitute an endorsement of Bolshevism on the part of the French Government.[2]

By mid-January 1939, the Radical-Socialist *L'Ere Nouvelle* had added its voice to the swelling chorus demanding the immediate appointment of an ambassador to Burgos, but without prejudice to French representation in Valencia, now once again the Republic's capital. France would thus remain impartial and at the same time thwart Italy's hopes of establishing a special relationship with Franco.[3] After the collapse of the Catalan front, the cry was raised even louder. Bailby in *Le Jour* asked Georges Bonnet how much longer he would procrastinate.[4] He subsequently called, not merely for the assignment of an ambassador, but for a military alliance with Franco which would spare France the need to defend her southwest frontier in the event of attack elsewhere, and would permit a combined operation to rid Spain of Italian troops if these should proceed to acts of provocation or should overstay their welcome.[5] Moreover, added d'Ormesson in *Le Figaro*, even Blum would admit that recognition was inevitable sooner or later; it was imperative, therefore, that it should be extended freely, before events should leave France no choice in the matter and her act of recognition would avail her nothing.[6] This argument, thought Buré in *L'Ordre*, was beside the point. Even if Franco's victory were inevitable, he wrote, France would be sacrificing her honour by approaching him.[7]

A new dimension was added to the argument by the arrival in France of Spanish Republican leaders. Even the liberal *La Dépêche* declared in bold type that France would not permit the Republican Government to convene on French soil.[8] *L'Époque*, though it had shuffled off some of the anti-Republican bias whence it sprang, also pointed out that the disintegrated Cabinet in Figueras could not reassemble in France, nor could the Spanish Foreign Ministry be allowed to install itself permanently in exile there. Such a permanency, added *L'Époque*, could not be justified by the need to solve the refugee problem; the question of finding asylum for the refugees could easily be handled by the Spanish Consulate in Perpignan.[9] Azaña replied on 7 February that the Republican Government would not establish itself in exile in France.[10] The arrival of Negrín and Álvarez del Vayo in Toulouse two days later passed unnoticed; and the meeting of the Cabinet in the Spanish Consulate was either unknown to, or more probably concealed by, *La Dépêche*.

Despite the plea of Buré, France now approached Franco and with ungainly haste. In the Senate on 7 February, Bonnet explained that the Nationalist Government had assured France that it would jealously maintain the independence of Spain and would allow no foreign enterprise to impinge upon it. Since there was no possibility that Jules Henry would be welcome in Burgos, a replacement was necessary and the choice fell upon Senator Léon Bérard, who was dispatched to the Nationalist capital to ingratiate himself as best he could.[11*] The selection of Bérard was generally approved; he was supported on the Right because he was a Catholic and a Basque, on the Left because he was a Basque and a member of the Académie Française. The result of his mission, however, won no such consensus. Nor did his mission itself win any respect from Léon Blum, who denounced the government's haste to humiliate itself. 'What impatience,' he wrote, 'how ungenerous, how undignified, how unwise! Can they really believe that in this way they will forestall the Duce's demands, rid Spain of foreign domination, and hold secure our Empire lifeline?'[12] Blum considered that it was now the duty of French Socialists neither to incite the Spanish Republicans to resist to the last man nor to betray them by extending recognition to Burgos, whether on the grounds that the transfer of power was a *fait accompli*, or that the Republic was incapable of further resistance, or that the Republic no longer existed and Franco was now sole master.[13] If this were really the case, added Blum, what were the Italian legionnaires and the German specialists still doing in Spain? If Franco's victory was beyond dispute, their presence was no longer necessary. Why, then, did Franco not invite them to leave?[14]

On his first return to Paris, Senator Bérard reported to the press that he was 'very satisfied with the courtesy shown by General Jordana,'[15]* Franco's Foreign Minister, and by the welcome extended to him in Nationalist Spain.[16] The Senator's report was a serious attempt to beguile the French public. There is every reason to believe Thomas' verdict that the Senator was 'treated coldly.'[17] But Bérard repeated his story to the Agence Havas, after his return to Burgos: 'I would like to report the charming welcome extended to me here.'[18]

Again in Paris, Bérard informed the press that he had seen several friends and that he had found the country 'calm' while it proceeded to 'sort out' the population. 'Have you seen Franco?' was the first question of reporters. 'No,' admitted Bérard sheepishly, 'he had other things to do; but I received the warmest welcome from Jordana.' What did the Senator think of the accounts of his visit published in the Spanish Nationalist press? 'I've seen certain local papers,' replied Bérard loftily. 'They're simply polemizing. What they think is certainly not the attitude of Burgos.'[19]

What the Spanish local papers thought was precisely the attitude of Burgos. Bérard—so high in hope, wrote L'Humanité, that he had left Burgos two days earlier than scheduled—had no sooner crossed the frontier than every paper in Nationalist Spain received orders to publish the following communiqué:

> Those nations that seek normal relations with us should now formally admit to the disappearance of the Red government, recognize its basic illegality and its powerlessness to impose authority, and attach no conditions to the re-establishment of such relations.

The mission, remarked L'Humanité, had already ended in total failure.[20]

The conditions to which the Spanish Nationalist press referred were the guarantee of no reprisals which Paris and London were desperately trying to secure before granting recognition. Burgos, as Le Populaire pointed out, was just as adamant that recognition should precede the guarantee.[21] And indeed, by announcing their agreement in principle to moving toward recognition, France and Britain, as Le Peuple observed, had forfeited their power to impose conditions.[22] The danger from failing to obtain such guarantees was unquestionably real. On 13 February, the Burgos government made public the 89 articles of the new laws. The decree defined 'subversive activity' as any action committed from 1 October 1934, or at the latest from 17 July 1936, 'in fact or in thought (*de hecho o pasivamente*),' against the Nationalist movement. Thus all those who had not joined the movement, even when the movement was underground or illegal, could be prosecuted, whether they were party leaders, civic officials, or ordinary policemen. Moderate journals such as L'Aube[23] and La Dépêche[24] bitterly denounced the vindictive spirit manifest in the decree. As if in direct reply to these responses, Franco assured the correspondent of the

News Chronicle that 'hatred and the spirit of revenge [had] no place in the new Spain. Between our former enemies and ourselves, there exists a common ideal.' As for French fears that the Axis could come to dominate the Spanish economy, the Caudillo set their fears at rest: 'Spain can win by its efforts alone the place in Europe that befits it.'[25] Even General Toussan, in *La Garonne*, was not reassured: 'Might not these efforts be directed against France? Might not a totalitarian Spain risk being moored to the Rome–Berlin axis by the very resemblance of their regimes?'[26]*

La Dépêche could only denounce bitterly the selfish indifference of the Right and the extreme Left alike toward the fate of the refugees.[27] *L'Oeuvre* still maintained that it was impossible for France to extend recognition until Franco had agreed to an amnesty, without which thousands of Spaniards whose only 'crime' was their loyalty to the Republic ran the risk of facing a court martial and an execution squad.[28] Such reflections in the world press had their effect on Nationalist policy. On 22 February Franco sent a telegram to Chamberlain, assuring him, on his honour as a soldier, that the vanquished would enjoy 'an equitable peace, . . . since the notion of reprisals is completely alien to the Nationalist movement.' Even those journals that downplayed the threat contained in the decree of 13 February shared in the concern that Franco was under the strong influence of his allies. Italy, wrote *La Dépêche*, was advising Franco not to amnesty anyone, for amnesty was simply a crooked manoeuvre to deny Franco the full reward of his victory; and what need had he of amnesty, when an entire wing of the political spectrum in France and a considerable segment of French public opinion were already won over to his cause?[29]

Indeed, by this time even the Socialist organs admitted that three quarters of the French press now favoured recognition of Franco,[30] and for these the question of guarantees was largely academic. *L'Époque*, despite its growing fears of Axis aggression, reminded its readers that the demand for over-precise guarantees in the affair of the Spanish Succession had been a direct cause of the Franco-Prussian War of 1870.[31] *L'Aube* still insisted that Franco had no right whatever to receive any homage from France.[32] But on this constitutional question, *L'Ere Nouvelle* indulged in the Machiavellian notion that legitimacy is always a question of fact. If a so-called legitimate government has disappeared, argued the chameleon Radical, and another is installed which is strong and guarantees order, who would prefer nothingness to what exists, especially when French interests were at stake?[33] But the legitimate government had not disappeared, replied Scelle in *La Dépêche*, and not until it had been totally eliminated could Franco be granted recognition. Even then, added Scelle, only de facto recognition could be extended. De jure recognition could properly be granted only after an eventual constitutionalization of Franco's de facto power, whatever form that constitutional power might assume.[34] In the same paper, the jurist Gaston Jèze took a slightly different position by conceding the government's right to grant Franco de facto recognition at once in respect to the territory he held, but not to the whole of Spain. Like Scelle, Jèze denied the government's right to extend de jure recognition to Franco as long as an organized Spanish Government exercised its authority over a part of that territory; *a fortiori*, the French Government could not appoint an ambassador to Burgos while such a situation obtained. The action therefore of Switzerland, added Jèze, in appointing a plenipotentiary to Burgos, was a violation of international law and an act of intervention.[35]

None opposed the government's initiative more fiercely than Léon Blum. For days his column in the Socialist press was headed 'Non! Non! Non!' The United States, wrote Blum, in an article he soon wanted to forget, would refuse recognition to Franco even if his forces should occupy the whole of Spain and even if Britain and France were to show America the way. The possibility of British recognition, added Blum, was equally remote. As long as German and Italian forces remained in the Peninsula, as long as the Republican Government held a fraction of Spanish soil, and as long as there was cause to fear reprisals, the British Government, in the opinion of the French Socialist leader, would never agree to 'unconditional' recognition.[36] In fact, Great Britain and France had declared, on 24 November 1938, that all foreign troops had to be withdrawn from Spain before belligerent rights could be granted. At the moment that hostilities were suspended, in February 1939, Axis forces were still present in Spain, with the result that, even then, neither those two powers nor others granted belligerent rights. This denial of belligerent rights, however, would not obstruct the recognition of the Franco regime as the *de jure* government of Spain.

Blum's reference to current U.S. policy was particularly unfortunate, since it corroborated a similarly inaccurate report published in *L'Ordre*. According to the latter, French recognition of Franco at this moment would tend to neutralize the new readiness of the United States to accept responsibility in Europe, as supposedly expressed in President Roosevelt's address a few days before.[37] A phrase taken from this speech, suggesting that the United States undertook to guarantee France's borders, was prominently displayed in the press. At the same time, the American Ambassador to London, Joseph Kennedy, was said to have made a similar statement to Chamberlain. According to *L'Ordre*, Kennedy had told the Prime Minister that the unconditional recognition of Franco, implying ipso facto the breaking of relations with the Republic, would create a most unfavourable reaction in Washington and would permanently discourage U.S. solidarity with the Western European democracies. Kennedy had allegedly added that, in the opinion of the majority of Americans, from the President down, the quickest way to push the United States 'back into irremediable isolationism' was for Britain and France to show signs of weakness and irresolution in the conduct of their foreign policy.[38] But

Roosevelt himself quickly showed, by flatly refuting the statement attributed to him, that the United States had not emerged from her isolationism.[39]* *La Dépêche*, for one, took the humiliation gracefully, wistfully, and even nobly, likening France to the heroine of La Fontaine who loses her milk and with it all her dreams.[40]

In *Gringoire*, Tardieu now took Blum to task on the question of the continued existence of the Republican Government. Writing with what his southern satellite *La Garonne* called 'an alert and vigorous pen,'[41] Tardieu remarked that 'the most backward child in kindergarten' knew that, when a government took refuge abroad, it forfeited ipso facto its validity and its existence. Instead of ordering its planes to Toulouse and being driven by car to Perpignan, continued Tardieu, the government in Barcelona could have flown to Valencia or Madrid. In this case, France's obligations to the Republican Government would have remained binding, and protocol would have required the French Ambassador to follow it to the new capital. As it was, Tardieu had only to quote Bonnet, Sarraut and Salvador de Madariaga who conceded that, by preferring Perpignan as a capital to a city in Spain, the Republican Government no longer existed in international law.[42] In point of fact, however, the Republican Government had by now transferred its seat back to Valencia. With the permission of the French authorities, Negrín and Álvarez del Vayo had returned from Toulouse to Alicante in an aircraft belonging to Air-France.

The arguments of the Right were vindicated by the widening division in the Republican ranks between those favouring capitulation and those calling for further resistance. Azaña, strongly urged by Álvarez del Vayo to return to Spain, flatly refused. *L'Oeuvre* expressed no surprise at the decision of a man it called an inveterate appeaser, whose views would have been known much earlier had it not been for his 'jailers at Montserrat.'[43] Negrín replied to Azaña by giving him the choice of returning or of resigning. His ultimatum was in accordance with the Constitution of the Republic, but the Constitution also stipulated that in such an event the presidential powers should pass to the president of the Cortes. Since the incumbent, Martínez Barrio, was similarly in exile in Paris and as reluctant as Azaña to return to a lost cause, Negrín's hopes of electing a 'die-hard' President hinged upon Martínez' resigning in favour of the vice-president of the Cortes, who was the Communist militant Dolores Ibarruri, known as Pasionaria. The result, as *Le Journal* pointed out, was a widening split in the Republican Cabinet.[44] Negrín therefore entrusted Álvarez del Vayo, according to *L'Epoque*, with a further mission of urging the French and British Governments to delay their recognition of Franco to save the Republic's face.[45]

Despite Franco's obvious snub to Daladier in disdaining to meet Bérard, the right-wing press pretended not to see it and encouraged the Senator in his mission. He was on the right track, wrote *L'Action Française*. Prospects were favourable, wrote *Le Journal*. *L'Excelsior* was 'definitely optimistic.'[46] In *Le Petit Journal*, La Rocque could offer the Premier the full support of his reactionary Parti Social Français.[47] Bérard completed his mission on 26 February, and France and Britain formally recognized the Franco regime the following day. Blum's predictions to the contrary, the United States followed suit on 3 April.

The French decision had followed a short debate in the Assembly and a vote which showed a majority of 60 in favour. Blum expressed his anguish in *Le Populaire* at such a disarray of his Front Populaire of May 1936. France had obtained nothing. She was agreeing to return 8 million pounds sterling in Spanish gold, all Republican war matériel in France, including all warships and merchant vessels, vehicles and rolling stock, and all documents and works of art. In return, Franco was agreeing merely to receive a French ambassador in Burgos. He had given no guarantees against repression, Italian divisions were parading at the head of triumphant processions in the streets of Barcelona,[48*] and the Spanish Republic was being buried alive.[49] It was the first time in history, added Blum's former Air Minister, Pierre Cot, that a rebel leader had obtained recognition without first occupying the capital.[50*] The victories of international Fascism, Blum resumed, had clearly revived the class hatred of the same forces of reaction that caused the blood baths of June 1848 and May 1871. 'I would swear,' wrote Blum, 'that the thought crossed more than one mind among those members seated on the right-wing benches that a massacre of the Reds in France would not be such a bad thing at all. In all sincerity, I do not think this to be an exaggeration.'[51]

It certainly would be an exaggeration, replied *L'Ère Nouvelle* to Blum's forebodings, to suggest that the 323 Deputies who had just voted their confidence in President Daladier were in any way the adversaries of democracy or of the Republic. Such a suggestion would be an insult to the millions of Frenchmen who had elected them and who asked only that they serve the national interest.[52] Writing in *Le Jour*, François Piétri, who was himself to serve as Vichy Ambassador to Spain, welcomed the act of recognition with words that spoke for many: 'Good sense has finally prevailed.'[53]

On 28 February 1939, the day following the recognition of Franco by France and Britain, Azaña resigned from the presidency of the Republic. Two conservative papers did not fail to pay homage to the departing leader. One of them was the editor of *L'Époque*,[54] the same Kérillis who long, long ago had presented a sword of honour to Franco. The other was *Le Petit Parisien*, which wrote: 'His action is indeed that which we could expect of a man who, in a régime where moderation is hardly the common currency, always showed himself relatively measured in his acts and conciliatory in his counsel, in the hope of hastening a peaceful solution to the Spanish Civil War.'[55*]

The nomination on 2 March of Marshal Pétain, already 82 years of age, as the new ambassador was widely acclaimed by the Right and Centre, who reminded Frenchmen that the hero of Verdun was not only Franco's old commandant at the École de Guerre and his comrade-in-arms in Morocco in 1925 but also a member of the Académie Française.[56] The Left generally thought the choice unfortunate, especially *L'Humanité*, which remarked that generals rarely made good diplomats. Blum considered that the selection of Pétain confirmed the failure of Bérard, and he deplored the flattery thus paid to Franco by sending him 'the noblest, the most human of our leaders.'[57]* In a subsequent slogan, *Le Midi Socialiste* scored a bull's-eye: 'PETAIN IS PREPARED TO TELL FRANCO HOW HE HELD VERDUN IF FRANCO WILL TELL HIM HOW HE TOOK MADRID.'[58] Pétain's counterpart was José Félix de Lequerica, one of the July conspirators in Madrid. *L'Ordre* responded to his appointment as ambassador to Paris with a full-scale indictment. The 'Lequerica affair,' as *L'Ordre* called it, reflected Franco's inchoate anti-French policy. According to Buré, Lequerica was a political prodigy of Maura, 'the most germanophile of Spanish germanophiles,' and was the author of the most virulently anti-French articles published by *ABC* of Seville. That the Quai d'Orsay could consider accepting the credentials of such an envoy was for *L'Ordre* a sorry indication of its state of mind.[59]

27

The End of Hostilities

Casado's coup d'état—Republican troops and matériel enter France—Marty explains to the Senate—Spain in Europe

Now that France and Britain had extended recognition to Franco with no guarantee that reprisals would not be taken, the knowledge of what lay in store for captured Republicans became more than ever their reason for resistance. But since the Republic no longer had the remotest chance of receiving further supplies from abroad,[1*] resisting was tantamount to dying. So it was that on the night of 5–6 March 1939, Colonel Casado overthrew the Negrín government—whose leaders had just made a final transfer from Valencia to Madrid for a last-ditch stand[2*]—in the hope of providing the Republic with a new image of moderation and thereby obtaining better peace terms from Franco. Casado's platform, still anti-Fascist but equally anti-Communist, was described by the pro-Fascist *Le Journal* as 'certainly the cleverest means of obtaining peace with honour from Franco.'[3]

The Catholic *L'Aube* welcomed the take-over. Since the Nationalists' principal argument had upheld the need to rescue Spain from the influence of Moscow, now that this influence had been eliminated Franco would no longer have the same reasons to refuse immediate peace talks.[4] *Le Peuple*, however, suspected that Franco, and his allies even more, needed a total military victory to save their prestige. The fearful difficulties of further resistance in the central zone suggested to the CGT organ that the hopes of the new Republican leaders, however sincere, were quite unfounded.[5]

The assumption that the Communists had been eliminated from power and influence was contested by *L'Époque*. If those like Negrín, Álvarez del Vayo and Líster had fled, wrote *L'Époque*, the 'hard-liners' remained, determined to sell their lives dearly, and ready for anything except pretty speeches in a time of revolution. While the majority of the people in Republican Spain supported the new Casado-Miaja régime, it added, the Republic had always been the victim of a militant minority and the Communists had alway succeeded in suppressing the advocates of peace.[6] And the Communist Party, according to the statement which *Les Échos* attributed to the Socialist Besteiro, had a single aim: to continue resistance until a world war was unleashed.[7] In any event, Franco's reluctance to accept Miaja's conditions of surrender, as *La Dépêche* accurately observed, reflected his constant intention to refuse an amnesty.[8]

The granting of recognition to Franco automatically raised the question of the Republican troops fleeing to France and the matériel they deposited with the French authorities. The matter was covered under Articles 11 and 12 of the Hague Convention (V) of 1907, respecting the Rights and Duties of Neutral Powers and Persons in Case of War on Land, which read:

> Article 11: A neutral Power which receives on its territory troops belonging to the belligerent armies shall intern them, as far as possible, at a distance from the theatre of war.
> It may keep them in camps and even confine them in fortresses or in places set apart for this purpose.
> It shall decide whether officers can be left at liberty on giving their parole not to leave the neutral territory without permission.
> Article 12: In the absence of a special convention to the contrary, the neutral Power shall supply the interned with the food, clothing and relief required by humanity.
> At the conclusion of peace the expense caused by the internment shall be made good.
> All the war matériel as well as military personnel shall be held by the neutral Power. The latter is entitled to withhold the return of such matériel to its owners at the conclusion of peace until such time as the expenses agreed upon for the maintenance of the interned have been made good.

This means that the Republicans' arms would remain in the confiscation of France until the end of hostilities, when only one government would exist in Spain. That government could demand the return of the matériel, but France in turn could demand indemnification of the expenses incurred by the maintenance of the internees, and the matériel could therefore serve as security. Meanwhile, vehicles seized by French Customs would be returned to their owners.

It was now evident that the cause of the Front Populaire was utterly discredited. In *Le Midi Socialiste*, Hudelle began a painful reappraisal of the entire Socialist outlook in foreign affairs. Should France now fortify her southern frontier, he asked, or should France rather remind Franco that he owed his victory largely to French neutrality and cooperate in the reconstruction of Spain? Despite his misgivings, Hudelle spoke for many Socialists in siding with the latter alternative.[9] On the credit side, it was understood that France and Britain were in closer agreement than at any time since the Civil War began. Events seemed to vindicate Blum's suggestion of July 1938[10] that, while the French attitude to Franco was softening, the British was hardening.

Le Journal's London correspondent reported that even now Britain would reply to any attempt by Nationalist forces to interfere with British shipping in the remaining Republican ports.[11] The two democracies were unanimous in their desire for a Mediterranean open to the free commerce of the world, which would require certainly the agreement of Spain as well as that of Italy. But there were indications, as Maurice Pernot pointed out in *Luxembourg*, that Spain had decided to play the role of a great power, which raised the specter of a Mediterranean restricted to the riparian states and divided into zones of influence.[12] Besides this, as *Les Échos* observed, Franco was more and more impressed by the growing power of the Axis.[13] Buré discouraged the hope that Franco would now shuffle off the Axis coil. A 'leading supporter' of Franco, not identified, allegedly informed *L'Ordre* on 7 March that Mussolini had intervened to remove *personae Duci non gratae* from the lists of the new Spanish Embassy staffs in Paris and London, their sympathies with the democracies being an embarrassment to him.[14] *Les Échos* believed that it was Franco's confidence in an imminent Axis victory that led him to his present treatment of Pétain; for weeks the Marshal had been awaiting the Caudillo's pleasure in order to present his credentials, with a growing inclination, *Les Échos* said, to demand his recall by the French Government.[15] The coolness of his reception was due to French delay in handing over the fifteen Republican warships which had mutinied and sailed for Bizerta, where on 6 March they were interned by the French authorities. The SFIO continued to oppose the return of these warships which it considered entrusted to French care, but it was to no avail. It was agreed on 26 March that the vessels would be returned to Franco on 2 April. The French Government had already authorized Nationalist agents to seize Republican property in France.[16]* Such was the price, as the Socialist press put it, of Franco's consent to receive Pétain, despite the denials of the Quai d'Orsay. 'It is more than humiliation this time,' wrote *Le Midi Socialiste*, 'it is a crime.'[17]*

Amid the encircling gloom, the Assembly hearing in March 1939 into the conduct in Spain of the Communist Député André Marty provided the Right and Centre with a refreshing diversion, while the Socialists, who felt that the nation had division enough without widening the schism with a witch-hunt, downplayed the affair. Marty was accused of having blocked the liberation of certain French prisoners who had served in the International Brigades and whose release had been arranged under the auspices of the League of Nations.[18]* He had continued to hold them in prison in Barcelona, where they were sentenced without trial. In particular, he was charged personally with the murder of Captain Gaston Delassale, commander of the 12th Battalion ('La Marseillaise,' renamed 'Henri Barbusse'), who after an unsuccessful engagement at Lopera (Jaén) in late December 1936 was accused of spying for the Nationalists; he was put on trial in front of Joseph Putz, found guilty and shot.[19]* Marty was further charged with the murder of a number of Nationalist prisoners, including the hero of Teruel, Colonel Domingo Rey d'Harcourt, and the Bishop of Teruel, who were held as hostages and found murdered near the French frontier after their release had reportedly been negotiated by an intermediary.[20]* The hearings, which opened on 10 March, were highlighted by the following exchanges:

> Député Ybarnegaray: 'I am going to speak to you frankly, Monsieur Marty. You played a leading role in the International Brigades. On the frontier at Le Perthus, you were seen reviewing the Brigades returning to France. But certain members of these Brigades accuse you. If their evidence is true, you are guilty of murder.'
> Député Xavier Vallat: 'At the Socialist Congress, Monsieur Marx Dormoy has accused you of having ordered the murder of Frenchmen.'[21]*
> Député Marty: 'Those who accuse me are Fascist agents. They were sent in from outside to destroy the International Brigades. I have nothing but contempt for their evidence.'[22]

This was the only rebuttal that Marty attempted up to this point. The hearings were adjourned until 16 March, when Député Tixier-Vignancour led the prosecution. In reading the evidence brought against Marty by Reserve Captain Marcel Clerc, a socialist, Tixier-Vignancour was interrupted by Député Ramette:

> Député Tixier-Vignancour (to Député Ramette): 'You have already faced a jury that found you guilty of slandering Monsieur Kléber Legay. You would do better to hold your tongue.' (Varied animation.) 'Captain Clerc was treated by Marty in an arrogant manner. His documents were torn up. He was imprisoned for lack of respect towards Marty, and Spanish Socialists had great difficulty in setting him free.' (Animation.) 'It was Marty's habit to tear up documents, including those of Frenchmen who volunteered as workers, in spite of which they were sent to the front; if they showed the slightest resistance they were sent to the disciplinary companies, from which they did not return. . . . As for the money taken from the dead, and collected in Albacete, it found its way back to Paris where it helped in the recruitment of new volunteers.' (Prolonged animation.) 'There was in Albacete a court of justice to hear mostly civil cases, for combatants were tried generally by the Brigades themselves and their verdict was afterwards submitted to the approval of Marty.'

Tixier-Vignancour then cited individual cases of French combatants whose execution the Senator imputed to Marty. Significantly, the Socialist benches were as silent as the remainder of the Assembly when Marty rose to his defence.

The End of Hostilities

Député Marty: 'What has been said against me in respect to the International Brigades is false.' (Animation.) 'Those who have returned to France to bring these charges against me are nothing more than deserters from the Brigades and traitors to the Spanish Republic.' (Expressions of stupefaction from several benches.) 'Among thousands of international heroes, could there not have been some deserters and traitors?[23*] Isn't the German Gestapo quite capable of having placed its agents in the International Brigades?' (Uproar.) 'Every language was spoken in the Brigades except Russian.' (Howls of derision.) 'It has been said that I sentenced hostages to the Karl Marx Prison in Barcelona. The name of Karl Marx has never been given to a prison.'

Karl Marx was in fact the name of the Barcelona barracks. Such nit-picking was Marty's best and only line of defence. The Assembly waited patiently:

Député Marty: 'If the hostages who were to be freed have not returned, it is unquestionably on Franco's side that they have been executed.' (Uproar.) 'Major Delassale was really a captain, but he did in fact command a battalion. It was the general in command of the army[24*] who discharged him at the front for treason, but the fact that he was a member of the Deuxième Bureau during the Great War was quite unknown at the time; if it had been known, he would not have been enlisted in Spain, at least not before he had been tested. He was taken before the military tribunal of the sector and allowed due process of law, not in accordance with the military code of Primo de Rivera but in accordance with the improved code of the Spanish Republic.' (Varied animation.) 'The Spanish judges did not uphold the charge that he had communicated with the enemy. They nonetheless sentenced him to death, and the general signed the death warrant. At this trial I was neither prosecutor nor witness.' (Prolonged applause from the Communist benches, joined this time by a section of the Socialists; additional applause from various other benches.)

Marty next undertook his defence on the subject of the Nationalist prisoners held as hostages:

Député Marty: 'I have never been mixed up in any negotiation concerning hostages. All I have done is sometimes to report some special cases. I have never had any dealings with the French Ambassador Monsieur Jules Henry. It is impossible that the Bishop of Teruel and his companions could have been executed by Spanish officials. The murders can only be the work of *agents provocateurs*.' (Uproar.)

Finally, Marty complained that the 'calumny' leveled against him, though it left him unmoved, had dealt cruelly with his father and mother. 'Clown!' cried out a voice from the Right.[25]

In summing up for the prosecution, Député Colomb probed the mind of the Communist member.

> Député Colomb: 'What he has done has been to obey the orders of the Communist Party and of the Third International, and the directives of Lenin and his successors.' (Interruptions from the extreme Left, varied animation.) 'In carrying out these orders and directives, there is blood everywhere.'

At this point a massive broadside of invectives was loosed at Député Colomb by the Communist members. 'Swine!' and 'Pig!' were the commonest epithets, though not the strongest, and Député Ramette's choice of 'You poor imbecile!' was moderate in contrast. Député Colomb continued his exploration of Député Marty's mind with a reference to the latter's touted anti-militarist record.

> Député Colomb: 'In order to save him from the sentence of death by court martial, his attorney revealed to the court 'a certain intellectual dimness' in his client.' (Bedlam, continued in the corridors outside.)[26]

The debate was adjourned *sine die*. Marty had put up a respectable—or recalcitrant—fight before the Assembly, though it wavered at times and he could not find the courage to answer the point-blank question: 'Monsieur Marty, are you or are you not a killer?' At the bar of history, however, he stands convicted by overwhelming evidence,[27*] and his final reward was to find himself expelled from the party he had served with blind devotion.[28*]

On 28 March 1939, Nationalist forces finally entered Madrid. After cabling President Lebrun to request that all Republicans who so wished be permitted to land in France, Casado left Gandía on 29 March in a British vessel bound for Marseilles. On the morrow of Franco's victory, *La Dépêche* gave its last word on the war: 'A MAN WHO HOPES TO BE A LEADER must show the world that HE DESERVES to be treated as such, by proclaiming now: FULL AND TOTAL AMNESTY FOR ALL SPANIARDS. THE DOOR IS OPEN, SPAIN IS HOME TO ALL.'[29*] But as the Toulouse daily observed the very next day, Franco would now refuse to acknowledge any obligation; if he chose to invite the Italian forces to remain, there was none now to gainsay it, and he would even seek a basis in law for his attitude by claiming that the entire non-intervention system was henceforth invalid. *La Dépêche* marked the occasion by publishing the address by Serrano Suñer, who as Franco's next Foreign Minister was to place Spain unequivocally in the Axis camp:

> Every Spaniard—at least every Spaniard of the better Spain—knows that the

responsibility for the blood spilt does not devolve upon the Spanish Reds alone, for they were merely stupid and docile tools. Those who talk so much about 'invasion forces' have been instruments of the implacable offensive unleashed by certain nations to ensure their economic and political hegemony in the world.

At the same time that we affirm our will, we affirm our unbreakable loyalty to those who have stayed with us faithfully since the first uncertain hours. And with these two asseverations, if other states have a sincere desire for international collaboration we shall contribute to peace in Europe.[30]

In France, the ending of the war came in no blaze of glory, even for partisans of the victors. The Nazi occupation of Bohemia and Moravia in mid-March, followed immediately by Lithuania's fear-crazed cession of Memel, gave the French Right cares enough.[31]* In all the obituaries written to commemorate the end of resistance in Spain, none was more significant than *L'Aube*'s Catholic appraisal of the Christian Crusade:

It has taken two and a half years of terrifying war to achieve the capture of Madrid, announced with pride and pomp ever since the autumn of 1936. At the close of this long trial, an exhausted Spain is overlain with ruins and the only thing that has grown in the conflict has been hate.

The victory of General Franco leaves Spain more divided than she was under the bad government of the Frente Popular. Not only weaker, not only more infiltrated by foreign influences but—we repeat—more divided and more vulnerable to convulsion in the future.[32]

Conclusion

The doctrine of non-intervention, to be a legitimate principle of morality, must be accepted by all governments. The despots must consent to be bound by it as well as the free States. Unless they do, the profession of it by free countries comes but to this miserable issue—that the wrong side may help the wrong, but the right must not help the right. Intervention to enforce non-intervention is always rightful, always moral, if not always prudent.'

JOHN STUART MILL
Essay on Liberty (1859)

'C'est un mot métaphysique et politique qui signifie à peu près la même chose qu'intervention.'

TALLEYRAND (1830)

It was pointed out in the Preface and the Introduction that the decisive moment in the Spanish Civil War came in the first month of hostilities, in the decision of the Blum Cabinet to deny the Spanish Republic its right to regular commercial intercourse with France, and, even more importantly, in December 1936, when the democracies sat hypnotized in the sessions of the London Committee before the contemptuous antics of Ribbentrop and Grandi. The Front Populaire leaders, in their defeat, could not with sincerity censure the Daladier government for continuing a policy of their own making. Daladier at Munich was in fact following the policy of Chautemps in the Anschluss, and he in turn was continuing that of Blum, with the Radicals' approval, over Spain. That policy—the policy of *éviter l'aventure*—was a triple failure: the Front Populaire failed to provide its sister government with the matériel it sorely needed; it failed to prevent the Fascist states from supplying arms to the rebels; and finally, by allowing a thin trickle of French and foreign arms to permeate the frontier—though the responsibility of France as a neutral was not engaged thereby under the terms of the Hague Convention[1*]—in the ambiguous situation of the time she forfeited her own integrity as a neutral. For although French aid to the Republic remained negligible,[2*] it was sufficient to 'justify' Axis intervention.

On the other hand, Blum was faced with enormous difficulties both at home and abroad. On the domestic scene, even with the support of the Communists and the rest of the Left, the SFIO could not remain in power without the backing of the Radical-Socialists and even the Radicals, most of whom agreed with the Conservatives in the arguments for non-intervention. Moreover, the

Socialists were anxious to strengthen these relations with the Radical-Socialists and the Radicals, even at the expense of the Communists, who were, after all, the guests of the Front Populaire. If it had ever come to a choice, Blum would not have hesitated to abandon them for the friendship of these centre forces, to bring about revolution within the law by means of the *politique du juste*. And for the Radicals, the 'radical' question, on the very eve of the insurrection in Spain, concerned their collaboration with the Communists. This question, asked each morning by journalists of the Right, was repeated in the Radical-Socialist organ *La République*. Marcel Déat, who still held an important post in the Front Populaire, wrote in *L'Europe Nouvelle*: 'If one half of France turns into Stalin's foot-soldier, the other half of France won't want anything to do with it.'[3] Equally alarming to the Radicals was the call in Bergery's *La Flèche de Paris*, at the beginning of July 1936, for a 'second' revolution.[4] The result was a new alignment of the Radicals: on the same day that the 'super-Radical' Bergery raised his standard, and only weeks before Spain erupted, Roche, Dominique and Frot joined battle with the Communist Party.

The question must be asked why the growing threat from Germany did not alert France to the need for unity. On his return to power in March 1938, Blum proposed to President Lebrun the creation of a government of 'Rassemblement National,' which would transcend the Front Populaire to include all forces ranging from the Communists to the moderate Conservatives, 'from Thorez to Reynaud.' The Communists and the Radicals were in agreement with the proposal. Thorez had himself advocated, in July 1936, the enlargement of the Front Populaire into a 'Front Français,' a suggestion which Blum had denounced as an appeal to nationalist feeling and destructive to the Front Populaire. The Radicals, for their part, would have accepted a national union in the knowledge that the Communists would thereby be submerged in the whole. Blum's project failed, however, for two reasons. On the one hand, Reynaud wanted the union to extend as far as the Conservative bloc of Louis Marin, for fear that his moderates would otherwise be held hostage for the Right. On the other hand, Blum was under pressure within his own party from Pivert's 'Revolutionary Left' not to compromise the program of the Front Populaire but rather to form a 'Front Populaire de Combat,' and it was in deference to Pivert that Blum allowed his SFIO members to bring down the Chautemps government. It was, therefore, a more modest Union Nationale that Blum inaugurated in March 1938. Its purpose was above all to oppose Fascism, the very principle upon which the Front Populaire was founded. The initiative, however, met with the almost unanimous opposition of the Right, headed by Flandin in the Chamber and Cailloux in the Senate. Thus, to the cry of '*Plutôt le fascisme que le socialisme*,' ended the last and best hope of creating an effective counterweight to the triumphant forces of Fascism, and, from this point on, Munich—and the débâcle in Catalonia—were inevitable.

This domestic stalemate consequently aggravated the situation of France in foreign affairs. The sorry disarray in the French system of alliances, though partly the fault of Chautemps, predated even the formation of the Front Populaire. Prior to 1936, the League of Nations had already failed over Manchuria and Abyssinia. The absence of a French response to the remilitarization of the Rhineland in 1936 led in April 1937 to Belgium's declaration of neutrality. The subsequent failure of France to respond by extending the Maginot Line west of the Ardennes encouraged the dissolution of the Petite-Entente and a new spirit in Poland of collaboration with Germany. The non-military pact between France and the Soviet Union was made even more tenuous by the damage done to the Russian General Staff by Stalin's purges of 1937. The United States had endorsed her Neutrality Act of May 1935 with further declarations in 1936 and 1937 dissociating herself from any future involvement in war in Europe. Great Britain, while bound to France under the Treaty of Locarno, had still not signed any military agreement with her, and it was common knowledge that Britain was at a stage of rearmament little more advanced than that of France. French rearmament, for its part, was dependent upon an industrial production that in 1938 stood below the level in 1913, making it so woefully inadequate[5*] that it made nonsense of French pretensions to guarantee the integrity of Czech and Polish territory.

In the case of the Spanish Republic, however, France was bound by no such treaty, but the government of the Front Populaire felt an even greater moral responsibility to go to the aid of a kindred régime. Bereft of any support from any other democracy, what last throw might Blum have tried? In the light of the balance of power, it must be considered that if France had decided to arm the Republic, the result would have been an arms-supply race between France and the Fascist states which France would have lost. To preclude that, it was in the French interest to prevent all provision to both camps. The failure of non-intervention stemmed of course from the failure of the London Committee to control maritime traffic.[6*] Could any other policy have succeeded? None surely except the most radical, involving a certain renunciation of national sovereignty. The French Government might have begun by sealing hermetically her Pyrenean border and inviting observers from the Fascist states to see for themselves the evidence of French good faith. France might then have proceeded at once to a demand for an equally rigorous adherence to non-intervention on the part of the Axis states. To achieve that would have required political will of the highest order. To place British and French warships in the international waters right outside the Nationalist-held ports, challenging the Italian and German troop and supply ships, would indeed be going to the brink, but that was the only strategy that had any real chance of success.

Such a strategy would have disturbed, of course, the policy of *éviter l'aventure*. If the Front Populaire was founded on the principle of resistance to

Fascism, it must not be forgotten that the SFIO was founded on the principle of pacifism. The difficulty lay in deciding where pacifism ended and appeasement began, when the pacifist is often at a loss to explain to himself the existence of evil in the world. Pacifists in France and Britain looked to the Great War as the war that ended wars. In France, the pacifist spirit of Geneva and the conciliatory spirit of Locarno expressed themselves in the cry of Briand: *'Plus jamais la guerre!'* There was no such thing as a just war, proclaimed the SFIO. In England, the desire for peace found its most misleading expression in the motion before the Oxford Union of 1933: 'This House will never again fight for King and Country,' and the motion was carried. Yet it was precisely these idealists, scorning patriotism and war between nations, who were the first to rally to the humanitarian ideal and to enlist in the service of the Spanish Republic. To such as these, the conflict in Spain represented the first international war of political ideologies; the issues were clear, the conflict 'clean,' and the war offered a welcome outlet to all who were weary of the cynicism of the Thirties and who sought freedom in the reality of the struggle. Pierre Mille pointed out in *La Dépêche* that the Spanish conflict marked a return from 'political' war to holy war and attributed it to the participation of women. But Suzanne Lacore, for one, in a speech given in Toulouse on 18 October 1936, suggested a different ideal both for women and Socialism: 'Every bourgeois government has spoken to you of nothing but hatred, war and death. We ourselves want to speak of life, joy and hope.'[7*]

If such elements as these aligned themselves with the cause of involving the democracies in Spain, and if the Left in general was pushing the government to take a stand, they faced the fundamental division in French society. The traditional roles, between 1933 and 1938, had simply been inverted: it was now the Right that was pushing toward pacifism. In the centre, the foreign policy of the Third Republic's ever dominant Party, the Parti Radical, combined in effect the traditional pacifism of the Left with the neo-pacifism of the Right. This policy was sustained by a very large fraction of public opinion that, being given over to apathy and appeasement, preferred to let things take their course.

There was thus a general readiness to underestimate the character of the Italian and German dictatorships, and a general reluctance to be involved. In his first public address after the capitulation of France in June 1940, Marshal Pétain remarked that responsibility for the attitude of *primum vivere* was not to be imputed to any single section of the press or public opinion. The fault was general: *'On a revendiqué plus qu'on n'a servi.'* Certainly, of the four major ideologies involved in the Spanish conflict, bourgeois democracy was by far the least dynamic. Indeed, we have seen that the apathy of the democracies was made the pretext for its suppression by the forces of Fascism.[8*] Charles Maurras applied his considerable weight to refuting the contention of Lincoln that democracy has the right to vote itself out[9*]—or, as Maurras called it, 'to commit suicide at its pleasure'—if its vote was for revolution. To Churchill's warning that security was threatened by the class struggle, Gaston Guèze replied that the class struggle was one of the fruits of democracy.[10] Bernard de Jouvenel announced baldly in *L'Emancipation Nationale* that Franco was entitled to power by the right of the strongest:

> 'The right of the strongest? For shame!' cry out our moralists. These worthy gentlemen quite forget what is the essence of a government—namely, a group of men who command and whose word is law ... Men who lack such authority may be admirable on the spiritual level, but on the political level they are negligible.[11]

The right wing's presentation was not only Machiavellian but Manicchean. The conflict was portrayed as a struggle to the death between Euro-Christian civilization and barbarism, between Asiatic Bolshevism and the Latin West. The Marquis de Palaminy described Spain as a tiltyard between materialism and the spirit.[12] The Civil War was 'sought, prepared and financed by Moscow'[13] or by 'international Zionism.'[14] Ridiculing the 'pseudo-threat of Fascism,'[15] the right wing could proceed to present the Army as the only solid base on which authority in Spain could rest.[16] The French historians Bodin and Touchard insist that the press clearly contributed to the failure of the Front Populaire: 'the right-wing press by the violence of its attacks, ... the left-wing press by its incapacity to arouse public opinion in support of Léon Blum.'[17]

The French press law of 29 July 1881, states in its Article 1: 'The press and publishing shall be free.' In 1936, however, responsible opinion in France was concerned by the increasing partisanship of the press. On 4 February of that year, President Lebrun, speaking at a Republican journalists convention, warned of the danger of abusing that freedom by the deliberate dissemination of false news, and on 8 February 1937 he again warned that the integrity of the press was threatened by the pursuit of selfish interest, passion and hatred.[18*] At the same time, Daladier denounced the unhealthy system of *arrosage*, under which no less than four-fifths of all French journals were subsidized for political ends.

It goes without saying that such extremist journals as *L'Humanité* and *L'Action Française*, in their reportage, indulged in the wildest fancies, publishing the news stories that their readers yearned to read and giving full vent to what Montaigne called '*l'art piperesse*' of their rhetoric. Even among the big information-dailies, very few strove to maintain a balance between the reports which reached them from the two camps in conflict.[19*] They believed that they were demonstrating their impartiality by granting equal space to the dispatches of their correspondents on each side of the barricade. Their policy

Conclusion

was doubtless motivated by the desire not to lose either their pro-Republican or their pro-Nationalist readers; but such a compromise could not have satisfied either group. Certain journals, such as *Le Journal* and *Le Matin*, did not burden themselves with anxiety over the loss of any pro-Republican readers. When it became clear that the insurrection could not be suppressed by the Republic in a matter of days, they joined *L'Action Française, Le Jour, L'Écho de Paris* and the rest of the right-wing press in openly demonstrating their sympathy with the rebels. The conflict within *L'Écho de Paris*, however, ran an opposite course, as we have seen,[20] to that within *Le Petit Parisien*. After opening his celebrated subscription fund to offer a sword of honour to a Spanish rebel general,[21] the impulsive Henri de Kérillis followed his editor-in-chief Simond in resigning from the paper, taking with them Henry Bordeaux, the Tharaud brothers and most of the staff to form the free-wheeling *L'Époque*. While Bailby incorporated *L'Écho* into his *Le Jour*, Kérillis drew ever closer to the sceptic Radical Emile Buré, and when in 1938 the day came for the French Right to stand up and be counted, Kérillis and Pertinax, with Buré, led whatever opposition there was, in the press of the Right and Centre, to that spirit of eager collaboration known in 1936 as *'coblenzard'* and now as *'munichois.'*[22*]

What was the principal cause of right-wing opposition to war in 1938? Was it a sign of a high level of civilization? Or was it the classical phenomenon that accompanies all decline, a loss of faith in the values and vitality of a society? Thierry Maulnier, a disciple of Maurras and the theoretician of the monarcho-fascist movement, explained it in these words: '[The reactionary parties] had the impression that, in the event of war, not only would the disaster be immense, not only were the defeat and devastation of France possible, but the reverse might be no better: a defeat of Germany would entail the collapse of the authoritarian system that constituted the principal rampart against the communist revolution, and perhaps the immediate bolshevization of Europe.'[23] In other words, a defeat of France would be a defeat of France; and a victory of France over Germany would be less a victory of France than the victory of principles that would lead straight to the ruin of France and of civilization itself. Charles Micaud, in his study of the Right in this period, attributes this confusion of the twin dangers—the immediate and the problematic—to the following factors: the Right put no trust in what they considered the Machiavellian policies of Moscow; they were very much aware of the class struggle—one voter in seven had voted communist in the last elections, and one in five, socialist; and they tended more toward conjecture than to pragmatic reasoning.[24]

The Socialist press was left to reflect on Blum's agony of frustration at being denied, after December 1936, any real room in which to manoeuvre. Once Italy had thrown in its fortunes with Germany, the logical response of France would have been to align itself with the Soviet Union. Fascism would then have faced the coalition it feared and hated: the union of communism and the democracies. A conservative government that defined its primordial duties in terms of the national interest could have brought the French people to accept, with reassuring conditions, a Russian alliance and a strengthening of the pact of mutual assistance. But a government of the Front Populaire could not hope to do so. Micaud writes: 'Divided France did not come across as sufficiently conservative or sufficiently revolutionary to face up to a situation that required not only military power but a strong dose of optimism and self-confidence. Victory might not only leave unresolved the problem of French security in the future, it might also raise fearful social problems that the Right neither wanted to resolve nor was able to resolve.[25] Under the Daladier régime, Blum could only express in his newspaper his bitter regret over the wasted opportunities of the democracies which, had they acted in concert in a common interest, might have written another story. No society, he would say, can remain neutral between those who live to defend it and those who live to destroy it. Too many those, placed in the middle of the road, who argued that extremes have their virtues, and that moderation requires an absence of passion, of conviction, or of social interest. Too few those who thought with passion that truth often lies somewhere near the centre; that extremist tactics are rarely the route to take in order to succeed; that a democratic society that grows accustomed to seeing things achieved by extremist methods quickly loses the concept of a democracy. Too many those whose centrist policies placed them in a simply neutral position, in neutral gear as it were. Too few those whose centrist position was positive and dynamic in itself, who could see through false slogans and expose them for what they were.

The art of lying, in which Anarchism is temperamentally unsuited, attained new levels of perfection in the care of Fascism and Communism. There was, however, a certain basic difference in their respective approaches, and it could be seen in their organs of the press. The Marxist lie was in the nature of an inversion, and was not, in the mind of the Marxist, a lie. If he preached that freedom was slavery, it was the logical conclusion of a doctrine that saw nothing honest in the pretensions of bourgeois democracy. The Fascist lie was quite different: it knew what it was concealing; it was both obscurantist and aware of being so. Though both ideologies were inflexible in their denial of dialogue, their propaganda revealed a further difference. Marxism showed itself as a gospel of perverted love, whose goal was, despite everything, some kind of peace. Fascism showed itself to need war as its natural food. It was driven by a form of Romanticism that perverted the concept of death as inspiration into a longing for death and a hatred of life; the Nazi's natural hatred was ultimately directed at himself.

One can generally rely on intellectuals to provide a small minority on whom the pursuit of power and extremist ideas exert a fascination. This was a time

Conclusion

when their number was increasing. It was against this danger that Julien Benda in 1927 published *La Trahison des clercs*. The treason which Benda portrayed did not consist of the disloyalty of intellectuals to their nations, but the fact that they had ceased to think independently and individually and had abandoned detachment for political passion. Benda's aim was directed mainly at those intellectuals who, in their reaction to war and Fascism, and in their dream of influence and the advance of justice, had turned herd-like to Marxism as the hope of the future. Benda then went further, and fell headlong into an imbroglio of his own. In his eyes, the defeat of the Spanish rebels, a fortiori the defeat of Nazi Germany, would mean the victory of the working class and of the Soviet Union. Such a victory must be opposed, whatever the price for the national security of France.[26] Benda thus provided the best example of the confusion in the mind of the majority between the immediate danger and the hypothetical danger facing France and democracy in general. Benda had it backward.

Where Benda was right was in seeing in 1936 that the centrifugal movement toward the two poles had intensified. The Irish poet Yeats had glimpsed the final nightmare into which the world was sliding:

> Things fall apart; the centre cannot hold; . . .
> The best lack all conviction, while the worst
> Are full of passionate intensity.[27]

Thomas Mann, who had his own personal experience whereof he spoke, sketched his *Achtung Europa!* in two exclusive articles for *La Dépêche*.[28*] Mann warned against the 'falsehood studiously organized by the dictatorships and the submergence of the individual in the mass, with its consequences for civilisation.' To safeguard human dignity, Mann, like Malraux, advocated greater personal involvement. 'In every humanism,' he wrote, 'there is an element of weakness engendered . . . by its predilection for the doubt . . . What we need at the present time is a militant humanism.' Jacques Maritain wrote in the same vein for the *Nouvelle Revue Française*: 'What is needed for peace in the world is not the opposition of one ideology to another but the operation of concrete intelligence, allowing the nations and historic forces that exist to support one another mutually along the path of time.'[29]

The operation of concrete intelligence was certainly not helped by the mood of easy optimism. Émile Vandervelde, the Belgian Socialist leader, wrote in *La Dépêche* in the spring of 1937:

> I have said it on several occasions, I have written it in this very column, ever since the third day: such coups, when they do not succeed at once, do not succeed ever. I hold this firm conviction that they shall not pass![30*]

More realistically, Blum's editor Bracke preferred to concentrate on the supreme question of legitimacy: 'Neither victory nor defeat alters in any way the quality of Burgos and Madrid.'[31] Certainly the Right in Spain could claim that in 1936 it had done no more than emulate the Left when in 1934 it reacted to its own electoral defeat by staging the 'October revolution' and the Asturias uprising. Nothing, however, gainsays the fact that the elections of 1936, conducted by a centrist government, were reasonably fair and honest, and that the insurgent generals had sworn an oath of allegiance to the Republic.

On the international level, the moderate press insisted, *La Dépêche* in particular, that a Nationalist victory would launch Europe on adventure, while a Republican victory would allow the democracies to exorcise the spirit of war.[32] This was the crux of the matter. With the Front Populaire discredited and the Chamberlain government eager for any peace in Spain which would put an end to the Axis presence there, the true forces of democracy—the forces of militant humanism—were demoralized by failure and retreat. A Republican victory would undoubtedly have had a galvanizing effect throughout Europe upon the anti-Fascist cause. As it was, the defeat of the Republic brought Britain and France closer together, but at a point in time too late to prevent the onward march of war, for the solidarity between Hitler and Mussolini, in its turn, had been welded in the conflict, and this conflict was now concluded to the satisfaction of Hitler's timetable of war. Six months later, almost to the day, Hitler decided that the time had come. The role of Spain in the general war that followed has at last been carefully examined, by the present author among several. That Second World War, however, was in Churchill's simple phrase 'avoidable.'[33]* If the ending of Republican resistance in Spain convinced the last optimist that European war was imminent, no doubt it evoked memories of Blum's cry for unity against the growing Fascist danger, as when the SFIO press warned at the close of 1936: 'UNLESS THE DEMOCRACIES FORM A BLOC, HOW LONG DO YOU GIVE THEM?'[34] No doubt either that it brought back memories of hopes shattered and chances lost, as when at Nyon the democracies had acted in concert and with conviction, not setting themselves against the duty that befell them to stand up boldly to defend the right, even though their doing so seemed fraught with risk.

The world has moved on, and hatred fades in time. What lives forever are the memories lodged in the heart. Albert Camus later observed that the Republicans carried their sacrifice and defeat 'like an evil wound.' And understandably so. 'It was in Spain,' wrote Camus, 'that men learnt that one can be right and yet be beaten, that force can vanquish spirit, that there are times when courage finds no reward. It is this without a doubt that explains why so many men, the world over, regard the Spanish drama as a personal tragedy.'

Epilogue

The Fate of the Journals and the Journalists

Loss and gain alike lay in varied store for those who had been the principal contributors to the press of the French Third Republic. Both the far Left and the far Right were to undergo an agony of conscience: the former as a result of the Stalin-Hitler alliance, the latter in the call to patriotism after the worst defeat for France in all its two thousand years.

With the collapse of France in June 1940, *L'Aube, Les Échos, L'Époque, Excelsior, L'Intransigeant, L'Ordre, Le Petit Bleu,* and *Le Populaire* were among those that scuttled or were soon suppressed. When *Le Populaire* closed, its staff went in opposite directions. Jean Clavaud launched *Le Populaire du Centre,* and when Vichy banned it, Clavaud saved his workers by launching a new daily, *L'Appel du Centre,* in support of Vichy. Even so, some staff members were able from May 1942 to produce an underground edition of the same paper. Meanwhile, *Le Populaire*'s pre-war junior partner, *Le Midi Socialiste,* became ultra-collaborationist.

Le Petit Parisien, Le Petit Journal, Le Jour, Journal des Débats, Paris-Soir, Le Journal, Le Temps, Le Figaro, and *L'Action Française,* all set themselves up in the Free Zone of Vichy: the first four of them in Clermont-Ferrand, the last five directly or indirectly in Lyon, the new capital of the press. *La Croix* moved to Limoges. *Le Matin,* which had withdrawn to Angers, was the first to return to Paris, its owner Bunau-Varilla offering his services to the German authorities from day one of the Occupation. The decision of *Le Matin* to return to Paris was followed by *Le Petit Parisien.* With Operation *Torch* in November 1942, *Le Temps and Le Figaro* scuttled.

L'Oeuvre, now under the control of Marcel Déat, took a new turn to the right, thereby losing Jean Piot (editor in chief) and André Guérin (political editor).

The case of *L'Humanité* was unique. With the signing of the Molotov–Ribbentrop Pact on 23 August 1939, the French government had quickly suppressed it, but it continued to appear as an underground paper. With the French surrender and the German occupation, the editors of the PCF's central organ took advantage of the Pact to ask the German authorities to allow the newspaper to reappear, and the request was granted. It thus appeared freely in the first months of the Occupation. It later appeared, like *Le Populaire,* as an underground journal. With the Liberation, the PCF broke into libraries in order to destroy copies of *L'Humanité clandestine* and replace them with counterfeit issues; to counter this, the Bibliothèque Nationale proceeded to separate the authentic from the false, presenting the two versions in bound volumes for the public to view in the foyer.

At the opposite ideological extreme, the team of *L'Europe Nouvelle*, headed by Doriot and Déat, rushed into collaboration with the Nazis, but the temperamental difference between the metal worker Doriot and the academician Déat proved a more difficult collaboration.

La Dépêche, as the leading French journal of the Southwest and a prime observer of the war in Spain, requires a special attention. Its immediate reaction to the Armistice was to rally to Pétain, reopening on 23 June 1940. At the same time, several of its contributors and staff members suffered directly from the French defeat. That defeat had a special significance for the German and Italian antifascists who had taken up exile in France. Even if both of these exile groups had launched their own journals in Paris,[1*] some of the most renowned exiles wrote exclusively for *La Dépêche*, including the Italian historian Guglielmo Ferrero and the Germans Thomas and Heinrich Mann. Articles by the Mann brothers, and those by Pierre Mille, had so enraged Hitler in person that for several months during the war in Spain *La Dépêche* had been banned in Germany.[2] Heinrich Mann now had to escape across the Pyrenees to Spain; from there in 1940 he reached New York. Among the French contributors to the Toulouse daily, Albert Sarraut, Yvon Delbos and François de Tessan were deported to Germany; de Tessan, together with Georges Brousse (editor in chief of *L'Indépendant* in Perpignan) did not return from their captivity. As for the editorial team, Paul Bourniquel was killed in action in the Battle of France, and Armand Salvan was taken prisoner. Maurice Sarraut, the editor in chief, was to end his life murdered by the Milice.

A special place belongs in this Epilogue to those who contributed most to covering the war in Spain. Arrest warrants were issued, on 10 July 1940, against Émile Buré, Henri de Kérillis, Pertinax, and Geneviève Tabouis, but all four, together with Pierre Lazareff, had by then left the country. All four reached New York, where Kérillis and Tabouis co-founded the Gaullist monthly *Pour la Victoire*, which ran for 35 issues from 12 January 1942 to 25 August 1945.

=== ❖ ===

In examining the fate of the journalists individually, the logical end to the study is the Liberation, when those who had made their choice, in their individual definition of what patriotism meant, and what ultimate values meant, either won a place in the pantheon of heroes or met a traitor's end, or . . . . (no less important to history) found a way to play both sides of the street and emerge, at the end of the day, smudged, sullied, but alive.[3*]

The curious phenomenon of the Liberation was that the 'public intellectuals' of the Vichy government, who included the journalists, found themselves in the dock faster than the Vichy leaders themselves. This reflected the thinking of de Gaulle in 1944. As he told Stalin in 1945, when the Vozhd asked the General how quickly he planned to shoot Thorez now that Stalin was sending him home, 'Je vais refaire la France avec tous les Français!' 'Tous les Français' did not include those who had 'prostituted their pen.' His purpose was to restore French prestige, and that concerned more than anything else the role of its writers. The world must not look on France as if its *gens de lettres* had betrayed it. The guilty would be punished and glory go to those who, in the wake of the worst disaster in all French history, had not lost their way.

═ ❖ ═

The first point to note in this Glossary is the choice. The selection is based firstly, upon the importance of the individual writer to the press of the period 1936–1939, even when the writer was not primarily a journalist, and secondly, upon the significance of the writer's role in the period (pre-war and war) that followed. Persons such as Blum and Thorez are excluded because they are exclusively political figures. Equally excluded are men and women of letters such as Gide or Malraux who are not recognized as journalists. Excluded, too, are those journalists such as Pierre Mille who wrote on Spain but then disappeared from sight. Included, on the other hand, are journalists of modest renown, such as Jean-Maurice Herrmann, who still contributed much, and well, to the coverage of the war in Spain.

It will also be noted that the items in the Glossary are of varying length. This length is not based on the historical importance of the writer, but on the role the writer played in reaction to the Molotov–Ribbentrop Pact and in the war that followed. Hence, those such as Kérillis and La Rocque, whose roles were strangely nuanced, receive more coverage. Equally extended is the coverage of political leaders such as Marty and Maurras, due to their prominence in the press and the depth of their commitment to the war in Spain.

The logical close to events in such a Glossary comes with the purges (*Épuration*) that began in August 1944 with the Liberation.[4*]

═ ❖ ═

Bailby, Léon (1867–1964), *Le Jour—L'Écho de Paris*

After founding *Le Jour* in 1933 and *Le Jour-L'Echo de Paris* in March 1938, he abandoned this in 1939. Strongly pro-Mussolini, anti-Semitic, and anti-Masonic, he responded to the Armistice by supporting Vichy. In Nice in September 1940, he founded the weekly *L'Alerte*, but retired in 1942 and *L'Alerte* closed in 1943. The *Épuration* left him untouched.

Bardèche, Maurice (1907–1998), *L'Action Française*

Between 1936 and 1939 he had made several trips to Spain and co-authored with Brasillach their *Histoire de la guerre d'Espagne*. After June 1940, apart from a few articles on art for *Je Suis Partout*, he kept to literary work. At the Liberation, being close to his brother-in-law Brasillach, he was arrested, but while Brasillach was shot, Bardèche was quickly released.

Bardoux, Jacques (1874–1959), *Journal des Débats*, *Revue des Deux Mondes*

Under the Occupation, though appointed to Vichy's Conseil National, he remained an anglophile, escaping the *Épuration*.

Basch, Victor (1863–1944), *L'Oeuvre*

Born in Hungary and naturalized French in 1887, Basch was a co-founder in 1898 of the Ligue des Droits de l'Homme. As a professor of German at the Sorbonne, and editor at the Presses Universitaires de France, he was forced in 1941, being Jewish, to vacate his posts. On 10 January 1944, the Milice in Lyon under Paul Touvier broke into his home; his body, and that of his wife Ilona, were found outside the city, shot in the neck.

Bayet, Albert (1880–1961), *L'Oeuvre*

A professor of philosophy at the Sorbonne, he held the title, during the Occupation, of president of the underground press. With the Liberation he was made president of the Fédération Nationale de la Presse.

Belin, René (1898–1977), *Le Peuple*

As a leader of the Socialist CGT, he headed the minority group under Paul Faure that supported the Munich Agreement, adopting an anti-communist and anti-Soviet position. Rallying in 1940 to Pétain, he was appointed on 12 July to the post of Minister of Labour and (later) Industrial Production, with jurisdiction over Spanish immigrants. On 9 November 1940 Belin ordered the dissolution not only of the CGT but also of the Christian labour union, Confédération Française des Travailleurs Chrétiens (CFTC). At the Liberation he was brought to trial, but on 29 January 1949 he received an acquittal.

Benda, Julien (1867–1956), *La Dépêche*

The author of *La Trahison des clercs* (1927) and tireless opponent of *Action Française*, Benda responded to the Armistice by moving into seclusion, first in Carcassonne and then in Toulouse, living in a cloister or a maid's room. He thus spent the war writing: *La Grande Épreuve des démocraties,* that first came out in New York (Éditions de la Maison Française, 1942), and *La France byzantine* (Paris: Gallimard, 1945). While having taken no part in the Resistance, he showed, in the *Épuration*, no mercy to collaborators, and in the end, in his support of Stalin, Benda betrayed his own mission as guardian of truth and justice.

Béraud, Henri (1885–1958), *Gringoire*

His violently Anglophobic editorials, with their constant refrain ('Réduire l'Angleterre en esclavage'), had their natural place in *Gringoire*, 'the most anglophobe journal in the world,' until in 1943 the weekly's owner, Horace de Carbuccia, to Béraud's disgust, shifted his position. Arrested by the FFI in August 1944, in his elegant home on the Avenue de Wagram, he went on trial on 29 November and was sentenced to death for consorting with the enemy. The pardon he received from de Gaulle on 13 January 1945 came about from a request by King George VI. His sentence was commuted to 20 years at hard labour, then to 10 years' imprisonment on the Île de Ré. He was released for medical reasons in 1950.

Bergery, Gaston (1892–1974), *La Flèche de Paris*

Only six years after he had denounced fascism and advocated unity with the communists, this *député* of the Front Populaire rallied to Pétain, writing part of the Message to the French on 11 October 1940 in which the Maréchal proposed collaboration with Germany, and with Emmanuel Berl he launched the 'Appel aux travailleurs.' He subsequently served from April to June 1941 as Pétain's ambassador to Moscow, and from 1942 to 1944 as ambassador to Ankara. In 1949 he was arrested and put on trial, but won an acquittal.

Berl, Emmanuel (1892–1976), *La République*

On 17 June 1940, Berl, in Bordeaux, was invited to serve as speechwriter to Pétain, producing the speeches of 23 and 25 June that included the phrase: 'I hate the lies that have done you so much wrong.' After this brief stop in Vichy, he abandoned it for Cannes, then Argentat, where, in the company of André Malraux and Louis Bertrand, he devoted himself to history.

Bidault, Georges (1899–1983), *L'Aube*

An historian and co-founder of the Catholic *Aube*, he was taken prisoner of war in 1940 but freed in July 1941 as a veteran of 1914–1918. In Lyon he joined the Resistance network 'Combat' and in June 1943 he succeeded Jean Moulin as leader of the Conseil National de la Resistance (CNR). At the Liberation, he marched alongside de Gaulle on the Champs-Elysees, and like de Gaulle and Auriol, he sought to minimize the sentences and prison terms of the collaborators.

Bloch, Jean-Richard (1884–1947), *Ce Soir*

A thrice-wounded veteran of the First World War, and author of *Espagne! Espagne!* (1936), Bloch had joined Aragon in March 1937 in founding *Ce Soir*, and after Munich he joined the PCF. With the collapse of France he went underground, but in April 1941 he was able to reach the USSR where, from July 1941 to October 1944, he spoke as the Voice of France on Radio-Moscow. He has been called the poet of the Resistance. His daughter France Bloch, a Resistance heroine, was beheaded in Hamburg in 1943.

Bois, Élie-Joseph (dates unknown), *Le Petit Parisien*

As editor in chief of the biggest morning daily in Paris, Bois had sent two star reporters to the fronts in Spain: Andrée Viollis to the Republican side and André Salmon to the Nationalist. His response to the Armistice was to resign and to spend the war in exile in London.

Bonnard, Abel (1883–1968), *Le Figaro, La Garonne*

Originally a follower of Maurras, supporting his monarchism and anti-Germanism, Bonnard moved toward Doriot and fascism. Under Vichy he wrote editorials for *Je Suis Partout* and served, from April 1942 to 1944, as an anticlerical Minister of National Education and Youth. In 1944 he fled to Sigmaringen and from there to Spain, where Franco granted him asylum. On 4 July 1945 he was sentenced to death in absentia for collaboration with Germany, and hence automatically expelled from the Académie Française. In 1960 he returned to France to face retrial. He was given a sentence of banishment for ten years, with effect from 1945, and hence already purged. Dissatisfied with the verdict of guilty, he returned to Spain where he lived out the rest of his life.

Boris, Georges (1888–1960), *La Lumière*

A Jewish Radical-Socialist who had founded *La Lumière,* Boris served in the Ministry of Finance under Blum and opposed the Munich Agreement. Responding to the declaration of war by volunteering, at the age of 51, for military service, he served on the northern front as liaison officer with the British and was evacuated from Dunkirk on 28 May 1940. On 19 June he joined de Gaulle in London, and in 1941 was made responsible for liaison between the BBC and the Free French. It was his voice that carried the legendary code messages to the Resistance.

Botto, Georges (dates unknown), Agence Havas

A reporter for Agence Havas who is mostly remembered as the architect of the Guernica fabrication, Botto proved a willing collaborator after the French collapse, directing Radio-Journal in Paris to the end of the Occupation, when he left with the Germans for Sigmaringen.

Bourdet, Claude (1909–1996), *Temps Présent*

In Nice at the time of the Armistice, he quickly made contact with the British Intelligence Service, and in May 1941 he co-founded (with Georges Bidault) the underground *Combat*. Moving in July 1942 to Lyon, he merged in September 1943 with Albert Camus. In 1944 he was arrested by the Gestapo and deported to KL-Neuengamme, then KL-Sachsenhausen, finally KL-Buchenwald. He survived.

Brasillach, Robert (1909–1945), *L'Action Française, Je Suis Partout*

Brasillach responded to the Armistice in ecstasy, relaunching *Je Suis Partout* in 1941, but in 1943 he (like Béraud) broke with Carbuccia, abandoning that weekly (finding it now too extreme) to join *Révolution Nationale*, *La Gerbe* and *L'Écho de la France*. Among the very first after the Liberation to face trial, he was defended by Jacques Isorni, Pétain's counsel. No witnesses were called on either side. Chief among the accusations were his use of the bookshop Rive Gauche as a centre for Nazi propaganda, and his attendance in 1941 at the Nazi International Congress in Weimar. Beyond that, the prosecutor Reboul simply read out his articles, alternately anti-communist, anti-Semitic, and anti-British. In his summing-up, Maître Reboul presented it as the worst form of treason: 'A treason of pride against the Sorbonne and against this land of intellectual freedom. Talent carries responsibility.' No mercy was forthcoming from de Gaulle ('He prostituted his pen'). Brasillach was sentenced on 10 January 1945 and executed on 6 February, on the very anniversary of the 1934 riots he had inspired.

Brinon, Fernand Marquis de (1885–1947), *Journal des Débats, Le Matin*

As a contributor to *Le Matin* (in which he published in 1933 his first interview with Hitler, the first granted to a French journalist and for Brinon the first of six), the Marquis advocated rapprochement with Germany, founding in 1935 the Comité France-Allemagne. With the French defeat, Brinon moved fluently into collaboration, serving as the Vichy representative in the capital ('the French Ambassador to Paris'). In 1944 he was among the Vichy leaders to move to Sigmaringen where he presided over the 'Commission Gouvernentale,' or government in exile. In May 1945 he tried to fly to Spain before surrendering to US forces on the Austro-Swiss frontier. Brought to trial in France, charged with treason and espionage, he was sentenced to death on 6 March 1947 and executed on 15 April 1947 in the Fort de Châtillon.

Brisson, Pierre (1896–1964), *Le Figaro*

A former editor of *Le Figaro*, after the French collapse he took over its management but then closed the journal in November 1942 when the Germans invaded the south. The *Épuration* left him untouched.

Brosselette, Pierre (1903–1944), *Excelsior*

A member of the SFIO from 1929, he was originally a devotee of Briand's pacifism but changed his stance when he recognized fascism as a threat to peace. As foreign affairs editor for *Le Populaire* and a contributor to eight other journals, he denounced the Munich Agreement. In September 1939 he entered the Army and served as a captain. Rejecting the turn to Pétain, he joined Jean Cassou in the Resistance group *Musée de l'Homme*. In April 1942 he flew to London to meet de Gaulle. Between making 38 broadcasts on the BBC and working in liaison with the British SOE, he continued his Resistance activities in France until, on 3 February 1944, he was arrested by the Gestapo, tortured for 60 hours, attempted an escape, and died on 22 March.

Bunau-Varilla, Maurice (1856–1944), *Le Matin*

His journal *Le Matin* moved progressively in the 1930s in its sympathy toward Hitler, and after the French defeat it turned to collaboration. He died in Paris on 1 August 1944, on the eve of the Liberation, while *Le Matin* was still running (it closed on 17 August). His son and heir to *Le Matin*, Guy Bunau-Varilla, was sentenced on 3 January 1946 to imprisonment for life at hard labour.

Buré, Émile (1876–1952), *L'Ordre*

Almost alone on the political right and centre to oppose the Munich Agreement, Buré never wavered in his stand, closing publication of *L'Ordre* on 10 June 1940 and moving to New York where, with others, he launched *France Amérique*. On his death, Albert Bayet paid homage in *La Presse française* to the passing of a great French tradition that went back to Jean Jaurès and Clemenceau: 'the journal of opinion, albeit small in circulation, but one of the glories of our land.'

Cachin, Marcel (1869–1958), *L'Humanité*

A philosophy teacher in Bordeaux, Cachin became was one of the founders of the French Communist Party, serving as editor in chief of *L'Humanité* (1918–1958) and member of the Bureau Politique (1923–1958). As a member of the French Senate (1935–1940), he was forced to resign for his refusal to disavow the Molotov–Ribbentrop Pact. During the Occupation he lived underground, and after the Liberation and his reelection to the Assembly he became its dean, holding the title until his death.

Carbuccia, Horace de (1891–1975), *Gringoire*

Founder of the weekly *Gringoire* in 1928, he moved after the Armistice to the Zone Libre, supporting Pétain. With the Liberation he was sentenced in absentia to five years at hard labour. After ten years of hiding in Switzerland, he freely appeared in October 1945 before a military court which then dropped the charges against him.

Chamson, André (1900–1983), *Vendredi*
The founder of *Vendredi* (1935) and author of *Retour d'Espagne* (1937) took part in the Resistance under the name of Lauter. He edited an underground journal and joined the Maquis in Lot, where in 1944 he was made a battalion commander in the Malraux brigade.

Chaves Nogales, Manuel (1897–1944), *La Dépêche*
Born in Seville, Chaves was a Left Republican, militantly antifascist and antirevolutionary. In 1931 he became director of *Ahora*, supporting Manuel Azaña. In August 1936 he moved into exile in Paris, and in 1937 published *A Sangre y fuego: Héroes, bestias y martires de España* (Santiago de Chile: Ercilla, 1937) to portray the suffering on both sides of the war. In 1940 he reached London, where he directed the Atlantic Pacific Press Agency, wrote a regular column for the *Evening Standard*, collaborated with the BBC Overseas Broadcasts, and published *The Fall of France* (Montevideo: Claudio Garcia, 1941). He died in London, aged only 46.

Daudet, Léon (1867–1942), *L'Action Française*
Like his partner Maurras he welcomed Pétain's arrival in power, but the German occupation did not appeal to this resolutely Latin and viscerally anti-German patriot. He died in time to avoid sharing the fate of Maurras.

Déat, Marcel (1894–1955), *L'Oeuvre, L'Europe Nouvelle*
As founder of the far right Rassemblement National Populaire (RNP), he welcomed the Munich Agreement, writing a celebrated article in *L'Oeuvre* on 4 May 1939 entitled 'Mourir pour Dantzig?' and remaining throughout the Occupation the daily's political director. Allied to Laval and the Germans, contemptuous of Vichy's half-measures and in turn detested by Pétain, Déat moved to Paris in the hope of unifying the collaborationist movements in the Zone Nord into the spearhead of a national-socialist revolution in tune with the German and Italian. His 'collaborationistes de gauche,' however, failed to overcome the competition from Doriot. Under German pressure, Pétain installed him on 16 March 1944 as Minister of Labour and National Solidarity. In the flight to Sigmaringen in summer 1944, he kept his post in the 'government in exile.' When sentenced in April 1945 to death in absentia, he had already fled to Italy where, with a new name and as an overnight convert to Catholicism, he entered the convent of San Vito near Turin and there lived out the rest of his life.

Dominique, Pierre (1889–1973), *La République*

A doctor of medicine, he turned to politics, contributing to *L'Action Française* before becoming editor in chief of *La République*. Rallying to Pétain in June 1940, he became, on 18 December of that year, head of the press service in the Vichy Ministry of Information. A prolific historian, he was left untouched at the Liberation.

Doriot, Jacques (1898–1945), *L'Émancipation Nationale*

Formerly of the PCF, he deserted the Party no doubt because Stalin chose Thorez to lead it. Crossing the ideological street, he founded the PPF whose *Cri du Peuple* was to serve as its organ of xenophobia and anti-Semitism. After the French defeat, he reopened his weekly *L'Émancipation Nationale* in Marseilles and spoke out on Radio Paris in favour of collaboration. With Déat he founded the LVF, and in September 1941 he left for the eastern front in command of the first French contingent to fight for Hitler. After winning the Iron Cross in December 1943, he entered the Vichy government alongside Darnand and Déat, and in September 1944 he was granted a meeting with Hitler. After the 1944 exodus to Germany of Vichy's 'Commission Gouvernemental,' Doriot was near Memmingen on 22 February 1945 when the car in which he was travelling (in German uniform) was caught by a British fighter-plane. Doriot was machine-gunned to death.

Drieu La Rochelle, Pierre (1893–1945), *L'Émancipation Nationale*

This talented but unbalanced writer had emerged from a troubled childhood. From early thoughts of suicide he had moved into the life of a libertine. He then turned to politics, imagining a blend of Nietzsche and totalitarian government and seeing fascism as the only cure for the prevailing decadence of Europe. His marriage to the Jewess Colette Jéramec was soon ended. In 1936 he joined the PPF, writing editorials for its *Émancipation Nationale* before breaking with it in 1939. Under the Occupation, at the suggestion of the German Ambassador Otto Abetz, he became editor in chief of the *Nouvelle Revue Française* in which he pushed for a Fascist International. In 1943 he rejoined Doriot, writing for *La Gerbe,* but in his private diary he admitted, following El Alamein: 'Germany's screwed up, and so am I' (*'L'Allemagne est foutue, et moi aussi.'*) Then, in the same diary, he professed admiration for Stalin, and, in further self-contradiction, arranged with the help of Abetz for Colette, imprisoned in Drancy, to be released. With the Liberation he declined the suggestion of Malraux that he leave France by boat, proclaiming: 'Neither flight nor abnegation. We played, I lost. I call for death.' On 15 March 1945, at the height of the *Épuration*, Drieu was found gassed in a kitchen.

Duclos, Jacques (1896–1975), *L'Hamanité*

On 13 January 1939 Duclos was reelected vice-president of the Chambre des Députés, and as second in rank in the PCF he continued to make frequent visits to Spain. While too old to be called for military service, he responded to the Molotov–Ribbentrop Pact by leaving for Brussels on 10 October of that year. After attending a meeting with Belgian and Dutch communists under the aegis of Eugen Fried of the Comintern, Duclos stayed in Belgium until June 1940 when Stalin ordered him to join Thorez in Moscow. The order, however, arrived too late and he returned to Paris just after the Germans had occupied the city. In August Stalin gave him full control of the PCF in France. Under the aegis of the Hitler-Stalin Pact, he approached the German authorities with the request that *L'Humanité* be allowed to reopen. The Germans agreed, but Stalin did not. Instead, he drafted the tract known as the *Appel du 10 juillet*. Duclos remained in control of the Party in France until Thorez returned to Paris in November 1944. Throughout the Occupation, Duclos ('the Stakhanovite of letters') served as the prolific editor of the underground Communist press. In the *Épuration*, Duclos attacked any judge who showed moderation, demanding that justice show nothing but 'bottomless hatred' toward those who had 'betrayed France.'

García de la Barga, Andrés (1888–1975), *La Dépêche*

While editor in chief of *El Sol* (Madrid), he wrote for *La Dépêche* under the name of Corpus Barga. In 1939 he left Spain for Peru, and in 1944 he returned to France as an intellectual of the UNE, writing for the communist *El Patriota del Sud-Oeste*.

Gaxotte, Pierre (1895–1982), *Je Suis Partout*

Despite his virulent attacks on Blum, writing in *Candide* on 7 April 1938: 'Il est le mal, il est la mort,' Gaxotte was a nationalist who took more and more his distance from fascism. By January 1939 he had stopped writing editorials for *Je Suis Partout*. With the collapse of June 1940 he was neither for Vichy nor for collaboration, trying in vain to persuade his master Maurras to close down *Action Française*. In Clermont-Ferrand, Gaxotte continued to direct *Candide*, which was critical of Vichy. Told to change his tone or stop, he stopped, and was then hunted by the Gestapo. He fled to the country. The *Épuration* left him alone.

Gay, Francisque (1885–1963), *L'Aube*

Much influenced by the Christian Socialism of Marc Sangnier, Gay had founded *La Vie Catholique* in 1924, and then *L'Aube*, with Georges Bidault. With the Armistice, *L'Aube* closed shop. Gay moved quickly into the Resistance, working with Jean Moulin, Pierre Brossolette, and Estienne d'Orves to produce the underground reviews *La France Continue* and *Les Cahiers Politiques*. For this he was savagely attacked in *Au Pilori* and by Maurras in *Action Française*. On 23 March 1944, his bookshop Librairie Bloud & Gay was raided by the Gestapo. Gay escaped arrest and remained in hiding up to the Liberation, when he was elected honorary president of the new Fédération de la Presse Française and served on the Comité d'Épuration de l'Édition. He was later appointed Ambassador to Canada (1948–1949).

Henriot, Philippe (1889–1944), *Gringoire*

Henriot had opposed Hitler, but he gave strong support to the Munich Agreement. With the defeat of France he rallied to Pétain, and on Radio Paris, in *Gringoire* and in *Je Suis Partout* he made constant attacks on de Gaulle. After the German invasion of Russia, his anticommunism led him to support Germany and he joined the Milice. On 6 January 1944 he was appointed Secretary of State for Information and Propaganda, but on 28 June he was assassinated by a COMAC resistance team. The funeral was held in Nôtre Dame cathedral, in the presence of Emmanuel Cardinal Suhard, while in Bordeaux Archbishop Maurice Feltin contributed a eulogy.

Héricourt, Pierre (1895–1965), *L'Action Française*

A follower of Maurras, he published the pamphlet *Pourquoi Franco vaincra* (Paris: Baudinière, 1937). After the French collapse he became a fervent collaborator. In September 1940 he was appointed Director General of the Légion Française des Combattants, and in March 1943 Laval selected him to be Consul General in Barcelona. He escaped the *Épuration* by taking refuge and living out his life in Spain.

Hérold-Paquis, Jean (1912–1945), radio

A follower of Doriot, in Spain he had fought for Franco and been the voice of France, first on Radio Burgos and then, from April 1938 to March 1939, on Radio Saragossa. After June 1940, Vichy appointed him Delegate for Propaganda in Hautes-Alpes. From 4 January 1942 he broadcast daily on Radio Paris, copying from Cato and calling with brio: '*Britannia delenda est*!' Vichy, he insisted, was far too wishy-washy in its collaboration. With the Liberation he fled to Germany and then to Switzerland, but on 8 July 1945 he was handed over to the French and imprisoned in Fresnes, hitherto used for captured Resistants. At his trial the prosecution presented no witnesses: his recorded words sufficed. On 17 September 1945 he was sentenced to death for treason, and on 11 October he was executed in the Fort de Châtillon.

Herrmann, Jean-Maurice, *Le Midi Socialiste, Le Populaire*

A lead writer on Spain for *Le Populaire* and *Le Midi Socialiste,* Herrmann was in the infantry when, on 13 June 1940, he was severely wounded and taken prisoner. Released by the Germans in the autumn, he moved to the south, making contact with Pierre Bertaux, Jean Cassou and Georges Bidault and entering the France Combattante resistance network. He then entered the Brutus network, settling in Lyon and writing for *Le Populaire clandestin* and *L'Espoir.* Arrested in Paris by the Gestapo on 10 May 1943, he passed through Fresnes and Royallieu before being sent to KL-Neuengamme, then KL-Ravensbrück. From there he escaped and reached the Russians, who handed him over to the Americans. On 25 May 1945, he returned to Paris, close to death.

Jacob, Madeleine (1896–1985), *L'Oeuvre*

Although well established as a journalist in the 1930s and the contributor to five journals during the Spanish Civil War, nothing is known of her during the Axis Occupation. In the *Épuration,* however, she played a leading role, and defenders of the collaborators described her as 'a hate-filled tigress for whom a sentence of imprisonment for life at hard labour seems an inexcusable indulgence.'

Jouhaux, Léon (1879–1954), *Le Peuple*

Jouhaux served as secretary general of the CGT from 1909 to 1947, and then president of the CGT-FO from 1948 to his death. His many activities in pacifist causes earned him the Nobel Prize for Peace in 1951. With the collapse of France in 1940, a half of the CGT rallied to Pétain, but Jouhaux led the other half toward resistance. Vichy placed him under surveillance, and in November 1942, with the German occupation of the south, he was arrested. On 1 March 1943, he was transported (by car) to KL-Buchenwald where, together with Blum, Daladier and Gamelin, he was granted preferential treatment. On 1 May of that year, he and other French leaders were transferred to Schloss Itter, a dependency of KL-Dachau in the Austrian Tyrol. They were liberated on 5 May 1945 by units of the US 103rd Division under General McAuliffe.

Jouvenel, Bertrand de (1903–1987), *L'Émancipation Nationale, Paris-Soir, Le Petit Journal*

A member of the PPF and editor in chief of its journal *L'Émancipation Nationale*, he worked with the Comité France-Allemagne and thereby formed a close friendship with Otto Abetz, the future German ambassador. In February 1936 he interviewed Hitler for *Paris-Midi*, but in 1938, when Doriot supported the Munich Agreement, Jouvenel broke with the PPF. Under the

Occupation, he played both sides, and when threatened by the Gestapo in September 1943 he fled to Switzerland, withdrawing from politics. On his return to France, he escaped the *Épuration*.

Kérillis, Henri Calloc'h de (1889–1958), *L'Echo de Paris*, *L'Époque*

An outstanding figure in the French press during the Spanish Civil War. The son of an admiral, he had fought in 1914–1918, first as a cavalry officer, then as leader of a bomber squadron. In the 1920s he was chef du service politique with *L'Écho de Paris*; when it folded, he helped to create *L'Époque*.

As a *député* from 1936, his reaction to the war in Spain was to advocate French intervention on the side of Franco, to whom in December he offered the celebrated sword. He then changed his mind. In October 1938 he was one of only two non-communist *députés*, and the only *député* on the Right, to vote against the Munich Agreement. He told the Assembly: 'Germany is insatiable when confronted by the weak. Germany has not a shred of pity for the weak. Germany respects nothing but the strong, and we have just shown Germany that we are weak.' Denouncing the defeatists as well as the Extreme Right, and publishing *Français, voici la guerre* (Paris: Grasset, 1936), he called for a vast European coalition against Hitler that would include the USSR. With the collapse of France, *L'Époque* was closed. From Bordeaux Kérillis escaped to London in a small plane piloted by his brother, and on 18 June 1940, he offered his services to de Gaulle. In mid-July he left for New York where with Geneviève Tabouis he co-founded the Gaullist monthly *Pour la Victoire* and where he published his *Français, voici la vérité* (Éditions de la Maison française, 1942). In the quarrel between de Gaulle and Giraud in 1943, he urged them to reconcile, then sided with Giraud, deploring the intransigence that he saw more in de Gaulle than in Giraud. When his son Alain was captured by the Milice and executed, de Kérillis blamed de Gaulle. He never returned to France, dying on his farm on Long Island.

La Rocque, François de (1885–1946), *Le Petit Journal*

As a battalion commander in the First World War, he was seriously wounded. In 1929 he entered the Croix de Feu and became its president in 1932. While rejecting an alliance with the Extreme Right of Doriot, he founded the Parti Social Français in 1937 and launched its organ *Le Petit Journal* which then followed a pacifist line. The collapse of France left him confused. He was briefly a member of Pétain's council, and he is credited with providing the Marshal with his slogan: 'Travail, Patrie, Famille.' At the same time, on 16 June 1940, his journal launched the first refusal: 'No collaboration under occupation.' In August he entered the Resistance, collecting information on the enemy, and in January 1941 he suffered his first interrogation by the Gestapo, followed by his arrest. Meanwhile, the sheer strength

(350,000 members) of the PSF (now renamed the Progrès Social Français) forced Vichy to legalize it but it failed to win it over. In May 1942 La Rocque founded the Klan network that provided military information to the British intelligence services, routing the information through Colonel Charandeau in Madrid (the *Alibi* network). On 9 March 1943 the PSF was dissolved outright by Oberg (commanding the SS throughout France from November 1942) and La Rocque was imprisoned, first in Fresnes and then in Cherche-Midi. From there he was transferred to Eisenberg (Czechoslovakia) and thence to Schloss Itter in Austria. On his return to France on 8 May he found himself again under arrest, this time for his pre-war activities. On his release in July 1945, he founded the Parti de la Reconciliation Française, but captivity had ruined his health and he died soon afterwards (28 April 1946). It was not until April 1961 that he received the honour he deserved, when de Gaulle bestowed on his widow the Medal of the Resistance.

Lauzanne, Stéphane (1874–1958), *Le Matin*

The editor in chief of *Le Matin* responded to the French collapse by rallying to Vichy and continued his anti-Allied work right through to 14 August 1944. Though aged 70 in 1944, he was found guilty on 31 October for 'consorting with the enemy' (his long association with Abetz) and sentenced to 20 years of solitary confinement. ('Some five days of prison per article, commented *El Patriota de Sud-Oeste* on 3 November 1944, 'almost nothing.') Lauzanne was imprisoned on the Île de Ré. Released early, he returned to writing for the far-right press.

Lazareff, Pierre (1907–1972), *Paris-Soir*

The editor in chief of *Paris-Soir* left for New York in 1940 to work for the Office of War Information as director of the French services ('L'Amérique en guerre'). In New York he published *Dernière Édition* (Brentano's, 1942) and *De Munich à Vichy* (Brentano's, 1944). He was then sent to London to head the American Broadcasting System in Europe, sending radio bulletins to occupied Europe.

Lejeune, Albert (1915–1944), *Le Petit Journal*

Both before and after the French collapse, as managing editor of several provincial newspapers (*Lyon Républicain, Le Petit Marseillais, Le Petit Niçois*), Lejeune enjoyed close relations with Abetz at the German Embassy and his newspapers collaborated fully. His trial after the Liberation was the first of a major leader of the French press, and on 22 October 1944 he was sentenced to death and duly executed.

Leroux, André (1892–1960), *Le Midi Socialiste*

The prolific contributor to *Le Midi Socialiste* was sui generis among journalists. Born Angelo Tasca in Moretta, Italy, he travelled by the names of Ernesto Rossi and Amilcare Rossi. As a member of the PCI, he was called to Moscow in 1928 to serve in the Comintern as representative of Italy, France, Spain, Belgium, and South America. Within a year his association with Bukharin caused him to flee for his life to France. In Paris he joined *Le Populaire*, where Blum entrusted him with the international page. Under the name of André Leroux, and now a French citizen, Tasca carved out an original ideological position: anti-fascist, anti-communist, and anti-pacifist. In the Spanish Civil War he defended the POUM against the PCE. He was now leader of the Italian Socialist Party, backed by many Italians who had taken refuge in France. The Armistice of 1940 caught him in Bordeaux, where he declined the chance to take ship to North Africa. Instead, he offered his services to Vichy, launching the Socialist journal *L'Effort* and accepting a post under Paul Marion in the Ministry of Information. Arrested at the Liberation, his imprisonment was brutal but brief. His connections were many, and they included Pierre Bertaux in Toulouse. He finally emerged in the Cold War as co-editor with Georges Albertini of the review *Est et Ouest,* devoted to the exposure of Soviet crimes.

Luchaire, Jean (1901–1946), *Notre Temps*

As founder of the weekly *Notre Temps*, he first met Otto Abetz in 1930, and shortly afterwards the future German ambassador married Luchaire's secretary, Suzanne de Bruyker. A lasting friendship resulted. His *Cahiers franco-allemands* were intended to win over the young French intelligentsia to friendship with Nazi Germany. After the French collapse he founded, in November 1940, the collaborationist evening daily *Les Nouveaux Temps,* and in 1941 he became president of the Association de la presse parisienne. With the assassination of Henriot, Luchaire was selected to replace him. His support of Hitler never slackened, and in 1944 he called on the Germans to 'exterminate' the French Resistance. In August he followed the Commission Gouvernementale into exile in Sigmaringen, serving as its Commissaire à l'Information, directing its radio station, and editing its daily journal *La France* which continued until March 1945. Then, after vainly trying to win political asylum in Liechtenstein and Switzerland, he fled to Italy, where he was arrested in May and handed over to the French authorities. At his trial in January 1946, his friend Abetz appeared as a defence witness. Luchaire claimed that at the end of 1942 he had become disenchanted with Vichy and became a Resistant ('by listening to the BBC' he explained!). If he continued to serve Vichy, he added, it was only to hide his 'double game' from the Germans! Unimpressed by his humour, the court sentenced him to death on 21 January 1946; he was executed on 22 February.

Mandel, Georges (1885–1944), *L'Ami du Peuple*

Mandel began his journalistic career by joining Georges Clemenceau at *L'Aurore* and *L'Homme Libre*. On 18 May 1940 he was selected by Reynaud to be his Minister of the Interior. With the capitulation Mandel moved to Morocco, where he was arrested on 8 August 1940 and put on trial in Riom. The Vichy court sentenced him on 7 November 1941 to imprisonment for life, holding him in the Fort du Portalet which is where the Germans found him after the invasion of the South. He was sent first to KL-Sachsenhausen, then to KL-Buchenwald, and then brought back to the Santé in Paris. On 7 July 1944, the Gestapo and the Milice together took him into the forest of Fontainebleau where the *milicien* Mansuy murdered him alongside the road to Nemours.

Marion, Paul (1899–1954), *L'Europe Nouvelle*

Like Daudet, Marion served in the central committee of the PCF, and after working for the Comintern in Moscow in 1927–1929 he left the Party in 1936 to join Doriot's PPF. After working as editor in chief of *L'Émancipation Nationale* and then *La Liberté*, Marion found Doriot too sympathetic to Hitler and broke from the PPF. The collapse of France, however, and the intervention of Abetz, brought Marion back to Doriot's side. On 11 August 1941 he was appointed the Vichy Minister of Information and Propaganda until, in January 1944, he was replaced by Henriot. Then, following the latter's assassination, Marion returned to office, becoming Secrétaire d'État and accompanying the Vichy leaders to Germany. Brought to trial, he was sentenced on 14 December 1948 to 10 years in prison, but was released in 1953 on medical grounds.

Marty, André (1886–1956), *L'Humanité*

On the basis of his knowledge of Spanish and Catalan, and his service in the French Navy, the Comintern had selected him, in August 1936, to serve as inspector general of the International Brigades. He remained in Spain until the end of the war but not without an interruption. His unpopularity among the Republicans (only too well explained by the anarchist journal *Le Libertaire* in France) was such that he was recalled to Moscow, where Dimitrov gave him a new assignment in Latin America. But Marty insisted on returning to Spain, and this was accepted on condition that the Brigades form part of the regular Spanish Republican Army. Behind this matter was the hostility that never ended between comrades Marty and Thorez. Recalled to Moscow again in August 1939, Marty was there when the Molotov–Ribbentrop Pact was announced, and was given the task of spokesman for its justification. With the declaration of war, his open letter to Léon Blum, dated 5 September 1939 and distributed secretly in France, denounced the 'imperialist and anti-worker character' of the war, earning him in France a sentence in absentia of four years' imprisonment. Marty continued working for the Comintern until its dissolution in May 1943, and in September he finally got his wish to return home, if not to France, at least to Algiers. Arriving there in October, he represented the PCF in the Provisional Government of de Gaulle. With the Liberation, when he ranked third in the Party hierarchy after Thorez and Duclos, he reached Paris on 3 September 1944 in time to take part in the *Épuration*. The former 'Mutineer on the Black Sea' was among the most ferocious of accusers of the Vichy admirals, but it availed him little in the end. From 1947 he found himself isolated in the Bureau Politique of the PCF. On 1 September 1952 he was summoned before the Bureau, excluded from its membership on 7 December, and banished from the Party on 24 December. No proof was ever produced of Marty having 'liaisons with the police,' but that was precisely the accusation made first by Duclos and then in a published article signed by Étienne Fajon. Totally isolated, denied any kind word from Stalin to whom he frantically appealed, Marty in his agony turned to his arch-enemies, the Trotskyists and the anarchists, before dying, unlamented, of cancer of the lung.

Massis, Henri (1886–1970), *L'Action Française*
Under Vichy he served to the end as editor in chief of the *Revue Universelle*, serving the National Revolution also in the training of youth. Although he was included after the Liberation in the List of Undesirable Writers, the *Épuration* left him untouched.

Maulnier, Thierry (1908–1988), *L'Action Française, Combat*
Under Vichy he continued to write for *L'Action Française*, but stopped writing after the Allied landings in North Africa. He thus escaped the *Épuration*.

Maurras, Charles (1868–1952), *L'Action Française*
The defeat of France had the effect of dividing Action Française and those close to the movement into three opposing groups. There were the orthodox Maurrassiens, who supported Pétain but who were reticent about collaborating with Germany; there were those like Brasillach, who were openly pro-Nazi and collaborated; and there was a minority which included Honoré Estienne d'Orves, who held to another image of France and who moved into the Resistance. Maurras himself never hesitated, speaking of Pétain's arrival in power as a 'divine surprise,' and of the defeat of France as beneficial if it were to rid France of its democrats. Settling in Lyon, and deaf to the appeals of Pierre Gaxotte, he revived his daily *L'Action Française* under the new slogan 'La France seule.' Declaring himself the enemy of de Gaulle, he referred to the Resistants as 'terrorists' and called for the harshest measures to be taken against them. His proposals included hostage-taking and executions without trial, even of Gaullists taken prisoner. If that proved insufficient, he added, then

seize their family members as hostages and execute them. Maurras was arrested in September 1944 in the liberation of Lyon. At his trial there in January 1945, he was accused of high treason and consorting with the enemy, and the prosecution urged a sentence of death. Instead, on 27 January, he was sentenced to life imprisonment and national degradation, the second sentence incurring his automatic expulsion from the Académie Française to which he had been elected on 9 June 1938. 'The revenge of Dreyfus!' was Maurras's sardonic response. On 21 March 1952, he received a pardon on medical grounds from President Vincent Auriol, and died shortly afterwards in a clinic.

Mille, Pierre (1864–1941), *La Dépêche*

A writer of renown, and a major contributor to *La Dépêche*, Mille was already 76 at the time of the Armistice and died in the following year.

Mireaux, Émile (1886–1969), *Le Temps*

As a *député*, and co-director of *Le Temps,* he voted on 10 July 1940 for full powers to Pétain, receiving on 12 July the post under Laval of Minister of Education and Fine Arts. In September, on grounds of his previous service to the Third Republic, he was dismissed, but he continued to produce *Le Temps* until he closed it on 28 November 1942. With the Liberation he was able to argue *faits de résistance* and thus avoid the *Épuration*.

Mounier, Emmanuel (1905–1950), *Esprit*

A philosopher and the founder of the Catholic *Esprit*, he thought he saw in the Vichy regime a chance to give a new direction to youth, and so revived *Esprit*, but in August 1941 he closed his journal and joined the *Combat* resistance movement in Lyon. Arrested by the Vichy police in early 1942, he went on hunger strike to such a point that they released him. He took refuge in Drôme, returning to writing, and after the war he took a leading part in the movement for reconciliation with Germany.

Nizan, Paul (1905–1940), *Ce Soir*

Before the war he had been one of the leading literary lights of the PCF, but in August 1939 he denounced the Molotov–Ribbentrop Pact and broke with the Party. For this he was violently attacked by Thorez, writing in *Die Welt,* the German edition of the Third International, at the precise moment that Thorez was deserting his post in the field of combat. Nizan, referred by the PCF after the war as 'the traitor Nizan,' was killed in action on 23 May 1940 during the evacuation from Dunkirk.

Ormesson, Wladimir d' (1888–1973), *Le Figaro*

The most prominent editor of *Le Figaro* found a new career on 25 May 1940 when Reynaud appointed him Ambassador to the Holy See. On 3 October 1940 the Vichy government removed him from his post, and from all posts in February 1941, after which he rejoined *Le Figaro* in Lyon before going underground.

Péri, Gabriel (1902–1941), *Ce Soir, L'Humanité*

A journalist by profession, he became a member of the Central Committee of the PCF, foreign editor of *L'Humanité,* and *député* for Seine-et-Oise. He remained with *L'Humanité* up to its closure by the government on 25 August 1939, but his sense of patriotism led him to part ways with the Party's policy of accepting the Molotov–Ribbentrop Pact. This caused the Comintern leaders to be concerned about him, especially when he volunteered to serve in the military. At the time of the German arrival in Paris in June 1940, he was one of very few PCF leaders to be still in the capital. When the two residual PCF leaders (Duclos and Tréand) requested the Germans to allow *L'Humanité* to resume legal publication (to which the Germans agreed), Péri responded in vehement opposition. On 18 May 1941 he was denounced by Hermann Bertele ('Armand', *né* Edmond Foeglin), working for Duclos and Tréand. Péri was interned in the Santé, then in the Cherche-Midi. He was one of the 92 hostages shot by the Germans at Mont-Valérien on 15 December 1941.

Pertinax, *né* André Géraud (1882–1974), *L'Echo de Paris, L'Europe Nouvelle*

As a nationalist opposed to all fascist regimes, and foreign policy editor of *L'Écho de Paris,* his hostility to Franco marginalized him on the Right in France. Opposed to the Munich Agreement, he responded to the collapse in June 1940 by escaping from Bordeaux on board a British destroyer. Reaching New York, he wrote regular articles for the *New York Times* and published *Les Fossoyeurs* (Éditions de la Maison française, 1943), an account of the French defeat.

Pujo, Maurice (1872–1955), *L'Action Française*

As co-director with Maurras of *L'Action Française*, he welcomed the Vichy takeover and continued to direct the journal even after the German occupation of the south. With the liberation of Lyon on 5 September 1944, he was arrested and put on trial. Found guilty of consorting with the enemy, he was sentenced on 27 January 1945 to national degradation and five years in prison, serving his term first in Riom (for symbolic reasons) and then in Clairvaux.

Romier, Lucien (1885–1944), *Le Figaro*

As editor in chief of *Le Figaro,* he rallied to Pétain, serving the régime from 11 August 1941 to 31 December 1943 as Minister of State. He died in January 1944 just after he left office.

Sampaix, Lucien (1899–1941), *L'Humanité*

As secretary general of *L'Humanité*, he was arrested by the Gestapo and shot on 15 December 1941.

Sarraut, Maurice (1869–1943), *La Dépêche*

The elder brother of Albert Sarraut (Minister of the Interior), he had resigned his seat in the Senate to become publisher of *La Dépêche*, the leading journal of the Southwest. Like Albert, Maurice rallied to Pétain, and *La Dépêche* supported Vichy while strongly opposing the ultras. In 1943 he came out in opposition to Laval, and especially to the creation of the Milice. In January 1943 he was arrested by the Gestapo, but his friendship with René Bousquet, the head of the Vichy police, won him a quick release. On 28 November 1943, Henriot, as Minister of Information and speaking on radio, denounced him by name for inciting the Resistance to acts of terrorism. On 1 December, he left his office on rue Bayard in Toulouse to return home to the Villa des Tilleuls in Saint-Simon where his assassin was waiting. The killer, a member of the Milice, emptied his machine-gun into his body. Maurice died in the arms of his brother Albert. His two-day funeral on 4–5 December was attended by more than 30,000 Toulousains who marched past his remains, which were then buried in Carcassonne. With the Liberation, Henry Frossard, the regional chief of the Milice, was accused of arranging the murder; he was sentenced to death and executed on 14 May 1945.

Suarez, Georges (1890–1944), *Gringoire, Notre Temps*

Known prewar for his articles in *Gringoire* and *Notre Temps,* he rallied at once to Vichy, taking over in December 1942 the editorship of the daily *Aujourd'hui* and giving it a clearly pro-German stance. The Riom trials were trials he welcomed, and in his support of the collaboration he called it a sacred duty to denounce Resistance activities. Several times he encouraged the authorities to intensify the execution of Jews and communists, and went beyond even what the Germans were prepared to do when he proposed the wholesale taking of Anglophone hostages as protection against Allied bombing raids. Not surprisingly, with the Liberation he was the very first journalist to be sentenced to death (23 October 1944) and the first to be executed (5 November 1944).

Tabouis, Geneviève (1892–1985), *L'Oeuvre*

Née Geneviève Lequesne, she was the niece of two French ambassadors, Paul and Jules Cambon, and the wife of Robert Tabouis, director of Radio Luxembourg. At the time of the French collapse the editor of *L'Oeuvre* was in Bordeaux, where she was particularly vilified by Franco's press. She reached London, and then New York, where she became a close friend of Eleanor Roosevelt. On 12 January 1942, she and Kérillis launched the Gaullist monthly *Pour La Victoire.*

Taittinger, Pierre (1887–1965), *L'Ami du Peuple*

In 1924 he had founded the movement Jeunesses Patriotes, competing on the extreme Right with Action Française. As president of the Conseil muncipal de Paris from 1937, he remained in his post under the German occupation up to the moment he made a stultifying switch from collaboration to Resistance. Arrested at the Liberation, charged with consorting with the enemy, the household name brought him connections that saved him.

Tardieu, André (1876–1945), *Gringoire*

As a writer for *Gringoire*, Germany would have benefitted from his services during the Occupation, but in July 1939 he was paralyzed and took no part in the war.

Tixier-Vignancour, Jean-Louis (1907–1989), *La Garonne*

Rallying to Vichy in 1940, he volunteered at once to serve as director of propaganda, including Radio Vichy. With the Liberation he was imprisoned several times over a period of months. The prosecution led by Maître Boissarie tried to disbar him, but the legal profession came to his aid.

Valois, Georges

During the Occupation, the founder of *Le Nouvel Age* joined the resistance in Lyons. He was finally arrested by the Gestapo on 18 May 1944, and died of typhus in February 1945 in Bergen-Belsen.

Vandervelde, Émile (1866–1938), *La Dépêche*

A professor at the Université Libre de Bruxelles and a major contributor to *La Dépêche*, he was one of the founders of the Parti Ouvrier Belge and its leader from 1933. He joined the Belgian government under Paul-Henri Spaak, but resigned when Spaak, in 1936, spoke out for neutrality in Spain. In *Ce que nous avons vu en Espagne* (1938), Vandervelde warned that the threat of fascism was real. He died, however, before the Civil War ended.

Wurmser, André (1899–1994), *Ce Soir, Lumière, Regards, Vendredi*

The brother-in-law of Jean Cassou, leader of the Resistance group *Musée de l'homme*, Wurmser had joined the PCF in 1934 and contributed to several of its journals. He responded to the Armistice in 1940 by launching the underground newspaper *Le Patriote du Sud-Ouest*.

Ybarnégaray, Jean (1883–1956), *Le Petit Journal*

A *député* and supporter of La Rocque in the Parti Social Français, in 1940 he voted full powers to Pétain and served him, first as minister for veterans' affairs (17 June–11 July 1940), then as minister for youth, family and sports

(12 July–6 September 1940). After resigning from Vichy service, he became active in 1943 in aiding refugees to cross the Pyrenees. Arrested by the police, he was sent first to Planze (Tyrol) and then to KL-Dachau. Despite this, with the Liberation he was arrested again and put on trial as a former member of the Vichy government. On 18 March 1946 he was sentenced to national degradation, but the sentence was suspended for 'fait de résistance.'

Zyromski, Jean (1890–1975), *L'Espagne Socialiste, Le Midi Socialiste, Le Populaire, Regards*

Descended from a family of Polish Catholic nobles, and the son of a professor of literature in Toulouse, Zyromski had been wounded at the front in the First World War. He became a left-wing socialist eager to establish a union with the PCF, hence close to Marceau Pivert, but had broken with him in 1935. In 1936 Blum invited him to serve as his chief of staff; he declined, but continued to support him. He was now a major writer for *Le Populaire* and *Le Midi Socialiste*. Following the Armistice, in October 1940 he lost the post he held at the Préfecture, and from 7 August 1941 he lived on his farm in Lot-et-Garonne, where he made contact with the local Resistance. He was arrested as 'Jewish,' held in Fort du Hâ, then Mérignac, then Drancy from late 1943 to early 1944. He was released from Drancy only when his family proved his Catholic origins, but the treatment that he had received from his communist co-prisoners led him to join Pétain's Front National, which created problems for him at the Liberation. In September 1945 he joined the PCF, but then withdrew from political activity.

Appendix I
Principal Characters

Aguirre, José Antonio: President of the Basque Republic.
Alba y Berwick, Duke of: official representative of Franco in London.
Albornoz, Álvaro de: Spanish Ambassador to Paris under Largo Caballero.
Alcalá Zamora, Niceto: first President of the Second Spanish Republic.
Alfieri, Dino: member of the Italian Fascist Grand Council.
Álvarez del Vayo, Julio: Spanish Foreign Minister under Largo Caballero; representative at the League of Nations under Negrín; left-wing Socialist.
Antoniutti, Ildebrando: Apostolic delegate to the Salamanca government.
Araquistain, Luis: Spanish Ambassador to Paris under Largo Caballero.
Atger, Fréderic: Prefect of the Department of Haute-Garonne.
Attolico, Bernardo: Italian Ambassador to Berlin.
Avenol, Joseph: Secretary General of the League of Nations.
Azaña, Manuel: second President of the Second Spanish Republic.
Azcárate, Pablo de: Spanish Ambassador to London.
Baldwin, Stanley: British Prime Minister; Conservative.
Barbier, Jean-Baptiste: Counsellor at the French Embassy in Madrid.
Barcia, Augusto: Spanish Foreign Minister under both Casares Quiroga and Giral.
Bastianini, Giuseppe: Italian Under-Secretary of State.
Beigbeder, Colonel Juan: Spanish Resident Minister in Morocco.
Bingham, Robert Worth: American Ambassador to London (–December 1937).
Bismarck, Prince Otto von: Counsellor at the German Embassy in London; Germany's representative on the London Committee.
Blomberg, Generalfeldmarschall Werner von: German Minister of War (–February 1938).
Blondel, Jules: French Chargé d'Affaires in Rome.
Blum, Léon: French Premier, leader of the SFIO and the Front Populaire.
Bonjean, René: French chargé d'affaires in Madrid.
Bonnet, Georges: French Foreign Minister under Daladier.
Bowers, Claude: American Ambassador to Madrid.
Bullitt, William C.: American Ambassador to Paris.
Cachin, Marcel: French PCF Senator; editor-in-chief of *L'Humanité*.

Canaris, Admiral Wilhelm: head of the German military intelligence service (Abwehr).
Cantalupo, Roberto: Italian Ambassador to Salamanca (November 1936–April 1937).
Cárdenas, Juan de: Spanish Ambassador to Paris (–July 1936).
Casado, Colonel Segismundo: President of the Consejo Nacional de Defensa in Madrid (March 1939).
Cerrutti, Vittorio: Italian Ambassador to Paris.
Chamberlain, Neville: British Prime Minister, leader of the Conservative Party.
Chambrun, Charles de: French Ambassador to Rome.
Chautemps, Camille: French Minister of State under Blum; Premier; Deputy Premier under Daladier; Radical.
Chilton, Sir Henry: British Ambassador to Madrid.
Ciano, Count Galeazzo: Italian Foreign Minister.
Clerk, Sir George: British Ambassador to Paris (1934–1937).
Companys, Lluís: President of the Generalitat of Catalonia.
Corbin, Charles: French Ambassador to London.
Cot, Pierre: French Air Minister under Blum and Chautemps; Radical.
Coulondre, Robert: French Ambassador to Moscow (1936–1938); to Berlin (1938–1939).
Cranborne, Lord: British Under-Secretary of State, Britain's representative at the League of Nations.
Daladier, Édouard: French Minister of War under Blum and Chautemps; Premier; Radical.
Davies, Joseph E.: American Ambassador to Moscow (November 1936–June 1938).
Dekanosov, Vladimir G.: Soviet Deputy-Commissar for Foreign Affairs; Ambassador to Berlin (November 1940–June 1941).
Delbos, Yvon: French Foreign Minister under Blum and Chautemps; Radical.
Dimitrov, Giorgi: Bulgarian Secretary-General of the Third International.
Dirksen, Herbert von: German Ambassador to London (May 1938–).
Drummond, Sir Eric: British Ambassador to Rome.
Du Moulin-Eckart, Count Karl-Max: German counsellor at the Embassy in Lisbon.
Eden, Anthony: British Foreign Secretary (1935–February 1938); Conservative.
Faupel, General Wilhelm von: German Ambassador to Salamanca (–September 1937).
Fouques-Duparc, Jacques: French chargé d'affaires in Barcelona.
François-Poncet, André: French Ambassador to Berlin (1931–1938); to Rome (1938–1940).

Gaikins, Leon Y.: Soviet chargé d'affaires in Madrid (20 February 1937–May 1937).
Gambara, General Gastone: Chief of the Italian Military Mission in Spain.
Gil Robles, José María: leader of the CEDA.
Giral, José: Spanish Prime Minister; left-wing Republican.
Gomá y Tomás, Isidro, Cardinal and Primate of Spain; chargé d'affaires of the Holy See to Salamanca.
Göring, Reichsmarschall Hermann: German Air Minister and chief of the Luftwaffe.
Grandi, Count Dino: Italian Ambassador to London, Italy's representative on the London Committee.
Halifax, Edward, Lord: British Foreign Secretary (February 1938–).
Hassell, Ulrich von: German Ambassador to Rome (1932–February 1938).
Heberlein, Dr. Erich: German counsellor at the Embassy in Salamanca.
Henderson, Sir Neville Meyrick: British Ambassador to Berlin (1937–1939).
Henry, Jules: French Minister to the Spanish Republic.
Herbette, Jean: French Ambassador to Madrid under Blum and Chautemps.
Hodgson, Sir Robert: British representative to Franco.
Hoyningen-Huene, Dr. Baron Oswald von: German Minister at the Embassy in Lisbon.
Hull, Cordell: US Secretary of State.
Jiménez de Asúa, Luis: Spanish Republican Ambassador to Czechoslovakia, Poland and the League of Nations.
Jordana, Count: Spanish Nationalist Foreign Minister (March 1938–).
Jouhaux, Léon: Secretary-General of the French CGT; Socialist.
Kagan, Samuel B.: Counsellor in the Soviet Embassy in London; Soviet representative on the London Committee.
Kennedy, Joseph P.: American Ambassador to London (December 1937–).
Kindelán, General Alfredo: chief of Nationalist air forces.
Kleber, General Emil: commander of the International Brigades.
Kollontay, Alexandra (Soviet Minister in Sweden).
Krivitsky, General Walter: chief of Soviet Military Intelligence in Western Europe.
Labonne, Eirik: French Ambassador to Madrid under Chautemps, Blum, and Daladier.
Lagarde, Ernest: secretary general of the French delegation to the League of Nations.
Largo Caballero, Francisco: Spanish Premier, leader of the Socialist UGT.
Leche, John: British Minister Plenipotentiary at the Embassy in Barcelona.
Lequerica, José Félix de: Franco's Ambassador to Paris (1939–).
Litvinov, Maxim Maximovich.: Soviet People's Commissar for Foreign Affairs (1930–3 May 1939; Ambassador to Washington (1941–1943).
Mackensen, Hans Georg von: German Ambassador to Rome (April 1938–).

Principal Characters

Magaz y Pers, Admiral Antonio, Marquis of: Franco's Ambassador to Rome (1937); to Berlin (1937–).

Maglione, Luigi Cardinal: Apostolic Nuncio in Paris (1926–22 July 1938); Vatican Secretary of State under Pope Pius XII (10 March 1939–1944).

Magny, Charles: French Director-General, Sûreté Nationale.

Maisky, Ivan: Soviet Ambassador to London, Russia's representative on the London Committee.

Marcassin, Maurice: French Consul in Valencia.

Miaja, General José: Spanish Republican commander on the Madrid front.

Mola, General Emilio: Spanish Nationalist general, member of the Junta.

Monteiro, Armindo: Portuguese Foreign Minister.

Morand, Paul: *chef de service* in the French Foreign Ministry.

Moullec, Commander Raymond: French Naval Attaché at the Embassy in Barcelona.

Naggiar, Paul: French Ambassador to Moscow (1938–).

Negrín, Juan: Spanish Prime Minister; Socialist.

Neurath, Baron Constantin von: German Foreign Minister.

Neuville, Emmanuel: French Consul in Madrid.

Noguès, Charles Hippolyte: French Resident-General in Morocco (September 1936–June 1943).

Oshima, Baron Hiroshi: Japanese Military Attaché in Berlin (1934–1938; Ambassador to Berlin (October 1938–).

Ossorio y Gallardo, Ángel: Spanish Republican Ambassador to Paris under Negrín.

Pascua, Marcelino: Spanish Republican Ambassador to Moscow, later to Paris under Negrín.

Paul-Boncour, Joseph: French Foreign Minister under Blum; chargé d'affaires in Moscow (1938–March 1939).

Payart, Jean: Counsellor at the French Embassy in Valencia, then Barcelona; Ambassador to Moscow (March 1939–).

Pedrazzi, Orazio Croce: Italian Ambassador to Madrid (–1937).

Pétain, Marshal Philippe: French Ambassador to Nationalist Spain (1939).

Peyrouton, Marcel: French Resident-General in Morocco (March–September 1936).

Phipps, Sir Eric: British Ambassador to Berlin (1933–1937); to Paris (1937–1939).

Plessen, Baron Johann von: Counsellor in the German Embassy in Rome.

Plymouth, Lord: Chairman of the London Committee.

Potemkin, Vladimir Petrovich: Soviet Ambassador to Paris (1934–April 1937).

Prieto, Indalecio: Spanish Socialist leader.

Prunas, Renato: Italian chargé d'affaires in Paris.

Queipo de Llano, General Gonzalo: Spanish Nationalist general, member of the Junta.
Ribbentrop, Joachim von: German Ambassador to London; Foreign Minister (4 February 1938–).
Ríos Urruti, Fernando de los: Spanish Ambassador to Paris (1936); to Washington (1936–1939).
Rivière, Jean: counsellor at the French Embassy to the Holy See.
Rosenberg, Marcel: Soviet Ambassador to Madrid (30 August 1936–20 February 1937).
Rosso, Augusto: Italian Ambassador to Moscow (1936–1940).
Salazar, Antonio de Oliveira: Portuguese Prime Minister.
Sangróniz, José Antonio de: head of the diplomatic cabinet in Salamanca (–March 1938).
Schmidt, Dr. Paul Otto Gustav: head of bureau, German Foreign Ministry.
Schulenburg, Count Friedrich von der: German Ambassador to Moscow.
Schwendemann, Dr. Karl: counsellor at the German Embassy in Madrid (1936).
Seeds, Sir William: British Ambassador to Moscow (1939–1940).
Serrano Suñer, Ramón: leader of CEDA Youth, later Secretary-General of the Falange.
Stein, Boris: Soviet Ambassador to Rome.
Steinhardt, Laurence A.: American Ambassador to Moscow (23 March 1939–).
Stohrer, Dr. Eberhard von: German Ambassador to Salamanca (September 1937–).
Suritz, Yakov Zaharovich: Soviet Ambassador to Paris (1937–).
Thorez, Maurice: PCF *député*, secretary-general of the French Communist Party.
Valeri, Mgr. Valerio: Apostolic Nuncio to Paris (December 1938–).
Viénot, Pierre: French Under-Secretary of State for Foreign Affairs.
Viola di Campalto, Count Guido: Italian Ambassador to Salamanca (April 1937–).
Voelckers, Hans-Hermann: chargé d'affaires in the German Embassy in Madrid (April–November 1936).
Weizsäcker, Baron Ernst von: head of the Political Department of the Wilhelmstrasse (–1938), Secretary of State (1938–).
Welczeck, Count Johannes von: German Ambassador to Paris (1936–1940).

Appendix II
The Five French Cabinets of 1936–1939
Key Ministries

FIRST BLUM CABINET (4 June 1936–22 June 1937)
    Premier: Léon Blum, SFIO Deputy

    Vice-Premier and Minister of National Defence: Édouard Daladier, Radical député

    Ministers of State:
        Camille Chautemps, Radical Senator
        Paul Faure, SFIO (non-parliamentary)
        Maurice Viollette, USR Senator

    Ministers:
        Foreign Affairs: Yvon Delbos, Radical député
        Air: Pierre Cot, Radical député
        Commerce: Paul Bastid, Radical député
        Finance: Vincent Auriol, SFIO député
        Interior: Roger Salengro, SFIO député; Marx Dormoy, SFIO député

    Ambassador to Spain: Jean Herbette.

FIRST CHAUTEMPS CABINET (23 June 1937–18 January 1938)
    Premier: Camille Chautemps, Radical Senator

    Vice-Premier: Léon Blum, SFIO Premier

    Ministers of State:
        Paul Faure, SFIO (non-Parliamentary)
        Albert Sarraut, Radical Senator
        Maurice Viollete, USR Senator

Ministers:
    National Defence: Édouard Daladier, Radical député
    Foreign Affairs: Yvon Delbos, Radical député
    Air: Pierre Cot, Radical député
    Commerce: Fernand Chapsal, Radical Senator
    Finance: Georges Bonnet, Radical député.
    Interior: Marx Dormoy, SFIO député

Ambassador to Spain: Jean Herbette; (from 8 October 1937) Eilrich Labonne

SECOND CHAUTEMPS CABINET (18 January–13 March 1938)
Premier: Camille Chautemps, Radical Senator

Vice-Premier and Minister of National Defence: Édouard Daladier, Radical député

Ministers of State:
    Ludovic-Oscar Frossard, USR député
    Georges Bonnet, Radical député

Ministers:
    Foreign Affairs: Yvon Delbos, Radical député
    Air: Guy La Chambre, Radical député
    Commerce: Pierre Cot, Radical député
    Finance: Paul Marchandeau, Radical député
    Interior: Albert Sarraut, Radical Senator

Ambassador to Spain: Eilrich Labonne

SECOND BLUM CABINET (13 March–10 April 1938)
Premier: Léon Blum, SFIO député

Vice-Premier and Minister of National Defence: Édouard Daladier, Radical député

Ministers of State:
    Vincent Auriol, SFIO député
    Paul Faure, SFIO (non-Parliamentary)
    Albert Sarraut, Radical Senator
    Théodore Steeg, Radical Senator
    Maurice Viollette, USR Senator

Ministers:
- Foreign Affairs: Joseph Paul-Boncour, USR Senator
- Air: Guy La Chambre, Radical député
- Budget: Charles Spinasse, SFIO député
- Commerce: Pierre Cot, Radical député
- Interior: Marx Dormoy, SFIO député
- Propaganda: Ludovic-Oscar Frossard, USR député

Ambassador to Spain: Eilrich Labonne

DALADIER CABINET (10 April 1938–21 March 1940)*
Premier and Minister of National Defence and War: Édouard Daladier, Radical Deputy

Vice-Premier: Camille Chautemps, Radical Senator

Ministers:
Foreign Affairs: Georges Bonnet, Radical député
Air: Guy La Chambre, Radical député
Commerce: Fernand Gentin, Radical député
Finance (until 1 November 1938): Paul Marchandeau, Radical député; (from 1 November 1938): Paul Reynaud, moderate Conservative député
Interior: Albert Sarraut, Radical Senator

Ambassador to Spain: Eilrich Labonne; replaced by Jules Henry (Minister to Republican Spain) and Marshal Pétain (Ambassador to Nationalist Spain)

* The Front Populaire was officially dissolved only after Munich, when the PCF withdrew its support of the Daladier government.

Appendix III
The Four War Cabinets of the Frente Popular
Key Ministries

GIRAL CABINET (19 July–4 September 1936)
    Premier: José Giral, Republican Left

    Ministers:
    Foreign Affairs: Augusto Barcia, Republican Left
    War: General Luis Castelló. Juan Hernández Sarabia.
    Interior: General Sebastián Pozas.
    Finance: Enrique Ramos y Ramos, Republican Left
    Industry and Commerce: Plácido Álvarez Buylla, Republican Union
    Communications and Merchant Marine: Bernardo Giner de los Ríos, Republican Union
    Ambassador to France (until 22 July 1936): Juan de Cárdenas; (from 22 to 27 July 1936); Fernando de los Ríos (pro tempore); (from 27 July 1936): Alvaro de Albornoz

LARGO CABALLERO CABINET (4 September 1936–15 May 1937)*
    Premier and Minister of War: Francisco Largo Caballero, Socialist Party

    Ministers:
    Foreign Affairs: Julio Álvarez del Vayo, Socialist Party
    Finance: Juan Negrín, Socialist Party
    Navy and Air: Indalecio Prieto, Socialist Party
    Interior: Ángel Galarza, Socialist Party
    Communications: Bernardo Giner de los Ríos, Republican Union
    Commerce: Anastasio de Gracia, Socialist Party; Juan López Sánchez, anarchist CNT-FAI
    Ambassador to France: Luis Araquistain

FIRST NEGRÍN CABINET (17 May 1937–5 April 1938)
   Premier and Finance: Juan Negrín, Socialist Party

   Ministers:
   Foreign Affairs: José Giral, Republican Left
   Defence: Indalecio Prieto, Socialist Party
   Interior: Julián Zugazagoitia, Socialist Party
   Communications: Bernardo Giner de los Ríos, Republican Union
   Ambassador to France: Ángel Ossorio y Gallardo.

SECOND NEGRÍN CABINET (5 April 1938–5 March 1939).
   Premier and Minister of Defence: Juan Negrín, Socialist Party

   Ministers:
   Foreign Affairs: Julio Álvarez del Vayo, Socialist Party
   Interior: Paulino Gómez Sáinz, Socialist Party
   Communications and Transport: Bernardo Giner de los Ríos, Republican Union
   Finance and Economy: Francisco Méndez Aspe, Republican Left
   Ambassador to France: Marcelino Pascua.

* There were in fact two cabinets under Largo Caballero, the second including four anarchists, but the second involved no change in the appointments listed.

Appendix IV
The French Consulates in Spain

The officials listed below are those who occupied the post in 1937. In the case of a change of post, the name of his predecessor or successor is indicated in the respective note. Names given in italics indicate consular agents.

Key
B   Belgian
F   French
S   Spanish

Consulate in Madrid: Neuville[1]
    Daimiel: *Max Cassin*   F
    Salamanca[2]   —
    Valladolid: *Montaut*   F

Consulate General in Barcelona:[3] Garreau[4]
    Gerona: *Estève*   F
    Huesca: *Bert*   F
    Jaca and Canfranc: *Juan Lacasa*   S
    Lérida[5]   —
Mataró: *Miralpeix*   S
Palamós: *de Martimprey*   F
Portbou: *Dustou*[6]   F
Puigcerdá: *Grau*   F
Tarragona: *Merelo Barbero*   F
Valle de Arán   —
Zaragoza: *Tur*[7]   F

Consulate in Bilbao: Casteran
    Gijón and Oviedo: *Paquet*   S
    Santander: *Van den Brouk*   F
    Santoña: *Albó*   S

The French Consulates in Spain

Consulate in La Coruña[8]
    Corcubión: *Tanaro* — S
    El Ferrol[9] — —
    León: *Landeira* — S
    Lugo and Monforte de Lemos: *Merino Feijoz* — S
    Orense[10] — —
    Santiago de Compostela[11] — —
    Vigo: *Cazaux* — F
    Villagarcía de Arosa[12] — —
    Vivero: *Jesús Franco Fernández* — S

Consulate in Las Palmas: Dorange
    Arrecife: *Armas* — S
    Santa Cruz de la Palma: *Duque Martínez* — S
    Santa Cruz de Tenerife: *Lepesteur*[13] — F

Consulate in Malaga: Desmartis[14]
    Adra: *Arturo Ortrera Cuenca* — S
    Almería: *Cazard* — F
    Granada: *Serre*[15] — F
    Linares and Jaén: *Marty* — F

Consulate in Palma: Flandin[16]
    Alcudia: *Arrom Bibiloni* — S
    Ciudadela: *Mir Gener* — S
    Ibiza: *Wallis* — S
    Mahón: *Moysi y Seuret* — S

Consulate in San Sebastián: Émile Lasmartres
    Burgos: *Payno* — S
    Irún: *Ducourau* — F
    Logroño: *San Juan Yecora* — S
    Pamplona: *Celso Lorda* — S
    Vitoria: *Benito Yara Santillán* — S

Consulate in Sevilla: Moraud
    Algeciras: *Dupuy*[17] — F
    Badajoz[18] — —
    Cádiz: *Huart*[19] — B
    Córdoba: *Cantais* — F
    Huelva: *Banastier*[20] — F
    Jerez de la Frontera[21] — —

        Peñarroya-Pueblo Nuevo: *Le Rumeur*[22]   F
        Puerto de Santa María: *Sancho y Peñasco*   S

Consulate in Tetuán
        Cueta   S

Consulate in Valencia: Marcassin
        Alicante: *Neuville*[23]   F
        Benicarló[24]   —
        Cartagena: *Adam*   F
        Castellón de la Plana: *Alcón Fandos*   S
        Denia: *Andrés*   F
        Gandía: *Andrés,* manager   F
        Murcia: *Raphanel*[25]   F
        Torrevieja: *Carasa Arana*   S
        Vinaroz: *Ramoz Ten*   S

Notes to Appendix IV

1 In 1938, Pigeonneau.
2 In 1936, H. *Louis,* after *de Arteaga.*
3 In 1938, a consulate was opened in Figueres, in the charge of *Monneret.*
4 Up until 1937, Trémoulet; In 1938, René Binet.
5 In 1936, *Plana Subirà.*
6 In 1938, *Pujol.*
7 In 1936, *David*; in 1938, Rohrbach.
8 Up until 1937, Pérétié.
9 Up until 1937, *Palacios.*
10 Up until 1937, *Martinez.*
11 Up until 1937, *Villar Iglesias.*
12 In 1936, *Poyán.*
13 Up until 1937, *Bigourdan.*
14 Up until 1937, a consulate existed in Granada, in the charge of *Barueco.*
15 In 1936, *Delorme.*
16 In 1936, Goubin.
17 In 1936, *Pagnon.* Dupuy was consul in Gibraltar.
18 In 1936, *Planté*, then *Saavedra.*
19 Up until 1937, *Sandrier.*
20 In 1936, *de Fitte de Garies.*
21 Up until 1937, *Salvador Díez.*
22 Up until 1937, *Birón.*
23 Up until 1937, *de Laigue;* from 1938, Aníossy.
24 Up until 1937, *Boyer Canals.*
25 In 1936, *Viallet;* then *Vernet.*

Appendix V
Trans-Pyrenean Rail and Road Links between France and Spain

RAILWAYS

Département in France	French Rail Station	Corresponding Spanish Rail Station	Province in Spain
Basses-Pyrénées	Hendaye	Irún	Guipúzcoa
Basses-Pyrénées	Urdos	Canfranc	Huesca
Pyrénées-Orientales	Latour-de-Carol	Puigcerdá	Girona
Pyrénées-Orientales	Cerbère	Portbou	Girona

ROADS

Département in France	City or Town on the French Border	Corresponding Spanish City or Town	Province in Spain	Classification
Basses-Pyrénées	Hendaye	Irún	Guipúzcoa	First class
Basses-Pyrénées	Béhobie	Behovia	Guipúzcoa	First class
Basses-Pyrénées	Herboure	Paso de Ibardin (Vera)	Guipúzcoa	Second Class
Basses-Pyrénées	Sare	Echalar	Navarra	Second Class
Basses-Pyrénées	Dancharia	Urdax	Navarra	First class
Basses-Pyrénées	St-Etienne-de-B.	Errazu	Navarra	Second Class
Basses-Pyrénées	Arnéguy	Valcarlos	Navarra	First class
Basses-Pyrénées	Licq-Athérey	Isaba	Navarra	Second Class
Basses-Pyrénées	Urdos	Canfranc	Huesca	First class
Basses-Pyrénées	Eaux-Chaudes	Sallent-de-Gallego	Huesca	First class
Hautes-Pyrénées	Gavarnie	Bujaruelo	Huesca	Second Class
Hautes-Pyrénées	Tramezaïgues	Parzan	Huesca	Second Class

Hautes-Garonne	Portillon de Burbe	Bossost	Lleida	Second Class
Hautes-Garonne	Fos	Bossost	Lleida	First class
Ariège[1]	L'Hospitalet[2]	—		—
Andorra	Sant Julia de Loria[3]	Seo de Urgel	Lleida	Second Class
Pyrenées-Orientales	Bourg-Madame, ou Latour de C.	Puigcerdá	Girona	First class
Pyrenées-Orientales	Amélie-les-Bains Palalda	Massanet-de-Cabrenys	Girona	Second Class
Pyrenées-Orientales	Maureillas	La Bajol	Girona	Second Class
Pyrenées-Orientales	Le Perthus	La Jonquera	Girona	First class
Pyrenées-Orientales	Villelongue-dels-Monts	Espolla	Girona	Second Class
Pyrenées-Orientales	Cerbère	Portbou	Girona	First class

Notes to Appendix V

1 Although geographically bordering on Spain as well as Andorra, Ariège had no frontier post, and no asphalt road existed between Ariège and Spain. However, certain points on the frontier were traversible, including some that were open all year round.
2 French customs post.
3 Andorran police control.

Appendix VI
Spain and the Pyrenean Border

For maps of the Pyrenean Border, see the following websites

- The Peninsula: http://map-of-spain.co.uk/large-map-of-spain.htm

- Aragon and Catalonia / Midi-Pyrénées: http://www.google.fr

- Pyrenees coast to coast: http://commons.wikimedia.org

- Andorra: http://maps.google.fr

A Guide to Principal Place Names, moving from the Atlantic to the Mediterranean

San Sebastián / Fuenterrabía / Irún / Hendaye / Saint-Jean-de-Luz / Pamplona / Tudela / Biarritz / Bayonne / Pau / Huesca / Lourdes / Tarbes / Bagnères-de-Bigorre / Bagnères-de-Luchon / Saint-Gaudens / Viella / Saint-Girons / Muret / Toulouse / Andorra la Vella / Foix / Pamiers / Puigcerdá / Castelnaudary / Ripoll / Carcassonne / Prades / Céret / Gerona / Perpignan / Figueras / Narbonne / Argelès-sur-Mer / Port-Vendres / Port Bou / Cerbère/Béziers / Montpellier.

Départements (west to east): Basses-Pyrénées / Hautes-Pyrénées / Haute-Garonne / Ariège / Pyrénées-Orientales.

Provincias (west to east): Guipúzcoa / Navarra / Huesca / Lleida / Gerona.

Appendix VII
The French Press, 1936–1939

Global figures—Classification: the three main categories—Frequency and distribution—The 'Big Five' and their competitors—The evening press—Other leading conservative dailies—The right-wing organs and magazines—The business press—The Catholic press—The centrist press in decline—The radical dailies—The left-wing organs and magazines—Miscellaneous periodicals—The provincial press—The Toulouse press—The press of the Pyrenees—The press agencies—The foreign-language press—Liaison with the Anglophone press

Global figures

As the 20th century opened, the French press was of an astonishing size and variety. Even if, after 1912, it began to decline, in that year the Paris dailies alone amounted to 65, of which 39 printed fewer than 5,000 copies. In 1937 there were only 40, and in 1939, only 32, of which 14 printed more than 100,000 copies.[1*] It was especially the press of opinion that was suffering most from the new conditions.

The number of dailies is still remarkable. In 1937, for all of France, there were no fewer than 253 titles. The total daily print run was 11,500,000 copies,[2*] of which 6,000,000 were printed in Paris.[3*] The provincial press thus amounted to almost half the total.[4*] In 1938 it included 177 dailies and 860 weeklies. In 1939, 19 of these titles had a print run of over 100,000 copies, and the provincial press had moved up to some 6,500,000, out of a total circulation of 12,000,000–12,500,000.[5]

Classification: The three big categories

The French daily press, as regards content, fell roughly into three categories. First, the political daily was the organ of a political party or creed and was subsidized by the party or its sympathizers; the news it published gave a subjective rather than factual account of events. Second, the political information daily was not the official organ of a party, but its editorial policy reflected some political creed; the news it published was fairly free from political bias. Third, the general information daily was devoted almost entirely to news reports, without editorial comment or political interpretation; occasionally it carried signed political editorials.

Frequency and distribution

Of the Paris dailies, a few appeared only four or five times a week, a larger number six times a week, but the general rule was seven, several with a morning and an evening edition. Despite the appearance of more than one edition of some dailies, the Paris press had long consisted of two other very distinct categories: the morning press, sold in the capital and in the provinces; and the evening press, which hardly overstepped the inner suburban area. The first category was dominated by *Le Petit Parisien*, 'the paper with the highest circulation in the world,' while the second had long been led by *L'Intransigeant*. By the 1930s, however, the French press had undergone a deep change. For the first time, an evening paper on sale in Paris from two in the afternoon reached the suburbs and the outer suburbs the same evening and was distributed in the farthest corners of the provinces the following morning, at the same time as the provincial edition of the Paris morning papers. This newcomer was *Paris-Soir*, which might be considered the evening edition of *Paris-Midi*. Of a total daily runoff of 5,800,000 in Paris, *Paris-Soir* accounted for little under 2,000,000 on the eve of the Second World War;[6] it boasted therefore of having 'the widest circulation of evening newspapers worldwide,' and 'the widest circulation of all newspapers in France.'[7*]

The following table shows circulation figures[8*] for the leading Paris dailies in 1936 and 1939:

MORNING	1936	March 1939
La Petit Parisien, general information daily	1,312,129	1,022,401[9*]
Le Journal, general information daily	650,000[10*]	411,021
Le Matin, general information daily	500,000[11*]	312,597
L'Humanité, political daily	319,000[12*]	349,587[13*]
Le Populaire, political daily	300,000[14*]	157,837[15*]
L'Oeuvre, political information daily	230,000[16*]	236,045[17*]
Le Petit Journal, political information daily	220,000[18*]	178,327[19*]
Le Jour, political daily	not declared[20*]	183,844[21*]
Excelsior, general information daily	100,000	123,792
L'Écho de Paris, political information daily	100,000	__[22*]
L'Ami du Peuple, political daily	not declared[23*]	__[24*]
EVENING		
Paris-Soir, general information daily	1,709,632	1,739,584
L'Intransigeant, general information daily	200,000	134,462[25*]
Ce Soir, political information daily	__[26*]	262,347

Two observations can quickly be made: first, that the majority of these journals belonged to the right or to the right of centre; here a distinction should be made between the conservative journals, such as *L'Echo de Paris* and *L'Intransigeant*, and the reactionary papers such as *Le Matin* and *Le Jour*, if for no other reason than that they showed the greater sympathy for authoritarianism and fascism. That does not mean that the right-wing newspapers were in agreement on questions of foreign policy, even those that were linked directly or indirectly with the Steel Trust (Comités des Forges et des Houillères),[27*] such as *Le Temps*, *Le Journal des Débats* and *L'Information*. The second observation that can be made is that a large number of the journals mentioned above, and particularly those on the right, were in decline, at least from 1937, even when they passed into the hands of financial or industrial interests.

The 'Big Five' and their competitors

The so-called 'Big Five' (*Petit Parisien, Journal, Matin, Petit Journal, Echo de Paris*) made up the powerful 'Consortium' put together in the course of the First World War to ensure that the leading Paris journals would enjoy the common use, and practically the monopoly, of the advertising market. *Le Petit Parisien*, like *Paris-Midi/Paris-Soir*, was suffering from deep internal division between its conservative administration and some of its liberal star-reporters. Under the ownership and direction of Pierre Dupuy, *Le Petit Parisien* claimed to reflect no political bias. Nevertheless, its correspondent in Madrid, Andrée Viollis, found her dispatches diluted or discarded; exasperated beyond endurance, she resorted to sending telegrams to such papers as *La Dépêche* clarifying the position. It was to no avail; she was forced to resign from her paper which became, in the opinion of the Socialist press, the most official of the morning papers during the Daladier administration.

If *Le Petit Parisien* was still able to increase its circulation, it was one of the few. *Le Journal*, along with *Le Matin*, were steadily losing their leading places as general information dailies. The former, directed by its owner Pierre Guimier, followed a more literary line than that of *Le Petit Parisien* but claimed the same impartiality while leaning in the same way to the right. While *Le Journal* appealed especially to women and girls, with light and sentimental news stories, *Le Matin*, in the hands of the financier Bunau-Varilla, another on the right, sought its clients among the industrialists, merchants, those with little time to read, and those who sought sensational accounts in condensed form. He presented himself as an independent republican, but his ultra-conservative bent made him not only an anti-communist but also an anti-democrat.

Le Petit Journal, also styling itself independent republican, had been in steady decline since World War I and underwent a series of ephemeral transfers. Prior to the insurrection in Spain it had passed from Louis Loucheur to Raymond Patenôtre, a half-American who, as a candidate of the Front Populaire, ran for re-election on 3 May 1936 and won with ease. He then proceeded to put *Le Petit Journal* and his other newspapers at the service of the Blum government. From May 1936 to June 1937, the Patenôtre chain would provide the new government, in Paris and the provinces alike, with a press aiming for the middle classes.[28] This turn to the left, it was observed,[29] included support for the Frente Popular, but this ended on 8 July 1937 when Patenôtre sold the paper to Lieutenant-Colonel François de La Rocque, who promptly made it the organ of his reactionary Parti Social Français (PSF), formed in 1936 after the dissolution by the government on 18 June of the Croix-de-Feu.[30*] From then on it bore the epigraph 'Travail, famille, patrie,' which was soon to become a national motto. Its support of Franco was expressed notably in the column of *député* Jean Ybarnegaray (Basses-Pyrénées). La Rocque could do nothing, however, for the paper's circulation, which dwindled like the rest,[31*] including *Le Jour*, founded, owned and directed by Léon Bailby. Its epigraph proclaimed: '*Le Jour* does not serve interests, its serves ideas,' but the ideas it served were reactionary and even Fascist.

L'Humanité had been founded by Jean Jaurès a year before the creation, in 1905, of the Section Française de l'Internationale Ouvrière (SFIO), the French Socialist Party. Following the scission of Tours (December 1920), the daily had grown as the official organ of the Parti Communiste Français; while in 1935 its circulation was only 180,000, in 1937 it was already challenging *Le Matin* for third place and had the backing of 39 regional papers. Directed since 1918 by Senator Marcel Cachin, with Vaillant-Couturier as editor-in-chief, it took aim at both the Second International and the Fourth. Meanwhile, the scission of 1920 forced the Socialists to create a new organ for the SFIO. This was *Le Populaire*, founded by the *député* Jean Longuet (Paris), the son-in-law of Karl Marx and one of the most influential Socialists during the First World War; it had the support of a southern auxiliary, *Le Midi Socialiste* in Toulouse. At the time of the electoral victory of the Front Populaire in 1936, management passed from Léon Blum to 'Georges Bracke' (A.-M. Desrousseaux). Oreste Rosenfeld, one of Blum's secretaries, was given charge of foreign affairs; he was aided by député Vincent Auriol (Haute Garonne), who became Finance Minister in the first Blum Cabinet, and by Paul Faure, secretary general of the SFIO and Minister of State in the same Cabinet.

L'Oeuvre, founded by Gustave Téry, was directed by the wealthy banker Henry Raud. Its political position was on the left wing of the Radical Socialists, finding its clientele among government workers and the lower-middle class, especially in the provinces. It too supported the Frente Popular. Geneviève Tabouis, with family ties to diplomatic circles, was a leading light in the daily's foreign political coverage. She apparently enjoyed some highly personal contacts in Rome, to judge from the sensational accounts she frequently wrote. But her sources were sometimes quite unreliable.

L'Excelsior, L'Echo de Paris and *L'Ami du Peuple* were all conservative dailies. The independent moderate *L'Excelsior,* founded by Pierre Lafitte, had passed into the hands of Mme Paul Dupuy, an American who maintained the paper's independence even though she was the sister-in-law of Pierre Dupuy (owner of *Le Petit Parisien*). The decline in its circulation was reversed in 1937 when it benefitted from the disappearance of *L'Écho de Paris.*

L'Écho de Paris, the organ of General Castelnau, president of the reactionary Fédération Nationale Catholique,[32*] appealed to the conservative, Catholic and provincial bourgeoisie. At the outbreak of war in Spain, *L'Écho* was under the direction of Henry Simond. The resignation of Simond, on 13 May 1937, was followed by that of his impulsive political editor, *député* Henri de Kérillis (Neuilly, Seine), and several other leading contributors, notably Henry Bordeaux, Louis Gillet and Louis Nadellin, all three members of the Académie Française, and Jérôme and Jean Tharaud.[33*] With these seceders from *L'Écho,* Simond founded *L'Époque* on 7 June of that year as the official organ of the 'Jeunesses Patriotes.' Whereas this staff had had to support in *L'Écho* all the ramifications of the Nationalists' cause in Spain,[34*] the new publication allowed them to draw distinctions; without offering any support to the Spanish Republic, and while retaining their nationalistic and authoritarian sympathies, they began to present Hitler as the greatest threat to French national security. In 1939 *L'Époque* was printing at 70,000 copies. Meanwhile *L'Echo de Paris* was taken over by Léon Bailby, who incorporated it into *Le Jour.*

The case of Pertinax was special. He had spent his youth in England, where Paul Cambon, the French Ambassador, had strongly influenced his political ideas. Through the contacts he had maintained in the Quai d'Orsay and various embassies, he had become a veritable expert in foreign affairs. The *Manchester Guardian* described him at one point as an editor who 'habitually reports today what the Quai d'Orsay denies tomorrow and confirms the day after tomorrow.' The articles that he wrote on the second or third page of *L'Écho* contradicted most of the time what Kérillis and other editors were writing on page one. Relations between Kérillis and Pertinax thus became strained. Pertinax, an opponent of Hitler from the very start, broke in May 1937 with the political line of Kérillis, preferring to join his close friend Émile Buré and write for *L'Ordre.*[35]

L'Ami du Peuple, 'Grand quotidien d'information du Rassemblement Social et National,' had been founded by the Corsican perfume manufacturer François Coty, a Catholic Bonapartist and fervent admirer of Mussolini. In its fight against Communism, *L'Ami* became, in 1933, the official organ of Solidarité Française, a far-right movement that Coty had also founded and which was led by Major Jean-Renaud.[36*] While calling for 'a more effective government to rein in abuses,' *L'Ami* itself was selling at a loss. In 1933, Coty, bankrupt, was forced to sell his paper and died the following year. Bought up by Agence Havas and *Le Journal,* the paper's political line remained that of Solidarité Française. The administration passed to Pierre Bermond. Then, in June 1935—with funds supplied by Mussolini—it passed to François Le Grix, and finally, in spring 1936, to *député* Pierre Taittinger (Paris), president of 'Jeunesses Patriotes.' Thus the paper's tone, at the beginning of the war in Spain, is clearly anti-Communist and pro-rebel. At the end of September, however, Taittinger rents his paper to Georges Mandel, and even though Jean-Renaud, vehemently anti-Communist, remained as editor, the tone of the editorials changed completely. The paper now called for resistance to German demands and a strengthening of the alliance with the Soviet Union. In January 1937, with a new editorial team, *L'Ami* adopted an anodyne policy that provoked many an attack from the right, and Georges Mandel abandoned the paper in the early spring. Saved temporarily by its editors, *L'Ami* finally went into liquidation on 30 October 1937.

The evening press

The evening press, as already mentioned, was dominated by the newly arrived *Paris-Soir.* This had been founded by Eugène Merle and was now owned, like Georges Bonnet's *Paris-Midi,* by a group headed by industrialist Jean Prouvost. At the moment that it passed to Prouvost, both dailies were in fact moribund, with print runs of 4,000 (*Paris-Midi*) and 60,000 (*Paris-Soir*). The two dailies then formed the mid-day and evening editions of the same paper. The format that had succeeded for the first was copied for the second: they offered news and illustrations rather than editorials. *Paris-Midi* also carried a good financial news section and a digest of the leading articles in the Paris, provincial and foreign morning press. By special arrangement with the London *Daily Express, Paris Soir* could share the services of Lord Beaverbrook's ace correspondents Gallagher and Sefton Delmer. Although both *Paris-Midi* and *Paris-Soir* styled themselves moderate left-of-centre and boasted of their 'bold realism,' the slightly more conservative *Paris-Soir* experienced the same difficulties with its liberal star reporters[37]* as did *Le Petit Parisien* and refused to publish the more sensational dispatches of its correspondent in Madrid, Louis Delaprée.[38]* As for circulation, since the purchase by Prouvost in 1930, its print-run had increased from 60,000 to 1,500,000. Although nearly eclipsed by the later edition, *Paris-Midi* was also increasing its circulation, from 80,000 in 1937 to 120,000 in 1939.[39]

The other two leading evening papers, meanwhile, were in decline. *L'Intransigeant* had been, between 1905 and 1931, in the hands of Léon Bailby, on the far right. His editor in chief was Colonel Fabry, Minister of War in 1934 and again in 1936. The paper was chronically opposed to whatever Cabinet was in power. Be that as it may, it was in the 1920s that the paper reached its peak: Bailby was the first to introduce literary columns, a sports section, and theatre and cinema reviews. They did not save Bailby's paper, and in 1932 he sold it to the *député* and millionaire flour merchant Louis Louis-Dreyfus.[40*] Then, at the end of 1936, it was the main shareholders of *Paris-Midi* and *Paris-Soir*, headed by Prouvost, who took control. Bought up in October 1938 by Charles Ribardière, it became the mouthpiece of the statesman Camille Chautemps. But nothing reversed its decline.

Ce Soir, alone among the evening papers to represent the Left, was founded by the Communist Party on 1 March 1937 with help from Raymond Patenôtre and money sent from Barcelona by Negrín.[41] To compete with the redoubtable *Paris-Soir* and *L'Intransigeant*, *Ce Soir* simply imitated their format and enticed Élie Richard away from *Paris-Soir* to become its editor-in-chief. Although controlled by the Communists Louis Aragon and Jean-Richard Bloch, *Ce Soir* was served by contributors representing all factions of the Left. Its success was virtually immediate and significant: a run of 200,000 copies at the end of its first year.

Another evening paper, *Le Temps*, was the most dignified of the Paris newspapers. Until the advent of the Front Populaire Cabinet in May 1936, this moderate republican daily was considered a semi-official publication; after that date it was still frequently referred to as the organ of the Quai d'Orsay, and during the Daladier administration it resumed its semi-official role. It was backed, if not by the Comités des Forges et des Houillères as the Socialist press contended, at least by conservative bankers and industrialists. Under the joint management of Jacques Chastenet and Senator Émile Mireaux (Hautes-Pyrénées), it published more complete news dispatches than any other journal, together with the complete texts of speeches and bills, and a 'Revue de la Presse.' With the collaboration of such lights as Jacques Bardoux, its political, literary and art criticism (generally anonymous in the case of politics) was of a high order. While its appeal was limited to a readership of high cultural level, its circulation was growing, from 70,000 in 1936 to 90,000 in 1939.

Other leading conservative dailies

Two other conservative papers of high literary repute were *Le Figaro* and *Le Journal des Débats Politiques et Littéraires*. The morning *Figaro* aimed specifically at Paris and its upper bourgeoisie. On the death in 1922 of its director Gaston Calmette, it had passed in 1928 into the hands of François Coty, and in 1934, to his ex-wife, Mme Cotnareanu. Under her it enjoyed a collegial team that included Henri Dubois, Lucien Romier, André Maurois, Paul Morand, and Count Wladimir d'Ormesson), to be joined in October 1936 by Pierre Brisson.

On 13 May 1937, its managing-director, Henri Dubois, resigned and was replaced by Lucien Romier, who with Count Wladimir d'Ormesson set the tone with some rather haughty political editorials. *Le Figaro* also provided society news and literary and artistic criticism. In 1936 its circulation stood at 95,000, declining to 80,000 in 1939. Its contributors included several of the most celebrated writers in France.

Although François Mauriac expressed in *Le Figaro* the conscience of many Catholics, his opinions, like those of Jacques Maritain, were more at home in the monthly *Nouvelle Revue Française*, which was primarily devoted to literature and literary criticism. The criticism ran from the pro-fascist (Drieu La Rochelle) to the conservative (Thibaudet) and the Radical Socialist (Alain).

The highly respectable *Journal des Débats*, the oldest newspaper in France and the property of the Wendel family, also included among its contributors members of the Académie Française such as Joseph Bédier, Henri Bordeaux, Andre Chaumeix and Pierre de Nolhac), as well as distinguished politicians. Under the direction of Étienne de Nalèche, former diplomat and president of the Paris Press Union,[42*] it claimed to represent the republican centre and to remain neutral in politics, but in fact, like *Le Temps*, it tilted strongly to the right. Its circulation was mediocre, declining from 19,000 in 1937 to 10,000 in 1939.

The right-wing organs and magazines

Apart from the pre-eminence of rightist papers in the wide-circulation press, the most remarkable aspect of the Paris press of the time was the existence of so many journals with a circulation in some cases of 5,000 or even less, and whose viability rested upon their political bias or at least the shade in which they interpreted events. The Right especially was supported by various organs holding a combination of conservative or reactionary sympathies: Catholic, Monarchist, Fascist.[43*]

L'Action Française, founded by Henri Vaugeois, had its roots in Church and monarchy and its sympathies with fascism. Its directors, Charles Maurras and Léon Daudet, aided by Jacques Bainville, Maurice Bardèche, Robert Brasillach, Henri Massis y Thierry Maulnier, were engaged in outright war with republican and democratic institutions. Theoretically anti-German, while cordial toward Italian fascism, the paper worked to promote 'integral nationalism,' the banner of Maurras's eponymous movement. Even though it did not represent the political opinions of Jean, Duke of Guise, Pretender in exile to the throne of France,[44*] Maurras acted as though it did, carrying in his epigraph a proclamation of the Duke, 'heir to the forty kings who, over a thousand years, made France what she is':

As head of the House of France, I lay claim to all the rights inherent therein,

I assume all the responsibilities thereof, I accept all the duties attaching thereto.

L'Action Française wages total war against the democratic institutions whose malfeasance lies flagrantly revealed; to this purpose it calls upon every Frenchman in whom reason still holds sway.

Of the entire press, it is *L'Action Française* that gives the most reliable information . . . the inadequacy of the principles of democracy and of its servants has given birth to the oft-repeated maxim: '*L'Action Française* was right!'

But *L'Action Française* was to be disappointed. It failed to win the support it yearned for. Pope and Pretender repudiated it. A Papal decree in 1927 placed *L'Action Française* on the Index of Forbidden Books, for policies regarded as inimical to the Holy See, and it remained on the Index until 5 July 1939, when the Vatican had graver concerns. Despite its financial difficulties—shown by its appeal for funds in August 1936—the paper's circulation increased: 70,000 in 1936, 80,000 in 1937, perhaps 120,000 in 1938, but falling to 40,000 in 1939.

Maurras faced competitors whose philosophies were close to his, such as *Frontières,* a monthly review devoted exclusively to the analysis of foreign events.[45*] *La Victoire,* 'national socialist daily,' advocated an authoritarian republic, repeating each morning: 'What we need is Pétain!' But its press run was mediocre.[46*] More impressive was Jacques Doriot, who had broken with the Communists in 1934[47*] and founded, on 26 June 1936, the Parti Populaire Français (PPF), recruiting followers from both extremes who were discontented with the current offerings. Doriot also founded the weekly *Émancipation Nationale,* whose circulation in November 1936, according to its own count, was 210,000, but a maximum of 130,000 in 1937 is a safer figure.[48] Ever active, in April 1937 he launched the Front de la Liberté, an anti-communist movement, and on 24 May, with the help of a former minister, Désiré Ferry, he took over the evening journal *La Liberté,* up to then in the hands of André Tardieu, the founder of the republican centre, a close friend of Clemenceau, and a former prime minister. In June 1937 *La Liberté* absorbed *L'Assaut,* a weekly created in October 1936 and directed by Alfred Fabre-Luce. Its contributors included Pierre-Etienne Flandin, Henry Lémery, François Piétri, Paul Reynaud and Louis Rollin. From ultra-conservative, *La Liberté* steered toward fascism. From a circulation of 40,000 under Tardieu, it moved upward to 90,000 under Doriot, but when the Minister of the Interior closed it down on 1 October 1938 it suffered badly; when permitted to reopen, it had lost between a quarter and a half of its readers.

Meanwhile, Lémery, a senator and former minister of finance, launched his own weekly, *L'Indépendant.* Another dissident weekly, and a fierier one, was *La Flèche de Paris,* the voice of the Mouvement Frontiste, which was the first to conceive of the Front Commun. Created in 1933 by the former Radical *député* Gaston Bergery, who now preached 'the liberation of France from the tyranny of money,' *La Flèche*, whose maximum press run was 60,000, took aim equally at those calling for a Union Nationale and those calling for 'Soviets everywhere!'

Among other right-wing weeklies, *Aux Écoutes*,[49*] *Le Flambeau*,[50*] and *Je Suis Partout* were outright fascist, *pace* Arthème Fayard, founder of *Je Suis Partout*, who intended it to be 'the daily journal of the cultivated man.' It was Pierre Gaxotte, already editor in chief of *Candide*, who bought it up in May 1937 and hired Brasillach as its lead editorialist. Its print-run, which at its peak reached 100,000, fell to 45,000 by 1939. The much stronger weekly *Candide*, with a circulation in March 1936 of 339,440, presented political commentary and news of the cultural world in a newspaper format, but it similarly hid its reactionary sentiments under the epigraph 'parisien et littéraire.' *Gringoire,* with a print-run of 497,575 copies in January 1936 and of 640,000 in November of that year, shared with *Candide* its format and its sympathies. Under the direction of Eugène Frot and Horace de Carbuccia, son-in-law of Jean Chiappe, it was even more aggressive, specializing in defamation. Among its contributors were Henri Béraud, vehemently anti-Semitic and Anglophobic, and André Tardieu, the only member on the staff to oppose the Munich Agreement. Others on the far right included *Combat*, a monthly founded in January 1936 by Thierry Maulnier and Jean de Fabrègues, which also enlisted Brasillach. Its life was short.[51*] So too was that of *Contre-Révolution*, an international revue founded in 1937 by León de Poncins. Appearing first in Geneva, it moved to Paris, where it ran from July 1938 to April 1939. All these periodicals on the far right were designed especially for middle-class youth.

The weekly *L'Illustration* and the fortnightlies *Revue Hebdomadaire*, *Revue des Deux Mondes*, *Revue de Paris*, *Revue de France*, and *Revue Universelle*, were all conservative. *L'Illustration* was the world's first (1843) and possibly foremost illustrated journal. Certainly it had the widest circulation abroad of any French publication, selling 200,000 copies a week in France and in 126 foreign countries. Although known chiefly for its illustrations, it published well documented articles on all matters of current interest. *La Revue Hebdomadaire* was more conventional, publishing novels, stories, articles and criticism on current events; its editor-in-chief, François Le Grix, who handled the political section, was a monarchist and pro-fascist. *La Revue des Deux Mondes,* under the direction of René Doumic and, from 1938, André Chaumeix of the Académie Française, was regarded as the most venerable of the French magazines, covering literature and history as well as politics. Among its contributors were Pierre Benoit, Louis Bertrand, Henri Bordeaux, Maurice Donnay, François Mauriac, André Maurois and Paul Morand. The journal included a fortnightly review, edited by René Pinon, of foreign and domestic politics. *La Revue de Paris,* under the direction of Count de Fels and Marcel Thiébaut, restricted itself, like the *Nouvelle Revue Française,* largely to literature, imitating its rival's format and even character. *La Revue de France,* owned by Horace de Carbuccia and directed by Marcel Prévost and Raymond Recouly, combined literature and politics, drawing its contributors from the right and the far-right. Finally, *La Revue Universelle,* founded by Jacques Bainville and Henri Massis, shared its formula and its politics, publishing a section entitled 'Facts of the Month'.

The business press

Among the dailies specializing in business information, the independent *L'Information Financière, Économique et Politique,* controlled by the Lazard Bank, provided financial news and stock reports, and its circulation in 1937 stood at 75,000. Its editor in chief, Fernand de Brinon, was also chairman of the Comité France-Allemagne whose principal founder was the Comités des Forges et des Houillères. *La Journée Industrielle* represented big industry in the form of the Confédération Nationale du Patronat. Under the direction of C.-J. Gignoux it was the largest economic daily in Europe, with a circulation in 1937 of 25,000. Gignoux denied the charge of the CGT leader, Léon Jouhaux, that his paper sided with Franco, describing it instead as moderate conservative and republican. *Les Echos,* fundamentally anti-Hitler, published both a daily and a weekly edition, reaching some 10,000 readers in 1939. *Le Journal des Finances,* directed by Ernest Vincent, appeared weekly.

The Catholic press

The Catholic press tended toward an attitude of opposition to the insurrection. *La Croix,* founded by the Assumptionists, was the semi-official Catholic organ of France. It was chiefly a cultural publication for Catholics with information for the clergy and bore the epigraph: '*Adveniat regnum tuum; Dieu protégé la France.*' Though politically conservative, hostile to Communism and opposed to the Front Populaire, it nevertheless published articles, notably those of Victor Montserrat, which won no favour among the Spanish Nationalists. Serrano Suñer denounced *La Croix* as another new pacifist organ 'and, as such, our enemy.'[52] The ownership passed from Paul Féron-Vrau to the Count L'Épinois, and then, in 1939, to René Barteaux. With Abbé Merklen as its editor-in-chief, its circulation was growing from 84,000 in 1937 to over 100,000 in 1939,[53*] supported by nearly a hundred[54*] provincial newspapers of the same name which followed the policy of the Paris daily.

Among the Catholic periodicals, the weekly *Esprit* was founded and directed by Emmanuel Mounier, a founder of the 'Personalist' school of philosophy; it attracted mainly Catholics of the left, grouped in the Parti Démocrate Populaire whose goal was to reconcile Christianity with Revolution. *Les Études* was a Jesuit fortnightly under the direction of Marc Le Mondèque; its circulation in 1936 was 14,000. The weekly *Sept* had been created by the Dominican Fathers of Juvisy in 1934 as 'a *Candide* for ten million Catholic readers.' Indeed, certain special issues ran over 100,000 copies, but its usual run in 1936 was 55,000. Unequivocally opposed to the concept of a 'Holy War,' in Spain as elsewhere, the paper found itself suppressed on 27 August 1937.[55*] Its place was taken almost immediately (5 November 1937) by another Catholic weekly, this one within the laity. *Temps Présent*, directed by Ella Sauvageot and Stanislas Fumet, attracted a dazzling board of editors that included Daniel-Rops, Gabriel Marcel, Maritain and Mauriac; its contributors included Georges Bernanos, Paul Claudel, Charles Du Bos, Louis Gillet and Pierre-Henri Simon.

The Dominicans also published, under the direction of Père Bernardot, the fortnightly *La Vie Intellectuelle*, again with articles by Claudel, Daniel-Rops, Marcel and Mauriac. *La Vie Catholique* was the weekly of Francisque Gay, who propagated, as in *Études*, the thought of the Jesuits. Its circulation in 1936 was 30,000; on 7 May 1938 it too was bought up by *Temps Présent*, and the two journals were then fused.

La Jeune République, a weekly founded by Marc Sangnier and directed from 1934 by Georges Hoog, carried as its motto: 'As long as we have a monarchy in the factory, we will never have a republic in our society.'[56*] Anti-capitalist without being Marxist, anti-fascist without tolerating hatred toward Germany, it sought to reconcile Church and Republic, patriotism and pacifism. Most of its articles, however, were intended for intellectuals; it offered little to the Catholic masses faced with the reality of political events. Meanwhile *Terre Nouvelle*, the monthly organ of Christian revolutionaries in the Union Internationale des Communistes-spiritualistes, carried on its cover an amalgam of Hammer and Sickle and the Cross. It was placed on the Index in the same month that the insurrection broke out in Spain.

L'Aube, 'the organ of the Christian-inspired democratic movement,' was controlled by an extra-parliamentary political group and was therefore as much political as Catholic. Under the direction of Gay and Gaston Tessier, it represented the centrist and moderate forces then grouped around Georges Bidault that denounced the insurrection in Spain and called for a 'Front Français' to unite all those who opposed Germany, whether of the right or the left. Its circulation was falling, from 12,500 in 1936 to 11,500 in 1937 and 10,000 in 1938.

The centrist press in decline

Three dailies found themselves in full decline. *Le Petit Bleu de Paris*, organ of the republican left, had a print run in 1939 of only 1,500. The independent *Homme Libre*, centre left, created by Clemenceau, was resuscitated in September 1936 by Ludovic-Oscar Frossard. When in March 1938 Frossard became Minister of Propaganda in Blum's second Cabinet, *L'Homme Libre* passed into the hands of Georges Bonnet. Its circulation fell from 30,000 at its apogee to 3,000 in 1939. In January of that year, Frossard launched a new daily, *La Justice*, in which he pleaded, as Clemenceau had done in *L'Homme Libre*, for a French Army ready to stand up to Germany.

Le Quotidien, founded by Henri Dumay and 'created to defend and perfect republican institutions,' was at birth radical-socialist and the official organ of the Cartel des Gauches. Dumay, like François Coty, opposed the monopoly pressure of the 'Big Five,' which indeed tried to boycott sales of *Le Quotidien*. Dumay in his desperate need thus accepted an offer of help from Jean Hennessy, a member of Parliament and, more notably, a wealthy brandy manufacturer. The attempt to build a newspaper without the backing of large capital was thus a failure, just as Coty failed to survive without the help of the big advertising and distribution firms. For the editorial staff of *Le Quotidien*, to reach out to Hennessy was still a betrayal of its principles of remaining independent of pressure groups. The result was the resignation, in 1926, of its editor in chief, Georges Boris, followed by that of his colleagues Alphonse Aulard, Ferdinand Buisson and Albert Bayet. Their resignations doomed *Le Quotidien*. Hennessy, who bought out Dumay in 1929, shifted its slant markedly to the right, and when, on 17 September 1936, Hennessy let it die, it had practically no readership at all.

The Radical dailies

Among the Radical dailies, the most important was *L'Ordre*, alone among the rightist press to support the Loyalist cause in Spain, while it continued to oppose the Front Populaire of Blum. Under the direction of the sceptic Emile Buré, it appealed mainly to a reading public at once clear-sighted and restrained; this public was nevertheless limited to 12,000, and according to Manevy, no more than 5,000 in 1939. For the Radical-Socialists, front-running *L'Oeuvre* was supported by *L'Ere Nouvelle, La République* and *Le Quotidien*.

L'Ere Nouvelle, the unofficial mouthpiece of Édouard Herriot, was the organ of the right-wing of the Radical-Socialist Party and of the Entente des Gauches. Lukewarm in his support of the Front Populaire, Herriot declined a place in the Cabinet, accepting instead, on Blum's victory, the presidency of the Chambre des Députés. When defeat finally approached the Spanish Republicans in January 1939, the Socialist press dubbed this daily 'pro-Franco from the word go.' The cause of this bitterness was the support then given by *L'Ere Nouvelle,* starting in January 1939, to the campaign to extend recognition to Franco; but neither Herriot nor the jurist Gaston Jèze, among its principal contributors, was really culpable in this regard. In any event, under the direction of Gaboriau its circulation remained at a lowly 7,000, or 10,000 in 1939, though its reputation and influence were considerably greater.

La République, which offered greater news coverage than did *L'Ere Nouvelle,* styled itself "the daily of Radical and Socialist combat," reflecting the sympathies of the moderate faction of the Radical-Socialist Party, though Joseph Caillaux wrote for both papers. Drawn from the 'Young Turk' radicalism of the years 1928–1930, it was directed up to 1930 by Édouard Daladier, and after that by his deputy Émile Roche, with Pierre Dominique as editor-in-chief. Like *L'Ordre,* it felt greater sympathy with the Frente Popular than with the Front Populaire. At its zenith, in October 1936, its circulation reached 142,000, but in 1939 it hit its nadir, with a circulation of only 6,000.[57]

The left-wing organs and magazines

The official organ of the Confédération Générale du Travail (CGT), which claimed 4 million members, was *Le Peuple.* Inspired by Léon Jouhaux, who also served as French delegate to the League of Nations, and directed from 1936 by Raymond Bouyer, *Le Peuple* was opposed to Caillaux and the Radical-Socialists for voting *inter alia* against devaluation in 1936. Its circulation in 1937 amounted to 32,000, but in 1939 it fell to 15,000. The weekly *Messidor* was also under the direction of Jouhaux and the CGT. Its circulation was massive but short-lived: it ran for only 18 months, between 18 March 1938 and 1 September 1939. Another weekly, *La Vie Ouvrière,* under the direction of Gaston Monmousseau, was semi-independent of the CGT. Another of short life was the fortnightly *La Vague*: launched on 15 November 1936 by Marceau Pivert, who made it the organ of his Parti Socialiste Ouvrier et Paysan, it ran exactly a year.

Pivert stood out as a publisher who was alternately in and out of print. With Jean Longuet and Jean Zyromski, he formed a trio of recalcitrants within the SFIO that created the Comité d'Action Socialiste pour l'Espagne (CASPE), demanding of Blum the same involvement in Spain as did *L'Humanité* and *Ce Soir.* Their fortnightly organ, *L'Espagne Socialiste,* was no less ephemeral, running only from April to October 1937. From February 1938 Pivert published the fortnightly *Juin 36,* again the organ of his party and again a journal that quickly failed.

As for the Communist Party, it offered a range of publications in support of *L'Humanité*. Its theoretical organ was the fortnightly *Cahiers du Bolchevisme*. The monthly *Commune* first appeared as the 'Review of the Association of Revolutionary Writers and Artists,' and then as the 'Literary Review for the Defence of Culture.' Communist youth of the Third International also had a weekly, *L'Avanr-Garde*, that in 1937 had a circulation of 50,000.

Within the Communist opposition, a group calling itself Bolshevik-Leninist published the fortnightly *La Vérité*, 'Theoretical organ for the construction of the Fourth International' that disappeared in January 1936 as a result of the reunification of the labour unions. Its voice returned in two weeklies: *La Commune* ('the organ of regrouping and revolutionary action,' later 'the organ of the 'Internationalist Communist Party') and *La Lutte Ouvriere;* and a fortnightly, *Révolution*. These periodicals, in defence of the Ist and IVth Internationals and in opposition to the IInd and IIIrd, gave their support to the CNT-AIT-FAI in Spain, denouncing *Commune* and *L'Avant-Garde* as frauds.[58*]

In the Anarchist press, the most important journals were the weekly *Le Libertaire* and the fortnightly *La Révolution Prolétarienne*, both published in Paris; *Terre Libre,* the organ of the Fédération Anarchiste Française, published as a weekly in Paris and as a monthly in Nîmes; and *L'Espagne Antifasciste*, the organ of the CNT-AIT-FAI and founded in Paris at the beginning of the war in Spain. This last was replaced in 1937 by *L'Espagne Nouvelle,* published irregularly in Paris and Nîmes by Aristide Lapeyre. The most celebrated contributor to these journals, until his murder in May 1937, was the exiled Italian philosopher Camillo Berneri.[59*]

The success of the right-wing weeklies such as *Candide* and *Gringoire* left limited room for newcomers on the left that followed their format, such as *Germinal, Vendémiaire* and *Vendredi*. This last was founded, on 8 November 1935, at the initiative of dissident journalists such as Andrée Viollis who came to it from *Le Petit Parisien*. Although control of this weekly was officially in the hands of the Communist-leaning André Chamson, it allowed full liberty to its contributors, especially André Gide and Romain Rolland, and even styled these two among its directors. From late 1935 its circulation was around 100,000, but even so, its life was no longer than that of its contemporary *Sept*: it ceased publishing on 10 November 1938. With the death of these two weeklies, a new fortnightly appeared: in September 1938, to fight against the spirit of Munich, Mounier launched *Le Voltigeur*, giving the editorship to P.-A. Touchard.

Three other dissident journalists, Aulard, Boris and Buisson, had founded *La Lumière* at the time they broke with *Le Quotidien*. In calling upon republicans 'athirst to unite against political and social falsehood,' this new weekly identified itself, as *Le Quotidien* did before it, with the Radical-Socialist cause and the union of the Left against fascism, capitalism, and clericalism. Its contributors included Alain, Vincent Auriol, Pierre Cot and Pierre Mendès-France. Under the direction of Boris, who in 1938 became chief of staff in Blum's second Cabinet, *La Lumière* climbed from 24,000 copies in 1936 to 75,000 in early 1939. The weekly *Regards* styled itself 'The workers' illustrated.' Its eminent editorial board included Gide, Rolland, Maksim Gorky, André Malraux and Louis Aragon.[60*] *Regards* maintained its circulation at 100,000 between 1936 and 1939.

The monthly *Europa*, founded by Rolland and Jean-Richard Bloch, with Jean Guéhenno and Emmanuel Berl as editors-in-chief, offered articles on international politics and literary topics that inclined toward communism; among their contributors were Aragon, Chamson, Georges Duhamel, Guglielmo Ferrero, Gorky, Thomas Mann and Jules Romains.[61*] *La Patrie Humaine* was a pacifist weekly.

But of all the attempts to create the great leftist weekly, it was *Marianne*, launched by Gaston Gallimard and directed by Emmanuel Berl, that came the closest. When Gallimard sold it, on 13 January 1937, to Raymond Patenôtre, who changed its policies and gave its editorials to Caillaux, Romains and Paul Reynaud, Berl walked out, but its circulation increased from 60,000 to 120,000. In general, *Marianne* provided its readers not only with political news, commentary and illustrations but also with world coverage in literature and the arts. Its contributors included Georges Auric, J.-R. Bloch, Édouard Bourdet, Jean Cassou, Colette, Georges Duhamel, L.-O. Frossard, Jean Giraudoux, Édouard Herriot, Jacques Kayser, Joseph Kessel, André Malraux, Roger Martin du Gard, André Maurois, Jules Moch, Paul Morand, Jean Perrin and Antoine de Saint-Exupéry.

Miscallaneous periodicals

Among other periodicals, the weekly *L'Europe Nouvelle* was an independent of liberal persuasion that inclined toward the Radicals and offered articles across the board: political, economic, financial and literary. Its editorship passed from Alfred Fabre-Luce to Doriot, then to Bonnet and finally, in 1938, to Pertinax. The journal paid particular attention to foreign policy, publishing a supplement each fortnight with texts and documents. *La Tribune des Nations*, a weekly under the direction of Jean de Rovera, appeared in five languages, with articles by Edvard Beneš, Anthony Eden, Salvador de Madariaga, Paul Reynaud and Bertrand Russell. The fortnightly *Le Mercure de France*, directed by Georges Duhamel, offered general articles and a *tour d'horizon* on the political, literary and artistic scene. *L'Ordre Nouveau*, a monthly review founded by Arnaud Dandieu and directed by Robert Aron, appeared from May 1933 to June 1937, and again from June to September 1938. The weeklies *Vu* (1928) and *Lu* (1931), founded and directed by Lucien Vogel, were fused in May 1937 under the title *Vu et Lu*; while essentially an illustrated revue, it included articles from the foreign press. It disappeared, however, in March 1938,[62*] at which point the weekly *Match* appeared in a new form, no longer geared to sports.[63*] Thanks to the novelty of this genre—styled on *Life,* which had introduced the form in November 1936—it climbed from 80,000 copies in July 1938 to 900,000 copies in March 1939. Finally, *Le Recueil*, published in Quebec, offered a résumé of articles taken from the principal periodicals in the French-speaking world.

The Provincial Press

On the eve of World War I, *Le Petit Parisien* was planning to install printing works in the large provincial towns which would turn out an on-the-spot edition capable of competing with the local publications. The provincial journals, however, even if they were beaten on the electoral level,[64*] were still sufficiently strong to safeguard their sales.[65*] Nineteen of them had press runs, in 1939, of over 100,000. The four most successful were the Christian Democrat *L'Ouest-Eclair* (Rennes, 350,000), firmly opposed to the Front Populaire;[66*] *La Petite Gironde* (Bordeaux, 325,000), moderate, reflecting the Union Républicaine; *L'Echo du Nord* (Lille, 300,000), also moderate; and *La Dépêche* (Toulouse, 260,000), Radical.

Among the rest, *Le Nouvelliste de Lyon* (180,000) was one of the most important conservative and Catholic organs in France; its 12 daily editions were distributed in 25 *départements*. The city also had *Le Progrès*, 'Journal républicain quotidien' (220,000), and *Lyon Républicain*, socialist (40,000). Marseilles published three dailies: *Le Petit Provençal,* 'Organe de la démocratie du Sud-est,' Radical Socialist, with Vincent Auriol among its editors (120,000); *Le Petit Marseillais*, 'Républicain' (150,000); and *Marseille-Matin, Marseille-Soir,* conservative (60,000). In Lille, apart from *L'Écho*, there was also *Le Réveil du Nord, 'la plus forte vente de la región,'* socialist (200,000). Montpellier offered *Le Petit Meridional*, republican (80,000); and *L'Eclair*, monarchist (58,000). Bordeaux, apart from *La Petite Gironde*, produced *La France de Bordeaux et du Sud-Ouest*, 'Grande information radicalisante,' (180,000) and *La Liberté de Sud-Ouest*, 'Puissant organe de combat et d'action' (25,000).

Other leading provincial dailies deserve a mention. *Le Petit Dauphinois*, 'Le grand quotidien des Alpes françaises,' Grenoble, moderate (200,000); *Les Dernières Nouvelles de Strasbourg*, moderate (150,000); *L'Est Republicain*, Nancy, moderate (140,000); *La Dépêche du Centre*, Tours, radical (140,000); *L'Éclaireur de Nice et du Sud-Est* (130,000), moderate; *La Tribune Républicaine*, Saint-Etienne, socialist (120,000); *Le Phare de la Loire, de Bretagne et de Vendée*, moderate (102,000); *Le Courrier du Centre*, Limoges, moderate (100,000);

L'Éclaireur de l'Est, Rheims (100,000), centre-left; and *Le Journal de Rouen*, 'Républicain progressiste: doyen des grands quotidiens régionaux de France,' conservative (100,000).

The Toulouse press

The Toulouse press stands apart from the rest of the French provincial press, for two reasons. In the first place, the *départements* of the Pyrenees, and particularly Toulouse, showed a far greater interest in Spanish affairs, and the news coverage was correspondingly wider; Toulouse itself, labelled by the right wing as the "Reddest" city in France, Lille not excluded, provided an excellent observatory. In the second place, the Toulouse press included a daily which could take its place among the best in Europe.

La Dépêche: Le Petit Toulousain, 'Journal de la démocratie' was a remarkable example of a general information daily providing both international and regional news. With special telegraph and telephone links with its Paris offices, *La Dépêche* employed nearly 2,000 correspondents and operated 4,000 depots in the 30 *départements* served by its 23 editions (including 18 regional), especially in the 12 *départements* of the Southwest. A morning daily, *La Dépêche* was at first the organ of Jean Jaurès until his assassination on the eve of the First World War. In 1918 control passed into the hands of the Belgian Socialist Émile Vandervelde, and from him to the Sarraut brothers: Albert, Prime Minister in the turbulent period of January–June 1936, and Maurice, who left the Senate in 1932 to work on the journal. Liberal and moderate in its sympathies, *La Dépêche* became the official organ of the Radical-Socialists, especially of Herriot's faction, supporting the Blum and Chautemps Cabinets but transferring its backing to Édouard Daladier when the latter took power in April 1938. Few newspapers, if any, could claim such a range of celebrated contributors of exclusive articles: Álvarez del Vayo, Sir Norman Angell, Clement Attlee, Augusto Barcia, Paul Bastid, Julien Benda, Yvon Delbos, Marcelino Domingo, Georges Duhamel, Guglielmo Ferrero, Jean Giraudoux, Édouard Herriot, Gaston Jèze, Léon Jouhaux, Salvador de Madariaga, Heinrich Mann, Thomas Mann, Martínez Barrio, Ossorio y Gallardo, Joseph Paul-Boncour, Jules Romains, Herbert Samuel, Albert Sarraut, Count Sforza, François de Tessan, Albert Thibaudet and Émile Vandervelde. They were joined in 1936 by three Spanish editors, as a result of the destruction of their printing houses in Madrid: Antonio Gascón, managing director of *Informaciones*; Manuel Chaves Nogales, director of *Ahora*, whose print-run had been the highest in Madrid; and Andrés García de la Barga, former director of *El Sol* in Madrid, who wrote under the name of Corpus Barga.

The SFIO was well represented in Toulouse by the morning daily *Le Midi*

Socialiste, whose six editions circulated in 15 *départements* of the Southwest. Militantly Socialist, it campaigned on behalf of the proletariat of the Midi, but its relations with *Le Populaire* were so close, and its reproduction of the other's editorials so regular, that it can be considered an auxiliary of the central organ. Under the direction of *député* Vincent Auriol (Haute-Garonne), and the editorship of Léon Hudelle, *Le Midi* presented regular articles by Auriol and, after the fall of Blum's second Cabinet, an almost daily column by the ex-Premier. It did not, however, as did *La Dépêche*, transfer its support to Daladier.

The Right was represented in Toulouse by a daily and a weekly. The daily was the morning *L'Express du Midi*, 'Organe d'union nationale et patriotique de défense nationale,' one of the leading journals of the greater provincial press; it published several regional editions and operated an office in Paris, under the direction of Charles Ledré. Founded to replace the Monarchist journal *Les Nouvelles,* it became the property of the Marquis de Suffren and the organ of the Marquis de Palaminy. His editor-in-chief, Victor Lespine, resigned as a result of differences which were to the paper's 'unceasing regret.' He was replaced by Colonel de Franclieu and Gaston Guèze. The paper's original epigraph: 'Dieu et Patrie,' required definition, since it stood for an anti-Semitic God and a 'purified' France, to be restored to the exiled Pretender Jean, Duke of Guise, and his eldest son the Count of Paris, and committed to a Latin bloc. *L'Express* ceased publication on 18 January 1938, apparently for financial reasons. Its place was taken two days later by *La Garonne*, which used the same offices and followed the same line and format, but published a single edition, limited to Toulouse, the Garonne basin, the Cévennes and the Pyrenees. Styling itself an organ of national regrouping, it appealed also to a literary and international readership by engaging Abel Bonnard of the Académie Française and the Americanologist Firmin Roz. In 1939 its circulation stood at 21,000.

On leaving *L'Express du Midi*, Victor Lespine joined the Sunday weekly *Le Journal de Toulouse et de sa Région Languedoc*. A socio-political and literary journal, it shared the sympathies of *L'Express*: Monarchist, clerical and anti-Socialist. Considering the Front Populaire as the unwitting harbinger of Fascism, it invoked the mystique of patriotism and tradition in extolling the figure of Marshal Pétain. With *L'Express du Midi, Le Journal de Toulouse* organised a Centre de Propagande d'Action Latine et d'Union Méditerranéenne.

The press of the Pyrenees

Other journals of the Pyrenees also deserve a mention. In Basses-Pyrénées, Richard Chapon, director de *La Petite Gironde*, also controlled *L'Indépendant des Pyrénées* (Pau, 30,000) and *La Gazette de Bayonne*, which in 1937 became *La Gazette de Biarritz et de Bayonne* (20,000). These dailies were in competition with three conservative and Catholic dailies: *Le Patriote de Pyrénées, La Presse du Sud-Ouest* and *Le Courrier de Bayonne*. In the *départements* bordering Haute-Garonne, only *Le Républicain des Hautes-Pyrénées*, in Tarbes, with the help of *Le Petit Parisien*, could compete with *La Dépêche*. In Pyrénées-Orientales, the right-wing Radical *L'Indépendant,* in Perpignan (60,000), was in the process of eliminating the old-established weekly *Le Roussillon*, a mouthpiece of Action Française.

Press agencies

Among the press agencies, France Havas was practically alone, and in 1937 it incorporated Agence Radio, up to then in the hands of the Blum government, as a listening post on the Pyrenees frontier. The Spanish Republicans had the use of Agence Espagne, inaugurated in Paris in October 1936 by Jaume Miravitlles, a delegate of the Council of the Generalitat; the agency was entrusted to the Yugoslav Otto Katz. Other bureaus were subsequently opened in the capitals of the big European democracies; in London, Geoffrey Bing ran the Spanish News Agency. The first two correspondents sent by Agence Espagne to Spain were Arthur Koestler and William Forrest.[67*] The Spanish Nationalists made maximum use of the propaganda sheet *Occident*, directed by Juan Estelrich in offices at 20 rue de la Paix in the centre of Paris. Published fortnightly in French and Spanish, it ran from 25 October 1937 to 30 May 1939.[68*]

The foreign-language press

In Paris, the Spanish Republicans published, between July 1938 and April 1939, the weekly *Voz de Madrid.* The Basques in exile had already launched *Euzko Deya* ('the voice of the Basques'), which ran from 1936 and stopped only in 1977 when the Basque Government in exile returned to Spain; at first a monthly, it became a weekly in Basque, French and Spanish.

The Mussolini regime, since 1925, had published in Paris the bi-lingual weekly *La Nuova Italia,* which was countered in the 1930s by three weeklies published by Italian antifascists in exile. *Nuovo Avanti*, the organ of the Italian Socialist Party, ran from 1934, and *La Giovine Italia* from December 1937. *Giustizia e Libertà*, also Socialist and also from 1934, was directed by Carlo Rosselli. Following his assassination,[69] it was replaced in July 1937 by the daily *Voce degli Italiani*.[70*]

As for the German anti-Nazis, the *Pariser Tageblatt* appeared from 12

December 1933 to 12 June 1936, to be replaced on 1 January 1937 by the *Pariser Tagezeitung*, launched by Heinrich Mann and Max Braun.

In the English language, the dailies *New York Herald Tribune: European Edition* and the *Daily Mail: Continental Edition*, both published in Paris, had appeared, respectively, since 1887 and 1904.

Liaison with the Anglophone Press

The French press was in particularly close touch with the British press. Not only were articles in the one frequently reproduced in the other but several French papers worked in individual cooperation with British and even US papers. The British press was fairly evenly divided in its sympathies: the *Morning Post, Daily Mail, Daily Sketch* and *The Observer* supported the Nationalists, while the *News Chronicle, Daily Herald, Manchester Guardian, Daily Express* and *Daily Mirror* were generally pro-Republican. *The Times* and *Daily Telegraph* tried to be impartial.[71] Thus, *Paris-Soir* and *Paris-Midi* collaborated with the *Daily Express* and the Hearst press, *Le Petit Parisien* with *The Times* and the *New York Times*, *L'Excelsior* with the United Press, and *Le Figaro* with the *Morning Post*.[72*]

In sum, unlike the British press, the French press showed a bias, in terms of circulation figures, in favour of the Spanish Nationalists. This situation reflected to a degree the basic difference between the two democratic regimes: traditionally at least, in England the Right reigned while the Left governed, while in France it was the Right that governed while the Left reigned. But more than that, 'fair play' still had meaning on Fleet Street. In France, the question of the dissentient's loyalty was at this time constantly in dispute. The derogatory term *métèque* was commonly applied in reference to French leaders who were alleged to put some other good, whether of their ideals, their religion, or their race, before that of France. It bred a mutual distrust which was to prove fatal to the Third Republic.[73*]

Notes to Appendix VII

1. Against a total of 28 dailies, with a global run of 6 million copies, shortly after the Second World War; and against a total of 14 dailies, with a global run of 3.9 million, in 1972. Despite the increase in population, circulation continues to decline, with 2,012 million reported in 2004.
2. However impressive the figure for 1937 of 11,500,000 in France, consider the figure of 18,625,000 for dailies in Germany, which represents more than one copy per German family, the highest proportion in the entire world (Dénoyer, 84).
3. Boyer (108) gives the figure of 5.7 million for the year 1939; *Encyclopédie Française*, vol. XVIII, cites 6.7 million.
4. Against approximately 60 percent in 1972.

5   Bellanger et al., t. III, 456–458, 605.
6   Ledré, 360.
7   Although *Le Petit Journal* claimed to be 'the most read (5 million readers),' Manevy pointed out, pitilessly, that the claim to 5 million copies 'read' did not mean 5 million copies sold, or anywhere close to that; it meant that 'every copy sold was read by the entire family' (Manevy, 149).
8   The figures for 1936 are based entirely on those given in Bellanger et al., or where this work provides no figures, on those provided by Bodin and Touchard. The latter point out that only in the case of *Le Petit Parisien*, *L'Humanité*, *L'Oeuvre*, *Le Petit Journal* and *Paris-Soir* were the figures confirmed by the Office de Justification des Tirages. Even so, one can find contradictions between the two published works, as pointed out below.
   The figures for March 1939 are drawn entirely from Bellanger et al. In the notes that follow, figures are given from Mazedier; Micaud; and Mottin.
9   Mottin: 1,320,000.
10 Bodin and Touchard: 400,000.
11 Bodin and Touchard: 275,000.
12 In March, 198,914 (Bodin and Touchard); in June, 510,000 (Bellanger et al.); in December, 319,273 (Bodin and Touchard).
13 Mottin: 320,000; Micaud: 450,000 in 1938.
14 Bodin and Touchard: 99,767.
15 Mottin: 60,000; Micaud: 250,000 in 1936–1938.
16 Bodin and Touchard: 115,016.
17 Mottin: 115,000; Mazedier: 250,000.
18 Bodin and Touchard: 156,645.
19 Mottin: 160,000.
20 According to the French Information Center in New York, then located at 610 Fifth Avenue: 240,000 en 1937.
21 Mottin: 150,000; this journal had already become *Le Jour – L'Écho de Paris*.
22 From March 1938 incorporated into *Le Jour*.
23 Micaud: 150,000; according to Schor (117), between 200,000 and 300,000; according to the French Center of Information, 150,000 en 1937; and according to Schor, fewer than 100,000 from July of that year.
24 Out of circulation from 30 October 1937.
25 Mottin: 170,000.
26 In 1937, its first year of publication: 120,000 (Bellanger et al.).
27 The Comités des Forges et des Houillères, whose organ was the daily *Bulletin*, were largely responsible for creating the Comité France-Allemagne, a principal agency of Franco-German rapprochement; it sought also to develop the idea of a 'realist' policy toward the Reich.
28 Kupferman and Machefer, 21.
29 *Le Journal de Toulouse*, 2 August 1936.
30 La Rocque's new movement, this time under the sign of non-violence, brought him far better results. In one year he had doubled his following, passing from 1 million in April 1936 to 2 million.

31 On the other hand, *Le Petit Journal* was later one of the few journals of the centre-right to oppose the Vichy Government.
32 It had been founded in 1924 to oppose the anti-clerical position of Édouard Herriot. Its vice-president was the *député* Xavier Vallat.
33 Among those who resigned with Simond were the editors André Pironneau, Raymond Cartier, and Laurent Sisco, together with the contributors Gérard Bauer, Adolphe Boschot, José Germain, Robert d'Harcourt and François Porch.
34 It was an old Catholic general, de Castellanza, who, at *L'Écho de Paris*, coined the term 'Frente Crapular.'
35 Breen, 125–126.
36 *La Solidarité Française*, 'hebdomadaire de combat de la nation réveillée,' had first appeared between April and October 1934. It reappeared from January 1936 to July 1937 under the title *La Solidarité Nationale*, the only official organ of the Parti du Faisceau Français. These elements were reincorporated between August 1937 and May 1938 into *La Solidarité Française de Paris*. Under the political direction of Jean-Renaud, with Pierre Quimay as editor-in-chief, it thereafter appeared only twice a month.
37 It cannot be said that the impulsive Bertrand de Jouvenel counted among its liberal reporters. Cf. Manevy, 335.
38 Delaprée died in December 1936. The Air-France plane on which he was travelling from Madrid to Toulouse was shot down by unidentified aircraft. Cf. Pike, *Crise,* 99–100).
39 Mottin, 23.
40 *L'Intransigeant*'s most famous correspondents were Antoine de Saint-Exupéry and Baron Guy de Traversay. Saint-Exupéry, who also wrote for *Paris-Soir*, covered the war from Barcelona and recounted his experiences on the Republican side in his book *La Terre des hommes* (Paris: Gallimard, 1950): "On fusille plus qu'on ne combat, . . . on fusille comme on déboise"). De Traversay lost his life in Majorca in August 1936 in the Republican defeat. Cf. Bernanos, 243.
41 Madariaga, 443.
42 Its union was in the hands of the following directors:
Honorary presidents:
Étienne de Nalèche (*Le Journal des Débats*)
René Baschet (*L'Illustration*)
President:
Léon Bailby (*Le Jour*)
Vice-presidents:
Pierre Dupuy (*Le Petit Parisien*)
Henry Raud (*L'Oeuvre*)
Jacques Chastenet (*Le Temps*).
43 They came to be known under three labels: traditional and authoritarian (Maurras), conditional (La Rocque) and resigned (Doriot). The national-socialist Doriot was to turn against La Rocque for what he termed the latter's excessive conservatism. While Doriot would find the support of Tardieu, Déat and others, La Rocque would be backed by Taittinger and Kérillis.

44 The Pretender's own organ was *Le Courrier Royal*. Its circulation fell from 40,000 in 1935 to 4,000 en 1937, before climbing back to 32,000 in 1939.
45 In July 1937 it published a pamphlet, entitled 'Espagne, rempart de l'Occident', entirely devoted to Franco's Spain. It consisted of 100 pages and 180 photographs not previously published, and its contributors included Eduardo Aunós, Henry Lémery, Xavier de Magallon, André Nicolas, Léon de Poncins, and Count of Saint-Aulaire.
46 From a maximum of 13,000 in 1936 to no more than 500 in 1939.
47 He had been secretary-general of the PCF from 1924. He was excluded from the Party as a result of the riots of February 1934.
48 Breen, 190.
49 Nationalist but anti-German, *Aux Ecoutes* had called, as early as 1933, for a preventive war against Germany.
50 'Organe de la réconciliation française', it was in fact the organ of the Croix-de Feu.
51 *Combat* called itself a violent opponent of conservatives and moderates, but for Brasillach it was itself too moderate, which is why he broke with it (Breen, 99, 189).
52 *ABC* (Seville): 21 June 1938.
53 Other sources show a decline, from 150,000 in 1936 to 140,000 in 1939.
54 Other sources give a figure of about sixty.
55 The Vatican had given its support to the creation of this journal which described itself as 'neither right nor left ' (*Sept*: 10 March 1934) and 'Catholic, nothing else' (*Sept*: 6 March 1936). Nevertheless, *Sept* was very soon denounced by Catholic circles on the right, including the Fédération Nationale Catholique; the journal was accused of being 'Christian Red.' Its suppression followed, at the suggestion of Giuseppe Cardinal Pizzardo (Southworth, *Mythe*, 139). Cardinal Pizzardo, a member of the Curia since 1908, had been one of the principal negotiators of the Latran Agreement, signed in 1929 between Italy and the Holy See, and was to become Secretary of State of the future Pope John XXIII. A few days after the suppression of *Sept*, *Esprit* wrote: '*Sept*, a Christian journal, has been strangled by Christian hatred.'
56 Sangnier devoted his life also to creating a unified school system and a 'fourth estate,' which would be a society founded on labour.
57 Bellanger et al., 564.
58 In Barcelona, the POUM published, between September 1936 and May 1937, a weekly French edition, *La Révolution Espagnole*.
The political nuances between Trotsky and the POUM deserve clarification. Trotsky, banished by Stalin in 1929 from Soviet territory, and sentenced to death in absentia in 1936, was at this time in Norway, just before being expelled to Mexico by the Norwegian Government. His Paris organ, *La Commune*, even if it sympathized with the Anarchists, was strongly opposed to the collaboration of certain of its Spanish leaders with the bourgeois parties. 'What is needed in Spain,' it wrote, 'is a proletarian democracy in the form of soviets, class unity in the form of soviets.' As for the POUM, it was for Trotsky

and his IVth International too 'anarchist' in its reluctance to install dictatorship, and too 'naive' and 'stupid' in its readiness to participate—as the Anarchists were ready—with the bourgeois parties. *La Commune* wrote, on 8 January 1937: 'What the POUM lacks is what all centrist parties lack, clear Marxist ideas on how to take political power and how to destroy the bourgeois state by means of installing the dictatorship of the proletariat, which is the sole guarantee of assuring the victory of socialist revolution. It cannot therefore style itself a Bolshevik party or compare itself to the party of Lenin and Trotsky. What Maurín has constructed is a Catalan communism.' The POUM was also guilty of an abominable crime: 'The POUM has tried its very best to put a good face on Stalin's counter-revolution, in order to obtain arms from that same Stalinism.'

For the POUM, as for the Anarchists, the real 'naif', the real 'cretin' was he who imagined one could centralize power in a Trotsky without ineluctably creating a new Stalin. It is therefore wrong to call this party even semi-Trotskyst.

59 This former professor at the University of Florence was political delegate in the Enrico Malatesta battalion. The most detailed report on the subject of his arrest is that published in *Guerra di Classe*, in its special supplement no 15 of 9 May 1937, reproduced in *La Révolution Prolétarienne* of 10 June 1937. As for his murder, it was to remain unsolved. While living in Toulouse I put the question of the perpetrator to Federica Monseny. The last time we met, in Barcelona on 20 April 1979, she replied: 'Whether Stalin or Mussolini, we'll never know for sure. They equally wanted him dead.'

60 Gide, Rolland and Malraux, as well as Alain and Henri Barbusse, had all presided at sessions of the Congress of Writers for the Defence of Culture, held in Paris in 1935.

61 Romains was, between 1936 and 1939, president of PEN, the international writers' club.

62 The leading share-holder of these two journals had demanded Vogel's dismissal, following a report published in *Lu* that he was considered too favourable to the Spanish Republicans.

63 Cf. Bailby, as always ahead of the pack, *supra*, p. 286.

64 'In many cities, the leading journal of the region or *département*, or indeed the only journal of the region or *département*, rarely succeeded in getting its candidates elected. The reason for this is that these journals had not followed the evolution to the left of the majority of their readers, or had moved in a contrary direction' (Ledré, 357).

65 The decline in circulation of the 'Top Four' was directly related to the collapse of their sales in the provinces, where more and more people bought the Paris daily only as a supplement to the regional daily (Bellanger et al., t. III, 458). Albert Sarraut, while Prime Minister, paid homage to the worth of the provincial press in a speech he delivered on 15 April 1936.

66 *L'Ouest-Eclair* also published in Brest an edition for seamen, distributed in all French ports inhabited by Bretons.

67 Koestler interviewed Queipo de Llano on 25 July 1936 for the *News Chronicle*.

His report on the interview was followed by his arrest in Malaga, on orders of Luis Bolín.
68 The Spanish pro-Franco correspondents in Paris included Juan Pedro Luna, who from 1936 wrote under the name of Calderon Fonte (Groussard, 117).
69 *Infra*, p. 344.
70 The directorship of *La Voce degli Italiani* passed to Giuseppe de Vittorio who, under the name of Nicoletti and before his transfer to Paris, had played a leading role in the formation and early development of the International Brigades; Felice Platone served as its editor-in-chief until 1939, when he was replaced by Mario Montagnana. *La Giovine Italia*, a weekly published in Paris between December 1937 and September 1939, was also published in French.
71 Thomas, 347–348.
72 Prominent among the correspondents of the *Morning Post* was Sir Percival Philipps.
73 In the course of the parliamentary inquiry that followed the Liberation, Georges Boris, one of the few journalists to be invited to make a statement, denounced the venality of the pre-war press, and especially that of the Havas Agency. Certain newspapers, he added, especially in the Marseilles-Nice region—he singled out *L'Éclaireur de Nice et de Sud-Est*—were 'entirely in the pay of Mussolini.' Boris denounced equally the attitude of the French Senate in the face of this corruption in the Press. A bill drawn up by the Blum government, whose main purpose relative to newspapers was to make their accounts public, was adopted in 1937 by the Chamber but rejected by the Senate 'Audition de M. Georges Boris,' *Événements*, 2438–2448. Lazareff, *passim*; Bellanger et al., t. III, 505–509.

Notes

Preface

1. Micaud, 5.
2. In September 1937 there were in France no more than 4 million radio receiving sets, compared with 26 million in the United States, 8.4 million in Germany, and 8.3 million in the United Kingdom. However, public interest in radio programmes, in France as elsewhere, was increasing. The big journals in Paris and the provinces were therefore busy in launching and expanding private radio stations, resulting in a decline in public demand for the morning newspapers (Bellanger et al., vol. III, 472–473). These journals, however, did not lose in influence as much as they lost in circulation, because envious elements in the press would often berate the radio stations for disseminating overlong press reviews, of their competitors of course.

    In Spain the number of receiving sets, officially declared, was estimated at the beginning of 1936 at 300,000. This number would not include crystal sets, which were much more numerous (Arias Ruiz, unpaged).
3. 'L'historien et la presse,' *Revue historique* (Paris), October 1957, 301; cited by Pierre Renouvin, preface to Bellanger et al., I, x.
4. Al Laney, a celebrated reporter of the *Paris Herald*, called the French press 'the most venal press the world has known' and considered that the news columns were for sale in all but one or two of the Paris dailies (Laney, 74; cited by Hohenberg, 295). In estimating the number of Paris dailies as 'more than a hundred,' Laney showed he had a tendency to exaggerate. But Laney was by no means alone in denouncing the venality of the French press of this period. The New York weekly *Time* ran an issue in June 1939 (resulting in a collective libel suit against Henry R. Luce by the Syndicat de la Presse Parisienne) according to which: 'The Paris press has long been the sewer of world journalism. Few are the Parisian newsmen who cannot be bought, rare is the newspaper unwilling to be "subsidized". . . . The way some prominent Paris newspapers have handled their German "news" recently suggests that slush funds from the Third Reich are also being passed around.' Cf. Micaud, 6.
5. *La Nouvelle Revue Française*, 1 July 1935.
6. *La Nouvelle Revue Française*, 1 January 1937.
7. Thomas, 369.
8. Radio contact between France and Spain was mediocre. At the outbreak of the Civil War, radio stations in Spain were not yet powerful enough to cover all the national territory. There were only six broadcasting stations of any creditable power: in Madrid (7 kW), Barcelona (5 kW), San Sebastian (3 kW), Valencia, Seville and Oviedo (1.50 kW). All were therefore at a power lower than 10 kW,

while those of Budapest (to take an example) were of 120 kW. Thus the range of the Spanish radio stations was limited to 300–600 km, and radio sets had to be powerful to receive them. Very quickly, the governments in Madrid and Burgos set up their own broadcasting stations, while in Barcelona the Anarchists installed their own. The Nationalists benefitted also from information sent from broadcasting sets in the region of Seo de Urgel, and from the help they received from Lisbon, where a station was set up in the Hotel Avice to serve as liaison between Radio Burgos and Radio Seville. It also provided radio contact between the Nationalist forces in the north and those in the south in the opening period when Extremadura remained in Republican hands. Thereafter the station specialized in disinformation (Fonseca, Montpellier, 1986).

The big change for the Nationalists came on 19 January 1937 when Franco in Salamanca inaugurated the Radio Nacional de España. Constructed with German material, it had a power of 20 kW. Transported on trucks, it had the advantage of mobility in a conflict in which the battle lines were constantly redrawn, and its coverage was virtually country-wide. Meanwhile, Radio Zaragoza, put together by public donations, attained 30 kW, and the combination of the two, transmitted on E.A.J. 101, made it the most powerful transmitter in Spain (Arias Ruiz, unpaged). Radio Nacional, at first under the Ministry of Communications and then under the Delegación Nacional, was directed by Antonio Tovar, a professor of humanities, and under the control of Ramón Serrano Suñer.

On the Republican side, the German Communist Party (KPD) was able to maintain a service in Spain right through to March 1939. Broadcasting on 29.8 megacycles, it presented itself as Deutscher Freiheitssender (Dahlem, 58; Schlenstedt, 242).

9   General A. Niessel, 'La propagande par radio,' *Revue des Deux Mondes*, 15 October 1938.

10 According to Gaston Guèze, in *L'Express du Midi*, all mail for Spain deposited with the French post office after the fall of Irún on 5 September 1936, whether it was addressed to the Republican zone or the Nationalist, was routed from Toulouse by one of two trains; the 57, from Toulouse to Cerbère, or the 115, from Bordeaux to Cerbère. All mail addressed to Pamplona or San Sebastian (after its fall on 13 September to the Nationalists) never reached its destination, since it had to pass through Barcelona and Madrid. 'There is therefore only one way to correspond with Spain Redeemed,' wrote Guèze, 'and that is to deliver your own mail to the post office in Irún (*L'Express du Midi*, 12 October 1936). This report was apparently successful. One month later, the Ministry of Telecommunications (PTT) in Paris invited the public to mention how they wished their mail to be sent, if they were in a position to know: Bayonne, for the northern region controlled by the Madrid government; Cerbère, for the eastern provinces also controlled from Madrid; and Hendaye, for the Nationalist regions (*L'Express du Midi*, 18 November 1936).

Airmail services were negligible, whether through the Spanish state-owned Lineas Aéreas Postales Españoles (LAPE), founded in 1931, or through the French Air-Pyrénées, launched in January 1937 by a private company with a dozen

planes. This airline closed down within weeks with the collapse of the Basque front.
11 At the start of the war, telephone communications, no less than radio, favoured the Republicans. General Cabanellas, as head of the provisional government in Burgos, protested in mid-September 1936 to the International Commission of Telecommunications in Berne against the fact that communications had not yet been re-established between territories occupied by the Nationalists and the rest of Europe (*La Dépêche*, 17 September 1936). From June 1937, the Nationalists controlled the three principal Spanish centres in Vigo, Malaga (Italcable), and Bilbao (Eastern Cable). The complaints of Luis Bolín, that correspondents on the Nationalist side could rarely transmit their reports to their news editors in time for them to appear in the next issue and thus compete with their Republican rivals in the race to press (Bolín, pp. 221–222), are thus limited in their validity. Besides, Hugh Thomas accused Bolín, then at the head of the Spanish Nationalist press office, of worsening the situation by sending home a large number of journalists. The tortuous reply of Bolín, that 'certain foreign journalists were sometimes suspected, rightly or wrongly . . . ' (Bolín, 361) drew only a minor retraction from Thomas in his later editions.
12 Puzzo, 168.
13 See Pike, 'Guernica Revisited,' 133–141.

Introduction

1 Alfonso XIII decided to leave Spain to avoid a war. He never renounced the Crown, but on 15 January 1941, six weeks before his death, he abdicated in favour of his son.
2 It is curious that Puzzo admits this (Puzzo, 77) but quotes Krivitsky, without rebuttal, to the effect that 'the Spanish Republic, after five years of existence, still refused to recognize the Soviet Government (Krivitsky, 79; Puzzo, 40).
3 These were Anatoli Lunacharski and Julio Álvarez del Vayo. However, no Soviet ambassador actually submitted his credentials in Madrid until Marcel Rosenberg arrived in August 1936. Presumably there would have been a special opposition in Spain to Lunacharski's appointment, if the reports of his hysterical contempt for Christian charity (see Pike, *Crise*, xxxii) were believed.
4 This was followed on 16 May 1935, by a Soviet–Czech mutual assistance pact.
5 Such a policy of collaboration hardly bears out Puzzo's statement that 'the Soviet Union had left the "revisionist" camp' (Puzzo, 110).
6 The Sociedad Minera y Metalúrgica de Peñarroya had been founded in 1881. In 1893 it absorbed the powerful Bélmez company, which allowed it an easy takeover of the Spanish market.
7 British investments in Spain amounted to $194 million, and French investments to $135 million.
8 Four days earlier, Mussolini had expressed no opposition to the German–Austrian agreement. It should also be remembered that at the moment that Blum took power, France had no ambassador in Rome.

9   Jellinek, 282; quoted in Puzzo, 45.
10 Fal Conde was later forced into exile by Franco for plotting against him. According to Díaz-Alejo, the head of the Carlist party was waiting in Saint-Jean-de-Luz for the chance to avenge this insult (*La Dépêche*, 2 February 1937).
11 Álvarez del Vayo, 50; cited by Puzzo, 47. However, Angel Viñas, whose work on the German connection is without a peer, considers it 'absolutely impossible that Canaris offered a promise of future help' (Viñas, 300).
12 He was imprisoned from 20 October 1936 to 1 July 1937. Maurras nevertheless enjoyed sufficient facilities in his prison cell to continue to write, under the name of Pellisson, editorials for *L'Action Française*.
13 Communist strength in Spain in early 1936 is generally estimated at about 10,000, though the party claimed 35,000 members.
14 Its official organ was *El Noticiero*.

The fluctuating alliances, in the Cortes as in the French Chambre des Députés, lend themselves to an infinite number of combinations in the formation of blocs in both assemblies. The differences stem chiefly from the proclivity of the centrist and non-aligned representatives.

In the case of the Cortes, there was always a certain number of unfilled seats, for various reasons, which explains why the total number of members (473) is incomplete. After the second round in the 1936 elections, Cortes was composed of: Frente Popular, 266; Centre, 54; Frente Nacional, 153. Jackson gives: the Left, 4.700.000 votes; the Right, 3.997.000; the Centre, 449,000; and the Basque Nationalists, 130,000 (Jackson, 193).

I The Call to Arms

1   If tanks were not mentioned, it was for a reason. In June 1936 the French Army had only 34 (Amouroux, 43).
2   Germany first sent aid on 29 July 1936, Italy on 30 July. The report by *Paris Soir*'s Sauerwein, dated 26 July, to the effect that 'France . . . Britain, Germany and Italy [are all] giving discreet but nevertheless effective assistance to one group or another,' was premature. Italy's collusion was established by the capture on 30 July of three Italian aircraft in French North Africa (see *supra*, 29).
3   On the following day, 3 August, *La Dépêche* announced that the French Government, for its part, had held, 'scrupulously up to now,' to its decision to prohibit all shipments of arms to Spain, including shipments under contracts signed before the opening of hostilities.

In Carmaux, on the occasion of the 22nd anniversary of the death of Jean Jaurès, Marx Dormoy, as Under-Secretary of State in the Council of Ministers, spoke likewise: 'The French Government has not even consented to the delivery, to the regular government of Spain, of orders which that government had contracted with the private sector before the insurrection broke out.'
4   Puzzo, 88.
5   On that day, 4 August, von Neurath told François-Poncet, the French Ambassador to Berlin, that he knew nothing about German planes in Spanish Morocco. As for the concentration of German naval forces in the proximity of

Spain—which very soon comprised all three of Germany's pocket-battleships, supported by two of her six cruisers and six of her twelve torpedo-boats—the foreign minister told the ambassador that he could not understand the insinuations and the attacks in which a 'journal as important as *La Dépêche*' had chosen to indulge' (François-Poncet to Delbos: T. numbers 2399 to 2404, Berlin, dated 4 August 1936. Ministère des Affaires ètrangères, Paris, *Documents diplomatiques français*, 2nd series, t. II, 70.

The press of the Reich, for its part, suppressed all news concerning German aid.

6 Cf. *supra*, 55.
7 Puzzo, 106.
8 Cf. *supra*, 55.
9 The visit to London on 5 August of the chief of staff of the French Navy was a final attempt to sway the British. Darlan had a personal acquaintance with Lord Chatfield, First Sea Lord. The murder of the Spanish naval officers by Republican seamen had destroyed all sympathy at the British Admiralty, and indeed with the British Government. It was also known that Darlan had long been an Anglophobe, as Jules Moch stressed to me in an interview on 24 November 1973.
10 *Le Nouvel Observateur*, 3 August 1936.
11 Blázquez, 147; quoted in Puzzo, 90.

2 The Revolt of the Generals

1 It was *Paris-Midi* that broke the news of the insurrection to the French public. On 18 July, at about 11:00, it ran the headline: 'WHAT IS GOING ON IN SPAIN ? . . . MADRID DOES NOT REPLY.' *Paris-Soir* immediately assigned six special correspondents to the story.
2 *La Dépêche*, 22 July 1936.
3 *Le Midi Socialiste*, 26 July 1936.
4 *L'Humanité* , 20 July 1936.
5 *Le Peuple* , 2 September 1936.
6 *Le Midi Socialiste*, 28 July 1936; 29 July 1936.
7 *Le Journée Industrielle* , 22 July 1936.
8 *La Victoire*, 23 July 1936.
9 *La Garonne*, 27 April 1938.
10 *L'Express du Midi*, 24 July 1936.
11 *La Revue Hebdomadaire*, 8 de agosto de 1936.
12 *La Dépêche*, 31 July 1936.
13 *L'Express du Midi*, 30 July 1936.
14 Rotvand, 89.
15 *La Dépêche*, 31 July 1936.
16 *Le Petit Journal,* 20 July 1936
17 *L'Aube*, 23 July 1936.
18 *L'Express du Midi*, 1 November 1936.
19 *L'Ere Nouvelle*, 5 August 1936.
20 *La Dépêche*, 9 August 1936.

21 *Le Petit Journal*, 8 septiembre 1936.
22 Cf. *infra*, 385 n9.
23 Indeed, the Salazar regime had reason to fear its own overthrow. Reports reaching the Ministère des Affaires étrangères ten weeks earlier attested to Portuguese anxiety over the internal situation in Spain. According to the French ambassador in Lisbon, communist cells were rapidly being organized among tramway workers, dockworkers, and even in certain military units; he cited specifically, the Republican Guard.

The ambassador further reported that a Soviet merchantman, on arrival in Lisbon to take on board a cargo of cork, had succeeded in unloading a certain number of crates of weapons and ammunition, the operation being facilitated by the connivance of the police agents that were entrusted to its surveillance. In his summing up to Premier Blum, the French foreign minister wrote: 'The apprehensions of the [Portuguese] government circles over the possibility of a communist coup, supported financially by Spanish extremists and backed by certain Portuguese political emigrants, are such that the Government questions the loyalty of the Navy and fears defections in the Lisbon garrison' (Ministre des Affaires étrangères, to Président du Conseil and Ministre de l'Intérieur: n° 3683, Very Urgent, dated 4 April 1936 and 8 April 1936).
24 *La Dépêche*, 8 August 1936; 11 October 1936.
25 See Thomas, 309.
26 *La Dépêche*, 7 August 1936.
27 *Le Journal de Toulouse*, 4 October 1936.
28 *L'Intransigeant*, 26 July 1936.
29 *Le Midi Socialiste*, 27 July 1936; 30 July 1936.
30 *Le Midi Socialiste*, 28 July 1936.
31 *La Dépêche*, 13 August 1936.
32 In two remarkably ignorant accounts of this period, published two years later in *La Garonne*, General Toussan wrote that the Republican Government's Army (*sic*) was at the commencement larger and better armed that the insurgents' (*La Garonne*: 12 April 1938). Count Saint-Aulaire added that the government forces had at their disposal, from the outset, several hundred thousand militiamen who had for long been trained in arms (*La Garonne*: 27 April 1938).

In fact, the Republican forces amounted, on 20 July 1936, to 91,000 men. Three months later they had increased to 450,000 men.
33 *La Dépêche*: 24 July 1936.
34 *La Dépêche*, 29 July 1936.
35 *Le Midi Socialiste*, 29 July 1936.
36 *Le Midi Socialiste*, 30 July 1936.
37 *Le Midi Socialiste*, 30 July 1936.
38 *L'Aube*, 23 July 1936.
39 *L'Ordre*, 20 July 1936; *Le Quotidien*, 23 July 1936.
40 Franco himself admitted his predicament to Henri Massis in July 1938. 'At a moment especially dangerous and confusing,' said the Caudillo, 'Germany supplied us what we lacked, and we lacked everything' (Massis, 148).

41 The Socialist press envisaged the rebels taking refuge in Africa, if not in Portugal (*Le Midi Socialiste*, 29 July 1936). See Thomas, 1963 edition, 244n, a speculation he withdraws in his 1965 edition.
42 *Le Midi Socialiste*, 31 July 1936. According to the version of *La Dépêche,* Franco would even 'strive' to provoke such an incident (*La Dépêche*, 31 July 1936).

3 The Appeal of Giral

1 Cf. *supra*, 2–3.
2 *Les Echos*, 24 July 1936.
3 *Candide*, 16 August 1936.
4 *Les Echos*, 24 July 1936.
5 Cf. Thomas, 349, 350.
6 Cf. Thomas, 343.
7 *Le Journal de Toulouse*, 26 August 1936.
8 *L'Express du Midi*, 26 July 1936. The post of chargé d'affaires in Paris was immediately filled by Luis Jiménez de Asúa, the Socialist lawyer who was the author of the Constitution of the Second Republic.
9 *Le Figaro*, 25 July 1936.
10 *Le Figaro*, 24 July 1936.
11 *Le Figaro*, 30 July 1936.
12 *Le Figaro*, 31 July 1936.
13 *La Dépêche*, 26 July 1936.
14 *La Dépêche*, 26 July 1936.
15 *L'Express du Midi*, 27 July 1936.
16 *Le Journal de Toulouse*, 2 August 1936.
17 *La Dépêche*, 26 July 1936.
18 The requirements and practices of international law relative to rebellion are set forth in Puzzo, 78–79, who draws from Padelford: 'An armed assault on the duly established government of a state is, by the laws of all nations, an act of treason. However, when an armed disturbance assumes such proportions that it cannot be successfully dealt with by the police and must be met by the military forces of the established government, then a de facto situation of insurgency exists. By opening the arsenals and arming the workers' militias, the Madrid government had tacitly acknowledged that a state of insurgency had come to exist. However, throughout the stages of both pre- and post-admission of insurgency, the established government of the distraught state continues to enjoy its normal peacetime personality and status. It may continue its diplomatic relations with all friendly states and participate in international organizations as if no rupture of its domestic peace had occurred. Customarily, it has been permitted to purchase arms and war materials in the private markets of other states for the suppression of the revolt, a privilege often denied to insurgents by the domestic laws of foreign states' (Padelford, *International Law and Diplomacy*, 5–6). Only if France were to extend Franco belligerent rights would the international laws governing the freedom of actions of France as a neutral power be altered. But even in that event, the Hague Convention (V) of 1907 does not require (in its Article 7) that the

neutral power 'prevent the export or transport, on behalf of one or other of the belligerents, of arms, munitions of war, or, in general, of anything which can be of use to the army or fleet,' but merely (in its Articles 2 and 5) that the neutral power 'forbid belligerents to move troops or convoys of either munitions of war or supplies' across its territory. This situation was widely misunderstood. It was generally believed that the Convention was distinguishing in its Article 7 between the rights of the government of the neutral power and the rights of its private persons.

19 *La Dépêche*, 27 July 1939.
20 *La Dépêche*, 29 July 1936.
21 *La Dépêche*, 1 August 1936.
22 From a certain geographical point of view, French involvement was inevitable. Rebel artillery, positioned on the road leading from Ibardín to Vera de Bidasoa, was firing over the heights of Licarlan on Republican units drawn up along the Bidasoa river from Endarlaza to the outskirts of Irún. In *La Dépêche*, Gaston Dumestre remarked that General Mola's shells were crossing French air space. Dumestre suggested that the matter of territorial air space should be examined by the competent authorities and established as precisely as territorial waters (28 July 1936).
23 *Le Figaro*, 27 July 1936.
24 *La République*, 11 August 1936.
25 *La République*, 8 August 1936.
26 *La République*, 20 August 1936.
27 *La République*, 8 October 1936.
28 *Le Journal*, 27 July 1936.
29 *La Tribune des Nations*, 27 August 1936.
30 *L'Action Française*, 24 July 1936.
31 *L'Express du Midi*, 24 July 1936. Even *La Dépêche* sympathized with this sentiment, quoting the *Manchester Guardian* which recommended, all things considered, absolute neutrality. 'Despite their small chance of success,' it wrote, 'the insurgents might still win, and we desire to remain on friendly terms with Spain, whatever her government may be' (*La Dépêche*, 29 August 1936).
32 *Le Petit Bleu de Paris*, 24 July 1936.
33 *Le Petit Bleu de Paris*, 26 July 1936.
34 *L'Express du Midi*: 28 July 1936. *L'Oeuvre* and *Le Petit Journal* were apparently the more reviled by the right wing for the fact that their respective directors were both millionaires. See Appendix VII.
35 *L'Express du Midi*, 20 August 1936.
36 *L'Express du Midi*, 26 August 1936.
37 *Marianne*, 29 July 1936.
38 So too did Anthony Eden, the British Foreign Secretary, in a speech to the House of Commons on 20 January 1937.
39 Cf. *supra*, 52; Thomas, 387; Puzzo, 64.
40 *Le Figaro*, 8 August 1936.
41 *La République*, 9 August 1936.

42 According to *Le Matin*, Socialists and Anarchists in Barcelona were already threatening to come to blows at the beginning of September 1936. Cf. *supra*, 146 et seq.
43 *Le Matin*, 2 September 1936. *Marianne* of 5 August was of the same opinion: 'If other nations lose their heads, France, for her part, has to keep her own.'
44 *L'Action Française*, 26 July 1936.
45 *Journal des Débats*, 24 July 1936.
46 *L'Express du Midi*, 25 July 1936.
47 *L'Indépendant* (Paris), 5 August 1936.
48 *Le Petit Journal*, 10 October 1936.
49 *La Dépêche*, 24 November 1936. Cf. *supra*, 92, 178–181.
50 *L'Humanité*, 27 July 1936.
51 *Le Midi Socialiste*, 20 July 1933.
52 *Le Midi Socialiste*, 2 August 1933.
53 *Le Midi Socialiste*, 26 July 1936.
54 *Le Populaire*, 22 July 1936.
55 *Le Midi Socialiste*, 3 August 1936.
56 *Le Peuple*, 30 July 1936.
57 *La Dépêche*, 25 July 1936.
58 *Le Midi Socialiste*, 23 July 1936.
59 *L'Œuvre*, 25 July 1936.
60 *L'Œuvre*, 28 July 1936.
61 *L'Aube*, 26 July 1936.
62 *L'Echo de Paris*, 25 July 1936.
63 *Candide*, 30 July 1936.
64 *L'Express du Midi*, 25 July 1936.
65 *L'Action Française*, 26 July 1936.
66 *La Dépêche*, 27 July 1936.
67 *La Dépêche*, 29 July 1936.
68 *Le Journal*, 25 July 1936.
69 *L'Humanité*, 25 July 1936.
70 *La Dépêche*, 26 July 1936.
71 *Le Populaire*, 25 July 1936.
72 *L'Express du Midi*, 26 July 1936.
73 *Le Midi Socialiste*, 27 July 1936.
74 *Le Jour*, 27 July 1936.
75 *L'Action Française*, 27 July 1936.
76 *Le Quotidien*, 26 July 1936.
77 *Le Quotidien*, 1 August 1936.
78 *Le Midi Socialiste*, 29 July 1936.
79 *La Dépêche*, 28 July 1936.
80 *L'Echo de Paris*, 28 July 1936.
81 *La Dépêche*, 31 July 1936.
82 *La Dépêche*, 30 July 1936.
83 Cf. *supra*, 17.

84 *La Dépêche*, 30 July 1936.
85 *La Dépêche*, 31 July 1936.
86 *L'Ordre*, 30 July 1936.

4 Italo-German Intervention and the Cot Formula

1   See Pike, *Crise*, 161.
2   *La Dépêche*, 30 July 1936.
3   *La Dépêche*, 30 July 1936.
4   *La Dépêche*, 31 July 1936.
5   *A fortiori* from 5 September, when the Sultan of Morocco addressed a message to the French Resident General in Rabat in which he expressed his 'profound unhappiness' to see some of his subjects called upon to serve in the ranks of the rebels.
6   *L'Express du Midi*, 30 July 1936.
7   *L'Action Française*, 30 July 1936.
8   *L'Action Française*, 2 August 1936.
9   *L'Indépendant* (Paris), 5 August 1936.
10 *L'Oeuvre*, 31 July 1936.
11 *L'Ami de Pueple*, 4 August 1936.
12 *L'Ami de Peuple*, 8 August de 1936.
13 *L'Echo de Paris*, 1 August 1936.
14 *L'Echo de Paris*, 2 August 1936.
15 *L'Echo de Paris*, 4 August 1936.
16 *L'Echo de Paris*, 5 August 1936.
17 *Le Midi Socialiste*, 6 August 1936.
18 International Red Help had its seat in the Maison des Sindicats, at 8 rue Mathurin-Moreau, which was also home to the Association des Travailleurs Étrangers. The PCF had set up its central committee at 128 rue La Fayette.
19 *L'Echo de Paris*, 8 August 1936.
20 *Le Figaro*, 5 August 1936.
21 *Le Figaro*, 8 August 1936.
22 *Le Figaro*, 10 August 1936.
23 *Le Figaro*, 13 December 1936.
24 *Le Midi Socialiste*, 14 December 1936.
25 *La Dépêche*, 4 August 1936. Cf. Pétain, *supra*, 235.
26 *L'Aube*, 1 September 1936.
27 *Le Petit Journal* continued: 'Those people have never forgiven us, not only for '89 but for our entire history. They still take pleasure in recalling the captivity of François I in their capital and in reminding us that Spanish infantry, at the time when it was the best infantry in the world, occupied Paris. Aristocratic Spain, from the earliest times, has sought her inspiration in Germany. Alfonso XIII admitted it, with a certain cynicism. The intellectuals came to our libraries, but the General Staff fitted out the Army with matériel from arsenals across the Rhine' (*Le Petit Journal*, 14 September 1936).
28 *Le Quotidien*, 1 August 1936.
29 *La République*, 8 August 1936.

30 *La Dépêche*, 31 July 1936.
31 *La Dépêche*, 1 August 1936.
32 *La Dépêche*, 2 August 1936.
33 *La Dépêche*, 4 August 1936.
34 *L'Ordre*, 6 July 1937.
35 *La Dépêche*, 28 February 1938.
36 *La Dépêche*, 3 August 1936.
37 *La Dépêche*, 6 August 1936.
38 *La Dépêche*, 14 August 1936.
39 Up to that time, the largest-selling daily in Barcelona had been the moderate *La Vanguardia*.
40 *La Dépêche*, 21 August 1936.
41 *Le Quotidien*, 3 September 1936.
42 Krivitsky, 77; quoted in Puzzo, 39.
43 To which some Rightist jokers shouted back: 'Thorez to Spain!' (*L'Express du Midi*, 14 December 1936).
44 *La Dépêche*, 6 August 1936.
45 Sometimes unsuccessfully. A coded telegram (N° 9946.B, dated 16 August 1936), concerning the possible touchdown of French territory of two Fokker aircraft, was retransmitted *en clair* and found its way into the hands of *L'Action Française*, which published it on 17 August. Charles Magny, Director-General of the Sûreté Nationale, issued frantic instructions, dated 20 August 1936 and classified Top Secret, warning against jeopardizing the code by retransmitting *en clair*. The incident also suggests an early German experiment in selling arms to the Republic.
46 Director General, Sûreté Nationale: circular n° 9340-B, dated 5 August 1936.
47 *L'Action Française*, 7 August 1936.
48 In its legend of 9 August, *Le Midi* put this question directly to *L'Express*: 'WOULD YOU DENY FRANCE WHAT YOU GRANT ITALY?' To this Lalande replied on 11 August: 'The question is wrongly posited. Its "denial" and its "granted" do not correspond. We have nothing to "grant" Italy.' *L'Express* presumably had something to 'deny' the Soviet Union.
49 Dispatch of the aircraft was as follows:
    4 August 1936: 5 Dewoitine D.372
    5 August 1936: 4 Dewoitine D.372
    6 August 1936: 5 Dewoitine D.372, 2 Potez 54
    7 August 1936: 1 Dewoitine D.372, 1 Potez 54
    8 August 1936: 11 Dewoitine D.372, 9 Potez 54
    9 August 1936: 1 Dewoitine D.372.
50 In his report to the Minister of the Interior on 13 August 1936, Prefect Atger confirmed that a certain Roger Gaillac was trying to recruit pilots and mechanics for action in Spain and was one of the ferry pilots, flying a Dewoitine on 8 August. Cf. Carr, *Spanish Tragedy*, 140, who describes the welcome given to the French pilots on their arrival in Barcelona.
51 Prefect of Haute-Garonne, to Minister of the Interior, dated 7 August 1936. The

customs director in Montpellier reported that illegal shipments of arms to Spain had been carried out by planes taking off from private aerodromes such as Salvaza and Lézignan (Aude). The Prefect of Aude at once took all precautionary measures to forestall and eventually wipe out this traffic (Prefect of Aude, to Commissaire Spécial in Carcassonne, 11 August 1936).

5 The Delbos–Daladier Formula

1 *Le Midi Socialiste*, 1 August 1936.
2 *L'Humanité*, 25 August 1936.
3 *Le Journal de Toulouse*, 16 August 1936.
4 *L'Œuvre*, 2 August 1936.
5 *L'Express du Midi*, 21 October 1936.
6 Chief Inspector of Special Police, Toulouse, to Prefect of Haute-Garonne: n° 389, dated 26 August 1936.
7 Unexplained.
8 *Le Midi Socialiste*, 21 August 1936.
9 *Le Figaro*, 5 August 1936.
10 *L'Œuvre*, 11 August 1936.
11 *L'Ere Nouvelle*, 17 August 1936.
12 *L'Ere Nouvelle*, 11 August 1936.
13 *L'Ordre*, 1 November 1936.
14 Many of these planes were in poor condition and were sold at 300,000 francs each.
15 A certain retired naval lieutenant, Quedru, was reported responsible for the dispatch of the aircraft (Chief Inspector of Special Police, Toulouse, to Prefect of Haute-Garonne: n° 389, dated 26 August 1936).
16 Prefect of Haute-Garonne, to Minister of the Interior, classified Secret, dated 10 November 1936.
17 *La Dépêche*, 1 August 1936.
18 *La Dépêche*, 13 August 1936.
19 *Le Quotidien*, 7 August 1936.
20 *Le Quotidien*, 20 August 1936.
21 *L'Intransigeant*, 11 August 1936.
22 *L'Intransigeant*, 13 August 1936.
23 *L'Œuvre*, 4 August 1936.
24 *Le Temps*, 13 August 1936.
25 *La Concorde*, 18 August 1936.
26 *L'Œuvre*, 24 August 1936. Cf. *supra*, 49.
27 *Le Populaire*, 13 August 1936.
28 *Le Populaire*, 19 August 1936.
29 *Le Midi Socialiste*, 15 August 1936.
30 *La Dépêche*, 30 August 1936.
31 *Le Midi Socialiste*, 23 August 1936.
32 *La Journée Industrielle*, 9 August 1936.
33 *Le Midi Socialiste*, 4 August 1936.
34 *Le Petit Bleu de Paris*, 16 August 1936.

35 *L'Ordre*, 7 August 1936.
36 *L'Ordre*, 2 August 1936.
37 *L'Ordre*, 9 August 1936.
38 *L'Ere Nouvelle*, 25 August 1936.
39 *L'Ere Nouvelle*, 3 August 1936.
40 *L'Ere Nouvelle*, 28 August 1936.
41 *L'Humanité*, 30 August 1936.
42 *Le Peuple*, 10 August 1936.
43 *Le Peuple*, 19 August 1936.
44 *Le Peuple*, 19 August 1936.
45 *Le Peuple*, 22 August 1936.
46 *Le Peuple*, 4 August 1936.
47 *Le Midi Socialiste*, 10 August 1936.
48 *Le Populaire*, 11 August 1936.
49 *Le Midi Socialiste*, 21 August 1936.
50 *Le Populaire, Le Midi Socialiste*, 14 August 1936; while Gallus, in *L'Intransigeant*, considered Bracke "clumsy" (*L'Intransigeant*, 12 August 1936). As Gallus saw it, Bracke was presenting Blum in an unfavorable light. World opinion would suppose from Bracke's statements, wrote Gallus, that Blum was only proposing neutrality because he had no choice, but he (Blum) personally thought it deplorable; such an image would provide the German press with good grounds to accuse France of hypocrisy (*L'Intransigeant*, 13 August 1936).
51 *Le Populaire, Le Midi Socialiste*, August 1936.
52 *Le Midi Socialiste*, 2 August 1936.
53 *L'Œuvre*, 3 August 1936.
54 *Le Midi Socialiste*, 7 August 1936.
55 *Le Midi Socialiste*, 9 August 1936.
56 *La Dépêche*, 3 August 1936.
57 *L'Humanité*, 10 August 1936.
58 *L'Humanité*, 12 August 1936.
59 *Le Peuple*, 12 August 1936.
60 *Le Petit Journal*, 13 August 1936.
61 *Le Petit Journal*, 11 August 1936.
62 *Le Midi Socialiste*, 21 August 1936.
63 *Le Populaire*, 30 August 1936.
64 *L'Oeuvre*, 30 August 1936.
65 *Le Peuple*, 7 September 1936.
66 *L'Express du Midi*, 20 August 1936.
67 *La République*, 20 May 1937.
68 *La Dépêche*, 18 February 1937.
69 *L'Action Française*, 11 August 1936.
70 *Candide*, 13 August 1936.
71 *L'Echo de Paris*, 10 August 1936.
72 *L'Echo de Paris*, 30 August 1936.
73 *Le Jour*, 10 August 1936.

74 *L'Express du Midi*, 22 August 1936.
75 *La Kermesse héroique* was one of the most popular films in France in 1936.
76 *La Dépêche*, 16 August 1936.
77 *La Dépêche*, 5 August 1936. However, even the United States abandoned its Madrid embassy on 26 November.
78 *Le Journal de Toulouse*, 20 September 1936.
79 *La Dépêche*, in reporting this incident on 4 September, added that it should not be exaggerated, if indeed it really occurred.
80 *La Dépêche*, 4 September 1936. In the debate in the Chamber of Deputies on 4 December 1936, the député Frédéric-Dupont (Paris) accused Ambassador Herbette of having 'alienated,' over the last five years, Spanish military leaders who up to then had been francophile (Breen, 43).
81 Puzzo, 131.
82 Marty had reached top rank in the PCF by the renown he had won, on the far Left, by the part he played in the mutiny on the Black Sea in 1919. A mechanical engineer in the French Navy, he was assigned to the *Protet* when it was sent into action against Bolshevik Russia. For having incited the crew to mutiny, Marty was sentenced to twenty years at hard labour. As a result of a widespread campaign, he was released in 1923. In 1935 he became the first Frenchman to occupy a seat on the executive committee of the Comintern.
83 Puzzo, 258. This action was vehemently denounced by Indalecio Prieto, in Santiago de Chile on 15 October 1938. According to Marty, who was at least on the spot, the French authorities blocked the trucks for 15 days just 100 metres from the frontier. According to other reports, four trucks were held up in Toulouse and Montauban so that they could not reach Irún until the day the city fell.
84 In the action against Irún, two Frenchmen were killed and 22 wounded.
85 *Le Midi Socialiste*, 9 September 1936.
86 *Le Midi Socialiste*, 24 September 1936.
87 *La Dépêche*, 16 October 1936.
88 *La Dépêche*, 21 October 1936.
89 *L'Express du Midi*, 21 October 1936.
90 *L'Express du Midi*, 19 October 1936.
91 Berneri Collection.
92 *Le Journal de Toulouse*, 20 September 1936.
93 *Le Midi Socialiste*, 24 September 1936.
94 *Le Midi Socialiste*, 23 October 1936.
95 *L'Express du Midi*, 23 October 1936.
96 *La Dépêche*, 12 November 1936.
97 *La Dépêche*, 20 November 1936.
98 *La Dépêche*, 30 November 1936.
99 Indeed, in the first month of the war, Roger Salengro, then Minister of the Interior, had forced Spanish Nationalists who had taken residence in French cities near the Pyrenees to either leave France or move to north of the River Loire. *L'Echo de Paris* responded on 8 September: 'The partiality of his behaviour amounts to cynicism.' By the end of 1936, however, all Spanish refugees resident in France

were uniformly ordered by the Special Police to move north of the Loire (*La Dépêche*, 31 December 1936).
100 *Le Petit Gironde*, 10 September 1936.
101 *L'Express du Midi*, 14 October 1936.
102 *L'Express du Midi*, 12 October 1936.
103 'Se comunica a todos los españoles de Toulouse que se ha constituido en esa localidad un comité español de acción antifascista con objeto de aportar al pueblo español en lucha abierta y heroica contra el fascista por la defensa de la libertad una ayuda inmediata y eficaz tanto moral como material. Rogamos encarecidamente a todos los españoles de Toulouse y su región adhieran sin demora a ese comité en la acción que se propone desarrollar.' This was followed by a notice in French: 'To reach the committee, contact Comrade Bonis, 14 rue Saint-Georges, Toulouse' (*La Dépêche*, 4 August 1936).
104 *Le Journal de Toulouse*, 6 December 1936.
105 *L'Express du Midi*, 16 August 1936.
106 *L'Echo de Paris*, 8 September 1936.
107 *L'Express du Midi*, 16 August 1936.
108 *L'Express du Midi*, 6 September 1936.
109 *L'Express du Midi*, 27 December 1936.
110 *La Dépêche*, 31 December 1936.
111 *La Dépêche*, 16 October 1936.
112 *Le Midi Socialiste*, 6 September 1936. For commentaries on Spaniards in France that were hostile as early as 1936, even in the columns of moderates such as Albert Milhaud in *L'Ère Nouvelle*, see Pike, *Crise*, 201 n.
113 *Le Midi Socialiste*, 5 September 1936.
114 Handwritten letter from the Public Prosecutor in Muret (Haute-Garonne), to Prefect, Haute-Garonne, dated 18 September 1936. Concerning French aid, Moch, *Front*, 230–237; Moch, *Rencontres*, 189–217.

6 Mediation Appeals and Fascist Consolidation

1 Berneri Collection.
2 *La Dépêche*, 7 August 1936.
3 *Le Figaro*, 17 August 1936.
4 *Le Figaro*, 19 August 1936.
5 *L'Ere Nouvelle*, 19 August 1936.
6 *Le Figaro*, 18 August 1936. *Sept* of 21 August 1936 expressed its appreciation to Mauriac for his intervention. Colonel John Nicoletis recounted to the author the experiences of the French viscount Jean d'Esme, who in 1936 was reporting for *Paris-Soir* and filming in forbidden areas of Nationalist Spain. He was taken prisoner by the Nationalists in Badajoz and kept in darkness and solitary confinement. When Nicoletis met him, on the plane home from Madrid to Paris, he was in a pitiful state, shaking and incoherent (interview). The Portuguese journalist Mario Neves reported that a priest, looking at the corpses, made the remark: 'The deserved it' (Mitchell, 56).
7 'Any war, or threat of war, whether immediately affecting any of the League or

not, is hereby declared a matter of concern to the whole League, and the League shall take any action that maybe deemed wise and ineffectual to safeguard the peace of nations. In case any such emergency should arise, the Secretary-General shall, on the request of any Member of the League, forthwith summon a meeting of the Council . . . '"
8   *L'Oeuvre*, 24 August 1936.
9   Though for different reasons of course. According to Daudet, it was necessary to intervene against 'those terrors for which a phantom government, outstripped by gangs of arsonists and thugs, must accept the responsibility (*L'Action Française*, 4 September 1936).
10 *L'Express du Midi*, 5 September 1936.
11 *L'Express du Midi*, 1 December 1936.
12 *La Dépêche*, 30 August 1936.
13 Castro had served in 1931–1932 as ambassador to Berlin. At this time he was serving the government as diplomat at large.
14 *Le Midi Socialiste*, 12 August 1936.
15 *Le Midi Socialiste*, 31 August 1936.
16 *La Dépêche*, 2 September 1936.
17 *Le Journal de Toulouse*, 25, 30 August 1936.
18 *Le Midi Socialiste*, 13 Novermber 1936.
19 *Le Midi Socialiste*, 10 December 1936.
20 *Le Figaro*, 8 August 1936.
21 Cf. *supra*, 106.
22 *L'Echo de Paris*, 8 September 136.
23 General Sanjurjo was killed in an air crash while taking off from Marinha Grande in Portugal on 20 July to lead the insurrection.
24 *L'Oeuvre*, 2 August 1936.
25 The *Manchester Gaurdian* asserted that Franco had promised Hitler the use of the naval base in the Balearics in exchange for immediate aid in capital and war matériel (*La Dépêche*, 5 August 1936).
26 The *Völkischer Beobachter* was discussing openly the need for a military intervention to 'protect German nationals' (*La Dépêche*, 5 August 1936).
27 Son of the statesman Hjalmar Branting and president of the Swedish Committee of Aid to Spain.
28 *L'Humanité*, 3 September 1936.
29 *Le Peuple*, 3 September 1936.
30 *Le Peuple*, 4 September 1936.
31 *Le Populaire*, 4 September 1936.
32 *Le Petit Journal*, 5 September 1936.
33 *Le Petit Journal*, 10 October 1936.
34 *Le Figaro*, 5 September 1936.
35 In an article on 9 August, cited *supra*, 23.
36 *La République*, 16 September 1936.
37 *Le Midi Socialiste*, 23 November 1936.
38 *L'Echo de Paris*, 4 August 1936. *L'Echo De Paris* could not, however, bring itself

to report the message sent by Cabanellas to the German people in mid-September 1936, in which the head *pro tempore* of the Junta of Burgos affirmed his solidarity with Hitler. The Socialist press commented sardonically on this 'understandable omission' (*Le Midi Socialiste*, 18 September 1936).
39. *Candide*, 13 August 1936.
40. *L'Action Française*, 6 August 1936.
41. *L'Ami du Peuple*, 8 August 1936.
42. *L'Ordre*, 4 August 1936.
43. *La Dépêche*, 1 August 1936.
44. *L'Oeuvre*, 9 August 1936.
45. *Paris-Midi*, 22 August 1936.
46. *Le Petit Journal*, 21 August 1936.
47. *Le Midi Socialiste*, 22 August 1936.
48. So it appeared also to the French Ambassador to Rome, Count de Chambrun (Puzzo, 117). Cf. *supra*, 55.
49. *Le Populaire*, 23 August 1936.
50. *Le Populaire*, 24 August 1936.
51. In 1937, *L'Express du Midi* published figures showing expenditure on arms by nation in the course of 1936, together with the respective rates of aircraft production in 1937:

	Expenditure (in billions of francs)	Aircraft Production (per month)
Soviet Union	89	Unknown
Germany	78	350
Italy	26	200
Great Britain	25	250
France	21	35–40

52. *Le Journée Industrielle*, 1 August 1936.
53. *Le Midi Socialiste*, 10 August 1936.
54. *Le Petit Journal*, 28 August 1936.
55. *L'Ere Nouvelle*, 6 September 1936.
56. *Le Dépêche*, 6 September 1936.
57. Cf. *supra*, 41.
58. Cf. *supra*, 100.
59. *Le Dépêche*, 26 October 1936.
60. *Le Dépêche*, 16 November 1936.
61. *Le Dépêche*, 13 November 1936.
62. *Le Midi Socialiste*, 29 December 1936.
63. *L'Express du Midi*, 23 November 1936.
64. *L'Express du Midi*, 16 December 1936.
65. *L'Express du Midi*, 20 December 1936. The Marquis of Palaminy's apprehensions were borne out by William Shirer. According to Shirer, Hitler admitted to his colleagues on November 5, 1937, that the continuation of tension in the Mediterranean would allow him a free hand in Central Europe (Shirer, 127).

According to Liddell Hart, Hitler also admitted that he hoped to divert the attention of the Western powers toward Spain, which would allow him to continue to rearm the Wehrmacht without being observed (Liddell Hart, 34).
66 *Le Petit Parisien*, 8 October 1936.

7 The London Committee

1 Cf. *supra*, 10.
2 See *Le Matin*, 6 August 1936; *New York Herald Tribune* (París), 7, 11 August 1936.
3 *Pravda*, 6 August 1936.
4 Cf. *supra*, 10.
5 Germany had adhered on August 17 on a minor condition (Puzzo, 113). Italy had adhered on August 21 subject to the proscription of 'indirect interference' (Puzzo, 127). *Le Petit Journal* remarked that the delay by Berlin and Rome in agreeing to the plan reflected their confidence both in the quality of their matériel and in the prospects of the rebels (*Le Petit Journal*, 5 September 1936).
6 *Le Populaire*, 3 September 1936.
7 *L'Intransingeant*, 10 September 1936. Following this report, Antoine was arrested on orders of Bolín (Koestler, 27).
8 *Le Peuple*, 3 September 1936.
9 *L'Oeuvre*, 3 September 1936.
10 *L'Humanité*, 3 September 1936.
11 *Le Journal*, 13 September 1936.
12 *Le Midi Socialiste*, 26 December 1936.
13 *Le Peuple*, 1 October 1936.
14 *L'Express du Midi*, 10 October 1936.
15 *L'Express du Midi,* 17 October 1936.
16 *L'Express du Midi*, 13 October 1936.
17 *Le Jour*, 12 October 1936.
18 *L'Express du Midi*, 6 November 1936.
19 The most carefully tabulated treatise on Soviet aid to the Republic prior to 15 October 1936 was that compiled and published by Jacques Bardoux in 1937. It was also among the most inaccurate. According to Bardoux, aid provided by the Comintern and the Soviet Government during the Asturias uprising of October 1934 included even tanks. Vessels from Odessa had been allegedly docking in Alicante twice a week since the beginning of September 1936 with cargoes of dismantled planes and anti-aircraft guns. (Bardoux, 29–30).

Certainly the Soviet steamer *Turquesa* had delivered arms to the Asturian miners in 1934, but the weapons for the most part had been buried by the miners for use on a future occasion.

The USSR continued to deny that it had sent aid to the Republic before October, and this is supported by Bolloten, 99 n. However, we saw above (p. 311) the report on the presence in Lisbon in April of a Soviet merchantman that was unloading crates of arms and munitions, and it appears that other forms of Soviet aid did reach Spain before Kagan gave his speech. According to the French commercial attaché in Turkey, four Soviet or Spanish vessels were seen crossing the straits between 15 August and 15 September, in provenance from Russia and bound for Spain, transporting a total of 30,000 tons of fuel. From 15 September to 3 October, four Soviet vessels passed through the straits (Herbette to Delbos: T. n° 1344, San Sebastian, dated 19 October 1936. Ministère des Affaires étrangères, 2nd series, t. III, § 374).

Whealey provides other information that supports this hypothesis. The first Soviet military and political advisers had apparently landed in Madrid on 16 September. Three Soviet vessels had allegedly weighed anchor in Spanish ports in the same month; the first (the *Neva*) reached Alicante on 25 September with the first Soviet arms. (Seventeen vessels followed in October and seven in November.) Whealey cites a report on 6 October from the French military attaché in San Sebastian, stating that the first Soviet planes entered service on the same day (Carr, 222–237).

20 Cf. *supra*, 68.
21 For another definition of non-intervention by another cynic, see Talleyrand, *supra*, 232.
22 *La Nouvelle Revue*, 1 September 1936.
23 *La Journée Industrielle*, 4 September 1936.
24 *Le Midi Socialiste*, 11 September 1936.
25 *Le Dépêche*, 13 September 1936.
26 *Le Dépêche*, 20 September 1936.
27 *Le Dépêche*, 13 November 1936.
28 *Le Petit Parisien*, 8 November 1936.
29 *Vendémiaire*, 1 November 1936.
30 At the time, the term was understood in the West only as the holy war of Islam, against the *giaours*.
31 *L'Ere Nouvelle*, 6 October 1936.
32 *L'Ere Nouvelle*, 8 September 1936.
33 *L'Ere Nouvelle*, 13 November 1936.
34 *Le Victoire*, 13 October 1936.
35 *Le Populaire*, 10 September 1936.
36 *Le Midi Socialiste*, 15 October 1936.
37 *Le Midi Socialiste*, 18 October 1936.
38 *Le Peuple*, 7 September 1936.
39 *L'Humanité*, 7 September 1936.
40 *L'Humanité*, 10 September 1936.
41 *L'Humanité*, 7 September 1936. See Gabriel Péri, *Regards*, 15 October 1936.
42 *L'Humanité*, 13 November 1936.
43 *L'Humanité*, 10 November 1936.
44 *Le Quotidien*, 3 September 1936.
45 *Le Quotidien*, 3 September 1936.
46 *Le Matin*, 6 September 1936.
47 *L'Echo de Paris*, 8 September 1936.
48 *Le Dépêche*, 7 September 1936.
49 *Le Dépêche*, 7 September 1936.

50 *Le Populaire*, 6 September 1936.
51 The question was taken in stride, however, by the Kremlin, which proceeded to exercise its incomparable skill in political gymnastics. *Investia* published a convenient 'letter' to show why, in the opinion of the Russian masses, France should do more than Russia. The letter, signed by a certain lady doctor by the name of Z. Babouchkina, of Moscow, ran in part as follows:

'The Franco Soviet agreement is more important for France than for us. In effect, if a war were to break out, Germany would probably attack France first . . . The friendship of the Soviet Union constitutes a genuine guarantee of security for France. The French Government should therefore show more logic . . . Why should we show France an indulgence so incomprehensible' (Berneri Collection).

It was in effect the first step in the campaign to neutralize the traditional Franco-Soviet friendship and to facilitate Russia's repudiation of her pledge to France inherent in the mutual assistance pact of 23 August 1939. Communist propaganda then proceeded to blame the expedient among the democracies, whose 'dismaying plan, drawn up and proclaimed, to attain the overthrow of the Soviet Union had to be thwarted at all costs' (*Epopée, passim*); cf. Litvinov to the French government (Thomas, 340n.); and Litvinov versus Dimitrov (Thomas, 1963 edition, 295n.).
52 *L'Humanité*, 6 September 1936.
53 *L'Humanité*, 10 September 1936.
54 *Le Midi Socialiste*, 9 December 1936.
55 Cf. *supra*, 68.
56 *La Dépêche*, 20 September 1936.
57 This committee, located at 26 Rue de la Pépinière, Paris 8th, became in 1937 the Comité International d'Aide à l'Espagne Républicaine, under the presidency of Martínez Barrio. Its purpose, which it pursued until February 1939, was to provide food supplies for the Republic.
58 The declaration was signed by the following: René Arcos, Claude Aveline, Jean-Richard Bloch, André Chamson, Gabriel Cudenet, Professor Cuvillier, Jacques Duclos, Elie Faure, Professor Hadamard, Augustin Hamon, Pastor J. Jézéquel, J. Jolinon, François Jourdain, Jacques Kayser, Guy de La Batut, René Lalou, Professor Paul Langevin, André Malraux, Pierre Mendès-France, Denise Moran, Jean Piot, Camille Planche, Professor Prenant, Romain Rolland, Henry Torrès, Professsor H. Wallon, Léon Werth, Jean Zyromski (*Le Midi Socialiste*, 18 September 1936).
59 *Le Midi Socialiste,* 18 September 1936.
60 *Le Midi Socialiste*, 5 November 1936.
61 *La Dépêche*, 6 November 1936.
62 *Le Peuple*, 27 October 1936; *Le Populaire*, 4 November 1936.

De Ureña, secretary-general at the Spanish Foreign Ministry, expressed his bitterness toward the Front Populaire in a conversation with René Bonjean, the French commercial attaché in Madrid. 'Its egoism will be its undoing,' said Ureña. 'Although it doesn't want to fight in defence of the Spanish Republic,

France will find itself four months from now dragged into a general war. I'll bet you on it' (Bonjean to Delbos: T. n° 503, Madrid, dated 25 October 1936, Ministère des Affaires étrangères, 2nd series, t. III, § 406).
63 *Le Midi Socialiste*, 5 November 1936.
64 *L'Express du Midi* had called in question the loyalty of certain Leftist journalists with names so un-Gallic as Herrmann, Zyromski and Rosenfeld (*L'Express du Midi*, 19 August 1936). Again, *L'Express* objected that the German and Hungarian Jewish origins of Longuet and Basch disqualified them from speaking in the name of France (*L'Express du Midi*, 26 November 1936); cf. *supra*, 86.
65 *Le Midi Socialiste*, 9 November 1936.
66 *Le Midi Socialiste*, 7 September 1936.
67 *Le Populaire*, 10 September 1936.
68 *La Dépêche*, 1 September 1936.
69 *L'Humanité*, 7 September 1936.
70 *Le Matin*, 11 September 1936. The proposal, opposing all intervention in Spain, was submitted by Sir Walter Citrine, as secretary general, and Ernest Bevin, as secretary, of the Transport Workers Union. The decision was approved in early October by the Labour Party Conference held in Edinburgh.
71 *La Dépêche*, 9 September 1936.
72 *L'Aube*, 10 September 1936.
73 *Le Populaire*, 8 November 1936.
74 *Les Echos*, 13 November 1936.
75 *La Dépêche*, 1 November 1936.
76 *L'Echo de Paris*, 1 November 1936.
77 *Le Journal*, 5 September 1936.
78 *L'Echo de Paris*, 8 September 1936.
79 *L'Express du Midi*, 6 September 1936.
80 *L'Echo de Paris*, 8 September 1936.
81 *L'Express du Midi*, 6 September 1936.
82 *Le Journal de Toulouse*, 6 September 1936.
83 *Le Jour*, 10 September 1936.
84 *L'Action Française*, 23 October 1936.
85 Pujo then proposed that legal proceedings be taken against the authors of all articles that carried false information. The government moved in compliance, taking similar action against *L'Action Française*'s managing editor, Joseph Delest.
86 *L'Action Française*, 11 December 1936.
87 Cf. *supra*, 35.
88 *Le Figaro*, 15 November 1936.

These figures would support Fischer's estimate of the total number of French aircraft delivered to the Republic in 1936 at 70, including 35 new fighters (Fischer, 449–449; quoted in Puzzo, 132).

According to Georges-Roux, in four months from August to November 1936, 35 heavily loaded vessels left Marseilles and Sète for Barcelona and Valencia; from August 1936 to April 1937, in seven months, the number of planes supplied came to 180 (Georges-Roux, 80).

The archives in Perpignan contain a single reference to the illicit traffic conducted through the Département of Pyrénées-Orientales. The report in question suggests either a super-meticulous inspection or a brand of sarcasm. The inspection in question brought to light . . . one rifle carrying the inscription 'Winchester, 1894', together with twenty cartridges. The arms were duly seized and the culprit arrested and imprisoned (Commissaire central, Pyrénées-Orientales, to Prefect of Pyrénées-Orientales: no. 20949, dated 21 September 1936).
89 *L'Express du Midi*, 18 September 1936.
90 Nevertheless, certain Anarchist elements discouraged the entry into Catalonia of foreign volunteers. Cf. *supra*, 72–74.
91 *La Dépêche*, 21 February 1936.
92 *La Dépêche*, 23 July 1936.
93 See Pike, *Crise,* 193 n.; Bernanos, 288.
94 *La Dépêche*, 25 July 1936.
95 *Le Midi Socialiste*, 26 August 1936.
96 *La Dépêche*, 12 October 1936.
97 Berneri Collection.
98 See Pike, *Vae,* 4. Among such gossip of impending revolution, Thomas refers to a rumour, picked up from Carlists by French journalists in Saragossa, that Thorez, helped by Blum and Daladier, had staged a coup d'état in France, that Pétain was fighting them in the South, and that, once the French civil war was over, Laval would place an army at the disposal of the Spanish rebels (Thomas, 1963 edition, 357).
99 Director General, Sûreté nationale, to the Prefects: no. 9409, Confidential, dated 8 October 1936.
100 *L'Express du Midi*, 7 October 1936.
101 *L'Express du Midi*, 11 November 1936.
102 *L'Express du Midi*, 23 November 1936.
103 *L'Echo de Paris*, 18 December 1936. The other six signatories to the manifesto were: députés d'Aillières (Sarthe), Michel (Haute-Loire), Poitou-Duplessy (Charente-Inférieure), Saint-Just (Pas-de-Calais), Soulier (Seine) and Tixier-Vignancour (Basses-Pyrénées).
104 *La Dépêche*, 19 December 1936.

8 The Soviet Ultimatum and Intervention

1 That the French Government understood this as early as November 1936 was corroborated by the American Ambassador to Paris, William Bullitt (Puzzo, 147).
2 Puzzo, 144–145.
3 This was reflected in Hitler's statement on 5 November 1937: 'A total victory of Franco is not desirable. It is in our interest to see the war prolonged in order to maintain tension in the Mediterranean.'
4 France had signed mutual assistance pacts with Poland in 1921 and then with the three States of the Petite-Entente: Czechoslovakia (1925), Romania (1926), Yugoslavia (1927).

5   *L'Action Française*, 10 October 1936.
6   Cf. *supra*, 59–61.
7   *L'Express du Midi*, 12 December 1936.
8   *L'Ere Nouvelle*, 3 September 1936.
9   *L'Humanité*, 10 September 1936.
10 It is not certain whether Thorez and Willi Münzenberg, the Comintern propaganda chief, contributed to Stalin's decision (Thomas, 450). According to some reports, they did not arrive in Moscow until the following day, 22 September. Münzenberg relied on Otto Katz, alias André Simon, as his chief lieutenant for Spain. Katz, a long-time Comintern official, set up the Spanish Relief Committee, directed the Spanish News Agency, and channelled whatever propaganda he could to the French press (Richardson, 12).

    Krivitsky and Münzenberg both defected in 1939 to the democracies, denouncing Stalinism. Münzenberg died in France in 1940, in mysterious circumstances (Koestler, *Scum*, 260). Krivitsky was murdered in Washington DC in 1941.
11 *Le Peuple*, 1 October 1936.
12 *Le Petit Journal*, 9 October 1936.
13 *L'Humanité*, 9 October 1936.
14 *L'Echo de Paris*, 11 August 1936.
15 *L'Ordre*, 10 October 1936.
16 *La Dépêche*, 9 October 1936.
17 *Le Matin*, 11 October 1936.
18 Cf. *supra*, 89.
19 *L'Express du Midi*, 14 October 1936.
20 *L'Express du Midi*, 17 October 1936.
21 *L'Express du Midi*, 14 October 1936. However, in discussing the possible blockade for the Portuguese ports, *L'Express du Midi* tacitly acknowledged, for the first time, the existence of an arms traffic with the rebels.
22 *La Dépêche*, 25 October 1936.
23 *La République*, 1 November 1936.
24 *L'Oeuvre*, 1 November 1936.
25 *Marianne*, 4 November 1936.
26 *L'Ere Nouvelle*, 9 October 1936.
27 *Le Midi Socialiste*, 1 October 1936. See Thomas, 571.
28 *Le Figaro*, 10 October 1936.
29 *Le Midi Socialiste*, 1 October 1936.
30 *L'Express du Midi*, 11 October 1936.
31 *L'Express du Midi*, 25 October 1936.
32 *La Victoire*, 10 October 1936.
33 *L'Echo de Paris*, 10 October 1936.
34 'The battle of Madrid—wrote Morel—is about to be joined. Short of a miracle, everything points to its fall, because Madrid does not have the will to resist to the end and because neither the people of Madrid nor the militiamen seem to want to fight [*n'a pas la volonté de résister jusqu'au bout, ni les miliciens ne semblent*

vouloir lutter]' (Morel to Daladier: D. n° 339/A. Secret, Madrid, dated 14 October 1936. Ministère des Affaires étrangères, 2nd series, t. III, § 350).

9 The Foreign Volunteers

1. *L'Oeuvre*, 27 July 1936.
2. *Le Temps*, 22 July 1936.
3. *La Dépêche*, 16 August 1936.
4. *La Dépêche*, 16 August 1936.
5. One of the volunteers, aged 58, had taken part in Cuba in the Spanish-American War of 1898. *La Dépêche* described them as 'poorly dressed, carrying no other baggage than a haversack with a little change of linen, going cheerfully to offer their lives, the only thing they have, in the defence of the Republic torn apart by the rebels' (*La Dépêche*, 30 September 1936).
6. *La Dépêche*, 13 August 1936.
7. *La Dépêche*, 16 August 1936.
8. *La Dépêche*, 16 August 1936.
9. *Le Midi Socialiste*, 17 August 1936. Rul was accompanied by correspondents of *L'Humanité*, *Vendredi*, *La Petit Parisien*, and *Le Petit Journal*.
10. *La Dépêche*, 1 September 1936.
11. *Le Matin*, 20 August 1936.
12. *La Dépêche*, 17 December 1936.
13. *La Dépêche*, 24 December 1936.
14. *La Dépêche*, 20 September 1936. However, according to a local journal, the only point that remained open from that moment was Port-Bou.
15. *La Dépêche*, 2 November 1936. The police were watching out especially for Danish passports. They often carried printer's errors, for example: Born, instead of Börn (Minister of the Interior, to Prefects, dated 11 February 1937).
16. *La Dépêche*, 20 October 1936; *Le Midi Socialiste*, 20 October 1936. In Perpignan, the volunteers were housed in the Maison du Peuple or in the former military hospital. After a wait of two or three days, they passed through the frontier in trucks or coaches without anyone asking them anything. According to Jacques Delperrie de Bayac, customs officials and frontier guards had received orders to close their eyes (Delperrie de Bayac, 130).
17. *L'Express du Midi*, 11 November 1936.
18. *L'Express du Midi*, 26 de November 1936. In an effort to malign the character of these volunteers, *L'Express* added: 'Some of these unwelcome guests . . . are afflicted with contagious diseases, the diagnosis of which we shall not discuss.'
19. *La Dépêche*, 9 November 1936.
20. *La République*, 17 December 1936.
21. *Le Matin*, 10 January 1937,
22. *L'Express du Midi*, 4 November 1936.
23. *La Dépêche*, 25 October 1936. La Fédération Anarquiste Française certainly existed; so too did the Anarchist Secours International Antifasciste, which provided limited help to the Spanish Anarchists throughout the war. Although Candiani remarked that things had changed by the time of her next visit a year

later, *Le Matin* reported that a certificate issued by the FAI was all that was required to enter France from Republican Spain (*Le Matin*, 1 October 1937). The French Government had nevertheless formally prohibited such procedure. It decreed that Spanish safe-conduct passes issued by the Generalitat of Catalonia were invalid; every [Spanish] person entering France had to carry a regular passport issued by the Spanish authorities (Ministry of the Interior, to Prefect, Pyrénées-Orientales, dated 22 February 1937).

24 *La Dépêche*, 18 November 1936.
25 André Legru, *La Dépêche*, 3 November 1936.
26 In mid-September, Franco was reported to have agreed to a territorial exchange: Spain would cede to France the Llivia enclave, 'which provided the passage for the contraband arms for the Frente Popular,' and France would cede two districts in Morocco from French to Spanish territory (*L'Indépendant*, Perpignan, 19 September 1936).
27 The first proposal submitted to the Conseil de la Principalitat failed to win a majority.
28 *L'Express du Midi*, 30 September 1936.
29 *La Dépêche*, 6 December 1936.
30 *La Dépêche*, 17 December 1936.
31 *Le Midi Socialiste*, 29 December 1936.
32 *La Dépêche*, 31 December 1936.
33 *La Dépêche*, 17 December 1936.
34 *L'Express du Midi*, 22 December 1936.
35 *La Dépêche*, 12 November 1936.
36 *L'Express du Midi*, 15 December 1936. Indeed, the volunteers protested against the term 'Foreign Legion' that certain moderate Republicans proposed. The volunteers insisted on not being treated as mercenaries.
37 Thomas, 1963 edition, 637 n.
38 *L'Express du Midi*, 22 November 1936.
39 *Le Figaro*, 17 February 1936.
40 Herbette to Delbos: T. n° 1470. Highly Confidential, San Sebastian (via Ciboure), dated 23 November 1936. Ministère des Affaires Étrangères, 2nd series, t. IV, § 22. See the Nationalist radio broadcasts in Russian, *infra*, 371.
41 *La Dépêche*, 8 December 1936.
42 Thomas, 983, estimates the total number of French volunteers at 10,000, while the Soviets numbered only 557. As for the XIVth Brigade ('La Marseillaise'), Dan Richardson, a leading authority on the subject of the Brigades, writes of a severe breakdown in morale and discipline that the brigade suffered in the wake of the Jarama fighting: 'Despite everything the officers and commissars could do, dissension, desertion, and drunkenness continued to plague the Brigade until it came to resemble more "a band of savages" than an elite military unit. The Brigade newspaper, *Le Soldat de la République,* alluded to this state of affairs in an article condemning what it called the "malcontent".' The directorate in Albacete, headed by André Marty, responded with a program of ruthless reprisals against the offenders. Richardson, 98–99.

43 Cf. *supra*, 17.
44 General Toussan made no mention whatever of any German or Italian aid to Franco (*La Garonne*, 12 April 1938).
45 *Le Matin*, 24 December 1936.
46 Geumann, whose name is given thus in *Documents diplomatiques français,* normally goes under the name of Gaymann. He took the Spanish name of Vidal and was appointed commander of the base at Albacete, under the authority of Marty. When Marty accused him of embezzlement, he returned to Paris, allegedly for reasons of health. Marty was finally accused of malversation himself, and had to leave for Moscow to explain his conduct.
47 *Le Journal de Toulouse*, 15 May 1938.
48 *L'Humanité*, 6 August 1936.
49 *L'Echo de Paris*, 6 August 1936.
50 *Le Jour*, 6 August 1936.
51 *Le Matin*, 6 August 1936.
52 *Le Journal*, 6 August 1936.
53 *La Dépêche*, 2 December 1936.
54 *L'Action Française*, 9 December 1936. Blue was the colour of the uniform of the Falange.
55 *L'Action Française*'s portrayal of the volunteers makes an interesting comparison with that of *La Dépêche* (cf. *supra*, 329 n5). According to the former, they were 'a bunch of poor wretches. Renault mechanics, suburban clerks, going to their deaths in the inhospitable sierras. And those who call themselves their leaders are guilty of real treachery toward these unhappy people. They are very careful not to tell them what is waiting for them down there . . . Probably the majority of them would like to come back' (*L'Action Française*, 13 December 1936).
56 *L'Action Française*, 13 December 1936.
57 *L'Express du Midi*, 13 December 1936.
58 *L'Express du Midi*, 14 December 1936.
59 *L'Express du Midi*, 15 December 1936.
60 Cf. *supra*, 69.
61 *L'Express du Midi*, 18 December 1936.
62 *L'Express du Midi*, 15 December 1936.
63 *L'Express* attributed to a member of the Brigades the comment: 'They ought to be very grateful to us. If we hadn't come, Franco would have made it a month ago' (*L'Express du Midi*, 18 December 1936). This argument is corroborated by Fischer but refuted by Buckley and Colodny (cited in Puzzo, 259).
64 *La Dépêche*, 2 December 1936.
65 *L'Express du Midi*, 18 December 1936.
66 *L'Ère Nouvelle*, 2 December 1936; 6, 14 January 1937.
67 Cf. *supra*, 67–68.
68 *L'Echo de Paris*, 25 July 1936.
69 *Le Jour*, 29 October 1936.
70 *Le Midi Socialiste*, 1 November 1936.
71 *Le Midi Socialiste*, 26 December 1936.

72 Cf. *supra*, 141. Recruitment was centred in Paris, at the Maison des Syndicats. Josip Broz, the future Marshal Tito, took charge, under the name of Tomanek, of ferrying volunteers to France from the Balkans and Central Europe, and under the name of Bronzev, of finding accommodation for them in small hotels on the Left Bank.

73 *L'Express du Midi*, 30 December 1936.

74 See Pike, *Crise*, 369–371.

75 *Le Midi Socialiste*, 21 December 1936.

76 Some of the estimates of Axis aid were as exaggerated as those of aid to the Loyalists. *Le Figaro* calculated the number of Germans in battle by February 1937 at 70,000–75,000 (*Le Figaro*, 17 February 1937). Similarly inflated were the figures published by the Valencia CNT organ *Fragua Social*, allegedly based upon official Nationalist documents which had fallen into Republican hands; the figures were reproduced by Dominique in *La République*, albeit with some reserve.

The Italians were estimated at 82,000, the Africans at 78,000, the Germans at 29,000, and the Irish, Poles and others at 12,000, giving a total of 201,000 (*La République*, 22 March 1937). See Thomas, who gives the following as maximum strength at any one time: Italians, 50,000; Africans, no estimate; Germans, 10,000; Irish, 600; Poles, no estimate; but Portuguese, 20,000 (Thomas, 980–981). In regard to the Irish Green Shirts, see Pike, *Crise*, 180.

77 *La Dépêche*, 3 September 1936.

78 *L'Express du Midi*, 3 November 1936.

79 Thomas, 568.

80 Cf. *supra*, 79.

81 *Le Figaro*, 14 September 1936.

82 The Bandera 'Jeanne d'Arc' was formed as part of the Tercio by Henri Bonneville de Marsangy and numbered some 180 French volunteers. Bonneville was killed on 10 February 1937 at Llanes in the Asturias, and the command passed to Captain Coursier. Undistinguished on the battlefield, the unit was dissolved on 23 November 1937 (Jacquelin, 114, 116).

83 Cf. *supra*, 141.

84 *L'Action Française*, 13 December 1936. However, Catherine Breen (109) cites an article in *La Croix* of 9 December 1936 which may have provoked the remonstrance of Gaudy. According to this anonymous article, Franco was in a state to admit to the effectiveness of Marxist aid and to complain about the lack of help he was receiving from 'all those international circles who value order and civilization.' He referred to their inaction as 'criminal indifference.'

85 Cf. *supra*, 141.

86 *La Dépêche*, 24 December 1936.

10 Axis Recognition of Franco

1 *L'Express du Midi*, 12 December 1936. Operation *Otto* (the second stage of the German intervention), which replaced Operation *Feuerzauber* and which consisted of the dispatch of arms), went into operation on 29 September.

2   *Le Midi Socialiste*, 15 November 1936.
3   *L'Echo de Paris*, 3 December 1936.
4   Christian de Vézins wrote with ill-concealed regret: 'Hitler is not thinking at all of invading Russia' (*L'Express du Midi*, 14 November 1936).
5   *L'Express du Midi*, 24 November 1936. The failure of the Madrid offensive had caused such a shock that *L'Express* even contemplated the defeat of the cause.

    As for the bombing attacks on the capital, two Soviet women-pilots who took part in the air defences performed so brilliantly that they were mentioned in the Nazi dispatches. Their mission was to stand ready beside their fighter-aircraft for immediate take-off, and in flight to watch for any Nationalist or German plane that got separated from the incoming squadron. The casualties they inflicted on the enemy were reported to be 'considerable,' and the German dispatch concluded: 'Attention must be given to wiping them out. We are seeking more information. This information has been supplied by the service inside the Soviet Embassy' (Generalpolitische Abteilung, Auskunftsbüro, Vienna III: n° 136, Secret, n.d.).
6   *La Dépêche*, 10 December 1936.
7   *Le Midi Socialiste*, 14 November 1936.
8   Cf. *supra*, 17, 28. *Le Temps* suggested a possible pretext: the Italian Government was reported to consider that the fortification of the Straits of Gibraltar, without the consent of all the nations signatory to the Montreux Convention of July 1936, constituted a violation of the agreement (*Le Temps*, 22 November 1936).
9   *L'Express du Midi*, 13 November 1936.
10 *La Griffe*, 13 December 1936.
11 *L'Oeuvre*, 15 November 1936.
12 *La Dépêche*, 9 November 1936.
13 See Pike, *Crise,* 133–134.
14 *Le Petit Journal*, 28 October 1936. On the other hand, the possibility that France might recognize such a republic revived the old argument of the unfriendly frontier (cf. *supra*, 23). For *Le Petit Parisien*, such a recognition would be the start of insuperable difficulties with the 'Nationalist Government of Madrid', as the paper prematurely assessed the outcome of Franco's November offensive (*Le Petit Parisien*, 8 October 1936). In any event, the Soviet policy then prevailing—to seek the support of the bourgeoisie, in Spain as elsewhere—could hardly have sought to establish a Soviet Catalonia separated from the rest of Spain. At the end of 1936, the crisis in Barcelona was slowly developing into a civil war within the Civil War. As Leroux pointed out, this crisis proved that the Soviet Union, on the contrary, opposed separatist leanings in favour of a single government and a single leadership in the war (*Le Midi Socialiste*, 22 December 1936). See Pike, *Crise,* 124–132.
15 *La Dépêche*, 28 November 1936.
16 *La Dépêche*, 22 December 1936.
17 *Le Midi Socialiste*, 16 November 1936.
18 *La Dépêche*, 22 December 1936.
19 *La Dépêche*, 1 December 1936.

20 *Le Midi Socialiste*, 18 October 1936.
21 *L'Oeuvre*, 23 December 1936.
22 *La Dépêche*, 24 December 1936.
23 Nevertheless, attention must be paid to a document in the possession of Herbert Southworth, according to which the exports of minerals from Nationalist Spain to Germany were considerably lower in relation to total exports, at least from September 1936 to the end of 1939, than what might be expected. The balance-sheet, drawn up and published by HISMA in 1939, on the three most important commodities exported to Germany during this period, shows the following figures:

Food and beverages	RM 94.191.973.89
Minerals and metals	RM 78.799.549.53
Tropical fruits	RM 54.260.918.52

24 *Excelsior*, 4 December 1936.
25 Herbette to Delbos: n° 1.470, Highly Confidential, San Sebastián (via Ciboure), dated 23 November 1936. Ministère des Affaires étrangères, 2nd series, t. IV, § 22.
26 *Les Echos*, 23 December 1936.
27 The real basis for it was the German–Japanese Anti-Comintern Pact, signed by Italy on 6 November 1937, by Japan on 25 November 1937, and by Spain on 27 March 1939.
28 *La Dépêche*, 11 December 1937.
29 *Le Midi Socialiste*, 31 December 1936.
30 The difference between *de facto* and *de jure* recognition is sufficiently misunderstood for a clarification to be useful. In granting de facto recognition, a government is affirming that power over a given occupied territory belongs provisionally to the occupant. In passing from *de facto* to *de jure* recognition, the same government affirms that the occupation is durable and that there is no reason to suppose that it will end; such a situation obtains when the legitimate government has ceased to exist, or when it no longer holds any national territory at all. It is wrong, therefore, to assume that a government that grants *de jure* recognition is attesting to the legitimacy or the right of the occupant; it is attesting only to the permanent nature of the occupation.
31 A few days earlier, the Spanish vice-consul in Hamburg had been arrested by the Gestapo (*La Dépêche*, 14 November 1936).
32 *Le Midi Socialiste*, 26 October 1936.
33 The diplomatic corps in Madrid met on 19 November under the deanship of the Ambassador of Chile. It subsequently expressed to the press in Madrid 'its revulsion at seeing, in the use of air bombardment, the blatant disregard for precepts and norms that are universally adopted.'
34 *Le Midi Socialiste*, 30 September 1936.
35 *L'Oeuvre*, 23 November 1936.
36 *L'Oeuvre*, 23 November 1936.
37 *Le Midi Socialiste*, 21 November 1936.

38 The prevailing rumour, fostered by the right-wing press, that the South American republics had decided to recognize Franco from the moment of his entry into Madrid was categorically denied in Buenos Aires. A *fortiori*, then, they would not confer recognition before the capture of the capital. Few journals of the Right bothered to record the denial.

As things turned out, Uruguay recognized Franco *de facto* on 6 December 1937, and *de jure* on 19 February 1939. Brazil did not confer recognition until 1 March 1939. Peru gave *de facto* recognition in May 1938, *de jure* on 15 February 1939; Bolivia, on 24 February 1939; Venezuela, on 25 February 1939; and Argentina, on 26 February 1939. In Central America, there was a greater readiness to grant Franco recognition (cf. *supra*, 86–87).

39 *L'Echo de Paris*, 8 November 1936.
40 *Le Matin*, 8 November 1936.
41 *Le Jour*, 20 November 1936.
42 *Le Petit Parisien*, 20 November 1936.
43 *L'Express du Midi*, 20 November 1936.
44 Puzzo, 129.
45 Cf. *supra*, 66, Puzzo, 147.
46 Puzzo, 147.
47 *L'Ordre*, 8 November 1936.
48 *Le Petit Parisien*, 20 November 1936.
49 Cf. *supra*, 82.
50 *L'Echo de Paris*, 8 November 1936.
51 *Journal de Débats*, 7 November 1936.
52 *L'Echo de Paris*, 21 November 1936.
53 *Journal des Débats*, 9 December 1936.
54 This motivation, according to *Le Matin*, stemmed from the growing hostility among the British people toward Soviet aspirations. According to the conservative journal, the Baldwin government informed Foreign Minister Litvinov of this attitude in no uncertain terms; if true in essence, it makes an interesting parallel with the Russian attitude toward France published in *Izvestia* (cf. *supra*, 325).

'The reserves of sympathy, or shall we say tolerance, available to Soviet Russia in the United Kingdom are already scanty indeed. If the Soviet Union wishes to reduce these reserves to zero, or even to transform them into a negative amount, she has merely to continue in her attitude. Come what may, Great Britain will tolerate no disturbance to the peace of the Mediterranean, and will range herself against all aggressors, whosoever they may be' (*Le Matin*, 9 December 1936.)

55 *The Times*, 17 July 1936.
56 The Madrid government itself had tacitly recognized that a state of insurgency indeed existed by its very act of opening the arsenals and in arming the workers' militias. That is to say, the government admitted, from that moment on, that the armed attack launched against it was no longer a simple act of treason that could be handled by the police; it had to call in the military.
57 The eminent jurist John Bassett Moore defines the problem in these terms: 'If it is a war, the commissioned cruisers on both sides may stop, search, and capture

the foreign merchant vessel; and that vessel must make no resistance, and must submit to adjudication by a prize court. If it is not a war, the cruisers of neither party can stop or search the foreign merchant vessel; and that vessel may resist all attempts in that direction, and the ships of war of the foreign State may attack and capture any cruiser persisting in the attempt ... If it is a war, the insurgent cruisers are to be treated by foreign citizens and officials, at sea and in port, as lawful belligerents. If it is not a war, those cruisers are pirates, and may be treated as such' (John Bassett Moore, 'International Law,' II. *The Collected Papers of John Bassett Moore* (1944), p. 227, 287–288, n. 4; reprinted from V Progress, no. 10, July 1900).

58 *L'Ere Nouvelle*, 22 November 1936.
59 Thomas disagrees, arguing that the British Government would have liked to confer belligerent status on the Nationalists, in the belief that this would more easily keep Britain out of the conflict, but it was prevented from so doing by the French government (Thomas, 567). It is true that the British compromise plan of 14 July 1937 proposed the granting of belligerent rights at sea to both parties in Spain by all governments party to the Non-intervention Agreement, but in his speech to Commons the following day the Foreign Secretary stressed that the granting of belligerent rights would be conditional.
60 *L'Humanité*, 22 November 1936. While *L'Humanité* thus objected to an equation of the two Spanish Governments by denying to the Republic as well as to the Nationalists the quality of belligerent, it goes without saying that it described the proposal to confer on Franco alone the title of belligerent as a 'criminal act' (*L'Humanité*, 12 December 1936).
61 *L'Oeuvre*, 27 November 1936.
62 Cf. *supra*, 335, n.38.
63 *La Dépêche*, 2 December 1936.
64 This league was served also by Georges Altman, André Breton, Albert Camus, René Clair and Jean-Paul Sartre. During the German Occupation, Altman was one of the founders of *Franc-Tireur*, just as Camus was of *Combat*.
65 *L'Express du Midi*, 26 November 1936. Cf. *supra*, 61.
66 *Le Midi Socialiste*, 19 December 1936.

11 The Three Anglo-French Peace Initiatives

1 *Le Midi Socialiste*, 11 October 1936.
2 *Le Midi Socialiste*, 22 October 1936.
3 *Le Midi Socialiste*, 22 October 1936.
4 *Le Midi Socialiste*, 13 October 1936.
5 For approximate equivalents, see Author's Remarks.
6 *La Dépêche*, 26 December 1936.
7 *Le Journal*, 10 December 1936.
8 *L'Aube*, 16 December 1936.
9 *La Dépêche*, 15 December 1936.
10 Provided that mediation did not involve the United States (cf. *supra*, 49). Secretary of State Hull described the U.S. policy as one of 'moral aloofness,' which

had, however, no official objection to the sending of aid to Spain (Thomas, 434). A coded telegram from the Minister of the Interior to the Prefect of Haute-Garonne, dated October 26, 1936, reported a dispatch of dismantled aircraft from 'North America' to Barcelona (Item n° 7.067, dated 4 December 1936, in the archives of Special Police in Toulouse).

11 *L'Ere Nouvelle*, 13 December 1936.
12 *Le Midi Socialiste*, 11 December 1936.
13 *L'Oeuvre*, 15 December 1936.
14 *L'Express du Midi*, 15 December 1936.
15 *Le Journal de Toulouse*, 27 December 1936.
16 *L'Express du Midi*, 15 December 1936.
17 *L'Humanité*, 12 December 1936.
18 *L'Humanité*, 26 December 1936.
19 *La Dépêche*, 17 December 1936.
20 *La Dépêche*, 17 December 1936.
21 *La Dépêche*, 2 December 1936. In point of fact, on 27 November Foreign Minister Álvarez del Vayo had telegraphed the secretary general of the League of Nations, affirming that the Axis recognition of the insurgents was the crowning touch of the German–Italian intervention in Spain. He appealed to the League by virtue of Article 11 in the Pact and called on the Council to take action.
22 *La République*, 13 December 1936.
23 The Partido Obrero de Unificación Marxista was created by a combination of two organizations: the workers' and peasants' bloc, whose leader Maurín was arrested in rebel territory and imprisoned, and the Spanish Trotskyists under the leadership of Nin. The merger was strongly denounced by Trotsky, who called it a betrayal of Leninism, and for this reason it is a misnomer to call the party even semi-Trotskyist. Nevertheless, the party was influenced by his ideas (see Pike, *Crise,* 128). It was in Barcelona, where the party published its journals *La Batalla* and *Juventud*, that it had its greatest strength.
24 *La Dépêche*, 16 December 1936.
25 *Excelsior*, 13 December 1936.
26 *Excelsior*, 13 December 1936.
27 *L'Express du Midi*, 17 November 1936. According to Thomas, Portugal, like the Soviet Union, was willing to support any mediation plan that could be agreed (Thomas, 571).
28 See Pike, *Crise,* 336.
29 According to Bracke in the Socialist press, it was again the Soviet Government, through the voice of Maisky in London, that introduced this last proposal on 4 December, calling for 'the prohibition of all possible means of the dispatch and transit of volunteers' and for 'the implementation of control by all governments to enforce this prohibition' (*Le Populaire*, 8 December 1936). In point of fact, the Soviet Union did not accept the Anglo-French proposal submitted by Lord Plymouth until 27 December; Russia was certainly not the prime mover of this proposal.
30 El *Berliner Börsen-Zeitung*, explaining the reasoning of the Wilhelmstrasse, wrote

that there was only one great power with no interest either in Spain or in the Mediterranean and that power was Germany. 'But the Bolshevik side of the Spanish question,' added the Berlin daily, '[that] interests Germany . . . [Thus] the two authoritarian states have reached agreement to defend European civilization.' (*L'Express du Midi*, 29 December 1936).

31 *L'Express du Midi*, 8 August 1936. Cf. *supra*, 41, 71.
32 *Le Petit Parisien*, 15 August 1936. Cf. *supra*, 76–77.
33 *L'Express du Midi*, 5 December 1936.
34 *La Dépêche*, 19 December 1936.
35 *L'Oeuvre*, 14 December 1936; *La République*, 17 December 1936.
36 *Le Journal de Toulouse*, 20 December 1936.
37 *Le Matin*, 9 December 1936.
38 *L'Humanité*, 10 December 1936.
39 *L'Ami du Peuple*, 30 December 1936.
40 *La Dépêche*, 29 December 1936.
41 *Le Midi Socialiste*, 24 December 1936.
42 *Le Petit Parisien*, 24 December 1936.
43 *La Dépêche*, 28 December 1936.
44 *L'Express du Midi*, 30 December 1936.
45 *L'Express du Midi*, 30 December 1936.
46 *L'Écho de Paris*, 24 December 1936.
47 Cf. *supra*, 72–73, 76–77.
48 *L'Humanité*, 19 December 1936.
49 *Le Midi Socialiste*, 20 December 1936.
50 *Le Midi Socialiste*, 24 December 1936.
51 *L'Oeuvre*, 23 December 1936.
52 *L'Express du Midi*, 31 December 1936.
53 *L'Express du Midi*, 31 December 1936.

12 The Democracies Outmanoeuvred

1 *L'Humanité*, 6 December 1936.
2 *Journal des Débats*, 12 December 1936.
3 *L'Information Financière, Economique et Politique*, 12 December 1936.
4 *La Dépêche*, 29 December 1936.
5 *Le Temps*, 12 December 1936.
6 *L'Aube*, 15 December 1936.
7 *La Dépêche*, 21 December 1936.
8 *La Dépêche*, 28 December 1936.
9 Cf. *supra*, 17.
10 *L'Écho de Paris*, 26 December 1936.
11 *L'Ordre*, 13 December 1936.
12 *La Dépêche*, 30 December 1936.
13 *La République*, 26 December 1936.
14 *L'Express du Midi*, 28 December 1936. None of the journals was aware of the indemnity demanded by the Kremlin, in the form of Spanish gold (cf. *supra*, 56).

15 *L'Ami du Peuple*, 13 December 1936.
16 *L'Express du Midi*, 28 December 1936.
17 *La Victoire*, 13 December 1936.
18 Cf. *supra*, 64.
19 *L'Écho de Paris*, 20 December 1936.
20 *L'Aube*, 23 December 1936.
21 Cf. *supra*, 40.
22 *L'Ere Nouvelle*, 8 January 1937.
23 *Les Échos*, 6 January 1937.
24 Spanish gold entering France between 26 August 1936 and 26 February 1937, amounted to 46,326 Kg., valued at 900,405,000 francs (Chief Inspector, Special Police to Director-General, Sûreté Nationale: n° 831, dated 1 March 1937). Spanish paper money, entering France between 19 January 1937 and 17 September 1937, amounted to 4,996 Kg., and being unsigned, was worth no more than its weight in paper (Chief Inspector, Special Police to Director-General, Sûreté Nationale: n° 1271, dated 17 September 1937).
25 *L'Ere Nouvelle*, 2 December 1936; 6, 14 January 1937.
26 *L'Action Française*, 15 January 1937. See Herbette to Delbos: T. numbers 1169–1171, dated 8 September 1936. Ministère des Affaires Étrangères, 2nd series, t. III § 237. Cf. *supra*, 139.
27 *Le Populaire*, 16 January 1937.
28 He used several names, but he was born Rajani Palme Dutt in Cambridge, England; his father was an Indian surgeon and his mother Swedish. At Balliol College Oxford he received a First in classics. In 1922 he married the Estonian Salme Murrik, who served as a representative of the Comintern, and from 1922 he served as chief theoretician to Harry Pollitt, leader of the British Communist Party, as well as editor of the *Workers Weekly* and later (1936–1938) *the Daily Worker*. He later broke with Pollitt, when Pollitt supported Britain's declaration of war on Germany. Dutt hued to Stalin's line. Stalin had Pollitt ousted, with Dutt taking his place. After June 1941, Stalin reappointed Pollitt. Dutt remained a Stalinist to his death in 1974, rejecting Khrushchev's 'Secret Speech' and applauding the Soviet invasions of 1956 and 1968.
29 Colonel Nicoletis, a member of the Fédération Nationale des Officiers de Réserve Républicains (an organization formed after the convulsion of 6 February 1934) was the chief representative in France of the British industrial giant Imperial Chemical Industries. On his own initiative he had contributed in 1936 to setting up the Ministry of Armaments in Madrid and to creating the first Spanish production of explosives. To this end he had recommended to the Republican Government that it import 7,000 tons of ammonium nitrate from the Kuhlmann factory in Odomez and the national factory in Toulouse, together with 30 tons of white phosphorous and a large quantity of aluminium from a Belgian subsidiary of ICI. When Dutt accused Nicoletis of working against the British Government's non-intervention policy, Nicoletis sued him for libel, but Bolaños warned him that justice would never catch up with anyone as slippery as Dutt (Antonio Fernández Bolaños, to John Nicoletis, letter from Saint-Cloud, dated

21 August 1939; interviews with John Nicoletis, 26 November 1975; 11 February 1976).
30 Antonio Fernández Bolaños (Subsecretario del Ejército de Tierra, Ministerio de Defensa Nacional, Valencia), to John Nicoletis: letter dated 28 August 1937. Dutt was finally shot by the French in Algeria.
31 *Le Figaro*, 6 February 1937.
32 *L'Ere Nouvelle*, 2 December 1937.
33 *Le Midi Socialiste,* 26 December 1937.
34 *L'Ordre,* 12 December 1937.
35 *L'Ordre,* 9 December 1937.
36 Chosen by Hitler in 1933 as his Finance Minister, Schacht had used his ability to finance the Führer's rearmament program. In 1937, however, he became uneasy about Hitler's ultimate plans and resigned his post. His loyalty was in question from the time of the Anschluss, and in 1944 Hitler had him arrested and sent to a concentration camp, which he survived. Put on trial as a war criminal, he was acquitted and returned to banking.
37 *La Dépêche*, 12 December 1936.
38 *L'Ordre,* 9 December 1936.
39 *L'Oeuvre*, 26 October 1936.
40 *La République*, 29 December 1936.
41 *Le Petit Parisien*, 30 December 1936.
42 *L'Oeuvre*, 27 January 1937.
43 *La République*, 29 December 1936.
44 *L'Oeuvre*, 26 October 1936.
45 Cf. Kérillis, *supra*, 79; Pays, *supra*, 100.
46 *Excelsior*, 27 December 1936.
47 *Le Midi Socialiste,* 29 December 1936.
48 *L'Express du Midi*, 10 January 1937.
49 *L'Oeuvre,* 26 December 1936.
50 *La Dépêche*, 29 December 1936.
51 *L'Oeuvre*, 26 December 1936.
52 *Le Matin*, 4 January 1937; *L'Humanité*, 4 January 1937.
53 *Le Journal*, 5 January 1937.
54 *Le Journal*, 9 January 1937.
55 *Le Journal de Toulouse*, 10 January 1937.
56 *L'Humanité*, 8 January 1937.
57 *Le Petit Journal*, 9 January 1937. It was, in fact, being fought in the more immediate area of the Casa de Campo in Madrid.
58 Cf. *supra*, 113.
59 *L'Écho de Paris*, 6 February 1937.
60 *L'Ordre*, 9 December 1936.
61 *L'Oeuvre*, 27 December 1936. Mme. Tabouis based her opinion on the 'total reliability' of certain foreign circles in Rome, according to which Mussolini would not persevere seriously in the war in Spain.
62 *La Dépêche*, 28 December 1936.

63 Pike, *Crise,* 133–134. The argument of Marcel Pays in *L'Excelsior* (cf. *supra,* 101), that Italy had no desire to see Germany installed as well as she in the Mediterranean, can lead to the opposite conclusion, that Italy could feel encouraged to pursue her own intervention.
64 *Le Matin,* 27 December 1936.
65 Cf. *supra,* 148; Pike, *Crise,* 119–120, 126–127.
66 *L'Express du Midi,* 30 December 1936.
67 *L'Express du Midi,* 30 December 1936.
68 Cf. *supra,* 51.
69 *Le Midi Socialiste,* 21 December 1936.
70 *Le Midi Socialiste,* 29 December 1936.
71 Cf. Kérillis, *supra,* 79; *Excelsior, supra,* 98.
72 *Excelsior,* 26 December 1936. See Cudenet, *supra,* 52; Maurras, *supra,* 67.
73 *Le Midi Socialiste,* 29 December 1936.
74 *L'Oeuvre,* 15 January 1937.
75 *Le Figaro,* 7 January 1937.
76 *La Lumière,* 9 January 1937.
77 *L'Oeuvre,* 19 January 1937.
78 Corbin to Delbos: D. n° 40, Confidential, London, dated 14 January 1937. Ministère des Affaires étrangères, 2nd series, t. IV, § 302.
79 *Le Figaro,* 19 January 1937.
80 *L'Aube,* 8 January 1937.
81 Cf. *supra,* 22–24.
82 *La Dépêche,* 30 January 1937.
83 In his statement to the post-war parliamentary commission of inquiry, Georges Boris referred to this matter of the arrival of the German volunteers in Spanish Morocco and the campaign launched at that moment against Pierre Viénot, Under-Secretary of State for Foreign Affairs, who was acting on behalf of Blum and Delbos. A communiqué from the Senate, to the effect that Blum's energetic protest had been approved by the senators irrespective of party, was truncated in the versions published in *Le Matin, Paris-Midi* and *Le Petit Journal.* It was totally ignored by *L'Ami du Peuple, L'Écho de Paris, L'Ère Nouvelle, Excelsior, Le Figaro, Le Jour, Le Journal, Le Petit Parisien,* and *La République* (*Les Événements survenus en France de 1933 à 1945,* t. VIII, 2442; cf. *La Lumière,* 23 January 1937).

13 The Committee Implements Control

1 Unamuno had at first sided with the Nationalists. 'It is the struggle of civilization against barbarism,' he told André Salmon, of *Le Petit Parisien.* Then, in his celebrated address at the University of Salamanca on the Fiesta de la Raza, 12 October 1936, in front of an audience passionately pro-Franco, Unamuno declared: 'You will win, because you have at your disposal the brute force necessary to win, but you will never convince. Because to convince, you would need the two things you lack: reason, and right in the struggle.'
2 *Le Journal,* 10 February 1937.
3 *L'Humanité,* 10 February 1937.

4 Cf. *supra*, 50.
5 *L'Humanité*, 11 February 1937. On 13 February, Ambassador Araquistain handed Delbos a memoràndum suggesting—in prudent diplomatic language—that the Republic was prepared, after the fall of Malaga, to discuss with Britain and France the future of Spanish Morocco and to abandon the policy of neutrality in European affairs if these two Powers agreed 'to take all measures at their disposal to put an end, once and for all, to German–Italian intervention in Spanish affairs.' In its third paragraph, the memorandum read: 'Spain would be ready to examine, in a global discussion, the suitability of modifying the present status of its territories in North Africa (Spanish Morocco), on condition that this modification does not work to the benefit of any Power other than France and the United Kingdom' (Araquistain to Blum: Paris, dated 13 February 1937. Ministère des Affaires étrangères, 2nd series, t. IV, § 441).
6 *Le Figaro*, 10 and 18 February 1937.
7 *Journal des Débats*, 9 February 1937.
8 *Le Journal*, 10 February 1937.
9 *L'Ordre*, 2 March 1937.
10 *Le Jour*, 2 March 1937.
11 *L'Ordre*, 2 March 1937.
12 Cf. *supra*, 132.
13 *L'Ordre*, 19 February 1937.
14 *L'Oeuvre*, 15 March 1937.
15 Cf. Berneri, *supra*, 113.
16 *Le Peuple*, 8 January 1937.
17 *Le Figaro*, 8 January 1937.
18 *L'Humanité*, 15 February 1937.
19 *La République*, 21 December 1936. Camillo Berneri strongly criticized a section of these volunteers in a private letter: 'A class of people who really get on my nerves are these observer-volunteers, the majority of them French. They arrive here with their God Almighty airs and their cowboy outfits, to spend half the day in the cafés. Among these imbeciles, there are women who feel they have to wear trousers if they want to look like militia-women' *(L'Espagne Nouvelle,* 10 June 1936). Berneri could hardly have been aiming at Simone Weil, though her outfit matched the description.
20 Barbier to Delbos: D. n° 3, Valencia, dated 4 March 1937, received on 12 March 1937. Ministère des Affaires étrangères, 2nd series, t. IV, § 259.
21 *Le Figaro*, 20 February 1937.
22 Herbette to Delbos: D. n° 235, Ciboure, dated 4 March 1937, received 12 March 1937. Ministère des Affaires Étrangères, 2nd series, t. III, § 66. Herbette confirmed his report that the volunteers wanted to return home (T. n° 387, Saint-Jean-de-Luz, dated 25 March 1937) but were prevented from doing so (T. n.° 293, Ciboure, dated 10 March 1937. Ministère des Affaires étrangères, 2nd series, t. V, § 176, § 87).
23 *Le Jour*, 22 May 1937. The volunteers were to receive a premium of 10,000 to 15,000 francs, payable in part on departure and in part on arrival in Spain. The

salary was to be 50 to 55 francs a day. Married men and those with families received the promise that, in the case of their death, the Spanish Government would provide their families with an annuity based on a rate of 10 to 25 francs for every day they had been in service.

24 Presumably by the special services brigade of the War Ministry, then run by the Anarchist Manuel Salgado.
25 *Le Populaire*, 2 February 1937.
26 See *Trentennio*.
27 The 27 States were the following: Albania, Austria, Belgium, Bulgaria, Czechoslovakia, Denmark, Estonia, Finland, France, Germany, Great Britain, Greece, Hungary, Ireland, Italy, Latvia, Lithuania, Luxemburg, the Netherlands, Norway, Poland, Portugal, Romania, Sweden, Turkey, USSR, Yugoslavia.
28 Cf. *supra*, 98.
29 *L'Humanité*, 5 February 1937.
30 *L'Humanité*, 9 February 1937.
31 This order prohibited the opening and the operating of recruitment offices, recruiting through public gatherings or visits to homes, and the sending of circular letters.
32 *Le Figaro*, 17 February 1937.
33 The Partit Socialista Unificat de Catalunya, and its organ *Las Noticias*, were under the control of the Communists.
34 *Le Matin*, 20 February 1937.
35 *Le Petit Parisien*, 27 February 1937.
36 Chief Inspector of Special Police, to Director General, Sûreté Nationale: n° 827, dated 27 February 1937.
37 Chief Inspector of Special Police, Toulouse, to the Director General, Sûreté Nationale: n° 816, dated 23 November 1937. In a subsequent report, the Chief Inspector of Special Police informed the Sûreté Nationale of the case of a certain Lamouroux, who was allegedly engaged in Saint-Etienne in the supply of arms and munitions to the Republic, in exchange for sacred treasures stolen from the cathedral in Lérida and handed over by the Spanish revolutionary committees. The conduct of Lamouroux, who was the son of a senior officer in the French Army, allegedly hastened his father's death (Chief Inspector of Special Police, Toulouse, to the Director-General, Sûreté Nationale, n° 881, dated 18 March 1937).
38 Prefect of Haute-Garonne to the Ministry of the Interior: dated 11 March 1937.
39 Ministry of the Interior, to Prefect of Pyrénées-Orientales: n° 3.481, dated 13 March 1937.
40 *L'Action Française*, 24 July 1937.
41 Command of the column was given to the Italian Socialist Carlo Rosselli, who had joined the Italian historian Gaetano Salvemini in launching the first antifascist underground journal in Italy. Imprisoned by Mussolini for helping Filippo Turati to flee to France, he succeeded in escaping. He too reached France, and in Paris he founded the daily *Giustizia e Libertà*. In Spain he was wounded on the Aragon front and repatriated to France to convalesce. On 9 June 1937, Rosselli

and his brother Nello were murdered in Bagnoles-de-l'Orne by a team of Cagoulards led by Jean Filliol. The American secret agent Donald Downes reported to Washington that the murder of the Rosselli brothers had been authorized by Marshal Badoglio in Rome. The order to assassinate passed from the Servizio di Intelligenza Militare to a Colonel Santo, who was Mussolini's contact with the CSAR (Downes, 171).

42 *L'Action Française*, 24 July 1937.
43 Commissaire de Police, to Prefect of Ariège: n° 340, Confidential, dated 8 May 1937.
44 *Le Petit Parisien*, 12 May 1937.
45 *Le Petit Journal*, 2 April 1937.
46 *Le Journal*, 30 May 1937.
47 Chief Inspector of Special Police, to Director General, Sûreté Nationale: n° 941, 24 April 1937.
48 *L'Humanité* offered sarcastic congratulations to a certain Louis de Condé for 'following a family tradition and enlisting in the army of the enemies of France,' having been told that the fighting would soon be in Toulouse (*L'Humanité*, 29 March 1937).
49 *L'Ordre*, 30 March 1937.
50 Cf. *supra*, 37.
51 *L'Humanité*, 27 February 1937.
52 *Le Populaire*, 28 February 1937.
53 *L'Oeuvre*, 19 February 1937.
54 *L'Humanité*, 3 March 1937.
55 Cf. *supra*, 307.
56 *L'Humanité*, 5 March 1937.
57 Bolloten, 181.

14 Guadalajara and Fascist Reaction

1 In an interview, Franco set out to put an end to false reports: 'These friends [Italy, Germany, Portugal] have provided help, but only moral help. . . . Not a single foreigner has entered the ranks of the Nationalist armies, unless it were a true volunteer, and in such case, only in the ranks of the Spanish Foreign Legion ('Pourquoi nous avons déclenché le mouvement nationaliste,' *La Revue Universelle*, 15 March 1937).
2 *L'Oeuvre*, 21, 23 March 1937.
3 *La Dépêche*, 21 March 1937.
4 *L'Oeuvre*, 21, 26 March 1937.
5 *Le Figaro*, 26 March 1937.
6 *L'Aube*, 26 March 1937.
7 *Le Petit Journal*, 26 March 1937.
8 *La Dépêche*, 5 April 1937.
9 For other such letters, see Thomas, 601 n.
10 Its circulation was approximately 200,000. Pike, *Crise*, 339.
11 *La Vanguardia*, 26 March 1937.

12 *Guerra di Classe*, 25 May 1937.
13 *L'Oeuvre*, 23 March 1937. Much of the victory was owed to the participation of Luigi Longo (later head of the Partito Comunista Italiano), who organized the propaganda. Loud-speakers and pamphlets dropped by plane appealed to the Black Flames not to fire on their 'brother workers' and urged them to desert and join the Republican ranks.
14 *Le Populaire*, 24 March 1937.
15 Cf. *supra*, 114.
16 *Le Petit Journal*, 25 March 1937.
17 *Le Petit Parisien*, 21 March 1937.
18 *L'Humanité*, 8 April 1937.
19 *L'Humanité*, 24 March 1937.
20 Vigo and Corunna were also used by Germany for unloading supplies, according to *L'Humanité*.
21 *L'Humanité*, 29 March 1937.
22 *L'Humanité*, 22 April 1937.
23 Cf. *supra*, 97–99.
24 Cf. *supra*, 113.
25 *L'Écho de Paris*, 6 February 1937.
26 *L'Oeuvre*, 27 March 1937.
27 *L'Écho de Paris*, 6 February 1937.
28 *L'Oeuvre*, 27 March 1937.
29 *La Dépêche*, 1 April 1937.
30 *L'Écho de Paris*, 4 April 1937.
31 *L'Oeuvre*, 18 April 1937.
32 *L'Ere Nouvelle*, 9 March 1937.
33 *La Dépêche*, 9 March 1937.
34 *La Journée Industrielle*, 30 April 1937.
35 *La Dépêche*, 9 March 1937.
36 *La Dépêche*, 29 April 1937.
37 *La Dépêche*, 9 March 1937.
38 *L'Aube*, 16 April 1937.
39 *L'Oeuvre*, 9 April 1937.
40 *La Dépêche*, 2 August 1937.
41 *La République*, 17 April 1937.
42 The left-wing Socialist Jean Zyromski had suspected, even in early March 1937, that political, diplomatic, and even official circles in Britain and France entertained an attitude toward reconciliation summed up in the simple formula: neither Franco nor Largo Caballero. Peace negotiations predicated on such a formula, wrote Zyromski in his denunciation of this attitude, would spell not only the end of the Spanish Revolution but also the annulment of the social reforms already introduced (*Le Populaire*, 3 March 1937).
43 *La République*, 17 April 1937.
44 *Le Temps*, 12 March 1937.
45 *Le Matin*, 16 September 1937.

46 *Le Journal de Toulouse*, 26 September 1937.
47 *Le Matin*, 25 September 1937.
48 *L'Écho de Paris*, 25 September 1937.
49 *L'Oeuvre*, 28 April 1937.

15 Gernikato Arbola and the Catholic Agony

1   The Condor Legion moved into action on 31 October 1936. This action, known as Operation *Winterübung Hansa,* constituted the third stage of German intervention, following Operations *Feuerzauber* and *Otto.*
2   *The Star* (London) also ran an article on Guernica on 27 April. The article was unsigned, but the dateline showed Bilbao, where a certain Watson was *The Star's* correspondent.
3   It should be noted that *Ce Soir* had been in circulation only since 1 March.
4   The first account in the Franco press, that of General Martínez Esparza, who wished to show that 'Guernica had been destroyed before the Nationalist forces reached it' (Bolín, 358), is precisely what is not in question. The second refers to the destruction of the town 'by our enemies . . . before we occupied it' (Bolín, 358), a comment which, looked at from the point of view of the tension in vogue between the Nationalists and the Germans (see Pike, *Crise,* 165, as well as the tensión between the Nationalists and the Italians, could be interpreted in more ways than one.
5   Vaillant-Couturier gave unstinted support in *L'Humanité* to the Ligue des Droits de l'Homme, which in May appealed to the League of Nations for the application of international law. 'That is all we ask,' added the Communist spokesman, unconvincingly (*L'Humanité*, 23 May 1937).
6   Durango, a small town 20 kilometres to the south of Guernica, had been bombed on 31 March by planes of the Condor Legion. The raid had inflicted 248 civilian casualties, but the event had passed relatively unnoticed in the world press. Up to the event of 26 April, this action could be passed off as another accident of war.
7   *L'Aube*, 29 April 1937.
8   *L'Aube*, 30 April 1937.
9   Among the buildings destroyed, as the Basque Minister Manuel de Irujo pointed out to *La Dépêche*, was the house where Don Carlos had sworn, a century earlier, to defend the Basque *fueros* (*La Dépêche*, 6 May 1937).
10 *L'Ordre*, 29 April 1937.
11 *La Dépêche*, 29 April 1937.
12 *La Dépêche*, 6 May 1937.
13 *L'Oeuvre*, 30 April 1937.
14 *L'Express du Midi*, 28 April 1937.
15 *L'Écho de Paris*, 28 April 1937.
16 *La Dépêche*, 3 April 1937; Montserrat, 95.
17 'Aguirre,' stated the first such communiqué, 'declares that Nationalist Spain's foreign air arm'—perhaps the first admission that such a force existed—'has bombed Guernica and burned it down. Aguirre is lying. It is not we who have set fire to Guernica. Franco's Spain sets fire to nothing. Arson is only for those

who burned down Irún and Eibar and who tried to burn alive the defenders of Toledo. We have respected Guernica not simply because it was Guernica. We have respected it as we respect everything that is Spanish. The Basque country knows that we respect it, that we wish to maintain its traditions. If we have not machine-gunned those militiamen fleeing like cowards towards Bilbao, it is because we respect the civilian population, which is being evacuated by force . . . Basques! Give yourselves up to the justice of Franco, which is serene and noble' (*La Dépêche*, 29 April 1937).

Similar pamphlets were distributed in the Basque Country even in 1938, when all resistance had ended. One of them ran: 'With the victors, or with the vanquished. You still have time to choose.'

18 *L'Écho de Paris*, 29 April 1937.
19 Kemp; cited in Bolín, 280–281.
20 *Le Jour*, 30 April 1937.
21 *L'Ordre*, 30 April 1937.
22 *L'Express du Midi*, 30 April 1937.
23 'Admit to its mistake' is what *The Times* certainly did not do. What it did was to publish the contradictory account of its second correspondent, which had to pass through the Nationalist censor, which in the eyes of all, was far more rigorous on the northern front than the Republican.
24 *Le Journal de Toulouse*, 9 May 1937.
25 *La Dépêche*, 15 November 1936.
26 *L'Express du Midi*, 11 May 1937.
27 *L'Express du Midi* asserted that the tree was completely in cement anyway, 'and therefore fireproof, fortunately' (*L'Express du Midi*, 3 May 1937).
28 *L'Action Française*, 11 May 1937.
29 More precisely, it was for 27 April that the Nationalist authorities denied any air action (Thomas, 625).
30 *Le Petit Journal*, 12 May 1937.
31 *L'Action Française*, 11 May 1937. Nationalist denials of responsibility for the destruction of Guernica continued right through the war and beyond. In his radio address on the second anniversary of the insurrection, Franco again referred to the 'arsonists of Guernica' (*La Garonne*, 20 June 1938). 'Guernica could not have been bombed,' wrote Jean Baudry in *La Garonne*; 'the Reds dynamited it, house by house' (*La Garonne*, 1 August 1938).

The unceasing efforts to 'explode the Guernica myth' attest to the embarrassment it continued to cause the Franco regime. In 1967, Bolín chose to repeat the arguments and 'evidence' of the right-wing press in 1937. Bolín alluded to a dispatch from Mackensen and a telegram from Faupel (Bolín, 359). Presumably, his purpose was to show that since neither Mackensen nor Faupel admitted to German responsibility for the attack, the Germans were not responsible. It would appear from these dispatches that the Germans, in their turn, were quite willing to let the Spanish Nationalists shoulder the blame and bear the recriminations of a horrified world public. Bolín adopts the exegesis that Guernica 'had been bombed intermittently [by the Germans] for several days before it was given up'

(Bolín, 278); cf. Thomas, 624): '[Prior to 26 April] Guernica had not been bombed'. But, insisted Bolín, the destruction of the town was the work of Republican arsonists. All the evidence provided by the Mayor of Guernica, by the Basque Vicar-General, and by the Basque priests who were eye-witnesses to the bombing, whose evidence was corroborated by the correspondents of *Ce Soir*, *The Times*, the *Daily Telegraph*, the *Daily Express*, *The Star*, and Reuter's agency—all this weight of evidence is almost entirely ignored. As for the confessions of Luftwaffe chief Hermann Göring, Luftwaffe ace Adolf Galland, and other Germans, Bolín blandly remarks that 'we have no right whatever to accept the reports of their evidence' (Bolín, 278). His final argument posits the question '*cui bono?*', contending—correctly—that 'Franco had nothing whatever to gain by destroying [Guernica]' (Bolín, 279). History's long catalogue of error and confusion in operations of war, of course, makes nonsense of the argument of *cui bono?* Apart from that, Franco's objectives were one thing, and the experiments of the young Luftwaffe were another.

Bolín's categorical statement was finally contradicted in 1970 by Ricardo de la Cierva, an official in the Spanish Ministry of Information. De la Cierva refers to the 'senseless and anti-historical posturing of the national propaganda of that time and in the post-war years' and to the '*insensato alarde* [of the propaganda of Salamanca] *de negar lo que acababa de suceder; ni comprende al historiador cómo pudieron emperrarse los servicios de Bolín en aplicar la táctica del avestruz a un hecho para el que podrían encontrarse centenares de testigos . . . Un hecho ya es incontrovertible: la aviación alemana bombardeó Guernica.*' On the other hand, Cierva claims that the Republican position is no more valid than the '*postura inmovilista y recalcitrante de la propaganda nacional*' (Cierva, vol. II, 153–156, passim). The entire presentation by Indaleccio Prieto in his *Convulsiones,* vol. I, 351–357, is based—according to Cierva—on arguments devoid of proof. De la Cierva maintains that after the destruction of Guernica by German planes, the Anarchists and other Republicans set into motion, there as elsewhere, the scorched-earth policy.

In spite of Cierva's confession, and as long as Franco was alive, the denials did not stop. In February 1973, *ABC* (Madrid) published an article entitled 'Guernica no fue destruida por la aviación.' In reply, Augusto Unceta, who was Mayor of Guernica between 1961 and 1967, and was an eye-witness to the events of 26 April 1937, asked *ABC* to stop publishing this 'stupidity,' assuring the newspaper that there are today 'several thousand' witnesses. And in February 1975, workmen digging a foundation for a new apartment building in Guernica uncovered an unexploded 500-pound bomb, which Air Force technicians identified as German-made. Though this was one of the few pieces of tangible evidence of German culpability, the discovery of the bomb was virtually ignored by the press and television. Then came the bomb that blew apart the Franco camp with the publication of Herbert Southworth's *Guernica! Guernica!* Even so, even after the death of Franco, there were still those who would argue any point to save a point. In its critique of the Southworth text, the *Boletín de Orientación Bibliográfica* (Madrid) wrote (numbers 113–114, January-February 1976, 35) that the population of Guernica in 1936 came to fewer than 4,000 inhabitants, and not the 7,000 given by Southworth (p. 355). If this figure of 4,000 can be vindicated, ran the *Boletín*'s argument, then the figure of 1,654 killed and 889 wounded as reported by Republican sources (Southworth, 365), is open to doubt. However, José Ramón González, in his thesis on the population of Guernica, states that 'the parish and judicial archives were reconstructed, and anomalies can be observed. In the catalogues listing the dead, the decade of the 1930s is missing. Equally missing are the records of the dead for the year 1937 in the parish of Santa María, and 17 files are also missing.' On 25 April 1976, three hundred eye-witnesses to the bombing, all in advanced age, gathered for the very first time in a public reunion to present their recollection of what happened on 27 April 1937. '¿Por qué fue destruida Guernica? Entre tantas posibilidades, una que no desaparece: por odio' (*Cambio 16*, Madrid, 10 May 1976, 18–19). Gannon, 113–117.

32   Cf. Vice Admiral Joubert, *supra*, 126.
33   Bolín denies this (Bolín, 282).
34   Alcoléa, 18.
35   The Sinn-Feiners even received official rebuke. Mauriac later recalled the message of the Pope to the Mexican bishops on 2 February 1926: 'In these difficult times, it is more than ever necessary for you, for your clergy, and for Christian associations to remain outside politics, lest your adversaries identify you after victory as partisans of the other side' (*Le Figaro*, 30 June 1938).
36   *Sept*, 21 August 1936.
37   *La Vie Catholique*, 26 September 1936.
38   *Esprit*, January 1937.
39   Isidro cardinal Gomá y Tomás, *Le Cas de l'Espagne* (Paris, 1937).
40   *La Vie Intellectuelle*, 25 February 1937.
41   *La Croix*, 8 January 1937.
42   *La Jeune République*, 28 March 1937.
43   *La République*, 11 April 1937.
44   See Pike, *Crise*, 333–338.
45   For an account of this fraud, see Pike, *Crise*, 336.
46   Cardinal Gomá could not see the conflict except in Manichean terms. Engraved on the Monumento de los Muertos de la Cruzada, in Pamplona, are his words summing up the war: 'Aquí se han enfrentado las dos civilizaciones, las dos formas antitéticas de la vida social. Cristo y el Anticristo se dan la batalla en nuestro suelo.'
47   *Le Journal*, 30 April 1937.
48   *La Croix*, 8 May 1937. Caret concluded: 'What is certain is that if a [Nationalist] regime should be installed in Spain to the detriment of the sacred rights of the Church, the latter would enter into combat with it just as it had entered into combat with National Socialism.' The conclusion carried an ironic twist, considering the Church's secular advancement in Spain as a result of the Nationalist victory, and the Vatican's powerlessness to rescue the Church in Germany.
49   The League sought to obtain employment for Basque refugees, and by November 1939 was successful in finding them jobs even in French arsenals, work hitherto

closed to foreign labour. Verdier, Feltin and Mathieu also made up the executive of the Comité National Catholique de Secours aux Réfugiés d'Espagne, with its headquarters in Bordeaux. The Comité did its best, with the help of a vast archive that in June 1939 contained more than 120,000 names, to reunite the families of refugees who had been separated.

50   Southworth, 208.
51   Padre Alberto de Onaindía, canon of the cathedral of Valladolid, happened to be passing through Guernica on the afternoon of 26 April.
52   *La Dépêche*, 7 May 1937. Signing the manifesto were: André Bellivier, Georges Bidault, Charles du Bos, Claude Bourdet, Stanislas Fumet, Francisque Gay, Georges Hoog, Hélène Iswolsky, Olivier Lacombe, Maurice Lacroix, Jacques Madaule, Gabriel Marcel, Jacques Maritain, François Mauriac, Pierre van der Meer de Volkeren, Maurice Merleau-Ponty, Emmanuel Mounier, Boris de Schloezer, Pierre-Henri Simon, Paul Vignaux. Twenty-eight students of the École Normale Supérieure also signed. Support from abroad came from: Élie Beaussart, editor of the *Pays Wallon*, Dom Luigi Sturzo, V.M. Crawford, and the British group Pope and Freedom.
53   *L'Aube*, 2 June 1937.
54   *L'Aube,* 31 July 1937.
55   Claudel's hundred-stanza poem was an ultra-Catholic lament over the execution by the Republicans of 11 bishops and '16,000' priests. It appeared in pamphlet form under both the above title and that of *Aux martyrs d'Espagne*, and under the former title appears as a prologue to the work of Juan Estelrich, *La Persécution religieuse en Espagne*. Translated into Spanish by Jorge Guillén, under the title 'A los mártires españoles,' it was published by the Secretaría de Ediciones de la Falange in Seville in 1937.

Estelrich was editor of the pro-Franco propaganda journal *Occident* in Paris. Its issue of 10 December 1937 included a proclamation of loyalty signed by a group of intellectuals.
56   Montserrat had witnessed the horrors in Barcelona on 19 July 1936. When, therefore, he toured all Nationalist Spain in October 1936, as special correspondent of *La Croix*, he did so with no Republican bias. Nevertheless, he was revolted as much by the White terror as by the Red and described the former as a 'rule of brutal intolerance, less savage than in Republican Spain, but officially condoned' (Montserrat, 16–17). Montserrat together with Maritain and *La Croix*, were singled out for attack by Serrano Súñer in his address of 19 June 1938, the anniversary of the fall of Bilbao, in which the Minister of the Interior referred to 'the pedantic prattle of the one-worlders on the rights of peoples' (*ABC* [Seville], 21 June 1938).
57   *Le Figaro*, 17 June 1937.
58   *Le Figaro*, 13 October 1937.
59   *La Nouvelle Revue Française*, July 1937.
60   Joubert, *Guerre,* 32, 34–35, 41. The truth was that Maritain, born Protestant, converted to Catholicism in 1906, together with his Jewish wife Raissa.
61   Joubert, *L'Espagne*. The Comité pour la Paix Civile et Religieuse en Espagne was

also the target of Padre Venancio D. Carro, who, in his book *La Verdad sobre la guerra española*, addressed a letter to him brimming with contempt.

62 *Euzko-Deya*, 12 December 1937. *Euzko-Deya* was published in Paris by the Basque Government in exile. José Aguirre, who had visited Paris in August 1936, remained its president until his death. Its issues of 2 and 9 May 1937 published expressions of outrage from French intellectuals.
63 See Pike, *Crise,* 329–338.
64 *Temps Présent*, 18 March 1938.
65 *Le Figaro*, 30 June 1938.
66 Cf. *supra*, 183.
67 Souchère, 9–10.
68 See above note (56). Serrano had written: 'I despise Maritain . . . What does the learning of Maritain mean to us? Maritain speaks in the accents of the lips of Israel; he has the false manners of the Jewish democrat. We may well doubt the sincerity of his conversion' (*ABC* [Seville]: 21 June 1938).

Mauriac's reply to Serrano's ignorance and malice bore that mark of dignity and restraint which, like Dr. Johnson's letter to Lord Chesterfield, makes the recipient better remembered in the stream of time than he would else have been. 'Maritain is not a converted Jew. We nonetheless believe that she whom God gave to him was instrumental in the making of that exemplary Christian who, like his Master, makes no distinction among human beings but instead reveres the redeemed soul of each, and on the countenance of men of every race sees the image of the Father' (*Le Figaro*, 30 June 1938).

69 Cf. *supra*, 19.
70 *Le Figaro*, 30 June 1938.
71 *L'Aube*, 19 March 1938; 16 February 1939.
72 *La Croix*, 7 April 1938.
73 Cf. *supra*, 133.
74 *La Croix*, 8 May 1938.
75 Bernanos addressed Bailby personally, informing the editor of *Le Jour* of how Guy de Traversay came to die. He stated, 'without fear of contradiction,' that the Nationalists had shot Traversay because he had been carrying on his body a brief letter of introduction to Captain Bayo, written and signed by officials of the Generalitat (Bernanos, 243).
76 Bernanos, 150; *L'Aube*, 13 May 1938.
77 Maret busied himself with presenting Europe's oldest civilization as 'not really a people.' The predicament of the Basques, he explained, was the result of their inferiority complex, which was reflected in the mediocrity of their intellectuals. (Not even Unamano earned a mention.) Warning against any excessive compassion for these people 'who, like the Jews, excel in tears,' Maret turned upon 'internationalist, materialist, Masonic Liberalism, often termed "democracy"' (Maret, 159–186, *passim*).

In a final address to Bernanos, dated 5 November 1938, Maret described the latter's book as a work of poison, devoid of reason and contrary to truth. It was necessary to take sides, whatever the cost, contended Maret; the delay in the

Nationalist victory proved that in July 1936 the Nationalists were as much without a plan as the government was equipped with one. On the other hand, Maret welcomed the protraction of the war as the means of forging the Spanish national spirit, and held that hatred was indispensable to the making of a good soldier. Professing to see no danger in the Anschluss, Maret argued that if Dollfuss and Schuschnigg had failed in Austria, it was due less to the intervention of a powerful neighbour that to the sensual and frivolous character of the Viennese who had failed in their responsibilities.

78   *La Croix*, 20 January 1939.
79   'The fear here in the Vatican,' wrote Cochin, 'is that if it is found, on the morrow of Franco's victory, that too much blood was spilt in his name for him to remain in power, then power will pass to the Falange, which is considered in Rome as no less pagan and idolatrous than its Nazi and Fascist masters' (*L'Époque*, 21 January 1939).
80   Bidault noted that their labour unions ('the only unions in Spain to represent the social doctrine of the encyclicals') had already been disentailed of their property by the Falange, wile their former members were henceforth under threat of imprisonment (*L'Aube*, 16 February 1939).
81   It was thus to Pius XII and not Pius XI that the Carlists turned in choosing a message from the Vatican to accompany the message from Cardinal Gomá on the Monumento a los Muertos en la Cruzada in Pamplona.

Thirty two years later, on 15 September 1971, the first-ever synod of Spanish bishops and priests was held in Madrid. In a retrospective examination of conscience, the Church of Spain adopted a resolution (with 137 in favour, 78 opposed, 19 expressing reservations, and 10 abstaining) imploring pardon—in general terms—for its partisan position during the Civil War. The resolution opened with a quotation from St John on the need for those who have sinned to acknowledge their sin, then continued with this passage: 'We thus humbly recognize our faults and beg for our forgiveness, for at that time we did not realize that our task as true ministers was to work for the reconciliation of our people, locked in fratricidal war.'

On 19 April 1975, the bishops followed up on this resolution by issuing their first collective pastoral letter since the one they wrote in Franco's support in 1937. The letter, approved by 70 of the 81 bishops voting, did not repudiate the letter of 1937 but called for reconciliation and pardon on victors and vanquished alike, urging a special care for the rights of minorities such as the Basques.

No writer on Guernica was bolder than the English historian Brian Crozier. As late as 1996, at the Stanford Conference on War Crimes and War Criminals, Crozier dragged out for a final flogging the long-dead horse of Sir Archibald James. See Pike, 'Guernica Revisited,' 133–141.

16   The Pamphlet War and the Battle of the Minds

1   Cf. *supra*, 239.
2   Berneri, 33, 35.

3 Berneri, 21.
4 Berneri, 20.
5 Berneri, 34.
6 Berneri, 23.
7 Bergamín was the editor of the Madrid daily *Cruz y Raya*, which claimed to be Catholic.
8 Rieger, 10.
9 Rieger, 11.
10 Rieger, 20. The POUM's organ, *La Batalla*, had admittedly published some dangerous or equivocal editorials. On 28 March 1937, it called for a policy of attack. The advice was sound enough, but Rieger chose to interpret this as 'an attempt to convince the troops of the uselessness of their sacrifices and struggle.' On 28 August 1937, *La Batalla* announced as the sad truth that everybody was tired of the war. Though the purpose of the POUM was to evoke a new revolutionary spirit, the report, while not inaccurate in itself, was certainly dangerous in the hands of Rieger, who could accuse the POUM of spreading defeatism (Rieger, 208).
11 *L'Écho de Paris*, 14 January 1937.
12 'Le complot russo-communiste,' *Revue des Deux Mondes*, 1 October 1937.
13 Bardoux, 29–41. The celebrated documents presented by Bardoux were given a close inspection by Herbert Rutledge Southworth.
14 'Cent heures chez Hitler', *La Revue Universelle*, 1 October 1937.
15 'Après deux ans de guerre: la nouvelle Espagne,' *La Revue Universelle*, 1 August 1938. This journal had already published, on 15 March 1937, an article by Franco: 'Pourquoi nous avons déclenché le mouvement nationaliste.'
16 Robert Brasillach, with Maurice Bardèche, *Histoire de la Guerre d'Espagne* (Plon, Paris 1939). *La Revue Universelle*, 15 October 1938; 1st, 15 March and 15 April 1939. Brasillach returned to Spain in May 1939 for Franco's victory parade.
17 Interviewed by Catherine Breen, 97–98. This explains the obvious jealousy that Brasillach felt for Malraux. Malraux the writer had converted into Malraux the man of action, in action in Spain. Brasillach stayed calmly in Paris, limiting his activity to visits of this kind.
18 Rotvand, 56.
19 Rotvand, 69.
20 Massis, 154–155.
21 Massis, 152.
22 Massis, 161.
23 Massis, 164.
24 Massis, 173. See Franco and the foreign press, *supra*, 158.
25 *La Nouvelle Revue Française*, November 1937.
26 Picon, 91.
27 In praising the novel, Pierre Mille remarked that it revealed Italy's hand in a 'Venezuelan' type of *pronunciamiento*, visible not only at the time of the insurrection but even prior to it (*La Dépêche*, 13 January 1938).
28 *La Nouvelle Revue Française*, July 1937.

29. Simone Téry was the daughter of Gustave Téry, founder of *L'Oeuvre*, and of Andrée Viollis. She left France in June 1940, on the last ship to sail from Bordeaux before the arrival of the Germans (see Pike, *Vae*, 104).
30. Jean Lansard, 'Drieu La Rochelle', address at the University of Montpellier, 13 June 1986.
31. Drieu also wrote in *Le Figaro* of 11 September and 10 November 1936; in *L'Emancipation Nationale* of 16 January 1937; and in *La Nación* (Buenos Aires) of 21 September 1936 and 19 September 1937.
32. The prologue was published in *Vendredi* at the end of 1936. Paul Nizan, the foreign editor at *Ce Soir*, then launched an attack on Gide.
33. See Garosci, 300–302; Caute, 137–138.
34. A group of these writers signed a manifesto that they sent to the editors of *Vendredi*, urging them to redouble their efforts in the struggle they had undertaken 'to bring the truth to light and show where justice sits.' The signers of the manifesto included, besides Alberti and Spender: Max Aub, Malcolm Cowley, Vincente Huidobro, Mikhail Koltsov, José Mancisidor, Juan Marinello, Pablo Neruda, Martin Andersen Nexo, Carlos Pellicer, Aleksei Tolstoy, César Vallejo and Sylvia Townsend Warner.
35. In reprisal, the Comité Intellectuel d'Amitié France-Espagne, a pro-Franco group formed at the end of 1937, published in *Occident* on 10 December 1937 its own manifestó, 'Aux intellectuels espagnols.'

For a full analysis of French literature on the war in Spain, see Bertrand de Muñoz.

17 Incidents in France

1. Cf. *supra*, 116.
2. Prefect, Haute-Garonne, to Minister of the Interior, dated 11 May 1937.
3. Prefect, Haute-Garonne, to Minister of the Interior, dated 14 May 1937.
4. Thomas states that their machine guns were first removed (Thomas, 680), but no mention of this appears in the Prefect's reports.
5. Chief Inspector, Special Police, Toulouse, to Director-General, Sûreté Nationale: n° 1966, dated 9 May 1937.
6. *Le Jour*, 27 May 1937. *L'Express du Midi*, 20, 21 May 1937.
7. *L'Écho de Paris*, 19 May 1937.
8. Director General, Sûreté Nationale, to Prefect, Haute-Garonne: n° 5477, dated 4 May 1937. He was formerly an anti-Fascist member of the Italian Parliament and had even served in the Death Battalion of Barcelona. Equally active at this time, especially in Toulouse and Marseilles, were the members of the Reischach Agency, a branch of the Deutsches Nachrichten Büro.
9. Minister of the Interior, to Prefect, Haute-Garonne: n° 5804. B, dated 11 June 1937.
10. *L'Action Française*, 24 July 1937. Bolín, 350–353.
11. *L'Action Française*, 31 July 1937.
12. Minister of the Interior, to Frontier Prefects, n° 7018, dated 15 June 1937.
13. Prefect, Aude: F.O.4, dated 11 June 1937.

14 Special Inspector, Carcasonne, to Prefect, Aude, dated 5 July 1937.
15 Prefect, Haute-Garonne, to Chief Administrator of Non-intervention Control (Colonel Lunn), dated 2 June 1937.
16 Chief Inspector, Toulouse, to Prefect, Haute-Garonne: n° 17236, dated 31 July 1937.
17 Cf. *supra*, 147–148.
18 It seems that the French intelligence agencies were too quick to identify this organization as an Anarchist international, since no proof was provided.
19 Commissaire, surveillance du territoire, to Contrôleur, surveillance du territoire, in Paris: n° 263, dated 26 August 1937.
20 *L'Humanité*, 27 May 1937.
21 *L'Action Française*, 31 July 1937.
22 *L'Humanité*, 24 June 1937.
23 Special Inspector, Sète, to Special Inspector, Carcasonne: n° 1298, dated 4 August 1937.
24 Its espionage centre in France was located in Saint Jean de Luz (*Historia 16*, December 1978, 84–5).
25 Note n° 135, dated 28 July 1937. Cf. *supra*, 96.
26 Commissaire, surveillance du territoire, in Nice: n° 181, Secret, dated 20 October 1937.
27 Special Commissaire, Carcasonne, to Prefect, Aude: n° 305, dated 18 February 1938. Despite that, Marthe Richard, 191–192, mentions the steamer *Carmen* as engaged in arms traffic.
28 Herbette to Delbos: T. numbers 1304 to 1307. San Juan de Luz, dated 30 August 1937. Ministère des Affaires étrangères, 2nd series. i. VI, § 371.

Among the Spanish nationals resident in France who returned to Spain during this period was the submarine commander Luis Carrero Blanco. The future Spanish Vice-President had found refuge in Madrid in the Mexican Embassy, and then in the French Embassy, before making his way to Toulon and finally, in June 1937, rejoining the Nationalist forces in San Sebastian.
29 Director General, Sûreté Nationale, to Prefect, Aude, dated 7 August 1936.
30 Cf. *supra*, 143.
31 *Le Populaire*, 20 September 1937; *La Dépêche*, 21, 22, 24 September 1937. A similar incident, again involving Troncoso, was reported in the same year in Le Havre, where Spanish Nationalists attempted to seize the Spanish Republican destroyer *José Luis Diez* (Archives Nationales, Paris: F^7 14722).
32 *L'Express du Midi*, 22 September 1937.
33 *L'Écho de Paris*, 22 September 1937.
34 *La Dépêche*, 21 September 1937.
35 *L'Humanité*, 21 September 1937. There was more to this story than what was told in *L'Humanité*. General Eugene Miller was president of the Federation of Czarist Army Veterans, with its seat in Paris. In 1935 Marshal Tukhachevsky was on his way to London to represent Stalin at the funeral of King George V. Passing through Paris he contacted Miller. Then in 1936 came the first of Stalin's purge trials, the Trial of the Sixteen, headed by Tukhachevsky. Miller knew how the

Gestapo had manufactured the evidence that duped its Soviet counterpart, the NKVD. On 22 September 1937, Miller was kidnapped in Paris. It is probable that he was put aboard the Soviet cargo vessel *Maria* at Le Havre. An investigation, including a search of the ship, was begun but called off (so it was later claimed) by none other than Léon Blum, then Deputy Prime Minister. The logical reason for the kidnapping was to induce Miller to testify against Tukhachevsky. This theory was advanced by Mauricio Carlavilla del Barrio, a fascist intellectual (not necessarily Spanish) who wrote and acted under the name of Mauricio Karl. Carlavilla claimed, quite implausibly, that he held documents attesting to Miller's arrival in Kronstadt that had been found by a Spanish soldier fighting in the Blue Division on the Leningrad front (French television channel ORTF, 8 December 1977). Carlavilla is untrustworthy, if for no other reason than that he refused to allow anyone to examine the documents he claimed were passed on to him. Walter G. Krivitsky, "Why Stalin shot his generals," *Saturday Evening Post* (Philadephia), 22 April 1939, 16–17.

36 *L'Humanité*, 24 September 1937. See Orlov, 233.
37 *Le Populaire*, 4 September 1937.
38 *Le Populaire*, 21 September 1937.
39 *La Dépêche*, 22 September 1937.
40 *Le Populaire*, 23 September 1937.
41 *L'Humanité*, 10 February 1938.
42 Director General, Sûreté Nationale, to Prefects: D/BE 1st section, circular 259, dated 22 November 1937.
43 Director General, Sûreté Nationale, to Prefects: n° Ch. 257, dated 10 December 1937.
44 Special Commissaire, Carcassonne, to Prefect, Aude: n° 917, dated 9 June 1938.
45 *L'Humanité*, 22 March 1938.
46 Divisional Commissaire, Montpellier, to Special Commissaire, Carcassonne: n° 2662, Secret, dated 22 December 1938.
47 *L'Express du Midi*, 8 October 1937.
48 Cf. *supra*, 4.
49 Cf. *supra*, 116.
50 Cf. *supra*, 115.
51 *L'Echo de Paris*, 29 April 1937.
52 *La Dépêche*, 30 April 1937.
53 *L'Humanité*, 4 May 1937.
54 *L'Écho de Paris*, 5 May 1937.
55 *L'Humanité*, 6 May 1937.
56 *L'Humanité*, 11 May 1937.
57 His former organization, the Mouvement Social Français, founded in October 1935, had been dissolved in 1936. The Parti Social Français replaced it.
58 The membership of the PPF had increased rapidly, from 25,000 in July 1936 to 66,000 in August, 101,000 in October, 120,000 in January 1937, and 180,000 in April. Despite this, on 25 May 1937 Doriot was removed from office as Mayor of Saint-Denis, losing the post to Marx Dormoy. In consequence of this and of his

failure in local elections, Doriot resigned on 29 June 1937 from his seat in the Assembly (Breen, 89, 169).
59 L'Écho de Paris, 13 May 1937.
60 Cf. supra, 284.
61 L'Époque, 9 June 1937.
62 L'Ordre, 14 May 1937.
63 Gringoire, 16 April 1937.
64 Breen, 119. Breen adds: 'However, the damage was done, and a large part of the reading public continued to believe in German innocence in this matter, and in the irresponsibility of certain journalists frantic for scoops and driven by bellicose ideas.'
65 For the unusual composition of the editorial staff of Vendredi, cf. supra, 294.
66 Valois, from 1924, had been a dissident in the Maurras camp. He had therefore experienced, between 1925 and 1928, during the life of his Nouveau Siècle, the rancour and the wrath of the editor of L'Action Française, who had never wanted any collaboration with the other movements on the Right. Maurras's journal observed a cold reserve toward the PPF, and was openly opposed to the Croix-de-Feu and the PSF.
67 Cf. supra, 173.
68 Cf. supra, 173.
69 La Dépêche, 23 December 1937.
70 Cf. supra, 133, 158.

18 British Mediation and the Deutschland Incident

1 La Dépêche, 6 May 1937.
2 In fact, membership in the Partido Comunista Español in July 1936 did not exceed 40,000. The number soon increased markedly, to 250,000 in March 1937, and to 650,000 in 1938.
3 Le Figaro, 2 January 1937.
4 L'Humanité, 23 March 1937.
5 Their correspondents in Spain were, respectively, Mikhail Koltsov and Ilya Ehrenburg. In his memoirs, Ehrenburg describes the moment when, in front of Anarchists, he projected Soviet films showing proper behaviour for a revolutionary; at all the key moments, the Anarchists exploded in laughter. As for Koltsov, his memoirs (Ispanskii dnevnik) appeared in 1938, a few months before he fell victim to a new Stalinist purge, this one aimed at antifascist elements that wanted to see the USSR enter the war in Spain.
6 Hans-Erich Kaminski, Ceux de Barcelone (Denoël, París 1937).
7 Cf. supra, 130–131.
8 Up to that moment, the Communists held only two portfolios, those of Agriculture and National Education.
9 La Dépêche, 17 January 1937.
10 La Dépêche, 1 May 1937.
11 But even the pro-Nationalist d'Ormesson had written that no respect for legality existed in Spain, on one side or the other (Le Figaro, 2 January 1937).

12 *L'Express du Midi*, 11 May 1937.
13 *Le Journal*, 5 May 1937.
14 *La Dépêche*, 6 May 1937.
15 *L'Aube*, 5 May 1937.
16 *L'Ordre*, 6 May 1937.
17 *Le Peuple*, 6 May 1937.
18 See Thomas, 502; Pike, *Crise,* 360–362.
19 *La Dépêche*, 8 May 1937.
20 Less than a month later, André Marty published a pamphlet entitled *Espagne heroïque*, in which he openly attacked the 'Trotskysts' for advocating a dictatorship of the proletariat instead of throwing their support to the democratic republic.
21 *La Dépêche*, 2 June 1937.
22 *La Dépêche*, 18 May 1937.
23 *La Dépêche*, 26 May 1937.
24 *La Dépêche*, 19 May 1937.
25 *La Dépêche*, 9 June 1937. Many official French reports refer to a revanchist Anarchist movement in Catalonia, and especially to a plot in the previous September in Valencia, Madrid and Barcelona. It was said that on 15 September the Republican Government had ordered the arrest in Valencia and Cartagena of twenty-seven high-ranking officers, who had been shot on the following day (Commissaire de la Surveillance du Territoire, Toulouse, to Inspector General, Surveillance du Territoire, Paris: n° 303, Secret, dated 10 September 1937; Chief Inspector, Special Police, to Director General, Sûreté Nationale: n° 1321, dated 14 October 1937).
26 Morel to Daladier: D. n° 491-A. Secret, Valencia, dated 21 June 1937. Ministère des Affaires étrangères, 2nd series, t. IV, § 100.
27 The preceding Chautemps Cabinet had fallen in 1934 as a result of the Stavisky scandal.
28 *La République*, 29 May 1937.
29 *La Lumière*, 4 June 1937.
30 *L'Oeuvre*, 25 May 1937.
31 *L'Oeuvre*, 4 May 1937.
32 The legality of the blockade could be challenged on another principle of international law. A blockade, to be legal, requires a presence on the spot of sufficient vessels to carry out a full control of all ships arriving and leaving. This condition of 'effectiveness' had been drawn up in order to put an end to blockades 'on paper', such as that decreed by Napoleon in 1806 in his attempt to force other nations to cease their commerce with Britain. Jurists in international law finally set up a common agreement in the Declaration of Paris (1856), requiring that whosoever wishes to instigate a blockade must have the necessary forces available.
33 However, *Le Temps* reported that, on a single day (1 April 1937), Nationalist ships had captured two vessels (*Magdalena* and *Cap Falcon*), 'without any other reaction from the French Government than a platonic protest' (Broué and Témime, 449 n.).

34 *L'Express du Midi*, 30 April 1937.
35 *L'Express du Midi*, 6 May 1937.
36 *L'Express du Midi*, 3 May 1937.
37 'If we run into difficulties—wrote Herbette—the operations we envisage could not be successfully carried out without the protection of the British battleships *Royal Oak* and *Resolution*. Perhaps we should inform these vessels in advance that the French ships may have need of their services' (Herbette to Delbos: T. nos. 659 to 661, San Sebastian, dated 4 May 1937. Ministère des Affaires Etrangeres, 2nd series, t. V, § 394.
38 Herbette to Delbos: T. n° 628, San Sebastián, dated 1 May 1937. Ministère des Affaires étrangères, 2nd series, t. V § 382.
39 *L'Oeuvre*, 16 May 1937.
40 Cf. *supra*, 116.
41 *La Dépêche*, 13 June 1937.
42 *Le Figaro*, 18 February 1937.
43 Puzzo, 190.
44 *Le Petit Journal*, 28 May 1937.
45 *Le Petit Journal*, 24 May 1937.
46 *L'Humanité*, 22 May 1937.
47 *L'Humanité*, 24 May 1937.
48 *Le Matin*, 2 June 1937.
49 *Le Journal*, 23 May 1937.
50 *La Dépêche*, 2 June 1937.
51 *La Dépêche*, 27 May 1937.
52 Álvarez de Vayo, 58–59.
53 Puzzo, 191.
54 *L'Oeuvre*, 23 May 1937.
55 *L'Ordre*, 11 June 1937.
56 *Le Journal*, 2 June 1937.
57 *L'Oeuvre*, 11 June 1937.
58 *Le Journal*, 31 May 1937.
59 *L'Écho de Paris*, 1 June 1937.
60 *L'Humanité*, 31 May 1937.
61 *La République*, 31 May 1937. Mussolini deliberately left Minorca in Republican hands to soothe the anxieties of the British and French admiralties.
62 *L'Oeuvre*, 31 May 1937.
63 *L'Ere Nouvelle*, 1 June 1937. However, the German cruiser *Leipzig* was attacked on 15 and 18 June by submarines.
64 *L'Humanité*, 2 June 1937.
65 *La Journée Industrielle*, 3 June 1937.
66 *Revue des Deux Mondes*, 1 October 1937. Indalecio Prieto, then Minister of National Defence, admits in his account that the airman responsible for the 'mistake' was Russian (Prieto, 100).
67 *Le Petit Journal*, 1 June 1937.
68 *La Lumière*, 4 June 1937.

69 *Le Journal*, 4 June 1937.
70 *L'Humanité*, 6 June 1937.
71 *L'Express du Midi*, 7 June 1937.
72 *Le Petit Journal*, 5 June 1937.
73 *Le Peuple*, 29 June 1937.
74 *La Dépêche*, 13 July 1937.
75 *Le Peuple*, 28 June 1937.
76 Puzzo, 191.
77 Salamanca now became for a time the official seat of the Nationalist Government before it returned to Burgos.
78 *Le Petit Parisien*, 8 July 1937.
79 *La Dépêche*, 24 June 1937.
80 *L'Humanité*, 6 July 1937.
81 *La Dépêche*, 13 June 1937.
82 *La République*, 2 August 1937.
83 *La République*, 4 November 1937.
84 *L'Oeuvre*, 3 November 1937.
85 *La Dépêche*, 18 October 1937.
86 *La Dépêche*, 24 October 1937.
87 *L'Oeuvre*, 25 October 1937.
88 *Le Petit Parisien*, 8 July 1937.
89 *L'Écho de Paris*, 1 June 1937.
90 Vaillant-Couturier died shortly afterwards, in October 1937.
91 *L'Écho de Paris*, 29 May 1937.
92 Cf. *supra*, 284.
93 It should be remembered that in the French edition authorized by the Führer, the anti-French diatribes were deleted.
94 *L'Époque*, 17 July 1937.
95 *L'Époque*, 25 November 1937.
96 *Le Figaro*, 22 July 1937.
97 *Le Figaro*, 31 July 1937.
98 *Le Populaire*, 28 July 1937.

19 The Nyon Arrangement

1 *L'Express du Midi*, 16 July 1937.
2 *L'Express du Midi*, 16 July 1937.
3 *La République,* 18 July 1937.
4 *L'Ordre*, 20 July 1937.
5 *La Dépêche*, 21 July 1937.
6 *L'Ordre,* 24 July 1937.
7 *L'Ordre*, 23 July 1937.
8 *L'Ordre*, 3 November 1937.
9 *Le Figaro*, 3 July 1937.
10 *Le Temps*, 20 July 1937.
11 *L'Humanité*, 6 May 1937.

12 Director General, Sûreté Nationale, to Prefect, Haute-Garonne: n° DF 14 614/2, dated 12 May 1937.
13 Chief Inspector, Special Police, Toulouse, to Director General, Sûreté Nationale: n° 1031, Buena Fuente, dated 5 June 1937.
14 Chief Inspector, Special Police, Toulouse, to Director General, Sûreté Nationale: n° 1044, dated 8 June 1937.
15 *L'Ordre*, 9 June 1938. Among such donations was the gift of ten ambulances delivered to General García Escámez by Countess du Luart (de la Cierva, vol. II, 316, photo).
16 Another study of the military lessons to be learnt was published in the same year by Helmuth Klotz, a German émigré living in Paris, who reached his conclusions after a few brief weeks in Spain. His work, which was liberally illustrated with photographs, analyzed aircraft and anti-aircraft defence, as well as tank and anti-tank warfare. His belief that the tank had been mastered by the anti-tank gun was not so much erroneous (see Thomas, 945) as misleading. What the French General Staff failed to take into account in its strategic planning against German armor was the fact that improvements in weapons of assault had more than redressed the balance in the period following the publication of Klotz' work.

Klotz was executed by the Gestapo in Berlin in February 1943.
17 *La Dépêche*, 9 June 1937.
18 *La Dépêche*, 16 June 1937.
19 This specialist general surprises by the paucity of his sources. Clearly missing from his study are some fifteen marks in general use, including some French such as the Blériot-Spad 510; above all, the Heinkel 111, the first thirty of which had arrived in February 1937 and created a sensation on the Madrid front from their first action on 9 March. The Caproni 310 fighter-bombers, for their part, did not reach Spain until July 1938. As for the Arado 68 and Fairey fighters, there were no more than two and three, respectively; the Fairey was not even in mass production. Selecting the Katiuska and the Dornier as the best of the bombers, Armengaud was unaware of the worth of the Savoia 79, for this Italian three-engine bomber was, at 475 km/h, by far the fastest bomber in the world. The Russian Katiuska—with two engines and a crew of three—could not possibly 'serve as an interceptor aircraft;' in Soviet aviation it was classified as SB, meaning medium bomber, and was certainly the best performing bomber on the Republican side. The Dornier, on the other hand, had a speed of only 330 km/h (information provided by Sr. Santiago Albertí). Cf. Bolín, 353–354; and *Life*, 10 April 1939. According to the latter, the Potez 54, the principal attack aircraft in the French Air Force, had proved itself 'a total failure.' As for small arms, the best rifles and light machine guns were of Czechoslovak manufacture: the Muser and the Bren, which were used primarily by the Republicans.
20 *La Dépêche*, 28 June 1937.
21 *Vu-Lu*, 2 June 1937 ('L'Espagne, polygone international d'expérience', 739–740). Kérillis, no friend of the Soviet Union, corroborated this estimate and accredited Russia with the greatest gains at this time in fighter-aircraft development (*L'Echo de Paris*, 1 April 1937).

22 *La Liberté*, 1 April 1937.
23 *La Dépêche*, 15 December 1937.
24 *L'Echo de Paris*, 13 July 1937.
25 *L'Echo de Paris*, 22 July 1937.
26 *L'Echo de Paris*, 23 July 1937.
27 *Le Figaro*, 20 August 1937.
28 A meeting had been held in Rome on 17 November 1936, attended by two Italian admirals (Deputy Chief of Naval Staff Vladimiro Pini and Oscar di Giamberardino) and two German naval captains (Lange and Heye). They agreed to express, in all cases of international inquiry into shipwrecks, 'total ignorance and extreme surprise' (German Naval Records: T-426, PG 80 773, U.S. National Archives, Washington, D.C.).
29 Thomas, 720–721.
30 *L'Aube*, 4 September 1937.
31 Fischer, 445; cited in Puzzo, 197.
32 *L'Ere Nouvelle*, 14 September 1937.
33 *Le Populaire*, 14 September 1937.
34 Puzzo, 199. Juan García Durán calculates, on the basis of his ample collection of documents, that British losses amounted to 235 cases of interference, 19 vessels sunk, 52 seamen killed, and 105 seamen wounded (private information).
35 *L'Humanité*, 19 September 1937.
36 *Le Peuple*, 19 September 1937. It is undeniable that the Axis, after the Nyon Arrangement and for a brief period, found itself on the ropes, without the democracies being able to understand the reason why. Grandi confessed privately to Eden, and also to Corbin, that Italy wanted to put an end to its Spanish expedition. The Italian people had had enough, he said. No more volunteers were signing up, and a large number of those at the front wanted to be sent home (Ministère des Affaires étrangères, 2nd series, t. VII, § 129). However, some articles, such as that published in the *Daily Telegraph* of 13 October 1937, show the frantic rush of British Conservatives to return to their position of non-intervention. Eden, for his part, expressed his doubts to Corbin about the capacity of the Republicans to continue their resistance until the onset of winter (*ibid.*, § 137).

20 The London–Burgos Exchange of Agents

1 See Pike, *Crise*, 133.
2 *Le Journal de Toulouse*, 3 October 1937.
3 *La Dépêche*, 1 October 1937.
4 *La Dépêche*, 26 September 1937.
5 *La Dépêche*, 26 September 1937.
6 *La République*, 19 February 1938.
7 In Madrid in September 1936, in Saint-Jean-de-Luz in November 1936, in Catalonia in September 1937; 'in exile' in February 1938 (*La Dépêche*, 26 September; 22 November 1936; 1 October 1937; and 11 February 1938).
8 *L'Ordre*, 10 February 1938.

9 *La Tribune des Nations*, 3 February 1938.
10 *L'Express du Midi*, 30 September 1937.
11 *L'Express du Midi*, 2 October 1937.
12 *L'Epoque*, 1 October 1937.
13 *L'Homme Libre*, 22 October 1937.
14 Abbé Lambert, Mayor of Oran, raised a minor furore by his ungodly rush to be the first to congratulate Franco on his capture of Gijón. After expressing his joy in a telegram to the Caudillo, he was invited to speak over Radio Seville, an offer he flew at. The left-wing press at once demanded to know, without success, who had issued the Abbot a passport and at the same time called for his resignation from the mayoralty (*La Dépêche*, 26 October 1937).
15 *La Dépêche*, 23 October 1937.
16 *L'Humanité*, 23 October 1937.
17 *Le Jour*, 23 October 1937.
18 *L'Oeuvre*, 15 September 1937.
19 The reconciliation in 1839 between the Carlists and the Liberals, as a result of which the Basques lost their liberties. This presentation of the history of the Basque people, popular among the Basques, does not go unchallenged. Among those who have challenged it are Herminio Morales Fernández, a former Consul Adjunto de España in Paris, and the historian Javier Rubio, who both attended a luncheon on 22 January 1983 at the Maison de l'Amérique Latine in Paris. Morales refuted almost every point: the Basques never beat the Romans; the Moors, not the Basques, repulsed Charlemagne; the Spaniards who helped Wellington to win at Vitoria were Castilians, not Basques. Rubio attributed the errors in the Basque approach to their history to their idea of racial superiority.
20 Rieu Vernet, *La Dépêche*, 18 October 1937.
21 *Le Populaire*, 18 December 1937.
22 *La Dépêche*, 1 October 1937.
23 Cf. *supra*, 123–124.
24 *Revue de Paris*, 15 December 1937.
25 *La Garonne*, 6 February 1938; Saint-Aulaire, 89.
26 *La Dépêche*, 10 October 1937.
27 Garosci mocks the pretentiousness of Chamson in his suggestion that if he was leaving Spain it was in the interest of world peace. 'If I am killed,' suggests Chamson, in Garosci's words, 'then France will intervene in Spain, and the result will be the Second World War. Then, I am responsible' (Garosci, 315).
28 *La Dépêche*, 1 November 1937.
29 *L'Ordre*, 24 October 1937.
30 The name derives from the city associated with the remilitarization of the Rhineland in February 1936 and the apathy of France to this first major challenge by Germany.
31 *Le Figaro*, 31 August 1937.
32 *Le Figaro*, 19 October 1937.
33 *L'Homme Libre*, 4 September 1937.
34 *L'Express du Midi*, 16 October 1937.

35 See Appendix IV.
36 *L'Oeuvre*, 8 October 1937.
37 *La République*, 4 November 1937.
38 *La République*, 4 November 1937.
39 Japan too had just granted recognition to Franco, on 1 December 1937.
40 *La République*, 20 November 1937.
41 *Le Figaro*, 4 November 1937.
42 *L'Ere Nouvelle*, 4 November 1937.
43 *L'Oeuvre*, 31 July 1937.
44 *Le Populaire*, 4 November 1937.
45 Ossorio y Gallardo, who had replaced de los Ríos as Ambassador to Paris, was reported negotiating at this time with Nationalist agents in Brussels (Thomas, 786).
46 *La Dépêche*, 15 December 1937; 21 January 1938.
47 *La Dépêche*, 25 March 1938.
48 Sir Norman had been awarded the Nobel Prize for Peace in 1933. Part pacifist and part pragmatist, he published *The Grand Illusion* in 1910 in an effort to prove that modern warfare is economically disastrous to all participants and that any victory is an illusion. His counsel was for peace through collective security.
49 *La Dépêche*, 22 May 1938.

21 The Threat to French Security

1 *L'Oeuvre*, 6 November 1937.
2 *La Dépêche*, 13 January 1938.
3 *L'Epoque*, 20 December 1937.
4 *L'Humanité*, 8 January 1938.
5 In *L'Ordre*, an American Colonel Sweeney, who had just returned from Teruel, belittled Franco's chances of recovering the town, while he pointed out that a more important Nationalist offensive had been planned in the Guadalajara sector. Sweeney added, however, that Franco's reserves were being whittled away in the snows between Teruel and Soria, and that the offensive was now contingent upon the arrival of fresh reinforcements from Italy (*L'Ordre*, 11 January 1938).
6 *Le Peuple*, 23 December 1937.
7 *La Dépêche*, 14 January 1938.
8 The Republican battleship *Jaime Primero* had blown up in June 1937.
9 Thomas classifies the *Miguel de Cervantes* as a destroyer (Thomas, 1963 edition, 680). The *Cervantes* was torpedoed on 22 November 1936 by an Italian submarine while anchored in Escombreras. At that time the Axis had not yet consulted Franco on the subject of naval operations.
10 *La Dépêche*, 22 January 1938. By November 1937, Italy had given Franco four destroyers and two submarines. Italian authorities denied this as late as February 1938 (*Manchester Gaurdian*, 4 February 1938).
11 *Journal de Finances*, 2 February 1938.
12 *La Garonne*, 27 April 1938. The exchange rate thus fluctuated around 8 French francs to the Swiss franc. *La Garonne*'s figures actually show a slight improvement

for the Republican peseta in April 1938 over the February quotation. This is highly improbable in the light of three interim disasters for the Republic: Teruel, the Anschluss, and Vinaroz.

This ratio of approximately 4:1 in favour of the Nationalist peseta gradually widened, until by February 1939 the Nationalist peseta was worth seventy times the Republican on the Paris Bourse.

13 The first of Chautemps' two Front Populaire Cabinets fell because it had lost the support of the Socialists and the Communists on financial issues. The death sentence was pronounced when Blum, as Vice-Premier, announced the resignation of the SFIO députés.
14 *Occident*, 10 January 1938.
15 *L'Ordre*, 1 January 1938.
16 *L'Ordre*, 25 February 1938.
17 *L'Ordre*, 18 April 1938.
18 *L'Ordre*, 23 April 1938.
19 *L'Ordre*, 7 May 1938.
20 The Institution was founded by Francisco Giner de los Ríos, after the death of Sanz del Río in 1869 and the Restoration of 1875.
21 *La Garonne*, 13 June 1938.
22 Banse was a free-lance geographer, psychologist, political theorist and military scientist. *Raum* created a world-wide sensation and accurately forecast the technique of German psychological warfare to be employed on both the military and home fronts. Banse held that geography (space) and psychology (people) are more important in modern warfare than traditional military science. The Nazis considered the publication of this book untimely and withdrew it from sale—though not from circulation—with the explanation that it was 'merely the senseless babblings of an irresponsible armchair strategist.' Indeed, his ideas seemed eccentric, incoherent and reckless, but they accidentally reflected the more carefully hidden plans of the German General Staff. Whether or not he had connections with the High Command, Banse received official recognition when Hitler appointed him to the important position of Professor of Military Sciences at the Brunswick Institute of Technology. His subsequent theories on bacterial warfare, which he was mistakenly believed to advocate unconditionally, won him a reputation as Germany's foremost 'strategist of terror.' Two of his theories, on the psychology of collapse and of the opponent, had appeared in the German press ('Psychologie des Zusammenbruchs', *Völkischer Beobachter*, 19 June 1932; 'Psychologie des Gegners', *Völkischer Beobachter*, 29 June 1932).
23 *Le Populaire*, 10 May 1938.
24 Cf. *supra*, 193.
25 *La Dépêche*, 25 March 1938.
26 According to André Marty, on 14 March 1938, the day after Blum returned to office, the French Ambassador in Barcelona asked Negrín to capitulate to Franco. Allegedly, he even offered his services to effect the surrender. Three hundred thousand Barcelona workers, again according to Marty, rejected this offer by parading on the same day under the windows of the Cabinet ministers,

carrying the slogans 'Spain is not Austria!' 'Better to die on your feet than live on your knees!'

27 Blum, once again convulsed, consulted the French military attaché Henri Morel, who responded: 'I can tell you only this: a King of France would go to war.' 'I am not the King of France,' replied Blum.

28 *Journal des Débats*, 27 April 1938. Jules Moch, at that time the Minister of Public Works, assured the author that Bardoux's talk of France sending three divisions to Catalonia was pure fiction (interview, 24 November 1973). The official minutes for the meeting of 17 March show that if Blum supported the action, no one else did.

29 Bailby, *Le Jour—L'Echo de Paris:* 25 June 1938. The question was raised on 2 June at a hearing of the Foreign Minister in front of the Foreign Affairs Committee of the House. Georges Bonnet told the committee that no confidential order existed, and that, on the contrary, the order of August 1936 remained in force (*Le Temps*: 4 June 1938). But the confidential order did indeed exist (Ministère des Affaires étrangères, 2nd series, volume IX § 520).

30 *L'Humanité*, 24 March 1938.
31 *L'Action Française*, 30 April 1938.
32 Cf. *supra*, 60, 283.
33 *Le Populaire*, 19 April 1938.
34 *Le Matin*, 20 March 1938.
35 *L'Action Française*, 25 March 1938.
36 *L'Epoque*, 20 March 1938.
37 *Le Jour*, 25 March 1938.
38 *L'Ere Nouvelle*, 9 May 1938.
39 *La Dépêche*, 10 May 1938.
40 *La Dépêche*, 4 June 1938.
41 *L'Epoque*, 30 January 1938.
42 *L'Epoque*, 18 April 1938.
43 *Le Figaro*, 20 March 1938.
44 *La Dépêche*, 23 March 1938.
45 *L'Epoque*, 20 March 1938.
46 *L'Echo de Paris*, 19 March 1938.
47 *Le Jour*, 25 March 1938.
48 *Le Figaro*, 22 March 1938.
49 *La Dépêche*, 1 April 1938.
50 John Nicoletis, Bulletin du Centre Polytechnicien d'Études Economiques, n° 40, July 1937.
51 *L'Oeuvre*, 30 May 1938.
52 *L'Epoque*, 20 March 1938. It is unclear what these guarantees were (cf. *supra*, 200). Meanwhile, the *New York Times* published a photo, reproduced in *La Dépêche* on 3 January 1938, of a letter mailed in Vigo bearing the postmark '¡Viva España! ¡Heil Hitler!' *L'Ordre* maintained, on 8 July, that the Germans controlled not only the telegraphs and telephones but also the Nationalists' maritime commerce and the secret pólice.

53 *Paris-Midi*, 1 April 1938.
54 *L'Action Française*, 26 March 1938.
55 *L'Ordre*, 28 May 1938.
56 *L'Action Française*, 31 May 1938.
57 But see Thomas: 'The possibility of a general war [in mid-1938], and one which he might have to fight against France, caused [Franco] to send 20,000 prisoners to work on border fortifications, both in the Pyrenees and in Spanish Morocco' (Thomas, 696; 848).
58 *El Heraldo de Aragón*, 11 July 1938 (from British United Press, Saragossa); *L'Ordre*, 12 July 1938.
59 *La Garonne*, 14 July 1938.
60 Labonne to Bonnet: D. n° 261, Barcelona, dated 26 May 1936. Ministère des Affaires étrangères, 2nd series, t. IX, § 460.

22 The Daladier–Bonnet Formula

1 *L'Epoque*, 15 May 1938.
2 *L'Oeuvre*, 15 May 1938.
3 *Il Corriere della Sera* (Milan), 16 May 1938.
4 *L'Humanité*, 17 May 1938.
5 Information provided by Sr. Santiago Albertí, an eye-witness to the raid on 17 March. He adds that people were caught in the open, because no air-raid alert had been sounded prior to the attack. Max Gallo writes of seventeen raids in ten hours, causing 1,300 dead and 2,000 wounded (*Historia Hors Série*, n° 22, p. 172). Among the dead, according to *La Dépêche* of 20 March 1938, were two French consuls. In the photograph of Barcelona given in my French edition, 302, taken on 17 March 1938, there were no survivors in the tramcar destroyed in the attack (Santiago Albertí, Barcelona, private correspondence).
6 *L'Aube*, 19 March 1938. Bidault recalled that in the Middle Ages, however barbaric the customs were, the Church had imposed the Peace of God, forbidding injury to non-combatants.
7 *L'Oeuvre*, 2 June 1938.
8 *Le Jour-L'Echo de Paris*, 1 June 1938.
9 *L'Epoque*, 28 June 1938.
10 *L'Oeuvre*, 28 June 1938.
11 *La République*, 13 June 1938.
12 *L'Epoque*, 13 June 1938.
13 *La République*, 13 June 1938.
14 *La Dépêche*, 30 June 1938.
15 In July 1938 Franco told Henri Massis in Burgos that Nationalist air raids were strictly limited to military objectives. 'There is no question', the Caudillo explained, 'of destroying towns systematically. We leave that for the Reds .... And yet it is we whom they accuse of such heinous crimes' (Massis, 173).
16 Eden and his Under-Secretary of State, Lord Cranborne, had resigned on 20 February 1938, in opposition to the policy of discrimination against the Republic now clearly immanent in the Non-intervention Agreement.

17 *Le Journal*, 1 June 1938.
18 *Le Matin*, 1 June 1938.
19 *La Dépêche*, 6 June 1938.
20 *Le Journal de Toulouse*, 28 August 1938.
21 *Le Journal de Toulouse*, 14 November 1937.
22 *La Liberté*, 29 May 1938.
23 *Le Journal*, 28 May 1938.
24 *La Garonne*, 30 May 1938.
25 *L'Humanité*, 6 June 1938.
26 *Le Populaire*, 6 June 1938.
27 *Le Peuple*, 6 June 1938.
28 *La Dépêche*, 7 June 1938.
29 *L'Ordre*, 6 June 1938.
30 *Le Journal*, 6 June 1938.
31 *L'Epoque*, 6 June 1938.
32 *L'Action Française*, 6 June 1938.
33 *Le Jour-L'Echo de Paris*, 6 June 1938.
34 *Le Figaro*, 6 June 1938.
35 *Le Journal*, 7 June 1938.
36 *La Garonne*, 8 June 1938.
37 *Le Matin*, 7 June 1938.
38 *Le Figaro*, 6 June 1938.
39 *Le Figaro*, 7 June 1938.
40 *L'Epoque*, 7 June 1938.
41 *La Dépêche*, 9 June 1938.
42 *Le Matin*, 7 June 1938.
43 *L'Action Française*, 7 June 1938.
44 *La Liberté*, 11 June 1938.
45 *La Dépêche*, 8 June 1938. *La Garonne* nonetheless claimed that *La Dépêche* refrained from imputing the blame to the Nationalists (*La Garonne*, 9 June 1938).
46 *Le Petit Parisien*, 7 June 1938.
47 *L'Ordre*, 8 June 1938.
48 *Le Populaire*, 7 June 1938.
49 *La Garonne*, 8 June 1938.
50 *L'Humanité*, 7 June 1938.
51 *Le Populaire*, 7 June 1938.
52 *Le Populaire*, 11 June 1938.
53 Cf. *supra*, 193.
54 *La Garonne*, 26 April 1938.
55 *Le Petit Bleu*, 3 March 1938.
56 *Le Figaro*, 28 May 1938.
57 In this there was one notable voice of dissent. Chaves Nogales expressed the view in *La Dépêche* that the Spanish military class considered war the natural state and was in no hurry to end the conflict. Chaves based this questionable theory on the Spanish record of protracted engagements: the Reconquista had dragged on for

nearly eight centuries, and even the Morocco campaign had taken twenty years (*La Dépêche*, 22 November 1938).
58 Bonjean to Paul-Boncour: *La Dépêche,* n° 136, Saint-Jean-de-Luz, dated 18 March 1939. Ministère des Affaires étrangères. 2nd series, VIII, § 924–925.
59 *La Dépêche*, 22 December 1938.
60 *L'Epoque*, 13 December 1938.
61 *La Garonne*, 14 December 1938. A report by Luis de Bermeo in *L'Ordre* showed that the Germans fared no better than the Italians in current popular esteem. According to Bermeo, a considerable section of the Nationalist officer corps, headed by Quiepo de Llano, were disgusted with the reputation of common murderers they had acquired through their association with the Germans as well as with the Italians. Bermeo referred to a 36-hour uprising in Cádiz, to an attack on two German officers in Montilla (Córdoba), to similar disturbances in Andalusia at Antequera, Utrera, La Línea and Estepona, and to an incident at Cáceres which delayed for two hours the departure of two troop-trains for the Madrid front (*L'Ordre*, 22 June 1938).
62 *Le Populaire*, 9 July 1938.
63 *News Chronicle*, 20 May 1938.
64 Stohrer to Wilhelmstrasse: telegram, Salamanca, 27 April 1938, n° 218, stamped Secret. Document n° 5 *Documents secrets du ministère des Affaires étrangères d'Allemagne. La politique allemande (1936–1943): Espagne.* Paul Dupont, Paris, 1946, p. 28.
65 These statements made by Franco to Admiral Canaris, chief of the Abwehr (military intelligence), were based, according to Stohrer, on the following considerations: 'It is possible that, for reasons of political expediency (the London Committee), or as a result of international complications, we and the Italians may find ourselves obliged to put an end to our action in Spain. In this case, it would be necessary to take all precautionary measures to avoid serious damage. Franco has taken care in advance for Spanish airmen to make immediate use of the materiel, even though, as Franco has emphasized on several occasions, "there is no way to replace, even remotely, the excellent German pilots" (Stohrer to Wilhelmstrasse: telegram, San Sebastian, 4 May 1938, n° 4, stamped Secret/ Urgent. Document n° 6, *ibid.* 29–30). According to Ian Colvin, 149, Canaris, an old friend of Franco's, informed the Caudillo that Hitler thought he would inevitably lose the war (quoted by Downes, 128).

Paradoxically, Generalfeldmarschall Wilhelm Keitel, whom Hitler in February 1938 had appointed supreme commander of the Wehrmacht, disclosed that German military equipment was below par, particularly in regard to aircraft and artillery. (Report from Keitel to Weizsäcker, head of the political section of the Wilhelmstrasse: Berlín, 2 June 1938, stamped Secret. Document n° 8, *Documents secrets du Ministère des Affaires étrangères d'Allemagne,* 34). In the same month, according to Geneviève Tabouis, General von Reichenau, whom Hitler would appoint in 1940 as head of Operation *Felix* against Gibraltar, stated in a private meeting that the German anti-aircraft guns and anti-tank guns were excellent (*L'Oeuvre*, 25 June 1938).

66 Whealey draws from a Gestapo report a reference to 84 Soviet planes, and an equivalent number of French aircraft, about to be sent via Marseilles to Barcelona (Carr, 226). Whealey estimates the number of French aircraft supplied to the Republic at 282, and Soviet planes at 932 (Carr, 232).
67 *La Garonne*, 23 June 1938.
68 *Le Matin*, 24 May 1938.
69 *La République*, 19 May 1938. *L'Ordre* reported at this time the discovery in Catalonia of British machine guns, presumably supplied to the Nationalists (*L'Ordre*, 9 June 1938).
70 *La Dépêche*, 21 May 1938.
71 The order was implemented at once. When the "Lost" 43rd Division retreated into France on 16 June 1938, the *New York Times* reported the following day that the French authorities had refused to allow ammunition for the isolated Loyalists to cross the border.
72 *La Garonne*, 23 June 1938.
73 *La Garonne*, 28 September 1938. *La Garonne* proceeded to enumerate the four "myths" which had been built around the New Spain. According to these "myths," which *La Garonne* 'exploded' as it went, Nationalist Spain was: the enemy of democracy; military and Fascist; fanatical and clerical; and germanophile. Legendre later described Spain (that is to say, the 'true' Spain, or Nationalist Spain), as 'the most tolerant nation in the world' (*La Garonne*, 16 October 1938).
74 *Le Populaire*, 24 June 1938.
75 *Le Populaire*, 24 June, 7 July 1938.
76 *Le Populaire*, 7 August 1938.
77 *Le Populaire*, 11 August 1938.
78 *La Dépêche*, 17 June 1938.
79 *La Dépêche*, 6 July 1938.
80 *La Dépêche*, 6 July 1938.
81 *La Dépêche*, 6 July 1938.
82 *La République*, 28 June 1938.
83 *Le Populaire*, 23 June 1938.

23 The Republic in Isolation

1 *Le Dépêche*, 3 June 1938.
2 *Le Dépêche*, 4 June 1938.
3 *L'Aube*, 3 June 1938.
4 However, for an account of the Republicans' efforts to protect Spanish art treasures from destruction by Spain's nihilists, see Camille Mauclair (*La Dépêche*, 1 March 1938).
5 Cf. *supra*, 174.
6 *La République*, 4 April 1938.
7 *L'Oeuvre*, 8 March 1938.
8 Cf. *supra*, 176.
9 *Le Populaire*, 18 April 1938.

10 *Le République*, 19 April 1938.
11 *La Garonne*, 26 April 1938. Did Franco sincerely believe in the existence in Spain of a large number of Soviets? According to *Tchassovoi* ('The Sentry'), a fortnightly published in Paris by Russian emigrants, in its issue of 12 February 1938, Franco was broadcasting propaganda in the Russian language. But cf. Marty, *supra*, 228–229.
12 Cf. *supra*, 133.
13 *L'Action Française*, 2 May 1938. Even a pro-Franco French writer attested to Spanish Nationalist indifference toward the support offered by Maurras (cf. *supra*, 210).

  In *La Garonne*, Jean Baudry presented the new Spain in terms similar to those of the Académicien. The new Spain, Baudry explained, constituted a nation tied together, not on the basis of counting up votes, but instead on freedom of conscience and force of will; not on the basis of general assent but on individual assent. The new Spain was a country 'free from all equality based on weakness,' a country 'where sorrow has its share' (*La Garonne*, 1 August 1938).
14 Cf. *supra*, 312.
15 Massis, 149.
16 *L'Époque*, 12 May 1938.
17 *L'Humanité*, 8 July 1938.
18 *La République*, 9 July 1938.
19 *La Garonne*, 1 July 1938.
20 *La République*, 7 May 1938.
21 *La République*, 2 May 1938.
22 *L'Époque*, 30 July 1938.
23 *L'Époque*, 13 December 1938.
24 *La République*, 2 January 1939. The Portuguese had good reason to fear for their independence. On 7 May 1941, the Air Attaché at the German Embassy in Madrid wrote a report (n° 268/41 com. secr.) to the Wilhelmstrasse stating: 'The opinion is expressed openly among Spanish military officers that a country as small as Portugal does not have the right to exist in a new Europe, and that from the geographical point of view, Portugal belongs to Spain . . . The majority openly voice the need for a military intervention against Portugal in the near future (*Documents secrets du ministère des Affaires étrangères d'Allemagne*, 74).
25 Cf. *supra*, 190.
26 *L'Oeuvre*, 28 May 1938.
27 *L'Oeuvre*, 28 May 1938.
28 *L'Action Française*, 22 June 1938. Among the most important were: Colonel Hans von Funck, German military attaché in Salamanca since 1937. Funck, together with Major Hans Wilhelmi, were implicated in 1939 in espionnage operations in the Southwest of France (see Pike, *Vae*, 100). Funck was later appointed General der Panzertruppen, and Wilhelmi, military attaché at the embassy in Madrid.
29 Cf. *supra*, 183.
30 *Le Jour – L'Écho de Paris*, 29 June 1938. *Le Journal de Toulouse* reported the crea-

tion of a new French merchant fleet named France-Navigation, comprising 21 vessels plying between Marseilles and Spanish Republican ports (*Le Journal de Toulouse*, 25 November 1938). The Republican Government had paid for the ships, but it was the French Communist Party that controlled the line (Madariaga, 232).
31 *L'Action Française*, 1 July 1938.
32 *Le Journal*, 25 January 1939. *Le Journal* was pleased, however, to announce that, Axis propaganda to the contrary, it was not France that followed the Soviet Union in the volume of aid supplied to the Republic but Great Britain, the United States, Czechoslovakia, Switzerland, and Sweden, whose individual consignments all far exceeded the French.
33 Tixier-Vignancour consequently appealed for an inquiry (*La Dépêche*, 17 March 1939).
34 *La Dépêche*, 22 December 1938.
35 *L'Oeuvre*, 25 June 1938. In 1940, Reichenau was given command of Operation *Felix* against Gibraltar.
36 The contents of the crates unloaded from the steamship *Midol* were evaluated, according to Antoine Delenda, assistant director in the commercial relations department of the Quai d'Orsay, at more than 1 million francs (11 April 1938: *Ministère des Affaires étrangères*, 2° serie, t. X, § 163).
37 *La Dépêche*, 31 July 1938.
38 *Le Jour- L'Écho de Paris*, 1 July 1938.
39 *Le Matin*, 8 July 1938.
40 *Le Populaire*, 8 July 1938.
41 *La Garonne*, 20 July 1938.
42 *Le Figaro*, 11 August 1938.
43 *L'Ordre*, 28 June 1938.
44 O.K. Simon, *Hitler en Espagne* (Paris 1938). O. K. Simon was the pseudonym of the Yugoslav Otto Katz.
45 *L'Ordre*, 1 June; 9 July 1938.
46 *La Dépêche*, 6 June 1938.
47 See Pike, *Crise,* 147, 192–3.
48 *L'Europe Nouvelle*, 30 July 1938.
49 *Le Figaro*, 28 May 1938.
50 *La République*, 23 June 1938.
51 Cf. *supra*, 128.
52 Bernanos had broken with Maurras in 1932. Garosci writes: 'L'ordine, l'onore, la Francia no erano per lui come stavano per Maurras coperture di una disposizione di guerra civile, ma ideali, sentimenti e quasi persone vere' (Garosci, 407).
53 *La Dépêche*, 5 August 1938.
54 *La Marsellaise*, 1 March 1938.
55 *Le Journal de Toulouse*, 6 March 1938.

24 The Shadow of Munich

1 Cf. *supra*, 190.

2 *La Dépêche*, 28 February 1938.
3 *La Dépêche*, 25 March 1938.
4 *Le Matin*, 25 March 1938.
5 Cf. *supra*, 67, 105.
6 Pivert proceeded to found the Parti Socialiste Ouvrier et Paysan, which supplied aid to the Spanish Republicans.
7 *La Dépêche*, 17 September 1938.
8 *La Dépêche*, 17 September 1938.
9 The fleet consisted of 19 mine-sweepers. Vice-Admiral Terreux, in Rochefort, to whom the offer was made, duly expressed his thanks for this gesture in a letter dated 5 October 1938.
10 *Le Journal*, 14 September 1938.
11 *Le Petit Bleu*, 21 September 1938.
12 *La Garonne*, 23 September 1938.
13 *Gringoire*, 7 October 1938.
14 Massis, 167.
15 *La Dépêche*, 23 October 1938.
16 In reprisal, politically minded pranksters in Paris replaced the signs above the Métropolitan station at Solférino with others reading Caporetto.
17 *La Garonne*, 1 October 1938.
18 *Le Jour – L'Écho de Paris*, 1 October 1938.
19 *Temps Présent*, 7 October 1938.
20 *L'Époque,* 30 September 1938.
21 Cf. *supra*, 64.
22 *L'Époque*, 2 October 1938.
23 *L'Époque*, 7 October 1938.
24 *La Garonne*, 12 October 1938.
25 *La Dépêche*, 4 October 1938.
26 *L'Humanité*, 3 October 1938.
27 But Blum, at the time of Munich, had praised Daladier in *Le Populaire* as a leader 'deserving of our gratitude' (Tiersky, 68).
28 *Regards*, 6 October 1938.
29 *La Garonne*, 23 October 1938. For further alleged slanders, see *La Garonne*, 13, 14, 15 and 20 October 1938.
30 Cf. *supra*, 205.
31 Letter from Muret (Haute-Garonne), dated 25 October 1938.
32 *La Garonne*, 4 November 1938.
33 Letter from Paris, dated 21 November 1938; published in *La Garonne*, 28 November 1938.
34 *La Garonne*, 31 December 1938.
35 *Le Petit Bleu*, 9 April 1938.
36 *L'Époque*, 7 June 1938.
37 *L'Oeuvre*, 7 June 1938.
38 *L'Action Française*, 18 August 1938.
39 *L'Eclaireur de Nice et du Sud-Est,* 27 August 1938.

40 *L'Oeuvre*, 9 October 1938.
41 *La Dépêche*, 22 December 1938.
42 *Le Figaro*, 7 November 1938.
43 *Le Populaire*, 4 November 1938.
44 *La Dépêche*, 8 November 1938.
45 *L'Ordre*, 15 October 1938.
46 Lord Runciman had been sent as a mediator to Prague in July 1938 at the beginning of the Czech crisis.
47 *L'Ordre*, 15 December 1938.
48 *Le Petit Parisien*, 9 October 1938. An attempt at such mediation consisted of creating a commission of prisoner exchange under the chairmanship of the British Field Marshal Sir Philip Chetwode, who set up his headquarters in Toulouse in August 1938. His adjuncts, Cowan in the Republican zone and Mosley in the Nationalist Zone, remained in Spain from September 1938 to April 1939. According to Brian Crozier, they achieved little (Crozier, 284), but Broué and Témime consider they organized 'numerous exchanges' and suggest that they probably helped in laying the groundwork for putting an end to the conflict (Broué and Témime, 459).
49 *L'Oeuvre*, 1 November 1938.
50 Koestler wrote: 'Stalin dropped Spain into the hands of fascism as a bridal gift, long before anyone could foresee the marriage' (Koestler, *Scum*, 121).
51 On their return to Paris in November 1938, the ex-volunteers marched in parade from the Gare d'Austerlitz to the Maison des Métallos. Meanwhile, a veterans' association was founded in Paris known as the Amicale des Anciens Volontaires Français en Espagne Républicaine. Under the leadership of Pierre Rebière, as member of the Central Committee of the Communist Party, and Fongarnand, it was affiliated to the Association Républicaine des Anciens Combattants, but it failed to secure government pensions for the French ex-volunteers, See Delperrie de Bayac, *Brigades*, 376.
52 The total number of deaths in the Brigade lines is roughly 10,000 of which 3,000 were French.
53 *La Garonne*, 5 November 1938; *Le Journal de Toulouse*, 13 November 1938.
54 On 7 November 1938, Franco told James Miller, vice-president of the United Press: "No habrá mediación. No habrá mediación porque los delincuentes y sus víctimas no pueden vivir juntos." Franco, *Palabras*, 476. Information from Paul Preston.
55 The Republican Government had transferred its seat from Valencia to Barcelona on 31 October 1937.
56 In place of this, Labonne was named high commissioner of Tunisia.
57 *Le Populaire*, 13 October 1938.
58 *Le Petit Parisien*, 18 December 1938. Ireland, followed by Switzerland, had been the first after the Axis States to grant recognition to Franco.
59 *Le Figaro*, 5 December 1938.
60 *Le Journal*, 25 November 1938.
61 *La Dépêche*, 22 December 1938.

62 *La République*, 26 December 1938.
63 *L'Ordre*, 22 December 1938.
64 *L'Époque*, 26 December 1938.
65 *L'Ordre*, 29 December 1938.
66 *La Revue Universelle*, 15 March 1937.
67 Franco, *Palabras*, 476. Information from Paul Preston.
68 *L'Ordre*, 11 November 1938.
69 *La Dépêche*, 21 December 1938.
70 Cf. *supra*, 198.
71 *La Dépêche*, 24 December 1938. Polls are always of uncertain value, but a poll conducted in December 1938 as to whether France should intervene in Spain produced an astounding result: 75 percent were in favour, and 21 percent opposed (Amouroux, 49).
72 *La Dépêche*, 22 December 1938.
73 See Pike, *Crise*, 25.
74 *Le Midi Socialiste*, 1 January 1939.

25 The War at the Gates of France

1 Although Marty returned to Spain about this time, his presence in Catalonia may not yet have been reported.
2 Reports in the press in early 1938 had attested to a return to freedom of religion in Catalonia, expressed notably at a session of Cortes held in February in the Montserrat monastery. Two thousand masses a day were being celebrated in Barcelona alone, wrote Pierre Mille, and there were as many Catholics fighting on the Republican side as there were Catholics with the Nationalists. Alcoléa affirms that there were three thousand priests in Catalonia at this time, with several hundred serving as chaplains on the eastern front (Pierre Mille, *La Dépêche*, 13 January 1938; *La Croix*, 22 February 1938; Alcoléa, 80). In sharp contrast, François Charles-Roux, France's Ambassador to the Holy See, claimed that 'religious worship remained underground, barely tolerated by the police even in private homes (Charles-Roux to Bonnet: D. n° 271, Rome, dated 29 August 1938. *Ministère des Affaires Étrangères*, 2nd series, t.X, § 496).
3 *La Dépêche*, 15 January 1939.
4 *La Dépêche*, 20, 24 January 1939.
5 *L'Ordre*, 16 January 1930. Ironically, Léon Bailby now reported in *Le Jour* that, at the moment of investing the city, Franco withdrew the Italian troops. The reasons for this, according to Bailby, were that the Italians had *not* taken a direct part in the operations, and that it was necessary to 'correct the popular misconception' that the war on the Nationalist side was being fought by foreign troops.'Even if the proportion had been as high as one in twenty,' wrote Bailby, 'it would be absurd to dignify this ludicrous myth' (*Le Jour*, 12 February 1939).
6 *La Dépêche*, 7 February 1939.
7 *La Dépêche*, 7 February 1939.
8 *Le Midi Socialiste*, 28 March 1939.
9 *La Dépêche*, 21 January 1939.

10 *Le Populaire*, 13 February 1939.
11 *L'Oeuvre*, 17 January 1939.
12 *L'Ordre*, 26 January 1939.
13 *L'Oeuvre*, 17 January 1939.
14 *L'Époque*, 24 January 1939.
15 *L'Oeuvre*, 18 January 1939.
16 *L'Action Française*, 22 February 1939.
17 *La Dépêche*, 11 February 1939.
18 *Le Journal*, 16 February 1939.
19 *L'Époque*, 18 January 1939.
20 Cf. *supra*, 64.
21 *L'Époque*, 23 January 1939.
22 The possibility of an attack on France across the Belgian border seemed totally to escape French attention. Such was French faith in Hitler's agreement to honour Belgian neutrality, which Belgium had declared in April 1937, that no decision was made to extend the Maginot Line north-westward beyond the Ardennes.
23 *L'Époque*, 19 January 1939.
24 Cf. *supra*, 133 and 193.
25 Maret, 214.
26 This undying resentment felt by the Spaniards toward the French had been observed early in the conflict by *Le Petit Journal*. Bernanos, 135: 'only the rabble and I love France', said Alfonso XIII.
27 Maret added that others drew a distinction between "legal" France and the "real" France of Maurras, a distinction similarly delivered by Pierre Laval in 1937.
28 *Le Midi Socialiste*, 17 January 1939.
29 *Le Midi Socialiste*, 17 January 1939.
30 In the front rank of the bad counsellors to Prime Ministers Baldwin and Chamberlain was Sir Horace Wilson. Sir Horace was so well disposed to the German point of view that von Dirksen, the German ambassador to London, spoke of him in May 1938 as 'the foreign minister of the German Chancellery' and considered him to be the dominant force in Chamberlain's foreign policy. He alone accompanied the British Prime Minister when he flew to Berchtesgaden on 15 September. On 26 September he flew to Berlin, alone. Hitler was not in a mood to listen to Chamberlain's accusations that he had broken his promises, and he broke out in anger when Chamberlain's envoy expressed them. Sir Horace was again at Chamberlain's side at the time of Munich.
31 However, Britain was so anxious to see an end to the war that the *Devonshire* was given a second assignment. In accordance with a secret bargain between Chamberlain and Franco, the destroyer was sent to organize, on 8 February, the surrender of Minorca to the Nationalist forces. The *Devonshire* disembarked Nationalist troops at the same time that it evacuated Republican refugees.
32 Note from Assistant Director of Political and Commercial Affairs [Robert Renom de La Baume], to Foreign Ministry, dated 11 April 1938. Ministère des Affaires étrangères. 2nd series, t. IX, § 164.
33 *Le Midi Socialiste,* 17 February 1939.
34 *La Dépêche*, 19 February 1939.

35 Although he had contributed significantly to drawing up the Munich Pact, and although he later served in the Vichy Government, Bonnet was acquitted in 1949 of the crime of collaboration with the enemy.
36 *Le Midi Socialiste,* 5 January 1939.
37 *L'Oeuvre,* 14 December 1938.
38 The pastor Lengereau had his own answer for any famine ravaging Republican Spain: the trucks transporting supplies from France carried signs saying, 'Handle carefully,' and 'No smoking' (*Le Journal de Toulouse,* 25 December 1938).
39 *La Dépêche,* 23 January 1939.
40 The last correspondent to remain in Barcelona was Gallagher, writing for the *Daily Express* and *Paris-Soir.* Some hours before the arrival of the insurgents, in the middle of the night of 25–26 January, he dictated by candlelight his account of the Republican resistance.
41 Silvia Mistral shows that the factories had long shut down for lack of electricity and raw materials. Morale was so low that a Fifth Column would be pointless (Mistral, *passim*). Solano Palacio, a member of the CNT-FAI, reveals one of the chief factors that led to this demoralization: in the last months, Líster had ordered the shooting of six hundred Anarchists, Socialists and Republicans (Solano Palacio, 45).
42 *Le Jour – L'Écho de Paris*: 25 January 1939. In an exclusive article for *La Dépêche,* published posthumously, Marcelino Domingo, Minister of Education in Azaña's Cabinet of February 1936, attributed the collapse in Catalonia to three main causes: the war did not exist for all too many Catalan Anarchists who talked only of the Revolution of July 1936; news of the Anglo-Italian Mediterranean Agreement, under which Chamberlain gave Mussolini a free hand in Spain, discouraged further assistance to the point that it appeared thereafter like Numantine suicide; famine and incessant bombing. 'No city in the world would have resisted the air attacks,' wrote Domingo, who died a year too soon to see his error. In conclusion, Domingo found that the spirit of Catalonia had been destroyed as early as 1936 (*La Depêche,* 6 March 1939).
43 *Le Midi Socialiste,* 4 February 1939.
44 Thomas, 871.
45 *Le Journal,* 24 January 1939.
46 Constancia de la Mora, the Communist wife of Hidalgo de Cisneros, the Republican air force chief, arrived at this time in Toulouse by air. The first sight she saw on the tarmac were three US-built planes, paid for by the Republic but prevented by the French authorities from crossing the frontier (Mora, 431).
47 *Ce Soir,* 1 February 1939.
48 *La Dépêche,* 6 February 1939.
49 *Le Midi Socialiste,* 1 February 1939.
50 *La Dépêche,* 5 February 1939.
51 *La Dépêche,* 1 February 1939. However, two days later, on 2 February 1939, Negrín and Álvarez del Vayo approached the French and British Ministers, Jules Henry and Stevenson, to try to arrange a mediation. With Henry pressing Negrín to surrender, the latter would certainly have liked to reach an agreement with

Franco on the following three points: the departure from Spanish territory of all foreign elements; the free determination by the Spanish people, without foreign pressure, of their political regime; the absence of reprisals.

52 *La Dépêche*, 5 February 1939.
53 *Le Populaire*, 4 February 1939.
54 *Le Midi Socialiste*, 4 February 1939. Solano Palacio writes that in Barcelona there was indeed available a more than sufficient stock of up-to-date arms, but they were in the hands of the Guardias de Asalto and not in the hands of the Militia (Solano Palacio, 45).
55 *Le Midi Socialiste*, 11 February 1939. The longer range of the bombers had allowed them to reach the Republican lines on the Valencia front.
56 Cf. *supra*, 218.
57 *La Garonne*, 16 March 1939.
58 *L'Oeuvre*, 20 February 1939.
59 *La Dépêche*, 15 February 1939.
60 *La Dépêche*, 18 February 1939.
61 *Le Midi Socialiste*, 14 February 1939.
62 *Le Midi Socialiste*, 16 February 1939.
63 *Le Peuple*, 21 January 1939.
64 *L'Époque*, 22 January 1939.
65 *New York Times*, 23 January 1939.
66 *Les Échos*, 25 January 1939. The Neutrality Act of 1 August 1935, did not apply to civil wars, but to fill the gap a special Embargo Resolution had been rushed through Congress on 6 January 1937. Stimson and former American Ambassador to Germany William Dodd had already circulated the petition, supported by and other scientists, to end the U.S. Government's embargo on arms to Spain. The petition was thwarted largely by the action of the new American Ambassador to London, Joseph Kennedy, a fervent supporter of Chamberlain (Thomas, 824–825).
67 *L'Oeuvre*, 19 January 1939.
68 *La République*, 16 January 1939.
69 *Le Matin*, 19 January 1939.
70 *Le Figaro*, 23 January 1939.
71 *Le Journal*, 23 January 1939.
72 *La Garonne*, 24 January 1939.
73 *L'Ordre*, 26 February 1939.
74 *L'Homme Libre*, 7 January 1939.
75 *L'Homme Libre*, 19, 20, 23 January 1939.
76 *La Dépêche*, 26 January 1939.
77 *Le Populaire*, 20 February 1939.
78 *La Dépêche*, 22 February 1939. A year earlier, the Duke of Saragossa, former chamberlain of Alfonso XIII, had arrived in Port-Vendres as a simple refugee, half-starved (*La Dépêche*, 24 March 1938).
79 *La Garonne*, 22 February 1939.
80 *Le Midi Socialiste*, 24 February 1939.

26 Anglo-French Recognition of France

1. *Le Petit Parisien*, 22 January 1939.
2. *Le Petit Parisien*, 22 February 1939.
3. *L'Ere Nouvelle*, 19 January, 12 February 1939.
4. *Le Jour – L'Écho de Paris*, 19 January 1939.
5. *Le Jour – L'Écho de Paris*, 25 January 1939.
6. *Le Figaro*, 29 January 1939.
7. *L'Ordre*, 19 January 1939.
8. *La Dépêche*, 6 February 1939.
9. *L'Époque*, 6 February 1939.
10. *La Dépêche*, 8 February 1939.
11. Bérard observed with anxiety the predominance of the pro-Nazi Falange over the pro-French Carlists and Alfonsists.
12. *Le Midi Socialiste*, 11 February 1939.
13. *Le Populaire*, 16 February 1939.
14. *Le Populaire*, 16 February 1939.
15. Up to the appointment of Jordana, in March 1938, as Foreign Minister, Franco had entrusted foreign affairs to Sangróniz, his chief of staff, who was thus de facto Foreign Minister. He lost his post because the Axis considered him too sympathetic to the British.
16. *La Dépêche*, 5 February 1939.
17. Thomas, 884.
18. *La Dépêche*, 7 February 1939.
19. *La Dépêche*, 9 February 1939.
20. *L'Humanité*, 8 February 1939.
21. *Le Populaire*, 21 February 1939.
22. *Le Peuple*, 21 February 1939.
23. *L'Aube*, 15 February 1939.
24. Paul Bastid, *La Dépêche*, 1 March 1939.
25. *La Garonne*, 6 March 1939.
26. One aspect of the new Spain was clearly of special interest to *La Garonne*: the survival of regionalism. The Toulouse daily was as anxious to see Catalan survive in Catalonia as see Langue d'oc survive in the French Midi. Franco, it proclaimed in a headline, had not banned the use of the Catalan language. In smaller type, it admitted that the Catalan language was authorized only in private. It was forbidden in 'public meetings or demonstrations'—as if demonstrations were to be permitted in the new Spain—for fear that the language might serve to further the cause of separatism (*La Garonne*, 20 February 1939).
27. *La Dépêche*, 21 February 1939. Georges Suarez, *Notre Temps*, 12 February 1939.
28. *L'Oeuvre*, 25 February 1939.
29. *La Dépêche*, 21 February 1939.
30. *Le Midi Socialiste*, 17 February 1939.
31. *L'Époque*, 20 February 1939.
32. *L'Aube*, 26 February 1939.
33. *L'Ere Nouvelle*, 21 February 1939.

34 *La Dépêche*, 21 February 1939.
35 *La Dépêche*, 17 February 1939.
36 *Le Midi Socialiste*, 20 February 1939.
37 *L'Ordre*, 21 February 1939.
38 *L'Ordre*, 19 February 1939.
39 According to a news report, Roosevelt had declared America's frontier to be in France or on the Rhine. The phrase quickly became world famous. At a press conference on 3 February 1939, Roosevelt denounced the report as 'a deliberate lie', saying (on the record) that 'some boob got that off' and that he 'would like to meet the author of the report face to face.' Roosevelt denied categorically that there had been any reference to the 'Rhine frontier' during the secret meeting of the Senate Military Affairs Committee. 'U.S. policy,' he declared, 'shuns entangling alliances.'
40 *La Dépêche*, 22 February 1939.
41 *La Garonne*, 27 February 1939.
42 *Gringoire*, 25 February 1939.
43 *L'Oeuvre*, 17 February 1939.
44 *Le Journal*, 17 February 1939.
45 *L'Époque*, 17 February 1939.
46 *Excelsior*, 22 February 1939.
47 *Le Petit Journal*, 16 February 1939.
48 Franco decided at the last minute to exclude the Italians from the parade, to avoid adverse publicity and the affront to Spanish pride. The Italians were subsequently allotted a place in the victory parade in Gerona, and of course, after the war, in Madrid.
49 *Le Populaire*, 25 February 1939.
50 *Le Midi Socialiste*, 28 February 1939. In a letter addressed to the American journalist Richard Sanders Allen, Pierre Cot stated: 'In the course of 1936–1937, we were able to deliver some 150 planes. We were able later to send some 30–50 more. The Soviet Union, in supplying planes through the Black Sea or the Atlantic route, ran into great difficulty, but the Russians succeeded, and we were then able, by transporting Soviet matériel, especially planes, through the French Southwest, to provide Soviet aid in place of our own and thus maintain the flow to the Spanish Republic.' Pierre Cot followed this with an article published in *Le Monde* on 21 November 1975 entitled 'Ce que fut la "non-intervention relâchée".' It was only after his death in 1977 that it was revealed he had been a secret member of the PCF.
51 *Le Populaire*, 26 February 1939.
52 *L'Ere Nouvelle*, 26 February 1939.
53 *Le Jour – L'Écho de Paris*, 27 February 1939.
54 *L'Époque*, 1 March 1939.
55 *Le Petit Parisien*, 27 February 1939. The next week Azaña left the Spanish Embassy in Paris, where he had been living, and travelled by train to the village of Collonges, near Gex on the Swiss border, there to continue in exile. The Nationalist representative Quiñones de León at once moved into the Paris Embassy.

56 *Le Midi Socialiste*, 4 March 1939.
57 The hero of Verdun referred to the Caudillo as 'the noblest sword in Europe.' Pétain's noble sword and noble spirit would be subjects for juridical debate in times ahead. Some indications were present earlier in Madrid. The German historian Klaus-Jörg Ruhl sent me the following information: 'I recently found out that Pétain in Madrid, just after the declaration of war [3 September 1939], at a time when French ambassadors in neutral countries were under orders to give only the slightest nod of recognition to their German counterparts at official receptions, to the astonishment of everybody present, went straight across a floor to shake von Stöhrer warmly by the hand' (Klaus-Jörg Ruhl, private correspondence). The present author concedes that Ruhl did not name his source, and Ruhl is now deceased.
58 *Le Midi Socialiste*, 9 March 1939.
59 *L'Ordre*, 7 March 1939.

27 The End of Hostilities

1 Now, with the Pyrenees frontier truly closed, huge quantities of Soviet war supplies were waiting in Marseilles for shipment to the Republic's remaining ports. By mid-March, the French Government had closed French ports to all supplies bound for the Republic. Food supplies from the United States were being shunted about the Mediterranean (Thomas, 1963 edition, 588 n.).
2 Negrín and his supporters assembled at Dakar before flying to France. At the very same moment, at a national meeting of the SFIO in Paris, a speaker called for armed intervention in favour of the Negrín government. 'We would smile,' wrote *Le Petit Parisien,* a little piously, of the coincidence, 'if the times were not so cruel' (*Le Petit Parisien*, 8 March 1939).
3 *Le Journal*, 8 March 1939.
4 *L'Aube*, 7 March 1939.
5 *Le Peuple*, 7 March 1939.
6 *L'Époque*, 10 March 1939.
7 *Les Échos*, 9 March 1939.
8 *La Dépêche*, 13 March 1939.
9 *Le Midi Socialiste*, 9 March 1939.
10 Cf. *supra*, 189.
11 *Le Journal*, 10 March 1939.
12 *La Garonne*, 6 March 1939.
13 *Les Échos*, 23 March 1939.
14 *L'Ordre*, 8 March 1939.
15 *Les Échos*, 23 March 1939.
16 The Franco government had appointed a commission, under the directon of Colonel Alfonso Barra Camer, to recover war matériel and cattle transferred to French territory. Chaveriat, Minister Plenipotentiary, and director of Political and Commercial Affairs, made an exception only for war matériel 'whose return [could] not be carried out until the end of hostilities' (Foreign Minister, to Minister of the Interior: n.° 570, dated 25 March 1939).

17 *Le Midi Socialiste*, 27 March 1939. Pierre Daguerre, Sub-Prefect of Basses-Pyrénées, later commented on the situation confronting Marshal Pétain on his arrival as Ambassador. He was met at Hendaye by the Carlist General Baïgorry. The Marshal soon found the situation not only delicate but confusing. Apart from what he could expect after briefing by Senator Bérard, Pétain was quickly made aware of the pro-German pressure being exerted on Franco by the Falange. When, on 10 August 1939, Jordana was replaced as Foreign Minister by the anglophile but francophone Colonel Beigbeder, the Falange strove to have the latter replaced by the anglophobe and even more francophobe Serrano Suñer, who Pétain believed would provoke border incidents necessitating the deployment of several French divisions along the Pyrenees. (By the time this replacement was put into effect, on 16 October 1940, such provocations were unnecessary.) Senior Spanish officers even reported that the Falange was preparing to remove Franco, whom it considered too pro-French, in favour of Serrano. According to Daguerre, Pétain told him that his task as Ambassador was made easier as a result of Daguerre's work of reconciliation during the Civil War. The Deputy-Prefect claimed to be the only French official who had maintained contact with the rebels 'Aspects nouveaux de l'ambassade du maréchal Pétain en Espagne', *Le Monde et la Vie*, February 1966).

On at least one occasion, Marshal Pétain took an active part in the extradition of Spanish Republicans in France who were accused of war crimes in Spain. Even after the declaration of war against Germany, Ambassador Pétain requested the French Foreign Minister to launch a search for Ramón González, a former police agent employed in October 1936 at the Ministry of War in Madrid. González was allegedly involved in the supposed death of Don Jaime de Borbón, who had been taken prisoner in Madrid on 10 October 1936 and subsequently shot (A. Chiappe, Prefect of Basses-Pyrénées, to Sub-Prefect, Oloron: Very Urgent, dated 14 November 1939). This Don Jaime who was the subject of the search was apparently none other than Don Jaime de Borbón y Battenberg, Duke of Segovia, who was still alive and resident in Paris. (He died in Switzerland in 1975.) The second son of Alfonso XIII, Don Jaime had left Spain for Italy in 1931, at the age of 22, at the time of the proclamation of the Second Republic. As a result of the haemophilia of his elder brother the Prince of Asturias, Don Jaime, albeit a deaf mute, was made first in line to the throne, until in 1934 his father removed him too from the succession in favour of his third son, Don Juan. Soon after the death of the king, in 1941, Don Jaime formally renounced his rights in favour of his younger brother.

As for Ange Chiappe, who was the author of the misreport on Don Jaime, he was the brother of Jean Chiappe, Prefect of Paris. In late 1944 he would be arrested on charges of having consorted with the enemy, and executed in Nimes on 28 January 1945.

18 Marty had already admitted, within the confines of the PCF, to more than that. The Party had recalled him from Spain to explain his actions, and in the report he gave them, Dan Richardson tells us, he freely admitted to the execution of some 500 from the ranks of the International Brigades. "These bandits," he said,

"have committed all sorts of crimes: rape, robberies, murders, kidnappings . . . ." Richardson, 175, citing the Marty Archives (Harvard University). Hemingway, 417–426, who presents Marty, addressing him by name, as "crazy as a bedbug, [one who] kills more than the bubonic plague."

19 Thomas, 491; Skoutelsky, 71, 73, 252–253. Jordi Arquer, a leader of the anti-Stalinist POUM, gives a very different account, based on what he heard from Hans Storck, who was then the 12th Battalion's political commissar. Storck was with Delassale in Andújar when one morning (Storck gave the date as 5 or 6 January 1937) Delassalle was walking out of the school for girls. As he came down the two steps he received a bullet in the back of the neck. Storck could not identify the murderer, but stated that he visited his bedroom on the day of the murder and "saw money in every corner." Arquer, Annexe 3; Antony Beevor, *The Times* (London), 24 May 2006.

20 Marty was only narrowly prevented from perpetrating further crmes against members of his old staff at Albacete, for fear that they would disclose the enormities he had already committed (Thomas, 881).

21 A leading member of the former Croix de Feu, Vallat had nevertheless refused to join its successor, the PSF. He was to become Commissioner for Jewish Affairs in the Vichy government. His activities during the Second World War would earn him, in 1947, a sentence of ten years' imprisonment, but he was released in 1950.

22 *La Dépêche*, 11 March 1939.

23 Henri Dupré, who for a short time was quartermaster of the I Brigade, boasted in 1942 of having been chief of the group of spies and saboteurs that the Cagoule had infiltrated into the ranks of the foreign volunteers. He further claimed responsibility for certain provocations, arrests and executions. Dupré continued along these lines during the German Occupation, working for the Abwehr. After the Liberation he was sentenced to death by a court in Paris and executed in 1951.

24 The Pole Karol Swierczewski, known as Walter, had commanded the XIV Brigade up to 15 February 1937. The command had passed to Putz, then in spring 1937 to Jules Dumont. Marty did not mention, of course, that Putz, who had a reputation as a courageous and competent combat commander, had been replaced on the basis that he was not a communist (Richardson, 99). Dumont, albeit a communist, was in turn replaced, in December 1937, by another, Marcel Sangnier. The political commissar of this brigade was the Communist André Heussler, then Marcel Renaud, then François Vittori, and finally, from June 1938, Colonel Henri Tanguy.

25 *La Dépêche*, 17 March 1939.

26 *La Dépêche*, 18 March 1939.

27 Marty had already admitted these crimes in a report to the Central Committee of the Communist Party on 15 November 1937, though presumably the report was not generally known to the Assembly. Marty wrote: 'The executions which I ordered did not exceed five hundred.' These did not include summary executions for drunkenness or disorderly conduct, for insubordination toward Marty, or for suspected espionage, which Marty admitted separately.

28 Marty was not the only political commissar to be denounced as a murderer. Otto

Flatter, born Ferenc Münnich, who served from June to August 1938 as commander of the XI International Brigade ('Thaelmann') of the 35th Division, had a reputation for extreme cruelty. He was later appointed president of the military tribunal of the 21st Corps, with its seat in Cambrils, a village 18 kilometres west of Tarragona, in a castle that served as a prison. A certain Alessandro Spreafico, who with a friend named Carreri was sentenced to death for anti-communism, managed to escape. According to Spreafico, Flatter was sentencing people to death at the rate of five to eight every two days. These individuals were conducted to the beach, and there they were shot. Spreafico had personally taken part in the execution of 60 to 70 prisoners, whose crimes were varied. Five men were executed for having stolen a rabbit, and another five, who held political ideas at variance with those of the Communist Party, were dropped into a well and left to die (Inspector of Special Police R. Bats, of the special sub-section at Mauléon, to the Special Commissioner, Pau: n.° 676, dated 1 June 1939. Cf. Rubio, vol. 1, 73; vol. 3, 839–840.

29 *La Dépêche*, 29 March 1939. The text conforms to the original.
30 *La Dépêche*, 30 March 1939.
31 Between these two German annexations (of 15 and 22 March 1939), the Senate on 19 March gave Daladier, by a vote of 286 to 17, dictatorial powers.
32 *L'Aube*, 29 March 1939.

Conclusion

1 As we have seen, the responsibility of a neutral power in regard to the movement of war matériel through its territory is determined by the identity of the party moving the material. Article 7 of Convention (V) respecting the Rights and Duties of Neutral Powers and Personas in Case of War on Land declares: 'A neutral Power is not called upon to prevent the export or transport, on behalf of one or other of the belligerents, of arms, munitions of war, or, in general, of anything which can be of use to an army or fleet.' A neutral power is bound only—under Article 5—to prevent violation of Articles 2 and 4 from occurring on its territory. And Article 2, concerning the movement of troops or convoys of either munitions of war or supplies across the territory of a neutral power, proscribes such practice only to belligerents.
2 Shortly after the end of the Second World War, Blum wrote: 'We offered arms without admitting it, and above all—because our means at that time were very limited—we got them through the frontier. We practised permissive non-intervention, meaning we organized a virtually official contraband.' In exactly the same period, André Marty was denying that the French Government had ever sent anything at all to the Spanish Republic. In 1945 he wrote: The French Government did not supply any arms to Republican Spain between 1936 and 1939.' (Both sources lost.)
3 *L'Europe Nouvelle*, 25 July 1936.
4 *Journal Officiel de la République Française*, 31 July 1936.
5 The situation would have been worse had it been left entirely to such unimaginative generals as Pétain, Weygand and Gamelin, who as successive Army Chiefs

of Staff were obsessed with static and defensive strategy. The General Staff's request in 1936 for a mere 9 billion francs for defence was considered particularly inadequate by War Minister Daladier, and with Blum's backing the appropriation was increased to 14 billion.
6 According to Admiral Carrero Blanco, Nationalist Spain had imported 8,543,768 tons of war matériel and had transported 316,151 men (Carrero Blanco, 108).
7 *La Dépêche*, 5 August 1936; *Le Midi Socialiste*, 20 October 1936. As Under-Secretary of State for the Protection of Children, Suzanne Lacore was the first Frenchwoman to obtain a seat in a Cabinet.
8 Frossard, among others, had remarked very much earlier, in *Marianne* of 24 October 1934, that democracy had lost its mystique. To recreate it, he sought to transform the Front Commun, brand new but too restricted, into a broader 'Front Républicain.'
9 'This country [the United States], with its institutions, belongs to the people who inhabit it. Whenever they shall grow weary of the existing government, they can exercise their constitutional right of amending it, or their revolutionary right to dismember or overthrow it' (First inaugural address, Chicago, 4 March 1861).
10 *L'Express du Midi*, 26 September 1936.
11 *L'Emancipation Nationale*, 19 September 1936.
12 *L'Express du Midi*, 13 August 1936. Cf. Verdier (Muñoz, 14).
13 *Le Journal de Toulouse*, 2 August 1936; *L'Express du Midi*, 2 December 1936.
14 *L'Express du Midi*, 8 September 1936.
15 *L'Express du Midi*, 11 August 1936.
16 *L'Express du Midi*, 12 September 1936.
17 Bodin and Touchard, 230–231.
18 The most popular invectives used in France to describe the opposite camp were 'Front Antipopulaire' and 'Front Crapulaire.' The arguments of the Right showed a remarkable inconsistency in regard to the Axis, being as they were motivated largely by hatred of the French left.
19 According to Manevy, only *Le Petit Parisien* and *Paris-Soir* attained this balance (Manevy, 323–324). It must be remembered, however, that the conflict on *Le Petit Parisien* between editor André Salmon and correspondent Andrée Viollis resulted in her resignation. Similarly, the impartiality of *Paris-Soir* was in no way served by the passionate dispatches of its correspondent Bertrand de Jouvenel (see Pike, *Crise*, 372; Manevy, 335).
20 Cf. *supra*, 144–145, 284.
21 Cf. *supra*, 64.
22 Rare indeed were the disclosures in the right-wing press that anything was wrong with the Right. But once at least *L'Express du Midi* remarked that the 'splendid indifference' of Conservative elements in France constituted a grave national danger (*L'Express du Midi*, 23 August 1936).
23 *Combat*, November 1938.
24 Micaud, 230.
25 Micaud, 230.

26 *L'Europe Nouvelle*, 18 July 1936.
27 William Butler Yeats, *The Second Coming*, 1920–1921.
28 'Européen, prends garde' (*La Dépêche*, 19 November 1936; 20 November 1936). The French edition, under the title *Avertissement à l'Europe,* preceded by a year the German edition published in Stockholm, entitled *Achtung Europa! Aufsätze zur Zeit.*
29 *La Nouvelle Revue Française*, 1 July 1937.
30 *La Dépêche*, 2 March 1937. In the same way, during Franco's counter-offensive on the Ebro in late 1938 with Barcelona as the target, Vandervelde wrote he was convinced that the Nationalist forces would never reach Tarragona. He died shortly afterwards, at the moment the Italians entered the Catalan port.
31 *Le Populaire*, 22 November 1936.
32 *La Dépêche*, 31 October 1936.
33 Although Churchill was already calling for a Grand Alliance with the Soviet Union, the leaders of the Spanish Republic had not forgotten his refusal to meet with the Republican Ambassador up to April 1938.
34 *Le Midi Socialiste*, 30 November 1936.

Epilogue

1 The Germans had produced the weekly *Pariser Tagezeitung* (1937), with Heinrich Mann and Max Braun as editors. The Italians had published three weeklies: *La Nuova Italia* (1925), *Nuovo Avanti* (1934), and *La Giovine Italia* (1937), together with the daily *La Voce degli Italiani* (1937).
2 'La Résistance antifasciste allemande,' Goethe Institut, Paris, 11 December 1984.
3 The total number of French citizens imprisoned for collaboration is estimated at 40,000. Only 13,000 were still in prison in December 1948, only 8,000 in 1949, and fewer than 4,000 at the beginning of 1951 (Novick, 297).
4 A final mention should be made of Otto Abetz, a close friend to many of the French journalists on the Right both during his long residence in Paris before the war and as German Ambassador during the Occupation. Abetz held the rank of SS-Brigadeführer. He left Paris in September 1944 as the German armies withdrew. In 1945 he was captured by Allied authorities in Baden-Württemberg, and went on trial in Paris in July 1949. Sentenced to 20 years of hard labour for war crimes, he was imprisoned in Loos but released on 17 April 1954. He died with his wife in a car accident near Langenfeld, Germany, on 5 May 1958.

Bibliography

The Bibliography is structured as follows:
I. PRIMARY SOURCES
   A. Documents
      1. Official
         a) Non-published
         b) Published
      2. Non-official
   B. The Media
      1. Journals and Revues
      2. News Agencies

II. SECONDARY SOURCES
   A. Works and articles pertaining to International Law
   B. Works and articles pertaining to the Spanish Civil War and published in that period.
   C. General Bibliography
   D. Bibliography of the Press

I. PRIMARY SOURCES
A. Documents
1. Official
a) Non-published

I   Archives départementales de l'Ariège (Foix)

5M	Esprit public
5M72	Rapports sur la situation générale du département de l'Ariège: 3 (1934–1936)
5M73	Déclarations du gouvernement: affiches imprimées (1910–1938)
5M90	Réfugiés français d'Espagne (1936–1940)
5M103	Surveillance du territoire et de la frontière franco-espagnole; régime frontalier; circulation et surveillance des étrangers à la frontière (1887–1940)
5M104	Surveillance de la frontière franco-andorrane et franco-espagnole: affaires générales et diverses (1939–1940)
5M138	Mouvements révolutionnaires espagnols: affaires générales et diverses
5M139	Informations inexactes; manifestations; correspondance avec la SNCF; vice-consul d'Espagne; hébergement ; vendangeurs; départ d'Espagnols résidant en France, etc. (1936–1938)
5M140	Mesures de sécurité à la frontière franco-espagnole ; plan de barrage (1937–1939)

5M141 Frontière franco-espagnole. Instructions, contrôle international, passeports volontaires, violation de la frontière, Brigades internationales, affaires diverses, etc. (1937–1939)

5M142 *Ibid.* Contrôle international, rapports au Ministère, dispositifs de surveillance, cantonnements des Gardes mobiles, subventions aux communes (1937–1940)

5M143 *Ibid.* Rapports des officiers de non-intervention (1937–1939)

5M144–146 Miliciens espagnols. Instructions, identification, recherche des évadés des camps, liste des miliciens ayant quitté le camp du Vernet d'Ariège (1939)

5M149 Refugiés politiques espagnols. Avis de passage à la frontière, rapports spéciaux de police, notices individuelles, correspondance (1937)

II Archives départementales de l'Aude (Carcassonne)

6M27 Camp de Bram. Divers sous-dossiers du commissariat spécial de police de Carcassonne comprenant la documentation générale du cabinet du préfet, les listes de réfugiés espagnols hébergés au camp, les volontaires français et les miliciens étrangers rapatriés, Divers rapports relatant le passage de miliciens et autres formations, le mouvement insurrectionnel anarchiste contre la Catalogne et autres complots subversifs sur divers points du département; aux rapatriements et aux réquisitions concernant des réfugiés espagnols du camp mutés dans d'autres départements (1927–1941) [Ces dossiers contiennent aussi des rapports des agents nationalistes espagnols au sujet du moral et des opérations militaires des Républicains, en recommandant le bombardement de certaines cibles en Espagne républicaine]

6M29–31 Dossiers relatifs au contrôle postal, à la censure de la correspondance, aux visites des camps d'internement de détenus politiques, au contrôle des messages et communications officielles par les commissions italo-allemandes (1938–1941)

6M147 Camps d'hébergement. Emploi de la main-d'œuvre des camps. Formation des groupes de Travailleurs étrangers. 318' groupe de Travailleurs étrangers. Incorporation de catégories de travailleurs: inaptes, reformes, déserteurs, etc. (1938–1943)

6M155 Recrutement de la main-d'œuvre étrangère et des oisifs pour la zone nord, l'Organisation Todt et l' Allemagne (1942–1944)

6M165 Rapports et messages télégraphiques, renseignements statistiques relatifs au dénombrement et à la situation des réfugiés espagnols dans les camps d'hébergement adressés respectivement par le préfet aux ministères de l'Intérieur et de la Santé publique (extrait du bordereau 902). (1938–1940).

III Archives départementales de la Haute-Garonne (Toulouse)

M1146 Rapports des agents du comité de non-intervention (1937)

M1262 Passages de réfugiés espagnols (1935–1938)

1912/55 Surveillance de l'aérodrome de Francazal et des terrains privés d'aviation du département. Instructions ministérielles et préfectorales. Transit d'avions destinés aux autorités gouvernementales espagnoles. Rapports du préfet et des services de police. Coupures de presse (1936)

1912/60 Police de l'air: aérodromes de Toulouse-Francazal et de Toulouse-Montaudran; mesures de surveillance rendues nécessaires par les événements d'Espagne ; rapports de police et de gendarmerie concernant le survol du territoire par des avions non identifiés; relations d'accidents; rapports relatifs à l'arrivée d'or de la Banque d'Espagne (1937–1939)

1912/61 Atterrissage en Espagne d'avions partis de Toulouse pour une destination métropolitaine. Enquête de police. Poursuites judiciaires. Disparition d'un avion. Recherches (1937)

1960/9 Surveillance de I' aérodrome de Montaudran. Trafic d'armes et de munitions. Cargaisons de caisses suspectes. Atterrissage d'avions gouvernementaux espagnols (1937)

1960/63 Situation intérieure de l'Espagne. Notes de renseignements des services de police et du service départemental des renseignements généraux (1940–1943)

1960/64 Surveillance par la police des personnalités espagnoles républicaines refugiées en France et d'organisations de secours (1939–1943)

1960/65 Instructions ministérielles relatives à la non-intervention de la France dans les affaires d'Espagne.
Mesures d'exécution.
Surveillance de la frontière. Cartes relatives à l'implantation des forces de surveillance (1937–1938)

IV Archives departernentales des Pyrénées-Atlantiques (Pau)

3Z237 Rapports de la commission internationale de non-intervention en Espagne (1937)

3Z238 Dépenses relatives aux réfugiés espagnols ; nourriture, soins, logement (1939)

3Z239 Demandes d'Espagnols désirant héberger des compatriotes réfugiés (1939)

3Z240 Réfugiés espagnols et étrangers des Brigades internationales; divers (1938–1939)

3Z241 Réfugiés espagnols et miliciens des Brigades internationales; rapatriements et affaires diverses (1939)

3Z242 Réfugiés espagnols au camp de Gurs et dans l'arrondissement d'Oloron (1939)

3Z243 Réfugiés espagnols; affaires diverses (1939–1940)

3Z244 Réfugiés espagnols; listes, statistiques, laissez-passer (1939–1940); rapatriements (1941–1942)

V Archives départementales des Pyrénées-Orientales (Perpignan)

Bordereau daté du 13 septembre 1951
- 56   Divers (Espagne)
- 83   Sureté nationale: notes des fonctionnaires (1939–1940)
- 87   Interventions militaires diverses (1942–1943)
- 91   Ligues dissoutes et activités des Ligues (1935–1936)
- 106 Internes (secours)
- 112 Personnel; dossiers d'internes (camps)
- 135 Avant 1939 (ministère)
- 160 Ligue Action française (1938)
- 161 Anarchistes étrangers (1936)
- 164 Anarchistes (1938–1939)
- 165 Surveillance frontière ; anarchistes espagnols; affaires d'Espagne
- 167 Partis politiques (1935–1939)
- 171 Anarchistes (1936–1937)
- 184 Brigades internationales
- 185 Brigades internationales dossiers avant 1939

Bordereau daté du 27 mai 1953
N° 73, 74, 75, 78, 80, 83, 92, 93

a) Published

Les Archives secrètes de la Wilhelmstrasse. Tome III: *L'Allemagne et la guerre civile espagnole.* Documents translated from the German by Michel Tournier. Paris: Plon, 1952.

Documents diplomatiques: Conférence internationale de la Paix, 1899. 8 vols. Paris: Imprimerie Nationale, 1900.

Documents on British Foreign Policy, 1919–1939. 5 vols. Edited by Sir Llewellyn Woodward and Rohan Butler. Third Series, vols. I–IV. London: Her Majesty's Stationery Office, 1968–1969.

Documents on German Foreign Policy, 1918–1945: From the Archives of the German Foreign Ministry. Series D, vol. III: *Germany and the Spanish Civil War.* Washington: Department of State, 1950; London: His Majesty's Stationery Office, 1951.

Documents secrets du ministère des Affaires étrangères d'Allemagne. La politique allemande (1936–1943): Espagne. Translated from the Russian by Madeleine and Michel Eristov. Paris: Paul Dupont, 1946.

Les Événements survenus en France de 1933 à 1945: Témoignages et documents recueillis par la Commission d'enquête parlementaire. Tomes I (events from 7 March 1936), II (documents on the period 1936–1945), III–IX (depositions). Paris: Presses Universitaires de France, n.d.

Ministère des Affaires étrangères. *Documents diplomatiques français, 1932–1939.* Second series (1936–1939). Tomes III (19 July–19 November 1936), IV (20 November 1936–19 February 1937), V (20 February–31 May 1937), VI (1 June–29 September 1937), VII (29 September 1937–16 January 1938), VIII (17 January–20 March 1938), IX (21 March–9 June 1938), X (10 June–2 September 1938), XI (3 September–2 October 1938), XII (3 October–30 November 1938), XIII (1

December 1938–31 January 1939), XIV (1 February–15 March 1939), XV (16 March–30 April 1939). Paris: ImprimerieNationale,1966/1967/1948/1970/1972/ 1973/1974/1976/1977/1978/1979/1980/1981

Ministère des Affaires étrangères. *Le Livre jaune française: Documents diplomatiques, 1938–1939.* Paris: Imprimerie Nationale, 1939.

2. Non-official

Berneri Collection, library of the Federazione Anarchica Italiana, Genoa. An unclassified collection of letters, memoranda, postcards, leaflets, pamphlets, tracts, and journals.

B. The Media
1. Journals and Revues

The date in parentheses after the name of the journal is its year of birth. Unless it is followed by another date, before 1939, it indicates that the journal continued to appear until the end of the Civil War.

All journals were published in Paris until otherwise indicated.

L' *Action Française* (1908), daily.
L' *Ami du Peuple* (1928–1937), daily.
L' *Aube* (1932), daily.
Aux Ecoutes (1918), weekly.
L' *Avant-Garde* (1920), weekly.
Bulletin de la Société d'Études et d'Informations Économiques (1920), daily.
Cahiers du Bolchevisme (1924), fortnightly.
Candide (1924), weekly.
Le Capital (1913), daily.
Ce Soir (1937), daily.
Combat (1936), monthly.
Commune (1933), monthly.
La Commune (1935–1938), weekly.
La Concorde (1930), daily/biweekly.
Le Courrier de Bayonne (1852), daily.
Le Courrier du Centre (Limoges, 1905), daily.
Le Courrier Royal (1934), monthly/weekly.
La Croix (1883), daily.
La Dépêche (Toulouse, 1870), daily.
La Dépêche du Centre (Tours, 1890), daily.
Les Dernières Nouvelles de Strassbourg (1877), daily.
L'Echo de Paris (1884), daily.
L' *Echo d'Indre-et-Loire* (Tours, 1928), weekly.
L'Echo du Nord (Lille, 1819), daily.
Les Echos (1908), daily/weekly.
L'Eclair (Montpellier, 1881), daily.

L'Eclaireur de l'Est (Reims, 1888), daily.
L'Eclaireur de Nice et du Sud-Est (Nice, 1883), daily.
L'Emancipation Nationale (1936), weekly.
L'Epoque (1937), daily.
L' Ere Nouvelle (1919), daily.
L'Espagne Antifasciste (1936), fortnightly.
L'Espagne Nouvelle (1937), irregular.
L'Espagne Socialiste (1937), fortnightly.
Esprit (1932), monthly.
L'Est Républicain (Nancy, 1889), daily.
Etudes Religieuses (1856), fortnightly.
Europe (1923), monthly.
L'Europe Nouvelle (1918), weekly.
Excelsior (1910), daily.
L'Express du Midi (Toulouse, 1891), daily.
Le Figaro (1854), daily.
Le Flambeau (1929–1937), weekly.
La Fléche de Paris (1934), fortnightly/weekly.
La France Catholique (1906), weekly.
La France de Bordeaux et du Sud-Ouest (1887), daily.
Frontières (1933), monthly.
La Garonne (Toulouse, 1938), daily.
La Gazette de Bayonne (1930–1936), daily.
La Gazette de Biarritz et de Bayonnne (Biarritz, 1893–1931, 1937), daily.
La Griffe (1918), weekly.
Gringoire (1928), weekly.
L'Homme Libre (1913), daily.
L'Homme Nouveau (1934–1937), monthly.
L'Homme Reel (1934–1938), monthly.
L'Humanité (1904), daily.
L'Illustration (1843), weekly.
L'Indépendant (1936), weekly.
L'Indépendant (Perpignan, 1846), daily.
L'Indépendant des Pyrenees (Pau, 1934), daily.
L'Information Financiere, Economique et Politique (1899), daily.
L'Intransigeant (1880), daily.
Je Suis Partout (1930), weekly.
La Jeune République (1920), weekly.
Le Jour (1933), daily.
Le Journal (1892), daily.
Le Journal de Rouen (1762), daily.
Le Journal de Saint-Gaudens (1839), weekly.
Journal des Débats (1789), daily.
Journal des Finances (1867), weekly.
Le Journal de Toulouse (1920), weekly.

Journal Officiel de la République Française (1869), daily.
La Journée Industrielle (1918), daily.
Juin 36 (1938), fortnightly.
La Justice (1939), daily.
Le Libertaire (1895), weekly.
La Liberté (1865), daily.
La Liberté du Sud-Ouest (Bordeaux, 1909), daily.
La Libre Parole (1930), weekly.
La Lumière (1927), weekly.
La Lutte Ouvriere (1936), weekly.
Lyon Républicain (1878), daily.
Marianne (1932), weekly.
La Marseillaise (1936), weekly.
Marseille-Matin (1931), *Marseille-Soir* (1932), daily.
Match (1927), weekly.
Le Matín (1884), daily.
Le Mercure de France (1889), fortnightly.
Messidor (1938), weekly.
Le Midi Socialiste (Toulouse, 1908), daily.
Monde Libre (1938), trimestral.
La Nation (1926), weekly.
Notre Temps (1927), weekly.
Nouvel Age (1931), monthly.
La Nouvelle Revue (1879), fortnightly.
La Nouvelle Revue Française (1909), monthly.
Le Nouvelliste (Lyon, 1879), daily.
Occident (1937), fortnightly.
L'Oeuvre (1904), daily.
L'Oeuvre Latine (1928), monthly.
L'Ordre (1929), daily.
L'Ordre Nouveau (1933–1938), monthly.
L' Ouest -Eclair (Rennes, 1899), daily.
Paris-Midi (1911), daily.
Paris-Soir (1923), daily.
La Patrie Humaine (1933), weekly.
Le Patriote des Pyrenees (Pall, 1896), daily.
Le Petit Bleu de Paris (1898), daily.
Le Petit Dauphinois (Grenoble, 1878), daily.
La Petite Gironde (Bordeaux, 1872), daily.
Le Petit Journal (1863), daily.
Le Petit Marseillais (1868), daily.
Le Petit Méridional (Montpellier, 1876), daily.
Le Petit Parisien (1876), daily.
Le Petit Provençal (Marseille, 1880), daily.
Le Peuple (1921), daily.

Le Phare de la Loire, de Bretagne et de Vendée (Nantes, 1815), daily.
Le Populaire (1918), daily.
La Presse du Sud-Ouest (Biarritz, 1930), daily.
La Production Française (1927), weekly.
Le Progrès de Lyon (1859), daily.
Le Quotidien (1923), daily.
Regards (1932), weekly.
Le Républicain des Hautes-Pyrérnées (Tarbes, 1917), weekly.
La République (1929), daily.
Le Réveil du Nord (Lille, 1889), daily.
Révolution (1933), fortnightly.
La Révolution Espagnole (1936), weekly.
La Révolution Prolétarienne (1925), fortnightly.
Revue de France (1921), fortnightly.
Revue de Paris (1864), fortnightly.
Revue des Deux Mondes (1829), fortnightly.
La Revue Hebdomadaire (1892). fortnightly/monthly.
Revue Politique et Parlementaire (1894), monthly.
La Revue Universelle (1920), bimonthly.
Le Roussillon (Perpignan, 1870), weekly.
Sept (1934), weekly.
Service d'Inforamtion du Comité Franco-Espagnol (1937–1938), fortnightly.
La Solidarité Française de Paris (1937–1938), monthly.
La Solidarité Nationale (1936–1937), weekly.
Le Temps (1861), daily.
Temps Présent (1937), weekly.
Terre Libre (1934), weekly (Paris); monthly (Nimes).
Terre Nouvelle (1927), monthly.
La Tribune des Fonctionnaires (1913), monthly.
La Tribune des Nations (1934), weekly.
La Tribune Républicaine (Saint-Etienne, 1899), daily.
Unité (1936–1938), monthly.
La Vague (1936–1937), fortnightly.
Vendémiaire (1934), weekly.
Vendredi (1935), weekly.
La Vérité (1926–1936), fortnightly.
La Victoire (1916), daily/weekly.
La Vie Catholique (1924), weekly.
La Vie Intellectuelle (1928), fortnightly.
La Vie Ouvrière (1909), weekly.
La Volonté (1925–1936), daily.
Le Voltigeur (1938), fortnightly.
Vu et Lu (1937), weekly.

2. News Agencies

Agence Économique et Financière (Paris, 1912).
Agence Espagne (Paris, 1936).
Agence Fournier (Paris, 1879).
Agence Havas (Paris, 1879).
Agence Radio (Paris, 1904).
Agence Reischach (Berlin, 1933, affiliated to the Deutches Nachrichten Büro).
Agence Stefani (Rome, 1924).
Agence Tass (Moscow, 1925).
Associated Press (New York, 1848).
Inter-France (Paris, 1937).
International News Service (New York, 1909).
Reuter's Agency (London, 1851).
Spanish News Agency (London, 1936).
United Press (New York, 1907).

II. SECONDARY SOURCES

A. Works and articles pertaining to International Law

Bestieu, André. *Droit d'asile dans les ambassades et légations en tours de la guerre d'Espagne, 1936–1939*. Montpellier: Causse, Graille & Castelnau, 1942.

Jessup, Philip C. 'The Spanish Revolution and International Law,' *Foreign Affairs* (New York), 1937, pp. 270 et seq.

Padelford, Norman J., 'The Non-Intervention Agreement and the Spanish Civil War,' *American Journal of International Law*, 1937, pp. 578 et seq.

Padelford, Norman J., 'International Law and the Spanish Civil War,' *American Journal of International Law* (Washington, D.C.), 1937, pp. 2226 et seq.

Padelford, Norman J. *International Law and Diplomacy in the Spanish Civil Strife*. New York: Macmillan, 1939.

Pagnoux, Henri. *Guerre civile et droit international: le conflit espagnol, 1936–1939*. Paris: A. Pedone 1939.*

Raiestad, Arnold. 'Guerre civile et droit international,' *Revue de droit international et de législation comparée* (Paris), 1938, pp. 809 et seq.

Rousseau, Charles. 'La non-intervention en Espagne,' *Revue de droit international et de législation comparée* (Paris), 1939, pp. 217, 473, 700 et seq.

Rousseau, Charles. *Jurisprudence française en matière de droit international public (1937)*. Paris: A. Pedone, 1939.

Smith, H. A. 'Some problems of the Spanish Civil War,' *British Year Book of International Law* (London), 1937, pp. 17 et seq.

Wehberg, Hans. *La Guerre civile et le droit international*. Rec. A.D.I., vol. LXVIII. Paris: no pub., 1938.

* All copies of this book were destroyed in 1940 by the printer (information given to the present author by the publisher).

B. **Works and articles pertaining to Spain and the Civil War and published in that decade** (they are selected for the impact they made on the press and the public)

Alcoléa, Raymond, *Le Christ chez Franco*. Paris: Denoël, 1938.
Álvarez del Vayo, Julio, *Freedom's Battle*, transl. Eileen E. Brooke London: William Heinemann, 1940.
Banse, Ewald, *Raum und Volk im Weltkrieg*. Oldenburg: Gerhard Stalling Verlag, 1931.
Bardoux, Jacques, *Le Chaos espagnol: Éviterons nous la contagion?* Paris: Ernest Flammarion, 1937.
Berjón, Don Antonio, *La Prière des exilés espagnols à la vierge du Pilier*. Liège: H. Dessain, 1938.
Bernanos, Georges, *Les Grands cimetières sous la lune*. Paris: Plon, 1938.
Berneri, Camillo, *Guerre des classes en Espagne*. Nimes: Les Cahiers de *Terre Libre*, 1937.
Bloch, Jean-Richard, *Espagne, Espagne!* Paris: Éditions Sociales Internationales, 1936.
Blázquez, José Martín, *Guerre civile totale*. Paris: Denoël, 1938.
Brasillach, Robert, with Maurice Bardèche, *Histoire de la guerre d'Espagne*. Paris: Plon, 1939.
Buckley, Henry, *Life and Death of the Spanish Republic*. London; Hamish Hamilton, 1940.
Carrera, B., *L'Europe aveugle devant l'Espagne martyre*. Paris: Maison du livre français, 1939.
Carro, Padre Venancio D., *La verdad sobre la guerra española*. Zamora: Tipografía Comercial, 1937.
Chamson, André, *Rien qu'un témoignage: Retour d'Espagne*. Paris: Bernard Grasset, 1937.
Delaprée, Louis, *Le Martyre de Madrid: Témoignages inédites de Louis Delaprée*, Madrid: no pub., 1937.
Delaprée, Louis, *Mort en Espagne*. Paris: Editions Pierre Tisné, 1937.
Le Drame du Pays Basque. Paris: Les Amis de l'Espagne nouvelle, S.G.I.E., 1937.
Drieu La Rochelle, Pierre, *Gilles*. Paris: Gallimard, 1939.
Estelrich, Juan, *La Persécution religieuse en Espagne*. Verse preface by Paul Claudel. Paris: Plon, 1937.
Gay, Francisque, *Dans les flammes et dans le sang: les crimes contre les églises et les prêtres en Espagne*. Paris: Bloud et Gay, 1937.
Gide, André, *Retour de l'URSS*. Paris: Gallimard, 1936.
Gomá y Tomás, Isidro cardinal, *El caso de España. Introducción a sus diocesanos y respuesta a unas consultas sobre la guerra actual*. Pamplona: Diputación Foral de Navarra, 1936.
Gomá y Tomás, Isidro cardinal, *Le Cas de l'Espagne*. Malakoff (Seine): Impr. G. Durassié, 1937.
Guérin, Daniel, *Fascisme et grand capital*. Paris: Gallimard, 1937.
Hitler, Adolf, *Ma doctrine*. Transl. and ed., François Dauture and Georges Blond. Paris: Arthème Fayard, 1938.
Hitler, Adolf, *Mon combat*. Unabridged transl., J. Gaudefroy-Demombynes and A. Calmettes. Paris: Fernand Sorlot, 1934.
Hitler, Adolf, *Hitler's Secret Book*. New York: Grove Press, 1983.

Jellinek, Frank, *The Civil War in Spain.* London: Victor Gollancz, 1938.

Joubert, Vice-amiral H., *La Guerre d'Espagne et le catholicisme: Réponse à M. Jacques Maritain.* Paris: Les Amis de l'Espagne Nouvelle, S.G.I.E., 1937.

Joubert, Vice-amiral H., *L'Espagne de Franco: Synthèse de trois conférences données du 17 janvier au 10 février 1938.* Paris: Les Amis de l'Espagne Nouvelle, Fernand Sorlot, 1938.

Kaminski, Hans-Erich, *Ceux de Barcelone.* Paris: Denoël, 1937.

Klotz, Helmuth, *Les Leçons militaires de la guerre civile en Espagne.* Paris: by the author, 1937.

Koestler, Arthur, *Spanish Testament.* London: Gollancz, 1937.

Koestler, Arthur, *Menschenopfer unerhoert. Ein Schwarzbuch ueber Spanien.* Paris: Éditions du Carrefour, 1937.

Krivitsky, Walter G., *In Stalin's Secret Service.* New York: Harper & Bros., 1939.

Landau, Katia, *Le Stalinisme en Espagne. Témoignages de militants révolutionnaires sauvés des prisons staliniennes.* Paris: Impr. Cerbonnet, 1938.

La Souchère, Hélène de, *Guerre et religion.* Paris: Éditions des Archives Espagnoles, 1938.

Malaparte, Curzio, *Viva la muerte !* Special issue of *Prospettive* (Rome), 1939.

Malraux, André, *L'Espoir.* Paris: Gallimard, 1937.

Mann, Thomas, *Avertissement à l'Europe.* Preface by André Gide. Paris: Gallimard, 1937.

Maret, François, *Les Grands chantiers au soleil,* with a letter to Georges Bernanos. Paris: Fernand Sorlot, 1938.

Maritain, Jacques, *Rebeldes españoles no hacen una 'guerra santa.'* Madrid: Ediciones Españolas, 1937.

Martín Blázquez. José, *I Helped to Build an Army.* Transl., Franz Borkenau and E. Mosbacher. Introduction by Franz Borkenau. London: Secker & Warburg, 1939.

Massis, Henri, *Chefs.* Paris: Plon, 1939.

Mendizábal, Alfredo, *Aux origines d'une tragédie: La politique espagnole de 1923 à 1936.* Preface by Jacques Maritain. Paris: Desclés de Brouwer, 1937.

Mistral, Silvia, *Éxodo: Diario de una refugiada española.* Mexico City: Minerva, 1940.

Montserrat, Victor, *Le Drame d'un peuple incompris: la guerre au pays basque.* Paris: H.-G. Peyre, 1937.

Morrow, Felix, *Revolution and Counter-Revolution in Spain.* New York: Pioneer Publishers, 1938.

Ollivier, Marcel, *Les Journées sanglantes de Barcelone: le Guépeou en Espagne.* Paris: Les Humbles, 1937.

Orwell, George, *Homage to Catalonia.* London: Secker & Warburg, 1938.

Quero Morales, José, *El bombardeo de las ciudades abiertas.* Barcelona: Ediciones Españolas (Subsecretaria de Propaganda), 1938.

Richard, Marthe, *Mes dernières missions secrètes, 1936–1938.* Paris: Éditions de France, 1939.

Rieger, Max, *Espionnage en Espagne,* transl. by Jean Cassou. Preface by José Bergamín. Paris: Denoël, 1938.

Rioland, F., *Avec l'abbé Lambert à travers l'Espagne nationaliste.* Oran: Imprimerie Plaza, 1938.

Riotte, Jean, *Arriba España !* Tarbes: Imprimerie des Orphelins-Apprentis, 1936.
Rocker, Rudolf, *Extranjeros en España*. Buenos Aires: Imán, 1938.
Rotvand, Georges, *Franco et la nouvelle Espagne*. Paris: Denoël, 1938.
Rous, Jean, *Espagne 1936 – Espagne 1939*. Paris: Librairie du travail, 1939.
Saint-Aulaire, Auguste-Félix-Charles de Beaupoil, Comte de, *La Renaissance de l'Espagne*. Paris: Plon, 1938.
Sartre, Jean-Paul, *Le Mur*. Paris: Gallimard, 1939.
Schor, Ralph, 'Xénophobie et extrême-droite: l'exemplaire de *L'Ami du Peuple*, 1928–1937', *Revue d'Histoire Moderne et Contemporaine* (Paris), January–March 1976.
Simon, O.K., *Hitler en Espagne*. Foreword by Émile Buré. Paris: Denoël, 1938.
Solano Palacio, *El éxodo: por un refugiado español*. Valparaiso: Editorial Más Allá, 1939.
Téry, Simone, *La Porte du soleil*. Paris: Éditeurs Français Réunis, 1939.
Tharaud, Jérôme et Jean. *Cruelle Espagne*. Paris: Plon, 1937.
Togliatti, Palmiro 'M. Ercoli,' *Particularités de la révolution espagnole*. Paris: Bureau d'Éditions, 1936.
Toledo, Angel de, *Le Jour pointe en Espagne*. Liège: Dessain, 1937.
Toynbee, Arnold J., *Survey of International Affairs 1939*. London: Oxford University Press, 1941.
Wullens, Maurice, *L'assassinat politique et l'URSS*. Paris: 'Les Humbles,' 1938.

C. General Bibliography

Abendroth, Hans-Henning, *Hitler in der spanischen Arena. Die deutsch-spanischen Beziehungen 1936–1939*. Paderborn: F. Schöningh, 1973.
Adamthwaite, Anthony, *Britain and France, 1919–1945*. London: Macmillan, 1979
Adamthwaite, Anthony, *Grandeur and Misery: France's Bid for Power in Europe, 1914–1940*. London: Arnold, 1995.
Ageron, Charles-Robert, *L'Opinion française pendant les crises internationales de septembre 1938 à juillet 1939*. Tours: Cahiers de l'Institut d'histoire de la Presse et de l'Opinion publique, 1975.
Alberti, Rafael, *La Futaie perdue (Mémoires)*. Livres III–IV. Paris: Éditions Belfond, 1991.
Alpert, Michael, *A New International History of the Spanish Civil War*. London: Macmillan; New York: St. Martin's Press, 1994.
Álvarez del Vayo Julio, *Les Batailles de la liberté (mémoires d'un optimiste)*. Paris: Masperó, 1963.
Álvarez del Vayo, Julio, *The Last Optimist*. London: Putnam, 1950.
Amouroux, Henri, 'Les coupables de 40', *Historia*. Madrid, no. 366, May 1977.
Araquistain, Luis, *Sobre la guerra civil y en la emigración*. Madrid: Ediciones Espasa-Calpe, 1983.
Arias Ruiz, Aníbal, *50 años de radiodifusión en España*. Madrid: Ministerio de Información y Turismo, 1973.
Arquer, Jordi, 'L'action du Parti communiste d'Espagne en France' (manuscript). Barcelona: Centre d'Estudis Histórics Internacionals, n.d.
Avilés Farré, Juan. *Pasión y farsa franceses y británicos ante la Guerra Civil Española*. Madrid: Eudema, 1994.

Azcarate, Pablo de, *Mi embajada en Londres durante la Guerra Civil Española*. España: Ariel, 1976.
Bayac, Jacques Delperrie de, *Les Brigades internationales*. Paris: Fayard, 1968.
Berdah. Jean-François, *La Démocratie assassinée: la République espagnole et les grandes puissances 1931–1939*. Paris: Berg International, 2000.
Bernecker, Walther L., 'L'intervention allemande: l'aigle à deux têtes, Madrid 1936–1939' in: *Un peuple en résistance, ou l'épopée ambigüe*. Paris: Autrement, 1994.
Berneri, Camille and Luce Fabbri, *Guerre de classes en Espagne: Camille Berneri, l'homme d'action et l'homme d'étude*. Paris: Spartacus, 1946.
Bertrand de Muñoz, Maryse, *La Guerre civile espagnole et la littérature française*. Montreal: Didier, 1971.
Beumelburg, Werner, *Kampf um Spanien*. Oldenburg: Stalling, 1939.
Bolín, Luis, *Spain: The Vital Years*. Foreword by Sir Arthur Bryant. London: Cassell, 1967.
Bolloten, Burnett, *The Spanish Civil War: Revolution and Counterrevolution*. Foreword by Stanley G. Payne. Chapel Hill and London: The University of North Carolina Press, 1991.
Borrás Llop, José María, *Francia ante la Guerra civil española: Burguesía, interés nacional et interés de clase*. Madrid: Centro de Investigaciones sociológicas, 1981.
Boyer, Jean-Paul, *La Liberté de la presse*. Paris: Au fil d'Ariane, 1963.
Breen, Catherine (Muller-Bapst), *La Droite française et la Guerre d'Espagne (1936–1937)*. Geneva: Éditions Médecine et Hygiène, 1973.
Brome, Vincent, *The International Brigades: Spain, 1936–1939*. New York: William Morrow, 1966.
Broué, Pierre and Témime, Émile, *La Révolution et la Guerre d'Espagne*, Paris: Les Éditions de Minuit, 1961.
Broué, Pierre, *Staline et la Révolution, Le cas espagnol (1936–1939)*. Paris: Fayard. 1993.
Buchanan, Tom, *Britain and the Spanish Civil War*. Cambridge: Cambridge University Press, 1997.
Cameron, Norman et al., *Hitler's Table Talk 1941–1944*. New York: Enigma Books. 2000.
Carr, Raymond, ed. *The Republic and the Civil War in Spain*. London: Macmillan, 1971.
Carr, Raymond, *The Spanish Tragedy: The Civil War in Spain in Perspective*. London: Weidenfeld & Nicolson, 1977.
Carr, Raymond, *The Civil War in Spain, 1936–39*. London: Weidenfeld & Nicolson, 1986.
Carrero Blanco, Luis, *Ideas básicas sobre la guerra marítima*. Madrid: Escuela de Guerra Naval, 1945.
Casanova, Marina, *La diplomacia española durante la guerra civil*. Madrid: Ministero de Asuntos Exteriores, 1996.
Castells, Andreu, *Las Brigadas Internacionales en la Guerra de España*. Barcelona: Ariel, 1974.
Catala, Michel, 'L'attitude de la France face à la guerre d'Espagne. L'échec des négociations pour la reconnaissance du gouvernement franquiste en 1938,' in: *Mélanges de la Casa de Velázquez*, vol. 29, 1993.

Cattell, David T., *Communism and the Spanish Civil War*. Berkeley: University of California Press, 1955.
Cattell, David T., *Soviet Diplomacy and the Spanish Civil War*. Berkeley: University of California Press, 1957.
Caute, David. *Le Communisme et les intellectuels français*. Paris: Gallimard, 1967.
Churchill, Winston, *The Gathering Storm*. London: Houghton Mifflin Harcourt, 1948.
Cierva, Ricardo de la, *Historia ilustrada de la guerra civil española*. Madrid: Ediciones Danae, 1970.
Colodny, Robert Garland. *The Struggle for Madrid: The Central Epic of the Spanish Conflict (1936–37)*. New York: Paine-Whitman, 1958.
Colvin, Ian, *Master Spy*. New York: McGraw Hill, 1951.
Coverdale, John F., *Italian Intervention in the Spanish Civil War*. Princeton, NJ: Princeton University Press, 1975.
Crozier, Brian, *Franco: A Biographical History*. London: Eyre & Spottiswoode, 1967.
Dahlem, Franz, *Am Vorabend des zweiten Weltkrieges: Erinnerungen*. Berlin: Dietz, 1977, vol. 1.
Delperrie de Bayac, Jacques. *Les Brigades internationales*. Paris: Fayard, 1968.
Demidjuk, Stanislav, and Skoutelsky, Rémi, *Nouveaux regards sur les Brigades Internationales: Espagne 1936-1939*. Montpellier: Indigène Éditions, 2010.
Díaz-Plaja, Fernando, *La historia de España en sus documentos: el siglo XX, la guerra 1936–1939*. Madrid: EDAF, 1994.
Downes, Donald, *The Scarlet Thread: Adventures in Wartime Espionage*. London: Derek Verschoyle, 1953.
Dreifort, John E. *Yvon Delbos at the Quai d'Orsay: French Foreign Policy during the Popular Front, 1936–1938*. Lawrence: University Press of Kansas, 1973.
Droz, Jacques, *Histoire de l'antifascisme en Europe 1923–1939*. Paris: La Découverte, 1985.
Dupré, Henri, *La 'Legion Tricolore' en Espagne, 1936–1939*. Preface by Pierre Constantini. Paris: Éditions de la Ligue Française (Mouvement social européen), 1942.
Edwards, Jill, *The British Government and the Spanish Civil War*. London: Macmillan, 1979.
Epopée d'Espagne: Brigades Internationales 1936–1939. [A collection of eye-witness accounts and historical documents compiled by the Amicale des Anciens Volontaires en Espagne Républicaine (AVER)]. Paris, 1957.
Ehrenburg, Ilia, *Memorias, 1921–1941*. Barcelona: Planeta, 1985.
Esenwein, George, and Shubert, Adrian, *Spain at War: The Spanish Civil War in Context, 1931–1939*. London/New York: Longman, 1995.
Fischer, Louis, *Men and Politics*. New York: Duell, Sloan & Pearce, 1941.
Fonseca, Carlos de, 'Le Portugal et la guerre d'Espagne,' Université de Montpellier: 14 June 1986.
Franco Bahamonde, Francisco, *Palabras del Caudillo 19 abril 1937–7 diciembre 1942*. Madrid: Ediciones de la Vicesecretaría de Educación Popular, 1943.
Gannon, Franklin Reid, *The British Press and Germany, 1936–1939*. Oxford: Clarendon Press, 1971.

García Durán, Juan, *La guerra civil española. Fuentes (Archivos, bibliografía, filmografía)*. Prologue by Gabriel Jackson. Barcelona; Crítica, 1985.

García Pérez, Rafael, *Franquismo y Tercer Reich. Las relaciones económicas hispano-alemanas durante la Segunda Guerra mundial*. Madrid: Centro de Estudios Constitucionales, 1994.

Garosci, Aldo, *Gli intellettuali e la guerra di Spagna*. Milan: Giulio Einaudi, 1959.

Georges-Roux, *La Guerre civile d'Espagne*. Paris: Arthème Fayard, 1963.

Gorkín, Julián, *Caníbales politicos: Hitler y Stalín en España*. Mexico City: Ediciones Quetzal, 1941.

Groussard, Serge, *Solitude espagnole*. Paris: Plon, 1948.

Halstead, Charles R., 'Spanish Foreign Policy 1936–1978,' in: James W. Cortada (ed.), *Spain in the Twentieth-Century World*. Westport Connecticut: Greenwood Press, 1980.

Haslam, Jonathan, *The Soviet Union and the Struggle for Collective Security in Europe, 1933–1939*. New York: St. Martin's Press, 1984.

Hemingway, Ernest, *For Whom the Bell Tolls*. New York: C. Scribner's Sons, 1940.

Hodgson, Sir Robert, *Spain Resurgent*. London: Hutchinson, 1953.

Howson, Gerald, *Arms for Spain: The Untold Story of the Spanish Civil War*. London: John Murray, 1998.

Jackson, Gabriel, *The Spanish Republic and the Civil War*. New Jersey: Princeton University Press, 1965.

Jäckel, Eberhard, *Hitler Idéologue*. Paris: Gallimard, 1993.

Jacquelin, André, *Espagne et Liberté: le second Munich*. Preface by Èmile Buré. Paris: Kérénac, 1945.

Kemp, Peter, *Mine Were of Trouble*. London: Cassell, 1957.

Koestler, Arthur, *Scum of the Earth*. New York: Macmillan, 1941.

Krop, Pascal, *Les Secrets de l'espionnage français*. Paris: Lattes, 1995.

Lacouture, Jean, *Léon Blum*. Paris: Le Seuil, 1979.

Lefebvre, Michel, and Skoutelsky, Rémi. *Les Brigades internationales: Images retrouvées*. Paris: Le Seuil, 2003.

Lefranc, Georges, *Histoire de Front popluaire (1934–1938)*. Paris: Payot, 1965, 1975.

Legarreta, Dorothy, *The Guernica Generation: Basque Refugee Children of the Spanish Civil War*. Reno: University of Nevada Press, 1984.

Liddell Hart, Basil H., *The Other Side of the Hill*. London: Cassell, 1948.

Łukasiewicz, Juliusz, *Diplomat in Paris, 1936–1939: Papers and Memoris of Juliusz Łukasiewicz, Ambassador of Poland*. New York: Columbia University Press, 1970.

de Madariaga, Salvador, *España*. Buenos Aires: Editorial Sudamericana, 1944.

Maisky, Ivan M., *Spanish Notebook*. London: Hutchinson, 1966.

Merkes, Manfred, *Die deutsche Politik im spanischen Bürgerkrieg*. Bonn: Röhrscheid, 1969.

Miralles, Ricardo, 'La diplomatie de la République espagnole face à la non-intervention (1936–1939),' *Guerres mondiales et Conflits contemporains* (Paris), no 186, April–June 1997, 51–72.

Mitchell, David. *The Spanish Civil War*. London: Granada, 1982.

Moch, Jules, *Rencontres avec Léon Blum*. Paris: Plon, 1970.

Moch, Jules, *Le Front Populaire*. Paris: Perrin, 1971.
Mora, Constancia de la, *Doble esplendor: Autobiografía de una mujer española*. Mexico: Editorial Atlante, 1944.
Moradiellos, Enrique, *Neutralidad benévola*. Oviedo: Pentalafa, 1990.
Moradiellos, Enrique, *La perfidia de Albión: el Gobierno británico y la Guerra civil española*. Madrid: Siglo XXI de España Editores,1999.
Moradiellos, Enrique, *1936: Los mitos de la guerra civil*. Barcelona; Península, 2004.
Olaya, Francisco, *La comedia de la 'no intervención' en la Guerra civil española*. Madrid: G. del Toro, 1976.
Orlov, Alexander, *The Secret History of Stalin's Crimes*. London: Jarrolds, 1954.
Orwell, George, *Homage to Catalonia*. London: Secker & Warburg, 1938.
Palencia, Isabel, *Smouldering Freedom*. London: Victor Gollancz, 1946.
Parker, R.A.C., *Chamberlain and Appeasement. British Policy and the Coming of the Second World War*. London: Bedford/St. Martins, 1993.
Paselli, Luigi, 'L'illusion déçue de Manuel Azaña Vich, 29 juillet 1938' in: *Azaña et son temps,* eds. Paul Albert and Jean-Pierre Amalric. Madrid: Casa de Velázquez, 1993.
Payne, Stanley G., *The Franco Regime, 1936–1975*. Madison: University of Wisconsin Press, 1987.
Paz, Armando, *Los Servicios de espionaje en la guerra civil española (1936–1939)*. Madrid: San Martín, 1976.
Picon, Gaëtan, *Malraux par lui-même*. Paris: Le Seuil, 1953.
Pike, David Wingeate, *La Crise espagnole de 1936*. Toulouse: Imprimerie de l'Arsenal, Université de Toulouse, 1966.
Pike, David Wingeate, 'Aspects nouveaux du rôle de l'Espagne dans la Seconde Guerre mondiale,' *Revue d'Histoire moderne et contemporaine*, Paris, t. XIX, July–September 1972, 510–518.
Pike, David Wingeate, 'Les Républicains espagnols incarcérés en URSS dans les années 1940,' *Matériaux pour l'Histoire* (Nanterre), July–December 1985, 99–103.
Pike, David Wingeate, 'Guernica Revisited', *International Journal of Iberian Studies* (Glasgow). vol. 12, no 3, January–March 1999, 133–141.
Preston, Paul, *Franco: A Biography*. London: HarperCollins, 1993.
Prieto, Indalecio, *Convulsiones de España*. Mexico City: Ediciones Oasis, 1967.
Puzzo, Dante A., *Spain and the Great Powers, 1936–1941*. New York: Columbia University Press, 1962.
Quatrefages, René, 'La politique française de non-intervention et le soutien matériel à la République espagnole pendant la Guerre Civil,' *Les Armées espagnoles et françaises. Modernisation et réforme entre les deux Guerres mondiales*. Madrid: Casa de Velázquez, 1989.
Rama, Carlos M., 'La misteriosa muerte de Camillo Berneri,' in: *Nueva Historia* (Barcelona), no. 12, January 1978, 42–49.
Richardson, R. Dan, *Comintern Army: The International Brigades and the Spanish Civil War*. Lexington: The University Press of Kentucky, 1982.
Rubio, Javier. *La emigración de la Guerra civil de 1936-1939: Historia del Éxodo que se produce con el fin de la II República española*. 3 vols. Madrid: Editorial San Martín, 1977.

Rubio, Javier. 'Le Parti communiste d'Espagne en exil dans l'immédiate après-guerre civile (1939–1941),' *Matériaux* (Nanterre), July–December 1985, 93–99.

Rufat, Ramón, *Espions de la République. Mémoires d'un agent secret pendant la guerre d'Espagne*. Paris: Éditions Allia, 1990.

Ruhl, Klaus-Jörg, '*L'alliance à distance: les relations économiques germano-espagnoles de 1936 à 1945*', *Revue d'histoire de la Deuxième Guerre mondiale* (Paris), 118, April 1980.

de Saint-Exupéry, Antoine, *Terre des hommes*. Paris: Gallimard, 1950.

Salas Larrazábal, Jesús, *Intervención extranjera en la guerra de España*. Madrid: Editora Nacional, 1974.

Schlenstedt, Sylvia, 'Exil und antifaschistischer Kampf in Spanien', in: *Exil in den Niederlanden und in Spanien*. Leipzig: Frankfurt am Main, 1981.

Schwartz, Fernando, *La Internacionalización de la guerra civil española*. Barcelona: Planeta, 1999.

Shirer, William L., *La Guerre civile d'Espagne*. Paris: Arthème Fayard, 1963.

Skoutelsky, Rémi. *L'Espoir guidait leurs pas: les voluntaires français dans les brigades internationales*. Foreword by Antoine Prost. Paris: Bernard Grasset, 1998.

Soria, Georges, *Guerre et révolution 1936–1939*. Vol. III. Paris: Livre club Diderot, 1976.

Southworth, Herbert Rutledge, *Le Mythe de la croisade de Franco*. Paris: Ruedo ibérico, 1964.

Southworth, Herbert Rutledge, *Guernica! Guernica! A Study of Journalism, Diplomacy, Propaganda, and History*. Berkeley: University of California Press, 1977.

The Soviet Union in the Spanish Civil War, edited by Ronald Radosh, Mary R. Habeck, and Grigory Sevostianov. New Haven/London: Yale University Press, 2001.

Suárez, Andrés, *Un episodio de la revolución española: el proceso contra el POUM*. Paris: Ruedo ibérico, 1974.

Thomas, Hugh. *The Spanish Civil War*. Third ed., revised and enlarged. Harmondsworth/New York: Penguin Books/Hamish Hamilton, 1977.

Tillon, Charles. *Un « procès de Moscou » à Paris*. Précédé de l'Interrogation par Raymond Jean. Paris: Le Seuil, 1971.

Un Trentennio di attività anarchica, 1914–1945. Cesena: Edizioni l'Antistato, 1953.

Tuñón de Lara, Manuel (ed.), *Historia de España, tomo IX: La crisis del Estado: dictadura, republica, guerra (1923–1939)*. Madrid: Editorial Labor, 1982.

Viñas, Ángel, *La Alemania nazi y el 18 de julio*. Madrid: Alianza Editorial, 1974.

Viñas, Ángel et al., *Política comercial exterior en España (1931–1975)*. Madrid: Servicio de Estudios Económicos, 1979.

Viñas, Ángel, *Guerra, dinero, dictadura: ayuda fascista y autarquía en la España de Franco*. Barcelona: Crítica/Grijalbo, 1984.

Viñas, Ángel, 'Rivalidad anglo-germana,' *Guerra, dinero, dictadura: Ayuda fascista y autarquía en la España de Franco*. Madrid: Editorial Crítica, 1984.

Viñas, Ángel, 'Las relaciones hispano-francesas, el Gobierno Daladier y la crisis de Munich,' in: *Españoles y franceses en la primera mitad del siglo XX*. Madrid: Consejo superior de investigaciones científicas. CSIC, Centro de estudios históricos, 1986.

Viñas, Ángel, *Franco, Hitler y el estallido de la guerra civil: Antecedentes y Consecuencias*. Madrid: Alianza, 2001.

Viñas, Ángel et al., *Política comercial exterior en España (1931–1975)*. Madrid: Servicio de Estudios Económicos, 1979.

Viñas, Ángel, and Fernando Hernández Sánchez, *El desplome de la República*. Barcelona: Crítica, 2009.

Watkins, Kenneth William, *Britain Divided. The effects of the Spanish Civil War on the British political opinion*. London: T. Nelson, 1963.

Watt, Donald Cameron, 'Britain, France and the Italian problem, 1937–1939,' in: *Les relations franco-britanniques de 1935–1939*. Paris: Éditions du Centre national de la recherche scientifique, 1975.

Whealey, Robert H., *Hitler and Spain: The Nazi Role in the Spanish Civil War, 1936–1939*. Kentucky: University Press of Kentucky, 1989.

Zugazagoitia, Julian, *Guerra y vicisitudes de los españoles*. Barcelona: Crítica, 1977.

D. Bibliography of the Press

Annuaire de la presse française, et étrangère et du monde politique: 1936 (54 ed.) *1937* (55 ed.), *1938* (56 ed.), *1939* (57 ed.). Director: Maurice Roux-Bluysen. Paris–London–Liège, n.d.

Armero, José, *España fue noticia: Corresponsales extranjeros en la guerra civil española*. Madrid: Sedmay Ediciones, 1976.

Bellanger, Claude ; Godechot, Jacques ; Guiral, Pierre ; and Terrou, Fernand, *Histoire générale de la presse française*, vol. III. Paris: Presses Universitaires de France, 1972.

Bodin, Louis, and Touchard, Jean, *Front populaire, 1936*. Paris: Armand Colin, 1961.

Boyer, Jean-Paul, *La Liberté de la presse*. Paris: Au Fil d'Ariane, 1963.

Calvet, Henri, *La Presse contemporaine*. Paris: Fernand Nathan, 1958.

Cointet, Michèle and Jean-Paul, directors, *Dictionnaire historique de la France sous l'Occupation*. Paris: Tallandier, 2000.

Denoyer, Pierre, *La Presse contemporaine*. Paris: Centre de documentation universitaire, 1948.

Encyclopédie française, vol. XVIII ("La Civilisation écrite"): Troisième partie: "La Revue et le Journal". Paris, 1939.

Estier, Claude, *La Gauche hebdomadaire*. Paris: Armand Colin, 1962.

Europa Year Book: 1929. London: Europa Publications, 1929 (denotes last year of publication).

Foucher, Jean-André, and Noël Jacquenart, *Le quatrième pouvoir: la presse française de 1830 à 1960*. Hors série de *L'Echo de la Presse et de la Publicité* (Paris) 1968.

Gannon, Franklin Reid, *The British Press and Germany, 1936–1939*. Oxford: Clarendon Press, 1971.

Gérome, Pierre, *La Presse et Franco*. Paris: Comité de vigilance des intellectuels antifascistes, 1937.

Handbuch der Weltpresse: Eine Darstellung des Zeitungswesens aller Länder. Leipzig/Frankfurt am Main: Armanen-Verlag, 1937.

Hatin, Eugène, *Bibliographie historique et critique de la presse périodique française*. Paris: Éditions Anthropos, 1966.

Hohenberg, John, *Foreign Correspondence: The Great Reporters and their Times*. New York and London: Columbia University Press, 1964, 1965.

Hourdin, Georges, *Le Presse catholique.* Paris: Arthème Fayard, 1957.
Kayser, Jacques, *La Presse de province sour la IIIème République.* Foreword by François Goguel. Paris: Armand Colin, 1958.
Kupferman, Fred, and Machefer, Philippe, 'Presse et politique dans les années trente: le cas du *Petit Journal,*' *Revue d'Histoire Moderne et Contemporaine* (Paris) January–March 1975.
Lacroix, Jean-Paul, *La Presse indiscrète.* Paris: René Julliard, 1967.
Laney, Al, *Paris Herald: The Incredible Newspaper.* London: Greenwood Press, 1947.
Lazareff, Pierre, *Dernière edition.* New York: Brentano's, 1942.
Ledré, Charles, *Histoire de la presse.* Paris: Arthème Fayard, 1958.
Le Nan, Danielle and Darmon, Norbert, *Bibliographie de la presse française politique et d'information générale, 1865–1944.* 31-Haute-Garonne. Prologue by Jacques Godechot. Paris: Bibliothèque Nationale, 1967.
Livois, René de, *Histoire de la presse française.* Lausanne: Editions Spes, 1945.
Manevy, Raymond, *Histoire de la presse: 1914 à 1939.* Paris: Editions Corréa, 1945.
Manevy, Raymond, *La Presse de la Troisième République.* Paris: J. Foret, 1955.
Mazadier, René. *Histoire de la presse parisienne, 1631–1945.* Paris: Éditions du Pavois, 1945.
Micaud, Charles A., *The French Right and Nazi Germany, 1933–1939: A Study of Public Opinion.* Durham, North Carolina: Duke University Press, 1943.
Mottin, Jean, *Histoire politique de la presse: 1944–1949.* Paris: Éditions "Bilans Hebdomadaires", 1949.
Nomenclature des journaux et revues en langue française du monde entier: 1936–37. Paris: L'Argues de la Presse, n.d. (prob. 1937).
Novick, Peter, *The Resistance versus Vichy: The Purge of Collaborators: Liberated France.* London: Chatto & Windus, 1968.
Political Handbook and Atlas of the World: Parliaments, Parties and Press as of January 1, 1936. Ed. Walter H. Mallory. New York: Harper and Bros., 1936.
Political Hanbook and Atlas of the World: Parliaments, Parties and Press as of January 1, 1938. Ed. Walter H. Mallory. New York: Harper & Bros., 1938.
La Presse catholique en France, 1936: Guide-mémorial de l'Exposition internationale, instituée à la Cité du Vatican par S.S. Pie XI. Paris/Colmar: Éditions "Alsatia", 1936.
Rémond, René, *La Droite en France: De la première restauration à la Ve République.* Paris: Aubier, 1968.
Schor, Ralph, 'Xénophobie et extrême-droite: l'exemple de *L'Ami du Peuple* (1928–1937),' *Revue d'histoire moderne et contemporaine* (Paris), January–March 1976.

Index

ABC (Madrid), 348
ABC (Seville), 303
Abetz, Otto (1903–1958), 250, 253, 256, 386
Abyssinia, 3, 32, 81, 100–1, 112, 163, 234
Académie française, 124, 133, 218, 224, 246, 259, 284, 287, 289, 298
Action française, 4, 96, 143, 258, 262, 299
Action Française (Paris daily), 4, 18, 22, 25, 27, 30, 34, 43, 49, 51, 62, 67, 75, 78, 95, 97, 109, 121, 127, 137, 139, 143–5, 154, 177–8, 180, 185–6, 193, 195, 202, 209, 222, 236–7, 241, 244, 247, 249–52, 258, 260, 287–8, 309, 316, 321, 326, 331–2, 339, 347, 357, 371
Africa, 22, 51, 112–14, 159, 163, 177–9, 194, 196, 203, 214, 256, 258, 309, 312, 332, 342
Agadir Crisis (1911), 40, 158
Agence Espagne (Paris), 299
Agence Havas (Paris), 47, 121, 219, 246, 285
Agence Radio (Paris), 299
Agence Reischach (Berlin), 354
Ahora (Madrid), 249, 297
Aillières, d' (*député*, Sarthe), 327
aircraft, 19, 20, 26, 28–33, 35, 37, 43, 45, 51, 56–7, 62, 81, 109, 114, 124, 136, 139, 153, 160–1, 164, 177, 183, 185–8, 190, 193–6, 222, 302, 309, 316–17, 322–3, 326, 333, 337, 361, 369–70
  British,
    Fairey, 161, 361
  Dutch
    Koolhoven, 109
  French
    Bloch, 63, 160, 177, 186
    Brack, 136
    Dewoitine, 34–5, 63, 160, 316
    Loire, 63
    Potez, 30, 34–5, 63, 160, 316, 361
  German
    Arado, 160, 361,
    Dornier, 160–1, 361
    Fokker, 316
    Heinkel, 139, 160–1, 361
    Junkers, 29, 74, 110, 122, 183, 195
    Messerschmitt, 109, 161
  Italian
    Caproni, 74, 160, 361
    Fiat, 160–61
    Savoia-Marchetti, 29, 160, 361
  Soviet
    I-15, 161
    I-16, 161
    Katiuska, 136, 161, 361
    MM3
Air France, 28, 109, 136, 222, 302
Air-Pyrénées, 138–9, 308
Ajam, Maurice (journalist), 82
Albacète, 107, 228, 330–1, 383
Albañá (Gerona), 139
Albania, 343
Alberti, Rafael (1902–1999), 135
Albertini, Georges (1911–1983), 256
Alcalá Zamora, Niceto (1877–1949), 1, 4, 49, 77, 176
Alcoléa, Raymond (author), 375
L'Alerte (Nice), weekly, 243
Alès (Gard), 137
Alfonso XIII, King of Spain (1886–1941), 1, 3, 50, 96, 139–40, 200, 215, 308, 315, 376, 378, 382
Algeciras, 162
Algeciras Conference (1906), 81, 111
Algeria, 14, 29, 340
Algiers, 50, 184, 258
Alhucemas Bay, 162
Alibi network, 255
Alicante, 57, 64, 183, 195, 222, 323–4

Alliance Française in Valencia, 107
Almería, 114, 146, 153–5, 159
Almirante Cervera (Nationalist cruiser), 151, 174
Alps, 210
Altman, Georges (1901–1960), 236
Álvarez del Vayo, Julio (1891–1975), 70, 76, 86, 107, 130, 153, 167, 197, 212–13, 218, 222, 225, 297, 308, 337, 377
Amélie-les-Bains (Pyrénées-Orientales), 107, 109
American Broadcasting System in Europe, 255
Amicale des anciens volontaires français en Espagne républicaine, 374
L'Ami du Peuple (Paris daily), 30, 51, 92, 95, 144, 257, 262, 281, 284, 341
Ancelet-Hustache, Jeanne (journalist), 123
Andalusia, 15, 369
Andes, Francisco, Marquis de los (pro-Franco agent), 140
Andorra, 74, 108
Andrieu, François (journalist), 34, 54
Angell, Sir Norman (1873–1967), 172, 297
Angers, 241
Anglo-Italian Agreements
Anglo-Italian 'Gentleman's Agreement,' 37, 89, 91, 164
Anglo-Italian Mediterranean Agreement, 180, 182, 190, 377
Ankara, 245
Anschluss, 128, 176, 232, 340, 352, 365
Antequera (Malaga), 369
Anti-Comintern Pact (1936), 334
Antoine, Jean (journalist), 56
Antwerp, 26, 124, 137
L'Appel du Centre, 241
Appel du 10 juillet, 251
Aragon, Louis (1897–1982), 286, 295
Arán Valley (Lérida), 74, 138
Araquistáin y Quevedo, Luis (1886–1959), 77, 113, 342
Archimbaud, Léon (journalist), 23, 42, 82
Arcos, René (1881–1959), 325
Ardennes, 22, 234
Arellano, Carlos de (Nationalist agent), 142
Argentat (Corrèze), 245
Argentina, 49, 335
Ariège, 58, 108, 110, 139, 185, 203
Arles-sur-Tech (Pyrénées-Orientales), 139

Armengaud, Major-General Paul (Fr. Air Force), 160–1, 168, 174, 179, 361
Arnaud-Bernard (journalist), 20, 37
Arriba España (Pamplona), 45, 210
Asociación Monárquica Española, 215
Association de la presse parisienne, 256
Association des travailleurs étrangers, 315
Association républicaine des Anciens combattants et victimes de guerre, 374
Asturias, 240, 323, 332, 382
Atger, Prefect Frédéric (1881–1976), 35–6, 38, 316
Atlantic Pacific Press Agency, 249
Atlantic Ocean, 54, 111, 162, 380
Attlee, Major Clement (later Prime Minister, later 1st Earl; 1883–1867), 85, 171, 297
Aub, Max (1903–1972), 354
Aude, 74, 137, 317
Auden, Wystan Hugh (1907–1973), 135
Au Pilori, 252
L'Aube (Paris daily), 17, 32, 61, 94–5, 102, 112–13, 115, 118, 128–9, 147, 163, 220, 225, 245, 251
Aujourd'hui, 261
Aulard, Alphonse (journalist), 292, 294
Aunós Pérez, Eduardo (1894–1967), 176, 303
Auriol, Vincent (1884–1966), 132, 200, 202–3, 245, 259, 283, 295–6, 298
L'Aurore (Paris daily), 257
Austria, 16, 101, 128, 176, 253, 255, 308, 343, 352, 366
Austruy, Henry (journalist), 57
Aux Écoutes (Paris weekly), 289, 303
L'Avant-garde (Paris weekly), 294
Aveline, Claude (1901–1992), 325
Axis, 3, 53, 81–5, 89, 100–1, 111, 116, 131, 136, 143, 153, 158–9, 161, 164, 173, 177–8, 180, 185, 188, 192, 195, 205, 207, 210, 214, 220–1, 227, 230, 232, 234, 240, 253, 332, 337, 362, 364, 372, 374, 379, 385
Ax-les-Thermes (Ariège), 186
Azaña y Díaz, Manuel (1880–1940), 1, 4, 13, 25, 33, 53, 102, 130, 213–14, 218, 222–3, 249, 377, 380
Azcárate y Flórez, Pablo de (1890–1971), 176, 184
Azores, 194

Babouchkina, Dr. Z. (Moscow resident), 325
Badajoz, 49, 105, 149, 320
Baden-Württemberg, 386
Badoglio, Marshal Pietro (1871–1956), 168, 344
Bagnères-de-Luchon (Haute-Garonne), 138
Bagnoles-de-l'Orne (Orne), 344
Baigorry, General, 382
Bailby, Léon (1867–1854), publisher, 27, 43, 56, 62, 75, 77, 83, 178, 185, 195–6, 201, 211, 217, 237, 243, 283–6, 351, 375
Bainville, Jacques (1879–1936), 287, 290
Bakunin, Mikhail Alexandrovich (1814–1876), 133
Baldwin, Stanley (later 1st Earl of Bewdley; 1867–1956), 9, 37, 150, 335, 376
Baleares (Nationalist cruiser), 174, 192
Balearic Islands, 23, 27, 37, 42, 51, 80–1, 100, 173, 179, 203, 321
Balk, Théodore (journalist), 33
Balkan Entente (Greece, Romania, Turkey, Yugoslavia: 1934), 101
Balkans, 332
Banque de France, 196
Bank of Spain, 57, 174, 196
Banque Lazard Frères, 160
Banse, Professor Ewald (1883–1953), 176, 365
Barbier, Jean-Baptiste (Fr. diplomat), 106
Barbusse, Henri (1873–1935), 227, 304
Barcelona (*qua* city), 3, 4, 10, 27, 34–5, 47, 72–4, 76–7, 90, 96, 107, 113, 127, 130, 138, 147, 150, 170, 178, 181, 183, 193, 195, 202–3, 205–6, 208, 217, 223, 227, 229, 252, 286, 302–4, 306–7, 314, 316, 326, 333, 337, 350, 354, 365, 370, 374–5, 377–8, 386
Barcia y Trelles, Augusto (1881–1961), 53, 101, 158, 297
Bardèche, Maurice (1907–1998), 132, 244, 287, 353
Bardoux, Jacques (Senator, Puy-de-Dôme; 1874–1959), 106, 132, 154, 177, 244, 286, 323, 366
Barra Camer, Colonel Alfonso, 381
Barroso Sánchez-Guerra, Major (later Lieutenant General) Antonio (1893–1982), 18–19
Basch, Victor (1867–1944), 2, 39, 49, 86, 244, 326

Basle, 124
Basque Government, 151, 200, 299, 351
Basque Provinces, 46–7, 63, 72–3, 91, 93, 117–20, 122–4, 127–9, 139, 142, 150, 153, 155–6, 168, 211, 308, 346–7, 349
Basques, 44, 48, 99, 118–20, 122, 124, 125–7, 151, 299, 347, 351–2, 363
Bassens (Gironde), 63
Basses-Pyrénées, 45–6, 108, 283, 298, 327, 382
Bastid, Paul (journalist), 297
Batalla, Major (aide to Muñoz Grandes), 64
La Batalla (Barcelona), 337, 349, 353
Batlle, José Antonio (Sp. Nationalist agent), 139
Bats, R. (Inspector of Special Police), 384
Battalion 'Enrico Malatesta,' 304
Battalion 'Garibaldi,' 113
Battalion 'La Marseillaise,' 227, 230
Bauer, Gérard Henri (1888–1967), 302
Baudry, Jean (journalist), 347, 371
Bausén (Lérida), 138
Bavaria, 200
Bayet, Albert (1880–1961), 99, 115, 149, 203, 244, 248, 292
Bayo Giroud, Captain (later General) Alberto (1892–1967), 351
Bayonne, 46–7, 63, 110, 139, 141, 155, 180, 307
BBC (British Broadcasting Corporation), 246, 248, 256
BBC Overseas Broadcasts, 249
Beaumarchais, Pierre Augustin Caron de (1732–1799), 71
Beaussart, Élie (journalist), 350
Bédier, Joseph (Académie Fr.; 1864–1938), 287
Béhobie (Basses-Pyrénées), 44–5, 64, 140, 142
Beigbeder Atienza, Colonel Juan (1888–1957), 264, 282
Belgium, 2, 67, 92, 101, 107, 122, 128, 251, 256, 343, 376
Belin, René (1898–1977), 244
Bellivier, André, 350
Benda, Julien (1867–1956), 32–3, 135, 239, 244, 245, 297
Beneš, Edvard (1884–1948), 295
Bérard, Félix Léon (Senator, Basses-Pyrénées; 1876–1960), 218–19, 222–4, 379, 382

Béraud, Henri (1885–1958), 200, 245, 247, 289
Berchtesgaden (Bavaria), 80, 99, 200, 376
Bergamín y Gutiérrez, José (1895–1983), 131, 135, 353
Bergery, Gaston (*député*, Seine-et-Oise; 1892–1974), 233, 245, 289
Bergonzoli, General Annibale (1884–1974), 112
Berkane (Oujda), 29
Berl, Emmanuel (1892–1976), 23, 170–1, 245, 295
Berlin (*qua* city), 50, 92, 116, 361, 376
Berliner Börsen-Zeitung (Berlin daily), 90, 175, 186, 207, 338
Bermeo, Luis de (journalist), 369
Bermond, Pierre (journalist), 285
Bernadot, Père Marie-Vincent (1883–1941), 127
Bernanos, Georges (1888–1948), 128, 198, 291, 351, 372
Berneri, Camillo (1897–1937), 113, 130–1, 146, 294, 342
Berneri Collection (Genoa), 319–20, 325, 327
Berniard, Georges (journalist), 117
Bernoville, Gaëtan (journalist), 123
Bernus, Pierre (journalist), 24, 83–4, 106, 154
Bersaglieri *Italy
Bertaux, Pierre (1907–1986), 253, 256
Bertele, Hermann, né Edmond Foeglin, 260
Berthod, Aimé (Senator, Jura; 1878–1944), 16, 38–9, 53, 208
Bertrán y Musitu, José (1875–1957), 139
Bertrand, Louis (journalist), 245, 289
Besteiro, Professor Julián (1870–1940), 176, 225
Bevin, Ernest (1881–1951), 326
Biarritz, 63, 139–40, 180
Bidassoa River, 45
Bidault, Georges Augustin (1899–1983), 89, 124, 127, 129, 245, 247, 251, 253, 291, 350, 352, 367
Bilbao, 4, 47, 99, 117–18, 120, 122, 125, 136–7, 139–40, 146, 149–56, 158, 175, 210, 308, 346–7, 350
Billoux, François (*député*, Bouches-du-Rhône; 1903–1978), 75
Biriatou (Basses-Pyrénées), 45
Biscay, Bay of, 163

Bizerta, 227
Black Sea, 164, 258, 319, 380
Blanc, François-Edmond, 145
Blanc, Jean-Marcel (Air France), 136, 138
Blaye (Gironde), 141
Bloch, France (Fr. Resistance heroine, 1913–1943), 246
Bloch, Jean-Richard (1884–1947), 42, 60, 130, 246, 286, 295, 325
Bloud & Gay (Paris bookshop), 252
Blum, Léon (1872–1950), 22, 25–8, 30, 32, 37, 39–40, 43, 47, 53, 61–3, 71, 74–5, 77, 90, 92, 95, 111, 131, 134, 171, 189–91, 200, 205–6, 209, 217, 221–2, 226, 232–4, 236–8, 240, 243, 246, 251, 253, 256, 292–3, 297–9, 308, 311, 318, 327, 341, 356, 365–6, 384–5
  and Congress of Tours, 1
  forms first Cabinet, 3
  physically assaulted, 4
  receives plea from Giral, 9
  visits London, 9, 18
  dispatches French arms, 10
  suspends French arms, 10–11
  and fall of the Giral government, 11
  follows counsel of Cot, 18
  and pacifism, 24, 105
  conceals operations, 33–34
  implements Cot formula, 35
  fails to secure Br. support, 36
  turns to Delbos-Daladier formula, 38, 55
  supports neutrality policy, 57
  and the Radicals, 58–59
  agrees to allow volunteers to leave, 72
  restrictions on volunteers, 73
  refuses to confer belligerency on either camp, 86
  invokes Morocco treaty (1912), 98
  replaced by Chautemps, 148
  visited by Prieto, 155
  forms second Cabinet, 176
  secretly authorizes passage of Fr. arms, 177
  and the Sp. gold, 196
  and Munich, 202, 373
  and Radical Congress in Marseilles, 204
  and pyrites, 211
  cries 'Still time to save the Rep.,' 213
  admits the game is lost, 214–15
  denounces mission of Bérard, 218
  denounces recognition of Franco, 223

denounces appointment of Pétain, 224
receives letter from Marty, 257
and Zyromski, 263
and Rosenfeld, 283
and Boris, 295, 305
Blun, Georges (journalist), 99
Bodin, Louis (historian), 236, 301
Bohemia, 231
Bois, Élie-Joseph (journalist), 246
Boissarie, Maître, 262
Bolaños, Major (Sp. military attaché), 95–6, 339
Bolín Bidwell, Luis (1897–1969), 305, 308, 323, 347–9
Bolivia, 335
Bolloten, Burnett (1909–1987), 111, 323
Boncour, Joseph Paul (1873–1972), 176–7, 200, 297
Bonis (anti-fascist militant), 320
Bonjean, René (chargé d'affaires, Madrid), 187, 325
Bonnard, Abel (1883–1968), 246, 298
Bonnet, Georges (1889–1973), 188, 199, 212, 215, 217–18, 222, 292, 295, 366, 377
Borbón, Don Carlos María Isidro de (1788–1855), 346
Borbón y Battenberg, Don Jaime de; Duke of Segovia (1908–1975), 382
Borbón y Battenberg, Don Juan de; Count of Barcelona (1913–1993), 382
Borchgrave, Baron Jacques de (Belg. diplomat), 107
Bordeaux, 44, 124, 126, 141, 179–80, 188, 245, 248, 252, 254, 256, 260–1, 296, 307, 350, 354
Bordeaux, Henry Camille (Académie Fr.; 1870–1963), 237, 284, 287, 289
Boris, Georges (1888–1960), 101, 149, 154, 246, 292, 294–5, 305, 341, 350
Bos, Charles du (1882–1939), 291, 350
Boschot, Adolphe (1871–1955), 302
Bosost (Lerida), 138
Botto, Georges (journalist), 246
Bouja (Gerona), 139
Boulineau (escort), 138
Bourdet, Claude (1909–1996), 124, 247, 350
Bourg-Madame (Pyrénées-Orientales), 73
Bourniquel, Paul (journalist), 242
Bousquet, René (1909–1993), 261

Bouyer, Raymond (journalist), 293
Bowers, Claude G. (1878–1958), 44
Boyer, Jean-Pul (historian), 300
Bracke, Georges (Alexandre-Marie Desrousseaux; *député*, Lille; 1861–1955), 1, 40–2, 53, 58, 60–1, 67, 192–3, 240, 283, 318, 337
Branting, Senator Karl-Hjalmar (1860–1925), 321
Brasillach, Robert (1909–1945), 132, 244, 247, 258, 287, 289, 303, 353
Braun, Max (publisher), 300, 386
Brazil, 83, 194, 335
Brecht, Bertholt (1898–1956), 135
Bremen, 81
Brest, 141, 304
Breton, André (1896–1966), 336
Briand, Aristide (1862–1932), 200, 235
Brigade Malraux, 249
Brighton, 124
Brinon, Fernand de (1885–1947), 247, 290
Brisson, Pierre (1896–1964), 247, 287
British Intelligence Service, 96, 247
British Labour Party, 61, 70–1
Brossolette, Pierre (1903–1944), 251
Brouckère, Louis de (1870–1951), 41, 52
Bourgués, Lucien (journalist), 83, 98, 206, 217
Brousse, Georges (journalist), 242
Broz, Josip (1892–1980) *Tito
Brunswick Institute of Technology, 365
Brussels (*qua* city), 52, 73, 251, 364
Brutus (Fr. Resistance network), 253
Bruyker, Suzanne de (wife of Otto Abetz), 256
Bucard, Marcel (1895–1946), 2
Bucharest, 106
Budapest, 307
Buenos Aires, 86, 335
Buisson, Ferdinand (journalist), 292, 294
Bukharin, Nikolai Ivanovich (1888–1938), 256
Bulgaria, 164, 343
Bullitt, William Christian (1891–1967), 77, 83, 188, 327
Bunau-Varilla, Guy, 248
Bunau-Varilla, Maurice (1856–1944), 241, 248, 282
Burat, peak of (Haute-Garonne), 138
Buré, Émile (1876–1952), 33, 40, 58, 97, 100, 106, 110, 145, 153, 158–9, 167,

169, 175, 180–1, 197, 201, 204–7, 212, 218, 224, 227, 237, 242, 248, 284, 292
Burgalays (Haute-Garonne), 138
Burgos (*qua* city), 50, 94, 123, 129, 133, 139, 142, 170, 187, 203, 205, 218–19, 221, 223, 308, 322, 360, 367

La Cabana (Lérida), 138
Cabanellas y Ferrar, General San Miguel (1862–1938), 16, 308, 322
Cáceres, 369
Cachin, Marcel (Senator, Seine; 1869–1958), 1, 26, 37, 90, 132, 146, 202, 248, 283
Cadaujac (Gironde), 126
Cádiz, 3, 81, 113, 177, 369
Cagoulards, 141, 344
Les Cahiers Politiques, 252
Cahiers franco-allemands, 256
Caillaux, Joseph (Senator, Sarthe) (1863–1944), 41, 293, 295
Calderón, Fonte, né Juan Pedro Luna, 305
Calvo Sotelo, José (1893–1936), 4
Cambon, Jules (1845–1935), 261
Cambon, Paul (1843–1924), 284
Cambrils (Tarragona), 384
Camel, François (*député*, Ariège; 1893–1941), 58
Camelots du Roi, 2, 4
Camprodón (Gerona), 109
Camps, José (Sp. Nationalist agent), 139
Camus, Albert (1913–1959), 240, 247, 336
Canada, 2, 252
Cañada-Hermosa, Marquis de, 215
Canal du Midi, 188
Canarias (Nationalist cruiser), 174
Canaris, Admiral Wilhelm (1887–1945), 3, 309, 369
Canary Islands, 162
Candiani, Clara (journalist), 73, 330
Candide (Paris weekly), 18, 25, 43, 51, 251, 289, 291, 294
Canfranc (Huesca), 45–6
Cannes, 245
Cap Falcon (French cargo ship), 358
Caporetto, Battle of (1917), 373
Carbuccia, Horace de (1891–1975), 145, 245, 247–9
Carcassonne, 138, 244, 261, 317
Cárdenas y Rodríguez de Rivas, Juan Francisco (1881–1966), 19

Cardiff, 124
Cardozo, Harold (journalist), 119
Caret, Jean (journalist), 123, 349
Carmaux, 309
Carmen (French yacht), 140, 355
Carrascal (Navarre), 107
Carreri (International Brigader), 384
Carrero Blanco, Admiral Luis (1903–1973), 355, 385
Carro, Padre Venancio D. (Sp. author), 351
Cartagena, 96, 192, 358
Cartel des Gauches, 1, 202, 292
Casado Lopez, Colonel Segismundo (1893–1968), 225, 230
Casares Quiroga, Santiago (1884–1950), 4, 53
Cassou, Jean (1897–1986), 248, 253, 262, 295
Castagnez, *député* de Castellanza, General, 302
Castelnau, General Édouard de Curières de (1851–1943), 157, 284
Castillo, Cristóbal del (Sp. diplomat), 19
Castillo, Lieutenant José (1901–1936), 4, 48
Castillon-en-Couserans (Ariège), 139
Castro, Américo (1885–1972), 49, 321
Catalonia, 45–8, 73, 80, 91, 136–7, 147, 177, 183, 186, 188, 196, 206, 208, 213–14, 233, 327, 330, 333, 358, 362, 366, 370, 375, 377, 379
Cato the Elder (234–149 BC), 252
Centre de propagande d'Action latine et d'Union méditerranéenne, 298
Cerbère (Pyrénées-Orientales), 47, 62, 72–4, 109, 137, 139, 184, 186–7, 307
Cerdagne, 181, 185, 203
Céret (Pyrénées-Orientales), 109
Cerruti, Vittorio (1881–1961), 77
Cervantes (Republican light cruiser), 174, 364
Ce Soir (Paris daily), 117, 213, 246, 259–60, 262, 281, 286, 293, 346, 348, 354
Ceuta, 18, 23, 52, 99, 162
Ceva, Major, 107
Cévennes, 298
Chamberlain, Sir Austen Joseph (1863–1937), 38
Chamberlain, Neville (1869–1940), 156, 171, 180, 182, 190–1, 199–200, 206, 209, 220–1, 240, 376–8

and Anglo-Italian Agreement of 1938, 182
visits Hitler in Bavaria, 200
Chambrun, Charles de Pineton, Count (1873–1952), 322
Chamson, André Louis Jules [*Lauter*] (1900–1983), 60, 135, 249, 294–5, 325, 363
Chapon, Richard (journalist), 299
Charandeau, Colonel, 255
Charentier, Gauthier (Bordeaux merchant), 63
Charlemagne (742–814), 168, 363
Chastenet, Jacques (journalist), 286, 302
Châteauroux, 105
Chatfield, Admiral of the Fleet Sir Alfred Ernle Montacute [later 1st Baron] (1873–1967), 310
Châtillon, Fort de (Montrouge), 247, 252
Chaumeix, André (Académie Fr.), 287, 289
Chautemps, Camille (1885–1963), 148, 170, 174, 176, 199, 202, 209, 232, 234, 286, 297, 358, 365
Chaveriat (Minister Plenipotentiary of Political and Commercial Affairs), 381
Chaves Nogales, Manuel (1897–1944), 152–3, 168, 188, 196–8, 204, 206–7, 215, 249, 297, 368
Chesterfield, Philip Dormer Stanhope, 4th Earl (1694–1773), 351
Chetwode, Field Marshal Sir Philip Walhouse [later 1st Baron] (1869–1950), 374
Chiappe, Ange (Prefect, Basses-Pyrénées), 382
Chile, 334
Chilton, Sir Henry Getty (1877–1954), 170
China, 159, 183, 194
Chioula, col de (Ariège), 186
Churchill, [later Sir] Winston Spenser (1874–1965), 116, 151, 172, 386
Ciano di Cortellazzo, Count Galeazzo (1903–1944), 55, 195, 212
Cier-de-Luchon (Haute-Garonne), 138
Cierp (Haute-Garonne), 138
Cierva y Hoces, Ricardo de la (1926–), 348
Cisneros, General Ignacio Hidalgo de (1896–1966), 377
Citrine, Sir Walter McLennan [later 1st Baron] (1887–1983), 326
Clair, René (1898–1981), 336

Claire, Lieutenant-Colonel Prosper Camille, 110
Clairvaux, 260
Claridad (Madrid), 41
Claudel, Paul (1868–1955), 125, 132, 291
Clavaud, Jean (publisher), 241
Clemenceau, Georges (1841–1929), 248, 257, 288, 292
Cléon (journalist), 34, 204
Clermont-Ferrand, 241, 251
Clerc, Captain, 228
Clerk, Sir George (1874–1951), 265
CNE (*Pro Movimiento Nacional*), 142
Cochin, F. (journalist), 129, 352
Colera (Gerona), 72, 74
Collonges (Ain), 380
Colodny, Robert Garland (1915–1997), 331
Colomb, Pierre (*député*, Vienne), 230
COMAC Resistance team, 252
Combat (Paris monthly), 258, 289
Combat (Resistance network), 245, 247, 259, 303, 336
Comintern, 10, 34, 111, 131, 251, 256–7, 260, 319, 323, 328, 334, 339
Comité Amsterdam-Pleyel, 2
Comité d'action socialiste pour l'Espagne (CASPE), 293
Comité d'Épuration de l'Édition, 252
Comité de vigilance des intellectuels antifascistes, 2, 72, 135
Comité d'organisation du Rassemblement populaire, 2
Comité France-Allemagne, 247, 253, 290, 301
Comité international d'aide à l'Espagne républicaine, 325
Comité international d'aide au peuple espagnol, 39
Comité national catholique de secours aux réfugiés d'Espagne, 350
Comité national d'Entente contre la Guerre, 143
Comité pour la paix civile et religieuse en Espagne, 351
Comité secret d'Action révolutionnaire (CSAR), 143
Comités des Forges et des Houillères, 282, 286, 290, 301
Comminges (Haute-Garonne), 46
Companys i Jover, Lluís (1883–1940), 74, 130

Compère-Morel (journalist), 215
Concordat of 1851, 129
La Concorde (Paris fortnightly), 39
Condé, Louis de (Fr. volunteer for Franco), 344
Condor Legion *Germany
Confédération générale du travail (CGT), 293
Confédération française des travailleurs chrétiens (CFTC), 244
Confédération nationale du Patronat français, 290
Congrès de Royan (1938), 24
Congrès de Tours (1920), 1
Corbin, Charles (1882–1970), 101, 362
Corman, Mathieu (journalist), 117
Cornez, Georges (pilot), 109
El Correo Español (Bilbao), 210
Il Corriere della Sera (Milan), 182
Corsica, 208–9, 284
Cortes españolas, 1, 15, 95, 222, 309, 375
Costa Rica, 86
Cot, Pierre (1895–1875), 9, 11, 18, 30, 33, 35, 38, 58, 63, 71, 186, 188, 200, 223, 295, 380
Cotnareanu, Yvonne, 286
Coty, François Spoturno (1874–1934), 2, 284–6, 292,
Coulondre, Robert (1885–1959), 205
Court, J. Félicien (journalist), 13
Cowan (aide to Sir Philip Chetwode), 374
Cowley, Malcolm (1898–1989), 354
Cranborne, Robert Cecil, Lord (1893–1972), 37, 367
Cristeros (Mexico), 123
La Croix (Paris daily), 122–3, 127–8, 241, 290, 332, 350
Croix de Feu, 2, 110, 254, 283, 303, 357, 383 *Mouvement social français des Croix de Feu
Crozier, Brian (1918–), 352, 374
Cruz Marín, A. (Republican Consul-General in Paris), 19
Cruzel, Julien (Mayor of Cerbère), 74, 109
Cruz y Raya (Madrid), 353
Cuba, 329
Cudenet, Gabriel (1894–1948), 42, 52, 80, 325
Cuvillier, Professor Armand (1887–1973), 325
Cyrano (journalist), 120

Cyrenaica, 112
Czechoslovakia, 50, 105–6, 194–5, 199–200, 209, 214, 255, 328, 343, 372

Daguerre, Pierre (Sub-Prefect, Basses-Pyrénées), 382
Daily Express (London), 117, 121, 285, 300, 348, 377
Daily Herald (London), 300
Daily Mail: Continental Edition (Paris), 300
Daily Mirror (London), 300
Daily Sketch (London), 300
Daily Telegraph (London), 92, 300, 348, 362
Daladier, Édouard (1884–1970), 2, 3, 9, 11, 33, 38, 55, 57, 148, 156, 186–9, 203, 212–13, 215, 217, 232, 236, 238, 253, 282, 286, 293, 297–8, 327, 384–5
 appointed Premier, 182
 and Munich, 199, 210
 snubbed by Franco, 222
 receives vote of confidence, 223
 praised by Blum, 373
Dakar, 381
Daniel-Rops (journalist), 291
Danzig, 14, 201
Darlan, Admiral François (1881–1942), 11, 210, 310
Daudet, Léon (1867–1942), 23, 25, 49, 51, 145, 154, 198, 249, 257, 287, 321
Dax, Bishop of *Mathieu
Déat, Marcel (1894–1955), 201, 233, 241–2, 249–50, 302
Death Battalion (Barcelona), 354
De Graaf, Admiral (Royal Netherlands Navy), 108
Delaprée, Louis (1902–1936), 130, 285, 302
Delarbre, Louis Raymond, 109
Delassale, Captain Gaston, 227
Delbos, Yvon (1885–1956), 9–11, 21, 26, 32–3, 38–9, 46, 55, 57–8, 62, 66, 88–91, 120, 155, 171, 190, 242, 297, 310, 324, 341
 receives message from Araquistáin, 342
 counsels cautious policy, 10, 21, 34
 upholds the rights of the Spanish government, 15
 submits plan for 'Gentlemen's Agreement,' 89
 defends Pertinax, 145
 presides at Nyon Conference, 164

out of office, returns to *La Dépêche*, 209
Delebecque, Jacques (journalist), 178, 195
Deleplanque, Roger (journalist), 39–40
Delest, Joseph (journalist), 326
Delmer, Sefton F. (1890–1944), 285
Deloncle, Eugène (Cagoule), 143
Delperrie de Bayac, Jacques (author), 329
De Munich à Vichy, 255
Denain, General Victor (1880–1952), 29
Denmark, 343
Denville, Alfred (1876–1955), 77
La Dépêche (Toulouse daily), 13–14, 16, 20–1, 24–9, 32–4, 39, 42, 44–8, 50, 52–4, 58, 60–3, 65, 68–9, 71–4, 79– 83, 86, 89, 91–2, 94–5, 99–100, 102, 112, 114–15, 118, 121, 130, 141, 143, 144–8, 151–3, 155–6, 158, 160, 166, 168–9, 172–3, 176, 178–9, 183–6, 190, 196–8, 200, 204, 206–7, 209, 213–15, 218–20, 222, 225, 230, 235, 239–40, 242, 244, 249, 251, 259, 261–2, 282, 286, 297–9, 308–10, 312–313, 329, 331, 346, 366–8, 375, 377
Desmartis (Fr. consul), 142
Deutsches Nachrichten Büro (Berlin), 354
Deutschland (German pocket battleship), 23, 52, 153, 154
Devau, Jean (journalist), 180
Devonshire (British destroyer), 211, 376
El Diario Vasco (San Sebastian), 211
Díaz Alejo, R. (journalist), 166, 309
Díaz Ramos, José (1896–1942), 194
Dibos Frères (South American suppliers), 160
Didkowski, Raoul (Prefect, Pyrénées-Orientales), 74
El Diluvio (Barcelona), 113
Dimitrov, Georgi (1882–1949), 132, 194, 257, 325
Dirksen, Herbert von (1882–1955), 376
Documents diplomatiques français, 310, 331
Dodd, William (1869–1940), 378
Dollfuss, Engelbert (1892–1934), 352
Domingo San Juan, Marcelino (1884–1939), 31, 205, 297, 377
Domingo (San Sebastian), 208, 210
Dominicans, 122, 291
Dominique, Pierre (1889–1973), 22–3, 42, 51, 69, 73, 90–2, 98, 149, 154, 156,

158, 167, 170, 192–4, 206, 212, 233, 250, 293, 332
Doriot, Jacques (1888–1845), 133–4, 141, 144, 186, 242, 246, 249–50, 252–4, 257, 288, 295, 302, 356–7
Doriotistes, 141, 250, 252
Dormoy, Marx (*député*, Allier; 1888–1941), 136, 141–3, 228, 309, 356
Doumer, President Paul (1857–1983), 141
Doumic, René (journalist), 289
Drancy, 250, 263
Drieu La Rochelle, Pierre (1893–1945), 134, 250, 287, 354
Drôme, 259
Du Bos, Charles (1882–1939), 291, 350
Dubois, Henri (journalist), 286–7
Duclos, Jacques (*député*, Montreuil; 1896–1975), 40–1, 60–1, 251, 258, 260, 325
Ducourau (Fr. consular agent), 142
Duhamel, Georges (1884–1966), 53, 295, 297
Duke of Parma, Prince François-Xavier de (1889–1977), 3
Dunkirk, 246, 259
Dumay, Henri (journalist), 292
Dumestre, Gaston (journalist), 45, 313
Dumont, Jules (comm. International Brigades), 383
Duployé, Père (journalist), 123
Dupré, Henri (Cagoule; ?-1951), 283
Dupuy, Mme. Paul (journalist), 284
Dupuy, Pierre (journalist), 282, 284, 302
Durango (Vizcaya), 118, 120–1, 346
Dutt, Rajani Palme [*Edward Eric*] (1896–1974), 95–6, 339

Eastern Cable (Bilbao), 308
L'Éclair (Montpellier daily), 203, 296
L'Éclaireur de Nice et du Sud-Est (Nice daily), 305
Est et Ouest, 256
Ebro River, 2, 22, 180–1, 189, 197, 209, 212, 386
Echevarrieta shipyards (Cádiz), 3
L'Écho de la France, 247
L'Écho de Paris (Paris daily), 18–19, 22, 25, 27, 29–31, 43, 47, 51, 59, 62, 64, 68, 70, 75, 77, 82–3, 93, 99, 105, 106, 114–16, 118–19, 132, 136, 141, 143–4, 153, 156, 161–2, 178, 201,

237, 243, 254, 260, 281–2, 284, 302, 319, 322, 341, 366
Les Échos (Paris daily), 18, 61, 81, 95, 214, 225, 227, 241, 290
Eden, Anthony (later Earl of Avon; 1897–1977), 9, 80, 84, 86, 150, 152, 171, 184, 295, 313, 362, 367
Edinburgh, 326
Edmond-Blanc, François (publisher), 145
L'Effort, 256
Egler, 160
Egypt, 164
Ehrenburg, Ilya Grigorevich (1891–1967), 135, 357
Eibar (Guipúzcoa), 118–20, 121, 347
Eisenberg, 255
Eldin (Inspector of Special Police), 109
El Salvador, 86
L'Émancipation Nationale (Paris weekly), 134, 138, 236, 250, 253, 257, 354
Ems dispatch (1870), 52
Enderiz, Ezechiel (journalist), 113
Entente cordiale (1904), 81
Entente des Gauches, 292
Entente, Petite- (Romania, Czechoslovakia, Yugoslavia: 1919), 101, 210, 234, 328
Épinois, Comte de l' (journalist), 290
L'Époque (Paris daily), 145, 156, 167, 173, 178, 180, 182, 185–6, 194, 201, 203, 209–10, 218, 220, 222–3, 225, 237, 241, 254, 284, 352
Épuration (1944–), 243–5, 247, 250, 251–4, 258–9
Ercoli, Ercole *Togliatti
L'Ère Nouvelle (Paris daily), 22–3, 38, 40–1, 49, 52, 58, 67, 69, 76, 86, 89, 95, 97, 115, 154, 164, 171, 178, 186, 210, 217, 220, 223, 292–3, 341
Escombreras (Murcia), 364
Esme, Jean d' [Viscount Jean Marie Henri d'Esmenard] (1894–1966), 320
L'Espagne Antifasciste (Paris fortnightly), 294
L'Espagne Nouvelle (Paris irregular), 294
L'Espagne Socialiste (Paris fortnightly), 263, 293
Espinosa de los Monteros y Bermejillo, General Eugenio (1880–1953), 64
L'Espoir, 133, 253
Esprit (Paris monthly), 122–3, 176, 259, 290, 303
Estelrich, Juan (publisher), 299, 350

Estepona (Malaga), 369
Estonia, 339, 343
Étampes-Mondésir (Seine-et-Oise), 30
L'Europe Nouvelle (Paris weekly), 197–8, 233, 242, 249, 257, 260, 295
Euzkadi *Basque Government
Euzko Deya (Paris monthly/weekly), 299, 351
Les Événements survenus en France de 1933 à 1945, 341
Evening News (London), 101
Evening Standard (London), 101, 213, 249
Excelsior (Paris daily), 81, 91, 98
L'Express du Midi (Toulouse daily), 101, 211, 223, 241, 248, 281, 284, 300, 341

Fabry, Colonel Jean (*député*, Seine; then Senator, Doubs; 1876–1968), 286
Fabrégues, Jean de (journalist), 289
Fajon, Étienne (1906–1991), 258
Falange, 144, 153, 198, 210, 331, 350, 352, 379, 382
Fal Conde, Manuel (1894–1975), 3, 309
Farinet, Émile (journalist), 39
Farnham (British cargo ship), 183
Faupel, Lieutenant-General Wilhelm (1873–1945), 92, 347
Faure, Élie (1873–1937), 325
Faure, Paul (1878–1960), 1, 24–5, 199–200, 244, 283
Fayard, Arthème (publisher), 289
Federación Anarquista Ibérica (FAI), 73
Fédération anarchiste française, 294
Fédération nationale catholique, 284, 303
Fédération nationale des étudiants d'Action française, 4
Fédération nationale de la Presse, 244
Fels, [Édouard Frisch], comte de (journalist), 290
Feltin, Mgr Maurice, Archbishop of Bordeaux (later Cardinal) (1883–1975), 124, 126, 252, 350
Ferdinand II, 'The Catholic' (1452–1516), 118
Fernández Peña (PCE envoy), 77
Féron-Vrau, Paul (journalist), 290
Ferrando, Commander José Luis (Nationalist Navy), 141
Ferrero, Guglielmo (1871–1942), 16, 53, 156, 169, 242, 295, 297
Ferry, Désiré (1886–1940), 288

Le Figaro (Paris daily), 19, 22–3, 31, 38, 49, 62, 70, 75, 77, 97, 101, 106–8, 112, 125, 127, 146, 152, 154, 157, 159, 169, 171, 178, 185, 187, 198, 201, 204, 206, 214, 217, 241, 246–7, 259–60, 286–7, 300, 332, 341
Figueras (Gerona), 109, 213, 218
Filliol, Jean (Cagoule), 344
Finland, 206, 343
Fischer, Louis (1896–1970), 331
Flandin, Pierre-Étienne (*député*, Yonne; 1889–1958), 177, 188–9, 201, 233, 288
Flatter, né Ferenc Munnich, Otto (political commissar), 384
La Flèche de Paris (Paris weekly/fortnightly), 233, 245
Flix Electrical (Barcelona), 96
Florence, 304
Foix (Ariège), 110, 186
Fongarnand (International Brigader), 374
Fontainebleau, 257
Fontanelle, Mgr, 124
Fontenay, Maurice (journalist), 161
Fort de Châtillon, 247, 252
Fort du Hâ (Gironde), 263
Fort du Portalet (Pyrénées-Atlantiques), 257
Les Fossoyeurs, 260
Fourques (Pyrénées-Orientales), 109
Français, voici la vérité, 254
France
  Air Ministry, 20, 36, 138
  Army, 11, 292, 309, 343
  Bank of France, 196
  Chambre des Députés (Palais Bourbon), 177, 251, 293, 309
  Deuxième Bureau, 229
  Garde Républicaine Mobile, 38
  General Staff, 200, 211, 361
  Ministry of Foreign Affairs (Quai d'Orsay), 38, 60, 105, 120, 140, 155, 177, 224, 227, 284, 286, 372
  Ministry of the Interior, 35, 38, 137, 147
  Ministry of Posts, Telegraphs and Telephones (PTT), 307
  Senate (Palais du Luxembourg), 9–11, 64, 189, 206, 225, 227, 233, 248, 261, 297, 305, 341, 383–4
  Sûreté Nationale, *Magny, 35, 74, 109, 141, 160, 316, 343
France-Amérique (New York), 248

France Combattante resistance network, 253
La France Continue, 252
France Navigation, 372
Franchet d'Esperey, Marshal Louis (1856–1942), 143
Francistes, 2
Franclieu, Colonel Henri de, 298
François I (1494–1547), 210, 315
François-Poncet, André (1887–1978), 309
Franco-Prussian War (1870–1871), 92, 220
Franco-Soviet Pact of Mutual Assistance (1935), 69, 189
Franco-Spanish Treaty (1912), 31
Franco-Spanish Treaty (1935), 10
Franc-Tireur, 336
Franco y Bahamonde, General Francisco (1892–1975), 4, 10–11, 14–15, 31–2, 43, 51–3, 71, 78, 80, 82–6, 89–90, 92–5, 97–101, 105–6, 108, 111–12, 115, 118, 120–3, 125, 127–9, 131–4, 137, 139–143, 145, 149, 151–3, 156–7, 160, 170–1, 174–6, 178, 180, 183–9, 192–8, 200, 203–5, 207–10, 213–17, 219–22, 225–6, 231, 236, 246, 252, 254, 260, 283, 290, 293, 307, 309, 311–12, 325, 327, 330–2, 335–6, 344–8, 353, 363–7, 369, 371, 374–7, 379–82
  the coup, 9
  receives Ital. and Ger. aid, 26–30
  receives Fr. aid, 63–4
  receives support from Laval, 64
  responds to Fr. volunteers for the Rep., 72
  orders destruction of Port-Bou, 74
  bids for Ital. volunteers, 77
  fails before Madrid, 79
  recognized by Axis, 81
  denies responsibility for Guernica, 119
  receives recognition from Vatican, 126
  attempts to blockade Basque ports, 150
  gives first reception to the foreign press, 150
  signs secret commercial protocol with Germany, 158
  forbids export of pyrites to France, 162–3
  captures Gijón, 167–8
  loses and recaptures Teruel, 173
  congratulates Hitler on Munich, 202
  launches offensive in Catalonia, 206
  takes Barcelona, 212
  receives Bérard, 218

receives Fr. and Brit. recognition, 223
appoints Lequerica ambassador to France, 224
receives Pétain, 227
enters Madrid, 230
Franco y Bahamonde, Ramón (1896–1938), 77, 79–80, 93
Frankfurter Zeitung, 197
Free French Forces, 246
French Communist Party, 1, 31, 39–40, 59–62, 67, 131, 248, 268, 372
French Foreign Legion, 72, 330
French Information Center (New York), 301
French North Africa, 22, 309
French Press Law, 236
French West Africa, 178
Fresnes, 252–3, 255
Fried, Eugen (1900–1943), 251
Front commun, 289, 385
Front de la Liberté, 144, 288
Front populaire de Combat, 199, 233
Front social Mouvement frontiste, 289
Frontières (Paris monthly), 288
Frossard, Henry, 261
Frossard, Ludovic-Oscar (*député*, Haute-Saône; 1889–1946), 1, 69, 176, 199, 202, 292
Frot, Eugène (journalist), 106, 233, 289
Fuenterrabía (Guipúzcoa), 142
Fumet, Stanislas (1896–1983), 124, 291, 350
Funck, Colonel [later General] Baron Hans von (1891–1979), 371

Gabet, Lieutenant-Colonel, 64
Gaikins, Leon Y. (Sov. diplomat), 266
Gaillac, Roger (Fr. pro-Rep. agent), 316
Galarza y Gogo, Ángel (Sp. Minister of the Interior), 212
Galerna (Nationalist armed trawler), 110, 151
Gallagher, O'Dowd (journalist), 285, 277
Galland, Major-General Adolf (1912–1996), 348
Gallimard, Gaston (journalist), 244, 295, 302
Gallo, Max (1932–), 367
Gambier, Brigadier-General, 187
Gamelin, General Maurice-Gustave (1872–1958), 177, 210, 253, 385

Gamero Cívico, Duke of (pro-Franco agent), 143
Gandia, 230
García de la Barga, Andrés (1888–1975), 34, 36, 251, 297
García Durán, Juan (1915–1986), 362
García Escámez, General Francisco (1893–1951), 361
García Oliver, José (1901–1980), 132
Garibaldi Battalion, 113
Garibaldi, Léon (journalist), 203
La Garonne (Toulouse daily), 168, 176, 181, 184–9, 193, 200, 202–3, 213, 215, 220, 222, 246, 262, 298, 311, 337, 370–1, 379
Garonne River, 49, 298
Garosci, Professor Aldo (1907–2000), 363, 372
Gascón, Antonio (publisher), 297
Gascony, Gulf of, 200
Gaudy, Georges (journalist), 75–6, 78, 332
Gaulle, General Charles de (1890–1970), 243, 245–8, 252, 254–5, 258
Gaxotte, Pierre (1895–1982), 25, 43, 133, 251, 258, 289
Gay, Francisque (1885–1963), 125, 251–2, 291, 350
Geneva (*qua* city), 70, 76, 90, 235, 289
*League of Nations
Genoa, 200
'Gentlemen's Agreement' *Anglo-Italian Agreements
George VI, King of the United Kingdom and Emperor of India (1895–1952), 245
Georges-Roux (historian), 326
Gerarchia (Milan), 197
La Gerbe, 247, 250
Germain, José (1884–1964), 302
Germany
  Abwehr, 3, 369, 383
  Condor Legion, 196, 346
  Foreign Ministry, 52, 98, 155, 163, 338, 369, 371
  General Staff, 99, 112, 114–15, 149, 200, 211, 234, 315, 361, 365
  Gestapo, 141, 229, 247–8, 251–4, 257, 261–2, 334, 356, 361
  Luftwaffe, 348
  National Socialist Party, 97
  Reichswehr, 93, 98

Wehrmacht, 11, 115, 323, 369
Wilhelmstrasse *Foreign Ministry
Gerona, 74, 109, 380
Gestapo *Germany
Geumann, Lucien (*Vidal*), 331
Gex (Ain), 380
Giamberardino, Admiral Oscar, 362
Gibel Zerjon (British cargo ship), 52
Gibraltar, 3, 18, 42, 51, 54, 100, 162, 194, 333, 369, 370
Gide, André (1869–1951), 130, 134, 243, 294–5, 304, 354
Gignoux, Claude-Joseph (journalist), 39, 57, 290
Gijón, 167–8, 173, 363
Gillet, Louis (1876–1943), 124, 284, 291
Gil Robles y Quiñones, José María (1898–1980), 63, 197
Giménez Caballero, Ernesto (1899–1988), 210
Giner de los Ríos, Francisco (1839–1915), 365
Il Giornale d'Italia (Rome), 26, 46
La Giovine Italia (Paris weekly), 299, 305
Giral y Pereira, José (1880–1962), 4, 23, 34, 53, 62, 90, 148
  sends message to Blum, 9, 18–19
  fails to secure French aid, 11–12
  resigns, 12
  and transition to Largo Caballero, 66
Giraud, General Jean Henri (1879–1949), 254
Girette, peak of (Ariège), 139
Giustizia e Libertà (Paris irregular), 299, 344
Goicoechea Cosculluela, Antonio (1876–1953), 3
Gomá y Tomás, Isidro Cardinal; Archbishop of Toledo (1869–1940), 122–3, 349, 352
Gómez-Jordana y Souza, General Count Francisco (1876–1944), 188, 193, 211, 219, 379, 382
González Peña, Ramón (1888–1952), 40, 349, 382
Göring, Reichsmarschall Hermann Wilhelm (1893–1946), 100, 116, 348
Gorky, Maksim [Aleksei Maksimovich Peshkov] (1868–1936), 295
Gouxa, ras (Abyssinia), 81
Grandi, Count Dino (1895–1988), 56–7, 80, 88, 92, 113, 232, 362

Granollers (Barcelona), 183
Greece, 162, 164, 343
Grenoble, 124, 296
La Griffe (Paris weekly), 80
Gringoire (Paris weekly), 132, 144–5, 200, 202, 222, 245, 248, 252, 261–2, 289, 294
Guadalajara, 112–13, 125, 146, 173, 187, 364
Guadalupe, Fort (Fuenterrabía), 142
Guadiana, 140
Guatemala, 86, 196
Guedde, Lothar (Ger. resident in Bilbao), 99
Guéhenno, Jean (journalist), 295
Guérin, André (journalist), 241
Guérin, Daniel (author), 130
Guernica (y Luno) (Vizcaya), 117–22, 124, 126, 147, 149, 151, 246, 346–50, 352
Guerra di Classe (Barcelona; 1904–1988), 113, 304
Guèze, Gaston (journalist), 14, 20, 22, 24–5, 37, 43, 49, 53, 57, 70, 74, 76, 83, 92, 121, 147, 203, 236, 298, 307
Guillén Álvarez, Jorge (1893–1984), 350
Guimera, Jean (Fr. pro-Franco agent), 110
Guimier, Pierre (journalist), 282
Guipúzcoa, 43, 45, 123, 139
Guise, Jean Pierre Clément Marie, Duke of (1874–1940), 198, 287, 298
Gyllenran, Captain (Swed. Navy), 108

Hadamard, Professor Jacques (1865–1963), 325
Hage, peak of (Haute-Garonne), 138
Hague Convention (1899), 85
Hague Convention (1907), 50, 71, 76, 169, 226, 313
Halifax, Edward Frederick Woods, 1st Earl of (1881–1959), 184
Hamburg, 26, 246, 334
Hamon, Augustin, 325
Hamsterley (British cargo ship), 150
Harcourt, Robert d' (1881–1965), 228, 302
Harmel, Maurice (journalist), 40, 42, 165
Haute-Garonne, 35–6, 38, 46, 108–10, 137–8, 160, 298–9, 317, 337
Haute-Pyrénées, 299
Hautes-Alpes, 252
Hearst Press, 300
Hedilla Larrey, Manuel (1902–1970), 153

Hegel, Georg Wilhelm Friedrich
    (1770–1831), 176
Helsey, Édouard (journalist), 200
Hemingway, Ernest (1898–1961), 135, 383
Hénaff, Senator Eugène (1904–1966), 50
Hendaye, 44–7, 63, 139–40, 142, 160, 170,
    194, 307, 382
Henderson, Sir Neville Meyrick
    (1882–1942), 152
Hennessy, Jean (journalist), 292
Henriot, Philippe (*député*, Gironde;
    1889–1944), 63, 252, 256–7, 261
Henry, Jules (1904–1969), 214, 218, 229
El Heraldo de Aragón (Saragossa), 137
El Heraldo de Madrid, 200
Hérault, 61
Herbette, Ambassador Jean (1978–1960),
    44, 75, 107, 140, 151, 170, 319, 359
Héricourt, Pierre (1895–1965), 109, 121,
    137, 139, 180, 252
Hernáez (anarchist), 137
Hernández, Miguel (1907–1942), 135
Hernández Tomás, Jesús (1907–1971), 148
Hérold-Paquis, Jean (1912–1945), 252
Herriot, Édouard (1872–1957), 2, 20, 69,
    124, 177, 200, 292–3, 295, 297, 302
Herrmann, Jean-Maurice (journalist),
    212–13, 243, 253, 326
Hervé, Gustav (journalist), 13, 58, 70, 154
Heussler, André (political commissar), 383
Heye, Captain (Kriegsmarine), 362
Hierro (Bilbao), 175
Hindenburg, Marshal Paul von
    Beneckendorff und von (1847–1934),
    176
Historia (Paris), 355
Hitler, Adolf (1889–1945), 25, 27, 61, 89,
    95, 101–2, 115, 154, 189, 195–8, 202,
    214, 252, 284, 290, 321, 333, 366
  and Banse, 365
  chooses Schacht, 340
  interviewed by Brinon, 247
  interviewed by Jouvenel, 253
  rages against Thomas and Heinrich Mann,
    242
  and support for him in France, 32, 45, 53,
    133, 201, 248, 250, 256
  and Morocco, 51
  and French neutrality proposal, 52
  and 'preventive counter-revolution', 79
  allegedly sends five divisions, 80
  and relations with Mussolini, 81, 240
  and recognition of Franco, 83, 153
  and volunteers for the Republic, 91
  and aid policy, 92–3, 97–8
  denies seeking territorial gains, 100
  and Czechoslovakia, 105–6, 322–3
  and capture of Bilbao, 155
  and Portugal, 194
  meets Chamberlain in Munich, 200
  and pact with Stalin, 241, 251, 257
  appoints Reichenau, 369
  and Belgian neutrality, 376
Hoche, General Lazare (1768–1797), 15
Hodgson, Sir Robert (1874–1956), 170
Holy Alliance, 64
Holy See *Vatican City
L'Homme Libre (Paris daily), 167, 170, 202,
    215, 257, 292
Honduras, 86
Hood (British battle-cruiser), 150
Hoog, Georges (journalist), 123–4, 291,
    350
Huesca, 107
Hudelle, Léon (journalist), 35, 87–9, 92–3,
    226, 298
Hungary, 244, 343
Huidobro, Vicente (1893–1948), 354
Hull, Cordell (1871–1955), 214, 337
L'Humanité (Paris daily), 13, 24, 26, 37, 40,
    53, 55–6, 59– 61, 63, 67–8, 75, 86,
    90, 92–4, 99, 105–8, 111, 113–14,
    117, 120, 134, 139, 141–2, 144, 146,
    152, 154–5, 160, 164, 168, 173, 177,
    182, 185, 187, 194, 202, 213–14, 219,
    224, 236, 241, 248, 251, 257, 260–1,
    281, 283, 293–4, 301, 336, 344, 346,
    355
L'Humanité clandestine (Paris), 241
Hutin, Jean (journalist), 43
Hyméréthée (French vessel), 64

Ibardín (Navarre), 313
Ibárruri Gómez, Dolores [*La Pasionaria*]
    (1895–1989), 62, 222
Iberia, 79, 115
Ibiza, 153–4
Ifni, 162
Île de Ré, 245, 255
L'Illustration (Paris weekly), 289
Imbert (police inspector), 140
L'Indépendant (Paris weekly), 24, 30

L'Indépendant (Perpignan daily), 242
Index of Forbidden Books, 288
Informaciones (Madrid), 200, 297
L'Information Financière, Économique et Politique (Paris daily), 290
Innitzer, Theodor Cardinal, Archbishop of Vienna (1875–1955), 128
Inquisition, 58
Institución Libre de Enseñanza, 176
Inter-American Conference for the Maintenance of Peace, Special (Buenos Aires, 1936), 86
International
  Second (Paris, 1889), 283
  Third (Moscow, 1919), 1, 2, 59, 146, 230, 259, 294
  Fourth (Trotsky in exile, 1938), 294, 304
International Brigades, 75, 106–7, 151, 197, 205, 208, 227–9, 257, 305
International Court of Justice (Tribunal of The Hague), 49
Internationale ouvrière socialiste (IOS), 39, 41, 58
International Red Help *Secours Rouge International
L'Intransigeant (Paris daily), 16, 39, 56, 241, 281–2, 285–6, 302, 318
Ireland, 343, 374
Irish Sinn Feiners, 123
Irigoyen, Antonio José (Sp. anarchist agent), 138
Irujo y Ollo, Manuel de (1891–1981), 118, 346
Irun (Guipúzcoa), 43–5, 47, 63, 72, 105, 119, 139, 141–2, 307, 313, 319, 347
Isorni, Jacques (barrister; 1911–1995), 247
Iswolsky, Hélène (1896–1975), 350
Italcable (Malaga), 308
Italian Socialist Party, 256, 299
Italy,
  Bersaglieri, 208
  Black Shirt (Camicia Nera) Division, 114
  Foreign Ministry (Palazzo Chigi), 163
  Legionnaires, 182, 218
  Presidential Palace (Palazzo Venezia), 116
Itter, Schloss (Austria), 253, 255
Izvestia (Moscow), 146, 335

Jackson, Gabriel (historian; 1921–), 309
Jacob, Madeleine (1896–1985), 253

Jaime Primero (Republican battleship), 192, 264
Japan, 66, 159, 334, 364
Jaurès, Jean (1859–1914), 46, 248, 283, 297, 309
Jéramec, Colette, 250
Je Suis Partout (Paris weekly), 244, 246–7, 251–2, 289
Jesuits, 291
La Jeune République (Paris weekly), 123, 291
Jeunesses patriotes *Parti national populaire
Jéze, Gaston (1869–1953), 21, 220–1, 293, 297
Jézéquel, Pastor J., 325
Jiménez, Mathilde (mistress of Juan March), 63
Jiménez de Asúa, Luis (1889–1970), 312
John XXIII, Pope [Angelo Giuseppe Roncalli] (1881–1963), 303
Johnson, Dr Samuel (1709–1784), 351
Jolinon, J., 325
Joliot-Curie, Professor Frédéric (1900–1958), 96
Jordana, Count *Gómez-Jordana
José Luis Diez (Spanish Republican destroyer), 355
Joubert, Vice-Admiral H., 126
Jouhaux, Léon (1879–1954), 25, 40, 56, 58, 71, 253, 290, 293, 297
Le Jour (Paris daily), 22, 27, 43, 56, 62, 75, 77, 83, 106–7, 119, 136, 138, 143–4, 168, 178, 183, 185, 187, 195–6, 211–12, 217, 223, 237, 241, 243, 281–4, 301, 351, 366, 375
Jourdain, Francis (1876–1958), 325
Le Jour-L'Écho de Paris (Paris daily), 243
Le Journal (Paris daily), 22, 26, 56, 62, 75, 89, 99, 105–6, 110, 123, 143, 147, 152–4, 184–5, 195, 200–1, 210–11, 213, 215, 222–3, 225, 237, 241, 281–2, 285, 341, 372
Le Journal des Débats Politiques et Littéraires (Paris daily), 24, 83,154, 177, 282, 286
Le Journal des Finances (Paris weekly), 174, 290
Le Journal de Toulouse (Toulouse weekly), 20, 37, 62, 120, 184, 187, 198, 298
Le Journal Officiel de la République Française (Paris daily), 177
La Journée Industrielle (Paris daily), 13–14, 22, 39, 52, 57, 115, 154, 290

Jouvenel, Bertrand de (1903–1987), 236, 253, 302, 385
Jover, Major (Republican Army), 107
Juin 36 (Paris fortnightly), 293
La Junquera (Gerona), 73
Jura, 38
Juventud (Barcelona/Madrid), 81

Kagan, Samuel B., 56–7, 68, 323
Kamerun (German cargo ship), 52, 56
Kaminski, Hans-Erich (1899–1963), 146
Kant, Immanuel (1724–1804), 176
Karlsruhe, 176
Katz, Otto [*André Simone*], 299, 328, 372
Kayser, Jacques (1900–1963), 295, 325
Kennedy, Joseph Patrick (1888–1969), 221, 378
Kérillis, Henri de (*député*, Seine ; 1889–1958), 18, 27, 31, 50, 59, 62, 64–5, 79, 84, 93–5, 136, 144–5, 156, 167, 178, 180, 183, 188, 194–5, 201–2, 206, 210, 214, 223, 237, 242–3, 254, 261, 284, 303, 361
Kindelán y Duany, General Alfredo (1879–1962), 43, 180
KL-Buchenwald, 247, 253, 257
KL-Dachau, 253, 263
KL-Neuengamme, 247, 253
KL-Ravensbrück, 253
KL-Sachsenhausen, 247, 257
Klan resistance network, 255
Klotz, Helmuth (1894–1943), 361
Koestler, Arthur (1905–1983), 299, 305, 374
Koltsov, Mikhail (1898–1942?), 354, 357
Krause, Karl Christian Friedrich (1781–1832), 176
Krivitsky, General Walter G. (1899–1941), 34, 68, 77, 308, 328, 356
Kronstadt, 148, 356

Labonne, Eirik (1888–1971), 170, 205, 374
La Batut, Guy de, 325
Lacombe, Olivier (1904–2001), 124, 350
Lacore, Suzanne (1875–1975), 235, 385
Lacroix, Maurice (1893–1989), 350
La Fayette, Marie Joseph Marquis de (1757–1834), 71
Lafitte, Pierre (journalist), 284
La Fontaine, Jean de (1621–1695), 222
Lagarde (Toulouse publisher), 203

Lagrange, Léo (*député*, Nord; 1900–1940), 97
Lalande (journalist), 35, 316
Lalou, René (1889–1960), 325
Lamartine, Alphonse Marie Louis de (1790–1869), 152, 155
Lambert, Abbé, Mayor of Oran, 363
Lambressat (Fr. agent), 142
Lamour, Philippe (journalist), 212
Lamouroux (French arms-dealer), 343
Lange, Captain (Kriegsmarine), 362
Langevin, Professor Paul (1872–1946), 2, 60, 80, 86, 96–7, 325
Langenfeld, 386
Lapeyre, Aristide (journalist), 294
Larache, 162
Largo Caballero, Francisco, 1, 41, 53, 61, 70, 89–90, 92, 97, 100, 107, 116, 130, 132, 212–13, 345
  succeeds Giral, 66
  replaced by Negrín, 148
La Rocque, Lieutenant-Colonel François de (1886–1946), 64, 144, 223, 243, 254–5, 262, 283, 302–3
Larralde, R. (journalist), 200
Las Haras, Commander José Miguel (Nationalist Navy), 141
La Souchère, Hélène de (1916–), 127
Latécoère factory (Toulouse), 137
Latour-de-Carol (Pyrénées-Orientales), 47
Latran, Agreement (1929), 303
Lattre de Tassigny, General Jean de (1889–1952), 11
Latvia, 343
Lauter *Chamson
Lauzanne, Stéphane (1874–1958), 116, 255
Laval, Pierre (1883–1945), 59, 64, 189, 206, 249, 252, 259, 261, 327, 376
Lazareff, Pierre (1907–1972), 242, 255
League of Nations, 2, 3, 15, 19, 49, 69, 82, 100, 116, 132, 149, 152, 154, 159, 163–4, 167, 227, 234, 293, 337, 347
Lebas, Jean-Baptiste (*député*, Nord), 178
Lebrun, Albert François (1871–1950), 179, 230, 233, 236
Ledré, Charles (historian), 298
Legay, Kléber (Secretary, UGT), 228
Legendre, Maurice (journalist), 189, 370
Légion Française des Combattants, 252
Le Grix, François (journalist), 14, 285, 289
Legru, André (journalist), 330

Lehmann, Lucien (journalist), 198
Leipzig (German cruiser), 359
Lejeune, Albert (1915–1944), 255
Lémery, Joseph Eugène Henry (Senator, Martinique), 24, 30, 187, 193, 288, 303
Le Mondèque, Marc (journalist), 291
Lenglois, Paul (journalist), 63
Lenin, Vladimir Ilyich (1870–1924), 1, 14, 67, 91, 217, 230, 294, 304, 337
Lequerica y Erquiza, José Félix de (1891–1963), 224
Lequesne, Geneviève, 261
Lérida, 74, 181, 330, 343
Leroux, André [*né* Angelo Tasca] (1892–1960), 13, 51, 56, 79–82, 97–8, 100–1, 256, 333
Lerroux García, Alejandro (1864–1949), 1
Lespine, Victor (journalist), 62, 203, 298
Levant, 82
Lézignan-Corbières (Aude), 317
Libertad (Republican cruiser), 174
Le Libertaire (Paris weekly), 257, 294
La Liberté (Paris daily), 144, 154, 161, 184, 186, 257, 288
La Liberté du Sud-Ouest (Bordeaux daily), 296
Libya, 173
Licarlan (Basses-Pyrénées), 313
Liddell Hart, Captain Sir Basil Henry (1895–1970), 323
Life (New York), 296, 361
L' Indépendant (Perpignan daily), 242, 288, 299
Ligue d'Action Française, 4
Ligue des Droits de l'Homme, 2, 86, 201, 244, 346
Ligue International des Amis des Basques, 124
Lille, 128, 296–7
Limoges, 241, 296
Limoux (Aude)
Linares, Marquis de [*Antonio Martín Montis*], 141
Lincoln, Abraham (1809–1865), 15, 128, 235
Lincoln Brigade, 92 *International Brigades
Lineas Aéreas Postales Españoles (LAPE), 138, 307
Lisbon, 56, 108, 110, 307, 311, 323
   Cardinal Archbishop of, 129
Líster Rodríguez, Colonel [later General]
   Enrique Jesús Forján (1907–1994), 212, 225, 377
Lithuania, 231, 343
Litvinov, Maksim Maksimovich (1876–1951), 163, 325, 335
Llansa (Gerona), 137
Llauro (Pyrénées-Orientales), 109
Llivia (Pyrénées-Orientales) *Lérida
Lloyd George, David (later 1st Earl of Dwyfor; 1863–1945), 156, 171
Locarno Pact (1925), 10, 58, 66, 234–5
Logroño, 180–1
Loire River, 140, 320
Loi sur la liberté de la presse (1881), 236
London (*qua* city), 9, 18, 48, 95, 122, 170, 246, 248–9, 254–5, 299, 355
London Agreement (1936), 113, 203–4
London Committee on Nonintervention, 56, 58, 68–70, 82, 84, 88, 90, 94, 106, 108, 111, 157, 159, 164, 168–9, 183, 215, 232, 234, 369
Long Island, N.Y., 254
Longo, Luigi (1900–1980), 345
Longuet, Jean (*député*, Seine; 1876–1938), 1, 37, 41, 50, 86, 283, 293, 326
Loos (Nord), 386
Lopera (Jaén), 227
Lot, 249
Lot-et-Garonne, 263
Loucheur, Louis (journalist; 1872–1931), 283
Louis XVIII (1755–1824), 49
Louis-Dreyfus, Louis (Senator, Alpes-Maritimes ; 1867–1940), 286
Luart, Countess du, 361
Luchaire, Jean (1901–1946), 256
Ludendorff, General Erich von (1865–1937), 98, 108, 176
Lufthansa, 110
La Lumière (Paris weekly), 101, 149, 154, 246, 294–5
Lunacharski, Anatoli Vasilievitch (1875–1933), 308
Lunn, Colonel Christian D. O. (Danish Army), 108, 136, 138, 189
Luque, José, Marquis de, 142
Luque, Romero de (1909–?), 142
Luxembourg, 227
Luxemburg, 261
Lyautey, Marshal Louis Hubert Gonzalve (1854–1934), 178

Lyon, 105, 241, 244–5, 247, 253, 258–60
Lyon Républicain (daily), 255, 296

MacDonald, James Ramsey (1866–1837), 200
MacGregor (British cargo ship), 150
Machado y Ruiz, Antonio (1875–1939), 135
Mackensen, Marshal August von (1849–1945), 195
Mackensen, Hans Georg von (1883–1947), 347
Madariaga y Rojo, Salvador de (1886–1978), 159, 214, 222, 295, 297
Madaule, Jacques (1898–1993), 124, 350
Madrid (*qua* city), 4, 10, 23, 26–7, 34, 80, 113, 130, 132, 135, 167, 193, 224, 306, 308, 324, 340, 352, 355
  French Embassy, 64, 106, 355
  French Lycée, 64
  University of, 48
Magdalena (French cargo ship), 358
Maginot Line, 234, 276
Magny, Charles (Sûreté Nationale), 35–6, 64, 137, 316
Mahon (Minorque), 50
Majorca, 114, 128, 132, 154, 161, 209, 302
Malaga, 4, 105–6, 108, 114–15, 142, 146, 305, 308, 342
Malatesta, Errico (1853–1932), 304
Malraux, André (1901–1976), 42, 97, 133, 135, 239, 243, 245, 250, 295, 304, 353
Malraux brigade, 249
Malvy, Jean-Louis (*député*, Lot; 1875–1949), 10
Manchester Guardian, 21, 26–7, 284, 300, 313
Manchuria, 234
Mancini, General (Italian Army), 142
Mancisidor, José (1895–1956), 354
Mandel, Georges (*député*, Gironde; 1885–1944), 199, 257, 285
Manevy, Raymond (historian), 292, 301, 385
Mann, Heinrich (publisher; 1871–1950), 80, 114, 242, 297, 300, 386
Mann, Thomas (1875–1955), 130, 239, 295, 297
Manresa, 212
Mansuy (Vichy Milice), 257
Marañón y Posadillo, Dr Gregorio (1887–1960), 168, 176

Mar Caspio (Republican ship), 110
Marcassin, Maurice (Fr. consul in Valencia), 107
Marcel, Gabriel (1889–1973), 127, 291, 350
March Ordinas, Juan (1884–1962), 63
Maret, François (author), 128, 210, 351–2, 376
Marianne (Paris weekly), 23, 53, 69, 295, 314, 385
Marienden, 114
Marignac (Haute-Garone), 138
Marin, Louis (*député*, Meurthe-et-Moselle; 1871–1960), 233
Marinello, Juan (1898–1977), 354
Marinha Grande (Leiria), 321
Marion, Paul (1899–1954), 154, 184, 256–7
Maritain, Jacques (1882–1973), 124–7, 239, 287, 291, 350–1
La Marseillaise (Marseilles weekly), 198
"Marseillaise" battalion, 227
Martimat (escort), 139
Martin-Chauffier, Louis (1894–1980), 145
Martin-Mamy (journalist), 116
Martínez Anido, General Severino (1862–1938), 128
Martínez Barrio, Diego (1883–1962), 4, 33, 115, 222, 297, 325
Martínez Esparza, General, 346
Martín Montis, Antonio *Linares
Marty, André, 45, 50, 75, 77, 84, 107, 123, 125, 130, 133, 197, 208, 229–30, 243, 257–8, 319, 331, 358, 365, 375, 382–4
  accused of blocking release of prisoners, 227
  charged with murder of prisoners, 227–8
Marx, Karl (1818–1883), 229, 283
Massanet de Cabrenys (Gerona), 109
Massis, Henri [*Agathon*] (1886–1970), 132, 193–4, 258, 287, 290, 311, 367
Mathieu, Mgr Clément; Bishop of Dax, 124, 350
Matignon Agreement (1936), 3
Le Matin (Paris daily), 22–3, 30, 59, 61, 69, 72–3, 75, 83, 93, 100, 108, 116, 152, 184–6, 189, 196, 199, 211, 214, 237, 241, 247–8, 255, 281–3, 314, 330, 335, 341
Matthews, Herbert (journalist), 213
Mauclair, Camille (journalist), 370
Maudinat (escort), 138

Mauléon-Licharre (Basses-Pyrénées), 64, 384
Maulnier, Thierry [Jacques Louis Talagrand] (1909–1988), 237, 258, 287–9
Maura y Gamazo, Miguel (1887–1971), 125, 167, 224
Mauriac, François (1885–1970), 19, 49, 124–5, 127, 201, 287, 290–1, 320, 349, 350–1
Maurín Juliá, Joaquín (1896–1973), 304, 337
Maurois, André (1885–1967), 286, 290, 295
Maurras, Charles (1868–1952), 2, 4, 27, 30, 67, 127–8, 132–3, 145, 180, 193, 195, 198, 202–3, 209–10, 235–7, 243, 246, 249, 251–2, 258–9, 260, 287–8, 302, 309, 357, 371–2, 376
Maxence, Jacques (journalist), 80
Mayrègne (Haute-Garonne), 138
Mazedier, René (historian), 301
McAuliffe, General Anthony C. (1898–1975), 253
Meer de Volkeren, Pierre van der 124, 350
Melilla, 162
Memel, 231
Memmingen, 250
Ménard, General André, 38
Mendès France, Pierre (*député*, Eure; 1907–1982), 60, 295
Méndez Núñez (Republican cruiser), 174
Mendizábal, Alfredo (historian), 125, 128
Mercier, Desiré-Joseph Cardinal; Archbishop of Malines (1851–1926), 128
Le Mercure de France (Paris fortnightly), 295
Mérignac, 263
Merle, Eugène (journalist), 285, 350
Merleau-Ponty, Maurice (1908–1961), 124
Merry Del Val, Paul Alfonso, Marquis de, 90
Messidor (Paris weekly), 212, 293
Mexico, 163, 303
Miaja Menant, General José (1878–1958), 115, 143, 206, 213, 225
Micaud, Professor Charles A. (1910–1974), 237–8, 301
Michel, Augustin (*député*, Haute-Loire; 1882–1970), 177
Le Midi Socialiste (Toulouse daily), 13, 35, 41, 45, 51, 56, 63, 87, 92, 97–8, 100, 207, 213, 224, 226–7, 241, 253, 256, 263, 283
Miguel de Cervantes (Republican light cruiser), 364

Milan, 110
Milhaud, Albert, 49, 89, 320
Millán Astray y Terreros, General José (1879–1954), 147
Mille, Pierre (1864–1941), 173, 207, 235, 242–3, 259, 353, 375
Miller, General Evgeny (1867–1939), 141–2, 355–6, 374
Minorca, 50, 154, 209, 211, 359, 376
Mintz & Fletcher (London), 160
Miramas, André, 45
Miravitlles, Jaume (journalist), 24, 53, 212, 299
Mireaux, Émile (Senator, Hautes-Pyrénées; 1885–1969), 259, 286
Mistral, Silvia (author), 377
Moch, Jules (*député*, Drôme; Hérault; 1893–1985), 295, 310, 366
Moitessier, C. (Sûreté Nationale), 141
Molló (Gerona), 109, 139
Molotov-Ribbentrop Non-Aggression Pact, 241, 243, 248, 251, 257, 259–60
Le Monde (Paris), 380
Le Monde et la Vie (Paris), 382
Monks, Noel (journalist), 117, 122
Monmousseau, Gaston (*député*, Seine; 1883–1960), 293
Montaigne, Michel Eyquem de (1533–1592), 236
Montalba (Pyrénées-Orientales), 139
Montauban, 319
Monteiro, Armindo R. De Sttau (1896–1955), 15
Montevideo, 86
Montgarri (Lérida), 139
Montilla (Córdoba), 369
Montpellier, 64, 296, 317
Montreux Convention, 333
Montserrat, 222, 375
Montserrat, Victor Tarrago (journalist), 123, 125, 290, 350
Mont-Valérien, 260
Monzie, Anatole de (*député*, Lot; 1876–1947), 22, 75, 199
Moore, John Bassett (1860–1937), 335
Mora, Constancia de la (author), 377
Moran, Denise, 325
Morand, Paul (1889–1976), 286, 290, 295
Moravia, 231
Morel, Lieutenant-Colonel Henri, 70, 148, 366

Morizet, André (Senator, Seine; 1876–1942), 86, 179–81
Moretta (Cuneo), 256
Morning Post (London), 101, 300, 305
Morrison, William Shepherd [later 1st Viscount Dunrossil] (1893–1961), 55
Morocco, 4,14, 18–19, 21, 23–4, 29–30, 33, 51, 80, 98–101, 134, 145, 156, 162, 173, 194, 200, 208, 211, 214, 224, 257, 310, 315, 330, 341–2, 367, 369
Moscardó Ituarte, Colonel [later General] José (1878–1956), 144
Mosley (aide to Sir Philip Chetwode), 374
Mottin, Jean (historian), 301
Moulin, Jean (1899–1943), 36, 245, 251
Mounier, Emmanuel (1905–1950), 259, 291, 294, 350
Mouvement d'Action Combattante, 2
Mouvement Frontiste, 289
Munich Pact (1938), 376
Munnich, Ferenc (1886–1967) *Flatter
Muñoz Grandes, Colonel [later General] Agustín (1896–1970), 64
Münzenberg, Willi (1889–1940), 328
Muret (Haute-Garonne), 110, 320, 373
Mureine, André (journalist), 39
Musée de l'homme (Resistance network), 248, 262
Mussolini, Benito, 25, 27, 53, 80, 83, 91, 97–8, 102, 106, 153, 156, 168, 173, 187–8, 190, 194–7, 206–9, 214–15, 227, 240, 243, 284–5, 299, 304–5, 340, 377
 and Miguel Primo de Rivera, 37
 supports Goicoechea, 3
 and Ramón Franco, 77
 and French non-intervention policy, 52
 and 'preventive counter-revolution,' 79
 and relations with Hitler, 81
 denies seeking territorial gains, 100, 182
 and Guadalajara, 112–13
 talks with Göring, 116
 and his spies in France, 142
 and Rosselli, 343–4
 and Berneri, 113
 and North Africa, 159
 and Nyon, 164
 and Anglo-Italian agreement, 195
 and German–Austrian agreement, 308
 and Minorca, 359

Nalèche, Etienne de (journalist), 287, 302
Nancy, 296
Naples, 80, 100
Napoléon I (1769–1821), 98, 168, 358
Narbonne, 72, 137, 140, 162
Naud, Albert (barrister), 144
Navarre, 47
Navarro (Spanish Naval Attaché), 95
Naychent, Georges (journalist), 72
Negrín López, Juan (1889–1956), 148, 153, 170–1, 177, 197, 202, 204, 213–15, 218, 222, 225, 286, 365, 377, 381
Nemours, 357
Nenni, Pietro (1891–1980), 13, 40, 77
Neruda, Pablo [Ricardo Reyes y Basoalto] (1904–1973), 354
The Netherlands, 80, 101, 137, 160, 176, 343
Neurath, Baron Constantin von (1873–1956), 10, 152–3, 309
Neva (Soviet cargo ship), 324
News Chronicle (London), 14, 17, 28, 80, 188, 220, 300, 305
New York, 242, 244, 248, 252, 255, 260, 261
New York Herald Tribune: European Edition (Paris daily), 300
New York Times, 208, 213–14, 260, 300, 366, 370
Nexo, Martin Andersen (1869–1954), 354
Nicaragua, 86
Nice, 140, 208, 243, 247, 305
Nicolas, André (journalist), 77, 303
Nietzsche, Friedrich (1844–1900), 250
Nîmes, 294, 382
Nin, Andrés (1892–1937), 337
Nizan, Paul (1905–1940), 259, 354
Nobel Prize for Peace, 172, 253, 364
Noel-Baker, Philip, M.P. (1889–1982), 171
Nolhac, Pierre Girauld de (Académie Fr.; 1859–1936), 287
North Africa, 22, 51, 114, 177–9, 196, 214, 256, 258, 309, 342
North Sea, 188
Norway, 162, 303, 343
Las Noticias (Barcelona), 343
Notre Temps, Paris weekly, 256, 261
Le Nouvel Observateur (Paris weekly), 11
Les Nouveaux Temps (Paris daily), 256
Nouvel Age (Paris fortnightly), 145, 262
La Nouvelle Revue (Paris fortnightly), 57

La Nouvelle Revue Française (Paris monthly), 125, 133–4
La Nuova Italia (Paris weekly), 299, 386
Nuovo Avanti (Paris weekly), 299, 386
Nuremberg, 165
Nyon (Vaud), 163, 240
Nyon Arrangement (1937), 163–5, 190, 362

Oak, Liston (journalist), 169
Oberg, General SS Karl, 255
The Observer (London), 101, 300
Occident (Paris fortnightly), 299, 350, 354
Odessa, 323
Odin, Jean (Senator, Gironde; 1889–1975), 209
Oels, Colonel (Danish Army), 108
L'Oeuvre (Paris daily), 23, 35, 37–8, 42, 49, 56, 71, 80, 93, 98, 100, 105–6, 112, 114, 118, 149, 153–4, 156, 168, 170–1, 173, 182–3, 192, 195, 203, 209, 212, 214, 220, 222, 244, 249, 253, 261, 292, 313
Office de Justification des Tirages (OJT), 301
Office of War Information (Washington DC), 255
Oms (Pyrénées-Orientales), 109
Onaindía y Zuluaga, Padre Alberto, 124, 350
Operation 'Felix,' 369, 372
Operation 'Feuerzauber,' 29, 332, 346
Operation 'Otto,' 332, 346
Operation 'Torch,' 241
Operation 'Winterübung Hansa,' 346
Oran, 184, 363
L'Ordre (Paris daily), 17, 28, 38, 83, 94, 110, 118, 147, 159–60, 169, 180, 185, 204, 206–7, 209, 224, 227, 248, 366, 369–70
Orgeix (Ariège), 184–7
Orlu (Ariège), 186
Ormesson, Wladimir d' (1888–1973), 19, 23, 31–2, 38, 50, 97, 106, 146, 154, 157, 159, 171, 185, 197, 206, 213, 217, 259, 287, 357
Orsten, Major von (Gestapo), 141
Ortega y Gasset, Eduardo (1882–1964), 15, 176
Orthez (Basses-Pyrénées), 179
Orves, Captain Estienne d' (1901–1941), 252, 258

L'Osservatore Romano (Vatican City), 128
Ossorio y Gallardo, Ángel (1873–1946), 15–16, 297, 364
Ostend, 124
L'Ouest-Éclair (Rennes daily), 296, 304
Oviedo, 40, 125, 306
Oxford Union, 235

Pacelli, Eugenio Cardinal [later Pope Pius XII] (1876–1958), 129
Paco (escort), 138
Padelford, Norman J. (legal scholar), 312
Palaminy, Marquis de, 53, 76, 98, 236, 298, 322
Palamos (Gerona), 137
Palm, Colonel (Royal Netherlands Army), 108
Palma, 154
Palmer, Mgr, 64
Palos (German cargo ship), 150
Pamplona, 123, 210, 307, 349, 352
Parant, Roger (journalist), 23
Paris
  Archbishop *Verdier
  Austerlitz, gare d', 73, 374
  Bibliothèque Nationale, 242
  Bourse, 365
  Cherche-Midi (prison), 255, 260
  Collège de France, 86, 96
  École normale supérieure, 350
  Fédération Nationale de la Presse, 244
  Luna Park, 57
  Maison des métallos, 374
  Maison des syndicats, 332
  Matignon, hôtel, 3
  Notre Dame, 252
  Orsay, gare d,' 139
  Palais de la Mutualité, 97
  Rive Gauche bookshop, 247
  Salle Bullier, 2
  Salle Pleyel, 64
  Solférino (metro station), 373
  Sorbonne, 244, 247
  Vélodrome d'hiver, 41
Paris Declaration (1856), 358
Pariser Tageszeitung (Paris daily), 300, 386
Paris-Midi (Paris daily), 52, 180, 253, 281–2, 285–6, 300, 310, 341
Paris-Soir (Paris daily), 130, 184, 241, 253, 255, 281–2, 285–6, 300–2, 310, 320, 377, 385

Parti communiste français, 283
Parti de la réconciliation française, 255
Parti démocrate populaire, 144, 291
Parti du faisceau français, 302
Parti national corporatif républicain (Solidarité française), 2, 284–5, 302
Parti national populaire (Ligue des jeunesses patriotes), 2, 262, 284–5
Parti ouvrier belge, 262
Parti populaire français, 288
Parti social français, 223, 254, 262, 283, 356
Parti socialiste ouvrier et paysan, 293, 373
Partido comunista español, 4, 357
Partido Obrero de Unificación Marxista, 337
Partido Socialista Unificado de Cataluña (PSUC), 108
Partito communista italiano, 345
Pasajes (Guipúzcoa), 177, 181
Pasionaria *Ibárruri
Patenôtre, Raymond (*député*, Seine-et-Oise; 1900–1951), 283
La Patrie Humaine (Paris weekly), 295
El Patriota del Sud-Oeste (Toulouse), 251
Le Patriote du Sud-Ouest (Toulouse), 262
Pau, 136, 299
Paul-Boncour *Boncour
Pays, Marcel (journalist), 101, 341
Le Pays Wallon (Charleroi), 350
Pedoussaut (Belg. observer), 110
Pedrazzi, Orazio (1889–1962), 81
Pellicer, Carlos (1897–1977), 354
PEN (international writers' club), 304
Peretti de la Rocca, Emmanuel; count of Emmanuel Marie Joseph, 211
Péri, Gabriel (*député*, Argenteuil; 1902–1941), 24, 86, 94, 131, 155, 164, 168, 200, 260
Perillou pass (Gerona), 139
Pernot, Maurice (journalist), 227
Perpignan, 34, 62, 64, 73–4, 109, 131, 142, 187, 218, 222, 299, 327, 329
Perrigault, Jean (journalist), 209
Perrin, Jean (1870–1942), 295
Le Perthus, (Pyrénées-Orientales), 73–4, 137, 228
Pertinax, né André Géraud (1882–1974), 31, 51, 70, 75, 99–100, 114, 145, 153, 161–2, 202, 237, 242, 260, 284, 295
Peru, 63, 251, 335
Pestaña, Ángel (1886–1937), 132

Pétain, Marshal Henri Philippe Omer (1856–1951), 143, 177, 223–4, 227, 235, 242, 244–5, 248–50, 252–3, 258–62, 288, 298, 327, 381–2, 385
Le Petit Bleu de Paris (Paris daily), 292
La Petite Gironde (Bordeaux daily), 46, 117, 296, 299
Le Petit Journal (Paris daily), 14–15, 24, 32, 42, 51–2, 68, 80, 99, 110, 113–14, 121, 144, 152, 154–5, 223, 241, 253–5, 262, 281–3, 301–2, 313, 315, 323, 333, 341, 376
Le Petit Marseillais (Marseilles daily), 255, 296
Le Petit Méridional (Montpellier daily), 296
Le Petit Niçois (Nice daily), 255
Le Petit Provençal (Marseilles daily), 296
Petite-Entente, 101, 210, 234, 328
Petrograd, 148
Le Peuple (Paris daily), 13, 25, 40, 42, 51, 56, 58, 68, 106, 147, 155, 165, 173, 210, 214, 225, 244, 253, 293
Picasso, Pablo Ruiz y (1881–1973), 135
Piétri, François (*député*, Corsica; 1882–1966), 223, 288
Pini, Admiral Wladimiro (1879–1959), 362
Pinon, René (journalist), 290
Piot, Jean (journalist), 241, 325
Pius XI, Pope [Achille Ratti] (1857–1939), 129, 352
Pius XII *Pacelli
Pivert, Marceau (1895–1958), 105, 199, 233, 263, 293, 373
Pizzardo, Giuseppe Cardinal (1877–1970), 303
Planche, Camille (*député*, Allier; 1892–1961), 325
Planze (Tyrol), 263
Plato (428–347 BC), 15
Plymouth, Ivor Miles Windsor-Clive, 2nd Earl of (1889–1943), 55, 57, 84, 89, 91, 337
Poitou-Duplessy (*député*, Charente), 327
Poland, 67, 101, 149, 210, 234, 327, 343
Poles, 201, 332
Pollastrini, General (Italian Milizia), 113
Pollestres (Pyrénées-Orientales), 109
Poncins, Léon de (journalist), 289, 303
Pont-du-Roi (Haute-Garonne), 138
Ponteilla (Pyrénées-Orientales), 109
Le Populaire clandestin, 253

Le Populaire de Paris (daily), 24, 26, 40, 53, 59–61, 95–6, 111–13, 116, 142, 157, 164, 171, 176–8, 185–7, 189, 191–2, 196, 215, 219, 223, 248, 253, 256, 263, 281, 283, 298, 373
Le Populaire du Centre, 241
Port-Bou (Gerona), 72–3, 87, 137, 166, 329
Portela Valladares, Manuel (1868–1952), 166–7
Portillon-de-Burbe pass (Haute-Garonne), 138
Port-la-Nouvelle (Aude), 137, 140
Portugal, 18, 55, 83, 89, 91, 108, 162, 194, 312, 321, 343, 371
Portuguese Africa, 194
Port-Vendres (Pyrénées-Orientales), 140, 184, 378
Pour la Victoire, 242, 264, 261
Pourquoi Franco vaincra, 252
Prado, Mariano (journalist), 210
Prague, 52, 106, 154, 374
Prat de Llobregat (Barcelona), 109
Prats-de-Mollo-la-Preste (Pyrénées-Orientales), 139
Pravda (Moscow), 146
Prenant, Professor Marcel (1893–1983), 325
Presses Universitaires de France, 244, 391
Prévost, Marcel (journalist), 290
Prieto y Tuero, Indalecio (1883–1962), 2, 17, 130, 139, 155, 182, 197, 319, 348, 359
Primo de Rivera y Orbaneja, General Miguel; Marquis d'Estella (1870–1930), 3, 37, 229
Primo de Rivera y Saenz de Heredia, José Antonio (1903–1936), 3, 37
Progrès Social Français, 255
Protêt (French battleship), 319
Prouvost, Jean (1885–1978), 285–6
Puigcerdá (Gerona), 63, 72–3
Pujo, Maurice (1872–1955), 18, 30, 62, 95–7, 145, 260, 326
Punic Wars (264–146 BC), 2
Pupier, Jean (journalist), 52
Putz, Joseph (commander, International Brigades; 1895–1945), 227, 383
Puzzo, Dante A. (historian), 66, 164, 308, 312
Pyrénées-Orientales, 46, 74, 108, 139, 299, 327, 330

Quebec, 296
Quedru, Lieutenant-Commander, 317
Queipo de Llano y Serra, General Gonzalo (1875–1951), 38, 43, 51, 53, 118, 134, 143, 305
Quiñones de León, Count José María (1873–1957), 86, 139, 381
Le Quotidien (Paris daily), 17, 27, 32, 34, 39, 59, 292, 294

Rabat, 315
Radical Party Congress (1938), 202, 204
Radio Burgos, 252, 307
Radio-Journal (Paris), 246
Radio Luxembourg, 261
Radio Moscow, 246
Radio Paris, 250, 252
Radio Salamanca, 111
Radio Seville, 307, 363
Radio Vatican, 128
Radio Vichy, 262
Radio Zaragoza, 307
Ramette, Arthur (*député*, Nord; 1897–1988), 228, 230
Ramírez, Andrés (Republican agent), 34
Rassemblement populaire, 2, 198, 202
Rassemblement social et national, 284
Raud, Henry (journalist), 283
Rebière, Pierre (PCF Central Committee), 374
Reboul (barrister), 247
Reconquista (718–1492), 368
Regards (Paris weekly), 202, 262–3, 295
Reichenau, General [later Field Marshal] Walter von (1884–1842), 196, 369, 372
Reinhards, Captain Paul (Latvian Army), 108
Renaud, Jean (Solidarité Française), 285, 302
Renaud, Marcel (Fr. political commissar), 383
Renault, 331
Rennes, 296
Renouvin, Pierre (1893–1974), 306
La République (Paris daily), 22–3, 32, 92, 95, 98, 106, 116, 123, 149, 154, 156, 158, 167, 170, 183, 186, 189, 192, 198, 206, 212, 214–15, 233, 245, 250, 292–3, 313, 332, 341
Requesens (Gerona), 109
Requetés, 45, 139

Resolution (British cruiser), 108, 359
Restoration of 1875, 365
Reuter's News Agency (London), 14, 28, 117, 122, 183, 348
Révolution (Paris fortnightly), 294
Révolution Nationale, 247
La Révolution Prolétarienne (Paris fortnightly), 294, 304
Revue de France (Paris fortnightly), 289–90
Revue de Paris (Paris fortnightly), 168, 289–90
Revue des Deux Mondes (Paris fortnightly), 132, 154, 244, 289
Revue Hebdomadaire (Paris weekly/fortnightly), 14, 289
La Revue Universelle (Paris fortnightly), 207, 290, 344, 353
Rey d'Harcourt, Colonel Domingo (1883–1939), 228
Reynaud, Paul (*député*, Seine) (1878–1966), 38, 60, 199–200, 233, 257, 260, 288, 295
Rheims, 297
Rhineland, 3, 234, 363
La Rhune (Basses-Pyrénées), 142
Ribbentrop, Joachim von (1893–1946), 57, 152, 232
Richard, Élie (journalist), 286
Richard, Marthe (1889–1982), 355
Rieger, Max (Comintern propagandist), 131, 353
Rieu-Vernet, Aubin (journalist), 14, 16, 73, 75, 89, 91–2, 94, 115, 146–8, 155, 166, 171
Rif, 50, 81
Rio de Oro, 162, 178
Riom, 257, 260–1
Ríos Urrutia, Fernando de los (1879–1949), 15, 19, 33, 62, 168, 365
Riotinto, mines of (Huelva), 80
Riou, Gaston (journalist), 95
Ripoll (Gerona), 74, 109
Ripoull, Théo (journalist), 186
Rivet, Professor Paul (1876–1958), 2
Robertico, Juan (PCE envoy), 77
Roche, Émile (1893–1990), 69, 212, 233, 293
Rochefer, Henri (journalist), 15
Rochefort, 373
La Rochelle, 155
Rodríguez, Francisco (Nationalist agent), 63

Rolland, Philippe (journalist), 62
Rolland, Romain (1866–1944), 134, 294–5, 304, 325
Rollin, Louis (*député*, Seine; 1879–1952), 76, 213, 215, 288
Rol-Tanguy (1908–2002) *Tanguy
Romains, Jules (1885–1974), 295, 297, 304
Romania, 164, 328, 343
Rome (*qua* city), 3, 29, 116, 129, 195, 200, 206, 208–9, 284, 340, 344, 352, 362
Romier, Lucien (1885–1944), 49, 51, 101, 163, 169–70, 178–9, 187, 198, 201, 207, 260, 286–7
Roosevelt, Eleanor (1884–1962), 261
Roosevelt, Franklin Delano (1882–1945), 86, 222, 380
Rosenberg, Marcel (1896–1937), 75, 197, 308
Rosenfeld, Oreste (journalist), 41, 52, 93, 107, 283, 326
Rosselli, Carlo (Ital. Anarchist), 299, 343–4
Rosselli, Nello (Ital. Anarchist), 344
Rossi, Amilcare *Leroux, André
Rossi, Ernesto, *Leroux, André
Rotvand, Georges (author), 132–3
Roubaix, 128, 137, 178
Roucayrol, Fernand (*député*, Hérault; 1894–1945), 61
Roussillon province, 64, 74
Le Roussillon (Perpignan weekly), 299
Rovera, Jean de (journalist), 295
Royal Oak (British cruiser), 359
Royallieu barracks (Compiègne), 253
Royan, 199
Roz, Firmin (1866–1957), 298
Rul, Georges, 72, 329
Runciman, Walter, 1st Viscount (1870–1949), 374
Russell, Bertrand, 3rd Earl (1872–1970), 295
Russia *Union of Soviet Socialist Republics

Saavedra Lamas, Carlos (1878–1959), 86
Sadowa, Battle of (1866), 201
Sahara, 29
Saïda, 29
Saint-Aulaire, Auguste de Beaupoil, count of (1866–1954), 14, 168, 303, 311
Saint-Brice, Louis de (journalist), 154–5, 201
Saint-Cyr, Duke of (Nationalist agent), 63

Saint-Étienne, 296, 343
Saint-Exupéry, Antoine de (1900–1944)
Saint-Jean-de-Luz (Basses-Pyrénées), 44, 49–50, 63, 110, 142, 362
Saint-Just, François de (*député*, Pas-de-Calais; 1896–1984)
Saint-Laurent-de-Cerdans (Pyrénées-Orientales), 139
Saint-Martory (Haute-Garonne), 46–7
Saint-Simon (Toulouse), 261
Sala (escort), 139
Salamanca (*qua* city), 94, 119, 133, 139, 149, 151, 307, 331, 360
Salazar, Antonio de Oliveira (1889–1970), 56, 311
Salengro, Roger (1890–1936), 62, 319
Salgado, Manuel (anarchist), 343
Salmon, André (journalist), 246, 341, 385
Salsas (engineer), 95–6
Salvan, Armand (journalist), 24, 242
Sampaix, Lucien (1899–1941), 63, 261
Samuel, Herbert, 1st Viscount (1870–1963), 151, 155–6, 297
Sangnier, Marc (1873–1950), 198, 251, 291, 303, 383
Sangróniz y Castro, José Antonio de; Marquis de Desio, 170, 379
Sanjurjo Sacanel, General José (1872–1936), 3, 50, 321
San Sebastián, 44–5, 47, 77, 105, 140–2, 180–1, 194, 196, 216, 306–7, 324, 355
Santander, 151, 155, 163
Santiago de Chile, 319
Sanz del Río, Julián (1814–1869), 365
Saragossa, 96, 180–1, 252, 327, 278
Sarajevo, 34
Sardinia, 29
Sarraut, Albert (1872–1962), 200, 222, 242, 261, 297, 304
Sarraut, Maurice (1869–1943), 242, 261
Sartre, Jean Paul (1905–1980), 134, 336
Sauerwein, Jules (journalist), 309
Savoy, 208
Scelle, Georges (journalist), 16, 39, 48–9, 94, 99, 115, 147–8, 152, 155, 184, 190, 196, 199, 220–1
Schacht, Dr Hjalmar Horace Greeley (1877–1970), 58, 97–8, 340
Schloezer, Count Boris de, 350
Scholl, Dr (Ger. Nationalist agent), 160

Schuschnigg, Kurt von (1897–1977), 56, 352
Scipio Africanus, Publius Cornelius (236–184 BC), 197
Secours rouge international, 31, 39, 315
Section française de l'Internationale ouvrière (SFIO), 1–2, 24, 31, 39–40, 53, 55, 59, 136, 177, 187–8, 199, 202, 204, 227, 232–3, 235, 240, 248, 283, 297, 365, 381
Segone, Georges (journalist), 210
Seine-et-Oise, 30, 260
El Sembrador (Puigcerdá), 63
Seo de Urgel (Lérida), 74, 181, 307
Sept (Paris weekly), 122–3, 145, 291, 294, 320
Serrano Suñer, Ramón (1901–2003), 127, 230, 290, 307, 350–1, 382
Servicios de Información de Fronteras del Norte de España (SIFNE), 139
Servizio di Intelligenza Militare, 344
Setil (Santarém), 56
Seven Seas Spray (British cargo ship), 149–50
Sévérac, J.-B. (journalist), 39–40, 58–9, 61, 88
Seville, 4, 114, 134, 249, 306, 350
Sforza, Count Carlo of (1873–1952), 102, 297
Shanghai, 163
Shirer, William Laurence (1904–1993), 322
Sigmaringen, 246–7, 249, 256
Silla, Gaston (anarchist commissar), 109
Silva, Major (Ital. Army), 113
Simon, O.K. *Katz
Simon, Pierre-Henri (1903–1972), 291, 350
Simond, Henry (journalist), 144–5, 237, 284, 302
Sinn Feiners, 123, 349
Sisco, Laurent (journalist), 302
Smorti, Filiberto (Ital. fascist agent), 136
El Socialista (Madrid), 184
Solano Palacio, Fernando (author), 377–8
Solidaridad Obrera (Barcelona), 34, 113
Solidarité des ouvriers basques, 126
Solidarité française *Parti national corporatif républicain
Soria, 364
Soule, region of, 63
Soulier, Édouard (*député*, Seine), 327
Soult, Marshal Nicolas Jean de Dieu, Duke of Dalmatia (1769–1851), 179

South America, 194, 256
Southworth, Herbert Rutledge (historian; 1908–1999), 334, 348–9, 353
Spaak, Paul-Henri Charles (1899–1972), 262
Spanish-American War (1898), 329
Spanish Foreign Legion *Tercio
Spanish News Agency (London), 299, 328
Spender, Stephen Harold (1909–1995), 135
Spreafico, Alessandro (International Brigader), 384
Stalin [Yossif Vissarionovich Dzhugashvili] (1879–1953), 31, 66, 110, 143, 146–9, 154, 233–4, 241, 245, 374
  and Trotsky, 303–04
  sends aid to Spain , 67–8, 188
  and Miller, 355
  and Tukhachevsky, 117
  and Koltsov, 357
  and Krivitsky, 328
  and Münzenberg, 328
  and Pollitt, 339
  and the POUM, 131
  and Berneri, 304
  and Gide, 134
  sends message to Díaz, 194
  and impact of Munich, 205
  recalls Marty, 208, 258
  recalls Duclos, 251
  and de Gaulle, 243
Stanbrook (British cargo ship), 150
La Stampa (Turin), 93
The Star (London), 346, 348
Stavisky, Aleksandr (1886–1934), 2, 358
Steer, George L. (journalist), 117, 119
Stevenson, (later Sir] Ralph (1895–1977), 377
Stimson, Henry Lewis (1867–1950), 214, 378
Stockholm, 386
Stolz (journalist), 53
Straperlo scandal (1934–1935), 2
Stresa Agreement (1935), 30
Sturzo, Dom Luigi (1871–1959), 124, 127, 192, 350
Suarez, Georges (1890–1944), 145, 261
submarines (Republican), 141, 174
Sudetenland, 201
Suffren, Marquis de, 298
Suhard, Emmanuel Cardinal, Archbishop of Paris (1874–1949), 252

Sunday Times (London), 97
Swierczewski, General Karol [*General Walter*] (1897–1947), 383
Switzerland (*qua* city), 96, 160, 248, 252, 254, 256, 382

Tabouis, Geneviève (1892–1985), 50, 52, 80, 90, 100, 112, 115, 151, 156, 196, 204, 242, 254, 261, 283, 340, 369
Tabouis, Robert (journalist), 261
Taillet (Pyrenées-Orientales), 109
Taittinger, Pierre (*député*, Seine; 1887–1965), 2, 30, 51, 64, 188–9, 201–2, 205–6, 213, 262, 285, 303
Talleyrand-Périgord, Charles-Maurice de; Prince of Bénévent (1754–1838), 324
Tangier, 28, 42, 53, 97
Tangier Agreements of 1923 and 1928, 31
Tanguy, Colonel Henri [*Rol*] (1908–2002), 383
Tapis (Gerona), 139
Tarascon-sur-Ariège, 186
Tarbes, 108, 179, 299
Tardieu, André (1876–1945), 144, 202, 222, 262, 288–9, 302
Tarragona, 212, 384, 386
Tasca, Angelo *Leroux, André
Tchassovoi ['The Sentry'] (Paris fortnightly), 371
Tech, River, 109
Témime, Émile (historian; 1926–2008), 374
Le Temps (Paris daily), 22, 39, 71, 94, 116, 159, 184, 241, 259, 282, 286–7, 333, 358
Le Temps Présent (Paris weekly), 127
Tercio (Sp. Foreign Legion), 77, 332
Terreux, Rear Admiral, 373
Terre Libre (Paris weekly/Nimes monthly), 130, 294
Terrible (Fr. destroyer), 151
Teruel, bishop of (Padre Anselmo Polanco y Fontecha; 1883–1939), 228–9
Téry, Gustave (1871–1928), 283, 354
Téry, Simone (1897–1967), 134, 354
Tessan, François de (journalist), 242, 297
Tessier, Gaston (journalist), 291
Tetuán, 14
Il Tevere (Rome), 208
Thaelmann, Ernst (1886–1944), 384
Tharaud, Jean (1877–1952), 237, 284
Tharaud, Jerome (1874–1953), 237, 284

Thibaudet, Albert (1874–1936), 287, 297
Thiébaut, Marcel (journalist), 290
Thomas Aquinas, Saint (1225–1247), 16, 122
Thomas, Hugh (historian; 1931–), 308
Thorez, Maurice (*député*, Ivry-sur-Seine; 1900–1964), 1, 60–1, 132, 233, 243, 250–1, 257–9, 316, 327–8
The Times (London), 92, 117, 120, 189, 192, 214, 300, 347–8, 383
Tito, Josip Broz [*Tomanek*], later Marshal (1892–), 332
Tixier-Vignancour, Jean-Louis (*député*, Basses-Pyrénées ; 1907–1989), 93, 196, 203, 228, 262, 327, 372
Togliatti, Palmiro [*Ercole Ercoli*] (1893–1964), 16
Toledo, 122, 347
Tolera, Roger (Sov. agent), 109
Tolosa (Guipúzcoa), 43, 168
Tolstoy, Aleksei Nicolayevich Count (1883–1945), 354
Tomanek *Tito
Torquemada, Tomás de (1420–1498), 91
Torrès, Henry (1891–1966), 325
Touchard, Jean (1918–1971), 236, 294, 301
Toulouse,
  Congress of (1936), 2
  Francazal (airport), 34–6, 38, 109, 138, 177
  Montaudran (airfield), 38, 109, 136
Tours, Congress of (1920), 1
Toussan, General, 75, 220, 311, 331
Touvier, Paul (1915–1996), 244
Tovar, Professor Antonio (1911–1985), 307
Trades Union Congress (1936), 61
Travailleurs étrangers *Commission Todt
Traversay, Guy de (journalist), 302, 351
Tréand, Maurice (1900–1949), 260
Un Trentennio di attività anarchica
La Tribune des Nations (Paris weekly), 22, 75, 167, 295
Triple Alliance, 30
Troncoso y Sagrado, Major Julián (1895–?), 139, 141–2, 355
Trotsky, Leo [Lev Davidovich Bronshtein] (1879–1940), 133, 303–4, 337
Tuesta, Ángel Díaz de (1890–1971), 46
Tukhachevsky, Marshal Mikhail Nikolaievich (1893–1937), 117, 149, 355–6

Tunis, 142, 208
Tunisia, 14, 197, 374
Turin, 110, 249
Turkey, 164, 324, 343
Turquesa (Soviet cargo ship), 323
Tyrol, 253, 263

Unamuno Jugo, Miguel de (1864–1936), 147, 341
Unidad (San Sebastián), 194
Union Commerciale Bordelaise (Bassens), 63
Union nationale, 60, 233, 289
Union républicaine, 296
Union of Soviet Socialist Republics (USSR), 30, 56–7, 66–9, 95, 98, 100–1, 106, 111, 131–2, 134, 147, 163, 202, 246, 252, 254, 319, 323–5, 333, 335, 337, 343, 357, 361
United Kingdom
  Admiralty, 11, 99, 163–4, 310
  Foreign Office (Whitehall), 55, 82, 105
  Parliament (Westminster), 37, 101
  House of Commons, 92, 150, 313
United Press, 192, 207, 300, 374
United States of America, 2–3, 18, 44, 49, 89, 110, 150, 214, 221–4, 306, 319, 336, 372, 381, 385
Ureña, de (Sp. Foreign Ministry), 325–6
Uruguay, 49, 83, 335
Utrera (Seville), 369

La Vague (Paris fortnightly), 293
Vaillant-Couturier, Paul (*député*, Seine; 1892–1937), 41–2, 59, 67, 139, 156, 283, 346, 360
Valencia (*qua* city), 4, 70, 73, 91, 96–7, 102, 135–6, 161, 163, 177, 214, 222, 306, 326, 358, 374, 378
  Alliance française, 107
Valladolid, 350
Vallat, Xavier (*député*, Ardeche; 1890–1972), 228, 302, 383
Valle, Captain (Republican Air Force), 136
Vallejo, Cesar (1892–1938), 354
Vallescà, Lluhí i (Cat. diplomat), 46
Valois, Georges (1878–1945), 145, 262, 357
Van der Schatte Olivier, Rear-Admiral J. (Royal Netherlands Navy), 108
Vandervelde, Émile (1866–1938), 42, 71, 75, 107, 169, 171, 176, 198–9, 239, 262, 297, 386

Van Dulm, Vice-Admiral M. H. (Royal Netherlands Navy), 108
La Vanguardia (Barcelona), 113, 316
Varko (Greek cargo ship), 137
Vatican, 56, 89, 98, 123, 126, 128–9, 260, 288, 303, 352, 375
Vaugeois, Henry (journalist), 287
Vautel, Clément (journalist), 62
Vendée counter-revolution (1793–1795), 15
Vendémiaire (Paris weekly), 58, 294
Vendredi (Paris weekly), 145, 249, 262, 294, 329, 354, 357
Venezuela, 335
Vera de Bidasoa (Navarre), 313
Verdier, Jean Cardinal, Archbishop of Paris (1864–1940), 124, 350, 385
Verdun, Battle of (1916), 224, 381
Vergara, Abrazo de (1839), 168
Verlomme, Roger (Fr. Ministry of the Interior; 1890–1950), 35–6
Versailles, 64, 136
Versailles, Treaty of (1919), 3
Vertex, Jean (journalist), 18, 51
Veuillot, François (journalist), 127
Vézins, Christian de (journalist), 333
Vichy Government (1940–1944), 243, 250, 260, 263, 302, 377, 383
La Victoire (Paris irregular/weekly), 13, 22, 58, 70, 95, 154, 288
Vidal *Geumann
Vidal, Jean (journalist), 27
La Vie Catholique (Paris weekly), 122–3, 251, 291
La Vie Intellectuelle (Paris fortnightly), 122–3, 291
La Vie Ouvrière (Paris weekly), 293
Viénot, Pierre (*député*, Ardennes; 1897–1944), 341
Vignaux, Paul (1904–1987), 350
Vigo, 51, 308, 345, 366
Villacoublay, 34
Vinaroz, 176, 182, 192–3, 365
Vincent, Ernest (journalist), 174, 290
Viollis, Andrée (journalist), 54, 246, 282, 294, 354, 385
Vitoria, 117–18, 120, 123, 168, 181, 363
Vittori, François (political commissar), 383
Vittorio Emmanuelle III (1869–1947), 3
La Voce degli Italiani (Paris daily), 305, 386

Vogel, Lucien (journalist), 295
Völkischer Beobachter (Munich/Berlin), 27, 99, 321, 365
Le Voltigeur (Paris fortnightly), 294
La Voz de España (San Sebastián), 210
Voz de Madrid (Paris weekly), 299
Vu et Lu (Paris weekly), 296

Wallden, Lieutenant-Colonel P. (Finnish Army), 108, 136
Wallon, Professor Henri (1879–1962), 325
Walter, General [Karol Wacław Wierczewski] (1897–1947), 383
Warnemunde (Rostock), 114
Warner, Sylvia Townsend (1893–1978), 354
War of the Spanish Succession (1701–1714), 51
Warsaw *qua* city, 57, 68
Washington, DC, 150, 328
Washington, Treaty of (1923), 86
Watson (journalist), 346
Weil, Simone (1909–1943), 342
Weimar, 247
Weimar Constitution (1919), 176
Wellington, Arthur Wellesley, 1st Duke of (1769–1852), 179, 363
Die Welt (Berlin), 259
Werth, Léon (1878–1955), 325
Wettre, Colonel (Norwegian Army), 108
Weygand, General Maxime (1867–1965), 385
Whealey, Robert H. (historian), 324, 370
Wigbert (German cargo ship), 56
Wilhelmi, Major Hans (1899–1970), 371
Wilkinson, Dr Ellen, M.P. (1891–1947), 171
Wilson, Sir Horace (1883–1972), 376
Woodford (British cargo ship), 163
Wurmser, André (1899–1994), 262

Ybarnegaray, Jean (*député*, Basses-Pyrénées; 1883–1956), 228, 262, 283
Yeats, William Butler (1865–1939), 239
Yugoslavia, 164, 328, 343

Zurich, 138
Zyromski, Jean (1890–1975), 40, 50, 60, 95, 146, 168, 214, 263, 293, 325, 345